6 대화를 듣고, 두 사람이 만날 시각을 고르시오.

① 6:00 a.m.   ② 6:30 a.m.   ③ 7:00 a.m.

④ 7:30 a.m.   ⑤ 8:00 a.m.

KB244297

7 대화를 듣고, 남자의 장래 희망으로 가장 적절한 것을 고르시오.

① 여행가   ② 역사교사   ③ 사진작가

④ 영상편집자   ⑤ 관광가이드

8 대화를 듣고, 여자의 심정으로 가장 적절한 것을 고르시오.

① 슬픔   ② 실망   ③ 질투

④ 안도   ⑤ 설렘

9 대화를 듣고, 남자가 대화 직후에 할 일로 가장 적절한 것을 고르시오.

① 시계 구매하기   ② 목적지로 출발하기   ③ 가구 밑을 찾아보기

④ 핸드폰에 전화하기   ⑤ 약속 시간 미루기

10 대화를 듣고, 무엇에 관한 내용인지 가장 적절한 것을 고르시오.

① 체육복 디자인   ② 시간표 변경   ③ 음악실 위치

④ 체육대회   ⑤ 시험 일정

11번~20번 문제는 다음 페이지에 ➡

11 대화를 듣고, 두 사람이 함께 이동할 방법으로 가장 적절한 것을 고르시오.

① 택시 　　② 도보 　　③ 지하철
④ 버스 　　⑤ 자동차

12 대화를 듣고, 남자가 커뮤니티센터에 가는 이유로 가장 적절한 것을 고르시오.

① 스포츠 강좌를 등록하려고 　　② 필요한 서류를 발급하려고
③ 마을 도서관을 이용하려고 　　④ 멘토링 봉사 활동을 하려고
⑤ 친구들과 모여 숙제를 하려고

13 대화를 듣고, 두 사람이 대화하는 장소로 가장 적절한 곳을 고르시오.

① 서점 　　② 병원 　　③ 사진관 　　④ 경찰서 　　⑤ 공항

14 Kids' Baking Class에 관한 다음 내용을 듣고, 표에서 일치하지 <u>않는</u> 것을 고르시오.

	Kids' Baking Class	
①	일시	this Saturday, 2 p.m.
②	주제	how to make pizza
③	수업 시간	2 hours
④	참가비	$10
⑤	장소	community center

15 대화를 듣고, 남자가 여자에게 부탁한 일로 가장 적절한 것을 고르시오.

① 스파게티 요리하기 　　② 채소 손질하기 　　③ 요리 가르쳐주기
④ 치즈 사오기 　　⑤ 냉장고 청소하기

16 대화를 듣고, 여자가 남자에게 제안한 것으로 가장 적절한 것을 고르시오.

① 미술관 가기　　　② 동아리 가입하기　　　③ 그림 모델 되어주기

④ 미술 대회 참가하기　　　⑤ 전시회 티켓 구해주기

17 대화를 듣고, 두 사람이 주말에 할 일로 가장 적절한 것을 고르시오.

① 공원 산책하기　　　　② 워터파크 가기

③ 게임 대회 참여하기　　　④ 콘서트 표 구매하기

⑤ K-Pop 공연 관람하기

18 대화를 듣고, 여자의 직업으로 가장 적절한 것을 고르시오.

① 경찰관　　　② 소방관　　　③ 건축가　　　④ 관광 가이드　　　⑤ 역사 선생님

[19~20] 대화를 듣고, 남자의 마지막 말에 이어질 여자의 말로 가장 적절한 것을 고르시오.

19 Woman: _____

① See you later.　　　② You're welcome.

③ I don't understand.　　　④ I hope you have fun.

⑤ Every Friday after school.

20 Woman: _____

① I like watching TV.　　　② It's my favorite.

③ I like classical music.　　　④ That's all right.

⑤ Thank you very much.

Dictation(받아쓰기)은 본문을 받아쓰면서 영어듣기의 집중력을 향상시키고 다양한 표현을 정리하기 위한 영어듣기 학습법입니다. 녹음을 다시 듣고, 빈칸에 알맞은 단어를 써 보세요.
※Dictation의 정답은 듣기 대본의 밑줄 친 부분을 확인하세요. 📖 정답 p. 1

맞은 개수 / 총117개

그림정보파악(담화)

1. 다음을 듣고, 'I'가 무엇인지 가장 적절한 것을 고르시오.

①  ②

③  ④

⑤

01 M: I have two hands, two legs and a long tail. I _____ _____ trees, and I use my hands and tail _____ _____ trees. I also have a red bottom. I am _____ _____. What am I?

그림정보파악(대화)

2025 영어듣기능력평가 1회 2번 변형

2. 대화를 듣고, 여자가 구입할 인형으로 가장 적절한 것을 고르시오.

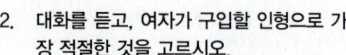

①  ②

③   ④

⑤

02 W: Excuse me. I want to buy a _____ _____ for my six-year-old son.

M: Sure. Astronauts and pilots are popular.

W: He wants to be an _____ one day.

M: Then, how about this one with a flag?

W: Great! The astronaut _____ _____ _____ looks cute. I'll take it.

날씨파악-그림

3. 다음을 듣고, 현재 세종의 날씨로 가장 적절한 것을 고르시오.

① ② ③ ④ ⑤

03 W: Good afternoon. This is Sejong's weather report. _____ _____ _____ stopped this morning, but now heavy rain is falling. It'll be rainy _____ this evening. So, bring an umbrella if you're going out. But it'll be sunny tomorrow. Thanks for _____ _____ the weather update.

마지막말의도파악

4. 대화를 듣고, 남자가 한 마지막 말의 의도로 가장 적절한 것을 고르시오.

① 거절 ② 축하
③ 사과 ④ 위로
⑤ 감사

04 W: Grandpa, can I talk to you?

M: Sure. What is it, Eva?

W: My pet hamster, Coco _____ _____ last night.

M: Oh, I'm so _____ to hear that. How are you feeling?

W: I'm really sad.

M: It's fine to feel sad. Let's _____ the happy times you had with Coco.

다음 페이지에 계속 ➡

5. 다음을 듣고, 남자가 자신의 여동생에 대해 언급하지 않은 것을 고르시오.

① 이름   ② 나이
③ 성격   ④ 취미
⑤ 좋아하는 음식

05 M: Hi, everyone. I'd like to introduce my younger sister. Her name is Lucy Kim. She's 9 years old. She's very _____ and friendly. Her favorite food is pizza, and she really likes chocolate ice cream. She always _____ _____ _____ when I feel sad.

6. 대화를 듣고, 두 사람이 만날 시각을 고르시오.

① 6:00 a.m.   ② 6:30 a.m.
③ 7:00 a.m.   ④ 7:30 a.m.
⑤ 8:00 a.m.

06 M: I'm so _____ _____ the Andong Mask Dance Festival tomorrow.

W: Me too. We're going to meet at the Daejeon Bus Terminal tomorrow morning, right?

M: Yes, we'll _____ _____ the 7:30 bus. What time should we meet?

W: How about 6:30?

M: Hmm, I think that's _____ _____.

W: Then, how about 7:00?

M: Sounds good. See you tomorrow!

장래희망추론

7. 대화를 듣고, 남자의 장래 희망으로 가장 적절한 것을 고르시오.
① 여행가
② 역사교사
③ 사진작가
④ 영상편집자
⑤ 관광가이드

07
W: Hey, how was your family trip?

M: It was great. We went to Gyeongju.

W: Did you have _____ _____ _____ fun?

M: Yes. I _____ videos to make a video clip. I'll show you.

W: Wow, that's awesome! You're so good at editing videos.

M: I'm really into video editing. I want to become a _____ _____ in the future.

고난도 심정추론

8. 대화를 듣고, 여자의 심정으로 가장 적절한 것을 고르시오.
① 슬픔
② 실망
③ 질투
④ 안도
⑤ 설렘

08
M: Sujin, why do you _____ _____ _____?

W: I lost my muffler yesterday.

M: You mean the red one?

W: Yes. It was my _____ muffler.

M: That's too bad. I thought it _____ _____ _____ you.

W: I know. My mother _____ _____ for me as a birthday present.

M: Oh, no. I'm sorry to hear that.

다음 페이지에 계속 ➡

9. 대화를 듣고, 남자가 대화 직후에 할 일
    로 가장 적절한 것을 고르시오.
    ① 시계 구매하기
    ② 목적지로 출발하기
    ③ 가구 밑을 찾아보기
    ④ 핸드폰에 전화하기
    ⑤ 약속 시간 미루기

09

W: Mark, we should get going.

M: Hmm... How much time do we _____

_____?

W: About 30 minutes. Is something wrong?

M: Yes, I can't find my cell phone.

W: _____ _____ _____ under the bed?

M: Yes, it's not there. Can I use your cell phone for a

minute? I'll have to call my phone.

W: Sure, _____ _____ _____.

10. 대화를 듣고, 무엇에 관한 내용인지 가장
    적절한 것을 고르시오.
    ① 체육복 디자인
    ② 시간표 변경
    ③ 음악실 위치
    ④ 체육대회
    ⑤ 시험 일정

10

M: Jenny, why are you wearing your sports uniform?

W: I got changed for _____ _____. Don't
   we have PE class now, Minjun?

M: No, today's _____ has been changed. We
   have music class now.

W: Really? I didn't know that.

M: Mrs. Kim told us about it yesterday.

W: Oh, I see. I'll _____ _____ then.

특정정보파악(교통수단)

11. 대화를 듣고, 두 사람이 함께 이동할 방법으로 가장 적절한 것을 고르시오.

① 택시
② 도보
③ 지하철
④ 버스
⑤ 자동차

11

W: Why is the traffic so _____ today?

M: I think there is a car accident up ahead. I heard about it on the radio before you _____ _____ _____.

W: Oh, really? I didn't hear that. Anyway, we have to hurry to get there _____ _____.

M: How about _____ _____ _____ at that parking lot and taking the subway?

W: I agree. Taking the subway will be faster than driving.

이유파악

12. 대화를 듣고, 남자가 커뮤니티센터에 가는 이유로 가장 적절한 것을 고르시오.

① 스포츠 강좌를 등록하려고
② 필요한 서류를 발급하려고
③ 마을 도서관을 이용하려고
④ 멘토링 봉사 활동을 하려고
⑤ 친구들과 모여 숙제를 하려고

12

W: David, where are you going?

M: I'm going to the community center _____ _____ for the Youth Mentorship Program.

W: What's that all about?

M: It's a program where I _____ _____ _____, helping them with their homework and _____ _____.

W: That's wonderful! You've always been great with kids.

M: Thanks! I'm excited to help them.

다음 페이지에 계속 ➡

13. 대화를 듣고, 두 사람이 대화하는 장소로 가장 적절한 곳을 고르시오.
① 서점　　　② 병원
③ 사진관　　④ 경찰서
⑤ 공항

13

W: Hello, I'd like you to take a photo of me.

M: Sure. May I ask _____ _____ _____ _____ _____?

W: It's for my passport.

M: Okay. Then, I need to make the background white.

W: Is there anything I need to do?

M: Just _____ _____ your ears are showing.

W: Okay. Shall I sit down here?

신유형 ｜ 2025 영어듣기능력평가 1회 14번 변형

14. Kids' Baking Class에 관한 다음 내용을 듣고, 표에서 일치하지 <u>않는</u> 것을 고르시오.

Kids' Baking Class		
①	일시	this Saturday, 2 p.m.
②	주제	how to make pizza
③	수업 시간	2 hours
④	참가비	$10
⑤	장소	community center

14

W: Hello, everyone! Let me introduce our Kids' Baking Class. It'll be held this Saturday at 2 p.m. In this class, kids will learn how to bake their own cupcakes and _____ them with fun toppings. The class will last 2 hours. The _____ is 10 dollars, including all _____. Please bring your own apron. The class will take place at the community center.

15. 대화를 듣고, 남자가 여자에게 부탁한 일로 가장 적절한 것을 고르시오.

① 스파게티 요리하기
② 채소 손질하기
③ 요리 가르쳐주기
④ 치즈 사오기
⑤ 냉장고 청소하기

15

W: What are you doing, honey?

M: I'm making some spaghetti. I learned the recipe at the cooking club.

W: I see. Wow! You have all the _____ _____.

M: Yes, but I _____ _____ _____ some cheese.

W: I think there's some in the refrigerator.

M: No, there isn't. Actually, could you _____ _____ _____ some for me?

W: Sure. No problem.

제안파악

16. 대화를 듣고, 여자가 남자에게 제안한 것으로 가장 적절한 것을 고르시오.

① 미술관 가기
② 동아리 가입하기
③ 그림 모델 되어주기
④ 미술 대회 참가하기
⑤ 전시회 티켓 구해주기

16

W: This is a beautiful drawing. Did you make it?

M: Yes, I'm practicing for _____ _____ _____ next month.

W: I didn't know you were interested in art.

M: I joined the art club _____ _____. It's really fun.

W: Oh, then how about going to an art museum together? I like art, too.

M: That _____ _____!

다음 페이지에 계속 ➡

할일파악

17. 대화를 듣고, 두 사람이 주말에 할 일로 가장 적절한 것을 고르시오.

① 공원 산책하기
② 워터파크 가기
③ 게임 대회 참여하기
④ 콘서트 표 구매하기
⑤ K-Pop 공연 관람하기

17

M: Mom, can we go to the K-Pop concert this Saturday?

W: I'm sorry, honey. But I don't think we can.

M: Why?

W: It's _____ _____ to get tickets.

M: Oh, okay. Then, how about going to the water park _____?

W: That's a good idea. You did say you wanted to try the new water slide.

직업추론

18. 대화를 듣고, 여자의 직업으로 가장 적절한 것을 고르시오.

① 경찰관
② 소방관
③ 건축가
④ 관광 가이드
⑤ 역사 선생님

18

W: Welcome to Bulguksa! I'm Jinny from Mother Tongue Travel.

M: Wow! It's so _____. How old is it?

W: It's about one _____, two hundred years old.

M: (pause) Oh, look! There are two towers. What are those?

W: They are Seokkatap and Dabotap. Please come this way and I'll _____ their history.

19. 대화를 듣고, 남자의 마지막 말에 이어질 여자의 말로 가장 적절한 것을 고르시오.

Woman: _____

① See you later.
② You're welcome.
③ I don't understand.
④ I hope you have fun.
⑤ Every Friday after school.

19

W: Kevin, how are you doing?

M: Hi, Ms. Lee. Classes are fine, but I still need to complete some volunteer hours.

W: Then, would you like to _____ my community service club? You can get volunteer hours there.

M: Oh, really? What kind of community service do you do?

W: We keep the streets and neighborhoods clean by _____ _____ _____.

M: I'm interested. When does your club meet?

W: Every Friday after school.

20. 대화를 듣고, 남자의 마지막 말에 이어질 여자의 말로 가장 적절한 것을 고르시오.

Woman: _____

① I like watching TV.
② It's my favorite.
③ I like classical music.
④ That's all right.
⑤ Thank you very much.

20

W: Edward, whose violin is this?

M: It's mine.

W: Can you _____ _____ _____?

M: Yes, I can. What about you?

W: I can't play the violin. But, I like to _____ _____ music a lot.

M: Oh, really? What's your _____ genre?

W: I like classical music.

Words & Expressions Review 01

● 다음 단어를 암기하세요.

문제	번호	단어	뜻
1	☐ 1	climb	오르다
	☐ 2	bottom	엉덩이
	☐ 3	clever	영리한
2	☐ 4	astronaut	우주 비행사
3	☐ 5	light	가벼운, (양 · 정도가) 적은
	☐ 6	fall	내리다, 떨어지다
4	☐ 7	pass away	죽다
	☐ 8	remember	기억하다
5	☐ 9	cheerful	명랑한
	☐ 10	friendly	친근한
6	☐ 11	be going to + 동사	~할 것이다, ~할 셈이다
	☐ 12	take	(교통수단, 도로 등을) 타다, 이용하다
	☐ 13	early	빠른, 이른
7	☐ 14	trip	여행
8	☐ 15	look down	의기소침해 보이다
	☐ 16	favorite	가장 좋아하는
	☐ 17	muffler	목도리
9	☐ 18	find	찾다
	☐ 19	for a minute	잠깐
	☐ 20	Here you go.	여기 있어.
10	☐ 21	wear	입다, 착용하다
	☐ 22	timetable	시간표

문제	번호	단어	뜻
11	☐ 23	traffic	교통량, 교통
	☐ 24	heavy	많은, 심한
	☐ 25	turn off	끄다
	☐ 26	on time	제시간에
12	☐ 27	volunteer	자원봉사하다
	☐ 28	mentor	지도하다, 조언하다
14	☐ 29	last	계속되다, 지속되다
	☐ 30	ingredient	재료
	☐ 31	apron	앞치마
15	☐ 32	have ~ ready	~을 준비해 두다
	☐ 33	vegetable	채소
	☐ 34	forget to + 동사	~할 것을 잊다
	☐ 35	refrigerator	냉장고
16	☐ 36	practice	연습하다
	☐ 37	be interested in ~	~에 관심이 있다
	☐ 38	join	가입하다, 함께 하다
17	☐ 39	instead	대신에
18	☐ 40	Come this way.	이쪽으로 오세요.
	☐ 41	explain	설명하다
19	☐ 42	How are you doing?	어떻게 지내니?
	☐ 43	neighborhood	지역, 인근
20	☐ 44	listen to music	음악을 듣다

● 왼쪽 단어장의 뜻이 보이지 않게 반으로 접고, 학습한 단어의 뜻을 아래 빈칸에 적어주세요.

1	light	_____	23 How are you doing?	_____
2	for a minute	_____	24 pass away	_____
3	look down	_____	25 instead	_____
4	listen to music	_____	26 early	_____
5	turn off	_____	27 astronaut	_____
6	be interested in ~	_____	28 vegetable	_____
7	apron	_____	29 fall	_____
8	forget to + 동사	_____	30 find	_____
9	practice	_____	31 volunteer	_____
10	last	_____	32 take	_____
11	bottom	_____	33 mentor	_____
12	wear	_____	34 remember	_____
13	favorite	_____	35 explain	_____
14	trip	_____	36 ingredient	_____
15	neighborhood	_____	37 Here you go.	_____
16	muffler	_____	38 have ~ ready	_____
17	friendly	_____	39 traffic	_____
18	be going to + 동사	_____	40 join	_____
19	climb	_____	41 heavy	_____
20	timetable	_____	42 cheerful	_____
21	clever	_____	43 Come this way.	_____
22	on time	_____	44 refrigerator	_____

02회 중학영어듣기 모의고사

M1(17)_02_US
모두 **미국식 발음(US)**
으로 녹음

M1(17)_02_UK
20문제 중 5문제에 **영국식 발음**
(US+UK)을 포함하여 녹음

정답 및 해석 p. 5

1 다음을 듣고, 'this'가 가리키는 것으로 가장 적절한 것을 고르시오.

① 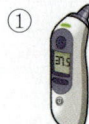　② 　③ 　④ 　⑤

2 대화를 듣고, 여자가 구입할 장화로 가장 적절한 것을 고르시오.

① 　② 　③ 　④ 　⑤

3 다음을 듣고, 현재 제주도의 날씨로 가장 적절한 것을 고르시오.

① 　② 　③ 　④ 　⑤

4 대화를 듣고, 여자가 한 마지막 말의 의도로 적절한 것을 고르시오.

① 허락　　② 거절　　③ 꾸중　　④ 충고　　⑤ 칭찬

5 다음을 듣고, 남자가 현장학습에 대해 언급하지 <u>않은</u> 것을 고르시오.

① 목적지   ② 날짜   ③ 모임 장소
④ 출발 시간   ⑤ 교통 수단

02 회 모의고사

6 대화를 듣고, 두 사람이 만날 시각을 고르시오.

① 5:00 p.m.   ② 5:15 p.m.   ③ 5:30 p.m.   ④ 5:45 p.m.   ⑤ 6:00 p.m.

7 대화를 듣고, 남자의 장래 희망으로 가장 적절한 것을 고르시오.

① 작가   ② 사서   ③ 교사
④ 대학 교수   ⑤ 사회복지사

8 대화를 듣고, 남자의 심정으로 가장 적절한 것을 고르시오.

① worried   ② bored   ③ jealous   ④ shy   ⑤ excited

9 대화를 듣고, 남자가 대화 직후에 할 일로 가장 적절한 것을 고르시오.

① 옷 갈아입기   ② 아침 식사하기   ③ 물 받아 놓기
④ 이불 정리하기   ⑤ 아빠에게 전화하기

10 대화를 듣고, 무엇에 관한 내용인지 가장 적절한 것을 고르시오.

① 학생회장 선거   ② 교내 사생대회   ③ 독서 퀴즈 대회
④ 새 학년 반 배정   ⑤ 도서관 새 이름

11번~20번 문제는 다음 페이지에 ➡

11 대화를 듣고, 두 사람이 함께 이용할 교통수단으로 가장 적절한 것을 고르시오.

① 택시   ② 기차   ③ 고속버스   ④ 비행기   ⑤ 배

12 대화를 듣고, 남자가 시립 공원에 가는 이유로 가장 적절한 것을 고르시오.

① 사진을 찍기 위해서   ② 조깅을 하기 위해서
③ 그림을 그리기 위해서   ④ 개를 산책시키기 위해서
⑤ 곤충을 관찰하기 위해서

13 대화를 듣고, 두 사람이 대화하는 장소로 가장 적절한 곳을 고르시오.

① 식당   ② 박물관   ③ 워터파크
④ 놀이터   ⑤ 백화점

14 대화를 듣고, 두 사람이 찾고 있는 손목시계의 위치로 가장 적절한 것을 고르시오.

15 대화를 듣고, 남자가 여자에게 부탁한 일로 가장 적절한 것을 고르시오.

① 동아리 추천해 주기   ② 피아노 연주하기
③ 경기 보러 와 주기   ④ 동아리 대신 가입해 주기
⑤ 탁구 연습 도와주기

16 대화를 듣고, 남자가 여자에게 제안한 것으로 가장 적절한 것을 고르시오.

① 창문 열기
② 방 청소하기
③ 창문에 커튼 달기
④ 누수 해결 업체 예약하기
⑤ 집주인에게 전화하기

17 대화를 듣고, 여자가 오늘 오후에 한 일로 가장 적절한 것을 고르시오.

① 쿠키 만들기
② 친구들 초대하기
③ 디저트 주문하기
④ 파티 참석하기
⑤ 홍보 전단 만들기

18 대화를 듣고, 여자의 직업으로 가장 적절한 것을 고르시오.

① 배달원
② 커피 농장주
③ 커피 바리스타
④ 식재료 공급업자
⑤ 주방용품 제조업자

[19~20] 대화를 듣고, 여자의 마지막 말에 이어질 남자의 말로 가장 적절한 것을 고르시오.

19 Man: _____

① No, that's all.
② I don't like cheese.
③ It's going to rain today.
④ That's very kind of you.
⑤ Here is my credit card.

20 Man: _____

① Many people were at the party.
② She is always a disappointment.
③ Sorry, I lost my phone yesterday.
④ We are going to be busy tomorrow.
⑤ No, you should talk to him directly.

Dictation Test 02

녹음을 다시
듣으면서 빈칸을
채워주세요

M1(17)_02_D

Dictation(받아쓰기)은 본문을 받아쓰면서 영어듣기의 집중력을 향상시키고 다양한 표현을 정리하기 위한 영어듣기 학습법입니다. **녹음을 다시 듣고, 빈칸에 알맞은 단어를 써 보세요.**
※Dictation의 정답은 듣기 대본의 밑줄 친 부분을 확인하세요.

📖 정답 p. 5

맞은 개수	/
	총115개

2024 영어듣기능력평가 2회 1번 변형

그림정보파악(담화)

1. 다음을 듣고, 'this'가 가리키는 것으로 가장 적절한 것을 고르시오.

①
②
③
④
⑤

01 M: This is small and has buttons with numbers and _____. When you press the buttons, you can _____ math problems quickly. Students and adults use it for _____. What is this?

그림정보파악(대화)

2. 대화를 듣고, 여자가 구입할 장화로 가장 적절한 것을 고르시오.

①
②
③
④
⑤

02 M: What can I do for you?

W: I want to buy _____ _____ for my daughter.

M: How about these ones _____ _____ _____ on them?

W: Hmm. Do you have _____ rain boots?

M: Sure. What about these ones _____ _____ _____ on them? They are shorter.

W: I'll buy those ones. I hope my daughter likes them.

날씨파악-그림

3. 다음을 듣고, 현재 제주도의 날씨로 가장 적절한 것을 고르시오.

①  ②

③  ④

⑤

03 W: Good evening. Here is today's weather report. In Seoul, it's cloudy _____ _____ _____ _____ light rain later tonight. Busan is warm and sunny, perfect for outdoor activities. In Jeju, _____ _____ will be blowing throughout the day. Temperatures will _____ tonight, so bring a light jacket if you go out!

마지막말의도파악

4. 대화를 듣고, 여자가 한 마지막 말의 의도로 적절한 것을 고르시오.
① 허락 ② 거절
③ 꾸중 ④ 충고
⑤ 칭찬

04 W: So, did you do what I said?

M: Yes, Mom. I just _____ my homework.

W: Good. _____ _____ your piano practice?

M: I finished that, too.

W: Great job. Always do what you _____ _____ do first.

M: OK, Mom. May I go out and play with Michael now?

W: Of course, you may.

다음 페이지에 계속 ➡

5. 다음을 듣고, 남자가 현장학습에 대해 언급하지 **않은** 것을 고르시오.
   ① 목적지   ② 날짜
   ③ 모임 장소   ④ 출발 시간
   ⑤ 교통 수단

05 M: Hello, students. Let me remind you about our upcoming _____ _____ to the Museum of Natural History. Don't forget that we are going on February 28th. We will _____ _____ 9:50 in the morning. A bus will _____ _____ to the museum. I hope you're excited about the trip!

6. 대화를 듣고, 두 사람이 만날 시각을 고르시오.
   ① 5:00 p.m.   ② 5:15 p.m.
   ③ 5:30 p.m.   ④ 5:45 p.m.
   ⑤ 6:00 p.m.

06 M: Hey, Jiyoung! Do you want to go to Burger Bites tonight?

W: Sure! I'm _____ a burger!

M: Same here.

W: What time?

M: They start _____ at 5 p.m. How about 5:30 p.m.?

W: I have piano practice until 5:15. Can we _____ _____ 6 p.m.?

M: Sounds good. See you at Burger Bites.

장래희망추론

7. 대화를 듣고, 남자의 장래 희망으로 가장 적절한 것을 고르시오.
   ① 작가 ② 사서
   ③ 교사 ④ 대학 교수
   ⑤ 사회복지사

07

W: Daniel, what's on your mind?

M: I'm thinking about what job to do in the future.

W: Any ideas?

M: I like how teachers help kids learn.

W: Teachers do make a big _____.

M: Exactly. I want to be like my _____ _____ who helped me learn.

W: That's a great _____!

심정추론

8. 대화를 듣고, 남자의 심정으로 가장 적절한 것을 고르시오.
   ① worried ② bored
   ③ jealous ④ shy
   ⑤ excited

08

M: Kelly, _____ _____! I'm going to Japan during summer vacation.

W: Sounds great! What are you going to do there?

M: I'm going to Disney World. _____ _____ _____!

W: Really? I'm so _____ _____ you!

M: I'm really looking forward to my trip.

다음 페이지에 계속 ➡

9. 대화를 듣고, 남자가 대화 직후에 할 일로 가장 적절한 것을 고르시오.
   ① 옷 갈아입기
   ② 아침 식사하기
   ③ 물 받아 놓기
   ④ 이불 정리하기
   ⑤ 아빠에게 전화하기

09

M: Good morning, Mom. I woke up late.

W: Good morning, Steve. How about _____ _____ for breakfast?

M: Now? What's up?

W: The water supply _____ _____.

M: On Sunday?

W: Just for a couple of hours. Can you _____ _____ _____ before we go?

M: Sure. I'll do it right now.

10. 대화를 듣고, 무엇에 관한 내용인지 가장 적절한 것을 고르시오.
   ① 학생회장 선거
   ② 교내 사생대회
   ③ 독서 퀴즈 대회
   ④ 새 학년 반 배정
   ⑤ 도서관 새 이름

10

W: Have you checked the new posting on the school website?

M: You mean the one about the new name for the school library?

W: Yes. There were three options. Which one _____ _____ _____?

M: I chose number two, 'Forest of _____.' I like the meaning of the name.

W: Me, too! The name is also _____.

M: You're right.

特정정보파악(교통수단)

11. 대화를 듣고, 두 사람이 함께 이용할 교통수단으로 가장 적절한 것을 고르시오.
① 택시 ② 기차
③ 고속버스 ④ 비행기
⑤ 배

11 W: John, I _____ _____ _____ from the airline. We cannot _____ today.

M: Why? Bad weather?

W: Yes. Should we stay here one more night?

M: Well, there's an _____ _____. If we leave now, we can be back tonight.

W: Let's hurry, then.

이유파악

2025 영어듣기능력평가 1회 12번 변형

12. 대화를 듣고, 남자가 시립 공원에 가는 이유로 가장 적절한 것을 고르시오.
① 사진을 찍기 위해서
② 조깅을 하기 위해서
③ 그림을 그리기 위해서
④ 개를 산책시키기 위해서
⑤ 곤충을 관찰하기 위해서

12 W: Hey, Daniel. Where are you going?

M: Hi, Mia. I'm going to the city park.

W: Oh, are you going to _____ there?

M: No, I'm meeting my science group there. We're _____ _____ for our project.

W: That's cool! I hope you find something interesting.

다음 페이지에 계속 ➡

13. 대화를 듣고, 두 사람이 대화하는 장소로 가장 적절한 곳을 고르시오.

① 식당
② 박물관
③ 워터파크
④ 놀이터
⑤ 백화점

13

W: Dad! I'm so excited right now.

M: _____ _____, honey. Don't run near the water.

W: Okay. Can we go on that water slide?

M: Of course, but let's do some warm-ups before we go in the water.

W: Sure. I _____ _____ _____ try it out!

M: I'm glad that you like it here.

14. 대화를 듣고, 두 사람이 찾고 있는 손목 시계의 위치로 가장 적절한 것을 고르시오.

14

W: Kevin, can you help me find my watch?

M: Sure. Where did you last see it?

W: I think I saw it _____ _____ _____, but it's not there now.

M: It's not on the desk, either. Oh, look! Isn't that your watch _____ _____ _____?

W: Ah, _____ _____ _____! I forgot that I had put it there.

15. 대화를 듣고, 남자가 여자에게 부탁한 일로 가장 적절한 것을 고르시오.

① 동아리 추천해 주기
② 피아노 연주하기
③ 경기 보러 와 주기
④ 동아리 대신 가입해 주기
⑤ 탁구 연습 도와주기

15

M: Maya, did you join any of the school clubs?

W: I'm on my way to join one now. Today is the _____, remember?

M: Yes, but I'm late for my piano lesson, so I _____ _____ _____.

W: You want me to _____ _____ _____?

M: Yes. Can you please sign me up for the table tennis club?

W: Sure. See you later!

제안파악

16. 대화를 듣고, 남자가 여자에게 제안한 것으로 가장 적절한 것을 고르시오.

① 창문 열기
② 방 청소하기
③ 창문에 커튼 달기
④ 누수 해결 업체 예약하기
⑤ 집주인에게 전화하기

16

M: Tanya, are you okay?

W: No. The rain _____ _____ my room last night. I was up all night dealing with it.

M: Oh, no. Did you forget to close the windows?

W: The windows were all closed. The water still came in, _____.

M: _____ _____ _____ _____ the owner of the house?

W: Yeah, I should ask the owner to _____ the leaky windows.

다음 페이지에 계속 ➡

17. 대화를 듣고, 여자가 오늘 오후에 한 일로 가장 적절한 것을 고르시오.
  ① 쿠키 만들기
  ② 친구들 초대하기
  ③ 디저트 주문하기
  ④ 파티 참석하기
  ⑤ 홍보 전단 만들기

17 (Cellphone rings.)

M: Hey, Yejin!

W: Hello, Daniel. Are you coming to the _____ bake sale this Saturday?

M: Of course. Do you need me to bring anything?

W: No need. I baked all the _____ this afternoon.

M: That's wonderful! What did you make?

W: I made some cookies and brownies.

M: Sounds _____! Then, I'll come with many friends.

18. 대화를 듣고, 여자의 직업으로 가장 적절한 것을 고르시오.
  ① 배달원
  ② 커피 농장주
  ③ 커피 바리스타
  ④ 식재료 공급업자
  ⑤ 주방용품 제조업자

18 (Telephone rings.)

W: Green Beans.

M: Ms. Carter, I'm _____ your order now. 40kg of coffee beans, right?

W: That's right. I'm _____ _____ _____ this week.

M: Well, your coffee is the best in town.

W: It's thanks to your beans. I'll have a _____ _____ for you.

M: That's very kind. I'll be there in an hour.

19. 대화를 듣고, 여자의 마지막 말에 이어질 남자의 말로 가장 적절한 것을 고르시오.

Man: _____

① No, that's all.
② I don't like cheese.
③ It's going to rain today.
④ That's very kind of you.
⑤ Here is my credit card.

19

W: What would you like to order?

M: Can I have a cheese and tomato sandwich, please?

W: Sure. _____ _____ _____ white bread or brown bread?

M: Brown, please.

W: Is it for here or _____ _____?

M: To go. And I'll also have a bottle of water.

W: OK. It's 7 dollars. How would you like to _____?

M: Here is my credit card.

20. 대화를 듣고, 여자의 마지막 말에 이어질 남자의 말로 가장 적절한 것을 고르시오.

Man: _____

① Many people were at the party.
② She is always a disappointment.
③ Sorry, I lost my phone yesterday.
④ We are going to be busy tomorrow.
⑤ No, you should talk to him directly.

20

M: Laura, where were you yesterday? I didn't see you at Matthew's birthday party.

W: Oh, no! Was that yesterday? I thought it was today.

M: Matthew is _____ because you didn't come.

W: I completely forgot. How can I _____ _____ _____ it?

M: Well, you should _____ first.

W: Should I send him a text message?

M: No, you should talk to him directly.

Words & Expressions Review 02

● 다음 단어를 암기하세요.

문제	번호	단어	뜻
1	☐ 1	symbol	부호, 기호
	☐ 2	press	누르다
	☐ 3	solve	(문제 등을) 풀다, 해결하다
	☐ 4	calculation	계산
2	☐ 5	rain boots	장화
3	☐ 6	outdoor	야외의
	☐ 7	blow	(바람이) 불다
	☐ 8	throughout	~동안 쭉
	☐ 9	temperature	온도, 기온
4	☐ 10	finish	끝내다, 마무리 짓다
	☐ 11	practice	연습
	☐ 12	upcoming	곧 있을, 다가오는
5	☐ 13	field trip	현장학습, 견학
	☐ 14	museum	박물관
7	☐ 15	make a difference	변화를 일으키다, 차이를 낳다, 도움이 되다
	☐ 16	goal	목표
8	☐ 17	jealous of ~	~가 부러운, ~를 질투하는
	☐ 18	look forward to ~	~이 기대되다
9	☐ 19	wake up	일어나다
	☐ 20	go out	나가다, 외출하다
	☐ 21	supply	공급
10	☐ 22	forest	숲, 삼림

문제	번호	단어	뜻
10	☐ 23	catchy	기억하기 쉬운
11	☐ 24	get a call	전화를 받다
	☐ 25	express bus	고속버스
12	☐ 26	observe	관찰하다
	☐ 27	insect	곤충
13	☐ 28	calm down	진정하다
	☐ 29	can't wait to + 동사	몹시 ~하고 싶다
14	☐ 30	bookshelf	책장
15	☐ 31	on one's way	~하는 중에
	☐ 32	deadline	마감, 기한
	☐ 33	need a favor	부탁이 있다
	☐ 34	sign ~ up	~을 등록하다
	☐ 35	leak	(액체·기체 등이) 새다
16	☐ 36	be up all night	밤을 새다
	☐ 37	deal with ~	~을 처리하다, 다루다
	☐ 38	repair	수리하다
17	☐ 39	charity	자선
18	☐ 40	customer	손님, 고객
	☐ 41	thanks to ~	~ 덕분에, ~ 때문에
19	☐ 42	order	주문하다
20	☐ 43	make up for ~	~을 만회하다
	☐ 44	apologize	사과하다

● 왼쪽 단어장의 뜻이 보이지 않게 반으로 접고, 학습한 단어의 뜻을 아래 빈칸에 적어주세요.

1	temperature		23	deal with ~
2	customer		24	make up for ~
3	need a favor		25	sign ~ up
4	blow		26	look forward to ~
5	observe		27	field trip
6	calculation		28	make a difference
7	can't wait to + 동사		29	bookshelf
8	leak		30	get a call
9	express bus		31	jealous of ~
10	practice		32	thanks to ~
11	insect		33	charity
12	be up all night		34	supply
13	forest		35	solve
14	symbol		36	deadline
15	repair		37	go out
16	rain boots		38	throughout
17	on one's way		39	catchy
18	upcoming		40	order
19	calm down		41	press
20	goal		42	outdoor
21	museum		43	wake up
22	finish		44	apologize

03회 중학영어듣기 모의고사

모두 **미국식 발음(US)** 으로 녹음

20문제 중 5문제에 **영국식 발음 (US+UK)**을 포함하여 녹음

정답 및 해석 p. 9

1 다음을 듣고, 'I'가 무엇인지 가장 적절한 것을 고르시오.

①  ②  ③  ④  ⑤

2 대화를 듣고, 여자가 구입할 망토 타월로 가장 적절한 것을 고르시오.

① 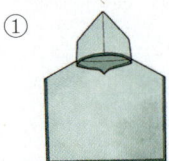 ②  ③  ④  ⑤

3 다음을 듣고, 내일의 날씨로 가장 적절한 것을 고르시오.

①  ②  ③  ④  ⑤

4 대화를 듣고, 남자의 마지막 말의 의도로 가장 적절한 것을 고르시오.

① 승낙   ② 거절   ③ 제안   ④ 칭찬   ⑤ 불평

5 다음을 듣고, 남자가 과학 캠프에 대해 언급하지 <u>않은</u> 것을 고르시오.

① 날짜　　　　　　② 장소　　　　　　③ 캠프 주제
④ 참가비　　　　　⑤ 신청 방법

6 대화를 듣고, 두 사람이 만날 시각을 고르시오.

① 3:00 p.m.　② 4:00 p.m.　③ 5:00 p.m.　④ 6:00 p.m.　⑤ 7:00 p.m.

7 대화를 듣고, 남자의 장래 희망으로 가장 적절한 것을 고르시오.

① 작가　　　② 배우　　　③ 아나운서　　　④ 영화감독　　　⑤ 만화가

8 대화를 듣고, 여자의 심정으로 가장 적절한 것을 고르시오.

① 난감함　　　② 행복함　　　③ 화남　　　④ 그리워함　　　⑤ 피곤함

9 대화를 듣고, 여자가 대화 직후에 할 일로 가장 적절한 것을 고르시오.

① SNS 팔로우하기　　② 셀카 찍는 법 알려주기　　③ 사진 편집 앱 보여주기
④ 핸드폰 수리하러 가기　　⑤ 새로운 메신저 가입하기

10 대화를 듣고, 무엇에 관한 내용인지 가장 적절한 것을 고르시오.

① 릴레이 달리기 요령　　② 달리기 대회 일정　　③ 응원 연습 계획
④ 경기 순서 결정　　　　⑤ 대회 상품 준비

11번~20번 문제는 다음 페이지에 ➡

11 대화를 듣고, 남자가 이용할 교통수단으로 가장 적절한 것을 고르시오.

① 자전거　　② 택시　　③ 버스　　④ 배　　⑤ 기차

12 대화를 듣고, 여자에게 얼음이 필요한 이유로 가장 적절한 것을 고르시오.

① 열을 내리기 위해서　　　　　　② 운동 후 찜질하기 위해서
③ 아이스박스에 넣기 위해서　　　④ 발목 통증을 줄이기 위해서
⑤ 과일 스무디를 만들기 위해서

13 대화를 듣고, 두 사람이 대화하는 장소로 가장 적절한 곳을 고르시오.

① 미용실　　② 지하철역　　③ 공항　　④ 소방서　　⑤ 백화점

14 Family Drawing Class에 관한 다음 내용을 듣고, 표에서 일치하지 <u>않는</u> 것을 고르시오.

Family Drawing Class		
①	일시	this Sunday, 1 p.m.
②	행사 내용	draw a picture of their family, and then their drawing will be printed on a T-shirt
③	소요 시간	2 hours
④	참가비	free
⑤	접수 방법	sign up online

15 대화를 듣고, 여자가 남자에게 부탁한 일로 가장 적절한 것을 고르시오.

① 모자 빌려주기　　　② 선크림 가져오기　　　③ 운동화 주문하기
④ 도시락 준비하기　　⑤ 점심 함께 먹기

16 대화를 듣고, 남자가 여자에게 제안한 것으로 가장 적절한 것을 고르시오.

① 우산 빌려주기　　② 창문 닫아주기　　③ 안부 전화하기
④ 하교 같이 하기　　⑤ 날씨 알려주기

17 대화를 듣고, 남자가 휴일에 한 일로 가장 적절한 것을 고르시오.

① 거실 청소하기　　② 소방서 견학하기　　③ 영화 감상문 쓰기
④ 좋아하는 영화 보기　　⑤ 여행 계획 짜기

18 대화를 듣고, 남자의 직업으로 가장 적절한 것을 고르시오.

① 사진작가　　② 전자제품 수리기사　　③ 화가
④ 건축가　　⑤ 웹 디자이너

[19~20] 대화를 듣고, 남자의 마지막 말에 이어질 여자의 말로 가장 적절한 것을 고르시오.

19 Woman: _____

① It's Saturday.　　② I got 100 points.
③ That's a good idea.　　④ He's 70 years old.
⑤ He's older than my grandmother.

20 Woman: _____

① I'm glad to help you.
② They don't have my size.
③ Don't worry, I can do it myself.
④ I'd like a simple and smart one.
⑤ I want to be a violinist in the future.

Dictation Test 03

전국 15개 시·도 교육청 공동주관 및 서울시 연합 내신 중학영어듣기 능력평가 대비

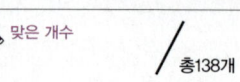

M1(17)_03_D

Dictation(받아쓰기)은 본문을 받아쓰면서 영어듣기의 집중력을 향상시키고 다양한 표현을 정리하기 위한 영어듣기 학습법입니다. 녹음을 다시 듣고, 빈칸에 알맞은 단어를 써 보세요.
※Dictation의 정답은 듣기 대본의 밑줄 친 부분을 확인하세요.

정답 p. 9

맞은 개수 / 총138개

그림정보파악(담화)

1. 다음을 듣고, 'I'가 무엇인지 가장 적절한 것을 고르시오.

①
②
③
④
⑤

01 M: I have four legs and a long tail. I have yellow fur with small _____ _____. I eat mostly meat. I can _____ _____ than any other _____ animal. What am I?

그림정보파악(대화)

2024 영어듣기능력평가 1회 2번 변형

2. 대화를 듣고, 여자가 구입할 망토 타월로 가장 적절한 것을 고르시오.

①
②
③
④
⑤

02 M: How can I help you?

W: I'm _____ _____ a poncho towel for my 5-year-old son.

M: How about this one with sharks on it?

W: It's nice, but he really _____ _____ these days.

M: What about this one with little dinosaurs on it? It has a _____, too.

W: I love it. I'll buy that one.

3. 다음을 듣고, 내일의 날씨로 가장 적절한
   것을 고르시오.

①  ②

③  ④

⑤

03 M: Good morning. This is the weather forecast. We can enjoy the beautiful clear sky now, but it will be _____ in the afternoon. Tomorrow, we will have _____ _____ _____ of this winter. So, _____ _____ warm clothes and gloves.

4. 대화를 듣고, 남자의 마지막 말의 의도로
   가장 적절한 것을 고르시오.

① 승낙   ② 거절
③ 제안   ④ 칭찬
⑤ 불평

04 W: Are you OK, Mike? You don't look very well.

M: Mom, I stayed home all day and I feel _____.

W: OK. How about doing some exercise?

M: I don't _____ _____ it.

W: Then, shall we go outside and _____ _____ _____?

M: Sure. I think getting some fresh air will help.

다음 페이지에 계속 ➡

5. 다음을 듣고, 남자가 과학 캠프에 대해 언급하지 <u>않은</u> 것을 고르시오.

① 날짜   ② 장소
③ 캠프 주제   ④ 참가비
⑤ 신청 방법

05 M: Hello, students. This is your science teacher, Bill Jones. Let me tell you about the _____ science camp. It'll be from January 20 to 22. It'll _____ _____ at the National Science Museum. The topic for this camp is smart cities, which are cities that use various ways to _____ _____. The fee is 100,000 won. This will be a great chance for students to learn about smart cities.

---

6. 대화를 듣고, 두 사람이 만날 시각을 고르시오.

① 3:00 p.m.   ② 4:00 p.m.
③ 5:00 p.m.   ④ 6:00 p.m.
⑤ 7:00 p.m.

06 M: Lily, would you like to help me buy Kenny's birthday present?

W: Sure. Is this afternoon OK?

M: Yes. _____ _____ _____ at 3 at the mall?

W: How about 4? I _____ _____ _____ my homework.

M: Oh, I forgot. I have to do my homework, too. Let's _____ _____ _____.

W: All right!

7. 대화를 듣고, 남자의 장래 희망으로 가장 적절한 것을 고르시오.

① 작가　　　② 배우
③ 아나운서　④ 영화감독
⑤ 만화가

07

M: How did you like the movie?

W: I thought it was awesome. The _____ _____ was great.

M: Wasn't he? He was very _____ in that role.

W: You are really into him. Have you seen any of his other movies?

M: I've seen most of them. I want to be _____ _____ _____ _____.

W: Really? I believe you will be _____ _____.

M: Thanks. That's very kind of you.

8. 대화를 듣고, 여자의 심정으로 가장 적절한 것을 고르시오.

① 난감함　　② 행복함
③ 화남　　　④ 그리워함
⑤ 피곤함

08

M: Hey, Emily.

W: Hi, Huey. Do you know that Ebony _____ last week?

M: What? I didn't know that.

W: She moved to San Francisco.

M: Oh, I am so sorry to hear that. Ebony is your _____ _____, right?

W: Yes. I _____ _____ very much.

다음 페이지에 계속 ➡

9. 대화를 듣고, 여자가 대화 직후에 할 일로 가장 적절한 것을 고르시오.

① SNS 팔로우하기
② 셀카 찍는 법 알려주기
③ 사진 편집 앱 보여주기
④ 핸드폰 수리하러 가기
⑤ 새로운 메신저 가입하기

09

M: Hey, Linda! I like your profile picture.

W: You mean the one on SNS? Thanks, I took it yesterday.

M: It's a nice photo. You look _____ _____ _____, though.

W: That's because I used a special app _____ _____ _____.

M: Really? I didn't notice. _____ _____ did you use?

W: Here, I'll show it to you. It's really handy.

🇺🇸🇬🇧

2025 영어듣기능력평가 1회 10번 변형

10. 대화를 듣고, 무엇에 관한 내용인지 가장 적절한 것을 고르시오.

① 릴레이 달리기 요령
② 달리기 대회 일정
③ 응원 연습 계획
④ 경기 순서 결정
⑤ 대회 상품 준비

10

W: Mr. Choi, we really want to _____ the relay race at the sports day.

M: That's great! Let me give you some _____.

W: Yes, please! What's the most important thing?

M: You need to pass the baton smoothly.

W: How can we do that?

M: Practice _____ _____ _____ while running at full speed.

W: Should we think about the order of the runners, too?

M: Absolutely. Put your fastest runner at the end to _____ _____!

11. 대화를 듣고, 남자가 이용할 교통수단으로 가장 적절한 것을 고르시오.

① 자전거   ② 택시
③ 버스   ④ 배
⑤ 기차

11

W: How are you enjoying your stay?

M: I'm enjoying it very much. The beach here is really nice.

W: There's another nice beach a few kilometers away called Higgs Beach.

M: Really? How do I _____ _____?

W: There's a bus, but I can _____ _____ _____ _____ if you want.

M: The bus will be fine. Thank you.

12. 대화를 듣고, 여자에게 얼음이 필요한 이유로 가장 적절한 것을 고르시오.

① 열을 내리기 위해서
② 운동 후 찜질하기 위해서
③ 아이스박스에 넣기 위해서
④ 발목 통증을 줄이기 위해서
⑤ 과일 스무디를 만들기 위해서

12

M: Jina, do you need anything from the supermarket?

W: Yes, honey. I need a bag of _____.

M: Okay. What do you need it for?

W: I _____ _____ _____ this morning, so I want to use it to _____ _____ _____.

M: I see. I'll make sure to buy it.

W: Thank you.

다음 페이지에 계속 ➡

13. 대화를 듣고, 두 사람이 대화하는 장소로 가장 적절한 곳을 고르시오.

① 미용실　　② 지하철역
③ 공항　　　④ 소방서
⑤ 백화점

13

M: Can I see your passport, please?

W: _____ _____ _____.

M: Why are you visiting Chicago?

W: I have a _____ _____ here.

M: How long will you stay?

W: For three days.

M: OK. _____ _____ _____ in Chicago.

14. Family Drawing Class에 관한 다음 내용을 듣고, 표에서 일치하지 <u>않는</u> 것을 고르시오.

Family Drawing Class		
①	일시	this Sunday, 1 p.m.
②	행사 내용	draw a picture of their family, and then their drawing will be printed on a T-shirt
③	소요 시간	2 hours
④	참가비	free
⑤	접수 방법	sign up online

14

W: Hello, Urban Heights Mall shoppers! Join our Family Drawing Class this Sunday at 1 p.m. Kids will draw a picture of their family, and then their drawing will be _____ on a T-shirt for them to keep. The class lasts 2 hours. You can join _____ _____. Spots are first come, first served. _____ _____, visit the information desk on the first floor. Thanks!

15. 대화를 듣고, 여자가 남자에게 부탁한 일로 가장 적절한 것을 고르시오.

① 모자 빌려주기
② 선크림 가져오기
③ 운동화 주문하기
④ 도시락 준비하기
⑤ 점심 함께 먹기

15 [Cellphone rings.]

M: Hi, Jessica.

W: Hey, Ha-jun. Today we're going on a school _____ _____ to the forest.

M: Yes! I've got my lunchbox and trainers ready.

W: I'll bring sun cream. But I don't have a hat.

M: I have _____ _____.

W: Can I borrow one? It's so sunny outside.

M: Sure. I'll _____ _____ _____ to school.

16. 대화를 듣고, 남자가 여자에게 제안한 것으로 가장 적절한 것을 고르시오.

① 우산 빌려주기
② 창문 닫아주기
③ 안부 전화하기
④ 하교 같이 하기
⑤ 날씨 알려주기

16 M: Hey, look out the window. It's raining!

W: That's true. Did you bring _____ _____?

M: No. My mom is picking me up after school. Did you?

W: No, I totally _____.

M: Then, why don't you let my mom _____ _____ _____, as well?

W: Thanks. That's very kind of you.

다음 페이지에 계속 ➡

17. 대화를 듣고, 남자가 휴일에 한 일로 가장 적절한 것을 고르시오.

① 거실 청소하기
② 소방서 견학하기
③ 영화 감상문 쓰기
④ 좋아하는 영화 보기
⑤ 여행 계획 짜기

17

M: Sarah, how was your holiday?

W: Great. I _____ _____ _____ watching my favorite movies. How about you?

M: I went on a tour of _____ _____ _____.

W: Sounds interesting. Did you learn anything?

M: Yes. The firemen _____ _____ what to do in a fire emergency.

18. 대화를 듣고, 남자의 직업으로 가장 적절한 것을 고르시오.

① 사진작가
② 전자제품 수리기사
③ 화가
④ 건축가
⑤ 웹 디자이너

18

W: Hi, Mike. You _____ _____.

M: I had to work all night.

W: Are you still _____ _____ the web page?

M: Yes. They liked my design, but I needed to _____ _____ _____.

W: What kind of changes?

M: _____ _____. Now the page is more blue-based.

19. 대화를 듣고, 남자의 마지막 말에 이어질 여자의 말로 가장 적절한 것을 고르시오.

Woman: _____

① It's Saturday.
② I got 100 points.
③ That's a good idea.
④ He's 70 years old.
⑤ He's older than my grandmother.

19
W: Next Friday is my grandfather's birthday.

M: Did you _____ _____ for him?

W: Not yet. Do you have any recommendations?

M: How about _____ _____ a birthday cake?

W: I don't think he likes sweets.

M: How about a hat, then? Your grandfather _____ _____ _____ all the time.

W: That's a good idea.

20. 대화를 듣고, 남자의 마지막 말에 이어질 여자의 말로 가장 적절한 것을 고르시오.

Woman: _____

① I'm glad to help you.
② They don't have my size.
③ Don't worry, I can do it myself.
④ I'd like a simple and smart one.
⑤ I want to be a violinist in the future.

20
W: Andy, I heard you're interested in fashion.

M: I am. I want to be a fashion designer in the future.

W: Then, can you help me _____ _____ _____?

M: Sure. What do you _____ _____ _____?

W: I have to wear a dress for my violin concert.

M: Okay. _____ _____ _____ _____ do you want?

W: I'd like a simple and smart one.

Words & Expressions Review 03

● 다음 단어를 암기하세요.

문제	번호	단어	뜻
1	1	tail	꼬리
	2	fur	털
	3	spot	반점
	4	mostly	주로, 대부분
	5	land animal	육지 동물
2	6	hood	모자
3	7	cloudy	흐린
	8	put on	입다, 끼다
4	9	bored	지루해하는
	10	exercise	운동
	11	feel like ~	~하고 싶다
	12	take a walk	산책하다
5	13	upcoming	다가오는
	14	take place	개최되다, 일어나다
	15	various	다양한
7	16	lead actor	주연 배우
	17	believable	그럴듯한
	18	be into ~	~에 빠져있다
	19	one day	언젠가
8	20	best friend	가장 친한 친구
	21	miss	그리워하다
9	22	edit	편집하다

문제	번호	단어	뜻
9	23	notice	알아채다
	24	handy	편리한
10	25	tip	조언
	26	order	순서
11	27	a few	몇, 조금
	28	call	부르다, ~에게 전화하다
12	29	sprain	삐다, 접지르다
	30	ankle	발목
13	31	reduce	줄이다
	32	passport	여권
14	33	print	인쇄하다
	34	keep	(자기 것으로) 갖다, 보유하다
15	35	field trip	현장학습
	36	trainer	운동화
16	37	umbrella	우산
	38	let	~하게 하다
17	39	relax	쉬다, 휴식을 취하다
	40	fire station	소방서
18	41	all night	밤새
19	42	recommendation	추천
20	43	choose	고르다
	44	need	필요로 하다

M1(17)_W_03

●왼쪽 단어장의 뜻이 보이지 않게 반으로 접고, 학습한 단어의 뜻을 아래 빈칸에 적어주세요.

1	passport		23	one day
2	take place		24	notice
3	need		25	various
4	ankle		26	exercise
5	print		27	a few
6	take a walk		28	miss
7	handy		29	feel like ~
8	umbrella		30	edit
9	trainer		31	put on
10	sprain		32	keep
11	believable		33	lead actor
12	call		34	upcoming
13	order		35	tip
14	fire station		36	best friend
15	spot		37	tail
16	bored		38	fur
17	land animal		39	be into ~
18	cloudy		40	reduce
19	hood		41	relax
20	recommendation		42	let
21	mostly		43	all night
22	choose		44	field trip

03 회 단어

전국 15개 시·도 교육청 공동주관 및 서울시 연합 내신

04회 중학영어듣기 모의고사

M1(17)_04_US
모두 **미국식 발음(US)**
으로 녹음

M1(17)_04_UK
20문제 중 5문제에 **영국식 발음**
(US+UK)을 포함하여 녹음

📖 정답 및 해석 p. 13

1 다음을 듣고, 'I'가 무엇인지 가장 적절한 것을 고르시오.

①  ②  ③  ④  ⑤

2 대화를 듣고, 남자가 구입할 케이크로 가장 적절한 것을 고르시오.

①  ② 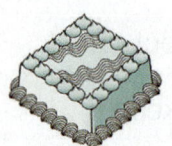 ③  ④  ⑤

3 다음을 듣고, 파리의 오늘 저녁 날씨로 가장 적절한 것을 고르시오.

①  ②  ③  ④  ⑤

4 대화를 듣고, 남자가 한 마지막 말의 의도로 가장 적절한 것을 고르시오.

① 거절 ② 확인 ③ 승낙 ④ 제안 ⑤ 격려

5 다음을 듣고, 여자가 세계 음식 축제에 대해 언급하지 <u>않은</u> 것을 고르시오.

① 날짜   ② 특별행사   ③ 입장료
④ 음식 가격   ⑤ 장소

6 대화를 듣고, 두 사람이 만날 시각을 고르시오.

① 4:00 p.m.   ② 4:30 p.m.   ③ 5:00 p.m.   ④ 5:30 p.m.   ⑤ 6:00 p.m.

7 대화를 듣고, 남자의 장래 희망으로 가장 적절한 것을 고르시오.

① 가수   ② 디자이너   ③ 화가   ④ 외교관   ⑤ 건축가

8 대화를 듣고, 남자의 심정으로 가장 적절한 것을 고르시오.

① shy   ② upset   ③ proud
④ happy   ⑤ thankful

9 대화를 듣고, 여자가 대화 직후에 할 일로 가장 적절한 것을 고르시오.

① 기념품 가게 가기   ② 롤러코스터 타기   ③ 열쇠고리 만들기
④ 음료 사러 가기   ⑤ 사진 인화하기

10 대화를 듣고, 무엇에 관한 내용인지 가장 적절한 것을 고르시오.

① 봉사활동 안내   ② 방과 후 수업   ③ 교내 체육 대회
④ 동아리 활동   ⑤ 진로 탐색 교육

11번~20번 문제는 다음 페이지에 ➡

11 대화를 듣고, 두 사람이 함께 이동할 방법으로 가장 적절한 것을 고르시오.

① 자전거　　　② 지하철　　　③ 택시　　　④ 버스　　　⑤ 자동차

12 대화를 듣고, 남자가 쇼핑몰에 가는 이유로 가장 적절한 것을 고르시오.

① 옷을 사려고　　　　　　　　② 물건을 교환하려고
③ 부모님과 식사하려고　　　　④ 친구와 영화를 보려고
⑤ 게임 대회에 참가하려고

13 대화를 듣고, 두 사람이 대화하는 장소로 가장 적절한 곳을 고르시오.

① 학교　　　　　　　② 버스 정류장　　　　　③ 양로원
④ 영화관　　　　　　⑤ 주민 센터

14 대화를 듣고, 아이스크림 매장의 위치로 가장 알맞은 곳을 고르시오.

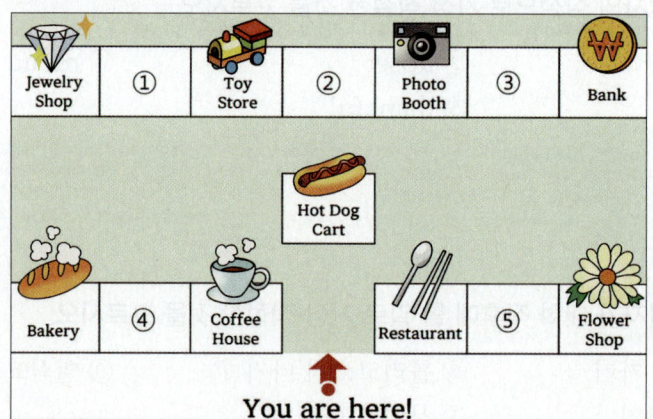

15 대화를 듣고, 여자가 남자에게 부탁한 일로 가장 적절한 것을 고르시오.

① 방 청소하기　　　　　　② 책 반납하기
③ 숙제 끝내기　　　　　　④ 음악 교재 챙기기
⑤ 바이올린 연습하기

16

대화를 듣고, 여자가 남자에게 제안한 것으로 가장 적절한 것을 고르시오.

① 파티 열기　　　　② 쿠키 만들기　　　　③ 선물 사기
④ 편지 쓰기　　　　⑤ 꽃다발 준비하기

17

대화를 듣고, 여자가 방학에 한 일로 가장 적절한 것을 고르시오.

① 악기 배우기　　　　② 수족관 관람하기　　　　③ 반려동물 키우기
④ 컴퓨터 게임하기　　　　⑤ 스쿠버 다이빙 배우기

18

대화를 듣고, 남자의 직업으로 가장 적절한 것을 고르시오.

① 변호사　　　　② 경찰관　　　　③ 농구 선수
④ 택배 배달원　　　　⑤ 핸드폰 수리 기사

[19~20] 대화를 듣고, 여자의 마지막 말에 이어질 남자의 말로 가장 적절한 것을 고르시오.

19

Man: _____

① Sure! I love salad.
② Okay, I'll try this once.
③ No, I didn't like the restaurant.
④ Yes, I'll have some Chinese food.
⑤ Thanks, but I'll pay for lunch today.

20

Man: _____

① Let's meet at 5.　　　　② I'll have a sandwich.
③ I can't walk anymore.　　　　④ I think I lost my ticket.
⑤ The map says it's on the third floor.

Dictation(받아쓰기)은 본문을 받아쓰면서 영어듣기의 집중력을 향상시키고 다양한 표현을 정리하기 위한 영어듣기 학습법입니다. **녹음을 다시 듣고, 빈칸에 알맞은 단어를 써 보세요.**
※Dictation의 정답은 듣기 대본의 밑줄 친 부분을 확인하세요.

📖 정답 p. 13

맞은 개수 / 총143개

고난도 그림정보파악(담화)

1. 다음을 듣고, 'I'가 무엇인지 가장 적절한 것을 고르시오.

①  ②

③  ④

⑤

01
W: I live in _____ _____ _____ places. You may find me on rainy days. I'm small and _____ _____. I have a soft body so I _____ _____ _____ on my back to protect my body. What am I?

그림정보파악(대화)

2. 대화를 듣고, 남자가 구입할 케이크로 가장 적절한 것을 고르시오.

① ② ③ ④ ⑤

02
M: Hi, I am looking for a cake for my friend's birthday party.

W: We have square-shaped and round-shaped cakes.

M: I would like a _____ one, please.

W: Would you like a cake _____ _____ on top or just a _____ _____? Oh, we have cakes with chocolate on top, too.

M: I will take the one with strawberries on top.

---

3. 다음을 듣고, 파리의 오늘 저녁 날씨로 가장 적절한 것을 고르시오.

①
②
③
④
⑤

03 W: Good morning, Paris. This is your daily weather forecast. Yesterday, it was _____ all day. It's a little _____ this morning. This evening, it will start to _____. Tomorrow is also going to be a rainy day, so _____ _____ to bring your umbrella.

4. 대화를 듣고, 남자가 한 마지막 말의 의도로 가장 적절한 것을 고르시오.
① 거절   ② 확인
③ 승낙   ④ 제안
⑤ 격려

04 W: Hajun, can you help me with my homework?

M: OK. What is it?

W: I have to go to the science museum and _____ _____ _____.

M: That sounds fun. I love science.

W: I'm going on Friday. Can you _____ _____ _____?

M: I'm _____ _____. I have a swimming lesson on Friday.

다음 페이지에 계속 ➡

04
회
딕
테
이
션

5. 다음을 듣고, 여자가 세계 음식 축제에 대해 언급하지 <u>않은</u> 것을 고르시오.

① 날짜　　② 특별행사
③ 입장료　　④ 음식 가격
⑤ 장소

05 W: Let me tell you about the World Food Festival which will be held on September 5. You can taste food from different countries at the festival. You can also experience different cultures through _____ _____, like playing traditional games. The food will be _____ _____ 4 to 8 dollars per dish. Come to Parkview Gardens and enjoy the day!

6. 대화를 듣고, 두 사람이 만날 시각을 고르시오.

① 4:00 p.m.　　② 4:30 p.m.
③ 5:00 p.m.　　④ 5:30 p.m.
⑤ 6:00 p.m.

06 W: You look like you're _____ _____ _____ _____.

M: I'm just _____ _____ _____ the baseball game tonight.

W: Me, too. The game starts at 6:00 p.m., right?

M: Yes, I'll pick you up _____ _____ _____ at 5:30 p.m. How's that?

W: Can you _____ _____ _____? Let's buy some fried chicken before we go to the game.

M: No problem. See you later.

7. 대화를 듣고, 남자의 장래 희망으로 가장 적절한 것을 고르시오.

① 가수　　② 디자이너
③ 화가　　④ 외교관
⑤ 건축가

07
W: Peter, what is your dream?

M: Well, I want to make people happy.

W: Then, you can be a singer since you're _____ _____ _____.

M: But I like to draw and build things.

W: Oh, I see. Then, what do you want to be when you _____ _____?

M: I'm thinking of _____ _____ _____ like my dad.

W: That sounds great! I'm sure your dad would be so happy.

8. 대화를 듣고, 남자의 심정으로 가장 적절한 것을 고르시오.

① shy　　② upset
③ proud　　④ happy
⑤ thankful

08
W: Rodney, why are you wearing an eye-patch?

M: I hurt my eye playing basketball yesterday.

W: Sorry to hear that. That must _____.

M: Yeah, it's _____ _____ and puffy.

W: We have a class _____ _____ tomorrow.

M: I know. I feel _____ _____ that I have to wear this patch.

다음 페이지에 계속 ➡

9. 대화를 듣고, 여자가 대화 직후에 할 일로 가장 적절한 것을 고르시오.
   ① 기념품 가게 가기
   ② 롤러코스터 타기
   ③ 열쇠고리 만들기
   ④ 음료 사러 가기
   ⑤ 사진 인화하기

09 M: Wow! That roller coaster was so fun!

W: I know! It was scary but really exciting.

M: Do you want to _____ _____ _____ now?

W: No, I'm not thirsty yet.

M: Then what do you want to do?

W: I want to buy _____ _____ from here.

M: How about getting a keychain or a mug?

W: Great idea. I'll go to the _____ shop now.

10. 대화를 듣고, 무엇에 관한 내용인지 가장 적절한 것을 고르시오.
   ① 봉사활동 안내
   ② 방과 후 수업
   ③ 교내 체육 대회
   ④ 동아리 활동
   ⑤ 진로 탐색 교육

10 W: Kevin, what are you looking at?

M: I'm _____ _____ club activities on our school website.

W: Which club do you _____ _____ _____?

M: I'm interested in the book club and the volunteer service club.

W: Sounds good!

M: Yeah, but I can't decide between the two. What about you?

W: I'm thinking of joining one of the school _____ _____.

11. 대화를 듣고, 두 사람이 함께 이동할 방법으로 가장 적절한 것을 고르시오.

① 자전거 ② 지하철
③ 택시 ④ 버스
⑤ 자동차

11 W: Hey, how are we going to get to the concert downtown?

M: Hmm, I'm not sure. Maybe we'll take the subway or _____ _____ _____.

W: Why don't we ride our bikes _____?

M: Really? Do you want to bike to the concert?

W: Yeah, it would be faster and more fun.

M: Okay, let's _____ _____ _____ then.

2024 영어듣기능력평가 2회 12번 변형

12. 대화를 듣고, 남자가 쇼핑몰에 가는 이유로 가장 적절한 것을 고르시오.

① 옷을 사려고
② 물건을 교환하려고
③ 부모님과 식사하려고
④ 친구와 영화를 보려고
⑤ 게임 대회에 참가하려고

12 W: Hey, David. Where are you going after school?

M: I'm going to the shopping mall.

W: Are you going there _____ _____ new clothes?

M: No, I'm going there _____ _____ the video game tournament.

W: That sounds fun! Can I come and watch you play?

M: Sure. Let's meet _____ _____ _____ the school at 3:30.

다음 페이지에 계속 ➡

13. 대화를 듣고, 두 사람이 대화하는 장소로
가장 적절한 곳을 고르시오.

① 학교
② 버스 정류장
③ 양로원
④ 영화관
⑤ 주민 센터

13

M: Hi, Miranda. Where are you going?

W: Hi, Sam. I'm _____ _____ _____

the nursing home.

M: Do you do volunteer work there?

W: Yes. What about you? Where are you _____?

M: I'm going to the movies. Oh, _____ _____

my bus.

W: OK. Have a good time. See you at school.

M: You, too!

2024 영어듣기능력평가 1회 14번 변형

14. 대화를 듣고, 아이스크림 매장의 위치로
가장 알맞은 곳을 고르시오.

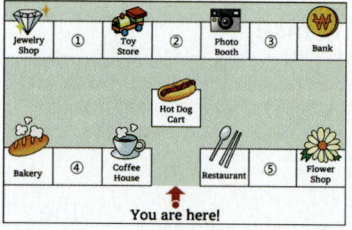

14

M: Hello. Can you tell me where the ice cream shop

is?

W: Sure. Do you see the hot dog cart over there?

M: Yes.

W: _____ _____ to the hot dog cart and

_____ _____.

M: Go straight and then turn left?

W: Yes. Then, you should see it on your left. It's

_____ the bakery and the coffee house.

M: Thank you.

15. 대화를 듣고, 여자가 남자에게 부탁한 일로 가장 적절한 것을 고르시오.

① 방 청소하기
② 책 반납하기
③ 숙제 끝내기
④ 음악 교재 챙기기
⑤ 바이올린 연습하기

15
W: Did you finish your homework?

M: Yes, Mom. I'm _____ _____ my homework.

W: That's awesome! Are you ready for your violin lesson?

M: Yes, I've been practicing all week.

W: Great job! Please don't _____ _____ _____ your music book.

M: Thanks for _____ _____, Mom.

16. 대화를 듣고, 여자가 남자에게 제안한 것으로 가장 적절한 것을 고르시오.

① 파티 열기   ② 쿠키 만들기
③ 선물 사기   ④ 편지 쓰기
⑤ 꽃다발 준비하기

16
W: What _____ _____ _____ for Mom's birthday?

M: Hmm… She didn't like the party very much last year, did she?

W: No, she likes to _____ _____. Do you think she would like a present?

M: Yes, but it doesn't have to be _____ _____. She liked our homemade cookies, remember?

W: Then how about writing a letter to her? I think she would like it _____ _____ _____ flowers.

M: Sounds good!

다음 페이지에 계속 ➡

17. 대화를 듣고, 여자가 방학에 한 일로 가장 적절한 것을 고르시오.

① 악기 배우기
② 수족관 관람하기
③ 반려동물 키우기
④ 컴퓨터 게임하기
⑤ 스쿠버 다이빙 배우기

17

W: Tom, what did you do _____ _____

_____?

M: I just played computer games. What about you?

W: I learned how to scuba dive.

M: That sounds interesting. Tell me more about it.

W: I saw _____ _____ _____ _____

underwater. It was amazing.

M: Good for you.

18. 대화를 듣고, 남자의 직업으로 가장 적절한 것을 고르시오.

① 변호사   ② 경찰관
③ 농구 선수   ④ 택배 배달원
⑤ 핸드폰 수리 기사

18

M: Hello, how can I help you?

W: Hi, I _____ my phone this morning and my

screen broke. Can I _____ _____ _____?

M: May I take a look?

W: Sure, here you go.

M: Hmm… I cannot fix this, but I can _____

_____ _____ with a new one if you'd like.

W: Yes, please. I'd like that.

19. 대화를 듣고, 여자의 마지막 말에 이어질 남자의 말로 가장 적절한 것을 고르시오.

Man: _____

① Sure! I love salad.
② Okay, I'll try this once.
③ No, I didn't like the restaurant.
④ Yes, I'll have some Chinese food.
⑤ Thanks, but I'll pay for lunch today.

19

W: Have you been to the new restaurant down the road?

M: No, I haven't. How about you?

W: _____ _____. Shall we have lunch there today?

M: That would be nice. What do they have?

W: They mainly sell organic sandwiches and salads.

M: I see. They _____ _____, but they're not my favorites.

W: Why don't you _____ _____? You might like it.

M: Okay, I'll try this once.

20. 대화를 듣고, 여자의 마지막 말에 이어질 남자의 말로 가장 적절한 것을 고르시오.

Man: _____

① Let's meet at 5.
② I'll have a sandwich.
③ I can't walk anymore.
④ I think I lost my ticket.
⑤ The map says it's on the third floor.

20

M: This museum is a huge place!

W: Yes, _____ _____ _____ for two hours and we still have many things to see.

M: I want to check out the Egyptian exhibit.

W: _____ _____ _____ says that it is on the second floor.

M: Before we go, how about taking a break and _____ _____ _____?

W: Good idea. Where is the cafeteria?

M: The map says it's on the third floor.

Words & Expressions Review 04

● 다음 단어를 암기하세요.

문제	번호	단어	뜻
1	1	humid	습한
	2	slowly	천천히
	3	carry	가지고 다니다
	4	shell	껍데기
	5	protect	보호하다
2	6	square-shaped	네모난 모양의
	7	plain	꾸미지 않은, 무늬가 없는
3	8	daily	매일 일어나는, 나날의
	9	forget	잊다, 잊어버리다
4	10	help A with B	A가 B하는 것을 돕다
5	11	taste	맛보다, 먹다
	12	traditional	전통의, 전통적인
6	13	in a good mood	기분이 좋은
	14	pick A up	A를 (차로) 데리러 가다
	15	place	집, 장소
7	16	since	~때문에, ~이므로
	17	be good at -ing	~을 잘하다
	18	build	만들다, 짓다
	19	grow up	(다) 크다, 성장하다
	20	architect	건축가
8	21	puffy	부어 있는
	22	photo shoot	사진 촬영

문제	번호	단어	뜻
9	23	souvenir	기념품
	24	search for	~을 찾다
10	25	have in mind	생각해 두다, 염두에 두다
	26	be interested in	~에 관심이 있다
	27	after school	방과 후
12	28	join	참가하다
	29	tournament	경기, 시합
	30	on one's way to	~로 가는 길에
13	31	nursing home	양로원
	32	head	가다, 향하다
14	33	cart	카트, 수레
	34	practice	연습하다
15	35	bring	~을 챙기다, 갖고 가다
	36	remind	상기시키다
16	37	homemade	집에서 만든
	38	even	(비교급 앞에서) 훨씬 더
17	39	lots of	많은
	40	underwater	물속에서
18	41	fix	고치다
19	42	organic	유기농의
20	43	floor plan	평면도
	44	snack	간식

M1(17)_W_04

●왼쪽 단어장의 뜻이 보이지 않게 반으로 접고, 학습한 단어의 뜻을 아래 빈칸에 적어주세요.

1	since		23	slowly
2	on one's way to		24	practice
3	lots of		25	remind
4	protect		26	daily
5	architect		27	have in mind
6	humid		28	souvenir
7	nursing home		29	square-shaped
8	homemade		30	plain
9	head		31	pick A up
10	join		32	cart
11	bring		33	shell
12	place		34	be interested in
13	tournament		35	photo shoot
14	even		36	underwater
15	carry		37	puffy
16	traditional		38	fix
17	snack		39	in a good mood
18	after school		40	grow up
19	search for		41	organic
20	taste		42	floor plan
21	be good at -ing		43	forget
22	help A with B		44	build

04
회
단어

05회 중학영어듣기 모의고사

M1(17)_05_US
모두 **미국식 발음(US)** 으로 녹음

M1(17)_05_UK
20문제 중 5문제에 **영국식 발음 (US+UK)**을 포함하여 녹음

📖 정답 및 해석 p. 18

1 다음을 듣고, 'this'가 가리키는 것으로 가장 적절한 것을 고르시오.

①  ② 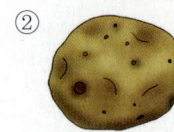 ③  ④  ⑤

2 대화를 듣고, 남자가 구입할 현관 매트로 가장 적절한 것을 고르시오.

①  ②  ③  ④  ⑤

3 다음을 듣고, 광주의 날씨로 가장 적절한 것을 고르시오.

①  ②  ③  ④  ⑤

4 대화를 듣고, 여자의 마지막 말의 의도로 가장 적절한 것을 고르시오.

① 충고 　　② 사과 　　③ 부탁 　　④ 축하 　　⑤ 거절

5 다음을 듣고, 여자가 쓰레기 줍기 행사에 대해 언급하지 <u>않은</u> 것을 고르시오.

① 행사 날짜   ② 소요 시간   ③ 복장
④ 준비물   ⑤ 단체사진 촬영

6 대화를 듣고, 두 사람이 이야기를 나누는 현재 시각을 고르시오.

① 4:00 p.m.   ② 4:30 p.m.   ③ 5:00 p.m.   ④ 5:30 p.m.   ⑤ 6:00 p.m.

7 대화를 듣고, 남자의 장래 희망을 고르시오.

① 의사   ② 작가   ③ 축구 선수   ④ 선생님   ⑤ 수의사

8 대화를 듣고, 여자의 심정을 고르시오.

① 슬픔   ② 평온함   ③ 기쁨   ④ 무서움   ⑤ 당황스러움

9 대화를 듣고, 남자가 대화 직후에 할 일로 가장 적절한 것을 고르시오.

① 아이와 놀아주기   ② 악기 연주하기   ③ 인터넷 검색하기
④ 강아지 산책시키기   ⑤ 동영상 보여주기

10 대화를 듣고, 무엇에 관한 내용인지 가장 적절한 것을 고르시오.

① 학교 공사 안내   ② 건물 출입 요건   ③ 도서 반납 방법
④ 제품 교환 요청   ⑤ 시험 응시 규칙

11번~20번 문제는 다음 페이지에 ➡

11 대화를 듣고, 남자가 이용할 교통수단으로 가장 적절한 것을 고르시오.

① 배   ② 자동차   ③ 비행기   ④ 자전거   ⑤ 기차

12 대화를 듣고, 여자가 지역 축제에 가는 이유로 가장 적절한 것을 고르시오.

① 친구를 만나려고   ② 공연을 구경하려고
③ 태권도 시범을 보이려고   ④ 행사 음식을 사 먹으려고
⑤ 행사 관련 봉사활동을 하려고

13 대화를 듣고, 두 사람이 대화하는 장소로 가장 적절한 곳을 고르시오.

① 매표소   ② 약국   ③ 은행
④ 버스 정류장   ⑤ 자동차 대여점

14 대화를 듣고, 두 사람이 찾고 있는 여권의 위치로 가장 적절한 것을 고르시오.

15 대화를 듣고, 여자가 남자에게 부탁한 일로 가장 적절한 것을 고르시오.

① 창문 열기   ② 빵 사오기
③ 물 갖다주기   ④ 토스터 청소하기
⑤ 공기청정기 켜기

16 대화를 듣고, 남자가 여자에게 제안한 것으로 가장 적절한 것을 고르시오.

① 옷 환불하기　　　　② 연고 바르기　　　　③ 아침 식사하기
④ 사과 문자 보내기　　⑤ 선생님과 상담하기

17 대화를 듣고, 남자가 지난 토요일에 한 일로 가장 적절한 것을 고르시오.

① 축구 연습하기　　　　② 과학 숙제하기　　　　③ 전시회 관람하기
④ 다큐멘터리 시청하기　⑤ 시험 공부하기

18 대화를 듣고, 남자의 직업으로 가장 적절한 것을 고르시오.

① 가전제품 판매원　　② 배관공　　　　　③ 경찰관
④ 에어컨 수리 기사　　⑤ 식당 점원

05 회 모의고사

19 대화를 듣고, 여자의 마지막 말에 이어질 남자의 말로 가장 적절한 것을 고르시오.

Man: _____

① It's for take-out.　　　　　② Five friends, please.
③ Can I order later?　　　　　④ They'll come by bus.
⑤ One burger is enough.

20 대화를 듣고, 남자의 마지막 말에 이어질 여자의 응답으로 가장 적절한 것을 고르시오.

Woman: _____

① I'm late for work.　　　　　② Sure, no problem.
③ Nice to meet you.　　　　　④ I like reading books.
⑤ The bus station is nearby.

Dictation Test 05

녹음을 다시 듣으면서 빈칸을 채워주세요.

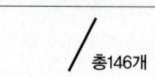

M1(17)_05_D

Dictation(받아쓰기)은 본문을 받아쓰면서 영어듣기의 집중력을 향상시키고 다양한 표현을 정리하기 위한 영어듣기 학습법입니다. **녹음을 다시 듣고, 빈칸에 알맞은 단어를 써 보세요.**

※Dictation의 정답은 듣기 대본의 밑줄 친 부분을 확인하세요.

📖 정답 p. 18

✏️ 맞은 개수 　　／　총146개

그림정보파악(담화)

1. 다음을 듣고, 'this'가 가리키는 것으로 가장 적절한 것을 고르시오.

① 　②
③ 　④
⑤

01 M: This is a _____ _____ that grows underground. This has a _____ _____ and taste. This has many white _____. This can make you _____ when you cut this. What is this?

그림정보파악(대화) 🇺🇸🇬🇧

2. 대화를 듣고, 남자가 구입할 현관 매트로 가장 적절한 것을 고르시오.

① 　②
③ 　④
⑤

02 W: Hello, can I help you?

M: Hi, I'm looking for a door mat.

W: How about this round one?

M: Well, I like _____ _____ _____ better.

W: Okay. We have this one _____ _____ _____ on it.

M: Oh, that's nice. It's very cute.

W: Yes, and it will make you feel _____.

M: Great! I'll _____ _____.

---

3. 다음을 듣고, 광주의 날씨로 가장 적절한 것을 고르시오.

① ② ③ ④ ⑤

03 W: Good morning! It's time for your Sunday _____ _____. If you are living in Seoul, you will need an umbrella because it is going to rain. In Gwangju, it will be cloudy but there is _____ _____ _____ _____. Busan, on the other hand, will be very sunny, so enjoy the sun.

4. 대화를 듣고, 여자의 마지막 말의 의도로 가장 적절한 것을 고르시오.
   ① 충고   ② 사과
   ③ 부탁   ④ 축하
   ⑤ 거절

04 M: Mom, you _____ _____.

W: Oh, I'm fine, honey. My throat just _____ _____ _____.

M: Why does it hurt?

W: The wind was pretty cold when I was outside.

M: Can I get you anything?

W: Well, can you please get me _____ _____ _____ _____?

다음 페이지에 계속 ➡

5. 다음을 듣고, 여자가 쓰레기 줍기 행사에 대해 언급하지 <u>않은</u> 것을 고르시오.

① 행사 날짜
② 소요 시간
③ 복장
④ 준비물
⑤ 단체사진 촬영

05 W: We'll have a clean-up event at our school soon. It will _____ _____ on May 10th. We'll walk around our neighborhood for an hour _____ _____ _____. You should wear comfortable shoes and clothing. Please bring a trash bag and gloves. Let's work together to make our community _____ _____ _____!

6. 대화를 듣고, 두 사람이 이야기를 나누는 현재 시각을 고르시오.

① 4:00 p.m.   ② 4:30 p.m.
③ 5:00 p.m.   ④ 5:30 p.m.
⑤ 6:00 p.m.

06 *[Cellphone rings.]*

W: Hi, Kevin. Are you almost here?

M: Yeah. I _____ _____ the bus at 4:30 p.m.

W: Okay. How's the traffic?

M: It's a bit slow today. I think it'll take about 30 more minutes to get there.

W: So, you'll arrive _____ 5:30?

M: Yes. It's 5:00 _____, so I should be there by then.

7. 대화를 듣고, 남자의 장래 희망을 고르시오.
① 의사   ② 작가
③ 축구 선수   ④ 선생님
⑤ 수의사

07
W: What do you want to be when you _____ _____, Craig?

M: I like all _____ _____ animals. I want to help them when they are sick.

W: You mean you want to be a vet?

M: Yes. A doctor _____ _____.

W: I think you will be a good vet.

8. 대화를 듣고, 여자의 심정을 고르시오.
① 슬픔   ② 평온함
③ 기쁨   ④ 무서움
⑤ 당황스러움

08
W: James, _____ _____ my puppy!

M: Really? That's good news!

W: Yes. I've been looking for the puppy for two days _____ _____ _____ it at the park.

M: How did you find it?

W: I _____ _____ _____ _____ all over the park. One woman called me.

M: That's great! I know how much you love your puppy.

다음 페이지에 계속 ➡

9. 대화를 듣고, 남자가 대화 직후에 할 일로 가장 적절한 것을 고르시오.

   ① 아이와 놀아주기
   ② 악기 연주하기
   ③ 인터넷 검색하기
   ④ 강아지 산책시키기
   ⑤ 동영상 보여주기

09

M: Jenny, have you seen this video online?

W: What is it about?

M: It's a video of _____ _____ _____ _____ playing together. It has more than three million views on YouTube.

W: Oh! That sounds so cute!

M: It sure is.

W: I want to see it.

M: Okay. I'll _____ _____ _____ _____ right away.

10. 대화를 듣고, 무엇에 관한 내용인지 가장 적절한 것을 고르시오.

   ① 학교 공사 안내
   ② 건물 출입 요건
   ③ 도서 반납 방법
   ④ 제품 교환 요청
   ⑤ 시험 응시 규칙

10

W: Steve, what are you doing?

M: I'm checking the library website on how to _____ books.

W: The library _____ _____ because of renovations.

M: Yes, but there's a return box outside the building.

W: Oh, then you can just _____ the books in.

M: Yes!

11. 대화를 듣고, 남자가 이용할 교통수단으로 가장 적절한 것을 고르시오.

① 배　　　② 자동차
③ 비행기　④ 자전거
⑤ 기차

11

M: Honey, I have a _____ _____ next week.

W: Again? Are you going overseas this time, _____ _____?

M: Not this time. I have a _____ _____ _____ in Busan.

W: That's great, considering it's only a three-hour drive from here.

M: Yeah, but I'm planning on taking the train. Driving makes me tired.

W: Sure. Do _____ _____ _____ best!

이유파악　🇺🇸🇬🇧　**2025 영어듣기능력평가 1회 12번 변형**

12. 대화를 듣고, 여자가 지역 축제에 가는 이유로 가장 적절한 것을 고르시오.

① 친구를 만나려고
② 공연을 구경하려고
③ 태권도 시범을 보이려고
④ 행사 음식을 사 먹으려고
⑤ 행사 관련 봉사활동을 하려고

12

M: Kate, where are you going?

W: I'm going to the _____ _____.

M: Are you going there to enjoy the _____ _____?

W: No, I'm going to do a taekwondo performance.

M: Really? So you'll show some taekwondo moves _____ _____?

W: Yes! I hope lots of people come and watch us.

다음 페이지에 계속 ➡

13. 대화를 듣고, 두 사람이 대화하는 장소로 가장 적절한 곳을 고르시오.

① 매표소   ② 약국
③ 은행   ④ 버스 정류장
⑤ 자동차 대여점

13

W: Hi, how can I help you?

M: Hi, I'll be going on a _____ _____ soon. And…

W: Are you worried about car sickness?

M: Yes. Can you give me something that will help?

W: Sure. _____ _____ _____ half an hour before you get in the car.

M: Thank you. I'll buy four packages of them.

14. 대화를 듣고, 두 사람이 찾고 있는 여권의 위치로 가장 적절한 것을 고르시오.

14

W: We have to leave now or we're going to _____ _____ _____.

M: I just need to find my _____.

W: Isn't it on your desk?

M: I remember putting it there, but I can't find it.

W: Oh, I see it! It's _____ _____ _____ on the floor. You must have _____ it.

M: Thanks. Let's go now.

15. 대화를 듣고, 여자가 남자에게 부탁한 일로 가장 적절한 것을 고르시오.

① 창문 열기
② 빵 사오기
③ 물 갖다주기
④ 토스터 청소하기
⑤ 공기청정기 켜기

15 M: What's that smell? Did _____ _____?

W: Yeah, I burnt the toast.

M: Did you take it out of the toaster?

W: I did. I _____ a good piece of bread.

M: Don't worry about it. Let's just _____

_____ _____ the smell.

W: Oh, right. Could you open the window for me?

M: Sure. I'll open it right now.

16. 대화를 듣고, 남자가 여자에게 제안한 것으로 가장 적절한 것을 고르시오.

① 옷 환불하기
② 연고 바르기
③ 아침 식사하기
④ 사과 문자 보내기
⑤ 선생님과 상담하기

16 M: Anna, _____ _____ _____ _____?

W: I had a fight with my sister this morning.

M: Why?

W: I wore her jeans the other day without her

_____, and she was upset.

M: Oh, I'm sorry to hear that. How about sending her

_____ _____ _____?

W: Yeah, texting sounds good.

다음 페이지에 계속 ➡

05
회
딕
테
이
션

17. 대화를 듣고, 남자가 지난 토요일에 한 일로 가장 적절한 것을 고르시오.

① 축구 연습하기
② 과학 숙제하기
③ 전시회 관람하기
④ 다큐멘터리 시청하기
⑤ 시험 공부하기

17

W: Did you watch the documentary last Saturday?

M: No, I _____ it. How was it?

W: It was very interesting. I _____ new things about AI.

M: Well, I _____ _____ soccer practice.

W: Oh, did you have a soccer practice on Saturday?

M: Yeah. I'll watch a _____ of the documentary on the Internet.

18. 대화를 듣고, 남자의 직업으로 가장 적절한 것을 고르시오.

① 가전제품 판매원
② 배관공
③ 경찰관
④ 에어컨 수리 기사
⑤ 식당 점원

18

W: Thank you for coming _____ _____ _____ _____.

M: No problem. I was in the neighborhood. What seems to be the problem?

W: The air conditioner isn't _____ _____. Customers are complaining that our restaurant is too hot.

M: Hmm… There seems to be some _____ from the pipe.

W: How long will it take to _____ _____ _____?

M: I can fix it within an hour.

19. 대화를 듣고, 여자의 마지막 말에 이어질 남자의 말로 가장 적절한 것을 고르시오.

Man: _____

① It's for take-out.
② Five friends, please.
③ Can I order later?
④ They'll come by bus.
⑤ One burger is enough.

19

W: Joel, we've _____ _____ the place to have your birthday party.

M: Where is it going to be, Mom?

W: It will be _____ _____ _____ _____.

M: You mean at Jamie's Burgers?

W: That's right.

M: Thank you so much, Mom! I love that restaurant.

W: _____ _____ _____ do you want to invite?

M: Five friends, please.

20. 대화를 듣고, 남자의 마지막 말에 이어질 여자의 응답으로 가장 적절한 것을 고르시오.

Woman: _____

① I'm late for work.
② Sure, no problem.
③ Nice to meet you.
④ I like reading books.
⑤ The bus station is nearby.

20

W: Honey, are you going to work?

M: Yes, I'm _____ _____ _____ _____. Why?

W: Can you _____ _____ _____ at the subway station on your way there?

M: Of course. Where are you going?

W: I need to go to the bookstore.

M: Okay, _____ _____ _____ in the car. Can you be down in five minutes?

W: Sure, no problem.

Words & Expressions Review 05

● 다음 단어를 암기하세요.

문제	번호	단어	뜻
1	1	vegetable	채소
	2	grow	자라다
	3	underground	지하에
	4	layer	막, 층, 겹
2	5	look for ~	~을 찾다
	6	round	둥근
	7	rectangular	직사각형의
	8	cozy	포근한
3	9	there is no chance ~	~할 가능성이 없다
	10	on the other hand	반면에
4	11	unwell	아픈, 몸이 편치 않은
	12	honey	얘, 자기, 여보
5	13	clean-up	대청소
	14	neighborhood	근처, 인근 지역
	15	trash	쓰레기
6	16	almost	거의
7	17	all kinds of	모든 종류의
	18	You mean ~?	~이라는 말이니?
	19	vet	수의사
8	20	find	찾다
	21	lose	잃어버리다, 분실하다
9	22	adorable	사랑스러운

문제	번호	단어	뜻
9	23	million	100만
	24	return	반납하다
10	25	renovation	수리, 수선
	26	toss	던지다
11	27	suit	적합하다, 어울리다
12	28	performance	공연, 시범
	29	stage	무대
13	30	car sickness	차멀미
	31	medicine	약
14	32	flight	항공편, 비행
15	33	burn	불에 타다
	34	long face	시무룩한 얼굴
16	35	permission	허락, 허가
	36	apology	사과
17	37	miss	놓치다, 빠지다
	38	rerun	재방송
	39	properly	제대로, 적절하게
18	40	customer	손님
	41	get ~ fixed	~을 고치다
19	42	take-out	가지고 가는 음식
20	43	in a minute	곧, 즉시
	44	drop A off	A를 내려 주다

M1(17)_W_05

● 왼쪽 단어장의 뜻이 보이지 않게 반으로 접고, 학습한 단어의 뜻을 아래 빈칸에 적어주세요.

1	rectangular		23	neighborhood	
2	get ~ fixed		24	vet	
3	all kinds of		25	burn	
4	cozy		26	miss	
5	unwell		27	almost	
6	trash		28	long face	
7	on the other hand		29	medicine	
8	in a minute		30	find	
9	underground		31	clean-up	
10	properly		32	honey	
11	round		33	return	
12	look for ~		34	suit	
13	rerun		35	there is no chance ~	
14	apology		36	car sickness	
15	customer		37	toss	
16	vegetable		38	grow	
17	performance		39	You mean ~?	
18	drop A off		40	permission	
19	take-out		41	renovation	
20	million		42	layer	
21	stage		43	lose	
22	flight		44	adorable	

05
회
단
어

06회 중학영어듣기 모의고사

M1(17)_06_US
모두 **미국식 발음(US)**
으로 녹음

M1(17)_06_UK
20문제 중 5문제에 **영국식 발음**
(US+UK)을 포함하여 녹음

정답 및 해석 p. 22

1 다음을 듣고, 'this'가 가리키는 것으로 가장 적절한 것을 고르시오.

① 　② 　③ 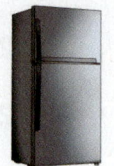　④ 　⑤

2 대화를 듣고, 여자가 만든 냉장고 자석으로 가장 적절한 것을 고르시오.

① 　② 　③ 　④ 　⑤

3 다음을 듣고, 포항의 오늘 오후 날씨로 가장 적절한 것을 고르시오.

① 　② 　③ 　④ 　⑤

4 대화를 듣고, 여자가 한 마지막 말의 의도로 가장 적절한 것을 고르시오.

① 감사　　② 사과　　③ 불평　　④ 거절　　⑤ 승낙

5 다음을 듣고, 여자가 음악 축제에 대해 언급하지 <u>않은</u> 것을 고르시오.

① 장르   ② 날짜   ③ 티켓 가격   ④ 장소   ⑤ 출연 가수

6 대화를 듣고, 두 사람이 만날 시각을 고르시오.

① 5:00 p.m.   ② 5:30 p.m.   ③ 6:00 p.m.   ④ 6:30 p.m.   ⑤ 7:00 p.m.

7 대화를 듣고, 남자의 장래 희망으로 가장 적절한 것을 고르시오.

① 군인   ② 요리사   ③ 선생님
④ 농구 선수   ⑤ 방송 작가

8 대화를 듣고, 여자의 심정으로 가장 적절한 것을 고르시오.

① shy   ② upset   ③ proud
④ worried   ⑤ thankful

9 대화를 듣고, 여자가 대화 직후에 할 일로 가장 적절한 것을 고르시오.

① 안약 넣기   ② 눈 씻어내기   ③ 마실 물 찾기
④ 안과에 가기   ⑤ 충혈된 눈 감고 있기

10 대화를 듣고, 무엇에 관해 이야기하고 있는지 고르시오.

① 봉사 활동   ② 환경 보호   ③ 주민 대표 선출
④ 분리수거   ⑤ 포장 이사

11번~20번 문제는 다음 페이지에 ➡

11 대화를 듣고, 여자가 이용할 교통수단으로 가장 적절한 것을 고르시오.

① 지하철   ② 자전거   ③ 걷기   ④ 버스   ⑤ 택시

12 대화를 듣고, 여자가 서점에 가는 이유로 가장 적절한 것을 고르시오.

① 책을 반품하려고   ② 문제집을 살펴보려고
③ 책 관련 기념품을 사려고   ④ 신간 만화책을 구매하려고
⑤ 작가의 사인회에 참석하려고

13 대화를 듣고, 두 사람이 대화하는 장소로 가장 적절한 곳을 고르시오.

① 영화관   ② 놀이공원   ③ 장난감 가게   ④ 아쿠아리움   ⑤ 수영장

14 대화를 듣고, 두 사람이 가족 사진을 둘 위치로 가장 알맞은 곳을 고르시오.

15 대화를 듣고, 여자가 남자에게 부탁한 일로 가장 적절한 것을 고르시오.

① 음식 재료 사오기   ② 설거지하기   ③ 방 청소하기
④ 아빠한테 전화하기   ⑤ 저녁식사 준비하기

16 대화를 듣고, 여자가 남자에게 제안한 것으로 가장 적절한 것을 고르시오.

① 농구 연습하기　　　　② 사인된 농구공 선물하기
③ 코치와 상담하기　　　　④ 팀원들과 축하 파티 하기
⑤ 농구 경기 보러 가기

17 대화를 듣고, 두 사람이 주말에 할 일로 가장 적절한 것을 고르시오.

① 소풍 가기　　　　② 카페에 가기
③ 영화 보기　　　　④ 디저트 만들기
⑤ 공연 보기

18 대화를 듣고, 남자의 직업으로 가장 적절한 것을 고르시오.

① 사진사　　② 공무원　　③ 교통 경찰　　④ 연극 배우　　⑤ 학교 선생님

[19~20] 대화를 듣고, 여자의 마지막 말에 이어질 남자의 말로 가장 적절한 것을 고르시오.

19 Man: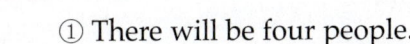

① Maybe next time.　　　　② That's a good idea.
③ I'm glad to hear that.　　④ Thank you for your help.
⑤ You'll do better this time.

20 Man: _____

① There will be four people.
② I can't make it at 7 o'clock.
③ We'll play for about an hour.
④ It takes 10 minutes to get there.
⑤ You don't need to pay any money.

Dictation Test 06

녹음을 다시 들으면서 빈칸을 채워주세요

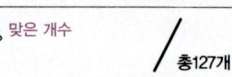

M1(17)_06_D

Dictation(받아쓰기)은 본문을 받아쓰면서 영어듣기의 집중력을 향상시키고 다양한 표현을 정리하기 위한 영어듣기 학습법입니다. 녹음을 다시 듣고, 빈칸에 알맞은 단어를 써 보세요.
※Dictation의 정답은 듣기 대본의 밑줄 친 부분을 확인하세요.

정답 p. 22

맞은 개수 / 총127개

그림정보파악(담화)

1. 다음을 듣고, 'this'가 가리키는 것으로 가장 적절한 것을 고르시오.

①
②
③
④
⑤

01

M: You can find this in a kitchen. It has one door. You put food _____ _____ _____ inside. The plate turns around and _____ _____ the food. What is this?

그림정보파악(대화)

2. 대화를 듣고, 여자가 만든 냉장고 자석으로 가장 적절한 것을 고르시오.

①
②
③
④
⑤

02

M: Hi, Erin. What's that?

W: It's a fridge magnet for my friend.

M: _____ _____ _____ shape looks cute. Did you make it?

W: Yes, I made it myself.

M: Wow, I want to have one, too. Can you make a _____-_____ _____ for me?

W: Okay, I will.

---

3. 다음을 듣고, 포항의 오늘 오후 날씨로 가장 적절한 것을 고르시오.

① ② ③ ④ ⑤

03 W: Hello! This is the weather report for Pohang. Yesterday, it was cloudy, but the clouds _____ by late afternoon. This morning, it will be nice outside with a light _____. It will be _____ sunny and warm this afternoon. Enjoy the _____ weather in Pohang today!

4. 대화를 듣고, 여자가 한 마지막 말의 의도로 가장 적절한 것을 고르시오.

① 감사 ② 사과
③ 불평 ④ 거절
⑤ 승낙

04 M: Jessica, are you alright? You look like you're _____ _____.

W: I have a toothache. It hurts so much!

M: I think _____ _____ see a dentist _____ _____.

W: Right. But to be honest, I'm afraid of the dentist.

M: Do you want me to come with you?

W: Thanks, but I can handle it on my own.

다음 페이지에 계속 ➡

06
회
딕
테
이
션

5. 다음을 듣고, 여자가 음악 축제에 대해 언급하지 **않은** 것을 고르시오.

① 장르　　② 날짜
③ 티켓 가격　　④ 장소
⑤ 출연 가수

05 W: Hello, music lovers. The London Jazz & Blues Music Festival is back. It _____ _____ _____ from July 8th to the 10th. Tickets are priced at £10 for each day. Come and enjoy live music performances at Hyde Park in London. _____ _____ _____ _____ there!

6. 대화를 듣고, 두 사람이 만날 시각을 고르시오.

① 5:00 p.m.
② 5:30 p.m.
③ 6:00 p.m.
④ 6:30 p.m.
⑤ 7:00 p.m.

06 M: Sophia, there's a free classical concert at the community center tonight.

W: Great! Why don't we go together and _____ _____ _____?

M: Okay. The concert starts at 7:00 p.m.

W: Then, I'll _____ _____ your place at 6:30.

M: If we're late, we won't _____ _____ _____ get good seats. How about 6?

W: 6 o'clock? Got it. See you then.

7. 대화를 듣고, 남자의 장래 희망으로 가장 적절한 것을 고르시오.

① 군인
② 요리사
③ 선생님
④ 농구 선수
⑤ 방송 작가

07

W: Ted, what are you watching on your phone?

M: I'm watching a _____ about a famous basketball player, Stephen Curry.

W: Oh, that looks fun. Do you like basketball?

M: Yes. In fact, I want to become a basketball player when I _____ _____.

W: I hope you _____ _____ _____.

M: Thank you.

8. 대화를 듣고, 여자의 심정으로 가장 적절한 것을 고르시오.

① shy   ② upset
③ proud   ④ worried
⑤ thankful

08

M: Jane, you're so talented at yoga!

W: I _____ _____ _____ _____ in the beginning.

M: You _____ _____ _____ hard.

W: Yes, I've gotten better little by little, and now I'm able to stay calm in difficult poses.

M: You must feel so good about yourself.

W: I do. I feel more confident now.

다음 페이지에 계속 ➡

9. 대화를 듣고, 여자가 대화 직후에 할 일로 가장 적절한 것을 고르시오.

① 안약 넣기
② 눈 씻어내기
③ 마실 물 찾기
④ 안과에 가기
⑤ 충혈된 눈 감고 있기

09

M: Whoa, your eyes are all red, Olivia.

W: Really? Well, I was just _____ them.

M: Do you want eye drops? I have some.

W: That's okay, thanks. I _____ just had something in my eyes.

M: Are you sure? You should at least _____ _____ with clean water.

W: That's a good idea. I'll do it now.

10. 대화를 듣고, 무엇에 관해 이야기하고 있는지 고르시오.

① 봉사 활동　② 환경 보호
③ 주민 대표 선출　④ 분리수거
⑤ 포장 이사

10

M: Do you live in this apartment?

W: Yes, I do. I moved in a few days ago.

M: Oh, I see. Well, please _____ _____ _____ before throwing it away.

W: Okay. Where do I put _____ _____ _____ and cans?

M: There are _____ _____ over there.

W: Oh, thank you.

11. 대화를 듣고, 여자가 이용할 교통수단으로 가장 적절한 것을 고르시오.

① 지하철
② 자전거
③ 걷기
④ 버스
⑤ 택시

11

W: Evan, aren't you _____ _____ the concert tomorrow?

M: I am! My favorite band is playing.

W: Mine, too. _____ _____ _____ _____ _____ the concert?

M: I'll take the subway. My bike is broken. You?

W: I'll be _____ _____. It's not far from my house.

2025 영어듣기능력평가 1회 12번 변형

12. 대화를 듣고, 여자가 서점에 가는 이유로 가장 적절한 것을 고르시오.

① 책을 반품하려고
② 문제집을 살펴보려고
③ 책 관련 기념품을 사려고
④ 신간 만화책을 구매하려고
⑤ 작가의 사인회에 참석하려고

12

M: Hey, Lily. Are you going out?

W: Yes. I'm going to the bookstore _____ the station.

M: Are you going to buy a new comic book again?

W: No. My _____ writer is coming to the store today. She will _____ _____ for her readers.

M: Wow, I hope you get it!

다음 페이지에 계속 ➡

13. 대화를 듣고, 두 사람이 대화하는 장소로 가장 적절한 곳을 고르시오.

① 영화관
② 놀이공원
③ 장난감 가게
④ 아쿠아리움
⑤ 수영장

13

M: I'm happy to see so many _____ _____ that I love!

W: You must be really happy to see your _____ sea animal, the beluga. Now, let's go touch some starfishes in that touch pool.

M: Okay, Mom! I'm so _____ to touch some starfishes!

W: But, David, before you touch them, you need to wash your hands first.

M: Okay! I will _____ _____ my hands.

W: Don't run, David!

14. 대화를 듣고, 두 사람이 가족 사진을 둘 위치로 가장 알맞은 곳을 고르시오.

14

W: Honey, look. I _____ our new family photo.

M: Oh, it's beautiful. The photo _____ _____ so nice.

W: I think so, too. Where should we put it?

M: We can put it on the bookshelf.

W: It's kind of _____ there. How about right _____ _____ the TV?

M: That would be nice.

15. 대화를 듣고, 여자가 남자에게 부탁한 일로 가장 적절한 것을 고르시오.

① 음식 재료 사오기
② 설거지하기
③ 방 청소하기
④ 아빠한테 전화하기
⑤ 저녁식사 준비하기

15
W: Jamie, did you _____ _____ _____ in the sink?

M: Of course, Mom. I even cleaned my room.

W: Wow, I'm _____.

M: Anyway, when is Dad coming home?

W: He should be here by now. Will you give him a _____ _____?

M: Okay, I will. I'm so hungry. What are we having for dinner?

W: We're having roast chicken and baked beans.

16. 대화를 듣고, 여자가 남자에게 제안한 것으로 가장 적절한 것을 고르시오.

① 농구 연습하기
② 사인된 농구공 선물하기
③ 코치와 상담하기
④ 팀원들과 축하 파티 하기
⑤ 농구 경기 보러 가기

16
W: Congratulations _____ _____ the basketball game yesterday.

M: Thanks. I _____ _____ _____ to my coach, Mr. Snaders.

W: He must be a great coach.

M: He is. I'd like to get him a gift as a thank-you.

W: How about a basketball _____ _____ _____ on the team?

M: That's a great idea.

다음 페이지에 계속 ➡

17. 대화를 듣고, 두 사람이 주말에 할 일로 가장 적절한 것을 고르시오.

① 소풍 가기
② 카페에 가기
③ 영화 보기
④ 디저트 만들기
⑤ 공연 보기

17
M: Hey, let's _____ _____ _____ in the park this Saturday.

W: I don't think that's a good idea.

M: Why not?

W: The weather forecast says it might rain, and _____ in the rain isn't fun.

M: True. How about trying some new sweets at a café instead?

W: Great idea! We can enjoy some _____ _____ together.

18. 대화를 듣고, 남자의 직업으로 가장 적절한 것을 고르시오.

① 사진사
② 공무원
③ 교통 경찰
④ 연극 배우
⑤ 학교 선생님

18
M: Hello, how can I help you?

W: Hi, I'm here to have an _____ _____ _____.

M: Sure. What's the photo for?

W: I need the photo for my driver's license.

M: Okay. Please sit over here and _____ _____ the camera.

W: Sure. Shall I sit like this?

M: Perfect! Now _____ _____ for a moment, please.

19. 대화를 듣고, 여자의 마지막 말에 이어질 남자의 말로 가장 적절한 것을 고르시오.

Man: _____

① Maybe next time.
② That's a good idea.
③ I'm glad to hear that.
④ Thank you for your help.
⑤ You'll do better this time.

19
M: What's the matter, Sujin?

W: _____ _____ _____ my math test tomorrow.

M: Do you want some help?

W: It's okay. I _____ _____ _____ today.

M: Then why are you so worried?

W: I got a really bad grade _____ _____ _____ _____.

M: You'll do better this time.

20. 대화를 듣고, 여자의 마지막 말에 이어질 남자의 말로 가장 적절한 것을 고르시오.

Man: _____

① There will be four people.
② I can't make it at 7 o'clock.
③ We'll play for about an hour.
④ It takes 10 minutes to get there.
⑤ You don't need to pay any money.

20
M: Nancy, do you want to play badminton tomorrow evening?

W: I'd love to, but I don't have a racket.

M: You can use mine. I have a _____ one.

W: Great. Thanks! What time shall we meet?

M: Is 7 o'clock okay? I have two other friends coming.

W: Oh, that's fine. How long are you _____ _____ _____?

M: We'll play for about an hour.

06
회
딕
테
이
션

Words & Expressions Review 06

● 다음 단어를 암기하세요.

문제	번호	단어	뜻
1	□ 1	plate	(둥근) 접시, 그릇
	□ 2	inside	안에
	□ 3	turn around	회전하다
	□ 4	heat up	~을 데우다, 뜨겁게 만들다
2	□ 5	fridge magnet	냉장고 자석
	□ 6	bird-shaped	새 모양의
3	□ 7	breeze	산들바람
	□ 8	to be honest	솔직히 (말해서)
4	□ 9	handle	처리하다, 다루다
	□ 10	on one's own	혼자 힘으로
5	□ 11	take place	(행사가) 열리다
	□ 12	performance	공연, 행사
	□ 13	community center	주민 센터
6	□ 14	check out	(흥미로운 것을) 살펴보다[보다]
	□ 15	come by	잠깐 들르다
	□ 16	be able to + 동사	~할 수 있다
7	□ 17	achieve	이루다, 성취하다
8	□ 18	talented	재능이 있는
	□ 19	little by little	조금씩
9	□ 20	rub	비비다, 문지르다
	□ 21	at least	적어도, 최소한
10	□ 22	a few days ago	며칠 전에

문제	번호	단어	뜻
10	□ 23	separate	분리하다, 나누다
	□ 24	trash	쓰레기
	□ 25	throw ~ away	~을 버리다
	□ 26	recycling	재활용
11	□ 27	broken	고장 난, 부서진
	□ 28	on foot	걸어서
	□ 29	near	~에 가까운
12	□ 30	station	역, 정류장
	□ 31	sign	사인하다
13	□ 32	starfish	불가사리
	□ 33	be excited to + 동사	~하게 되어서 신나다
14	□ 34	frame	액자에 넣다
	□ 35	crowded	붐비는
15	□ 36	impressed	감동받은
16	□ 37	owe A to B	A는 B의 덕분이다
	□ 38	How about ~?	~은 어때?
	□ 39	picnic	소풍, 피크닉 / 소풍[피크닉] 가다
17	□ 40	sweet	디저트
	□ 41	instead	대신에
18	□ 42	Shall I ~?	내가 ~할까요?
	□ 43	still	가만히 있는, 아직도
20	□ 44	spare	여분의, 예비용의

M1(17)_W_06

● 왼쪽 단어장의 뜻이 보이지 않게 반으로 접고, 학습한 단어의 뜻을 아래 빈칸에 적어주세요.

1	still		23	little by little
2	Shall I ~?		24	on foot
3	performance		25	instead
4	frame		26	community center
5	heat up		27	handle
6	spare		28	near
7	to be honest		29	sign
8	inside		30	throw ~ away
9	a few days ago		31	bird-shaped
10	rub		32	impressed
11	at least		33	come by
12	talented		34	turn around
13	broken		35	crowded
14	starfish		36	trash
15	on one's own		37	plate
16	owe A to B		38	check out
17	be excited to + 동사		39	station
18	recycling		40	breeze
19	be able to + 동사		41	fridge magnet
20	take place		42	separate
21	How about ~?		43	sweet
22	achieve		44	picnic

06
회
단
어

07회 중학영어듣기 모의고사

모두 **미국식 발음(US)**
으로 녹음

20문제 중 5문제에 **영국식 발음**
(US+UK)을 포함하여 녹음

📖 정답 및 해석 p.26

1 다음을 듣고, 'I'가 무엇인지 가장 적절한 것을 고르시오.

①  ②  ③  ④  ⑤

2 대화를 듣고, 여자가 구입할 동전지갑으로 가장 적절한 것을 고르시오.

①  ②  ③  ④  ⑤

3 다음을 듣고, 부산의 날씨로 가장 적절한 것을 고르시오.

①  ②  ③  ④  ⑤

4 대화를 듣고, 남자가 한 마지막 말의 의도로 가장 적절한 것을 고르시오.

① 칭찬 ② 거절 ③ 항의 ④ 충고 ⑤ 부탁

5 다음을 듣고, 남자가 가게에 대해 언급하지 <u>않은</u> 것을 고르시오.

① 이름   ② 위치   ③ 판매 상품
④ 할인 행사   ⑤ 분위기

6 대화를 듣고, 두 사람이 만날 시각을 고르시오.

① 1:30 p.m.   ② 2:00 p.m.   ③ 2:30 p.m.   ④ 3:00 p.m.   ⑤ 3:30 p.m.

7 대화를 듣고, 남자의 장래 희망으로 가장 적절한 것을 고르시오.

① 경찰   ② 조각가   ③ 운동 선수
④ 프로게이머   ⑤ 스포츠 기자

8 대화를 듣고, 여자의 심정으로 가장 적절한 것을 고르시오.

① 부러움   ② 화남   ③ 자랑스러움
④ 실망스러움   ⑤ 걱정스러움

9 대화를 듣고, 남자가 대화 직후에 할 일로 가장 적절한 것을 고르시오.

① 소포 보내기   ② 세탁물 찾아오기   ③ 헌 옷 가지러 가기
④ 봉사활동 하러 가기   ⑤ 친구들에게 전화하기

10 대화를 듣고, 무엇에 관한 내용인지 가장 적절한 것을 고르시오.

① 옷 환불   ② 택배 상자 포장
③ 인터넷 광고   ④ 어울리는 옷 선택
⑤ SNS에 사진 게시

07
회
모
의
고
사

11번~20번 문제는 다음 페이지에 ➡

11 대화를 듣고, 두 사람이 함께 이용할 교통수단으로 가장 적절한 것을 고르시오.

① 버스　　　　　② 택시　　　　　③ 기차
④ 지하철　　　　⑤ 비행기

12 대화를 듣고, 남자가 새 셔츠를 산 이유를 고르시오.

① 셔츠가 얼마 없어서　　　　　② 선물을 하고 싶어서
③ 색깔이 마음에 들어서　　　　④ 새 청바지에 잘 어울려서
⑤ 친구가 멋있다고 해서

13 대화를 듣고, 두 사람이 대화하는 장소로 가장 적절한 곳을 고르시오.

① 병원　　　　② 식물원　　　　③ 마트　　　　④ 카페　　　　⑤ 동물원

14 대화를 듣고, 슈퍼마켓의 위치로 가장 알맞은 곳을 고르시오.

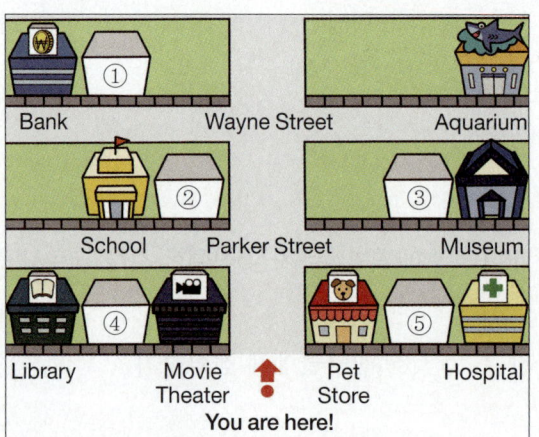

15 대화를 듣고, 여자가 남자에게 부탁한 일로 가장 적절한 것을 고르시오.

① 방 청소하기　　　　② 과일 사오기　　　　③ 개 먹이 주기
④ 개 산책시키기　　　⑤ 공원에 데려다주기

---

16 대화를 듣고, 남자가 여자에게 제안한 것으로 가장 적절한 것을 고르시오.

① 오렌지 주스 마시기　　② 엄마께 연락하기　　③ 레모네이드 함께 만들기
④ 과일 사오기　　⑤ 설거지 하기

17 대화를 듣고, 남자가 지난 주말에 한 일을 고르시오.

① 숙제하기　　② 쿠키 굽기　　③ 병문안 가기
④ 세차 도와주기　　⑤ 가족 여행 가기

18 대화를 듣고, 남자의 직업으로 가장 적절한 것을 고르시오.

① 경찰관　　② 택시 기사　　③ 택배 기사
④ 버스 기사　　⑤ 철도 승무원

[19~20] 대화를 듣고, 남자의 마지막 말에 이어질 여자의 말로 가장 적절한 것을 고르시오.

19 Woman: _____

① The online lecture is free.　　② Sure, let's do it together now.
③ My hobby is drawing pictures.　　④ The new poster looks interesting.
⑤ Let's go to the lecture after school.

20 Woman: _____

① Yes, I'd love to.
② No, I didn't eat them.
③ Yes, I'll try using your soap.
④ No, I'm not good at cooking.
⑤ Well, I don't like taking classes.

Dictation Test 07

녹음을 다시 들으면서 빈칸을 채워주세요

M1(17)_07_D

Dictation(받아쓰기)은 본문을 받아쓰면서 영어듣기의 집중력을 향상시키고 다양한 표현을 정리하기 위한 영어듣기 학습법입니다. 녹음을 다시 듣고, 빈칸에 알맞은 단어를 써 보세요.
※Dictation의 정답은 듣기 대본의 밑줄 친 부분을 확인하세요.

📖 정답 p. 26

맞은 개수 / 총135개

그림정보파악(담화)

1. 다음을 듣고, 'I'가 무엇인지 가장 적절한 것을 고르시오.

①  ②

③  ④

⑤

01 W: I live in Africa. I have _____ _____ _____ _____. I have four long legs. I am tall and I have a very long neck. I eat _____ _____ _____. What am I?

고난도 그림정보파악(대화)

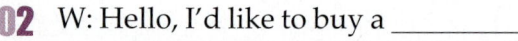

2024 영어듣기능력평가 2회 2번 변형

2. 대화를 듣고, 여자가 구입할 동전지갑으로 가장 적절한 것을 고르시오.

①  ②

③  ④

⑤

02 W: Hello, I'd like to buy a _____ _____.

M: We have round ones and square ones.

W: Could you show me the round ones?

M: Sure, how about this one _____ _____?

W: Hmm… Do you have any other designs?

M: We have this _____ one with hearts on it.

W: I like hearts. I'll take that one.

---

3. 다음을 듣고, 부산의 날씨로 가장 적절한
   것을 고르시오.

① ② ③ ④ ⑤

03

W: Good morning! Let's check the weather for today. In Seoul, it will be _____. There will be _____ _____ in Daegu. Busan will be very _____. If you're in Busan, don't forget to _____ a jacket when you go outside.

2025 영어듣기능력평가 1회 4번 변형

4. 대화를 듣고, 남자가 한 마지막 말의 의
   도로 가장 적절한 것을 고르시오.
   ① 칭찬　　② 거절
   ③ 항의　　④ 충고
   ⑤ 부탁

04

M: Hey, Emily. Who's that you're with?

W: Hey, Roger. She's a _____ _____. I'm showing her around the school.

M: But aren't you _____ _____ the student council?

W: It's okay. I like _____ people.

M: You're always there for others. That's amazing!

다음 페이지에 계속 ➡

07회 딕테이션

5. 다음을 듣고, 남자가 가게에 대해 언급하지 **않은** 것을 고르시오.

① 이름
② 위치
③ 판매 상품
④ 할인 행사
⑤ 분위기

05 M: I want to tell you about a nice store in our town. It's called Jeremy's Best Subs. It is on Elm Street, right _____ _____ the subway station. They sell _____ _____ _____ sandwiches, but ham and egg is my favorite. I love this place because they always _____ _____ at the beginning of the semester!

---

6. 대화를 듣고, 두 사람이 만날 시각을 고르시오.

① 1:30 p.m.　② 2:00 p.m.
③ 2:30 p.m.　④ 3:00 p.m.
⑤ 3:30 p.m.

06 (*Telephone rings.*)

M: Hello?

W: Dad, it's me. You are coming to _____ _____ _____, right?

M: Of course, sweetheart. I'll be at the station by 2:00 p.m.

W: No, I'm taking the next train. It arrives one and _____ _____ _____ _____.

M: No problem. I'll see you at 3:30.

W: Thanks, Dad. See you soon.

7. 대화를 듣고, 남자의 장래 희망으로 가장 적절한 것을 고르시오.

① 경찰 ② 조각가
③ 운동 선수 ④ 프로게이머
⑤ 스포츠 기자

07

W: Brad, what are you working on?

M: I'm writing a sports _____ for our school newspaper.

W: That _____ _____. You must like sports very much.

M: Yes, I want to become a _____ _____ in the future.

W: I'm sure you'll _____ _____!

M: Thank you!

8. 대화를 듣고, 여자의 심정으로 가장 적절한 것을 고르시오.

① 부러움
② 화남
③ 자랑스러움
④ 실망스러움
⑤ 걱정스러움

08

M: What are you reading?

W: I'm reading the school newspaper. My sister is on _____ _____ _____.

M: Your sister?

W: Yes. She _____ _____ _____ in the piano competition. I'm so _____ _____ her.

M: Wow, that's great!

W: I'm really happy for her. She did a great job.

다음 페이지에 계속 ➡

07회 딕테이션

9. 대화를 듣고, 남자가 대화 직후에 할 일로 가장 적절한 것을 고르시오.

① 소포 보내기
② 세탁물 찾아오기
③ 헌 옷 가지러 가기
④ 봉사활동 하러 가기
⑤ 친구들에게 전화하기

09
W: Chris, can you _____ _____ _____ these boxes?

M: Sure! What are they?

W: They're _____ _____ that I'm sending to people in developing countries.

M: How did you collect them?

W: I called all my friends and _____ _____ _____.

M: I have some clothes at home that I don't _____ _____.

W: Then can you give them to me?

M: Sure! I'll go get them right now.

대화화제추론

10. 대화를 듣고, 무엇에 관한 내용인지 가장 적절한 것을 고르시오.

① 옷 환불
② 택배 상자 포장
③ 인터넷 광고
④ 어울리는 옷 선택
⑤ SNS에 사진 게시

10
M: What are you looking at, Sojin?

W: I'm looking at how to _____ _____ _____ from this website.

M: What did you buy?

W: A T-shirt. But the sleeves are _____ _____ the pictures.

M: Okay. But it says you need to pay for _____ postage.

W: That's fine. This T-shirt doesn't suit me.

11. 대화를 듣고, 두 사람이 함께 이용할 교
통수단으로 가장 적절한 것을 고르시오.

① 버스
② 택시
③ 기차
④ 지하철
⑤ 비행기

11 W: Honey, how did you like the movie?

M: It was really great, especially _____ _____ _____. That was amazing.

W: It really was. By the way, it's 11:15. Do you think the subway is still running?

M: No, the _____ only runs until 11:00 p.m.

W: Then, I guess we should take a taxi _____ _____ _____.

M: Right! Look, there's an empty taxi coming.

W: All right, let's take that one.

12. 대화를 듣고, 남자가 새 셔츠를 산 이유
를 고르시오.

① 셔츠가 얼마 없어서
② 선물을 하고 싶어서
③ 색깔이 마음에 들어서
④ 새 청바지에 잘 어울려서
⑤ 친구가 멋있다고 해서

12 W: Jay! You look so nice! Did you _____ _____ _____?

M: Yes, I bought this red shirt.

W: It's really great. However, you already have a lot of shirts.

M: But I didn't have a red one and I _____ _____ _____ so much.

W: Oh, okay. Anyway, I think it _____ _____ _____ your new jeans.

다음 페이지에 계속 ➡

07회 딕테이션

13. 대화를 듣고, 두 사람이 대화하는 장소로 가장 적절한 곳을 고르시오.

① 병원   ② 식물원
③ 마트   ④ 카페
⑤ 동물원

13

W: Hi there! How can I help you?

M: I want to know when the animals _____ _____.

W: Sure! Just _____ _____ the signs around the zoo showing feeding times.

M: Thanks! I'll check them out.

W: We also have special times when you can help our staff feed the animals.

M: Cool! How can I join?

W: You can _____ _____ at the zoo entrance.

14. 대화를 듣고, 슈퍼마켓의 위치로 가장 알맞은 곳을 고르시오.

14

M: Excuse me. Is there a supermarket _____?

W: Yes, there is one not too far from here.

M: Good! Can you tell me where it is?

W: Sure. _____ _____ one block and _____ _____ on Parker Street.

M: On Parker Street?

W: Yes, it's _____ _____ _____. It's between the library and the movie theater.

M: Thank you.

15. 대화를 듣고, 여자가 남자에게 부탁한 일로 가장 적절한 것을 고르시오.

① 방 청소하기
② 과일 사오기
③ 개 먹이 주기
④ 개 산책시키기
⑤ 공원에 데려다주기

15
W: Sam, did you feed the dog?

M: Yes, Mom. I _____ him _____ _____

_____ ago.

W: Good. Then, can you _____ _____ _____

_____ _____?

M: Okay, I'll take him to the park.

W: Thank you.

16. 대화를 듣고, 남자가 여자에게 제안한 것으로 가장 적절한 것을 고르시오.

① 오렌지 주스 마시기
② 엄마께 연락하기
③ 레모네이드 함께 만들기
④ 과일 사오기
⑤ 설거지 하기

16
W: I'm going to make orange juice. Do you want

some?

M: We're _____ _____ _____. Mom will buy

some later. But, we have lemons.

W: Then, I'll make some _____.

M: Why don't we _____ _____ _____? I'm

thirsty, too.

W: Sounds good.

07
회
딕
테
이
션

다음 페이지에 계속 ➡

17. 대화를 듣고, 남자가 지난 주말에 한 일을 고르시오.

① 숙제하기 　　② 쿠키 굽기
③ 병문안 가기 　④ 세차 도와주기
⑤ 가족 여행 가기

17

M: Lisa, what did you do over the weekend?

W: I _____ _____ with my mom at home. How was your weekend?

M: I helped my dad wash his car at the _____ _____.

W: That sounds like hard work.

M: Yeah, I'm _____ _____ tired today.

W: Still, I think it's sweet of you to help your dad.

18. 대화를 듣고, 남자의 직업으로 가장 적절한 것을 고르시오.

① 경찰관
② 택시 기사
③ 택배 기사
④ 버스 기사
⑤ 철도 승무원

18

W: Hello. Do you go to Bakersville?

M: We stop _____ _____ _____ _____ the village. It's easy walking from there.

W: Oh, good. How long does it take?

M: About 40 minutes. There are four stops in between.

W: I see. Which bus should I take to _____ _____?

M: Bus 402. The same number. Would you like to _____ _____?

W: Yes! How much is the fare?

M: It's 4 dollars.

19. 대화를 듣고, 남자의 마지막 말에 이어질 여자의 말로 가장 적절한 것을 고르시오.

Woman: _____

① The online lecture is free.
② Sure, let's do it together now.
③ My hobby is drawing pictures.
④ The new poster looks interesting.
⑤ Let's go to the lecture after school.

19

W: Hey, Jinwoo.

M: Hi, Yujin. Did you see the new poster on the _____ _____?

W: Which one do you mean?

M: The one about the online _____ on art.

W: Oh, yes. It looks very interesting. I love art.

M: Then shall we _____ for the lecture? I'm interested in art, too.

W: <u>Sure, let's do it together now.</u>

20. 대화를 듣고, 남자의 마지막 말에 이어질 여자의 말로 가장 적절한 것을 고르시오.

Woman: _____

① Yes, I'd love to.
② No, I didn't eat them.
③ Yes, I'll try using your soap.
④ No, I'm not good at cooking.
⑤ Well, I don't like taking classes.

20

M: Hi, Harin. Did you have a good weekend?

W: Yes. I _____ a soap making class.

M: That's nice. I love making soap.

W: It was really fun. How was your weekend?

M: It was great. I went to a strawberry farm.

W: Did you _____ many strawberries?

M: Yes, I did. Do you want to _____ _____?

W: <u>Yes, I'd love to.</u>

07
회
딕
테
이
션

Words & Expressions Review 07

● 다음 단어를 암기하세요.

문제	번호	단어	뜻
1	1	spot	반점
	2	twig	잔가지
3	3	heavy	많은, 심한
	4	windy	바람이 많이 부는
4	5	amazing	놀라운
5	6	right	바로, 정확히
	7	semester	학기
6	8	station	역, 정류장
	9	arrive	도착하다
	10	article	(신문, 잡지의) 기사, 글
7	11	journalist	기자, 저널리스트
	12	make it	(바라던 일을) 해내다
	13	the front page	제1면
8	14	competition	경연, 대회
	15	be proud of ~	~를 자랑스러워하다
9	16	used	헌, 중고의
	17	ask for ~	~을 요청하다
	18	get a refund	환불받다
	19	different from ~	~과 다른
10	20	return postage	반송료
	21	suit	(~에게) 어울리다
11	22	especially	특히

문제	번호	단어	뜻
	23	by the way	그런데
11	24	run	운행하다, 운영하다
	25	take a taxi	택시를 타다
	26	empty	빈, 비어 있는
12	27	anyway	아무튼, 어쨌든
	28	go best with ~	~과 가장 잘 어울리다
	29	look for	~을 찾다
13	30	check ~ out	~을 확인하다
	31	sign up	신청하다
14	32	nearby	가까운 곳에, 인근에
	33	turn	몸을 돌리다
	34	feed	먹이를 주다, 먹이
15	35	half an hour	30분
	36	take A for a walk	A를 산책시키다
	37	car wash	세차장
17	38	a bit	조금, 약간
	39	still	그래도, 그럼에도 불구하고
18	40	hop on	(버스, 기차 등에) 타다
19	41	lecture	강의
	42	take	(수업·강의 등을) 듣다, 수강하다
20	43	soap	비누
	44	pick	(과일 등을) 따다

● 왼쪽 단어장의 뜻이 보이지 않게 반으로 접고, 학습한 단어의 뜻을 아래 빈칸에 적어주세요.

1	take a taxi	23	by the way
2	station	24	suit
3	turn	25	nearby
4	spot	26	half an hour
5	semester	27	arrive
6	empty	28	lecture
7	windy	29	article
8	journalist	30	hop on
9	make it	31	take A for a walk
10	get a refund	32	used
11	twig	33	feed
12	anyway	34	car wash
13	different from ~	35	the front page
14	check ~ out	36	a bit
15	look for	37	especially
16	return postage	38	still
17	amazing	39	competition
18	be proud of ~	40	take
19	heavy	41	go best with ~
20	right	42	soap
21	sign up	43	ask for ~
22	run	44	pick

07 회 단 어

전국 15개 시·도 교육청 공동주관 및 서울시 연합 내신

08회 중학영어듣기 모의고사

M1(17)_08_US
모두 **미국식 발음(US)**
으로 녹음

M1(17)_08_UK

20문제 중 5문제에 **영국식 발음**
(US+UK)을 포함하여 녹음

📖 정답 및 해석 p. 30

1 다음을 듣고, 'I'가 무엇인지 가장 적절한 것을 고르시오.

①  ②  ③  ④  ⑤

2 대화를 듣고, 여자가 구입할 잠옷으로 가장 적절한 것을 고르시오.

①  ②  ③  ④  ⑤

3 다음을 듣고, 서울의 내일 날씨로 적절한 것을 고르시오.

①  ②  ③  ④  ⑤

4 대화를 듣고, 마지막 말에 담긴 남자의 의도로 적절한 것을 고르시오.

① 요청   ② 수락   ③ 거절   ④ 사과   ⑤ 격려

5 다음을 듣고, 남자가 자신의 반려견에 대해 언급하지 <u>않은</u> 것을 고르시오.

① 이름　　　② 나이　　　③ 외모 특징　　　④ 크기　　　⑤ 성격

6 대화를 듣고, 두 사람이 만날 시각을 고르시오.

① 3:00 p.m.　　② 3:30 p.m.　　③ 4:00 p.m.　　④ 4:30 p.m.　　⑤ 5:00 p.m.

7 대화를 듣고, 남자의 장래 희망으로 가장 적절한 것을 고르시오.

① 교사　　　　　② 외교관　　　　　③ 패션 디자이너
④ 모델　　　　　⑤ 화가

8 대화를 듣고, 여자의 심정으로 가장 적절한 것을 고르시오.

① shy　　　② bored　　　③ calm　　　④ excited　　　⑤ nervous

9 대화를 듣고, 여자가 대화 직후에 할 일로 가장 적절한 것을 고르시오.

① 주제 정하기　　　② 과제 제출하기　　　③ 선생님 찾아가기
④ 온라인 강의 듣기　　⑤ 친구에게 전화하기

10 대화를 듣고, 무엇에 관한 내용인지 가장 적절한 것을 고르시오.

① 급식 만족도　　　② 어버이날 행사　　　③ 자원봉사활동
④ 학교 축제　　　　⑤ 수업 공개의 날

11번~20번 문제는 다음 페이지에 ➡

11 대화를 듣고, 두 사람이 함께 이용할 교통수단으로 가장 적절한 것을 고르시오.

① 기차　　　　② 택시　　　　③ 버스　　　　④ 자전거　　　　⑤ 지하철

12 대화를 듣고, 남자가 영화관에 갈 수 <u>없는</u> 이유로 가장 적절한 것을 고르시오.

① 감기에 걸려서　　　　　　　　② 용돈을 다 써서
③ 학원에 가야 해서　　　　　　　④ 심부름을 해야 해서
⑤ 엄마와 쇼핑을 가야 해서

13 대화를 듣고, 두 사람이 대화하는 장소로 가장 적절한 곳을 고르시오.

① 버스 매표소　　　　　② 경찰서　　　　　　③ 놀이공원
④ 공항　　　　　　　　⑤ 우체국

14 Kids' DIY Workshop에 관한 다음 내용을 듣고, 표에서 일치하지 <u>않는</u> 것을 고르시오.

		Kids' DIY Workshop
①	일시	this Saturday, 1 p.m.
②	내용	build and fly kites
③	소요 시간	2 hours
④	참가비	$5
⑤	장소	Central Park

15 대화를 듣고, 여자가 남자에게 부탁한 일로 가장 적절한 것을 고르시오.

① 공항 마중오기　　　　② 사진 보내주기　　　　③ 비행기 예약하기
④ 고양이 밥 주기　　　　⑤ 날씨 확인하기

16 대화를 듣고, 여자가 남자에게 제안한 것으로 가장 적절한 것을 고르시오.

① 사진 촬영하기　　　　　② 쇼핑 같이 가기
③ 옷 수선하기　　　　　　④ 점심 같이 먹기
⑤ 옷 기부하기

17 대화를 듣고, 여자가 지난 주말에 한 일을 고르시오.

① 청소하기　　　　② 낚시하기　　　　③ 영화 보기
④ 놀이동산 가기　　⑤ 가족사진 찍기

18 대화를 듣고, 여자의 직업으로 가장 적절한 것을 고르시오.

① 화가　　　　　② 사진 작가　　　　③ 수의사
④ 제빵사　　　　⑤ 버스 기사

19 대화를 듣고, 남자의 마지막 말에 이어질 여자의 응답으로 가장 적절한 것을 고르시오.

Woman: _____

① Let's go swimming.　　　　② Let's meet at the library.
③ I don't like taking quizzes.　④ Math is my favorite subject.
⑤ Tomorrow is Friday already!

20 대화를 듣고, 여자의 마지막 말에 이어질 남자의 응답으로 가장 적절한 것을 고르시오.

Man: _____

① Let's play tennis.　　② Nothing special.　　③ Don't mention it.
④ I can't play tennis.　　⑤ That sounds good.

Dictation Test 08

녹음을 다시 듣으면서 빈칸을 채워주세요

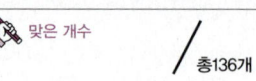

M1(17)_08_D

Dictation(받아쓰기)은 본문을 받아쓰면서 영어듣기의 집중력을 향상시키고 다양한 표현을 정리하기 위한 영어듣기 학습법입니다. **녹음을 다시 듣고, 빈칸에 알맞은 단어를 써 보세요.**

※Dictation의 정답은 듣기 대본의 밑줄 친 부분을 확인하세요.

📖 정답 p. 30

🏹 맞은 개수 ____ / 총136개

그림정보파악(담화)

1. 다음을 듣고, 'I'가 무엇인지 가장 적절한 것을 고르시오.

01 M: I live in the forest. I have large eyes, a flat face, and _____ _____. I hunt for small animals like mice _____ _____ _____ using powerful claws. I can turn my head and neck up to 270 degrees. I make a unique "_____" _____. What am I?

그림정보파악(대화)

2. 대화를 듣고, 여자가 구입할 잠옷으로 가장 적절한 것을 고르시오.

02 M: How can I help you?

W: Hi. I want to buy _____ for my son.

M: Okay. _____ _____ these ones with circles on them?

W: Hmm... I don't think he'll like those ones.

M: Then, how about these ones with _____?

W: Great! He loves stars.

M: I'm sure he'll like them.

W: Right. I'll _____ them.

---

3. 다음을 듣고, 서울의 내일 날씨로 적절한 것을 고르시오.

①    ②

③    ④

⑤

03 W: Good morning! It's Friday, February 12th. This is the weather report. It's sunny and warm all over the country now, but tomorrow _____ _____ _____ than today. Seoul will have very _____ _____. In Jeju and Daegu, there will be _____ in the afternoon.

4. 대화를 듣고, 마지막 말에 담긴 남자의 의도로 적절한 것을 고르시오.

① 요청   ② 수락
③ 거절   ④ 사과
⑤ 격려

04 W: Hey, do you have a biology textbook?

M: Yes, I do. Why?

W: Can I _____ _____ _____ today? I forgot to bring mine today.

M: Hmm. You tore my book last time.

W: Oh, that was my mistake. I promise I will _____ _____ this time.

M: Okay. _____ _____ _____.

08
회
딕
테
이
션

다음 페이지에 계속 ➡

담화미언급

5. 다음을 듣고, 남자가 자신의 반려견에 대해 언급하지 <u>않은</u> 것을 고르시오.
① 이름 ② 나이
③ 외모 특징 ④ 크기
⑤ 성격

05 M: Hello, everyone. I'd like to talk about my pet dog. His name is Max. He's three years old. I got him when he was a puppy. He has soft, _____ _____ and loves meeting new people. He's very friendly and _____ _____ _____ outside. He's like a little brother to me.

수치파악

6. 대화를 듣고, 두 사람이 만날 시각을 고르시오.
① 3:00 p.m. ② 3:30 p.m.
③ 4:00 p.m. ④ 4:30 p.m.
⑤ 5:00 p.m.

06 M: Hi, Sophie. I have an _____ ticket to the basketball game.

W: Really? Can I come?

M: Sure. It starts at 5 p.m. tomorrow.

W: Then, I'll come to your house at 4:00. Let's _____ _____ _____ on the way.

M: In that case, let's meet 30 minutes _____.

W: 3:30 at your house? Okay. I'll see you then.

7. 대화를 듣고, 남자의 장래 희망으로 가장
   적절한 것을 고르시오.
   ① 교사   ② 외교관
   ③ 패션 디자이너 ④ 모델
   ⑤ 화가

07
W: What are you doing, David?

M: I'm _____ _____. I want to speak English well.

W: Why? Do you want to become an English teacher?

M: No, I want to _____ _____. I want to go abroad and study fashion.

W: I see. Is that why you always practice drawing?

M: That's right. I have to study art and _____ _____ well.

W: Wow. You're working really hard to achieve your dream!

8. 대화를 듣고, 여자의 심정으로 가장 적절
   한 것을 고르시오.
   ① shy   ② bored
   ③ calm   ④ excited
   ⑤ nervous

08
M: Vacation time! Are you excited, Claire?

W: I would be… But our _____ has been talking for 20 minutes _____…

M: Yeah… He is making a particularly _____ _____ today.

W: It is _____ _____ _____. All I want to do is get out of here.

M: Just _____ _____ _____. Let's hope that he will be done soon.

W: Okay…

다음 페이지에 계속 ➡

08 회 딕테이션

9. 대화를 듣고, 여자가 대화 직후에 할 일로 가장 적절한 것을 고르시오.

① 주제 정하기
② 과제 제출하기
③ 선생님 찾아가기
④ 온라인 강의 듣기
⑤ 친구에게 전화하기

09

W: Lorrie, who's your group project partner?

M: It's Patrick. Why do you ask?

W: My partner Margaret is moving to another school, so I _____ _____ have a partner.

M: Do you want to _____ us?

W: Can I?

M: Sure. Patrick will be glad to have you, too.

W: Just to _____ _____, I'll call and ask him right now.

10. 대화를 듣고, 무엇에 관한 내용인지 가장 적절한 것을 고르시오.

① 급식 만족도
② 어버이날 행사
③ 자원봉사활동
④ 학교 축제
⑤ 수업 공개의 날

10

W: James, did you see this new _____ on the school website?

M: No, what is it about?

W: It's about the _____ _____ next Wednesday. It says that our parents should come.

M: Then, what are we doing on that day?

W: We just _____ _____ as usual _____ our parents are watching. And then, they will have some time with our teacher to talk about us.

11. 대화를 듣고, 두 사람이 함께 이용할 교통수단으로 가장 적절한 것을 고르시오.

① 기차   ② 택시
③ 버스   ④ 자전거
⑤ 지하철

11

M: Where do you want to go today?

W: Let's go to Gyeongbokgung Palace.

M: Okay. Shall we _____ _____ _____?
There's a subway station near the palace.

W: Hmm… I was hoping to do some sightseeing on our way there.

M: Why don't we _____ bicycles then?

W: Great idea! Let's _____ _____ to the palace.

12. 대화를 듣고, 남자가 영화관에 갈 수 없는 이유로 가장 적절한 것을 고르시오.

① 감기에 걸려서
② 용돈을 다 써서
③ 학원에 가야 해서
④ 심부름을 해야 해서
⑤ 엄마와 쇼핑을 가야 해서

12

M: Mom, can I go to the movies with my friends today?

W: Today? No, _____ _____ you can't.

M: Why not?

W: You _____ _____ _____ _____ with me today so we could buy you a new coat.

M: Oh, I'm sorry. I forgot about that.

W: Why don't you go to the movies _____ _____?

M: Okay, I will.

다음 페이지에 계속 ➡

08 회 딕테이션

13. 대화를 듣고, 두 사람이 대화하는 장소로 가장 적절한 곳을 고르시오.

① 버스 매표소   ② 경찰서
③ 놀이공원   ④ 공항
⑤ 우체국

13
M: Hi, how can I help you?

W: I'd like to buy a ticket to Seoul, please.

M: Sure. What time would you like to _____?

W: I'd like to leave _____ _____ _____

_____.

M: There's a _____ bus that leaves _____

10 minutes.

W: I'll take that one. Thank you.

---

14. Kids' DIY Workshop에 관한 다음 내용을 듣고, 표에서 일치하지 <u>않는</u> 것을 고르시오.

Kids' DIY Workshop		
①	일시	this Saturday, 1 p.m.
②	내용	build and fly kites
③	소요 시간	2 hours
④	참가비	$5
⑤	장소	Central Park

14
W: Hello, everyone! Let me tell you about our Kids'

DIY Workshop. It'll _____ _____ this

Saturday at 1 p.m. In this workshop, kids will

build their own kites, and then test them outside.

The event will be 2 hours _____ _____.

The fee is 10 dollars, including all materials. The

workshop will _____ _____ at Central

Park. Thanks.

15. 대화를 듣고, 여자가 남자에게 부탁한 일로 가장 적절한 것을 고르시오.

① 공항 마중오기
② 사진 보내주기
③ 비행기 예약하기
④ 고양이 밥 주기
⑤ 날씨 확인하기

15 (*Telephone rings.*)

M: Hello.

W: Hi, Jamie. This is Hailey.

M: Hi, Hailey. Are you _____ _____ _____ _____?

W: No, my flight has been _____ because of bad weather.

M: Oh, I'm sorry to hear that.

W: I won't be home until tomorrow. So, could you _____ _____ _____ for one more day?

M: No problem. She's in good hands, so don't worry.

제안파악

16. 대화를 듣고, 여자가 남자에게 제안한 것으로 가장 적절한 것을 고르시오.

① 사진 촬영하기
② 쇼핑 같이 가기
③ 옷 수선하기
④ 점심 같이 먹기
⑤ 옷 기부하기

16 M: Hailey, nice jeans!

W: Thank you. I _____ _____ yesterday.

M: Where did you get them?

W: A new store just opened in my town. It has _____ _____ _____ _____.

M: Good for you! Does it have jeans for men, too? I really need to buy some.

W: Yes. Why don't we _____ _____ together?

M: That sounds great!

다음 페이지에 계속 ➡

08 회 딕테이션

17. 대화를 듣고, 여자가 지난 주말에 한 일을 고르시오.

① 청소하기
② 낚시하기
③ 영화 보기
④ 놀이동산 가기
⑤ 가족사진 찍기

17

W: Fred, how did you spend your _____?

M: I watched a movie with my friends. How was your weekend?

W: I _____ _____ with my Dad.

M: Wow, that sounds awesome! Did you catch many fish?

W: No, I couldn't catch any, but I _____ had fun.

M: Great! I'd _____ _____ give fishing a try _____ _____.

2025 영어듣기능력평가 1회 18번 변형

18. 대화를 듣고, 여자의 직업으로 가장 적절한 것을 고르시오.

① 화가
② 사진 작가
③ 수의사
④ 제빵사
⑤ 버스 기사

18

W: How can I help you today?

M: My dog, Rocky, hasn't been able to _____ _____ since yesterday.

W: Let's take a look. [Pause] He has a sharp piece of wood stuck in his _____.

M: Oh, can you take it out?

W: Sure. I'll also clean his wound and _____ _____ _____ on it.

M: Thank you.

19. 대화를 듣고, 남자의 마지막 말에 이어질 여자의 응답으로 가장 적절한 것을 고르시오.

Woman: _____

① Let's go swimming.
② Let's meet at the library.
③ I don't like taking quizzes.
④ Math is my favorite subject.
⑤ Tomorrow is Friday already!

19
W: Jake, _____ _____ _____ studying for the math quiz?

M: No, not yet. How about you?

W: Me, neither. Why don't we study together?

M: Sounds good. The quiz is next week, isn't it?

W: Yes, it's next Friday. Let's start studying tomorrow after school.

M: Great idea! _____ _____ _____ _____?

W: Let's meet at the library.

20. 대화를 듣고, 여자의 마지막 말에 이어질 남자의 응답으로 가장 적절한 것을 고르시오.

Man: _____

① Let's play tennis.
② Nothing special.
③ Don't mention it.
④ I can't play tennis.
⑤ That sounds good.

20
M: Who is that girl? She's so good at tennis.

W: She's a _____ _____ in my class.

M: What do you think of her?

W: She's very nice. By the way, _____ _____ _____ _____ tennis, too?

M: Yes, I am.

W: Then why don't you _____ _____ _____?

M: That sounds good.

08회 딕테이션

Words & Expressions Review 08

● 다음 단어를 암기하세요.

문제	번호	단어	뜻
1	□ 1	flat	평평한
	□ 2	broad	넓은
2	□ 3	pajamas	잠옷
	□ 4	be sure	확신하다
3	□ 5	all over the country	전국적으로, 전국에
4	□ 6	tear	찢다
5	□ 7	soft	부드러운, 푹신한
	□ 8	golden	금빛의
	□ 9	friendly	친근한
6	□ 10	extra	여분의
	□ 11	grab a snack	간식을 먹다
	□ 12	on the way	가는 길에
	□ 13	earlier	더 일찍
7	□ 14	go abroad	외국에 가다
8	□ 15	principal	교장 선생님
	□ 16	already	이미, 벌써
	□ 17	make an announcement	소식을 전하다, 발표를 하다
9	□ 18	project	과제, 연구 프로젝트
	□ 19	no longer	더 이상 ～하지 않는
	□ 20	make sure	확실하게 하다
10	□ 21	notice	공지사항, 공고문
	□ 22	as usual	평소처럼, 늘 그렇듯이

문제	번호	단어	뜻
10	□ 23	while	～하는 동안
11	□ 24	sightseeing	관광
	□ 25	on one's way ～	～에 가는 중에
	□ 26	Why don't we ~?	～하는 게 어때?
	□ 27	borrow	빌리다
12	□ 28	another day	다른 날
13	□ 29	depart	출발하다, 떠나다
	□ 30	as soon as possible	가능한 한 빨리
14	□ 31	build	만들다
	□ 32	include	포함하다
	□ 33	material	재료
15	□ 34	cancel	취소하다
	□ 35	in good hands	잘 관리되는
16	□ 36	all kinds of	모든 종류의
	□ 37	Good for you!	너에게 잘됐다!
17	□ 38	still	그런데도, 그럼에도 불구하고
	□ 39	would like to + 동사	～하고 싶다
	□ 40	as well	～도, 또한
18	□ 41	properly	제대로
	□ 42	stick	찔리다, 박히다
19	□ 43	quiz	(간단한) 시험
20	□ 44	What do you think of ~?	～에 대해 어떻게 생각해?

M1(17)_W_08

● 왼쪽 단어장의 뜻이 보이지 않게 반으로 접고, 학습한 단어의 뜻을 아래 빈칸에 적어주세요.

1	as usual	23	build
2	soft	24	include
3	sightseeing	25	make sure
4	Good for you!	26	on the way
5	while	27	extra
6	pajamas	28	another day
7	principal	29	stick
8	depart	30	borrow
9	project	31	tear
10	be sure	32	properly
11	as well	33	material
12	friendly	34	cancel
13	make an announcement	35	flat
14	Why don't we ~?	36	all kinds of
15	go abroad	37	earlier
16	already	38	grab a snack
17	in good hands	39	would like to + 동사
18	on one's way ~	40	as soon as possible
19	broad	41	still
20	golden	42	all over the country
21	notice	43	quiz
22	no longer	44	What do you think of ~?

08
회
단
어

1 다음을 듣고, 'I'가 무엇인지 가장 적절한 것을 고르시오.

①  ②  ③  ④  ⑤

2 대화를 듣고, 여자가 구입할 쿠션으로 가장 적절한 것을 고르시오.

①  ②  ③  ④  ⑤

3 다음을 듣고, 오늘 오후의 날씨로 가장 적절한 것을 고르시오.

①  ②  ③  ④  ⑤

4 대화를 듣고, 마지막 말에 담긴 여자의 의도로 적절한 것을 고르시오.

① 사양　　② 격려　　③ 사과　　④ 감사　　⑤ 부탁

5 다음을 듣고, 남자가 친구에 대해 언급하지 <u>않은</u> 것을 고르시오.

① 이름　　② 고향　　③ 취미　　④ 성격　　⑤ 싫어하는 음식

6 대화를 듣고, 두 사람이 만날 시각을 고르시오.

① 8:00 a.m.　　② 9:00 a.m.　　③ 10:00 a.m.　　④ 11:00 a.m.　　⑤ 12:00 p.m.

7 대화를 듣고, 여자의 장래 희망으로 가장 적절한 것을 고르시오.

① 디자이너　　　　　② 컴퓨터 프로그래머　　　③ 가수
④ 배우　　　　　　　⑤ 영화감독

8 대화를 듣고, 여자의 심정으로 가장 적절한 것을 고르시오.

① 지루함　　② 수줍음　　③ 슬픔　　④ 감사함　　⑤ 화남

9 대화를 듣고, 남자가 대화 직후에 할 일로 가장 적절한 것을 고르시오.

① 지갑 주문하기　　② 신용카드 찾기　　③ 참고서 구매하기
④ 코트 수선 맡기기　　⑤ 서점에 데려다 주기

10 대화를 듣고, 무엇에 관한 내용인지 가장 적절한 것을 고르시오.

① 공연장 에티켓　　② 긴급상황 대피 요령　　③ 식품 안전 교육
④ 대중교통 에티켓　　⑤ 대중교통 수단

11번~20번 문제는 다음 페이지에 ➡

11 대화를 듣고, 두 사람이 함께 이용할 교통수단으로 가장 적절한 것을 고르시오.

① 택시   ② 기차   ③ 비행기

④ 지하철   ⑤ 공항 버스

12 대화를 듣고, 남자가 꽃을 구입한 이유로 가장 적절한 것을 고르시오.

① 사촌의 졸업을 축하하기 위해서

② 할머니의 생신을 축하하기 위해서

③ 친구들의 공연을 축하하기 위해서

④ 동생의 대회 수상을 축하하기 위해서

⑤ 부모님의 결혼기념일을 축하하기 위해서

13 대화를 듣고, 두 사람이 대화하는 장소로 가장 적절한 곳을 고르시오.

① 호텔   ② 공항   ③ 도서관   ④ 음식점   ⑤ 영화관

14 대화를 듣고, 여자가 찾고 있는 편지의 위치로 가장 적절한 것을 고르시오.

15 대화를 듣고, 남자가 여자에게 부탁한 일로 가장 적절한 것을 고르시오.

① 음식 데우기   ② 식당 예약하기   ③ 선물 골라주기

④ 동생 숙제 도와주기   ⑤ 저녁 식사 준비하기

16 대화를 듣고, 남자가 여자에게 제안한 것으로 가장 적절한 것을 고르시오.

① 일찍 출발하기　　② 숙소 예약하기　　③ 방 청소하기
④ 역까지 태워 주기　　⑤ 기차표 예매하기

17 대화를 듣고, 여자가 토요일에 할 일로 가장 적절한 것을 고르시오.

① 옷 교환하기　　② 자전거 타기　　③ 케이크 만들기
④ 축구 연습하기　　⑤ 야구경기 관람하기

18 대화를 듣고, 남자의 직업으로 가장 적절한 것을 고르시오.

① 화가　　② 미용사　　③ 사진 작가
④ 디자이너　　⑤ 네일 아티스트

[19~20] 대화를 듣고, 남자의 마지막 말에 이어질 여자의 말로 가장 적절한 것을 고르시오.

19 Woman: _____

① You did a good job!
② I hope he gets better soon.
③ I'm glad he likes our dance.
④ Don't worry, you'll be great.
⑤ Thank you for understanding.

20 Woman: _____

① No, it's free.
② It's not on sale.
③ I don't play baseball.
④ That's a good choice.
⑤ Yes, you can try it on.

Dictation Test 09

녹음을 다시 들으면서 빈칸을 채워주세요

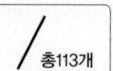

M1(17)_09_D

Dictation(받아쓰기)은 본문을 받아쓰면서 영어듣기의 집중력을 향상시키고 다양한 표현을 정리하기 위한 영어듣기 학습법입니다. **녹음을 다시 듣고, 빈칸에 알맞은 단어를 써 보세요.**
※Dictation의 정답은 듣기 대본의 밑줄 친 부분을 확인하세요.

📖 정답 p. 35

맞은 개수 / 총113개

2024 영어듣기능력평가 1회 1번 변형

그림정보파악(담화)

1. 다음을 듣고, 'I'가 무엇인지 가장 적절한 것을 고르시오.

①  ②

③   ④

⑤

01 W: I am an insect. I have large eyes. I have six legs and I also have _____. I am yellow and black. I _____ _____ from flower to flower and make honey. What am I?

그림정보파악(대화)

2. 대화를 듣고, 여자가 구입할 쿠션으로 가장 적절한 것을 고르시오.

①  ②

③   ④

⑤

02 M: Can I help you?

W: Yes. I'm looking to buy a sofa cushion.

M: How about this one with the _____ picture?

W: Hmm… Do you have anything else?

M: We have this one _____ _____ _____ on it.

W: Oh… I like that one!

M: I'm glad that you like it.

W: Great! I'll take it.

날씨파악–그림

3. 다음을 듣고, 오늘 오후의 날씨로 가장 적절한 것을 고르시오.

①
②
③
④
⑤

03 W: Good morning. Here's the _____ _____. We are having a little bit of rain right now. The rain will _____ _____ snow this afternoon. The snow will continue until tomorrow morning. So, please be careful on the road.

마지막말의도파악

4. 대화를 듣고, 마지막 말에 담긴 여자의 의도로 적절한 것을 고르시오.

① 사양 ② 격려
③ 사과 ④ 감사
⑤ 부탁

04 M: Kelly! What happened to the camera?

W: I'm sorry, Dad. I _____ _____.

M: How did it happen?

W: I _____ on the floor when I tried to take a photo of our puppy yesterday.

M: Oh, didn't you _____ _____?

W: I'm OK. I _____ for the camera trouble again.

다음 페이지에 계속 ➡

5. 다음을 듣고, 남자가 친구에 대해 언급하지 <u>않은</u> 것을 고르시오.

① 이름　　　② 고향
③ 취미　　　④ 성격
⑤ 싫어하는 음식

05 M: Hello, everyone. Let me tell you about my best friend. His name is John. He is my _____ _____ friend. He likes to play soccer and video games for fun. He is kind and _____. He likes to eat everything, _____ _____ vegetables.

6. 대화를 듣고, 두 사람이 만날 시각을 고르시오.

① 8:00 a.m.
② 9:00 a.m.
③ 10:00 a.m.
④ 11:00 a.m.
⑤ 12:00 p.m.

06 W: Sam, did you do the reading and writing homework?

M: No, I can't decide which book I want to read.

W: _____, _____. Why don't we go to the library together?

M: Okay. Let's meet tomorrow morning at 9.

W: Um... That's a little _____ _____ _____. Can we meet at 10 a.m.?

M: No problem. See you tomorrow.

7. 대화를 듣고, 여자의 장래 희망으로 가장 적절한 것을 고르시오.

① 디자이너
② 컴퓨터 프로그래머
③ 가수
④ 배우
⑤ 영화감독

07

M: I love these videos _____ _____ _____.

Did you make them?

W: Yes. I used my cell phone. Which video is your favorite?

M: The one with your sister dancing. It's like a movie.

W: Really? _____ _____ _____? I want to become _____ _____ _____.

M: Wow. That's wonderful!

8. 대화를 듣고, 여자의 심정으로 가장 적절한 것을 고르시오.

① 지루함   ② 수줍음
③ 슬픔   ④ 감사함
⑤ 화남

08

M: Mary, these are for you.

W: Oh, new shoes! I love them, Dad. But, it's not my birthday.

M: Your shoes are _____ _____. And, I saw you _____ _____ these ones at the shop.

W: Really? Dad, you are amazing!

M: Also, they are green, your _____ _____.

W: Thank you so much, Dad. I love you.

다음 페이지에 계속 ➡

9. 대화를 듣고, 남자가 대화 직후에 할 일로 가장 적절한 것을 고르시오.
   ① 지갑 주문하기
   ② 신용카드 찾기
   ③ 참고서 구매하기
   ④ 코트 수선 맡기기
   ⑤ 서점에 데려다 주기

09 W: Dad, I need to go to the bookstore and buy some new workbooks.

M: Sure, take my _____ _____ with you.

W: I can't find your _____, Dad!

M: It's in the front _____ of my coat.

W: I don't know which coat you're _____ _____.

M: Oh, I'll go find it for you.

W: Thank you, Dad!

10. 대화를 듣고, 무엇에 관한 내용인지 가장 적절한 것을 고르시오.
    ① 공연장 에티켓
    ② 긴급상황 대피 요령
    ③ 식품 안전 교육
    ④ 대중교통 에티켓
    ⑤ 대중교통 수단

10 M: Amy, when you're on _____ _____, always keep these rules in mind.

W: What rules, Dad?

M: Keep your voice down, line up in an orderly fashion, and _____ _____ _____.

W: I understand the first two, but why can't I eat?

M: Because the smell can be _____ to others.

W: Okay. I will always keep those things in mind.

11. 대화를 듣고, 두 사람이 함께 이용할 교통수단으로 가장 적절한 것을 고르시오.

① 택시　　　② 기차
③ 비행기　　④ 지하철
⑤ 공항 버스

11

W: How should we get to the airport tomorrow?

M: Since we have some _____, why don't we grab a taxi?

W: I'm not sure about that. Isn't it too expensive?

M: Then let's take the _____ _____ instead.

W: Hmm... Is the bus stop near our house?

M: Yes, and it'll take us _____ to the airport.

W: Great!

12. 대화를 듣고, 남자가 꽃을 구입한 이유로 가장 적절한 것을 고르시오.

① 사촌의 졸업을 축하하기 위해서
② 할머니의 생신을 축하하기 위해서
③ 친구들의 공연을 축하하기 위해서
④ 동생의 대회 수상을 축하하기 위해서
⑤ 부모님의 결혼기념일을 축하하기 위해서

12

W: Hi, Victor. Those flowers are so pretty! Where did you _____ _____ _____?

M: I bought them from the flower shop down the road.

W: Oh, what are they for?

M: They're for my parents' _____ _____. It's today.

W: I see. How nice _____ _____ to buy flowers for them!

M: Well, I just hope they'll like them.

W: I'm sure they will.

다음 페이지에 계속 ➡

09
회
딕테이션

13. 대화를 듣고, 두 사람이 대화하는 장소로 가장 적절한 곳을 고르시오.
   ① 호텔   ② 공항
   ③ 도서관   ④ 음식점
   ⑤ 영화관

13

W: Good morning, sir. May I help you?

M: Yes, please. I made a reservation two _____

_____.

W: Okay. What is your name?

M: Thomas Boyles.

W: You _____ a double room for three days, right?

M: Yes.

W: Here is the key. Please leave your key at the

_____ _____ when you go out.

14. 대화를 듣고, 여자가 찾고 있는 편지의 위치로 가장 적절한 것을 고르시오.

14

W: Ted, did you see my letter from Sarah?

M: Didn't you put it _____ _____ _____ the books?

W: I did, but it's not there.

M: Then look _____ _____ _____ or on the chairs.

W: I still can't find it. Can you look _____ the flower vases?

M: It's not there. Wait a minute. Oh, it's next to the left one _____ _____ _____!

15. 대화를 듣고, 남자가 여자에게 부탁한 일로 가장 적절한 것을 고르시오.

① 음식 데우기
② 식당 예약하기
③ 선물 골라주기
④ 동생 숙제 도와주기
⑤ 저녁 식사 준비하기

15
W: Happy anniversary, Dad. Have a great dinner with Mom.

M: Thanks, sweetie. You know what to eat for dinner, right?

W: Yes, Mom told me how to _____ _____ the food.

M: And your little sister needs help with her _____ after dinner.

W: Her math homework?

M: Yes. Could you _____ _____ _____ _____?

W: Sure, no problem.

16. 대화를 듣고, 남자가 여자에게 제안한 것으로 가장 적절한 것을 고르시오.

① 일찍 출발하기
② 숙소 예약하기
③ 방 청소하기
④ 역까지 태워 주기
⑤ 기차표 예매하기

16
M: Rebecca, when are you _____ _____ Pohang?

W: Tomorrow. I'll stay just for one night.

M: Did you _____ a room?

W: Not yet. I'll do that on my cellphone on the way.

M: Why don't you do it now? It can be hard to _____ _____ _____.

W: Okay, I will. That's a good idea.

다음 페이지에 계속 ➡

17. 대화를 듣고, 여자가 토요일에 할 일로 가장 적절한 것을 고르시오.

① 옷 교환하기
② 자전거 타기
③ 케이크 만들기
④ 축구 연습하기
⑤ 야구경기 관람하기

17

W: What do you think of this t-shirt?

M: It's nice, but I don't think it _____ you very well.

W: Don't worry. I bought it for my brother. It's his birthday this weekend.

M: Oh, okay. Do you _____ _____ _____?

W: We're planning to _____ a baseball game at the stadium this Saturday.

M: Sounds fantastic! Have fun.

고난도　직업추론

18. 대화를 듣고, 남자의 직업으로 가장 적절한 것을 고르시오.

① 화가　　② 미용사
③ 사진 작가　④ 디자이너
⑤ 네일 아티스트

18

M: Hello. What can I help you with?

W: I made an _____ to get my hair colored today.

M: Sure. Sit here, please. So what color were you thinking?

W: Can you _____ _____ _____ light brown?

M: Okay. Do you want to _____ your hair _____, too?

W: Yes. Just a _____, please.

M: Alright. Let's begin.

19. 대화를 듣고, 남자의 마지막 말에 이어질 여자의 말로 가장 적절한 것을 고르시오.

Woman: _____

① You did a good job!
② I hope he gets better soon.
③ I'm glad he likes our dance.
④ Don't worry, you'll be great.
⑤ Thank you for understanding.

19
W: Hi, Mark. You're coming to tonight's dance practice, right?

M: Oh, Sally, I'm afraid I can't.

W: Why not? Our contest is next week.

M: I know. I have to go visit my grandpa _____ _____ _____.

W: Oh, I see. Is he very _____?

M: I think so. I'd better go and see how he is.

W: I hope he gets better soon.

20. 대화를 듣고, 남자의 마지막 말에 이어질 여자의 말로 가장 적절한 것을 고르시오.

Woman: _____

① No, it's free.
② It's not on sale.
③ I don't play baseball.
④ That's a good choice.
⑤ Yes, you can try it on.

20
W: May I help you?

M: I'm looking for a baseball cap for my daughter.

W: OK. How old is she?

M: She's 14. Can you _____ one for me?

W: Sure. This one is very _____ among girls that age.

M: That looks nice. I'll take it.

W: Would you like it gift-wrapped?

M: Is there an _____ _____?

W: No, it's free.

Words & Expressions Review 09

● 다음 단어를 암기하세요.

문제	번호	단어	뜻
1	1	insect	곤충
	2	from A to B	A에서 B로
2	3	butterfly	나비
3	4	a little bit of	약간의, 조금의
	5	turn into ~	~으로 변하다
4	6	slip	미끄러지다
	7	floor	바닥, 층
	8	take a photo of ~	~의 사진을 찍다
5	9	elementary school	초등학교
	10	for fun	취미로
	11	outgoing	외향적인, 사교적인
	12	except for	~을 제외하고
6	13	neither	(부정문에서) ~도 아니다
7	14	movie director	영화감독
	15	wonderful	아주 멋진, 훌륭한
8	16	worn out	닳아서 못 쓰게 된
	17	amazing	놀라운
9	18	credit card	신용카드
	19	wallet	지갑
	20	pocket	주머니
	21	talk about	~에 대해서 이야기하다
10	22	public transit	대중교통

문제	번호	단어	뜻
10	23	in an orderly fashion	질서 있게
	24	allowed	허용된
	25	disturbing	방해가 되는
11	26	airport	공항
	27	grab a taxi	택시를 잡다
	28	straight	바로, 곧장
12	29	anniversary	기념일
	30	hope	바라다
	31	May I help you?	무엇을 도와드릴까요?
	32	make a reservation	예약하다
13	33	book	예약하다
	34	front desk	안내데스크
	35	go out	외출하다
14	36	on top of ~	~ 위에
	37	warm up	(식은 음식을) 데우다
15	38	homework	숙제
	39	give ~ a hand	~를 도와주다
16	40	leave for ~	~로 떠나다
	41	suit	어울리다
17	42	plan	계획
	43	stadium	경기장
18	44	appointment	예약, 약속

M1(17)_W_09

● 왼쪽 단어장의 뜻이 보이지 않게 반으로 접고, 학습한 단어의 뜻을 아래 빈칸에 적어주세요.

1	straight		23	take a photo of ~
2	plan		24	except for
3	butterfly		25	in an orderly fashion
4	a little bit of		26	insect
5	disturbing		27	movie director
6	suit		28	give ~ a hand
7	turn into ~		29	amazing
8	elementary school		30	allowed
9	appointment		31	wonderful
10	slip		32	on top of ~
11	book		33	make a reservation
12	floor		34	public transit
13	leave for ~		35	credit card
14	for fun		36	pocket
15	anniversary		37	warm up
16	outgoing		38	homework
17	worn out		39	go out
18	May I help you?		40	wallet
19	grab a taxi		41	airport
20	stadium		42	talk about
21	neither		43	from A to B
22	front desk		44	hope

전국 15개 시·도 교육청 공동주관 및 서울시 연합 내신

10회 중학영어듣기 모의고사

M1(17)_10_US
모두 **미국식 발음(US)**
으로 녹음

M1(17)_10_UK
20문제 중 5문제에 **영국식 발음**
(US+UK)을 포함하여 녹음

📖 정답 및 해석 p.39

1 다음을 듣고, 'this'가 가리키는 것으로 가장 적절한 것을 고르시오.

①  ②  ③ 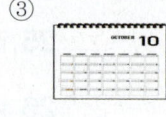 ④  ⑤

2 대화를 듣고, 여자가 구입할 도시락통으로 가장 적절한 것을 고르시오.

①  ②  ③ 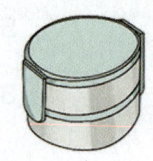 ④ 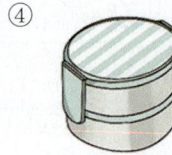 ⑤

3 다음을 듣고, 다음 주 금요일 날씨로 적절한 것을 고르시오.

①  ②  ③  ④  ⑤

4 대화를 듣고, 마지막 말에 담긴 여자의 의도로 적절한 것을 고르시오.

① 사과　　　② 허락　　　③ 권유　　　④ 거절　　　⑤ 위로

5 다음을 듣고, 남자가 체육대회에 대해 언급하지 <u>않은</u> 것을 고르시오.

① 시작 시간　　　　② 장소　　　　　　③ 경기 종목
④ 날씨　　　　　　⑤ 준비물

6 대화를 듣고, 두 사람이 이야기를 나누는 현재 시각을 고르시오.

① 5:30 p.m.　　② 6:00 p.m.　　③ 6:30 p.m.　　④ 7:00 p.m.　　⑤ 7:30 p.m.

7 대화를 듣고, 남자의 장래 희망으로 가장 적절한 것을 고르시오.

① 영상 편집자　　　　② 영화 감독　　　　③ 프로 게이머
④ 운동선수　　　　　⑤ 유튜버

8 대화를 듣고, 남자의 심정으로 가장 적절한 것을 고르시오.

① bored　　② relaxed　　③ excited　　④ angry　　⑤ worried

9 대화를 듣고, 남자가 대화 직후에 할 일로 가장 적절한 것을 고르시오.

① 간식 사 오기　　　　　　② 자전거 대여하기
③ 공원에 주차하기　　　　④ 일기예보 확인하기
⑤ 졸업 선물 구입하기

10 대화를 듣고, 무엇에 관한 내용인지 가장 적절한 것을 고르시오.

① 통학버스 안전 수칙　　　　② 대중교통 탑승 예절
③ 안전벨트 착용 방법　　　　④ 안전사고 대처 요령
⑤ 버스요금 할인 혜택

11번~20번 문제는 다음 페이지에 ➡

11 대화를 듣고, 남자가 이용할 교통수단으로 가장 적절한 것을 고르시오.

① 자전거   ② 걷기   ③ 자동차   ④ 버스   ⑤ 지하철

12 대화를 듣고, 여자가 카페에 가는 이유로 가장 적절한 것을 고르시오.

① 책을 읽으려고   ② 친구를 만나려고   ③ 쿠키를 구매하려고
④ 일자리를 알아보려고   ⑤ 샌드위치를 먹으려고

13 대화를 듣고, 두 사람이 대화하는 장소로 가장 적절한 곳을 고르시오.

① 놀이공원   ② 문구점   ③ 스키장   ④ PC방   ⑤ 식료품점

14 대화를 듣고, 남자가 가려고 하는 장소를 고르시오.

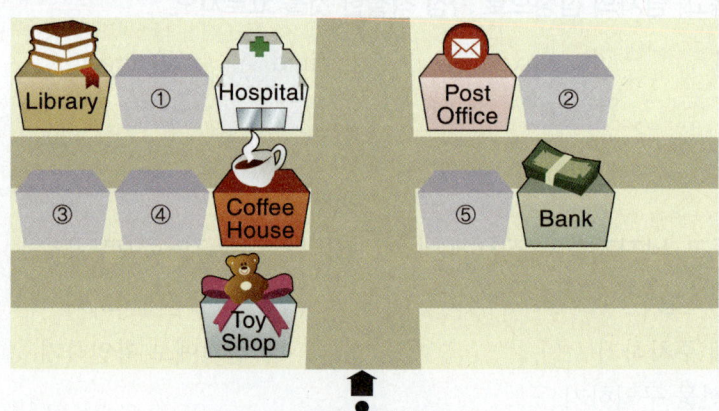

15 대화를 듣고, 남자가 여자에게 부탁한 일로 가장 적절한 것을 고르시오.

① 피아노 연습하기   ② 학교 축제 준비하기   ③ 창문 닫기
④ 음악실 청소하기   ⑤ 문 잠그기

16 대화를 듣고, 여자가 남자에게 제안한 것으로 가장 적절한 것을 고르시오.

① 책 읽기　　　　② 운동하기　　　　③ 얼음물 마시기
④ 도서관에 가기　　⑤ 에어컨 수리하기

17 대화를 듣고, 남자가 여름방학에 한 일로 가장 적절한 것을 고르시오.

① 캠핑 가기　　　　② 춤 배우기　　　　③ 자원 봉사하기
④ 드럼 배우기　　　⑤ 사촌 집 방문하기

18 대화를 듣고, 여자의 직업으로 가장 적절한 것을 고르시오.

① 화가　　　　　　② 사진 작가　　　　③ 배구 선수
④ 영화 배우　　　　⑤ 동물 사육사

[19~20] 대화를 듣고, 남자의 마지막 말에 이어질 여자의 말로 가장 적절한 것을 고르시오.

19 Woman: _____

① I'll try for ten.　　　　　② You should try it.
③ It looks delicious.　　　　④ I have eaten enough.
⑤ Two apple pies, please.

20 Woman: _____

① I enjoy swimming in summer.　　② The wind is strong.
③ It is sunny outside.　　　　　　④ Winter is my favorite season.
⑤ The flowers bloom in the spring.

Dictation Test 10

녹음을 다시 들으면서 빈칸을 채워주세요

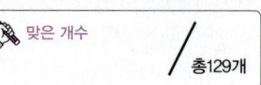

M1(17)_10_D

Dictation(받아쓰기)은 본문을 받아쓰면서 영어듣기의 집중력을 향상시키고 다양한 표현을 정리하기 위한 영어듣기 학습법입니다. **녹음을 다시 듣고, 빈칸에 알맞은 단어를 써 보세요.**
※Dictation의 정답은 듣기 대본의 밑줄 친 부분을 확인하세요.

📖 정답 p. 39

✎ 맞은 개수 / 총129개

그림정보파악(담화)

1. 다음을 듣고, 'this'가 가리키는 것으로 가장 적절한 것을 고르시오.

①
②
③
④
⑤

01 W: You can find this _____ _____ a desk or on the wall. This is a system for _____ _____ _____ days, months, or years. You can use this to _____ _____ important events, like friends' birthdays, so you don't forget them. What is this?

고난도 **그림정보파악(대화)** 🇺🇸🇬🇧

2. 대화를 듣고, 여자가 구입할 도시락통으로 가장 적절한 것을 고르시오.

①
②
③
④
⑤

02 W: Hi, I am looking for a lunch box for my daughter.

M: We have _____ ones and _____ ones.

W: I think a round one would be nice.

M: Okay. Any _____ _____ for the lunch box?

W: My daughter likes cats. Do you have one with _____ _____ _____?

M: Yes, we do! This one would be perfect! Isn't it cute?

W: Great! I will take it. Thank you.

날씨파악–그림

3. 다음을 듣고, 다음 주 금요일 날씨로 적절한 것을 고르시오.

① ② ③ ④ ⑤

03 W: Here is the weather forecast for next week. It will be rainy until next Wednesday evening and start to _____ _____ Wednesday night. It will be _____ and _____ Thursday and Friday. However, we will have very cloudy skies again and be _____ _____ _____ this weekend.

마지막말의도파악

4. 대화를 듣고, 마지막 말에 담긴 여자의 의도로 적절한 것을 고르시오.

① 사과 ② 허락
③ 권유 ④ 거절
⑤ 위로

04 M: Mom, can I _____ _____ at David's house?

W: Why?

M: He has got an awesome toy robot. It's very _____ _____ _____ alone.

W: I guess it can be fun.

M: Yes! And he asked for my help.

W: OK. Don't forget to _____ _____ _____ and phone number.

다음 페이지에 계속 ➡

5. 다음을 듣고, 남자가 체육대회에 대해 언급하지 **않은** 것을 고르시오.
① 시작 시간　② 장소
③ 경기 종목　④ 날씨
⑤ 준비물

05 M: Good morning, students! Let me remind you about tomorrow's Sports Day. The events _____ _____ at 9 a.m. Please _____ _____ the soccer field before then. The weather will be very hot tomorrow. _____ _____ to bring a water bottle, hat, and sunscreen.

6. 대화를 듣고, 두 사람이 이야기를 나누는 현재 시각을 고르시오.
① 5:30 p.m.　② 6:00 p.m.
③ 6:30 p.m.　④ 7:00 p.m.
⑤ 7:30 p.m.

06 M: Esther, I've got two tickets to a concert tonight at Lincoln Center. _____ _____ _____ _____ come?

W: Sounds great! When does the concert start?

M: It starts at 7 p.m.

W: Then we _____ _____ there by 6:30 p.m.

M: Right. So we have to _____ _____. It's 6 p.m. now.

W: Is it 6 already? Let's hurry!

7. 대화를 듣고, 남자의 장래 희망으로 가장 적절한 것을 고르시오.

① 영상 편집자　② 영화 감독
③ 프로 게이머　④ 운동선수
⑤ 유튜버

07
W: Daniel, what are you watching?

M: I'm watching game-playing videos.

W: But don't you _____ _____ the actual game more than watching it?

M: I _____ _____. I want to be a pro gamer someday.

W: I believe you will be a great pro gamer.

M: Thank you!

8. 대화를 듣고, 남자의 심정으로 가장 적절한 것을 고르시오.

① bored　　② relaxed
③ excited　④ angry
⑤ worried

08
W: Tony, what's wrong?

M: I got a _____ _____ on my math test.

W: Well, you will do better next time.

M: But my mom will be _____ _____.

W: I'm sure your mom will understand.

M: No, you don't know my mom. She will _____ _____ for weeks.

다음 페이지에 계속 ➡

9. 대화를 듣고, 남자가 대화 직후에 할 일로 가장 적절한 것을 고르시오.
   ① 간식 사 오기
   ② 자전거 대여하기
   ③ 공원에 주차하기
   ④ 일기예보 확인하기
   ⑤ 졸업 선물 구입하기

09
M: Isn't the weather lovely, Annie?

W: Yes, Dad. It's beautiful and I love this park.

M: I'm glad you like it. Look! There are people _____ _____.

W: It looks so fun. Can we ride bicycles, too? There's a _____ _____ over there.

M: Sure. I'll go and _____ two bicycles now.

W: Great! Thanks, Dad.

10. 대화를 듣고, 무엇에 관한 내용인지 가장 적절한 것을 고르시오.
   ① 통학버스 안전 수칙
   ② 대중교통 탑승 예절
   ③ 안전벨트 착용 방법
   ④ 안전사고 대처 요령
   ⑤ 버스요금 할인 혜택

10
M: Sandy, here are some _____ _____ for your school bus.

W: What are they, Dad?

M: First, you should always wear your _____.

W: I already know that. What else?

M: Also, don't _____ your seat before the bus stops.

W: Why not?

M: It's dangerous to stand up on a moving bus.

W: Okay. I'll remember the rules.

🇺🇸🇬🇧

11. 대화를 듣고, 남자가 이용할 교통수단으로 가장 적절한 것을 고르시오.

① 자전거   ② 걷기
③ 자동차   ④ 버스
⑤ 지하철

11 W: Ed, aren't you _____ _____ _____

_____?

M: No, Mom. My appointment is at 5 p.m. It's only 4:30.

W: That's my point. It'll take more than 30 minutes to get there _____ _____.

M: Ah, Dad's going to _____ _____ _____ by car.

W: Oh, that's good. It'll save a lot of time.

2024 영어듣기능력평가 2회 12번 변형

12. 대화를 듣고, 여자가 카페에 가는 이유로 가장 적절한 것을 고르시오.

① 책을 읽으려고
② 친구를 만나려고
③ 쿠키를 구매하려고
④ 일자리를 알아보려고
⑤ 샌드위치를 먹으려고

12 M: Hi, Ella! Where are you going?

W: Hi! I'm going to a café.

M: Are you going to _____ _____

_____ there?

W: Actually, no. They sell delicious cookies there, and I'm going to buy some.

M: Sounds good! Can I _____ _____ you?

W: Of course you can!

다음 페이지에 계속 ➡

13. 대화를 듣고, 두 사람이 대화하는 장소로 가장 적절한 곳을 고르시오.

① 놀이공원   ② 문구점
③ 스키장   ④ PC방
⑤ 식료품점

13
M: Wow, let's ride the roller coaster! It looks _____ _____!

W: It looks scary. I'm afraid it's too fast.

M: Come on. It's safe. It's the most _____ _____ in this park.

W: Let's try the merry-go-round first.

M: Okay. First, ride the merry-go-round, and then _____ _____ the roller coaster.

14. 대화를 듣고, 남자가 가려고 하는 장소를 고르시오.

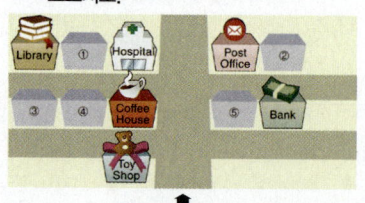
You are here!

14
M: Excuse me. How can I get to the art gallery?

W: Oh, it's not far. _____ _____ for two blocks, and then turn left.

M: Turn left?

W: Yes. Walk down _____ _____ _____, and you'll see it on your left. It's _____ _____ _____ the coffee house.

M: Okay, thanks a lot.

부탁(요청)한일파악

15. 대화를 듣고, 남자가 여자에게 부탁한 일로 가장 적절한 것을 고르시오.

① 피아노 연습하기
② 학교 축제 준비하기
③ 창문 닫기
④ 음악실 청소하기
⑤ 문 잠그기

15

M: Mary, can I talk to you?

W: Sure, Mr. Johnson.

M: Are you going to _____ _____ _____ in the music room?

W: Yes. The school festival is next week.

M: Then, can you _____ _____ _____ when you leave the room?

W: Yes, I'll do that.

제안파악

16. 대화를 듣고, 여자가 남자에게 제안한 것으로 가장 적절한 것을 고르시오.

① 책 읽기
② 운동하기
③ 얼음물 마시기
④ 도서관에 가기
⑤ 에어컨 수리하기

16

W: Tony, are you okay?

M: Not really. It's so hot in here. Is the _____ _____ _____ _____?

W: I'm afraid not. It'll be fixed this afternoon.

M: Oh, no. I can't study _____ _____ _____. What can I do?

W: Well, how about _____ _____ _____?

M: Sounds good. It won't be so hot in the library.

다음 페이지에 계속 ➡

17. 대화를 듣고, 남자가 여름방학에 한 일로
    가장 적절한 것을 고르시오.

    ① 캠핑 가기
    ② 춤 배우기
    ③ 자원 봉사하기
    ④ 드럼 배우기
    ⑤ 사촌 집 방문하기

17

M: Rose, did you have a good summer vacation?

W: Yes, I _____ _____ with my cousins.

M: That _____ fun! What did you do together?

W: We sang around the fire. What about you?

M: I learned to _____ _____ _____ at the
   community center.

W: Wow! That sounds wonderful.

18. 대화를 듣고, 여자의 직업으로 가장 적절
    한 것을 고르시오.

    ① 화가
    ② 사진 작가
    ③ 배구 선수
    ④ 영화 배우
    ⑤ 동물 사육사

18

M: Tiffany, how was the event with your fans?

W: It was amazing. They all _____
   me on winning the MVP award.

M: Great! You played really well this season.

W: I hope they'll _____ _____ me next
   season as well.

M: I'm sure they will. You're the best player in the
   women's volleyball league.

W: Thank you for _____ that.

19. 대화를 듣고, 남자의 마지막 말에 이어질 여자의 말로 가장 적절한 것을 고르시오.

Woman: _____

① I'll try for ten.
② You should try it.
③ It looks delicious.
④ I have eaten enough.
⑤ Two apple pies, please.

19

W: Have you heard about the peach festival happening next weekend?

M: Yeah, it'll be _____ _____ _____ fun. Are you thinking of going?

W: I'm _____ _____ the peach pie eating contest. I love peaches!

M: That's awesome! You'll have so much fun!

W: Thanks!

M: _____ _____ pies do you think you can eat?

W: I'll try for ten.

20. 대화를 듣고, 남자의 마지막 말에 이어질 여자의 말로 가장 적절한 것을 고르시오.

Woman: _____

① I enjoy swimming in summer.
② The wind is strong.
③ It is sunny outside.
④ Winter is my favorite season.
⑤ The flowers bloom in the spring.

20

M: It's _____ _____ these days.

W: Yeah. Summer is _____ _____.

M: Do you like summer?

W: Not really. It's too hot in summer.

M: What _____ do you like most, then?

W: Winter is my favorite season.

Words & Expressions Review 10

● 다음 단어를 암기하세요.

문제	번호	단어	뜻
1	□ 1	either A or B	A나 B
	□ 2	rectangular	직사각형의
2	□ 3	round	원형의
	□ 4	preferred	선호하는
3	□ 5	be caught in ~	~을 만나다
	□ 6	shower	소나기
	□ 7	sleep over	(남의 집에서) 자다
	□ 8	awesome	멋진, 굉장한
	□ 9	assemble	조립하다
4	□ 10	alone	혼자서, 혼자
	□ 11	ask for ~	~을 요청하다
	□ 12	address	주소
5	□ 13	remind	상기시키다
	□ 14	tonight	오늘 밤, 오늘 밤에
6	□ 15	Would you like to ~?	~할래?, ~하시겠습니까?
	□ 16	get going	출발하다, 시작하다
7	□ 17	actual	실제의
	□ 18	someday	언젠가, 훗날
	□ 19	beautiful	(날씨가) 화창한
9	□ 20	rental shop	대여점
	□ 21	rent	(사용료를 내고 단기간) 빌리다
10	□ 22	safety rules	안전 수칙

문제	번호	단어	뜻
10	□ 23	seatbelt	안전벨트, 안전띠
	□ 24	dentist	치과, 치과의사
11	□ 25	appointment	예약, 약속
	□ 26	save	절약하다, 구하다
	□ 27	meet	만나다
12	□ 28	actually	사실은
	□ 29	delicious	아주 맛있는
	□ 30	afraid	걱정하는, 두려워하는
13	□ 31	popular	인기 있는, 대중적인
	□ 32	merry-go-round	회전목마
15	□ 33	lock	잠그다, 자물쇠
	□ 34	fix	수리하다, 고치다
16	□ 35	heat	더위, 열기
	□ 36	sound + 형용사	~하게 들리다
17	□ 37	learn to + 동사	~하는 것을 배우다
	□ 38	congratulate	축하하다
	□ 39	win an award	상을 받다
18	□ 40	keep ~ing	계속해서 ~하다
	□ 41	support	지지하다
	□ 42	volleyball	배구
19	□ 43	consider	고려하다, 숙고하다
20	□ 44	bloom	꽃이 피다, 꽃

M1(17)_W_10

●왼쪽 단어장의 뜻이 보이지 않게 반으로 접고, 학습한 단어의 뜻을 아래 빈칸에 적어주세요.

1	tonight		23	rectangular
2	beautiful		24	bloom
3	afraid		25	keep ~ing
4	rental shop		26	meet
5	save		27	sound + 형용사
6	assemble		28	get going
7	actual		29	merry-go-round
8	heat		30	shower
9	address		31	lock
10	remind		32	support
11	awesome		33	either A or B
12	preferred		34	learn to + 동사
13	congratulate		35	round
14	Would you like to ~?		36	sleep over
15	win an award		37	seatbelt
16	alone		38	safety rules
17	someday		39	volleyball
18	dentist		40	consider
19	ask for ~		41	delicious
20	rent		42	popular
21	appointment		43	actually
22	fix		44	be caught in ~

10
회
단
어

전국 15개 시·도 교육청 공동주관 및 서울시 연합 내신

11회 중학영어듣기 모의고사

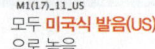
모두 **미국식 발음(US)**
으로 녹음

20문제 중 5문제에 **영국식 발음**
(US+UK)을 포함하여 녹음

정답 및 해석 p. 43

1 다음을 듣고, 'I'가 무엇인지 가장 적절한 것을 고르시오.

① 　② 　③ 　④ 　⑤

2 대화를 듣고, 여자가 구입한 컵으로 가장 적절한 것을 고르시오.

① 　② 　③ 　④ 　⑤

3 다음을 듣고, 현재 시카고의 날씨로 가장 적절한 것을 고르시오.

① 　② 　③ 　④ 　⑤

4 대화를 듣고, 마지막 말에 담긴 여자의 의도로 적절한 것을 고르시오.

① 사과　　② 감사　　③ 격려　　④ 충고　　⑤ 위로

5 다음을 듣고, 남자가 식목 행사에 대해 언급하지 <u>않은</u> 것을 고르시오.

① 행사 날짜   ② 식목 장소   ③ 제공품
④ 식재 나무 종류   ⑤ 신청 방법

6 대화를 듣고, 두 사람이 만날 시각을 고르시오.

① 2:00 p.m.   ② 3:00 p.m.   ③ 4:00 p.m.   ④ 5:00 p.m.   ⑤ 6:00 p.m.

7 대화를 듣고, 남자의 장래 희망으로 가장 적절한 것을 고르시오.

① 시인   ② 공무원   ③ 경찰관
④ 과학자   ⑤ 영화 감독

8 대화를 듣고, 여자의 심정으로 가장 적절한 것을 고르시오.

① 수줍음   ② 부러움   ③ 실망스러움   ④ 긴장함   ⑤ 미안함

9 대화를 듣고, 남자가 대화 직후에 할 일로 적절한 것을 고르시오.

① 저녁 먹기   ② 빵 굽기   ③ 상 차리기
④ 채소 썰기   ⑤ 손 씻기

10 대화를 듣고, 무엇에 관한 내용인지 가장 적절한 것을 고르시오.

① 동아리 모집   ② 소방 훈련   ③ 자전거 구매
④ 마라톤 행사   ⑤ 학교 축제

11번~20번 문제는 다음 페이지에 ➡

11 대화를 듣고, 여자가 이용할 교통수단으로 가장 적절한 것을 고르시오.

① 택시   ② 자전거   ③ 지하철   ④ 버스   ⑤ 오토바이

12 대화를 듣고, 여자가 장갑을 찾는 이유로 가장 적절한 것을 고르시오.

① 날씨가 추워서   ② 반품하기 위해서
③ 선물하기 위해서   ④ 세탁하기 위해서
⑤ 친구에게 돌려주기 위해서

13 대화를 듣고, 두 사람이 대화하는 장소로 가장 적절한 곳을 고르시오.

① 병원   ② 편의점   ③ 세탁소
④ 미용실   ⑤ 극장

14 대화를 듣고, Flower Shop의 위치로 가장 알맞은 곳을 고르시오.

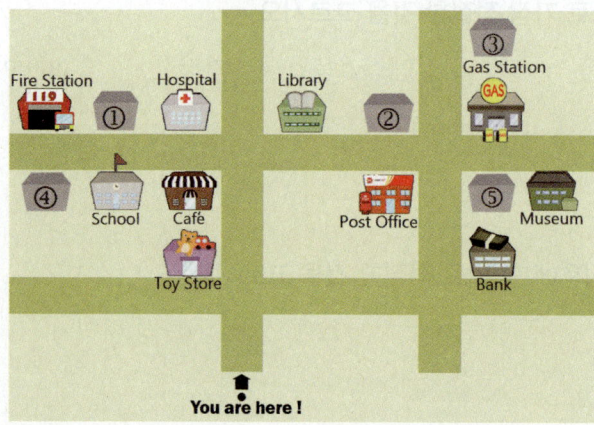

15 대화를 듣고, 여자가 남자에게 부탁한 일로 가장 적절한 것을 고르시오.

① 고기 굽기   ② 설거지하기   ③ 텐트 주문하기
④ 아버지 돕기   ⑤ 캠핑장 청소하기

16 대화를 듣고, 남자가 여자에게 제안한 것으로 가장 적절한 것을 고르시오.

① 병원 가기　　　　② 휴식 취하기　　　　③ 물 자주 마시기
④ 마스크 착용하기　　⑤ 따뜻한 차 마시기

17 대화를 듣고, 여자가 지난 주말에 한 일을 고르시오.

① 동생 돌보기　　　　② 친구 만나기　　　　③ 봉사활동하기
④ 개 산책 시키기　　　⑤ 가족 여행 다녀오기

18 대화를 듣고, 남자의 직업으로 가장 적절한 것을 고르시오.

① 교통 경찰관　　　　② 택배 기사　　　　③ 버스 기사
④ 자동차 정비사　　　⑤ 환경 미화원

19 대화를 듣고, 여자의 마지막 말에 이어질 남자의 응답으로 가장 적절한 것을 고르시오.

Man: _____

① It's 10 o'clock.　　　　　　② We can go there by bus.
③ I like eating popcorn.　　　　④ Thursday is fine with me.
⑤ We must hurry or we will be late.

20 대화를 듣고, 남자의 마지막 말에 이어질 여자의 응답으로 가장 적절한 것을 고르시오.

Woman: _____

① What is a kiosk?　　　　　② That is a big screen.
③ I prefer snacks to ice cream.　④ There's a scanner on the side.
⑤ It's the big blue one at the bottom.

Dictation Test 11

녹음을 다시 듣으면서 빈칸을 채워주세요

M1(17)_11_D

Dictation(받아쓰기)은 본문을 받아쓰면서 영어듣기의 집중력을 향상시키고 다양한 표현을 정리하기 위한 영어듣기 학습법입니다. **녹음을 다시 듣고, 빈칸에 알맞은 단어를 써 보세요.**
※Dictation의 정답은 듣기 대본의 밑줄 친 부분을 확인하세요.

📖 정답 p. 43

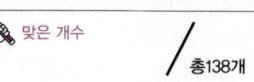
맞은 개수 / 총138개

그림정보파악(담화)

1. 다음을 듣고, 'I'가 무엇인지 가장 적절한 것을 고르시오.

①
②
③
④
⑤

01
W: I have four legs and a long tail. I can jump very
_____ _____ _____. I eat plants. I live
in Australia. I have _____ _____ _____
_____ _____ and carry my baby in it.
What am I?

그림정보파악(대화)

2. 대화를 듣고, 여자가 구입한 컵으로 가장 적절한 것을 고르시오.

①
②
③
④
⑤

02
M: Can I help you?

W: Hello. I'd like to buy a cup for my little brother.

M: OK. _____ _____ this one with a star on it?

W: It's nice, but my brother really likes animals.

M: Then how about this one with a pig _____
_____? It's very _____.

W: He'll like it very much. I'll _____ it.

날씨파악–그림

3. 다음을 듣고, 현재 시카고의 날씨로 가장 적절한 것을 고르시오.

① ② ③ ④ ⑤

03 M: Good morning. This is your weather report.
In Boston, it's sunny and clear. New York is
_____ light rain and strong winds.
In Chicago, it's not raining, but it is _____.
Expect cooler temperatures in the evening.
_____ _____ for changing weather!

고난도 마지막말의도파악

4. 대화를 듣고, 마지막 말에 담긴 여자의 의도로 적절한 것을 고르시오.
① 사과   ② 감사
③ 격려   ④ 충고
⑤ 위로

04 W: What's _____, Frank?
M: I am so tired. I want to sleep _____ _____.
W: Why? Didn't you sleep well last night?
M: No. I had to do my homework _____ _____
_____ because I played computer games until late.
W: So, did you finish your homework?
M: No. I didn't have _____ _____.
W: I think you should always do your homework first.

다음 페이지에 계속 ➡

11
회
딕
테
이
션

5. 다음을 듣고, 남자가 식목 행사에 대해 언급하지 않은 것을 고르시오.

① 행사 날짜
② 식목 장소
③ 제공품
④ 식재 나무 종류
⑤ 신청 방법

05 M: This spring, we're organizing a tree planting event. It will _____ _____ on April 22nd. We'll be _____ _____ in the local park to _____ Earth Day. The meeting point will be near the park entrance. We'll give volunteers shovels and small trees to plant. You can register to _____ _____ the event on our website.

6. 대화를 듣고, 두 사람이 만날 시각을 고르시오.

① 2:00 p.m. ② 3:00 p.m.
③ 4:00 p.m. ④ 5:00 p.m.
⑤ 6:00 p.m.

06 W: How about _____ _____ this afternoon?

M: OK. What time shall we meet?

W: How about at five?

M: I think that's _____ _____. Why don't we meet a little earlier?

W: What time do you say?

M: Let's _____ _____ at three.

W: All right. See you then.

장래희망추론

🇺🇸🇬🇧

7. 대화를 듣고, 남자의 장래 희망으로 가장 적절한 것을 고르시오.

① 시인   ② 공무원
③ 경찰관   ④ 과학자
⑤ 영화 감독

07

W: What's this notebook for? May I _____ _____ _____?

M: Sure. I practice _____ _____ in that notebook.

W: Wow! Did you really write these _____ by yourself? They're amazing.

M: Thanks. I'm _____ to become _____ _____ in the future.

W: I'm sure you'll _____ an amazing poet.

M: Thank you.

심정추론

8. 대화를 듣고, 여자의 심정으로 가장 적절한 것을 고르시오.

① 수줍음   ② 부러움
③ 실망스러움   ④ 긴장함
⑤ 미안함

08

M: Grace, _____ _____!

W: You look really excited. What's the news?

M: I got tickets to my favorite band's concert!

W: No way! Can I see the tickets?

M: Sure. Now I can finally see them _____ _____!

W: I'm _____ _____ _____! I've been wanting to see them for ages.

다음 페이지에 계속 ➡

9. 대화를 듣고, 남자가 대화 직후에 할 일로 적절한 것을 고르시오.

① 저녁 먹기
② 빵 굽기
③ 상 차리기
④ 채소 썰기
⑤ 손 씻기

09

M: I'm home, honey. Something _____ _____!

W: I'm making spaghetti. It's your favorite.

M: Do you need any help?

W: No, thanks. I'm _____ _____.

M: Then, do you want me to _____ _____ _____?

W: That would be great. The spaghetti will be done in a minute.

M: I'll go _____ _____ _____ first.

---

10. 대화를 듣고, 무엇에 관한 내용인지 가장 적절한 것을 고르시오.

① 동아리 모집 ② 소방 훈련
③ 자전거 구매 ④ 마라톤 행사
⑤ 학교 축제

10

W: Hey, James. What are you looking at?

M: I'm looking at this poster. It's about an event called the Untact _____ Run.

W: What's that?

M: It's a marathon to _____ money to help those _____ _____.

W: That's wonderful!

M: Isn't it? And to _____ large crowds, runners can choose their _____ course and date.

11. 대화를 듣고, 여자가 이용할 교통수단으로 가장 적절한 것을 고르시오.

① 택시　　　② 자전거
③ 지하철　　④ 버스
⑤ 오토바이

11

W: Gary, let's go home. This library will close soon.

M: Okay. How are you getting home, Amy?

W: I'll take the subway.

M: Why don't you _____ _____ _____? The stop is right outside the library, but the subway station is far away.

W: Okay, _____ _____ _____. How about you?

M: I _____ _____ _____.

2023 영어듣기능력평가 1회 12번 변형

12. 대화를 듣고, 여자가 장갑을 찾는 이유로 가장 적절한 것을 고르시오.

① 날씨가 추워서
② 반품하기 위해서
③ 선물하기 위해서
④ 세탁하기 위해서
⑤ 친구에게 돌려주기 위해서

12

M: Mom, what are you looking for?

W: I'm trying to find the new gloves I _____ yesterday.

M: The black ones? I saw them on the kitchen table.

W: Oh, there they are! I need to _____ them to the store.

M: Why? Are they too small?

W: Yes, and there's a small hole in one of them.

다음 페이지에 계속 ➡

13. 대화를 듣고, 두 사람이 대화하는 장소로
가장 적절한 곳을 고르시오.

① 병원　　② 편의점
③ 세탁소　④ 미용실
⑤ 극장

13

M: Hi, Sally. What can I do for you today?

W: I would like to _____ _____ _____.

M: Haircut? How short?

W: _____ _____ _____, please.

M: Around your neck?

W: No, _____ _____ _____.

M: Just let me know when you'd like to stop.

W: Okay.

14. 대화를 듣고, Flower Shop의 위치로 가
장 알맞은 곳을 고르시오.

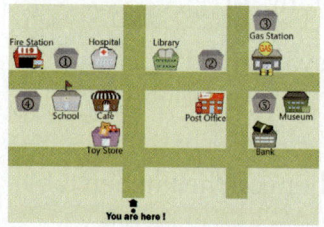

14

M: Amy, is there a flower shop around here? I need to
buy some flowers for my sister's birthday.

W: Yes, I know a _____ _____. First, walk
straight for two blocks and turn right.

M: OK.

W: Then, _____ _____ _____ one more
block and turn left.

M: Turn left?

W: That's right. _____ _____ _____ on your
right, next to the gas station.

M: I see. Thanks!

15. 대화를 듣고, 여자가 남자에게 부탁한 일로 가장 적절한 것을 고르시오.

① 고기 굽기
② 설거지하기
③ 텐트 주문하기
④ 아버지 돕기
⑤ 캠핑장 청소하기

15
W: This _____ is great. What do you think, Kevin?

M: I really like it, Mom.

W: I'll take the grill out and make some barbecue now.

M: So soon? I'm not hungry, yet.

W: It'll _____ _____. Your dad is still _____ _____ the tent. Can you go help him?

M: Sure. I'll do that.

2025 영어듣기능력평가 1회 16번 변형

16. 대화를 듣고, 남자가 여자에게 제안한 것으로 가장 적절한 것을 고르시오.

① 병원 가기
② 휴식 취하기
③ 물 자주 마시기
④ 마스크 착용하기
⑤ 따뜻한 차 마시기

16
M: Amy, are you okay? You don't _____ _____.

W: I have a _____ _____.

M: Did you drink some water?

W: A little bit. But my throat still _____.

M: How about drinking some _____ _____?

W: That sounds nice. I'll make some now.

다음 페이지에 계속 ➡

11
회
딕
테
이
션

17. 대화를 듣고, 여자가 지난 주말에 한 일을 고르시오.

① 동생 돌보기
② 친구 만나기
③ 봉사활동하기
④ 개 산책 시키기
⑤ 가족 여행 다녀오기

17
W: James, did you have a good weekend?

M: Yes, I _____ _____ _____ my baby brother. How about you?

W: I took care of my friend's dog. Her family _____ _____ for the weekend.

M: Oh, did you enjoy it?

W: Yeah. I _____ _____ _____.

M: Sounds like you had fun!

18. 대화를 듣고, 남자의 직업으로 가장 적절한 것을 고르시오.

① 교통 경찰관
② 택배 기사
③ 버스 기사
④ 자동차 정비사
⑤ 환경 미화원

18
W: How was your day, dear?

M: I'm feeling quite tired.

W: Did you have to _____ a lot of packages today?

M: No, but there was _____ _____ all day. It was hard to drive through it.

W: You're really good at making sure the packages get there _____ _____.

M: Thanks. I feel _____ _____ what I do.

19. 대화를 듣고, 여자의 마지막 말에 이어질 남자의 응답으로 가장 적절한 것을 고르시오.

Man: _____

① It's 10 o'clock.
② We can go there by bus.
③ I like eating popcorn.
④ Thursday is fine with me.
⑤ We must hurry or we will be late.

19

M: Riley, there's a new _____ _____ _____ _____ tomorrow.

W: Oh really? I hope it's good.

M: I heard it's really scary. The reviews are _____ _____ _____.

W: It sounds great. We should go see it.

M: Okay. Why don't we go see it next week?

W: Let's do that! How is Thursday for you?

M: Thursday is fine with me.

20. 대화를 듣고, 남자의 마지막 말에 이어질 여자의 응답으로 가장 적절한 것을 고르시오.

Woman: _____

① What is a kiosk?
② That is a big screen.
③ I prefer snacks to ice cream.
④ There's a scanner on the side.
⑤ It's the big blue one at the bottom.

20

W: Dad, let's buy some ice cream there.

M: Okay, sweetie. [pause] Is this an _____ store?

W: Yes.

M: Then how do we pay?

W: We use the _____ here.

M: Oh, do you know _____ _____ use it?

W: It's easy. Just scan the barcode and _____ the pay button on the screen.

M: Where is the pay button?

W: It's the big blue one at the bottom.

Words & Expressions Review 11

● 다음 단어를 암기하세요.

문제	번호	단어	뜻
1	1	pouch	(작은) 주머니
	2	carry	들고 있다, 나르다
2	3	popular	인기 있는
3	4	experience	겪다, 경험하다
	5	expect	예상하다
	6	temperature	기온, 온도
	7	prepare	준비하다
	8	changing	변화하는
4	9	finish	다 하다, 끝내다
	10	enough	충분한
5	11	organize	준비하다
	12	plant	심다
6	13	play tennis	테니스 치다
7	14	poetry	(집합적으로) 시
	15	poem	(한 편의) 시
	16	poet	시인
	17	finally	드디어, 마침내
8	18	jealous	부러워하는, 질투하는
	19	for ages	오랫동안
	20	delicious	맛있는
9	21	almost	거의
	22	set the table	상을 차리다

문제	번호	단어	뜻
10	23	untact	비대면, 비접촉
	24	donation	기부, 기증
	25	raise money	모금하다, 돈을 마련하다
	26	in need	어려움에 처한, 궁핍한
12	27	look for	~을 찾다
	28	return	반품하다, 반납하다
	29	hole	구멍
13	30	trim	다듬다, 손질하다
14	31	around	주위에
	32	campsite	야영지
15	33	take ~ out	~을 꺼내다
	34	take time	시간이 걸리다
	35	put up	(텐트 등을) 세우다
16	36	throat	목, 목구멍
	37	still	여전히
17	38	spend time with	~와 시간을 보내다
	39	take care of	~를 돌보다
	40	go away	(특히 휴가를 맞아) 집을 떠나다
18	41	quite	꽤
	42	deliver	배달하다
20	43	unmanned	무인의
	44	kiosk	키오스크(무인 주문 및 결제 기계)

● 왼쪽 단어장의 뜻이 보이지 않게 반으로 접고, 학습한 단어의 뜻을 아래 빈칸에 적어주세요.

1	take ~ out		23	unmanned
2	campsite		24	raise money
3	organize		25	throat
4	look for		26	expect
5	deliver		27	carry
6	set the table		28	trim
7	popular		29	hole
8	for ages		30	plant
9	around		31	kiosk
10	delicious		32	pouch
11	take care of		33	spend time with
12	quite		34	enough
13	temperature		35	donation
14	take time		36	poem
15	still		37	almost
16	poetry		38	jealous
17	go away		39	put up
18	untact		40	changing
19	in need		41	experience
20	poet		42	prepare
21	finally		43	play tennis
22	finish		44	return

12 회 중학영어듣기 모의고사

M1(17)_12_US
모두 **미국식 발음(US)**
으로 녹음

M1(17)_12_UK
20문제 중 5문제에 **영국식 발음**
(US+UK)을 포함하여 녹음

📖 정답 및 해석 **p. 47**

1 다음을 듣고, 'this'가 가리키는 것으로 가장 적절한 것을 고르시오.

①  ②  ③  ④  ⑤

2 대화를 듣고, 남자가 만든 브로치로 가장 적절한 것을 고르시오.

①  ②  ③  ④  ⑤

3 다음을 듣고, 파리의 오늘 날씨를 고르시오.

①  ②  ③  ④  ⑤

4 대화를 듣고, 남자의 마지막 말의 의도로 가장 적절한 것을 고르시오.

① 위로   ② 불평   ③ 축하   ④ 감사   ⑤ 부탁

5 다음을 듣고, 남자가 드론 교실에 대해 언급하지 <u>않은</u> 것을 고르시오.

① 수업 시간   ② 장소   ③ 강사 이름
④ 준비물   ⑤ 수강료

6 대화를 듣고, 남자가 여자를 만날 시각을 고르시오.

① 6:00 p.m.   ② 6:30 p.m.   ③ 7:00 p.m.   ④ 7:30 p.m.   ⑤ 8:00 p.m.

7 대화를 듣고, 여자의 장래 희망으로 가장 적절한 것을 고르시오.

① 요리사   ② 선생님   ③ 발레리나
④ 패션 모델   ⑤ 음향 감독

8 대화를 듣고, 남자의 심정으로 가장 적절한 것을 고르시오.

① sad   ② shy   ③ calm   ④ excited   ⑤ nervous

9 대화를 듣고, 남자가 대화 직후에 할 일로 가장 적절한 것을 고르시오.

① 지갑 찾기   ② 소파 옮기기   ③ 창문 닫기
④ 기차표 예약하기   ⑤ 우산 가져오기

10 대화를 듣고, 무엇에 관한 내용인지 가장 적절한 것을 고르시오.

① 셀프 계산대 사용법   ② 외국어 학습앱 추천   ③ 서빙 로봇 이용 방법
④ 코딩 교육용 로봇 도입   ⑤ 음성 인식 기술의 활용

11번~20번 문제는 다음 페이지에 ➡

11 대화를 듣고, 남자가 이용할 교통수단을 고르시오.

① 버스 　　② 비행기 　　③ 기차 　　④ 배 　　⑤ 자동차

12 대화를 듣고, 여자가 머리를 말리지 <u>못한</u> 이유로 가장 적절한 것을 고르시오.

① 드라이어가 고장 나서 　　② 수영장이 닫을 시간이 되어서
③ 소방 훈련에 참여하느라 　　④ 화재 대피를 해야 해서
⑤ 약속 시간에 늦어서

13 대화를 듣고, 대화가 이루어지고 있는 장소를 고르시오.

① 도서관 반납기 앞 　　② 동물원 매표소 　　③ 공항 환전소
④ 만남의 광장 　　⑤ 분실물 센터

14 Weekly Art Workshop에 관한 다음 내용을 듣고, 표에서 일치하지 <u>않는</u> 것을 고르시오.

Weekly Art Workshop		
①	일시	this Sunday, 2 p.m.
②	주제	how to paint with oil colors
③	소요 시간	2 hours
④	참가비	$18
⑤	장소	community hall

15 대화를 듣고, 여자가 남자에게 부탁한 일로 가장 적절한 것을 고르시오.

① 책 빌려주기 　　② 숙제 같이 하기 　　③ 저녁 식사 같이 하기
④ TV 함께 보기 　　⑤ 과제물 출력하기

16 대화를 듣고, 남자가 여자에게 제안한 것으로 가장 적절한 것을 고르시오.

① 창문 닫기　　　　② 일찍 자기　　　　③ 음악 감상하기
④ 반려동물 키우기　　⑤ 귀마개 사용하기

17 대화를 듣고, 여자가 지난 주말에 한 일을 고르시오.

① 극장 가기　　　　② 공부하기　　　　③ 도서관 가기
④ 뮤지컬 보기　　　⑤ 놀이공원 가기

18 대화를 듣고, 남자의 직업으로 가장 적절한 것을 고르시오.

① 목수　　　② 작가　　　③ 화가　　　④ 조각가　　　⑤ 사진작가

19 대화를 듣고, 남자의 마지막 말에 이어질 여자의 말로 가장 적절한 것을 고르시오.

Woman: _____

① Let's take a taxi.　　　　② You're already late.
③ I don't like walking.　　　④ You should wait here.
⑤ Thanks for telling me.

20 대화를 듣고, 여자의 마지막 말에 이어질 남자의 응답으로 가장 적절한 것을 고르시오.

Man: _____

① I did it yesterday.　　　　② How about three o'clock?
③ That's too bad.　　　　　④ I'd love to go.
⑤ That's too late.

Dictation Test 12

녹음을 다시 듣으면서 빈칸을 채워주세요

M1(17)_12_D

Dictation(받아쓰기)은 본문을 받아쓰면서 영어듣기의 집중력을 향상시키고 다양한 표현을 정리하기 위한 영어듣기 학습법입니다. **녹음을 다시 듣고, 빈칸에 알맞은 단어를 써 보세요.**
※Dictation의 정답은 듣기 대본의 밑줄 친 부분을 확인하세요.

📖 정답 p. 47

🖊 맞은 개수 / 총132개

그림정보파악(담화)

1. 다음을 듣고, 'this'가 가리키는 것으로 가장 적절한 것을 고르시오.

①  ②

③   ④

⑤

01 M: This can be worn _____ _____ _____.

This _____ _____ _____ and nose. This

can protect you from getting sick. You can also use

this on a smoggy day. What is this?

그림정보파악(대화)

2. 대화를 듣고, 남자가 만든 브로치로 가장 적절한 것을 고르시오.

①  ②

③  ④

⑤

02 W: Minho, what's that?

M: It's _____ _____ for my mom. It's a Parents'

Day _____.

W: The brooch _____ _____ your mom's face. I

like it.

M: Thanks. I hope she likes it, too.

W: I thought you were going to make a flower

brooch.

M: Yes, but I changed my mind.

---

3. 다음을 듣고, 파리의 오늘 날씨를 고르시오.

①
②
③
④
⑤

03 W: Hi, I'm Jenny Lee for the world weather update. Let's _____ _____ _____ _____ the weather in Europe. Stormy weather and thunderstorms _____ _____ _____ is forecasted in London. Paris is expected to be warm, but it will be very cloudy today. Berlin is mostly cloudy this morning but clearing later on, so it will be sunny _____ _____ _____.

4. 대화를 듣고, 남자의 마지막 말의 의도로 가장 적절한 것을 고르시오.

① 위로
② 불평
③ 축하
④ 감사
⑤ 부탁

04 W: Hey, Andy! What are you doing at the park?

M: I'm _____ to fly this kite, but I can't get it up.

W: Let me help you. Which _____ is the wind blowing?

M: It's coming from the east.

W: Let's change _____ we're holding the kite to make it fly better.

M: Thanks for _____ out.

다음 페이지에 계속 ➡

5. 다음을 듣고, 남자가 드론 교실에 대해 언급하지 **않은** 것을 고르시오.

① 수업 시간   ② 장소
③ 강사 이름   ④ 준비물
⑤ 수강료

05 M: Hello, students. Our school is starting a new drone class starting next week. It's from 9 a.m. to 12:00 p.m. every Saturday. The class will _____ _____ in the computer room. You must _____ your own smartphone or tablet PC. There is no fee to _____. In this class, you can learn what a drone is and _____ _____ _____ it. Hope to see you there!

6. 대화를 듣고, 남자가 여자를 만날 시각을 고르시오.

① 6:00 p.m.   ② 6:30 p.m.
③ 7:00 p.m.   ④ 7:30 p.m.
⑤ 8:00 p.m.

06 M: Jane, what are you _____ _____ _____ tonight?

W: I'm going to watch my favorite TV show. Shall we watch it together?

M: Sure. What time does it begin?

W: It _____ _____ 7 o'clock. Come to my house at 6:30.

M: Okay. _____ _____ _____.

7. 대화를 듣고, 여자의 장래 희망으로 가장 적절한 것을 고르시오.

① 요리사　　　② 선생님
③ 발레리나　　④ 패션 모델
⑤ 음향 감독

07
M: Tina, what are you doing _____ _____

_____ the mirror?

W: I was just practicing some of my ballet moves.

M: Wow, you're amazing! Do you like ballet?

W: Yeah, I want to become a ballerina when I

_____ _____.

M: You're definitely going to _____ _____.

W: Thanks, Paul.

---

8. 대화를 듣고, 남자의 심정으로 가장 적절한 것을 고르시오.

① sad　　　② shy
③ calm　　④ excited
⑤ nervous

08
M: Mom, _____ _____.

W: How was your day? Did you do anything

interesting at school today?

M: I made too many mistakes on my math quiz. I feel

like I've _____ _____ _____.

W: Don't say that! I know that you studied hard for

the quiz. _____ _____! You'll do better next

time.

M: Thanks, but I still _____ _____ about myself.

다음 페이지에 계속 ➡

9. 대화를 듣고, 남자가 대화 직후에 할 일로 가장 적절한 것을 고르시오.

① 지갑 찾기
② 소파 옮기기
③ 창문 닫기
④ 기차표 예약하기
⑤ 우산 가져오기

09
W: Hurry up, Mike! We're going to _____ _____ _____.

M: I'm sorry. I just can't _____ _____ _____.

W: It's on the sofa.

M: Oh, thanks. Now let's go.

W: Wait. Isn't it going to rain this evening?

M: I think you're right.

W: Then we should _____ _____ _____ before we go.

M: I'll do it right now.

대화화제추론

2024 영어듣기능력평가 2회 10번 변형

10. 대화를 듣고, 무엇에 관한 내용인지 가장 적절한 것을 고르시오.

① 셀프 계산대 사용법
② 외국어 학습앱 추천
③ 서빙 로봇 이용 방법
④ 코딩 교육용 로봇 도입
⑤ 음성 인식 기술의 활용

10
M: Look! That robot is bringing our food!

W: Yeah, it's my first time seeing a _____ _____ in a restaurant.

M: Do we need to do anything?

W: When the robot stops, _____ _____ _____ from it and press "Done."

M: Haha! Can it talk to us, too?

W: I wish! It just plays a short message and then leaves.

11. 대화를 듣고, 남자가 이용할 교통수단을 고르시오.

① 버스 ② 비행기
③ 기차 ④ 배
⑤ 자동차

11

W: Hey, Paul. I heard that you're going to China next week.

M: Yes. I always wanted to go there.

W: Did you buy a _____ _____?

M: No. That's too _____ for me.

W: Then how are you going to China?

M: I'm taking a _____ _____ Incheon.

W: I see. I hope you have a good trip!

12. 대화를 듣고, 여자가 머리를 말리지 못한 이유로 가장 적절한 것을 고르시오.

① 드라이어가 고장 나서
② 수영장이 닫을 시간이 되어서
③ 소방 훈련에 참여하느라
④ 화재 대피를 해야 해서
⑤ 약속 시간에 늦어서

12

M: Wendy, your hair is wet. Did you go swimming?

W: Yes, but I couldn't _____ _____ _____ there.

M: Was the dryer broken?

W: No. Before I could dry my hair, the _____ _____ _____ _____.

M: Oh, no. Was there a fire?

W: Just a small one, but I had to leave right away.

다음 페이지에 계속 ➡

13. 대화를 듣고, 대화가 이루어지고 있는 장소를 고르시오.

① 도서관 반납기 앞
② 동물원 매표소
③ 공항 환전소
④ 만남의 광장
⑤ 분실물 센터

13

M: I lost my bag in the _____ _____.

W: We have three bags here. Please tell me what your bag looks like.

M: My bag is big, green, and has a _____ _____.

W: What is your name?

M: James Benson.

W: Oh, you're _____. Here is your bag.

표불일치 🇺🇸🇬🇧 신유형 | 2025 영어듣기능력평가 1회 14번 변형

14. Weekly Art Workshop에 관한 다음 내용을 듣고, 표에서 일치하지 <u>않는</u> 것을 고르시오.

Weekly Art Workshop		
①	일시	this Sunday, 2 p.m.
②	주제	how to paint with oil colors
③	소요 시간	2 hours
④	참가비	$18
⑤	장소	community hall

14

W: Hello, everyone in Maplewood Village. Let me tell you about our Weekly Art Workshop. It'll be this Sunday at 2 p.m. In this workshop, you'll learn how to paint with _____. The workshop will be 2 hours in length. You need to pay 18 dollars _____ _____. The workshop will _____ _____ at the community hall. Thanks.

15. 대화를 듣고, 여자가 남자에게 부탁한 일로 가장 적절한 것을 고르시오.

① 책 빌려주기
② 숙제 같이 하기
③ 저녁 식사 같이 하기
④ TV 함께 보기
⑤ 과제물 출력하기

15 *(Telephone rings.)*

M: Hello?

W: Hello. This is Rina. May I _____ _____ Karl?

M: Speaking. What's up, Rina?

W: You have the book "Charlie and the Chocolate _____," don't you?

M: Yes, I do. Why?

W: I have to read it for my homework. Can you _____ _____ _____ me for three days?

M: Sure.

16. 대화를 듣고, 남자가 여자에게 제안한 것으로 가장 적절한 것을 고르시오.

① 창문 닫기
② 일찍 자기
③ 음악 감상하기
④ 반려동물 키우기
⑤ 귀마개 사용하기

16 M: Tia, what's wrong? You look so tired.

W: I _____ _____ too early this morning.

M: Why?

W: Well, the birds in the trees outside my window _____ _____ so early this morning.

M: Oh, really? Then why don't you _____ _____ _____?

W: Yeah, using earplugs sounds like a great idea.

다음 페이지에 계속 ➡

17. 대화를 듣고, 여자가 지난 주말에 한 일을 고르시오.

① 극장 가기
② 공부하기
③ 도서관 가기
④ 뮤지컬 보기
⑤ 놀이동산 가기

17

W: Oliver, did you do anything fun last weekend?

M: Yes, I _____ _____ _____ _____. What about you?

W: I went to the _____ _____ with my friends.

M: That's great! Did you have fun?

W: Some of the _____ _____ _____ _____ for me, but it was fun.

M: I should go there with my friends as well.

2024 영어듣기능력평가 **2회 18번 변형**

18. 대화를 듣고, 남자의 직업으로 가장 적절한 것을 고르시오.

① 목수   ② 작가
③ 화가   ④ 조각가
⑤ 사진작가

18

W: Owen, are you going to the countryside again?

M: Yes, Mia. I need some quiet time to write.

W: Are you _____ _____ your next book?

M: Yes. I'm writing about my _____ in nature.

W: That sounds great. I love your _____.

M: Thank you! I hope you enjoy the new one, too.

19. 대화를 듣고, 남자의 마지막 말에 이어질 여자의 말로 가장 적절한 것을 고르시오.

Woman: _____

① Let's take a taxi.
② You're already late.
③ I don't like walking.
④ You should wait here.
⑤ Thanks for telling me.

19

M: Emma, are you going to _____ _____ _____ now?

W: Yes, Jake. I have to go downtown.

M: Be careful. There's _____ _____ on Main Street.

W: Really? I didn't know that.

M: The bus might _____ _____ in traffic. Why don't you take the subway instead?

W: <u>Thanks for telling me.</u>

알맞은응답찾기

20. 대화를 듣고, 여자의 마지막 말에 이어질 남자의 응답으로 가장 적절한 것을 고르시오.

Man: _____

① I did it yesterday.
② How about three o'clock?
③ That's too bad.
④ I'd love to go.
⑤ That's too late.

20

W: It's a _____ day.

M: Hey, how about going to the zoo?

W: That's a _____ _____. What time shall we meet?

M: I have something to do in the morning. Let's go in the afternoon.

W: You _____ _____ _____.

M: <u>How about three o'clock?</u>

Words & Expressions Review 12

● 다음 단어를 암기하세요.

문제	번호	단어	뜻
1	1	cover	덮다, 가리다
	2	smoggy	스모그가 많은
2	3	brooch	브로치
	4	Parents' Day	어버이날
3	5	take a look at ~	~을 살펴보다
	6	thunderstorm	뇌우
	7	throughout the day	온종일
4	8	way	방향, 쪽
5	9	participate	참가하다
6	10	favorite	제일 좋아하는
	11	begin	시작하다
	12	in front of	~의 앞에서
7	13	definitely	분명히, 틀림없이
	14	make it	(바라던 일을) 해내다
8	15	let ~ down	~를 실망시키다
	16	nervous	초조한
9	17	miss	놓치다
	18	right now	바로, 지금 당장
	19	tray	쟁반
10	20	press	누르다
	21	leave	떠나다
11	22	expensive	비싼

문제	번호	단어	뜻
13	23	subway station	지하철역
	24	name tag	이름표
	25	lucky	운이 좋은
14	26	paint	그리다
	27	watercolor	수채화 그림물감
	28	be held	열리다, 개최되다
15	29	lend	빌려주다
	30	tired	피곤한, 지친
16	31	get up	(잠자리에서) 일어나다, 깨다
	32	earplug	귀마개
17	33	go to the movies	영화 보러 가다
	34	amusement park	놀이공원
	35	ride	놀이 기구
	36	as well	또한, 역시
18	37	countryside	시골
	38	nature	자연
	39	essay	수필
19	40	road work	도로 공사
	41	zoo	동물원
20	42	in the morning	오전에
	43	in the afternoon	오후에
	44	set the time	시간을 정하다

M1(17)_W_12

● 왼쪽 단어장의 뜻이 보이지 않게 반으로 접고, 학습한 단어의 뜻을 아래 빈칸에 적어주세요.

1	in the afternoon		23	press
2	lucky		24	go to the movies
3	ride		25	essay
4	miss		26	way
5	name tag		27	smoggy
6	favorite		28	take a look at ~
7	earplug		29	leave
8	begin		30	watercolor
9	nervous		31	definitely
10	thunderstorm		32	expensive
11	tired		33	make it
12	be held		34	cover
13	amusement park		35	in the morning
14	zoo		36	tray
15	brooch		37	as well
16	nature		38	participate
17	Parents' Day		39	countryside
18	let ~ down		40	road work
19	in front of		41	right now
20	throughout the day		42	lend
21	set the time		43	subway station
22	paint		44	get up

13 회 중학영어듣기 모의고사

M1(17)_13_US
모두 **미국식 발음(US)**
으로 녹음

M1(17)_13_UK
20문제 중 5문제에 **영국식 발음**
(US+UK)을 포함하여 녹음

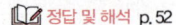 정답 및 해석 p. 52

1 다음을 듣고, 'this'가 가리키는 것으로 가장 적절한 것을 고르시오.

①  ②  ③  ④  ⑤

2 대화를 듣고, 여자가 선택할 꽃병으로 가장 적절한 것을 고르시오.

①  ②  ③  ④  ⑤

3 다음을 듣고, 일요일 날씨를 고르시오.

①  ②  ③  ④  ⑤

4 대화를 듣고, 남자가 한 마지막 말의 의도로 가장 적절한 것을 고르시오.

① 거절　　② 불평　　③ 축하　　④ 충고　　⑤ 감사

5 다음을 듣고, 여자가 건물에 대해 언급하지 <u>않은</u> 것을 고르시오.

① 이름   ② 모양   ③ 지어진 연도
④ 건축가   ⑤ 높이

6 대화를 듣고, 두 사람이 만날 시각을 고르시오.

① 9:00 a.m.   ② 9:30 a.m.   ③ 10:00 a.m.
④ 10:30 a.m.   ⑤ 11:30 a.m.

7 대화를 듣고, 여자의 장래 희망으로 가장 적절한 것을 고르시오.

① 지휘자   ② 작곡가   ③ 성악가
④ 플루트 연주자   ⑤ 바이올린 연주자

8 대화를 듣고, 여자의 심정으로 가장 적절한 것을 고르시오.

① angry   ② happy   ③ worried   ④ proud   ⑤ excited

9 대화를 듣고, 두 사람이 대화 직후에 할 일로 가장 적절한 것을 고르시오.

① 생일 파티에 가기   ② 서점 방문하기   ③ 제과점에 가기
④ 선물 포장하기   ⑤ 케이크 재료 구입하기

10 대화를 듣고, 무엇에 관한 내용인지 가장 적절한 것을 고르시오.

① 자기소개   ② 건강 검진   ③ 장래 희망
④ 시험 준비   ⑤ 주말 계획

11번~20번 문제는 다음 페이지에 ➡

11 대화를 듣고, 남자가 이용할 교통수단으로 가장 적절한 것을 고르시오.

① 택시   ② 기차   ③ 자전거
④ 비행기   ⑤ 셔틀버스

12 대화를 듣고, 남자가 슬퍼 보이는 이유를 고르시오.

① 길을 잃어서   ② 개를 잃어버려서   ③ 시험공부를 못해서
④ 시험을 못 봐서   ⑤ 가방을 잃어버려서

13 대화를 듣고, 두 사람이 대화하는 장소로 가장 적절한 곳을 고르시오.

① 네일 샵   ② 신발 가게   ③ 마트
④ 미용실   ⑤ 우체국

14 대화를 듣고, 두 사람이 찾고 있는 모자의 위치로 가장 적절한 것을 고르시오.

15 대화를 듣고, 여자가 남자에게 부탁한 일로 가장 적절한 것을 고르시오.

① 설거지하기   ② 청소기 돌리기   ③ 휴가 계획 짜기
④ 쓰레기 분류하기   ⑤ 화장실 청소하기

16 대화를 듣고, 남자가 여자에게 제안한 것으로 가장 적절한 것을 고르시오.

① 요리책 구입하기　　　　② 생일케이크 만들기
③ 컵케이크 판매하기　　　　④ 유기농 밀가루 사용하기
⑤ 블로그에 요리법 게시하기

17 대화를 듣고, 여자가 휴일에 한 일로 가장 적절한 것을 고르시오.

① 소풍 가기　　　　② 동생 돌보기　　　　③ 농구 연습하기
④ 컴퓨터 게임하기　　　　⑤ 보드게임 카페 가기

18 대화를 듣고, 남자의 직업으로 가장 적절한 것을 고르시오.

① 안경점 직원　　　　② 간호사　　　　③ 안과 의사
④ 치과 의사　　　　⑤ 물리 치료사

[19~20] 대화를 듣고, 남자의 마지막 말에 이어질 여자의 말로 가장 적절한 것을 고르시오.

19 Woman: _____

① I love K-pop music.　　　　② Sure, leave it to me.
③ I want to go to a concert.　　④ I'm sure you did your best.
⑤ Our presentation is tomorrow.

20 Woman: _____

① You're such a good cook!
② A blue dress will be good.
③ The wedding is on Sunday.
④ I want Vietnamese noodles.
⑤ We can take the bus home.

Dictation Test 13

녹음을 다시 들으면서 빈칸을 채워주세요

M1(17)_13_D

Dictation(받아쓰기)은 본문을 받아쓰면서 영어듣기의 집중력을 향상시키고 다양한 표현을 정리하기 위한 영어듣기 학습법입니다. **녹음을 다시 듣고, 빈칸에 알맞은 단어를 써 보세요.**

※Dictation의 정답은 듣기 대본의 밑줄 친 부분을 확인하세요.

📖 정답 p. 52

맞은 개수 / 총138개

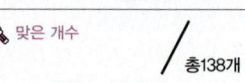

고난도 그림정보파악(담화)

1. 다음을 듣고, 'this'가 가리키는 것으로 가장 적절한 것을 고르시오.

①  ②

③  ④

⑤

01 W: This is usually _____. You can open this, put tissues inside, and then close it. This has a _____ on its top. You can _____ tissues _____ through the hole. What is this?

그림정보파악(대화)

2. 대화를 듣고, 여자가 선택할 꽃병으로 가장 적절한 것을 고르시오.

①   ②

③   ④

⑤

02 W: Hello. I am looking for a vase for my grandmother.

M: How about this one with a _____ _____ on it? It is our best seller.

W: That heart is way too big. I would like a vase with a _____ _____.

M: Okay. How about this one with smaller hearts?

W: That's nice. But I think my grandmother would prefer that one _____ _____ on it.

M: That's a good choice!

W: Thank you. I'll take it.

3. 다음을 듣고, 일요일 날씨를 고르시오.

①  ②

③  ④

⑤

03 W: Happy weekend! This is Carrie. It's Saturday, _____ _____ _____ _____. It was rainy all day long yesterday but it stopped this morning. Today's weather condition is perfect for _____ _____. Don't forget sunscreen, though. We can't enjoy clear skies tomorrow, because there's _____ _____ _____ _____ of showers.

4. 대화를 듣고, 남자가 한 마지막 말의 의도로 가장 적절한 것을 고르시오.
① 거절 ② 불평
③ 축하 ④ 충고
⑤ 감사

04 M: You _____ _____, Jisu. What happened?

W: Dad, you know I really wanted to win the speaking contest. But my friend Hojin _____ _____ _____.

M: I see. Did he do a good job?

W: He actually did. But I feel so jealous, and I don't even want to speak to him.

M: I understand why you are upset, but I think you should _____ _____.

다음 페이지에 계속 ➡

5. 다음을 듣고, 여자가 건물에 대해 언급하지 <u>않은</u> 것을 고르시오.

① 이름
② 모양
③ 지어진 연도
④ 건축가
⑤ 높이

05 W: This is one of the most famous and historic buildings in New York City. _____ _____ _____ the Flatiron Building. Its _____ _____ makes it different from other buildings. The building _____ _____ in 1902. It is about 97 meters tall.

6. 대화를 듣고, 두 사람이 만날 시각을 고르시오.

① 9:00 a.m.
② 9:30 a.m.
③ 10:00 a.m.
④ 10:30 a.m.
⑤ 11:30 a.m.

06 W: Sam, let's go see the new _____ _____ tomorrow.

M: Sounds good. Let's see the earliest show.

W: Um... It's at 9 in the morning. Isn't that _____ _____?

M: It is. Hey, there is one at 10:30.

W: Good. How about _____ _____ _____ at the theater?

M: Great. See you tomorrow.

7. 대화를 듣고, 여자의 장래 희망으로 가장 적절한 것을 고르시오.

① 지휘자
② 작곡가
③ 성악가
④ 플루트 연주자
⑤ 바이올린 연주자

07 [Orchestra sound]

M: I'm excited to be at a symphony concert.

W: Me, too. All the different musical instruments _____ _____ to make a beautiful harmony.

M: What are those _____? The players are all blowing on them.

W: They're flutes, oboes, and clarinets.

M: How do you know their names?

W: I'm studying classical music. I want to _____ _____ _____.

M: That's fantastic!

8. 대화를 듣고, 여자의 심정으로 가장 적절한 것을 고르시오.

① angry   ② happy
③ worried   ④ proud
⑤ excited

08 M: Amy, what's wrong?

W: Dad, Kevin _____ _____ my notes again.

M: I'm sorry to hear that. I'll tell him to _____ to you.

W: No. I don't even want to talk to him anymore.

M: But sweetie, he's only three years old. I hope you understand.

W: I'm trying. But he really gets on my _____!

다음 페이지에 계속 ➡

13회 딕테이션

9. 대화를 듣고, 두 사람이 대화 직후에 할 일로 가장 적절한 것을 고르시오.
   ① 생일 파티에 가기
   ② 서점 방문하기
   ③ 제과점에 가기
   ④ 선물 포장하기
   ⑤ 케이크 재료 구입하기

09 M: It's Heesu's birthday today. Did you know that?

W: Oh, I _____ _____ that.

M: How about buying a cake _____ _____?

W: That's a good idea. Should we go to the bakery now?

M: Sure. There's one _____ _____ the bookstore.

W: Okay. Let's go.

10. 대화를 듣고, 무엇에 관한 내용인지 가장 적절한 것을 고르시오.
    ① 자기소개   ② 건강 검진
    ③ 장래 희망   ④ 시험 준비
    ⑤ 주말 계획

10 W: What are your plans _____ _____ _____?

M: I'm going to Gapyung to see my aunt. How about you?

W: I'm going to a hospital with some friends. _____ _____ to the sick kids.

M: That's nice! _____ _____ _____ _____.

W: Thanks. You, too.

11. 대화를 듣고, 남자가 이용할 교통수단으로 가장 적절한 것을 고르시오.

① 택시   ② 기차
③ 자전거   ④ 비행기
⑤ 셔틀버스

11

W: Jihoon, how will you get to the ski resort this weekend?

M: I'm not sure, Mom.

W: How about _____ _____ _____?

M: The resort is _____ _____ _____ the train station.

W: Then, why don't you take a _____ _____? It'll get you right at the door.

M: A shuttle bus? That sounds good.

12. 대화를 듣고, 남자가 슬퍼 보이는 이유를 고르시오.

① 길을 잃어서
② 개를 잃어버려서
③ 시험공부를 못해서
④ 시험을 못 봐서
⑤ 가방을 잃어버려서

12

W: You look sad. What happened?

M: _____ _____ happened to me.

W: Did you mess up on your English exam?

M: Yes, but it's not because of that.

W: _____ _____ _____ with you, then?

M: I lost my dog yesterday. He _____ _____ from home. I can't find him.

다음 페이지에 계속 ➡

13. 대화를 듣고, 두 사람이 대화하는 장소로 가장 적절한 곳을 고르시오.
① 네일 샵 ② 신발 가게
③ 마트 ④ 미용실
⑤ 우체국

13

W: Hello. I have an appointment under the name Grace Lim.

M: Oh, yes! For 4 o'clock, right? Please, _____ _____ _____.

W: Thank you.

M: So, do you have _____ _____ _____ in mind? If not, we have monthly designs you could choose from.

W: I was thinking of just _____ _____ _____ and using one solid-color for my nails.

M: Sounds good. Let me see your nails.

14. 대화를 듣고, 두 사람이 찾고 있는 모자의 위치로 가장 적절한 것을 고르시오.

14

M: Mom, can I go and ride my bicycle?

W: Sure. It's _____ outside so don't _____ your cap.

M: OK. I put it on my bicycle this morning.

W: But it's not there. Can you check on the table?

M: It isn't there. Oh! Here it is _____ the table.

W: Great. Have fun.

15. 대화를 듣고, 여자가 남자에게 부탁한 일로 가장 적절한 것을 고르시오.

① 설거지하기
② 청소기 돌리기
③ 휴가 계획 짜기
④ 쓰레기 분류하기
⑤ 화장실 청소하기

15
W: Honey, let's clean the house today.

M: Since we don't have any plans today, that's a good idea.

W: _____ _____ _____. We haven't done any cleaning for a while.

M: You're right. We have so many other things _____ _____.

W: First of all, can you _____ _____ _____?

M: No problem.

16. 대화를 듣고, 남자가 여자에게 제안한 것으로 가장 적절한 것을 고르시오.

① 요리책 구입하기
② 생일케이크 만들기
③ 컵케이크 판매하기
④ 유기농 밀가루 사용하기
⑤ 블로그에 요리법 게시하기

16
M: Vicky, you are _____ _____ _____ _____.

W: Thank you. I'm glad you like my cupcakes.

M: Can you give me the recipe? I want to try it someday.

W: Sure. It's not difficult to follow.

M: I'm sure everyone _____ _____ your recipe. Why don't you upload it on your blog?

W: OK, I'll _____ _____ _____ _____.

다음 페이지에 계속 ➡

17. 대화를 듣고, 여자가 휴일에 한 일로 가장 적절한 것을 고르시오.

① 소풍 가기
② 동생 돌보기
③ 농구 연습하기
④ 컴퓨터 게임하기
⑤ 보드게임 카페 가기

17

W: Alfie, how was your holiday?

M: It was good. I _____ _____ with my brother at the park. What about you?

W: I went to the board game café with my friends.

M: That sounds nice! _____ _____ did you play?

W: _____ _____ Clue for an hour. It was fun.

---

18. 대화를 듣고, 남자의 직업으로 가장 적절한 것을 고르시오.

① 안경점 직원 ② 간호사
③ 안과 의사 ④ 치과 의사
⑤ 물리 치료사

18

M: What brings you here today?

W: I've been having headaches _____.

M: For how long?

W: About two weeks. It's only when I wear my glasses.

M: Hmm. Have you been _____ _____ _____ clearly when wearing them?

W: Not really. But I notice _____ _____ _____ _____ more easily than before.

M: I see. Well, let's start off with the eye chart again, just to check.

---

19. 대화를 듣고, 남자의 마지막 말에 이어질 여자의 말로 가장 적절한 것을 고르시오.

Woman: _____

① I love K-pop music.
② Sure, leave it to me.
③ I want to go to a concert.
④ I'm sure you did your best.
⑤ Our presentation is tomorrow.

19

W: Tony, we _____ _____ _____ on our group project.

M: I agree. We should choose a topic first.

W: Yeah. Do you have any good ideas?

M: Why don't we _____ _____ _____ about K-pop?

W: That's a great idea! Let's start doing some research.

M: Okay. Can you _____ _____ some K-pop photos online?

W: <u>Sure, leave it to me.</u>

20. 대화를 듣고, 남자의 마지막 말에 이어질 여자의 말로 가장 적절한 것을 고르시오.

Woman: _____

① You're such a good cook!
② A blue dress will be good.
③ The wedding is on Sunday.
④ I want Vietnamese noodles.
⑤ We can take the bus home.

20

W: Dad, I need a dress to wear to uncle's _____.

M: I know. Do you want to go shopping on Saturday?

W: Of course! Is Mom coming with us, too?

M: Yes. She'll help you _____ a dress.

W: Great. Can we _____ _____ on the _____ back?

M: Sure. What do you want to eat?

W: <u>I want Vietnamese noodles.</u>

Words & Expressions Review 13

● 다음 단어를 암기하세요.

문제	번호	단어	뜻
1	☐ 1	rectangular	직사각형의
	☐ 2	hole	구멍
	☐ 3	pull	뽑다, 빼다, 잡아당기다
2	☐ 4	vase	꽃병
	☐ 5	How about ~?	~은 어때요?
	☐ 6	way	너무, 훨씬
3	☐ 7	all day long	하루 종일
	☐ 8	condition	상태, 상황
4	☐ 9	do a good job	잘 해내다
5	☐ 10	triangular	삼각형의
	☐ 11	about	약, 대략
6	☐ 12	show	(극장에서 하는) 쇼, 영화
7	☐ 13	symphony	심포니, 교향곡
	☐ 14	come together	(하나로) 합치다, 모이다
8	☐ 15	tear up	갈기갈기 찢다
	☐ 16	apologize	사과하다
	☐ 17	understand	이해하다
	☐ 18	get on one's nerves	신경을 건드리다
9	☐ 19	forget about ~	~을 잊다
	☐ 20	bakery	제과점, 빵집
	☐ 21	next to ~	~ 옆에
10	☐ 22	plan	계획

문제	번호	단어	뜻
10	☐ 23	weekend	주말
	☐ 24	aunt	이모, 고모
11	☐ 25	sick	아픈, 병든
	☐ 26	get to	~에 도착하다
	☐ 27	far	먼, 멀리 떨어진
	☐ 28	terrible	끔찍한
12	☐ 29	mess up	망치다, 엉망으로 만들다
	☐ 30	run away	도망치다, 달아나다
13	☐ 31	have an appointment	예약이 되어 있다
	☐ 32	have a seat	자리에 앉다
	☐ 33	have ~ in mind	~을 생각하다, 염두에 두다
14	☐ 34	ride	타다
15	☐ 35	It's about time.	때가 됐다.
	☐ 36	for a while	한동안
16	☐ 37	give it a try	한번 해보다
18	☐ 38	have trouble ~ing	~하는 데 어려움이 있다
	☐ 39	clearly	또렷하게
19	☐ 40	get started	시작하다
	☐ 41	presentation	발표
	☐ 42	wedding	결혼식
20	☐ 43	pick	고르다
	☐ 44	on the way back	돌아오는 길에

M1(17)_W_13

● 왼쪽 단어장의 뜻이 보이지 않게 반으로 접고, 학습한 단어의 뜻을 아래 빈칸에 적어주세요.

1	come together		23	hole
2	How about ~?		24	condition
3	rectangular		25	far
4	vase		26	about
5	terrible		27	next to ~
6	symphony		28	sick
7	wedding		29	all day long
8	pull		30	clearly
9	get to		31	apologize
10	have ~ in mind		32	get on one's nerves
11	on the way back		33	have an appointment
12	bakery		34	It's about time.
13	way		35	have trouble ~ing
14	ride		36	forget about ~
15	tear up		37	pick
16	weekend		38	triangular
17	give it a try		39	show
18	mess up		40	aunt
19	understand		41	presentation
20	have a seat		42	run away
21	do a good job		43	get started
22	plan		44	for a while

13
회
단
어

전국 15개 시·도 교육청 공동주관 및 서울시 연합 내신

14회 중학영어듣기 모의고사

M1(17)_14_US
모두 **미국식 발음(US)**
으로 녹음

M1(17)_14_UK
20문제 중 5문제에 **영국식 발음**
(US+UK)을 포함하여 녹음

📖 정답 및 해석 p.56

1 다음을 듣고, 'I'가 무엇인지 가장 적절한 것을 고르시오.

①  ②  ③  ④  ⑤

2 대화를 듣고, 남자가 구입할 가방으로 가장 적절한 것을 고르시오.

①  ②  ③  ④  ⑤

3 다음을 듣고, 내일 아침의 날씨로 가장 적절한 것을 고르시오.

①  ②  ③  ④  ⑤

4 대화를 듣고, 남자가 한 마지막 말의 의도로 가장 적절한 것을 고르시오.

① 감사 ② 거절 ③ 당부 ④ 사과 ⑤ 항의

5 다음을 듣고, 남자가 가족여행에 대해 언급하지 <u>않은</u> 것을 고르시오.

① 목적지 ② 여행 기간 ③ 교통수단
④ 음식 ⑤ 숙소

6 대화를 듣고, 두 사람이 만날 시각을 고르시오.

① 1:00 p.m. ② 1:30 p.m. ③ 2:00 p.m.
④ 2:30 p.m. ⑤ 3:00 p.m.

7 대화를 듣고, 여자의 장래 희망으로 가장 적절한 것을 고르시오.

① 발레리나 ② 성악가 ③ 사진작가
④ 화가 ⑤ 패션 디자이너

8 대화를 듣고, 남자의 심정으로 가장 적절한 것을 고르시오.

① 실망 ② 걱정 ③ 부러움 ④ 수줍음 ⑤ 지루함

14 회 모의고사

9 대화를 듣고, 여자가 대화 직후에 할 일로 가장 적절한 것을 고르시오.

① 낮잠 자기 ② 전등 끄기 ③ 안약 갖다주기
④ 휴대전화 찾기 ⑤ 동영상 검색하기

10 대화를 듣고, 무엇에 관한 내용인지 가장 적절한 것을 고르시오.

① 체험학습 일정 ② 도서 판매 행사
③ 권장 도서 안내 ④ 여름 방학 계획
⑤ 도서관 이용 방법

11번~20번 문제는 다음 페이지에 ➡

11 대화를 듣고, 두 사람이 함께 이동할 방법으로 가장 적절한 것을 고르시오.

① 지하철   ② 버스   ③ 택시

④ 도보   ⑤ 자전거

12 대화를 듣고, 여자에게 매트가 필요한 이유로 가장 적절한 것을 고르시오.

① 짐을 옮기기 위해서   ② 소풍을 가기 위해서

③ 방을 꾸미기 위해서   ④ 물건을 올려두기 위해서

⑤ 집에서 운동하기 위해서

13 대화를 듣고, 대화가 이루어지고 있는 장소를 고르시오.

① 백화점   ② 우체국   ③ 박물관   ④ 서점   ⑤ 도서관

14 대화를 듣고, 남자의 휴대전화가 놓인 장소를 고르시오.

15 대화를 듣고, 남자가 여자에게 부탁한 일로 가장 적절한 것을 고르시오.

① 에어컨 켜기   ② 짐 들어주기   ③ 청소하기

④ 음료수 사오기   ⑤ 문 열어두기

16 대화를 듣고, 여자가 남자에게 제안한 것으로 가장 적절한 것을 고르시오.

① 문자 보내기　　　② 얼음 찜질하기　　　③ 스트레칭 하기
④ 목도리 구입하기　　⑤ 스마트폰 수리하기

17 대화를 듣고, 남자가 주말에 할 일로 가장 적절한 것을 고르시오.

① 캠핑 가기　　　② 서점 가기　　　③ 영화 보기
④ 기타 연습하기　　⑤ 음악 축제 가기

18 대화를 듣고, 남자의 직업으로 가장 적절한 것을 고르시오.

① 여행 가이드　　　② 수의사　　　③ 기상 캐스터
④ 동물원 사육사　　⑤ 야생 탐험가

[19~20] 대화를 듣고, 남자의 마지막 말에 이어질 여자의 말로 가장 적절한 것을 고르시오.

19 Woman: _____

① That's too bad.　　　② No way!
③ Good for you.　　　④ Help yourself.
⑤ Be careful.

20 Woman: _____

① It was a good try.　　　② You are a good cook!
③ I'll take pictures of the food.　　④ Can I have your recipe, please?
⑤ Sure, I'll cook it for you sometime!

Dictation Test 14

녹음을 다시 들으면서 빈칸을 채워주세요.

M1(17)_14_D

Dictation(받아쓰기)은 본문을 받아쓰면서 영어듣기의 집중력을 향상시키고 다양한 표현을 정리하기 위한 영어듣기 학습법입니다. **녹음을 다시 듣고, 빈칸에 알맞은 단어를 써 보세요.**

※Dictation의 정답은 듣기 대본의 밑줄 친 부분을 확인하세요.

📖 정답 p. 56

✒ 맞은 개수 / 총109개

그림정보파악(담화)

1. 다음을 듣고, 'I'가 무엇인지 가장 적절한 것을 고르시오.

①    ②

③   ④

⑤

01 M: I am large and very heavy. I have four short legs and two small ears. I have _____, _____ _____ skin. I also have two _____ on top of my nose. What am I?

그림정보파악(대화)

🇺🇸🇬🇧

2. 대화를 듣고, 남자가 구입할 가방으로 가장 적절한 것을 고르시오.

①    ②

③    ④

⑤

02 M: Hello, I want to buy a _____ for my daughter.

W: Sure, we have square ones and round ones.

M: I think she would prefer a round one.

W: Okay, then how about this one with the _____?

M: Hmm… Is there _____ _____?

W: Yes, of course. There is this one with a unicorn.

M: She will love it! I'll take this one.

---

3. 다음을 듣고, 내일 아침의 날씨로 가장 적절한 것을 고르시오.

①
②
③
④
⑤

03 W: Good morning! This is the weather report. Right now, it is snowing outside. And it looks like we will get more snow _____ the day. Fortunately, by tomorrow morning, the snow will have stopped but it will be very windy. So, _____ _____ to wear a jacket when you go outside.

2024 영어듣기능력평가 1회 4번 변형

4. 대화를 듣고, 남자가 한 마지막 말의 의도로 가장 적절한 것을 고르시오.
① 감사　② 거절
③ 당부　④ 사과
⑤ 항의

04 W: Excuse me, can I get a different table?

M: Of course. Is there _____ _____?

W: Yes, this table is too close to the kitchen, and it isn't quiet.

M: I understand. Let me find you a table in a quieter section _____ _____.

W: Thank you.

M: My _____ for the trouble.

다음 페이지에 계속 ➡

5. 다음을 듣고, 남자가 가족여행에 대해 언급하지 <u>않은</u> 것을 고르시오.

① 목적지　　② 여행 기간
③ 교통수단　　④ 음식
⑤ 숙소

05 M: Let me tell you about my plans for a family trip. My family will go to Gyeongju and visit _____ _____. We'll be there for 3 days. We'll take trains and buses to _____ _____. My family will stay at a hotel built in a traditional Korean style.

---

6. 대화를 듣고, 두 사람이 만날 시각을 고르시오.

① 1:00 p.m.　　② 1:30 p.m.
③ 2:00 p.m.　　④ 2:30 p.m.
⑤ 3:00 p.m.

06 M: It's really hot today. Let's _____ _____ this afternoon.

W: Okay. Let's meet at the indoor pool.

M: Can we _____ _____ 1:30?

W: I have lunch at 1.

M: Then, let's meet at 2:30. We shouldn't go into the water _____ _____ lunch.

W: Okay. See you then.

7. 대화를 듣고, 여자의 장래 희망으로 가장
적절한 것을 고르시오.

① 발레리나　　　② 성악가
③ 사진작가　　　④ 화가
⑤ 패션 디자이너

07
M: Emma, that's a nice poster on your desk.

W: Thanks. It's a _____ of a work by Leona Wilson, my favorite artist.

M: Cool. So, she's a _____?

W: Yes. I want to be able to create something that beautiful someday.

M: Wow! So, do you want to be like her in the future?

W: Yes. So I am _____ every day.

M: Great!

8. 대화를 듣고, 남자의 심정으로 가장 적절
한 것을 고르시오.

① 실망　　　② 걱정
③ 부러움　　　④ 수줍음
⑤ 지루함

08
M: Mom, the rock festival was _____.

W: What? Are you sure? But you really wanted to go to it.

M: I know. How could they do that? I've already _____ _____ for the ticket.

W: I'm so sorry, honey.

M: This is _____ _____.

다음 페이지에 계속 ➡

9. 대화를 듣고, 여자가 대화 직후에 할 일
   로 가장 적절한 것을 고르시오.

① 낮잠 자기
② 전등 끄기
③ 안약 갖다주기
④ 휴대전화 찾기
⑤ 동영상 검색하기

09 W: What's wrong, Isaac?

M: My eyes are _____.

W: You are watching videos on your phone too much.

M: Maybe. I put eye drops in, but they're not

_____.

W: How about closing your eyes and giving them

_____ _____?

M: That sounds good. Could you _____ _____

_____ _____ for me?

W: Sure. I'll do it right now.

10. 대화를 듣고, 무엇에 관한 내용인지 가장
    적절한 것을 고르시오.

① 체험학습 일정
② 도서 판매 행사
③ 권장 도서 안내
④ 여름 방학 계획
⑤ 도서관 이용 방법

10 W: Did you hear about the school book _____?

M: You mean the school _____ event?

W: Yes. We can buy used books at a _____ price

there.

M: Sounds great. When is it?

W: It starts this Friday and will _____ _____

_____.

M: Why don't we go together this Saturday?

W: Sure. I'd love to.

11. 대화를 듣고, 두 사람이 함께 이동할 방법으로 가장 적절한 것을 고르시오.
   ① 지하철　　② 버스
   ③ 택시　　　④ 도보
   ⑤ 자전거

11
M: Amy, do you want to go to the cinema today?

W: Sure. What movie do you want to see?

M: I'm _____ _____ watching *The Flying Man*.

W: Oh, _____ _____ _____ watch it! Shall we walk there?

M: It's too hot outside. Why don't we take a taxi?

W: A taxi _____ _____.

12. 대화를 듣고, 여자에게 매트가 필요한 이유로 가장 적절한 것을 고르시오.
   ① 짐을 옮기기 위해서
   ② 소풍을 가기 위해서
   ③ 방을 꾸미기 위해서
   ④ 물건을 올려두기 위해서
   ⑤ 집에서 운동하기 위해서

12
M: Sarah, do you need anything from the supermarket?

W: Yes, Dad. Can you buy me a mat?

M: Sure. _____ _____?

W: My friends and I are _____ _____ _____ _____ this weekend. Karen and Sophia will bring food and I will _____ a mat.

M: I see. I'll buy one for you.

W: Thank you.

다음 페이지에 계속 ➡

13. 대화를 듣고, 대화가 이루어지고 있는 장소를 고르시오.

① 백화점　　② 우체국
③ 박물관　　④ 서점
⑤ 도서관

13

M: Excuse me. I'd like to _____ some books.

W: OK. May I see your _____ _____, please?

M: Here it is. And these are the books I want to borrow.

W: Oh, you can't borrow all these books.

M: Why?

W: You can borrow only three books _____ _____ _____.

M: OK. I'll borrow these three books.

14. 대화를 듣고, 남자의 휴대전화가 놓인 장소를 고르시오.

14

M: Maria, _____ _____ _____ my cellphone?

W: I think it is on the table.

M: No, it's not there.

W: Well, look _____ _____ _____.

M: It's not there, either.

W: Hmm, that's weird. What about on the piano?

M: Oh, _____ _____ _____.

15. 대화를 듣고, 남자가 여자에게 부탁한 일로 가장 적절한 것을 고르시오.

① 에어컨 켜기
② 짐 들어주기
③ 청소하기
④ 음료수 사오기
⑤ 문 열어두기

15 W: David, you _____ _____.

M: It's so hot in here.

W: That's true. I think the air conditioner _____ _____.

M: Would you do me a favor?

W: Sure, what is it?

M: Please leave the door _____ _____ on your way out.

16. 대화를 듣고, 여자가 남자에게 제안한 것으로 가장 적절한 것을 고르시오.

① 문자 보내기
② 얼음 찜질하기
③ 스트레칭 하기
④ 목도리 구입하기
⑤ 스마트폰 수리하기

16 M: Sally, _____ _____ _____.

W: You must have text neck!

M: Text neck? What is that?

W: It is neck pain caused by _____ _____ at your phone for too long.

M: Oh, what should I do?

W: Why don't you _____ your neck more often?

M: Okay, I will. Thank you.

다음 페이지에 계속 ➡

17. 대화를 듣고, 남자가 주말에 할 일로 가장 적절한 것을 고르시오.

① 캠핑 가기
② 서점 가기
③ 영화 보기
④ 기타 연습하기
⑤ 음악 축제 가기

17
W: Hi, Brian. Do you have any plans for the weekend?

M: Yes, Amy. I'm going to practice the _____ at home.

W: Oh, are you learning a new song?

M: Yeah! I want to make sure I _____ _____ _____ for my school festival.

W: That's cool. I'd love to hear you play someday.

M: Sure! I'll play for you when I get better.

18. 대화를 듣고, 남자의 직업으로 가장 적절한 것을 고르시오.

① 여행 가이드
② 수의사
③ 기상 캐스터
④ 동물원 사육사
⑤ 야생 탐험가

18
W: How was your day, honey?

M: I'm _____ _____.

W: Were there many _____ at the zoo today?

M: No, but we had to move some animals to their winter homes. It was a lot of work.

W: Your effort to _____ the animals safe and healthy is _____.

M: Thank you. I feel good knowing they're happy and safe.

19. 대화를 듣고, 남자의 마지막 말에 이어질 여자의 말로 가장 적절한 것을 고르시오.

Woman: _____

① That's too bad.
② No way!
③ Good for you.
④ Help yourself.
⑤ Be careful.

19

W: Paul, did you go to your _____ house last New Year's Day?

M: Yes, I did. Did you?

W: No, _____ _____ _____, because I was sick.

M: Oh, no! That's too bad.

W: So, what did you do there?

M: I ate a lot of food and _____ _____. It was fun.

W: Good for you.

---

20. 대화를 듣고, 남자의 마지막 말에 이어질 여자의 말로 가장 적절한 것을 고르시오.

Woman: _____

① It was a good try.
② You are a good cook!
③ I'll take pictures of the food.
④ Can I have your recipe, please?
⑤ Sure, I'll cook it for you sometime!

20

M: Do you enjoy _____?

W: I love cooking! Here's a photo of a dish I made yesterday.

M: Amazing! What is it?

W: _____ lasagna with meat sauce.

M: Looks so yummy! Did you _____ a recipe?

W: Yes. It's a family recipe that I've been using for years.

M: Looks tasty! I want to _____ _____ someday.

W: Sure, I'll cook it for you sometime!

14
회
딕
테
이
션

Words & Expressions Review 14

● 다음 단어를 암기하세요.

문제	번호	단어	뜻
1	□ 1	thick	두꺼운
	□ 2	bookbag	책가방
2	□ 3	stripe	줄무늬
	□ 4	anything else	그 밖에 또 다른 것
3	□ 5	throughout	~동안, 내내
	□ 6	make sure	반드시 ~하다, 확실히 하다
	□ 7	go outside	외출하다, 밖으로 나가다
4	□ 8	wrong	문제가 있는
	□ 9	apology	사과
	□ 10	historical	역사적인, 역사의
5	□ 11	site	유적, 장소, 위치
	□ 12	get around	(여기 저기) 돌아다니다
	□ 13	traditional	전통적인, 전통의
	□ 14	go swimming	수영하러 가다
6	□ 15	indoor	실내의
	□ 16	pool	수영장
7	□ 17	photocopy	복사본
	□ 18	work	작품
	□ 19	painter	화가
	□ 20	someday	(미래의) 언젠가
8	□ 21	festival	축제
9	□ 22	sore	아픈, 따가운

문제	번호	단어	뜻
9	□ 23	eye drops	안약, 점안액
	□ 24	charity	자선, 자선 단체
10	□ 25	used	중고의
	□ 26	cheap	싼, 저렴한
11	□ 27	think of ~	~을 생각하다
	□ 28	would love to + 동사	너무 ~하고 싶다
12	□ 29	bring	가져오다, 데려오다
13	□ 30	at a time	한 번에
14	□ 31	weird	이상한
	□ 32	air conditioner	에어컨
15	□ 33	broken	고장 난, 부서진
	□ 34	wide open	활짝 열린
16	□ 35	look down	내려보다, 내려다보다
	□ 36	stretch	스트레칭 하다, 펴다
17	□ 37	practice	연습하다
	□ 38	home	시설
18	□ 39	effort	노력
	□ 40	impressive	인상적인, 감명 깊은
19	□ 41	New Year's Day	설날
	□ 42	follow	따라하다, 따르다
20	□ 43	recipe	요리법
	□ 44	try	먹어보다

M1(17)_W_14

📖 정답 p. 60

● 왼쪽 단어장의 뜻이 보이지 않게 반으로 접고, 학습한 단어의 뜻을 아래 빈칸에 적어주세요.

1	get around	____	23	New Year's Day	____
2	broken	____	24	photocopy	____
3	stretch	____	25	effort	____
4	apology	____	26	at a time	____
5	go outside	____	27	work	____
6	indoor	____	28	cheap	____
7	practice	____	29	throughout	____
8	bookbag	____	30	sore	____
9	make sure	____	31	follow	____
10	go swimming	____	32	air conditioner	____
11	stripe	____	33	thick	____
12	home	____	34	historical	____
13	pool	____	35	wrong	____
14	someday	____	36	charity	____
15	anything else	____	37	impressive	____
16	traditional	____	38	recipe	____
17	weird	____	39	used	____
18	try	____	40	site	____
19	think of ~	____	41	look down	____
20	eye drops	____	42	would love to + 동사	____
21	festival	____	43	painter	____
22	wide open	____	44	bring	____

14
회
단
어

15회 중학영어듣기 모의고사

M1(17)_15_US
모두 **미국식 발음(US)** 으로 녹음

M1(17)_15_UK
20문제 중 5문제에 **영국식 발음 (US+UK)**을 포함하여 녹음

📖 정답 및 해석 p.60

---

1 다음을 듣고, 'this'가 무엇인지 가장 적절한 것을 고르시오.

①  ②  ③  ④ 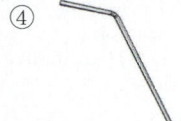 ⑤

---

2 대화를 듣고, 남자가 구입할 곰 인형으로 가장 적절한 것을 고르시오.

①  ②  ③  ④  ⑤

---

3 다음을 듣고, 내일 날씨를 고르시오.

①  ②  ③  ④  ⑤

---

4 대화를 듣고, 여자가 한 마지막 말의 의도로 가장 적절한 것을 고르시오.

① 당부　　　② 거절　　　③ 사과　　　④ 항의　　　⑤ 위로

---

5 다음을 듣고, 남자에 대해 알 수 없는 것을 고르시오.

① 이름　　　② 가족　　　③ 좋아하는 과목　　　④ 취미　　　⑤ 좋아하는 음식

---

6 대화를 듣고, 두 사람이 이야기를 나누는 현재 시각을 고르시오.

① 1:00 p.m.   ② 1:30 p.m.   ③ 2:00 p.m.   ④ 2:30 p.m.   ⑤ 3:00 p.m.

7 대화를 듣고, 여자의 장래 희망으로 가장 적절한 것을 고르시오.

① 가수   ② 발레리나   ③ 관광 가이드
④ 비행기 승무원   ⑤ 여행 작가

8 대화를 듣고, 여자의 심정으로 가장 적절한 것을 고르시오.

① bored   ② worried   ③ scared   ④ happy   ⑤ embarrassed

9 대화를 듣고, 남자가 대화 직후에 할 일로 가장 적절한 것을 고르시오.

① 서랍 수리하기   ② 배터리 구매하기   ③ 핸드폰 충전하기
④ 침대 위치 바꾸기   ⑤ 쇼핑 목록 작성하기

10 대화를 듣고, 무엇에 관한 내용인지 가장 적절한 것을 고르시오.

① 요리 실습   ② 현장 학습   ③ 급식 디저트 메뉴
④ 학교 매점 위치   ⑤ 축제 부스 운영

11번~20번 문제는 다음 페이지에 ➡

11 대화를 듣고, 두 사람이 함께 이용할 교통수단으로 가장 적절한 것을 고르시오.

① 기차   ② 택시   ③ 버스   ④ 자전거   ⑤ 비행기

12 대화를 듣고, 여자가 수영장에 갈 수 <u>없는</u> 이유로 가장 적절한 것을 고르시오.

① 감기에 걸려서   ② 치과에 가야 해서
③ 가족 모임이 있어서   ④ 수영복을 잃어버려서
⑤ 수영장이 보수 공사 중이어서

13 대화를 듣고, 두 사람이 대화하는 장소로 가장 적절한 곳을 고르시오.

① 서점   ② 식당   ③ 정육점
④ 제과점   ⑤ 놀이공원

14 대화를 듣고, 극장의 위치로 가장 알맞은 곳을 고르시오.

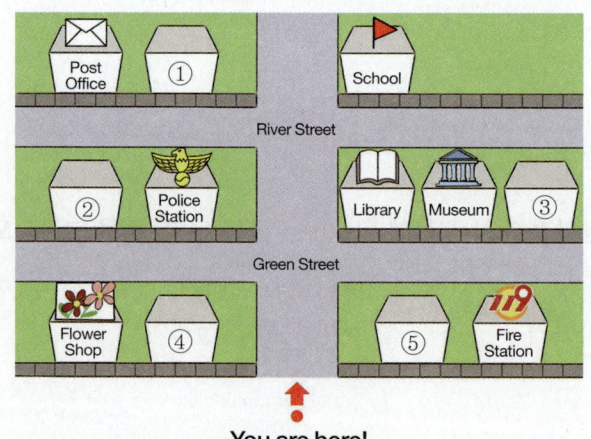

15 대화를 듣고, 남자가 여자에게 부탁한 일로 가장 적절한 것을 고르시오.

① 그림 그려주기   ② 길 알려주기   ③ 입장권 끊어주기
④ 사진 찍어주기   ⑤ 박물관 안내해주기

16 대화를 듣고, 여자가 남자에게 제안한 것으로 가장 적절한 것을 고르시오.

① 쿠키 굽기　　　　② 이웃 초대하기　　　　③ 감사 편지 쓰기
④ 오렌지 구입하기　　⑤ 제빵 수업 등록하기

17 대화를 듣고, 남자가 지난 주말에 한 일로 가장 적절한 것을 고르시오.

① 낚시 가기　　　　② 그림 그리기　　　　③ 봉사활동하기
④ 방 청소하기　　　⑤ 사진 촬영하기

18 대화를 듣고, 남자의 직업으로 가장 적절한 것을 고르시오.

① 변호사　　② 약사　　③ 치과 의사　　④ 백화점 직원　　⑤ 헬스장 트레이너

19 대화를 듣고, 남자의 마지막 말에 이어질 여자의 응답으로 가장 적절한 것을 고르시오.

Woman: _____

① I have already finished my project.　　② My hobby is reading books.
③ I'm sorry, but I can't.　　　　　　　　④ My place, at 2 p.m.
⑤ It's not my fault.

20 대화를 듣고, 여자의 마지막 말에 이어질 남자의 응답으로 가장 적절한 것을 고르시오.

Man: _____

① I'm so sorry. I'll pay next time.　　② My pleasure. See you later.
③ What do you think about the food?　　④ I'm hungry. Let's order now.
⑤ I'm going to be late.

Dictation Test 15

M1(17)_15_D

Dictation(받아쓰기)은 본문을 받아쓰면서 영어듣기의 집중력을 향상시키고 다양한 표현을 정리하기 위한 영어듣기 학습법입니다. **녹음을 다시 듣고, 빈칸에 알맞은 단어를 써 보세요.**

※Dictation의 정답은 듣기 대본의 밑줄 친 부분을 확인하세요.

정답 p. 60

맞은 개수 / 총131개

그림정보파악(담화)

 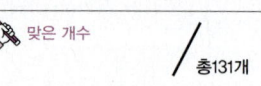

1. 다음을 듣고, 'this'가 무엇인지 가장 적절한 것을 고르시오.

① ② ③ ④ ⑤

01 W: You can use this when you drink something. This is usually long and thin. You _____ _____ _____ into your mouth with this. This is a tube usually _____ _____ plastic or _____ paper. What is this?

그림정보파악(대화)

2. 대화를 듣고, 남자가 구입할 곰 인형으로 가장 적절한 것을 고르시오.

① ② ③ ④ ⑤

02 M: Hi, I am _____ _____ a teddy bear for my daughter's birthday.

W: Oh, okay. _____ _____ this one with a big heart?

M: She already has that one.

W: Okay. How about this one with a moon on it? It's a new design.

M: That's cute. But do you have one with flowers on it?

W: We do! Here it is.

M: It's lovely! I'll _____ it.

---

3. 다음을 듣고, 내일 날씨를 고르시오.

①  ②

③  ④

⑤

03 W: Taking a look at today's weather, we have cloudy skies this morning with a _____ _____ _____ of showers this afternoon. Tomorrow _____ _____ _____ be warmer than today with clear, sunny skies. Please prepare an umbrella when you go out today.

2024 영어듣기능력평가 2회 4번 변형

4. 대화를 듣고, 여자가 한 마지막 말의 의도로 가장 적절한 것을 고르시오.
① 당부 ② 거절
③ 사과 ④ 항의
⑤ 위로

04 M: Did you say something, Nina?

W: Yes. I said, "_____ _____ the music a little."

M: Oh, I didn't hear that. Sorry.

W: You didn't hear what I said because the music was too loud. I'm _____ _____ _____ here.

M: Sorry again. I _____ the volume.

W: Thank you. Just try not to play the music too loudly.

다음 페이지에 계속 ➡

15
회
딕
테
이
션

5. 다음을 듣고, 남자에 대해 알 수 <u>없는</u> 것을 고르시오.

① 이름　　② 가족
③ 좋아하는 과목　　④ 취미
⑤ 좋아하는 음식

05 M: Hi, everyone. I'm Minsu. _____ _____ _____ meet you. Today is my first day at this school. I've _____ _____ _____ from Daegu. I live with my parents and an older brother. I like math. My hobby is playing baseball. I think we _____ _____ _____ _____ good friends. Thank you.

2024 영어듣기능력평가 2회 6번 변형

6. 대화를 듣고, 두 사람이 이야기를 나누는 현재 시각을 고르시오.

① 1:00 p.m.　　② 1:30 p.m.
③ 2:00 p.m.　　④ 2:30 p.m.
⑤ 3:00 p.m.

06 *[Cellphone rings.]*

W: Tyler, are you at the airport now?

M: Yes, I _____ _____ at 1 p.m.

W: What time is your _____?

M: It's at 3 p.m.

W: It's 2 p.m. now. So, you have about an hour before you _____ _____.

M: That's right. I'm just _____ at the gate now.

7. 대화를 듣고, 여자의 장래 희망으로 가장 적절한 것을 고르시오.

① 가수　　　② 발레리나
③ 관광 가이드　④ 비행기 승무원
⑤ 여행 작가

07 W: What do you want to be in the future?

M: You know that I _____ _____. I'd like to be a singer. What about you?

W: When I was young, I wanted to be a ballerina. However, now I like traveling, so I've _____ _____ _____.

M: You mean you want to be _____ _____ _____?

W: No, I want to be a flight attendant.

8. 대화를 듣고, 여자의 심정으로 가장 적절한 것을 고르시오.

① bored　　② worried
③ scared　　④ happy
⑤ embarrassed

08 M: What's up? You _____ _____.

W: My dad is back! It's his first day home from the hospital.

M: Oh, that's good. How's your dad feeling?

W: He is _____ _____. I can't wait to have dinner all together at home.

M: You must be _____! Have a wonderful evening with your family.

W: Thanks! I will.

다음 페이지에 계속 ➡

15
회
딕
테
이
션

9. 대화를 듣고, 남자가 대화 직후에 할 일로 가장 적절한 것을 고르시오.
① 서랍 수리하기
② 배터리 구매하기
③ 핸드폰 충전하기
④ 침대 위치 바꾸기
⑤ 쇼핑 목록 작성하기

09
M: Honey, do you remember where we _____ our spare batteries?

W: They're in our bedroom _____.

M: I checked the drawer, but they weren't there.

W: I guess we've _____ _____ _____ spare batteries, then.

M: Hmm… That's not good.

W: Let's buy some next time we're at the store.

M: It's _____. I'll head out and buy some right now.

10. 대화를 듣고, 무엇에 관한 내용인지 가장 적절한 것을 고르시오.
① 요리 실습
② 현장 학습
③ 급식 디저트 메뉴
④ 학교 매점 위치
⑤ 축제 부스 운영

10
W: Did you see the poster on the wall?

M: You mean the one about the new school lunch menu?

W: Yeah, we _____ _____ _____ a dessert menu for Christmas Eve.

M: Yes, I saw it. There are _____ _____ on the menu, chocolate cake and banana waffles.

W: I want the chocolate cake. I love sweet dessert.

M: I _____ _____ yet. They both look delicious.

11. 대화를 듣고, 두 사람이 함께 이용할 교통수단으로 가장 적절한 것을 고르시오.
    ① 기차　　② 택시
    ③ 버스　　④ 자전거
    ⑤ 비행기

11
W: Why don't we go to 'Happy Beach' this weekend?

M: Great idea. I'll _____ our train tickets.

W: It takes four hours by train, right? That's quite a _____ _____.

M: Do you want to take an airplane, then? It's only a one-hour flight and tickets are _____ these days.

W: Really? Let's take the plane then.

12. 대화를 듣고, 여자가 수영장에 갈 수 없는 이유로 가장 적절한 것을 고르시오.
    ① 감기에 걸려서
    ② 치과에 가야 해서
    ③ 가족 모임이 있어서
    ④ 수영복을 잃어버려서
    ⑤ 수영장이 보수 공사 중이어서

12
W: Dad, can I go to the swimming pool with my friends on Friday?

M: On Friday? No, I'm afraid you can't.

W: Why not?

M: You have to _____ _____ _____ _____ on Friday.

W: Do I? I thought it was Wednesday.

M: Your mom _____ _____ _____ on Wednesday so she changed your appointment to Friday.

W: Oh, I forgot. Then I'll have to go to the swimming pool on _____ _____.

M: Yes.

15
회
딕
테
이
션

다음 페이지에 계속 ➡

13. 대화를 듣고, 두 사람이 대화하는 장소로
가장 적절한 곳을 고르시오.

① 서점　　　② 식당
③ 정육점　　④ 제과점
⑤ 놀이공원

13
M: Can I _____ _____ _____, ma'am?

W: Yes. I'll have the vegetable soup and the beef
steak.

M: How do you want your steak?

W: I want it _____-_____.

M: Okay. Do you need _____ _____
drink?

W: Just water, please.

14. 대화를 듣고, 극장의 위치로 가장 알맞은
곳을 고르시오.

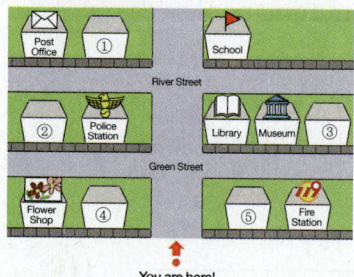

14
M: Excuse me. Is there a movie theater _____
_____?

W: Yes, there is one nearby.

M: How can I get there from here?

W: _____ _____ for one block and then
_____ _____ on Green Street.

M: On Green Street?

W: Yes. The movie theater will be _____ _____
_____. It's next to the police station.

15. 대화를 듣고, 남자가 여자에게 부탁한 일로 가장 적절한 것을 고르시오.
   ① 그림 그려주기
   ② 길 알려주기
   ③ 입장권 끊어주기
   ④ 사진 찍어주기
   ⑤ 박물관 안내해주기

15
M: Excuse me. Can you help me?

W: Sure. What do you need?

M: Would you _____ _____ _____ _____ me in front of the museum?

W: Okay. Do you want _____ _____ building in the picture?

M: That would be great. Thank you.

16. 대화를 듣고, 여자가 남자에게 제안한 것으로 가장 적절한 것을 고르시오.
   ① 쿠키 굽기
   ② 이웃 초대하기
   ③ 감사 편지 쓰기
   ④ 오렌지 구입하기
   ⑤ 제빵 수업 등록하기

16
M: Look. My new neighbors _____ these at the door.

W: Fresh oranges! _____ _____ of them!

M: There's this note saying hi, too.

W: They must be nice people.

M: I should do something. What can I buy them?

W: _____ _____ buying something, how about making cookies? You're _____ _____ _____.

M: That's a good idea.

15
회
딕
테
이
션

다음 페이지에 계속 ➡

17. 대화를 듣고, 남자가 지난 주말에 한 일로 가장 적절한 것을 고르시오.

① 낚시 가기
② 그림 그리기
③ 봉사활동하기
④ 방 청소하기
⑤ 사진 촬영하기

17

W: Phil, what did you do last weekend?

M: I did _____ _____ _____ in my room last weekend.

W: Nice! How was it?

M: It was _____ _____ . I even found some photos of me when I was a baby.

W: Cool! It _____ _____ _____ to have a clean room.

M: Yeah. I'm glad I did the cleaning.

18. 대화를 듣고, 남자의 직업으로 가장 적절한 것을 고르시오.

① 변호사
② 약사
③ 치과 의사
④ 백화점 직원
⑤ 헬스장 트레이너

18

M: Hello, Ms. Blake. What seems to be the problem today?

W: I have _____ _____ _____.

M: Okay, let me take a look first. Open your mouth, please.

W: Sure. Ah...

M: Hmm... It seems that you've got a bad tooth here.

W: Oh no! Do you have to pull the tooth out?

M: No need for that. It _____ _____ _____, though.

19. 대화를 듣고, 남자의 마지막 말에 이어질 여자의 응답으로 가장 적절한 것을 고르시오.

Woman: _____

① I have already finished my project.
② My hobby is reading books.
③ I'm sorry, but I can't.
④ My place, at 2 p.m.
⑤ It's not my fault.

19 [Cellphone rings.]

M: Hello.

W: Hello, Troy. This is McKenzie.

M: Hey, what's up?

W: We should _____ _____ for our group project.

M: Right. Did you talk to the others?

W: Yes. They are all _____ on Saturday afternoon. Can you _____?

M: Of course, I can. Where are we going to meet?

W: My place, at 2 p.m.

---

20. 대화를 듣고, 여자의 마지막 말에 이어질 남자의 응답으로 가장 적절한 것을 고르시오.

Man: _____

① I'm so sorry. I'll pay next time.
② My pleasure. See you later.
③ What do you think about the food?
④ I'm hungry. Let's order now.
⑤ I'm going to be late.

20 M: It was delicious.

W: Yes, it really was. Excuse me, can I _____ _____ _____, please?

M: Oh, no!

W: What's wrong, Larry?

M: I _____ _____ bring my wallet!

W: Don't worry. I'll treat you this time.

M: I'm so sorry. I'll pay next time.

Words & Expressions Review 15

● 다음 단어를 암기하세요.

문제	번호	단어	뜻
1	□ 1	drink	마시다, 음료
	□ 2	made of	~으로 만든
	□ 3	waterproof	방수의
2	□ 4	lovely	사랑스러운, 아름다운
	□ 5	take	선택하다, 사다, (시간이) 걸리다, (교통수단·도로 등을) 타다
3	□ 6	be expected to + 동사	~할 것으로 예상되다
	□ 7	prepare	준비하다
4	□ 8	turn down	(소리·온도 등을) 낮추다
	□ 9	here	지금, 이 순간에, 여기에
5	□ 10	pleased	기쁜
6	□ 11	airport	공항
	□ 12	take off	이륙하다
	□ 13	relax	느긋이 쉬다, 휴식을 취하다
	□ 14	gate	(공항의) 게이트, 탑승구
7	□ 15	change one's mind	마음을 바꾸다
8	□ 16	much better	훨씬 나은
9	□ 17	drawer	서랍
	□ 18	run out of ~	~을 다 써버리다, ~이 고갈되다
	□ 19	urgent	시급한, 긴급한
10	□ 20	option	선택지, 선택
11	□ 21	book	예약하다
	□ 22	quite	꽤, 상당히

문제	번호	단어	뜻
11	□ 23	flight	비행, 여행
12	□ 24	dentist	치과 의사
	□ 25	appointment	예약, 약속
13	□ 26	order	주문
	□ 27	vegetable	채소
	□ 28	well-done	완전히 익힌
14	□ 29	movie theater	영화관
15	□ 30	museum	박물관
	□ 31	whole	전체의, 완전히
	□ 32	neighbor	이웃, 가까이 있는 사람
16	□ 33	instead of	~ 대신에
	□ 34	be good at	~을 잘하다
	□ 35	spring cleaning	(봄에 하는) 대청소
17	□ 36	worth	~할 가치가 있는
	□ 37	refreshing	상쾌한, 산뜻한
	□ 38	severe	심한, 심각한
18	□ 39	toothache	치통
	□ 40	treatment	치료
19	□ 41	meet up	~와 만나다
	□ 42	group project	조별 과제
20	□ 43	treat	대접하다
	□ 44	pay	(돈을) 내다

●왼쪽 단어장의 뜻이 보이지 않게 반으로 접고, 학습한 단어의 뜻을 아래 빈칸에 적어주세요.

1	change one's mind	23	drink
2	lovely	24	be expected to + 동사
3	much better	25	pleased
4	toothache	26	turn down
5	prepare	27	flight
6	here	28	order
7	take	29	airport
8	dentist	30	severe
9	urgent	31	meet up
10	movie theater	32	quite
11	appointment	33	treat
12	book	34	take off
13	instead of	35	museum
14	drawer	36	made of
15	vegetable	37	run out of ~
16	well-done	38	group project
17	whole	39	waterproof
18	option	40	neighbor
19	be good at	41	pay
20	worth	42	spring cleaning
21	gate	43	relax
22	treatment	44	refreshing

15
회
단
어

전국 15개 시·도 교육청 공동주관 및 서울시 연합 내신

16회 중학영어듣기 모의고사

M1(17)_16_US
모두 **미국식 발음(US)**
으로 녹음

M1(17)_16_UK
20문제 중 5문제에 **영국식 발음**
(US+UK)을 포함하여 녹음

📖 정답 및 해석 p.64

1 다음을 듣고, 'I'가 무엇인지 가장 적절한 것을 고르시오.

①  ②  ③  ④  ⑤

2 대화를 듣고, 여자가 구입할 반바지로 가장 적절한 것을 고르시오.

①  ②  ③  ④  ⑤

3 다음을 듣고, 내일의 날씨로 가장 적절한 것을 고르시오.

①  ②  ③  ④  ⑤

4 대화를 듣고, 남자가 한 마지막 말의 의도로 가장 적절한 것을 고르시오.

① 축하　　② 감사　　③ 동의　　④ 후회　　⑤ 위로

5 다음을 듣고, 남자가 여름 댄스 대회에 대해 언급하지 <u>않은</u> 것을 고르시오.

① 장소   ② 날짜   ③ 참가 인원

④ 입장 제한 연령   ⑤ 공연 시간

6 대화를 듣고, 두 사람이 만날 시각을 고르시오.

① 8:00 a.m.   ② 9:00 a.m.   ③ 10:00 a.m.   ④ 11:00 a.m.   ⑤ 12:00 p.m.

7 대화를 듣고, 남자의 장래 희망을 고르시오.

① 경찰관   ② 의사   ③ 야구선수   ④ 요리사   ⑤ 교사

8 대화를 듣고, 남자의 심정으로 가장 적절한 것을 고르시오.

① 기쁨   ② 외로움   ③ 지루함   ④ 만족스러움   ⑤ 당황스러움

9 대화를 듣고, 두 사람이 대화 직후에 할 일로 가장 적절한 것을 고르시오.

① 쿠키 굽기   ② 디저트 사기   ③ 제과점 들르기

④ 재료 찾아보기   ⑤ 레시피 검색하기

10 대화를 듣고, 무엇에 관한 내용인지 가장 적절한 것을 고르시오.

① 쓰레기 분리 수거   ② 재활용 캠페인 준비   ③ 새 학기 교실 꾸미기

④ 학교 행사 간식 준비   ⑤ 예술 인재 발굴 프로그램

11번~20번 문제는 다음 페이지에 ➡

16 회 모의고사

11 대화를 듣고, 두 사람이 함께 이동할 방법으로 가장 적절한 것을 고르시오.

① 배　　　　② 기차　　　　③ 도보　　　　④ 버스　　　　⑤ 자동차

12 대화를 듣고, 여자가 쇼핑을 가려고 하는 이유를 고르시오.

① 어버이날 선물을 사려고　　　　② 귀걸이를 교환하려고
③ 새 신발을 사려고　　　　　　　④ 자신의 생일 선물을 고르려고
⑤ 친구의 생일 선물을 사려고

13 대화를 듣고, 두 사람이 대화하는 장소로 가장 적절한 곳을 고르시오.

① 법원　　　　　　　② 부동산 중개업소　　　　③ 편의점
④ 호텔　　　　　　　⑤ 여행사

14 대화를 듣고, 경찰서의 위치로 가장 알맞은 곳을 고르시오.

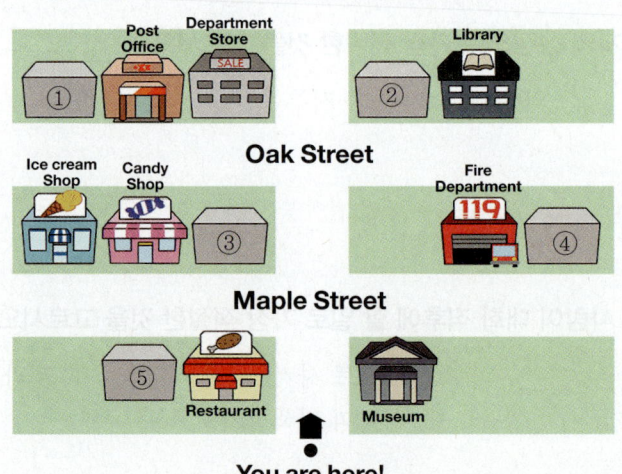

15 대화를 듣고, 여자가 남자에게 부탁한 일로 가장 적절한 것을 고르시오.

① 사진 촬영하기　　　　② 경기 심판 맡기　　　　③ 간식과 음료 준비하기
④ 개회식 인사말 준비하기　　⑤ 계주 주자로 뛰기

16 대화를 듣고, 여자가 남자에게 제안한 것으로 가장 적절한 것을 고르시오.

① 조퇴하기　　② 방과후 수업 신청하기　　③ 병원에 가기
④ 축구 연습하기　　⑤ 축구공 새로 사기

17 대화를 듣고, 남자가 토요일에 할 일로 가장 적절한 것을 고르시오.

① 깜짝 파티 준비하기　　② 생일 선물 사러 가기　　③ 생일 파티에 가기
④ 집에서 숙제하기　　⑤ Tammy네 집에 놀러 가기

18 대화를 듣고, 남자의 직업으로 가장 적절한 것을 고르시오.

① 요리사　　② 미용사　　③ 바리스타
④ 수영 선수　　⑤ 테니스 코치

[19~20] 대화를 듣고, 남자의 마지막 말에 이어질 여자의 말로 가장 적절한 것을 고르시오.

19 Woman: ＿＿＿＿＿＿＿＿＿＿＿＿＿＿＿＿＿＿＿＿＿

① I'll have ten.　　② You can't miss it.
③ Take number three.　　④ It will take half an hour.
⑤ It's over there.

20 Woman: ＿＿＿＿＿＿＿＿＿＿＿＿＿＿＿＿＿＿＿＿＿

① Of course! I'll try.　　② Sure! Come this way.
③ You can come any time.　　④ No, we don't have them.
⑤ Yes, the counter is over there.

Dictation Test 16

M1(17)_16_D

Dictation(받아쓰기)은 본문을 받아쓰면서 영어듣기의 집중력을 향상시키고 다양한 표현을 정리하기 위한 영어듣기 학습법입니다. 녹음을 다시 듣고, 빈칸에 알맞은 단어를 써 보세요.
※Dictation의 정답은 듣기 대본의 밑줄 친 부분을 확인하세요.

정답 p. 64

맞은 개수 / 총132개

그림정보파악(담화)

1. 다음을 듣고, 'I'가 무엇인지 가장 적절한 것을 고르시오.

①  ②

③  ④

⑤

01
M: I have six legs and _____ _____ _____
_____. I'm brown, but there are others who
are grey. I am _____ _____ _____ and fly
around bright lights. I look a lot like a butterfly.
What am I?

그림정보파악(대화)

2024 영어듣기능력평가 1회 2번 변형

2. 대화를 듣고, 여자가 구입할 반바지로 가장 적절한 것을 고르시오.

①  ②

③  ④

⑤

02
M: How can I help you?

W: I'm looking for cargo shorts for my son.

M: How about these checkered ones?

W: I think he would _____ something simpler.
Do you have any _____ ones?

M: Yes, how about these plain cargo shorts with
_____ _____?

W: Perfect! I'll take them.

---

3. 다음을 듣고, 내일의 날씨로 가장 적절한
   것을 고르시오.

①    ②

③    ④

⑤

03 W: Good morning. This is the daily weather report. Yesterday, it was cloudy and windy. But today, the sky will be sunny and clear _____ _____ _____. Starting tomorrow, it'll be rainy _____ _____ _____ of the week. Have a great day!

고난도 | 마지막말의도파악

4. 대화를 듣고, 남자가 한 마지막 말의 의도
   로 가장 적절한 것을 고르시오.
   ① 축하   ② 감사
   ③ 동의   ④ 후회
   ⑤ 위로

04 M: Congratulations, Somin. I heard your basketball team _____ _____ _____ at the championship game.

W: Thanks, Juho. But we _____ _____ the championship.

M: What do you mean?

W: I made _____ _____ _____ at the end of the game. I didn't know what to say to my teammates.

M: Well, everyone makes mistakes and second place is still something _____ _____ _____ _____.

다음 페이지에 계속 ➡

16 회 딕테이션

5. 다음을 듣고, 남자가 여름 댄스 대회에 대해 언급하지 <u>않은</u> 것을 고르시오.

① 장소　　② 날짜
③ 참가 인원　　④ 입장 제한 연령
⑤ 공연 시간

05 M: Let me tell you about the Summer Dance Contest at West Hill Park. It'll be on July 2. _____ _____ are participating and will put on wonderful performances. The contest will _____ _____ three hours between 5 p.m. and 8 p.m. It will be a great event, so don't _____ _____ _____ it!

6. 대화를 듣고, 두 사람이 만날 시각을 고르시오.

① 8:00 a.m.
② 9:00 a.m.
③ 10:00 a.m.
④ 11:00 a.m.
⑤ 12:00 p.m.

06 M: Anna, Mac's Smoothies _____ _____ _____ in our town!

W: Really? Their smoothies are famous!

M: Do you want to go there on Saturday?

W: Sure! I _____ _____ at 9 a.m. on weekends. So, let's meet at 10 a.m.

M: But they open at 11 a.m.

W: Let's _____ _____ 11 then.

M: Okay. See you at the shop on Saturday.

7. 대화를 듣고, 남자의 장래 희망을 고르시오.

① 경찰관   ② 의사
③ 야구선수   ④ 요리사
⑤ 교사

07

W: Tommy, what do you want to be when you

_____ _____?

M: Well, I want to help other people, just like my dad.

W: Oh, you want to be a _____ _____ like your

dad?

M: I'd like to. What about you, Lisa?

W: I want to help other people, just _____

_____. I want to be a doctor.

M: You'll be a wonderful doctor.

8. 대화를 듣고, 남자의 심정으로 가장 적절한 것을 고르시오.

① 기쁨   ② 외로움
③ 지루함   ④ 만족스러움
⑤ 당황스러움

08

W: Excuse me, sir. You cannot go into the pool

without a swimming cap.

M: Oh, but I _____ _____ _____ it here today.

Can I borrow one?

W: I'm sorry. We _____ _____ _____.

M: How much is it?

W: It's $50.

M: What! That's _____ _____. And I already

have lots of them at home.

16
회
딕
테
이
션

다음 페이지에 계속 ➡

9. 대화를 듣고, 두 사람이 대화 직후에 할 일로 가장 적절한 것을 고르시오.
  ① 쿠키 굽기
  ② 디저트 사기
  ③ 제과점 들르기
  ④ 재료 찾아보기
  ⑤ 레시피 검색하기

09
M: Oh no, the bakery is closed, Christine.

W: That's _____. What should we do for dessert?

M: How about making some cookies?

W: That sounds _____! Do you have a good recipe?

M: Yes, but I'm not sure if we have all the _____.

W: Let's _____ the kitchen and see what we have.

2024 영어듣기능력평가 **1회 10번 변형**

10. 대화를 듣고, 무엇에 관한 내용인지 가장 적절한 것을 고르시오.
  ① 쓰레기 분리 수거
  ② 재활용 캠페인 준비
  ③ 새 학기 교실 꾸미기
  ④ 학교 행사 간식 준비
  ⑤ 예술 인재 발굴 프로그램

10
W: Kevin, why are you _____ all these plastic bottles?

M: I'm helping with the school _____ _____, Mom.

W: Oh, that's great! What are you going to do with the bottles?

M: We're going to make a big _____ _____ with recycled materials.

W: That sounds fun. Do you need any help cleaning the bottles?

M: Yes, please. Thanks for helping me!

11. 대화를 듣고, 두 사람이 함께 이동할 방법으로 가장 적절한 것을 고르시오.

① 배   ② 기차
③ 도보   ④ 버스
⑤ 자동차

11
M: Mom, how are we getting to the restaurant this evening?

W: Well, we can't go _____ _____. Dad took it.

M: Then, let's go by bus.

W: In fact, I was thinking of getting there _____ _____.

M: Really?

W: It's only a 30-minute walk, and you need _____.

M: All right, then.

---

12. 대화를 듣고, 여자가 쇼핑을 가려고 하는 이유를 고르시오.

① 어버이날 선물을 사려고
② 귀걸이를 교환하려고
③ 새 신발을 사려고
④ 자신의 생일 선물을 고르려고
⑤ 친구의 생일 선물을 사려고

12
W: I'm going shopping now. Will you come with me?

M: Okay. What do you _____ _____ buy?

W: I want to buy a birthday present for Carol. But I don't know what to buy.

M: _____ _____ earrings? She's always wearing accessories. I think she'll like it.

W: That's a great idea! Thank you.

M: It's my _____.

다음 페이지에 계속 ➡

16 회 딕테이션

13. 대화를 듣고, 두 사람이 대화하는 장소로 가장 적절한 곳을 고르시오.

① 법원
② 부동산 중개업소
③ 편의점
④ 호텔
⑤ 여행사

13

M: Hi, how can I help you?

W: I'm looking for an apartment _____ _____.

M: Have a seat here. What area are you interested in?

W: I'm interested in the Seocho-dong area.

M: Can you tell me what kind of place you are _____ _____?

W: I need a _____-_____ apartment.

M: Okay, let me see what we have.

14. 대화를 듣고, 경찰서의 위치로 가장 알맞은 곳을 고르시오.

14

W: Oliver, I found this purse on the sidewalk. What should I do?

M: You should _____ _____ to the police station. There's one nearby.

W: Good idea. Can you _____ _____ _____?

M: Sure. _____ _____ two blocks and turn left on Oak Street.

W: Got it. Turn left on Oak Street.

M: Yes. It will be _____ _____ _____. It's next to the post office.

W: Thanks!

15. 대화를 듣고, 여자가 남자에게 부탁한 일로 가장 적절한 것을 고르시오.

① 사진 촬영하기
② 경기 심판 맡기
③ 간식과 음료 준비하기
④ 개회식 인사말 준비하기
⑤ 계주 주자로 뛰기

15 [Knock knock]

M: Come in.

W: Hello, Mr. Kim.

M: Hi, Yuna. What brings you here?

W: I have a _____ _____ _____. It's

    about our sports day next week.

M: Oh, I see. How can I help you?

W: Can you be the _____ for the relay race?

M: Sure! I'd be glad to help.

W: Thank you so much. It means _____

    _____ to us.

제안 파악

16. 대화를 듣고, 여자가 남자에게 제안한 것으로 가장 적절한 것을 고르시오.

① 조퇴하기
② 방과후 수업 신청하기
③ 병원에 가기
④ 축구 연습하기
⑤ 축구공 새로 사기

16 M: I don't feel good today.

W: Why? What's wrong?

M: I played soccer in the rain yesterday and now I

    _____ _____ and coughing.

W: Oh no! You _____ _____ _____

    _____.

M: Yeah, I think so, too.

W: Why don't you see a doctor after school?

다음 페이지에 계속 ➡

17. 대화를 듣고, 남자가 토요일에 할 일로 가장 적절한 것을 고르시오.

① 깜짝 파티 준비하기
② 생일 선물 사러 가기
③ 생일 파티에 가기
④ 집에서 숙제하기
⑤ Tammy네 집에 놀러 가기

17
M: What are you doing this Saturday, Kate?

W: I _____ Tammy and In-su to my house. We're _____ _____ _____ _____ for my birthday.

M: Oh, really? I didn't know this Saturday was your birthday.

W: It's OK.

M: Can I join you? I want to _____ with you.

W: Sure. I'd be happy if you came.

18. 대화를 듣고, 남자의 직업으로 가장 적절한 것을 고르시오.

① 요리사
② 미용사
③ 바리스타
④ 수영 선수
⑤ 테니스 코치

18
W: Can you _____ _____ _____ my backhand?

M: Sure, let's see how you hit the ball.

W: Like this?

M: You need to hold your racket _____ _____ _____.

W: Oh, I get it.

M: Yes, that's it! Now _____ _____ the ball again.

W: Wow, it feels much better!

M: Good job!

19. 대화를 듣고, 남자의 마지막 말에 이어질
   여자의 말로 가장 적절한 것을 고르시오.

   Woman: _____

   ① I'll have ten.
   ② You can't miss it.
   ③ Take number three.
   ④ It will take half an hour.
   ⑤ It's over there.

19
M: Excuse me. How can I _____ _____ the museum?

W: You can _____ _____ _____ or the subway.

M: Can't I just walk there?

W: No. It's _____ _____ to walk.

M: I see. How long will it take by bus?

W: It will take half an hour.

20. 대화를 듣고, 남자의 마지막 말에 이어질
   여자의 말로 가장 적절한 것을 고르시오.

   Woman: _____

   ① Of course! I'll try.
   ② Sure! Come this way.
   ③ You can come any time.
   ④ No, we don't have them.
   ⑤ Yes, the counter is over there.

20
W: Hello. May I help you?

M: Yes, please. I'm looking for _____ _____ _____ _____.

W: Oh, they are on this rack. What size do you need?

M: I wear a size 6.

W: Here they are.

M: Thank you. Can I _____ _____ _____?

W: Sure! Come this way.

16
회
딕
테
이
션

Words & Expressions Review 16

● 다음 단어를 암기하세요.

문제	번호	단어	뜻
1	☐ 1	active	활동적인
	☐ 2	look like	~와 비슷하게 생기다
	☐ 3	a lot	굉장히
2	☐ 4	shorts	반바지
	☐ 5	prefer	선호하다, 좋아하다
	☐ 6	plain	무늬가 없는, 수수한
	☐ 7	extra	추가의, 여분의
3	☐ 8	weather report	일기예보
	☐ 9	for the rest of	~내내, ~의 나머지 동안
4	☐ 10	make a mistake	실수하다
	☐ 11	second place	2등
5	☐ 12	participate	참가하다
	☐ 13	put on	상연하다
7	☐ 14	like	~처럼
8	☐ 15	forget to + 동사	~할 것을 잊다
9	☐ 16	disappointing	실망스러운
	☐ 17	delicious	맛있는
	☐ 18	ingredient	재료
10	☐ 19	collect	모으다
	☐ 20	piece	작품
11	☐ 21	take	가지고 가다
12	☐ 22	need to + 동사	~할 필요가 있다

문제	번호	단어	뜻
12	☐ 23	what to + 동사	무엇을 ~해야 할지
	☐ 24	accessory	액세서리
13	☐ 25	look for ~	~을 찾다
	☐ 26	be interested in ~	~에 관심이 있다
14	☐ 27	purse	지갑
	☐ 28	sidewalk	인도, 보도
	☐ 29	give A directions	A에게 길을 알려주다
15	☐ 30	sports day	운동회
	☐ 31	referee	심판
16	☐ 32	keep -ing	계속 ~하다
	☐ 33	sneeze	재채기하다
17	☐ 34	invite	초대하다
	☐ 35	join	함께 하다, 합류하다
	☐ 36	celebrate	축하하다, 기념하다
	☐ 37	help A with B	A가 B하는 것을 돕다
18	☐ 38	hit a ball	공을 치다
	☐ 39	hold	(손으로) 쥐고 있다
	☐ 40	racket	(테니스 등의) 라켓
19	☐ 41	try -ing	한번 ~해보다
	☐ 42	take a bus	버스를 타다
	☐ 43	take + 시간	(시간이) 걸리다
20	☐ 44	rack	선반, 받침대

M1(17)_W_16

●왼쪽 단어장의 뜻이 보이지 않게 반으로 접고, 학습한 단어의 뜻을 아래 빈칸에 적어주세요.

1	sports day		23	celebrate	
2	give A directions		24	ingredient	
3	plain		25	what to + 동사	
4	prefer		26	help A with B	
5	take + 시간		27	second place	
6	hold		28	rack	
7	active		29	join	
8	put on		30	purse	
9	invite		31	look like	
10	participate		32	delicious	
11	weather report		33	shorts	
12	need to + 동사		34	a lot	
13	make a mistake		35	be interested in ~	
14	piece		36	like	
15	accessory		37	sidewalk	
16	keep -ing		38	collect	
17	hit a ball		39	take	
18	extra		40	look for ~	
19	racket		41	referee	
20	try -ing		42	sneeze	
21	forget to + 동사		43	disappointing	
22	take a bus		44	for the rest of	

16
회
단
어

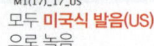

1 다음을 듣고, 'this'가 가리키는 것으로 가장 적절한 것을 고르시오.

① ② ③ ④ ⑤

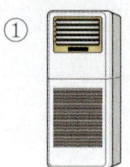

2 대화를 듣고, 남자가 선택할 물건으로 가장 적절한 것을 고르시오.

① ② ③ ④ ⑤

3 다음을 듣고, 다음 주 금요일 날씨로 적절한 것을 고르시오.

① ② ③ ④ ⑤

4 대화를 듣고, 마지막 말에 담긴 여자의 의도로 적절한 것을 고르시오.

① 사양   ② 충고   ③ 권유   ④ 감사   ⑤ 부탁

5 다음을 듣고, 남자가 동상에 대해 언급하지 <u>않은</u> 것을 고르시오.

① 위치   ② 모양   ③ 높이
④ 색상   ⑤ 설계자

17회 모의고사

6 대화를 듣고, 여자가 운동을 시작하는 시각을 고르시오.

① 5:30 p.m.   ② 6:00 p.m.   ③ 6:30 p.m.   ④ 7:00 p.m.   ⑤ 7:30 p.m.

7 대화를 듣고, 남자의 장래 희망으로 적절한 것을 고르시오.

① 스포츠 해설가   ② 야구 선수   ③ 농구 선수
④ 육상 선수   ⑤ 사진작가

8 대화를 듣고, 여자의 심정으로 가장 적절한 것을 고르시오.

① 감사함   ② 지루함   ③ 수줍음
④ 긴장함   ⑤ 편안함

9 대화를 듣고, 남자가 대화 직후에 할 일로 가장 적절한 것을 고르시오.

① 음료수 마시기   ② 커피 주문하기   ③ 손님 맞이하기
④ 재고 확인하기   ⑤ 청소용품 가지러 가기

10 대화를 듣고, 무엇에 관한 내용인지 가장 적절한 것을 고르시오.

① 동아리 홍보   ② 우승 팀 선정   ③ 댄스 대회 취소
④ 공연 순서 안내   ⑤ 학교 축제 참가

11번~20번 문제는 다음 페이지에 ➡

11 대화를 듣고, 두 사람이 함께 이동할 방법으로 가장 적절한 것을 고르시오.

① 도보   ② 택시   ③ 자전거
④ 지하철   ⑤ 버스

12 대화를 듣고, 여자가 신발가게에 가는 이유로 가장 적절한 것을 고르시오.

① 친구와 같이 쇼핑하기로 해서   ② 해당 매장에만 재고가 있어서
③ 바로 구매할 수 있어서   ④ 직접 신어볼 수 있어서
⑤ 할인 행사가 있어서

13 대화를 듣고, 두 사람이 대화하는 장소로 가장 적절한 곳을 고르시오.

① 극장   ② 호텔   ③ 반려견 미용실   ④ 옷가게   ⑤ 미술관

14 대화를 듣고, 여자가 찾고 있는 반지의 위치로 가장 알맞은 곳을 고르시오.

15 대화를 듣고, 남자가 여자에게 요청한 일로 가장 적절한 것을 고르시오.

① 날씨 확인하기   ② 비옷 구입하기   ③ 가방에 우산 넣기
④ 용돈 주기   ⑤ 도시락 준비하기

16 대화를 듣고, 여자가 남자에게 제안한 것으로 가장 적절한 것을 고르시오.

① 일기 쓰기　　　　② 신문 읽기　　　　③ 매일 독서하기
④ 대회에 참가하기　　⑤ 친구들과 토론하기

17 대화를 듣고, 남자가 주말에 할 일로 가장 적절한 것을 고르시오.

① 영화 보기　　　　② 빵집 가기　　　　③ 캠핑 가기
④ 자전거 타기　　　⑤ 호수에서 보트 타기

18 대화를 듣고, 여자의 직업으로 가장 적절한 것을 고르시오.

① 소설가　　　　　② 배우　　　　　　③ 게임 개발자
④ 테니스 선수　　　⑤ 비행기 조종사

[19~20] 대화를 듣고, 남자의 마지막 말에 이어질 여자의 말로 가장 적절한 것을 고르시오.

19 Woman: _____

① Let's meet at four.　　　　② Don't worry about it.
③ It takes two hours.　　　　④ He will help you a lot.
⑤ Sorry for being late.

20 Woman: _____

① Good idea!　　　　② You're right.　　　　③ That's too bad.
④ That's all right.　　⑤ Congratulations!

Dictation(받아쓰기)은 본문을 받아쓰면서 영어듣기의 집중력을 향상시키고 다양한 표현을 정리하기 위한 영어듣기 학습법입니다. 녹음을 다시 듣고, 빈칸에 알맞은 단어를 써 보세요.
※Dictation의 정답은 듣기 대본의 밑줄 친 부분을 확인하세요.

📖 정답 p. 69

맞은 개수 _____ / 총142개

그림정보파악(담화)

1. 다음을 듣고, 'this'가 가리키는 것으로 가장 적절한 것을 고르시오.

①
②
③
④
⑤

01 M: People's lives became _____ _____ when this was invented. This is an _____ _____ used with televisions and air conditioners. You can turn on the TV and turn up the volume wirelessly _____ _____ _____ _____ with this. What is this?

그림정보파악(대화)

2. 대화를 듣고, 남자가 선택할 물건으로 가장 적절한 것을 고르시오.

①
②
③
④
⑤

02 W: Can I help you, sir?

M: Yes, I need a _____ _____ _____ _____.

W: What about this one with the heart on it? Girls like hearts.

M: Well, she's really _____ _____ these days. I'll take this one.

W: _____ _____, sir.

3. 다음을 듣고, 다음 주 금요일 날씨로 적절한 것을 고르시오.

①  ②
③  ④
⑤

03 W: Here is the weather forecast for next week. It will _____ _____ until next Wednesday and _____ _____ be clear from Thursday morning. We can see blue skies on Thursday and Friday. But the weather condition for the weekend won't be good. There will be _____ _____ this weekend.

4. 대화를 듣고, 마지막 말에 담긴 여자의 의도로 적절한 것을 고르시오.
① 사양   ② 충고
③ 권유   ④ 감사
⑤ 부탁

04 W: At last, my online shopping mall opens tomorrow.

M: I know you have put _____ _____ _____ in this business. Congratulations!

W: Thank you.

M: I believe that it will be a _____ _____!

W: I couldn't launch it _____ _____ _____ about online business.

다음 페이지에 계속 ➡

17회 딕테이션

5. 다음을 듣고, 남자가 동상에 대해 언급하지 <u>않은</u> 것을 고르시오.

① 위치   ② 모양
③ 높이   ④ 색상
⑤ 설계자

05 M: Let me introduce a famous statue in my town. It is _____ _____ _____ of Central Park. It is in _____ _____ _____ a tiger, the mascot of our town. It is 3 meters tall. The statue was _____ _____ Laura Hopkins, the famous architect. Many visitors take photos in front of it.

6. 대화를 듣고, 여자가 운동을 시작하는 시각을 고르시오.

① 5:30 p.m.   ② 6:00 p.m.
③ 6:30 p.m.   ④ 7:00 p.m.
⑤ 7:30 p.m.

06 M: All our friends are meeting at the restaurant tonight. Can you _____ _____ _____ six?
W: No. I won't be able to be there until a half past seven.
M: Why? Do you have to work late?
W: No. I always _____ _____ from six to seven.
M: That's very _____. No wonder you are always _____ _____.
W: I'm sorry, I'll be late. I'll see you then!

7. 대화를 듣고, 남자의 장래 희망으로 적절한 것을 고르시오.

① 스포츠 해설가   ② 야구 선수
③ 농구 선수   ④ 육상 선수
⑤ 사진작가

07

W: Look how fast he is!

M: He is the fastest runner on that baseball team.

W: Is running _____ in baseball games?

M: Of course. _____ _____ hitting the ball _____ _____ running fast is important.

W: You know a lot about baseball.

M: I'm a big fan of baseball. I want to be a _____ _____ in the future.

W: I believe you can be.

8. 대화를 듣고, 여자의 심정으로 가장 적절한 것을 고르시오.

① 감사함   ② 지루함
③ 수줍음   ④ 긴장함
⑤ 편안함

08

M: Hey, Rosie. What's up?

W: Hey, Mark. I have to _____ _____ _____ next class.

M: Oh, right. You have a presentation in science class today.

W: I'm so worried because I'm _____ _____ _____ speaking in front of a lot of people.

M: Relax. You'll do just fine.

W: Will I? My heart is _____ and my palms are _____ _____ _____.

17회 딕테이션

다음 페이지에 계속 ➡

9. 대화를 듣고, 남자가 대화 직후에 할 일로 가장 적절한 것을 고르시오.

  ① 음료수 마시기
  ② 커피 주문하기
  ③ 손님 맞이하기
  ④ 재고 확인하기
  ⑤ 청소용품 가지러 가기

09
W: What happened here? This place is a mess!

M: I'm sorry. I _____ _____ on the floor.

W: Oh, that's why the floor is sticky.

M: _____ _____ _____ _____ before we open the store.

W: I'll help you clean this up. Can you go get some cleaning supplies?

M: Okay, I'll _____ _____ _____.

---

10. 대화를 듣고, 무엇에 관한 내용인지 가장 적절한 것을 고르시오.

  ① 동아리 홍보
  ② 우승 팀 선정
  ③ 댄스 대회 취소
  ④ 공연 순서 안내
  ⑤ 학교 축제 참가

10
W: Aaron, you and your team should join the school festival.

M: What are you talking about?

W: They are looking for a dance team for the opening.

M: Really? Isn't there already a team _____?

W: It's a singing group. They need dancers, too.

M: Then, I _____ _____ _____ _____.
    I should go see the teacher now.

11. 대화를 듣고, 두 사람이 함께 이동할 방법으로 가장 적절한 것을 고르시오.
   ① 도보   ② 택시
   ③ 자전거   ④ 지하철
   ⑤ 버스

11
W: Mike, how should we get to the library?

M: Why don't we ride our bikes? It will only take about 20 minutes.

W: But it's _____ _____.

M: Oh, really? I didn't know that.

W: Let's take the bus _____.

M: Sure. Taking the bus _____ _____ a better idea.

W: Good. Let's _____ in ten minutes.

---

12. 대화를 듣고, 여자가 신발가게에 가는 이유로 가장 적절한 것을 고르시오.
   ① 친구와 같이 쇼핑하기로 해서
   ② 해당 매장에만 재고가 있어서
   ③ 바로 구매할 수 있어서
   ④ 직접 신어볼 수 있어서
   ⑤ 할인 행사가 있어서

12
W: Dad, can you give me a ride to the shoe store, The Shoe Factory?

M: Sure, Lizzy, but I thought you liked to _____ online.

W: I do, but I have to go to the store today.

M: Why? Do you need to _____ _____ _____ _____?

W: No, they are having a huge sale today. It is even _____ than online shopping.

M: Really?

W: Yes. I can't _____ it.

다음 페이지에 계속 ➡

13. 대화를 듣고, 두 사람이 대화하는 장소로 가장 적절한 곳을 고르시오.

① 극장　　② 호텔
③ 반려견 미용실　④ 옷가게
⑤ 미술관

13

W: Hello! How can I help you?

M: Hi, I'm here to get my dog _____.

W: What services are you _____ _____?

M: I think my dog needs a _____ and a haircut.

W: Excellent! What's your dog's name?

M: Her name is Daisy.

W: OK. Daisy is _____ _____ _____.

　　Would you like to wait here or come back later?

M: I'll wait, thank you.

14. 대화를 듣고, 여자가 찾고 있는 반지의 위치로 가장 알맞은 곳을 고르시오.

14

W: Dad, there was a ring on my desk. _____ _____ _____ it?

M: No, nothing was on your desk.

W: I thought that I _____ it on the desk…

M: Did you look under the bed? Maybe you _____ it.

W: I _____ everywhere! I can't find it.

M: Well, did you also look on the bookshelf?

W: Ah, I found it. You were right.

부탁(요청)한 일 파악

15. 대화를 듣고, 남자가 여자에게 요청한 일로 가장 적절한 것을 고르시오.

① 날씨 확인하기
② 비옷 구입하기
③ 가방에 우산 넣기
④ 용돈 주기
⑤ 도시락 준비하기

15

M: Mom, I'm going to _____ _____

_____ tomorrow.

W: I know. Are you excited?

M: Of course! But I'm worried about the weather. It's

going to rain.

W: Do you want to _____ _____ _____?

M: No. Can you just _____ _____

_____ in my bag?

W: No problem.

제안 파악

16. 대화를 듣고, 여자가 남자에게 제안한 것으로 가장 적절한 것을 고르시오.

① 일기 쓰기
② 신문 읽기
③ 매일 독서하기
④ 대회에 참가하기
⑤ 친구들과 토론하기

16

M: Congratulations, Sumi! I heard you won a prize at

a writing contest.

W: Yes. Thanks, Jiho.

M: I wish I was good at writing, too.

W: Well, I believe anyone can have better _____

_____.

M: Really? How?

W: Why don't you try _____ _____

_____? It really helps.

M: Okay. I'll try it.

다음 페이지에 계속 ➡

17. 대화를 듣고, 남자가 주말에 할 일로 가장 적절한 것을 고르시오.

① 영화 보기
② 빵집 가기
③ 캠핑 가기
④ 자전거 타기
⑤ 호수에서 보트 타기

17

W: Hi, Tom. Any plans for the weekend?

M: Yes, Lucy. I'm going to ride my bike _____ _____ _____.

W: That sounds _____. Do you often go cycling?

M: Not really. I just bought a new bike, so I want to try it out.

W: Nice! Have fun and _____ _____.

M: Thanks! I'm really excited.

18. 대화를 듣고, 여자의 직업으로 가장 적절한 것을 고르시오.

① 소설가
② 배우
③ 게임 개발자
④ 테니스 선수
⑤ 비행기 조종사

18

M: Sarah, I've tried your _____ _____ of the game. It was so much fun!

W: Really? Are you sure the game wasn't too easy?

M: Not at all. I _____ _____ it.

W: How were the new characters?

M: They were well-designed.

W: I'm glad to hear it. Now I have to _____ _____ some graphics.

M: Good luck with the launch.

19. 대화를 듣고, 남자의 마지막 말에 이어질 여자의 말로 가장 적절한 것을 고르시오.

Woman: _____

① Let's meet at four.
② Don't worry about it.
③ It takes two hours.
④ He will help you a lot.
⑤ Sorry for being late.

19 *(Cellphone rings.)*

M: Hello, Lily. What's up?

W: Hey, did you finish your math homework?

M: No, I haven't even started. What about you?

W: _____ _____. I'll do it with Andy this afternoon.

M: That's a good idea. Can I _____ you?

W: Sure. _____ _____ I called you. Come to Andy's house.

M: Okay. _____ _____ should I be there?

W: Let's meet at four.

20. 대화를 듣고, 남자의 마지막 말에 이어질 여자의 말로 가장 적절한 것을 고르시오.

Woman: _____

① Good idea!
② You're right.
③ That's too bad.
④ That's all right.
⑤ Congratulations!

20

W: Dale, are you okay? You don't _____ so well.

M: I'm okay. I think I can _____ until school ends.

W: Are you sure? If you're not feeling well, you should go see a doctor.

M: Actually, you're right. I think I should go.

W: Did you _____ _____ _____?

M: No, I have a stomachache. I think I ate something _____.

W: That's too bad.

Words & Expressions Review 17

● 다음 단어를 암기하세요.

문제	번호	단어	뜻
1	1	invent	발명하다
	2	electronic	전자의
	3	turn on	(전등, 기계 등을) 켜다
	4	turn up the volume	소리를 키우다
2	5	diary	일기장
	6	be into ~	~에 빠지다, ~에 관심이 많다
	7	mermaid	인어
	8	choice	선택
3	9	weather forecast	일기 예보
	10	clear	(날씨가) 갠, 맑은
4	11	at last	마침내
	12	effort	노력
	13	launch	시작하다, 출시하다
	14	advice	조언, 충고
5	15	statue	조각상
6	16	work out	운동하다
	17	impressive	멋진, 감명 깊은
	18	no wonder ~	~하는 게 당연하다
7	19	important	중요한
	20	give a presentation	발표하다, 보고하다
8	21	be good at	~에 능숙하다
	22	sweat	땀을 흘리다

문제	번호	단어	뜻
9	23	spill	쏟다, 흘리다
	24	look for	~을 찾다
10	25	opening	개막식
	26	perform	공연하다, 연주하다
11	27	instead	대신에
	28	seem like	~인 것 같다, ~처럼 보이다
12	29	give A a ride	A를 태워주다
	30	groom	(머리, 털 등을) 다듬다
	31	interested in	~에 관심이 있는
13	32	bath	목욕
	33	haircut	이발, 미용
	34	be in good hands	안심해도 되다, 잘 관리되고 있다
	35	leave	~을 두고 오다, 남기다
14	36	drop	떨어트리다, 떨어지다
	37	check	확인하다, 조사하다
15	38	be worried about ~	~에 대해 걱정하다
	39	put A in B	A를 B에 넣다
17	40	along	~을 따라
18	41	pilot	시험하는, 시험적인
19	42	That's why ~	그래서 ~한 것이다
20	43	go see a doctor	병원에 가다
	44	stomachache	배탈, 복통

M1(17)_W_17

● 왼쪽 단어장의 뜻이 보이지 않게 반으로 접고, 학습한 단어의 뜻을 아래 빈칸에 적어주세요.

1	give a presentation		23	along
2	give A a ride		24	diary
3	work out		25	groom
4	spill		26	no wonder ~
5	mermaid		27	turn on
6	opening		28	be good at
7	leave		29	look for
8	interested in		30	launch
9	sweat		31	effort
10	statue		32	electronic
11	be into ~		33	perform
12	instead		34	seem like
13	drop		35	put A in B
14	be in good hands		36	at last
15	choice		37	haircut
16	invent		38	check
17	important		39	stomachache
18	advice		40	That's why ~
19	turn up the volume		41	bath
20	impressive		42	go see a doctor
21	weather forecast		43	be worried about ~
22	clear		44	pilot

전국 15개 시·도 교육청 공동주관 및 서울시 연합 내신

18회 중학영어듣기 모의고사

 M1(17)_18_US
모두 **미국식 발음(US)**으로 녹음

 M1(17)_18_UK
20문제 중 5문제에 **영국식 발음 (US+UK)**을 포함하여 녹음

📖 정답 및 해석 p. 73

1 다음을 듣고, 'this'가 가리키는 것으로 가장 적절한 것을 고르시오.

①  ②  ③  ④  ⑤

2 대화를 듣고, 여자가 구입할 치마로 가장 적절한 것을 고르시오.

① 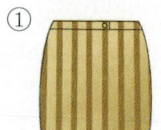 ② 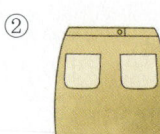 ③ 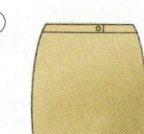 ④  ⑤

3 다음을 듣고, 수요일의 날씨로 가장 적절한 것을 고르시오.

①  ②  ③  ④  ⑤

4 대화를 듣고, 남자의 마지막 말의 의도로 가장 적절한 것을 고르시오.

① 제안 ② 경고 ③ 수락 ④ 거절 ⑤ 불평

5 다음을 듣고, 남자가 앱에 대해 언급하지 <u>않은</u> 것을 고르시오.

① 이름 ② 제작자 ③ 평점 ④ 기능 ⑤ 가격

6 대화를 듣고, 두 사람이 만날 시각을 고르시오.

① 12:00 p.m. ② 1:00 p.m. ③ 1:20 p.m. ④ 1:30 p.m. ⑤ 1:50 p.m.

7 대화를 듣고, 남자의 장래 희망으로 가장 적절한 것을 고르시오.

① 화가 ② 변호사 ③ 만화가 ④ 농구 선수 ⑤ 사진작가

8 대화를 듣고, 남자의 심정으로 가장 적절한 것을 고르시오.

① 슬픔 ② 지루함 ③ 화남 ④ 자랑스러움 ⑤ 당황스러움

9 대화를 듣고, 남자가 대화 직후에 할 일로 가장 적절한 것을 고르시오.

① 영화 관람하기 ② 친구 만나러 가기 ③ 영화관 가는 길 검색하기
④ 영화표 예매하기 ⑤ 책 구매하기

10 대화를 듣고, 무엇에 관한 내용인지 가장 적절한 것을 고르시오.

① 지진 대피 훈련 ② 감기 예방 요령 ③ 화재 안전 수칙
④ 교내 글쓰기 대회 ⑤ 엘리베이터 점검 안내

11번~20번 문제는 다음 페이지에 ➡

11 대화를 듣고, 두 사람이 함께 이동할 교통수단으로 가장 적절한 것을 고르시오.

① 자전거   ② 택시   ③ 버스   ④ 기차   ⑤ 비행기

12 대화를 듣고, 여자가 쿠키를 굽는 이유로 가장 적절한 것을 고르시오.

① 스트레스를 풀려고   ② 이웃에게 선물하려고
③ 바자회에서 판매하려고   ④ 다툰 친구와 화해하려고
⑤ 발렌타인데이를 기념하려고

13 대화를 듣고, 대화가 이루어지는 장소를 고르시오.

① 문구점   ② 헬스장   ③ 음식점   ④ 옷 가게   ⑤ 신발 가게

14 대화를 듣고, 남자가 찾고 있는 이어폰 케이스의 위치로 가장 알맞은 곳을 고르시오.

15 대화를 듣고, 여자가 남자에게 부탁하는 일을 고르시오.

① 시험공부 같이 하기   ② 잠 깨워 주기   ③ 시험 문제 풀어 주기
④ 간식 사 주기   ⑤ 시험 보러 같이 가기

16 대화를 듣고, 남자가 여자에게 제안한 것으로 가장 적절한 것을 고르시오.

① 옷 수선하기   ② 옷 기부하기   ③ 옷 구매하기   ④ 옷 세탁하기   ⑤ 옷 버리기

17 대화를 듣고, 여자가 주말에 한 일로 가장 적절한 것을 고르시오.

① 도서관 가서 책 빌리기   ② 친구들과 쇼핑하기   ③ 마트 가서 장보기
④ 휴대폰 수리 맡기기   ⑤ 병원 가기

18 대화를 듣고, 남자의 직업으로 가장 적절한 것을 고르시오.

① 영양사   ② 헬스 트레이너   ③ 의사
④ 소방관   ⑤ 경찰관

[19~20] 대화를 듣고, 남자의 마지막 말에 이어질 여자의 말로 가장 적절한 것을 고르시오.

19 Woman: _____

① You should be more careful.   ② Good luck to you!
③ I'm sorry to hear that.   ④ I'm glad we're on time.
⑤ That sounds exciting.

20 Woman: _____

① I want oranges.   ② We can take a taxi.
③ They look delicious.   ④ It will take 30 minutes.
⑤ Let's eat in a restaurant.

Dictation Test 18

M1(17)_18_D

Dictation(받아쓰기)은 본문을 받아쓰면서 영어듣기의 집중력을 향상시키고 다양한 표현을 정리하기 위한 영어듣기 학습법입니다. **녹음을 다시 듣고, 빈칸에 알맞은 단어를 써 보세요.**

※Dictation의 정답은 듣기 대본의 밑줄 친 부분을 확인하세요.

📖 정답 p. 73

맞은 개수 / 총132개

그림정보파악(담화)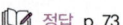

1. 다음을 듣고, 'this'가 가리키는 것으로 가장 적절한 것을 고르시오.

   ① ②
   ③ ④
   ⑤

01 W: You can see this in the kitchen. It has _____ _____ _____. You put different types of food in this to mix and _____ _____ _____ really fast. You can make smoothies or soups with this. What is this?

그림정보파악(대화)

2. 대화를 듣고, 여자가 구입할 치마로 가장 적절한 것을 고르시오.

02 M: What can I do for you?

   W: I need a skirt.

   M: What about this _____ _____?

   W: I'm not a fan of stripes. I prefer a _____ _____.

   M: Okay. How about this _____ _____ skirt with pockets?

   W: I love it. I'll buy that one.

---

3. 다음을 듣고, 수요일의 날씨로 가장 적절한 것을 고르시오.

①  ②
③ ④
⑤

03 W: Hello, New York. Here is the weather forecast for this week. It looks like a rainy week is _____ _____ us. It will rain on Monday and Tuesday. But, _____, the rain will stop and the sun will _____ _____ on Wednesday. It will be sunny but a little cloudy on Thursday. And then, on Friday, we will get rain again.

4. 대화를 듣고, 남자의 마지막 말의 의도로 가장 적절한 것을 고르시오.

① 제안 ② 경고
③ 수락 ④ 거절
⑤ 불평

04 *(Cell phone rings.)*

W: Hi, Ben. Are you home?

M: Yes. What's up?

W: Do you have any plans tonight?

M: No, nothing special. Why do you ask?

W: I have one _____ _____ for the Cardinals' basketball game tonight. Do you _____ _____ _____?

M: Are you kidding? I wouldn't _____ _____ for the world!

다음 페이지에 계속 ➡

5. 다음을 듣고, 남자가 앱에 대해 언급하지 않은 것을 고르시오.
① 이름　　　② 제작자
③ 평점　　　④ 기능
⑤ 가격

05 M: Hello. I'm Sandy Marks. _____ _____ _____ tell you about a new Korean learning app _____ Easy Korean. I created it with my friends. You can learn basic Korean _____ and test yourself with this app. You can download the app for free from the application market now.

6. 대화를 듣고, 두 사람이 만날 시각을 고르시오.
① 12:00 p.m.　　② 1:00 p.m.
③ 1:20 p.m.　　④ 1:30 p.m.
⑤ 1:50 p.m.

06 M: Let's _____ _____ tomorrow.
W: OK. What time shall we meet?
M: How about at noon?
W: But my class _____ _____ one.
M: Then _____ _____ at 1:20 in front of the school.
W: OK.

🇺🇸🇬🇧

7. 대화를 듣고, 남자의 장래 희망으로 가장 적절한 것을 고르시오.

① 화가
② 변호사
③ 만화가
④ 농구 선수
⑤ 사진작가

07

M: Mom, would you take a look at this movie character?

W: Wow! Did you draw this?

M: Yes, I did. I _____ _____ _____ show it to my friends.

W: I'm sure they will love it. You're really _____ _____ _____.

M: Thanks, Mom. I want to be a _____ someday.

W: I believe you can be.

---

8. 대화를 듣고, 남자의 심정으로 가장 적절한 것을 고르시오.

① 슬픔
② 지루함
③ 화남
④ 자랑스러움
⑤ 당황스러움

08

M: Minji, do you have a special plan for this weekend?

W: Yes, Dad. I'm _____ _____ _____ a nursing home.

M: Really? Are you going to _____ _____ _____?

W: Yes. I want to do something _____ _____ _____.

M: Oh! It's very important to help others. You are a wonderful girl!

다음 페이지에 계속 ➡

9. 대화를 듣고, 남자가 대화 직후에 할 일로 가장 적절한 것을 고르시오.

① 영화 관람하기
② 친구 만나러 가기
③ 영화관 가는 길 검색하기
④ 영화표 예매하기
⑤ 책 구매하기

09
W: Harry, what are you doing this weekend?

M: I'm going to go watch *The Good Guys* in the theater.

W: _____ _____?

M: Yes. I asked my friend Jack _____ _____ _____ _____, but he said that he had another appointment.

W: If you want, I can go with you.

M: That would be great. Thank you. Let me _____ two movie tickets online right away.

10. 대화를 듣고, 무엇에 관한 내용인지 가장 적절한 것을 고르시오.

① 지진 대피 훈련
② 감기 예방 요령
③ 화재 안전 수칙
④ 교내 글쓰기 대회
⑤ 엘리베이터 점검 안내

10
W: David, what are you looking at?

M: I'm checking the _____ _____ _____.

W: What are they?

M: First, when a fire _____ _____, get out fast.

W: We shouldn't use the elevators, right?

M: You're right! And it's important to _____ your mouth.

W: Cover my mouth?

M: Yes. You need to avoid _____ _____ too much smoke.

11. 대화를 듣고, 두 사람이 함께 이동할 교통수단으로 가장 적절한 것을 고르시오.

① 자전거   ② 택시
③ 버스   ④ 기차
⑤ 비행기

11
W: Tom, how should we get to Seoul next week?

M: _____ _____ _____ the train?

W: It sounds fun, but the train station is too _____ _____.

M: You're right. Then what shall we do?

W: Why don't we take the bus?

M: Good idea. The bus terminal is _____ _____ _____.

W: Yes. I'll _____ _____ _____, then.

이유파악

12. 대화를 듣고, 여자가 쿠키를 굽는 이유로 가장 적절한 것을 고르시오.

① 스트레스를 풀려고
② 이웃에게 선물하려고
③ 바자회에서 판매하려고
④ 다툰 친구와 화해하려고
⑤ 발렌타인데이를 기념하려고

12
M: Lucy, what are you baking?

W: I'm _____ _____ for Mrs. Brown, Dad.

M: Mrs. Brown? Our neighbor?

W: Yes, she's always been so kind to us, so I'm baking her cookies to _____ _____.

M: That's _____ of you! Why are you baking for her today?

W: She's moving away next week, so I want to give her something to _____ us by.

다음 페이지에 계속 ➡

13. 대화를 듣고, 대화가 이루어지는 장소를 고르시오.

① 문구점　　② 헬스장
③ 음식점　　④ 옷 가게
⑤ 신발 가게

13

M: What can I do for you?

W: I'm _____ _____ running shoes. Do you have any?

M: Yes. How about these? They are very _____ and _____.

W: Hmm, can I try them on?

M: Of course. _____ _____ do you wear?

W: I wear size six.

14. 대화를 듣고, 남자가 찾고 있는 이어폰 케이스의 위치로 가장 알맞은 곳을 고르시오.

14

W: What are you doing, Jack? _____ _____ _____ _____.

M: Mom, I can't find my earphone case. Did you see it?

W: No. Did you check the table?

M: I did. It's not there. I checked the sofa too, but I don't see it.

W: Then, did you _____ _____ the shelves?

M: [Pause] Oh, I found it. It's on the _____ _____ from the top.

15. 대화를 듣고, 여자가 남자에게 부탁하는 일을 고르시오.

① 시험공부 같이 하기
② 잠 깨워 주기
③ 시험 문제 풀어 주기
④ 간식 사 주기
⑤ 시험 보러 같이 가기

15

W: I am _____ _____ today.

M: Come on. We have a math test tomorrow.

W: I know. But I _____ _____ _____ at 2 a.m. last night.

M: Wow, you really studied hard yesterday.

W: Not really. Ted, could you _____ _____ _____ in 30 minutes?

M: Sure.

W: Thank you!

16. 대화를 듣고, 남자가 여자에게 제안한 것으로 가장 적절한 것을 고르시오.

① 옷 수선하기
② 옷 기부하기
③ 옷 구매하기
④ 옷 세탁하기
⑤ 옷 버리기

16

M: Hey, Jane. What are you doing?

W: I'm just _____ my old clothes _____.

M: Why? It looks like they are still _____ _____ _____.

W: I know, but they don't fit me anymore.

M: Why don't you _____ them instead?

W: That's a good idea.

다음 페이지에 계속 ➡

17. 대화를 듣고, 여자가 주말에 한 일로 가장 적절한 것을 고르시오.

① 도서관 가서 책 빌리기
② 친구들과 쇼핑하기
③ 마트 가서 장보기
④ 휴대폰 수리 맡기기
⑤ 병원 가기

17

W: Hi, John. How was your weekend?

M: It was terrible. I had to go to the hospital because I _____ _____ _____.

W: Oh no! That's too bad.

M: Don't worry. I'm _____ _____. What did you do last weekend, Jane?

W: I _____ _____ with my friends.

M: That sounds great.

18. 대화를 듣고, 남자의 직업으로 가장 적절한 것을 고르시오.

① 영양사　　② 헬스 트레이너
③ 의사　　　④ 소방관
⑤ 경찰관

18

M: You did that very well. How do you feel?

W: My legs are _____!

M: Keep your back _____ when you do your squat next time.

W: Okay. What do I do next?

M: Some stretches to _____ your muscles.

W: I'm glad I started to exercise. I feel so _____.

M: I'm glad to help you out.

19. 대화를 듣고, 남자의 마지막 말에 이어질 여자의 말로 가장 적절한 것을 고르시오.

Woman: _____

① You should be more careful.
② Good luck to you!
③ I'm sorry to hear that.
④ I'm glad we're on time.
⑤ That sounds exciting.

19 W: Hurry up! We are late.

M: Let's cross the street here.

W: No. This is not a _____.

M: Come on, Audrey. We don't have _____ _____.

W: Watch out! George, that car almost _____ _____.

M: Oh, my goodness!

W: You should be more careful.

20. 대화를 듣고, 남자의 마지막 말에 이어질 여자의 말로 가장 적절한 것을 고르시오.

Woman: _____

① I want oranges.
② We can take a taxi.
③ They look delicious.
④ It will take 30 minutes.
⑤ Let's eat in a restaurant.

20 M: Alyssa, I'm going _____ shopping. Do you want to come?

W: Okay, Dad. Can we buy some chocolate, too?

M: Sure.

W: Great! And can we also _____ some fruit?

M: Of course. I was going to buy some bananas.

W: Hmm. I don't _____ _____ _____ bananas.

M: Okay. Then what fruit do you want to eat?

W: I want oranges.

Words & Expressions Review 18

● 다음 단어를 암기하세요.

문제	번호	단어	뜻
1	1	container	용기, 그릇
	2	chop up	(잘게) 다지다, 썰다
2	3	striped	줄무늬가 있는
	4	plain	민무늬의
3	5	ahead of	(시간, 공간상으로) ~앞에
	6	thankfully	다행스럽게도, 고맙게도
	7	get rain	비가 오다
4	8	What's up?	무슨 일이야?, 잘 지냈어?
	9	extra	남는, 여분의
5	10	would like to + 동사	~하고 싶다
	11	expression	표현
	12	for free	무료로, 공짜로
7	13	cartoonist	만화가
	14	someday	언젠가, 훗날
	15	special	특별한
	16	nursing home	요양원
8	17	volunteer work	자원봉사
	18	important	중요한
	19	wonderful	멋진, 훌륭한
9	20	by yourself	너 혼자서
10	21	break out	발생하다, 발발하다
	22	breathe in	(숨을) 들이마시다

문제	번호	단어	뜻
11	23	far away	멀리 떨어진
	24	close	가까운, 근접한
12	25	bake	굽다
	26	thank	감사를 전하다
	27	thoughtful	사려 깊은, 친절한
	28	move away	이사 가다
13	29	light	가벼운
	30	comfortable	편안한
	31	It's time for ~	~할 시간이다
14	32	look through	살펴보다, 훑어보다
	33	shelf	선반, 책꽂이
15	34	wake up	(잠을) 깨우다, 일어나다
	35	throw away	버리다
16	36	condition	상태, 상황
	37	fit	(모양·크기가) 맞다
	38	keep ~ straight	~을 곧게 유지하다
18	39	squat	쪼그리고 앉은 자세, 스쿼트 동작
	40	energetic	활기에 찬, 정력적인
19	41	crosswalk	횡단보도
	42	watch out	조심하다
20	43	grocery shopping	장보기
	44	feel like -ing	~하고 싶다

M1(17)_W_18

●왼쪽 단어장의 뜻이 보이지 않게 반으로 접고, 학습한 단어의 뜻을 아래 빈칸에 적어주세요.

1	It's time for ~		23	plain	
2	for free		24	would like to + 동사	
3	light		25	thankfully	
4	volunteer work		26	nursing home	
5	feel like -ing		27	container	
6	shelf		28	close	
7	extra		29	squat	
8	expression		30	bake	
9	chop up		31	thank	
10	grocery shopping		32	move away	
11	watch out		33	break out	
12	thoughtful		34	ahead of	
13	wake up		35	get rain	
14	throw away		36	condition	
15	striped		37	important	
16	cartoonist		38	keep ~ straight	
17	far away		39	breathe in	
18	look through		40	special	
19	fit		41	someday	
20	energetic		42	comfortable	
21	What's up?		43	by yourself	
22	crosswalk		44	wonderful	

18
회
단
어

전국 15개 시·도 교육청 공동주관 및 서울시 연합 내신

19회 중학영어듣기 모의고사

M1(17)_19_US
모두 **미국식 발음(US)**
으로 녹음

M1(17)_19_UK
20문제 중 5문제에 **영국식 발음
(US+UK)**을 포함하여 녹음

📖 정답 및 해석 p.77

1 다음을 듣고, 'I'가 가리키는 것을 고르시오.

①  ②  ③  ④  ⑤

2 대화를 듣고, 여자가 구입할 자물쇠로 가장 적절한 것을 고르시오.

①  ②  ③  ④  ⑤

3 다음을 듣고, 경주의 오늘 오후 날씨로 가장 적절한 것을 고르시오.

①  ②  ③  ④  ⑤

4 대화를 듣고, 여자가 한 마지막 말의 의도로 가장 적절한 것을 고르시오.

① 감사 ② 사과 ③ 항의 ④ 칭찬 ⑤ 축하

5 다음을 듣고, 여자가 학교 캠핑 행사에 대해 언급하지 <u>않은</u> 것을 고르시오.

① 행사 날짜   ② 교육 내용   ③ 장소
④ 준비물   ⑤ 신청 방법

6 대화를 듣고, 두 사람이 만날 시각을 고르시오.

① 3:00 p.m.　　② 3:30 p.m.　　③ 4:00 p.m.　　④ 4:30 p.m.　　⑤ 5:00 p.m.

7 대화를 듣고, 여자의 장래 희망으로 가장 적절한 것을 고르시오.

① 수의사　　　　　② 요리사　　　　　③ 건축가
④ 사육사　　　　　⑤ 의상 디자이너

8 대화를 듣고, 남자의 심정으로 가장 적절한 것을 고르시오.

① 기쁨　　　② 화남　　　③ 슬픔　　　④ 지루함　　　⑤ 무서움

9 대화를 듣고, 여자가 대화 직후에 할 일로 가장 적절한 것을 고르시오.

① 실험 재료 사기　　② 인터넷 검색하기　　③ 선생님께 여쭤보기
④ 참고 도서 대출하기　　⑤ 화산 실험 영상 보기

10 대화를 듣고, 무엇에 관한 내용인지 고르시오.

① 가전 수리　　② 의류 세탁　　③ 가전 구매　　④ 의류 수선　　⑤ 의류 염색

11번~20번 문제는 다음 페이지에 ➡

11 대화를 듣고, 두 사람이 함께 이동할 방법으로 가장 적절한 것을 고르시오.

① 자동차   ② 버스   ③ 기차
④ 비행기   ⑤ 택시

12 대화를 듣고, 여자가 주문한 옷을 받지 <u>못한</u> 이유로 가장 적절한 것을 고르시오.

① 연휴로 배송이 늦어져서   ② 배송이 잘못되어서
③ 주문한 색상의 옷이 없어서   ④ 주문한 사이즈의 옷이 없어서
⑤ 집에 아무도 없어서

13 대화를 듣고, 두 사람이 대화하는 장소로 가장 적절한 곳을 고르시오.

① 놀이공원   ② 미용실   ③ 골프장   ④ 지하철역   ⑤ 스키장

14 Kids' Baking Event에 관한 다음 내용을 듣고, 표에서 일치하지 <u>않는</u> 것을 고르시오.

Kids' Baking Event		
①	일시	this Saturday, 11 a.m.
②	행사 내용	how to make rice cakes
③	소요 시간	1.5 hours
④	비용	$30
⑤	장소	Moonberry Mall event space

15 대화를 듣고, 여자가 남자에게 부탁한 일로 가장 적절한 것을 고르시오.

① 병원 알아보기   ② 선물 구입하기   ③ 옷 갈아입기
④ 음식 준비하기   ⑤ 친구 초대하기

16 대화를 듣고, 여자가 남자에게 제안한 것으로 가장 적절한 것을 고르시오.

① 치과 방문하기　　② 강아지 산책시키기　　③ 할 일 목록 만들기
④ 리포트 작성하기　　⑤ 일정 미루기

17 대화를 듣고, 여자가 주말에 한 일로 가장 적절한 것을 고르시오.

① 가족과 캠핑 가기　　② 수영 배우기　　③ 전자 상가 가기
④ 컴퓨터 수리하기　　⑤ 인터넷 쇼핑하기

18 대화를 듣고, 남자의 직업으로 적절한 것을 고르시오.

① 자동차 수리공　　② 소방관　　③ 운전기사　　④ 경찰　　⑤ 간호사

[19~20] 대화를 듣고, 여자의 마지막 말에 이어질 남자의 말로 가장 적절한 것을 고르시오.

19 Man: _____

① That sounds delicious.　　② There's a toilet nearby.
③ It takes an hour by car.　　④ Be careful with the fire.
⑤ We'll be there for 3 days.

20 Man: _____

① I believe in you.　　② I can't play that well.
③ You're always welcome.　　④ There will be a school festival.
⑤ Yes. And they take new members.

Dictation(받아쓰기)은 본문을 받아쓰면서 영어듣기의 집중력을 향상시키고 다양한 표현을 정리하기 위한 영어듣기 학습법입니다. **녹음을 다시 듣고, 빈칸에 알맞은 단어를 써 보세요.**
※Dictation의 정답은 듣기 대본의 밑줄 친 부분을 확인하세요.

📖 정답 p. 77

🖊 맞은 개수 / 총127개

그림정보파악(담화)

1. 다음을 듣고, 'I'가 가리키는 것을 고르시오.

01 M: I live in the _____ and eat plants. I help people cross the desert and _____ _____. I have humps on my back and there is a lot of fat in them. So, I can _____ _____ without food and water for a long period.

그림정보파악(대화)

2. 대화를 듣고, 여자가 구입할 자물쇠로 가장 적절한 것을 고르시오.

①  ②
③  ④
⑤

02 M: May I help you?

W: I want to _____ _____ _____.

M: We have 3-digit locks and 4-digit locks.

W: I want a 3-digit lock.

M: Okay, how about this 3-digit _____ _____?

W: Do you have anything else?

M: How about this _____-_____ _____?

W: I like hearts. I'll take it.

3. 다음을 듣고, 경주의 오늘 오후 날씨로 가장 적절한 것을 고르시오.

① ② ③ ④ ⑤

03 W: Hello! This is the Gyeongju weather report. Yesterday, we had some _____ _____ here and there, but by evening, the sky _____. Today, it's a cold but sunny day outside. Later in the afternoon, we _____ _____ some strong winds. So, dress warmly if you're going out.

2025 영어듣기능력평가 1회 4번 변형

4. 대화를 듣고, 여자가 한 마지막 말의 의도로 가장 적절한 것을 고르시오.

① 감사 ② 사과
③ 항의 ④ 칭찬
⑤ 축하

04 W: Eric, what are you doing?

M: I'm making a _____-_____ _____ for our school bus driver.

W: That's _____ of you. What made you want to do that?

M: He's always so kind, and I wanted to show my thanks.

W: I'm sure he'll love it. You're so sweet.

다음 페이지에 계속 ➡

5. 다음을 듣고, 여자가 학교 캠핑 행사에 대해 언급하지 **않은** 것을 고르시오.

① 행사 날짜
② 교육 내용
③ 장소
④ 준비물
⑤ 신청 방법

05 W: This spring we'll have a school camping event. It will _____ _____ on April 27th. You will learn to _____ _____ a tent, make a fire, and more. The school grounds will be our camping site. The event will _____ from the evening of April 27th until the next morning. You can _____ _____ _____ the event on the school website.

6. 대화를 듣고, 두 사람이 만날 시각을 고르시오.

① 3:00 p.m.   ② 3:30 p.m.
③ 4:00 p.m.   ④ 4:30 p.m.
⑤ 5:00 p.m.

06 M: Hey, Jennifer. Did you know that there is a _____ _____ at the community center today?

W: Yes, it's about jobs of the _____, isn't it?

M: Right. It starts at 5 p.m. Let's go together.

W: Sure, then I'll see you in front of the school at 4:30.

M: That'll be too _____. How about 4:00?

W: All right. See you then.

7. 대화를 듣고, 여자의 장래 희망으로 가장 적절한 것을 고르시오.

① 수의사
② 요리사
③ 건축가
④ 사육사
⑤ 의상 디자이너

07

M: Kathy, what do you usually do on the weekend?

W: I _____ _____ with my dogs and my hamsters.

M: Oh, you must love animals.

W: Yes, I want to _____ _____ _____ when I grow up.

M: Great. I'm sure your dream will come true.

W: Thanks, Mike. I will _____ _____ _____.

8. 대화를 듣고, 남자의 심정으로 가장 적절한 것을 고르시오.

① 기쁨
② 화남
③ 슬픔
④ 지루함
⑤ 무서움

08

M: Finally, our exams are all over!

W: Yay! The best thing is that we _____ _____ _____ _____ today!

M: You're right. What should we do today?

W: _____ _____ _____ go to the new coin noraebang?

M: Great idea! Let's go _____ _____ _____.

다음 페이지에 계속 ➡

9. 대화를 듣고, 여자가 대화 직후에 할 일로 가장 적절한 것을 고르시오.

① 실험 재료 사기
② 인터넷 검색하기
③ 선생님께 여쭤보기
④ 참고 도서 대출하기
⑤ 화산 실험 영상 보기

09
M: Did you decide what to make for the _____ _____?

W: Not yet. I'm thinking about making a model of a _____.

M: Have you read any books about how to make one?

W: I did, but I still don't know what _____ to use.

M: Why don't you ask the science teacher?

W: That's a good idea. I'll go ask her now.

대화화제추론

10. 대화를 듣고, 무엇에 관한 내용인지 고르시오.

① 가전 수리   ② 의류 세탁
③ 가전 구매   ④ 의류 수선
⑤ 의류 염색

10
M: Can I ask you something?

W: Sure, sir.

M: Can I _____ _____ this T-shirt?

W: No, you have to wash it _____ _____ in cold water with a gentle detergent.

M: What happens if I machine wash it?

W: All the color _____ _____ _____.

11. 대화를 듣고, 두 사람이 함께 이동할 방법으로 가장 적절한 것을 고르시오.

① 자동차　② 버스
③ 기차　④ 비행기
⑤ 택시

11
W: Dad, how are we going to Busan this weekend?

M: I was thinking of going in our car.

W: But it's the weekend. There'll be _____

_____!

M: That's true.

W: Can't we _____ _____ _____?

M: Sure, why not? Let's take the plane.

W: Great! I'll check _____ _____ _____.

12. 대화를 듣고, 여자가 주문한 옷을 받지 못한 이유로 가장 적절한 것을 고르시오.

① 연휴로 배송이 늦어져서
② 배송이 잘못되어서
③ 주문한 색상의 옷이 없어서
④ 주문한 사이즈의 옷이 없어서
⑤ 집에 아무도 없어서

12
M: You look _____. What's wrong?

W: I ordered a new dress online, but I _____

_____ _____ yet.

M: What happened?

W: I wanted a red one, but they were _____

_____ _____. I have to wait for another

week.

M: That must be annoying.

W: I wanted to wear it on my date this Friday, but

now my plans are ruined.

다음 페이지에 계속 ➡

13. 대화를 듣고, 두 사람이 대화하는 장소로 가장 적절한 곳을 고르시오.

① 놀이공원　　② 미용실
③ 골프장　　　④ 지하철역
⑤ 스키장

13

M: How can I help you?

W: I bought this _____ _____ yesterday, but I want to _____ it for a monthly pass.

M: Sure, do you want the monthly pass for the same area?

W: Yes, please. Can I also _____ _____ _____?

M: Absolutely! I'll do that for you.

W: Thanks a lot.

표불일치

🇺🇸🇬🇧　　　신유형　2025 영어듣기능력평가 1회 14번 변형

14. Kids' Baking Event에 관한 다음 내용을 듣고, 표에서 일치하지 <u>않는</u> 것을 고르시오.

Kids' Baking Event		
①	일시	this Saturday, 11 a.m.
②	행사 내용	how to make rice cakes
③	소요 시간	1.5 hours
④	비용	$30
⑤	장소	Moonberry Mall event space

14

W: Hello, Moonberry shoppers! Let me tell you about our Kids' Baking Event. It'll be held this Saturday at 11 a.m. _____ the event, kids will learn how to make tasty and colorful rice cakes with fun designs. The event will be 2 hours in length. The fee is 30 dollars, including all _____. It will _____ _____ at Moonberry Mall in the event space on the first floor. Thanks!

15. 대화를 듣고, 여자가 남자에게 부탁한 일로 가장 적절한 것을 고르시오.
　① 병원 알아보기
　② 선물 구입하기
　③ 옷 갈아입기
　④ 음식 준비하기
　⑤ 친구 초대하기

15 M: Honey, I'm so happy. Rachel is finally coming home with us.

W: I know. She was _____ _____ _____ for too long.

M: We should _____.

W: I think so, too. Shall we _____ _____ _____ _____?

M: Yes! How about new clothes?

W: Good idea. Can you go and buy them today?

M: Yes, I can.

16. 대화를 듣고, 여자가 남자에게 제안한 것으로 가장 적절한 것을 고르시오.
　① 치과 방문하기
　② 강아지 산책시키기
　③ 할 일 목록 만들기
　④ 리포트 작성하기
　⑤ 일정 미루기

16 W: Tommy, you look _____ _____.

M: I have so many things to do today.

W: _____ _____?

M: I have to write a report, clean my room, visit the dentist, walk my dog, and... Oh, I forget what else.

W: Why don't you _____ _____ _____ _____ of all the things you have to do today?

다음 페이지에 계속 ➡

17. 대화를 듣고, 여자가 주말에 한 일로 가장 적절한 것을 고르시오.

① 가족과 캠핑 가기
② 수영 배우기
③ 전자 상가 가기
④ 컴퓨터 수리하기
⑤ 인터넷 쇼핑하기

17

W: Ken, how was your weekend?

M: It was awful. My computer _____ _____, so I had to fix it.

W: Oh, that sounds terrible. Did you _____ _____ _____ it?

M: Yeah, I did. How did you spend your weekend?

W: I went camping with my family.

M: That sounds great.

18. 대화를 듣고, 남자의 직업으로 적절한 것을 고르시오.

① 자동차 수리공   ② 소방관
③ 운전기사   ④ 경찰
⑤ 간호사

18

M: Good morning. May I help you?

W: Yes. My car makes _____ _____ when I'm driving.

M: I see. Hmm, I think there is _____ _____ with the engine.

W: Oh, no. Is it serious?

M: I don't know yet. I'll have to look inside.

W: Can you finish by tomorrow?

M: I'm not sure, but I'll _____ _____ _____.

19. 대화를 듣고, 여자의 마지막 말에 이어질
남자의 말로 가장 적절한 것을 고르시오.

Man: _____

① That sounds delicious.
② There's a toilet nearby.
③ It takes an hour by car.
④ Be careful with the fire.
⑤ We'll be there for 3 days.

19
M: Emma, we're _____ _____ in
Gangwondo next week.

W: Really, Dad? Are we going to have a
_____?

M: Yes.

W: Awesome! Can we also have a barbecue?

M: Sure. What do you want to eat?

W: I want sausages and sweet potatoes.

M: OK. Let's have them both.

W: Great! How long are we going to _____ there?

M: We'll be there for 3 days.

20. 대화를 듣고, 여자의 마지막 말에 이어질
남자의 말로 가장 적절한 것을 고르시오.

Man: _____

① I believe in you.
② I can't play that well.
③ You're always welcome.
④ There will be a school
festival.
⑤ Yes. And they take new
members.

20
M: Maggie, how are you doing these days?

W: Hi, Mr. Baker. My classes are fine, but it's _____
_____ hard to make friends.

M: Then, why don't you _____ a club? Many
students _____ _____ there.

W: Really?

M: Really. And you play the guitar, _____ _____?

W: I do. Is there a guitar club?

M: Yes. And they take new members.

Words & Expressions Review 19

● 다음 단어를 암기하세요.

문제	번호	단어	뜻
1	1	cross	건너다, 가로지르다
	2	carry	나르다
	3	baggage	짐
	4	hump	혹, 툭 솟아 오른 것
2	5	lock	자물쇠
	6	digit	자릿수, 숫자
	7	square	사각형 모양의
	8	heart-shaped	하트 모양의
4	9	thoughtful	사려 깊은, 친절한
	10	show	보여주다
5	11	ground	운동장
6	12	lecture	강의, 강연
	13	community center	주민 센터
	14	tight	(여유가 없이) 빠듯한, 빡빡한
7	15	zookeeper	동물원 사육사
	16	come true	이루어지다, 실현되다
	17	do one's best	최선을 다하다
8	18	have fun	재미있게 놀다, 즐기다
9	19	volcano	화산
10	20	gentle	순한, 온화한
	21	detergent	세제
11	22	heavy traffic	교통 체증, 극심한 교통량

문제	번호	단어	뜻
11	23	schedule	시간표, 일정
	24	annoyed	짜증난
12	25	sold out	다 팔린, 매진된
	26	week	주, 일주일
13	27	exchange	교환하다
14	28	during	～동안
15	29	be in the hospital	입원해 있다
	30	stressed out	스트레스를 받은
	31	report	리포트, 보고서
16	32	dentist	치과, 치과 의사
	33	what else	그 밖의 다른 것
	34	make a list	목록을 만들다
17	35	break down	고장 나다
	36	manage to + 동사	어떻게든 ～하다
	37	make a sound	소리가 나다, 소리를 내다
18	38	strange	이상한
	39	engine	엔진
	40	serious	심각한
19	41	go camping	캠핑 가다
	42	sweet potato	고구마
20	43	believe in	～을 믿다
	44	kind of	약간, 어느 정도

정답 p. 82

M1(17)_W_19

● 왼쪽 단어장의 뜻이 보이지 않게 반으로 접고, 학습한 단어의 뜻을 아래 빈칸에 적어주세요.

1	be in the hospital		23	digit
2	strange		24	do one's best
3	gentle		25	during
4	manage to + 동사		26	sold out
5	annoyed		27	lock
6	schedule		28	week
7	heavy traffic		29	serious
8	lecture		30	stressed out
9	volcano		31	report
10	believe in		32	make a sound
11	go camping		33	hump
12	community center		34	detergent
13	come true		35	tight
14	heart-shaped		36	baggage
15	ground		37	exchange
16	engine		38	what else
17	sweet potato		39	carry
18	zookeeper		40	make a list
19	kind of		41	dentist
20	show		42	cross
21	break down		43	have fun
22	square		44	thoughtful

전국 15개 시·도 교육청 공동주관 및 서울시 연합 내신

20회 중학영어듣기 모의고사

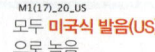

M1(17)_20_US
모두 **미국식 발음(US)**
으로 녹음

M1(17)_20_UK
20문제 중 5문제에 **영국식 발음
(US+UK)**을 포함하여 녹음

정답 및 해석 p. 82

1 다음을 듣고, 'I'가 무엇인지 가장 적절한 것을 고르시오.

①  ②  ③  ④  ⑤

2 대화를 듣고, 여자가 구입할 이어폰 케이스로 가장 적절한 것을 고르시오.

①  ②  ③  ④  ⑤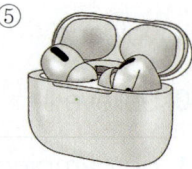

3 다음을 듣고, 오늘 날씨로 적절한 것을 고르시오.

①  ②  ③  ④  ⑤

4 대화를 듣고, 남자가 한 마지막 말의 의도로 가장 적절한 것을 고르시오.

① 위로 ② 사과 ③ 축하 ④ 거절 ⑤ 제안

5 다음을 듣고, 여자가 디자이너에 대해 언급하지 <u>않은</u> 것을 고르시오.

① 이름　　　② 거주지　　　③ 출신 학교　　　④ 나이　　　⑤ 고객

6 대화를 듣고, 두 사람이 이야기를 나누는 현재 시각을 고르시오.

① 8:00 a.m.　　② 8:30 a.m.　　③ 9:00 a.m.　　④ 9:30 a.m.　　⑤ 10:00 a.m.

7 대화를 듣고, 여자의 장래 희망으로 가장 적절한 것을 고르시오.

① 작가　　　② 가수　　　③ 성악가　　　④ 촬영 감독　　　⑤ 피아니스트

8 대화를 듣고, 여자의 심정으로 가장 적절한 것을 고르시오.

① excited　　② happy　　③ angry　　④ worried　　⑤ calm

9 대화를 듣고, 남자가 대화 직후에 할 일로 가장 적절한 것을 고르시오.

① 랜턴 챙기기　　　　② 침낭 구매하기　　　　③ 텐트 설치하기
④ 구급상자 준비하기　　⑤ 아이스박스 반품하기

10 대화를 듣고, 무엇에 관한 내용인지 고르시오.

① 박물관 규정　　② 교통 법규　　③ 콘서트 안내　　④ 컴퓨터 사용　　⑤ 길 안내

11번~20번 문제는 다음 페이지에 ➡

11 대화를 듣고, 남자가 이용할 교통수단으로 가장 적절한 것을 고르시오.

① 버스   ② 기차   ③ 지하철   ④ 자동차   ⑤ 자전거

12 대화를 듣고, 여자가 박물관에 가는 이유로 가장 적절한 것을 고르시오.

① 그림을 그리려고   ② 전시회를 보려고
③ 봉사활동을 하려고   ④ 무료 특강을 들으려고
⑤ 역사 과제 자료를 찾으려고

13 대화를 듣고, 대화가 이루어지는 장소를 고르시오.

① record store   ② bookstore   ③ restaurant   ④ library   ⑤ museum

14 대화를 듣고, 남자가 가려고 하는 장소를 고르시오.

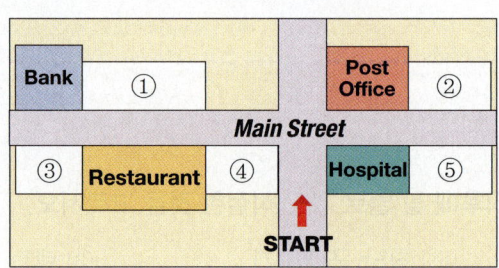

15 대화를 듣고, 남자가 여자에게 부탁하는 일을 고르시오.

① 같이 여행가기   ② 회의 준비하기   ③ 항공편 변경하기
④ 호텔 예약하기   ⑤ 보고서 제시간에 끝내기

16 대화를 듣고, 남자가 여자에게 제안한 것으로 가장 적절한 것을 고르시오.

① 친구 만나기　　② 집안 청소하기　　③ 음악 감상하기
④ 고양이 장난감 사기　　⑤ 강아지 산책 시키기

17 대화를 듣고, 여자가 어제 한 일로 가장 적절한 것을 고르시오.

① 서점 가기　　② 공원 가기　　③ 벼룩시장 가기
④ 식료품 사기　　⑤ 사진 현상하기

18 대화를 듣고, 남자의 직업으로 가장 적절한 것을 고르시오.

① 의사　　② 영양사　　③ 약사
④ 소방관　　⑤ 헬스 트레이너

[19~20] 대화를 듣고, 여자의 마지막 말에 이어질 남자의 말로 가장 적절한 것을 고르시오.

19 Man: _____

① Sounds great.
② You must have been disappointed.
③ I visited my friend in Busan.
④ I'm going to the library.
⑤ Everything will be fine.

20 Man: _____

① I'm hungry.　　② No, I didn't.　　③ An animal doctor.
④ Sounds interesting.　　⑤ A goldfish.

Dictation Test 20

녹음을 다시 듣으면서 빈칸을 채워주세요

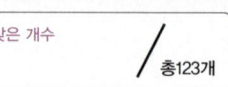

M1(17)_20_D

Dictation(받아쓰기)은 본문을 받아쓰면서 영어듣기의 집중력을 향상시키고 다양한 표현을 정리하기 위한 영어듣기 학습법입니다. 녹음을 다시 듣고, 빈칸에 알맞은 단어를 써 보세요.

※Dictation의 정답은 듣기 대본의 밑줄 친 부분을 확인하세요.

📖 정답 p. 82

맞은 개수 / 총123개

그림정보파악(담화)

1. 다음을 듣고, 'I'가 무엇인지 가장 적절한 것을 고르시오.

①  ②

③  ④

⑤

01 M: I live in a very cold area. I am black and white. I have small wings but I _____ _____. I can _____ _____ _____ fish very well. What am I?

그림정보파악(대화)

2. 대화를 듣고, 여자가 구입할 이어폰 케이스로 가장 적절한 것을 고르시오.

①  ②

③  ④

⑤

02 M: May I help you?

W: Yes, I am looking for a new EarPods case.

M: We have _____ _____ _____. How about this one with a heart on it?

W: No thanks. Do you have anything _____ _____ _____?

M: Oh, we have one with a bear and one with a rabbit.

W: The one with the rabbit on it sounds good. I will take that one.

---

3. 다음을 듣고, 오늘 날씨로 적절한 것을 고르시오.

① 　②

③ 　④

⑤

03 M: Good morning. It rained _____ yesterday. But today, you don't _____ _____ _____ your umbrella with you. It will be sunny and warm all day. _____ _____ wear light clothes. Have a nice day.

4. 대화를 듣고, 남자가 한 마지막 말의 의도로 가장 적절한 것을 고르시오.

① 위로　② 사과
③ 축하　④ 거절
⑤ 제안

04 W: Jake, do you have _____ _____ for tomorrow?

M: Hi, Kate. I am going to the mall to buy a birthday gift for Emily.

W: Oh, I forgot to buy her a gift!

M: Her birthday is _____ _____.

W: Right, there's not much time. Can I go with you?

M: Sure. Let's go and _____ together.

다음 페이지에 계속 ➡

20 회 딕테이션

5. 다음을 듣고, 여자가 디자이너에 대해 언급하지 **않은** 것을 고르시오.

① 이름　　　　② 거주지
③ 출신 학교　　④ 나이
⑤ 고객

05 W: Hi, everyone. Today, I will tell you about an amazing _____ _____. Her name is Marylin Chung. She was born in Canada, but now she lives in the UK. She is only 28 years old, but her hats are already very _____. Her customers _____ members of the European royal families.

6. 대화를 듣고, 두 사람이 이야기를 나누는 현재 시각을 고르시오.

① 8:00 a.m.　　② 8:30 a.m.
③ 9:00 a.m.　　④ 9:30 a.m.
⑤ 10:00 a.m.

06 M: Are you ready to leave, sweetie?

W: Yes, Dad. _____ _____ will it take to get to the resort?

M: It's a one-hour ride, but _____ _____ longer this morning.

W: Why is that?

M: There was _____ _____ on the road at 8:00 a.m.

W: It's 9:00 a.m. now. The road _____ _____ _____.

M: I hope so. Let's go.

7. 대화를 듣고, 여자의 장래 희망으로 가장 적절한 것을 고르시오.

① 작가 ② 가수
③ 성악가 ④ 촬영 감독
⑤ 피아니스트

07
M: Wow, you have a lot of _____ albums in your room.

W: Yes. I love listening to classical music.

M: Cool! Do you play a _____ _____ as well?

W: I play the piano. I actually want to become a pianist when I _____ _____.

M: Great! I'm sure you'll become a famous _____ one day.

W: Thanks!

8. 대화를 듣고, 여자의 심정으로 가장 적절한 것을 고르시오.

① excited ② happy
③ angry ④ worried
⑤ calm

08
M: Hey, Jane! What are you doing _____ _____?

W: I'm waiting for Emma. By the way, _____ _____ is it?

M: It's 2 o'clock.

W: _____ _____! She's 30 minutes late. She's always late.

M: Calm down! Why don't you sit down here and wait for her?

다음 페이지에 계속 ➡

9. 대화를 듣고, 남자가 대화 직후에 할 일로 가장 적절한 것을 고르시오.

① 랜턴 챙기기
② 침낭 구매하기
③ 텐트 설치하기
④ 구급상자 준비하기
⑤ 아이스박스 반품하기

09
M: Honey, are we almost _____ _____ the camping trip?

W: Almost! Did you pack the sleeping bags?

M: Yes, they're already in the car.

W: Great. What about the _____?

M: It's ready, too.

W: Perfect. Oh! I _____ about the lanterns.

M: Don't worry. I'll put them in the car right now.

---

10. 대화를 듣고, 무엇에 관한 내용인지 고르시오.

① 박물관 규정
② 교통 법규
③ 콘서트 안내
④ 컴퓨터 사용
⑤ 길 안내

10
W: Sir, you can't take pictures inside the _____.

M: I have to _____ _____ _____ of this old dish. This is my history homework.

W: The camera flash can damage the _____.

M: Then, what should I do?

W: There is a photo book. We sell it in the _____ _____.

M: Okay.

11. 대화를 듣고, 남자가 이용할 교통수단으로 가장 적절한 것을 고르시오.
  ① 버스　　② 기차
  ③ 지하철　　④ 자동차
  ⑤ 자전거

11
W: Jake, how are you going to get home? Your car is at the _____ _____, isn't it?

M: Yeah. I'll have to take the subway today.

W: I can _____ _____ _____ _____ home if you'd like.

M: Really? I'd _____ that.

W: Great! Meet me downstairs in 10 minutes.

M: Okay. Thanks, Rina!

고난도 **이유파악**

2025 영어듣기능력평가 1회 12번 변형

20 회 딕테이션

12. 대화를 듣고, 여자가 박물관에 가는 이유로 가장 적절한 것을 고르시오.
  ① 그림을 그리려고
  ② 전시회를 보려고
  ③ 봉사활동을 하려고
  ④ 무료 특강을 들으려고
  ⑤ 역사 과제 자료를 찾으려고

12
M: Megan, where are you going?

W: I'm going to the museum to help with the _____ _____.

M: That sounds interesting. What do you do on the tour?

W: I guide students and explain the history of Korean _____.

M: That's great! You really like history, right?

W: Yes. I'm so happy to _____ as a tour guide.

다음 페이지에 계속 ➡

13. 대화를 듣고, 대화가 이루어지는 장소를 고르시오.

   ① record store
   ② bookstore
   ③ restaurant
   ④ library
   ⑤ museum

13
W: Can I help you?

M: Yes, please. I'm _____ _____ a book. It's about Beethoven.

W: Do you know the _____ _____ the book?

M: It's *The Life of Beethoven*.

W: Oh, sorry. It's _____ _____ right now. But we'll have more on Monday.

M: Really? Thanks.

14. 대화를 듣고, 남자가 가려고 하는 장소를 고르시오.

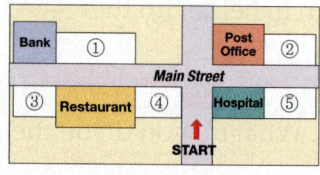

14
M: Excuse me. How do I get to the department store?

W: Go straight to Main Street and turn left.

M: Go straight and turn left?

W: Yes. Then, walk straight _____ _____ _____. You'll see it on your left _____ _____ the restaurant.

M: It will be on my left?

W: Yes. It's _____ _____ the bank.

M: Thank you.

15. 대화를 듣고, 남자가 여자에게 부탁하는 일을 고르시오.

① 같이 여행가기
② 회의 준비하기
③ 항공편 변경하기
④ 호텔 예약하기
⑤ 보고서 제시간에 끝내기

15 M: Grace, what time is my flight _____ _____ _____ tomorrow?

W: 11:50, sir.

M: I think I can't _____ _____. The meeting in the morning won't finish on time.

W: Do you want me to reschedule it?

M: Yes, please. One _____ _____ _____ for me.

제안파악

16. 대화를 듣고, 남자가 여자에게 제안한 것으로 가장 적절한 것을 고르시오.

① 친구 만나기
② 집안 청소하기
③ 음악 감상하기
④ 고양이 장난감 사기
⑤ 강아지 산책 시키기

16 M: Taylor, you look sad! _____ _____?

W: Well, I got a new cat last weekend, but she doesn't seem to like me.

M: Why do you think so?

W: Whenever she sees me, she tries to _____ or _____.

M: You should _____ _____ a cat toy. Why don't you buy one?

W: Good idea! I'll go buy a toy today.

다음 페이지에 계속 ➡

17. 대화를 듣고, 여자가 어제 한 일로 가장 적절한 것을 고르시오.

① 서점 가기
② 공원 가기
③ 벼룩시장 가기
④ 식료품 사기
⑤ 사진 현상하기

17

W: Harry, what did you do yesterday?

M: I went to the bookstore near Central Park. What about you, Linda?

W: I went to a _____ _____.

M: Cool! Did you buy _____ _____?

W: I bought a used camera. I love taking pictures.

M: Really? Can you _____ _____ _____ of me?

W: Sure. I will bring my camera tomorrow.

18. 대화를 듣고, 남자의 직업으로 가장 적절한 것을 고르시오.

① 의사   ② 영양사
③ 약사   ④ 소방관
⑤ 헬스 트레이너

18

M: May I help you?

W: Yes. I'd like to buy some medicine for a _____.

M: Here you are. _____ _____ _____ three times a day.

W: Do I have to take them after meals?

M: Yes. If you start to feel better, take one pill _____ _____ _____.

W: Okay. And can I get _____ _____, too?

M: Sure.

19. 대화를 듣고, 여자의 마지막 말에 이어질
남자의 말로 가장 적절한 것을 고르시오.

Man: _____

① Sounds great.
② You must have been
   disappointed.
③ I visited my friend in Busan.
④ I'm going to the library.
⑤ Everything will be fine.

19 M: Hi, Michelle. How was your weekend?

W: It was _____.

M: Oh, why? You _____ _____ _____ go

camping with your friends, weren't you?

W: Yes, I was, but we couldn't go.

M: What happened?

W: It _____ _____, so we had to cancel the trip.

M: You must have been disappointed.

알맞은응답찾기   🇺🇸🇬🇧

20. 대화를 듣고, 여자의 마지막 말에 이어질
남자의 말로 가장 적절한 것을 고르시오.

Man: _____

① I'm hungry.
② No, I didn't.
③ An animal doctor.
④ Sounds interesting.
⑤ A goldfish.

20 W: Do you have any _____ _____ this

afternoon?

M: Yes, I am going to the pet shop.

W: Wow, are you getting a pet?

M: Yes, I am. Will you come with me?

W: Of course, I will. _____ _____ _____ pet

do you want?

M: A goldfish.

Words & Expressions Review 20

● 다음 단어를 암기하세요.

문제	번호	단어	뜻
1	☐ 1	area	지역
	☐ 2	hunt	사냥하다
2	☐ 3	look for	~을 찾다
	☐ 4	several	여러 가지의, 몇몇의
	☐ 5	related to	~과 관련된
	☐ 6	take	선택하다, 사다
3	☐ 7	heavily	많이, 심하게, 세게
	☐ 8	all day	온종일
	☐ 9	had better + 동사	~하는 게 좋다
4	☐ 10	forget to + 동사	~할 것을 잊다
5	☐ 11	famous	유명한
6	☐ 12	be ready to + 동사	~할 준비가 되다
	☐ 13	accident	사고
	☐ 14	should	(아마) ~일 것이다
	☐ 15	clear	(장애물을) 제거하다, 치우다
7	☐ 16	classical	클래식의, 고전적인
	☐ 17	musical instrument	악기
8	☐ 18	Not again!	또야!
	☐ 19	calm down	진정하다, 진정시키다
	☐ 20	Why don't you ~?	~하는 게 어때?
9	☐ 21	pack	(여행) 짐을 챙기다, 싸다
	☐ 22	cooler	아이스박스

문제	번호	단어	뜻
10	☐ 23	history	역사
	☐ 24	homework	숙제
	☐ 25	damage	손상시키다
	☐ 26	artwork	예술품
11	☐ 27	sell	팔다
	☐ 28	gift shop	기념품점
	☐ 29	repair shop	정비소, 수리점
12	☐ 30	appreciate	고마워하다
	☐ 31	museum	박물관
	☐ 32	artifact	유물
13	☐ 33	sold out	다 팔린, 매진된
	☐ 34	more	더
14	☐ 35	a little	조금
	☐ 36	further	더, 더 멀리
15	☐ 37	be supposed to + 동사	~하기로 되어있다
	☐ 38	reschedule	일정을 변경하다
17	☐ 39	flea market	벼룩시장
18	☐ 40	medicine	약
	☐ 41	bandage	붕대
19	☐ 42	cancel	취소하다
	☐ 43	disappointed	실망한
20	☐ 44	pet	반려동물

● 왼쪽 단어장의 뜻이 보이지 않게 반으로 접고, 학습한 단어의 뜻을 아래 빈칸에 적어주세요.

1	pet	23	medicine
2	bandage	24	Not again!
3	take	25	flea market
4	be supposed to + 동사	26	cooler
5	be ready to + 동사	27	disappointed
6	damage	28	artifact
7	more	29	reschedule
8	should	30	calm down
9	accident	31	forget to + 동사
10	musical instrument	32	clear
11	further	33	famous
12	sold out	34	museum
13	all day	35	look for
14	had better + 동사	36	heavily
15	history	37	gift shop
16	appreciate	38	hunt
17	sell	39	a little
18	Why don't you ~?	40	several
19	related to	41	artwork
20	area	42	cancel
21	pack	43	classical
22	repair shop	44	homework

20
회
단
어

M1(17)_21_US
모두 **미국식 발음(US)**
으로 녹음

M1(17)_21_UK
20문제 중 5문제에 **영국식 발음**
(US+UK)을 포함하여 녹음

정답 및 해석 p. 86

1 다음을 듣고, 'I'가 무엇인지 가장 적절한 것을 고르시오.

①  ②  ③  ④  ⑤

2 대화를 듣고, 여자가 구입할 컵으로 가장 적절한 것을 고르시오.

①  ②  ③  ④  ⑤

3 다음을 듣고, 수요일 오전의 날씨로 가장 적절한 것을 고르시오.

①  ②  ③  ④  ⑤

4 대화를 듣고, 남자가 한 마지막 말의 의도로 가장 적절한 것을 고르시오.

① 위로　　② 사과　　③ 축하　　④ 거절　　⑤ 제안

5 다음을 듣고, 여자가 친구에 대해 언급하지 <u>않은</u> 것을 고르시오.

① 이름　　② 학년　　③ 외모　　④ 취미　　⑤ 성격

6 대화를 듣고, 두 사람이 이야기를 나누는 현재 시각을 고르시오.

① 5:00 p.m.　　② 5:30 p.m.　　③ 6:00 p.m.　　④ 6:30 p.m.　　⑤ 7:00 p.m.

7 대화를 듣고, 여자의 장래 희망으로 가장 적절한 것을 고르시오.

① 음악가　　　　　② 시나리오 작가　　　③ 영화 감독
④ 소설가　　　　　⑤ 배우

8 대화를 듣고, 여자의 심정으로 가장 적절한 것을 고르시오.

① 설렘　　　　　　② 슬픔　　　　　　　③ 부러움
④ 수줍음　　　　　⑤ 실망스러움

9 대화를 듣고, 여자가 대화 직후에 할 일로 가장 적절한 것을 고르시오.

① 대본 수정하기　　② 방송 녹음하기　　　③ 사진 찍으러 가기
④ 선생님 인터뷰하기　⑤ 학교 홈페이지 확인하기

10 대화를 듣고, 무엇에 관한 내용인지 가장 적절한 것을 고르시오.

① 환경 오염 원인　　② 동네 행사 일정　　　③ 분리수거 방법
④ 환경 보호 동아리　⑤ 쓰레기 재활용

11번~20번 문제는 다음 페이지에 ➡

11 대화를 듣고, 두 사람이 함께 이용할 교통수단으로 가장 적절한 것을 고르시오.

① 배　　　　② 버스　　　　③ 기차　　　　④ 지하철　　　　⑤ 자전거

12 대화를 듣고, 여자가 카드를 쓰는 이유로 가장 적절한 것을 고르시오.

① 엄마의 생신이어서　　　　　　② 영어 대회에서 입상해서
③ 교환학생이 올 예정이어서　　　　④ 반 친구들과 헤어지게 되어서
⑤ 선생님이 전근을 가게 되어서

13 대화를 듣고, 두 사람이 대화하는 장소로 가장 적절한 곳을 고르시오.

① 서점　　　　② 미용실　　　　③ 미술관　　　　④ 헬스장　　　　⑤ 영화관

14 대화를 듣고, 두 사람이 찾고 있는 리모컨의 위치로 가장 적절한 것을 고르시오.

15 대화를 듣고, 여자가 남자에게 부탁한 일로 가장 적절한 것을 고르시오.

① 차 태워주기　　　　② 저녁 요리하기　　　　③ 책 반납하기
④ 간식 사 오기　　　　⑤ 옷 찾아다 주기

16 대화를 듣고, 여자가 남자에게 제안한 것으로 가장 적절한 것을 고르시오.

① 운동하기　　　　② 집에서 일하기　　　　③ 퍼레이드에 참가하기
④ 걸어서 집에 가기　　⑤ 버스 노선 검색하기

17 대화를 듣고, 남자가 휴일에 한 일로 가장 적절한 것을 고르시오.

① 숙제하기　　　　② 요리 배우기　　　　③ 피아노 배우기
④ 공연 관람하기　　⑤ 가족 여행 가기

18 대화를 듣고, 여자의 직업을 고르시오.

① cook　　　　　　② teacher　　　　　　③ tour guide
④ computer programmer　　⑤ doctor

[19~20] 대화를 듣고, 여자의 마지막 말에 이어질 남자의 말로 가장 적절한 것을 고르시오.

19 Man: _____

① I'm so tired.　　　　　　② Let's hurry up.
③ That's not for me.　　　　④ You should take a break.
⑤ I don't like action movies.

20 Man: _____

① No. I don't like jogging.　　　② No problem. I'll call you later.
③ Okay. I'll be ready in 5 minutes.　④ You can use my laptop computer.
⑤ I don't like vanilla ice cream.

Dictation Test 21

M1(17)_21_D

Dictation(받아쓰기)은 본문을 받아쓰면서 영어듣기의 집중력을 향상시키고 다양한 표현을 정리하기 위한 영어듣기 학습법입니다. 녹음을 다시 듣고, 빈칸에 알맞은 단어를 써 보세요.
※Dictation의 정답은 듣기 대본의 밑줄 친 부분을 확인하세요.

📖 정답 p. 86

✏ 맞은 개수 / 총132개

그림정보파악(담화)

1. 다음을 듣고, 'I'가 무엇인지 가장 적절한 것을 고르시오.

① 　②

③ 　④

⑤

01 W: I am a bird. I have wings, but I cannot fly. Instead, I can _____ _____ _____. I can run at speeds of over 70 kilometers _____ _____. My legs are long and very strong. My neck is _____ _____, too. What am I?

그림정보파악(대화)

2. 대화를 듣고, 여자가 구입할 컵으로 가장 적절한 것을 고르시오.

① 　②

③ 　④

⑤

02 M: May I help you?

W: Yes, I'm _____ _____ a mug for a friend.

M: What about this one with a big heart on it? It's our _____ _____ one.

W: I like the heart, but I think it's too big.

M: Then, you may like this one. It has many _____ _____ on it.

W: It's great! I'll take it.

---

3. 다음을 듣고, 수요일 오전의 날씨로 가장
   적절한 것을 고르시오.

① 　②

③ 　④

⑤

03 M: Good morning, everyone! This is the _____
weather report. There will be _____ _____ on
Monday, but on Tuesday, we will have _____
_____. On Wednesday, it will _____ in the
morning, but the rain will stop in the afternoon.

4. 대화를 듣고, 남자가 한 마지막 말의 의
   도로 가장 적절한 것을 고르시오.
   ① 위로　　② 사과
   ③ 축하　　④ 거절
   ⑤ 제안

04 W: Hey, Kevin, what's up?

M: Hi, Wendy. Do you want to _____ _____
after school?

W: Oh, I don't think I can.

M: Why not?

W: I have _____ _____ _____ to attend. I
won first prize in a writing competition.

M: Good for you! That's an _____
_____.

다음 페이지에 계속 ➡

5. 다음을 듣고, 여자가 친구에 대해 언급하지 <u>않은</u> 것을 고르시오.

① 이름   ② 학년
③ 외모   ④ 취미
⑤ 성격

05 W: Hi, class. _____ _____ _____ my best friend to you. Her name is Da-won Kim. She goes to Suwon Middle School. She is very tall and I like her short hair very much. Her _____ is _____ _____ _____ _____. She is popular among her classmates because she is kind and _____.

수치파악

🇺🇸🇬🇧

6. 대화를 듣고, 두 사람이 이야기를 나누는 현재 시각을 고르시오.

① 5:00 p.m.
② 5:30 p.m.
③ 6:00 p.m.
④ 6:30 p.m.
⑤ 7:00 p.m.

06 W: Welcome, Josh. Was it hard to find my place?

M: Not at all. I'm late because I _____ the 5 p.m. bus. Sorry.

W: No worries. Dinner will be ready at 6:30 p.m., so you got here _____ _____.

M: That's a _____. And what a nice smell!

W: I have a pie in the oven. It'll be done at 6 p.m.

M: It's 6 p.m. now. You should _____ _____ _____.

7. 대화를 듣고, 여자의 장래 희망으로 가장 적절한 것을 고르시오.

① 음악가　　② 시나리오 작가
③ 영화 감독　④ 소설가
⑤ 배우

07

W: What would you like to be when you _____ _____?

M: I'm very interested in music. I want to be a musician.

W: It will be difficult to _____ _____ that field.

M: I know, but I really enjoy playing the piano and listening to music.

W: I understand. I _____ _____ _____ when I write something. My dream is to write screenplays.

M: That sounds wonderful! I look forward to seeing your stories _____ _____.

8. 대화를 듣고, 여자의 심정으로 가장 적절한 것을 고르시오.

① 설렘　　② 슬픔
③ 부러움　④ 수줍음
⑤ 실망스러움

08

M: Mona, what's up? You look different today.

W: Well, it's _____ _____ _____ _____.

M: You mean, the dance audition?

W: Yeah, I _____ _____ _____ the first round!

M: Really? I'm so happy for you. When is the second round?

W: Next week. I'm practicing really hard. I _____ _____ for it!

다음 페이지에 계속 ➡

9. 대화를 듣고, 여자가 대화 직후에 할 일로 가장 적절한 것을 고르시오.

① 대본 수정하기
② 방송 녹음하기
③ 사진 찍으러 가기
④ 선생님 인터뷰하기
⑤ 학교 홈페이지 확인하기

09 M: Did you finish writing the script for the school _____?

W: Not yet. I still need some comments from the event organizer.

M: Did you find any _____ on the school website?

W: I did, but it doesn't have any _____.

M: Then why don't you go and interview Mr. Kim? He planned the _____ event.

W: That's a good idea. I'll go and interview him now.

고난도　대화화제추론

10. 대화를 듣고, 무엇에 관한 내용인지 가장 적절한 것을 고르시오.

① 환경 오염 원인
② 동네 행사 일정
③ 분리수거 방법
④ 환경 보호 동아리
⑤ 쓰레기 재활용

10 W: Minsu, I heard about your environment club. Can I join?

M: Anyone _____ _____ protecting the environment is welcome.

W: What kind of activities do you guys do?

M: We meet every Saturday to _____ _____ the neighborhood.

W: Okay. I'll see you on Saturday then.

11. 대화를 듣고, 두 사람이 함께 이용할 교통수단으로 가장 적절한 것을 고르시오.
   ① 배   ② 버스
   ③ 기차   ④ 지하철
   ⑤ 자전거

11 *(Cell phone rings.)*

M: Hey, Gina!

W: Hey, Minho! Do you want to go to Island Park?

M: Sure. How do we get there?

W: We can _____ _____ _____.

M: Hey, there's _____ _____ _____ _____.
   How about trying it?

W: A ferry sounds a little scary.

M: It's _____ _____. Trust me.

W: Okay, then. Let's go now!

🇺🇸🇬🇧

12. 대화를 듣고, 여자가 카드를 쓰는 이유로 가장 적절한 것을 고르시오.
   ① 엄마의 생신이어서
   ② 영어 대회에서 입상해서
   ③ 교환학생이 올 예정이어서
   ④ 반 친구들과 헤어지게 되어서
   ⑤ 선생님이 전근을 가게 되어서

12 M: Hyomin, what are you doing?

W: I'm _____ a card to Ms. Newman, Dad.

M: You mean your English teacher?

W: Yes. She is _____ _____ a different
   school, so the whole class is _____
   _____ _____ _____.

M: The whole class? That's why the card is so big.

W: Yes, we are saying our thanks and good-byes.

다음 페이지에 계속 ➡

13. 대화를 듣고, 두 사람이 대화하는 장소로 가장 적절한 곳을 고르시오.

① 서점 ② 미용실
③ 미술관 ④ 헬스장
⑤ 영화관

13

M: Do you see that big _____ over there?

W: Yeah, and look at all those paintings on the wall.

M: They're really beautiful. But we _____ _____ _____ _____, okay?

W: Okay. There are so many people here.

M: Right, but I'm still glad we came today.

W: Yeah, me too.

M: Let's go _____ _____ the next _____.

14. 대화를 듣고, 두 사람이 찾고 있는 리모 컨의 위치로 가장 적절한 것을 고르시오.

14

W: Mark, can you _____ _____ the TV volume, please?

M: Sure, but I don't know where the TV remote control is.

W: I think I saw it on the sofa.

M: It's not there. It must be somewhere else.

W: Oh, it's right there, _____ _____ the flower vase.

M: I see it! I'll turn down the _____ now.

15. 대화를 듣고, 여자가 남자에게 부탁한 일
로 가장 적절한 것을 고르시오.

① 차 태워주기
② 저녁 요리하기
③ 책 반납하기
④ 간식 사 오기
⑤ 옷 찾아다 주기

15 *(Cell phone rings.)*

M: Hi, Kate. I'm at the supermarket. Do you need anything?

W: No, but can I ask you a favor?

M: Sure, _____ _____ _____ _____ for you?

W: Can you _____ _____ my shirt at the cleaner's on your way home?

M: Sure, no problem.

16. 대화를 듣고, 여자가 남자에게 제안한 것
으로 가장 적절한 것을 고르시오.

① 운동하기
② 집에서 일하기
③ 퍼레이드에 참가하기
④ 걸어서 집에 가기
⑤ 버스 노선 검색하기

16 W: Joel, what are you doing here?

M: I'm _____ _____ _____ _____ to go home. But it's taking so long.

W: Oh, the buses _____ _____ as usual. There's a big parade today.

M: Really? I didn't know that. What should I do?

W: How about _____ _____?

M: Yeah, walking home will be better.

다음 페이지에 계속 ➡

17. 대화를 듣고, 남자가 휴일에 한 일로 가장 적절한 것을 고르시오.
   ① 숙제하기
   ② 요리 배우기
   ③ 피아노 배우기
   ④ 공연 관람하기
   ⑤ 가족 여행 가기

17

M: Jessie, how was your holiday?

W: It was great. I _____ _____ _____ _____ with my family.

M: Oh, where did you go?

W: We went to Jeju Island. I had so much fun! How did you _____ _____ _____?

M: I learned how to play the piano.

W: That's wonderful!

18. 대화를 듣고, 여자의 직업을 고르시오.
   ① cook
   ② teacher
   ③ tour guide
   ④ computer programmer
   ⑤ doctor

18

M: You look tired. Did you _____ _____ last night?

W: Yes. I only got three hours of sleep because I had to work.

M: Oh, how's your work going?

W: Actually, very good. My team just _____ _____ a new educational software program.

M: Good for you. You are a very brilliant _____.

W: Thank you. This new computer software will help students _____ _____ math more easily.

19. 대화를 듣고, 여자의 마지막 말에 이어질 남자의 말로 가장 적절한 것을 고르시오.

Man: _____

① I'm so tired.
② Let's hurry up.
③ That's not for me.
④ You should take a break.
⑤ I don't like action movies.

19

W: Dad, when does the movie start?

M: In 10 minutes.

W: Oh, no! We still _____ _____ _____ the tickets.

M: And we need to get some popcorn, too.

W: Okay! Let's go now!

M: <u>Let's hurry up.</u>

20. 대화를 듣고, 여자의 마지막 말에 이어질 남자의 말로 가장 적절한 것을 고르시오.

Man: _____

① No. I don't like jogging.
② No problem. I'll call you later.
③ Okay. I'll be ready in 5 minutes.
④ You can use my laptop computer.
⑤ I don't like vanilla ice cream.

20

M: Mom, can we go get some ice cream later?

W: Sure, Sam. But why do you want to go later?

M: I want to _____ watching this movie first.

W: Well, you know it's going to _____ _____ in the afternoon.

M: Oh, I didn't think about that. I guess it's much cooler in the morning.

W: Yes. So, _____ we go now?

M: <u>Okay. I'll be ready in 5 minutes.</u>

21
회
딕
테
이
션

Words & Expressions Review 21

● 다음 단어를 암기하세요.

문제	번호	단어	뜻
1	□ 1	wing	날개
	□ 2	instead	대신에
	□ 3	strong	튼튼한
	□ 4	What's up?	잘 지냈어?, 요즘 어때?
	□ 5	awards ceremony	시상식
4	□ 6	win first prize	1등상을 타다
	□ 7	competition	대회, 시합
	□ 8	achievement	성취, 업적
	□ 9	introduce	~를 소개하다
5	□ 10	hobby	취미
	□ 11	gentle	온화한, 순한
	□ 12	place	집
6	□ 13	miss	놓치다
	□ 14	relief	안심
	□ 15	succeed	성공하다
7	□ 16	field	분야, 들판
	□ 17	look forward to ~	~을 기대하다
	□ 18	audition	(가수 · 배우 등의) 오디션
	□ 19	make it through	~을 통과하다
8	□ 20	round	(토너먼트 경기의) 라운드
	□ 21	practice	연습하다
	□ 22	can't wait for	~이 정말 기대되다

문제	번호	단어	뜻
	□ 23	broadcast	방송
9	□ 24	comment	의견
	□ 25	quote	인용문, 인용 어구
	□ 26	whole	전체의, 전부의
	□ 27	environment	환경
10	□ 28	interested in ~	~에 관심이 있는
	□ 29	protect	보호하다
11	□ 30	perfectly	완전히, 지극히
12	□ 31	leave	남기다
13	□ 32	statue	조각상
	□ 33	exhibit	전시품
	□ 34	turn down	(소리를) 낮추다
14	□ 35	volume	음량, 용량
	□ 36	flower vase	꽃병
15	□ 37	ask A a favor	A에게 부탁하다
16	□ 38	run	(버스 · 기차 등이) 운행하다, 다니다
	□ 39	as usual	평소처럼
17	□ 40	holiday	휴일, 휴가
	□ 41	develop	개발하다
18	□ 42	educational	교육용의
	□ 43	brilliant	능력 있는, 뛰어난
20	□ 44	get + 비교급	점점 더 ~해지다

M1(17)_W_21

● 왼쪽 단어장의 뜻이 보이지 않게 반으로 접고, 학습한 단어의 뜻을 아래 빈칸에 적어주세요.

1	gentle		23	run
2	introduce		24	miss
3	interested in ~		25	turn down
4	as usual		26	perfectly
5	What's up?		27	exhibit
6	field		28	succeed
7	awards ceremony		29	practice
8	look forward to ~		30	develop
9	educational		31	instead
10	wing		32	relief
11	audition		33	achievement
12	volume		34	get + 비교급
13	win first prize		35	ask A a favor
14	holiday		36	flower vase
15	protect		37	environment
16	leave		38	brilliant
17	make it through		39	broadcast
18	place		40	quote
19	round		41	comment
20	can't wait for		42	statue
21	hobby		43	strong
22	whole		44	competition

21
회
단
어

전국 15개 시·도 교육청 공동주관 및 서울시 연합 내신

22회 중학영어듣기 모의고사

모두 **미국식 발음(US)**
으로 녹음

20문제 중 5문제에 **영국식 발음
(US+UK)**을 포함하여 녹음

📖 정답 및 해석 p. 91

1

다음을 듣고, 'this'가 가리키는 것으로 가장 적절한 것을 고르시오.

①   ②   ③   ④   ⑤

2

대화를 듣고, 여자가 구입할 동전지갑으로 가장 적절한 것을 고르시오.

①   ②   ③   ④   ⑤

3

다음을 듣고, 7월 4일 오전의 날씨로 적절한 것을 고르시오.

①   ②   ③   ④   ⑤

4

대화를 듣고, 여자의 마지막 말의 의도로 가장 적절한 것을 고르시오.

① 거절   ② 축하   ③ 허락   ④ 초대   ⑤ 위로

5 다음을 듣고, 여자가 수영 경기에 대해 언급하지 <u>않은</u> 것을 고르시오.

① 날짜　　　② 종목　　　③ 장소　　　④ 신청 방법　　　⑤ 우승 상품

6 대화를 듣고, 두 사람이 만날 시각을 고르시오.

① 9:30 a.m.　　② 11:00 a.m.　　③ 11:30 a.m.　　④ 2:00 p.m.　　⑤ 6:30 p.m.

7 대화를 듣고, 남자의 장래 희망을 고르시오.

① 의사　　　② 소방관　　　③ 작가　　　④ 가수　　　⑤ 변호사

8 대화를 듣고, 남자의 심정으로 가장 적절한 것을 고르시오.

① 기쁨　　　② 수줍음　　　③ 당황스러움　　　④ 지루함　　　⑤ 자랑스러움

9 대화를 듣고, 남자가 대화 직후에 할 일로 가장 적절한 것을 고르시오.

① 포스터 붙이기　　　　　　　② 연설문 수정하기
③ 영화표 구매하기　　　　　　④ 연설하는 모습 녹화하기
⑤ 학생회장 선거 출마하기

10 대화를 듣고, 무엇에 관한 내용인지 가장 적절한 것을 고르시오.

① 자원 절약 방법　　　　　　② 여름철 보양 음식
③ 여름철 식중독 예방　　　　④ 인터넷 사용 예절
⑤ 예방 접종 안내

11번~20번 문제는 다음 페이지에 ➡

11 대화를 듣고, 두 사람이 함께 이동할 방법으로 가장 적절한 것을 고르시오.

① 택시   ② 도보   ③ 기차   ④ 버스   ⑤ 지하철

12 대화를 듣고, 여자가 도서관에 가는 이유로 가장 적절한 것을 고르시오.

① 책을 기증하려고   ② 봉사활동을 하려고
③ 자료를 검색하려고   ④ 그림책을 구매하려고
⑤ 무료 강좌를 수강하려고

13 대화를 듣고, 두 사람이 대화하는 장소로 가장 적절한 곳을 고르시오.

① 공원   ② 꽃집   ③ 동물 병원
④ 과일 가게   ⑤ 핸드폰 수리점

14 대화를 듣고, 편의점의 위치로 가장 알맞은 곳을 고르시오.

15 대화를 듣고, 남자가 여자에게 부탁한 일로 가장 적절한 것을 고르시오.

① 옷 수선하기   ② 서랍장 옮기기
③ 선물 포장하기   ④ 옷장 정리하기
⑤ 세탁물 찾아오기

16 대화를 듣고, 남자가 여자에게 제안한 것으로 가장 적절한 것을 고르시오.

① 베이킹 수업 듣기　　　　　② 제과점에서 일하기
③ 조리 도구 구입하기　　　　④ 수제 과자 판매하기
⑤ 요리 자격증 취득하기

17 대화를 듣고, 여자가 주말에 한 일로 가장 적절한 것을 고르시오.

① 미술 수업 듣기　　　　　　② 목도리 뜨개질하기
③ 극장에서 영화 보기　　　　④ 친구들과 쇼핑하기
⑤ 아빠 생신 파티 하기

18 대화를 듣고, 여자의 직업으로 가장 적절한 것을 고르시오.

① 간호사　　② 요리사　　③ 학원 강사　　④ 뮤지컬 배우　　⑤ 신발 가게 점원

[19~20] 대화를 듣고, 남자의 마지막 말에 이어질 여자의 말로 가장 적절한 것을 고르시오.

19 Woman: _____

① I like running.　　　　　② It's raining outside.
③ It's 8 dollars in total.　　④ They look good on you.
⑤ You can collect them on Friday.

20 Woman: _____

① I have to finish my homework.　　② Let's go swimming tomorrow.
③ I'm free in the afternoon.　　　　④ I had a good time.
⑤ It's snowing.

Dictation Test 22

녹음을 다시
들으면서 빈칸을
채워주세요

Dictation(받아쓰기)은 본문을 받아쓰면서 영어듣기의 집중력을 향상시키고 다양한 표현을 정리하기 위한 영어듣기 학습법입니다. **녹음을 다시 듣고, 빈칸에 알맞은 단어를 써 보세요.**
※Dictation의 정답은 듣기 대본의 밑줄 친 부분을 확인하세요.

📖 정답 p. 91

맞은 개수 　　　／
총137개

그림정보파악(담화)

1. 다음을 듣고, 'this'가 가리키는 것으로 가장 적절한 것을 고르시오.

① ② ③ ④ ⑤

01 W: You can find this in your _____. This is in the shape of human shoulders. This is _____ _____ _____ a coat, jacket, or dress. This _____ _____ in clothing. Sometimes, this has clips to hang skirts and pants. What is this?

그림정보파악(대화)

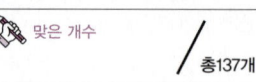

2. 대화를 듣고, 여자가 구입할 동전지갑으로 가장 적절한 것을 고르시오.

① ② ③ ④

⑤

02 W: Hi, I'm looking for a coin purse.

M: We have _____ ones and _____ ones.

W: I like square ones more.

M: Okay, how about this one with a _____ _____ _____?

W: Hmm… Do you have another one?

M: Sure, we also have this square one with a rabbit on it.

W: I like rabbits. _____ _____ _____.

---

3. 다음을 듣고, 7월 4일 오전의 날씨로 적절한 것을 고르시오.

①  ②

③  ④

⑤

03 W: If you were _____ _____ see the fireworks in the park this July 4th, don't worry because the weather will be beautiful. There will be early morning showers that will _____ _____ _____ sunny, clear skies in the afternoon. There will be winds coming in from the west to provide a nice, cool _____ by nightfall.

마지막말의도파악

4. 대화를 듣고, 여자의 마지막 말의 의도로 가장 적절한 것을 고르시오.

① 거절　　② 축하
③ 허락　　④ 초대
⑤ 위로

04 W: What did you do last night?

M: I watched the soccer game against Japan.

W: It must have been exciting.

M: Yes, I cheered for our victory _____ _____ _____ _____.

W: So, how did it go?

M: We won! I am so happy.

W: Congratulations! This _____ _____ a celebration.

다음 페이지에 계속 ➡

22 회 딕테이션

5. 다음을 듣고, 여자가 수영 경기에 대해 언급하지 <u>않은</u> 것을 고르시오.
   ① 날짜   ② 종목
   ③ 장소   ④ 신청 방법
   ⑤ 우승 상품

05 W: This summer, we're having a swimming race for middle school students. It's _____ for July 20th. There will be different swimming races like freestyle and backstroke. The competition will _____ _____ at the community pool. Students can _____ _____ _____ the competition through their school's sports _____ or on the community center's website.

6. 대화를 듣고, 두 사람이 만날 시각을 고르시오.
   ① 9:30 a.m.   ② 11:00 a.m.
   ③ 11:30 a.m.   ④ 2:00 p.m.
   ⑤ 6:30 p.m.

06 M: Let's go to Disneyland.

W: That's a _____ _____. What time shall we meet?

M: How about _____ _____ 9:30 tomorrow?

W: 9:30? I think that is _____ _____. I have something to do in the morning.

M: Then how about two hours later?

W: _____ _____? That will be fine.

7. 대화를 듣고, 남자의 장래 희망을 고르시오.

① 의사　　② 소방관
③ 작가　　④ 가수
⑤ 변호사

07
W: Bill, what do you want to be when you _____ _____?

M: Well, when I was little, I wanted to be a doctor.

W: Really? I didn't know that you were _____ _____ medical science.

M: I'm not interested in that _____. Now, I want to become a singer.

W: I'm sure you will be a good singer. You sing very well.

8. 대화를 듣고, 남자의 심정으로 가장 적절한 것을 고르시오.

① 기쁨　　② 수줍음
③ 당황스러움　　④ 지루함
⑤ 자랑스러움

08
W: Wake up, Brian! You're late _____ _____! It's already 9:30.

M: No, it's seven o'clock. _____ _____ the clock.

W: The clock is broken. Look at my watch. It's 9:30.

M: Oh, no! I'm so late for school. It's embarrassing!

W: Come on. Don't cry _____ _____ _____. I'll drive you to school now.

22
회
딕
테
이
션

다음 페이지에 계속 ➡

9. 대화를 듣고, 남자가 대화 직후에 할 일
   로 가장 적절한 것을 고르시오.
   ① 포스터 붙이기
   ② 연설문 수정하기
   ③ 영화표 구매하기
   ④ 연설하는 모습 녹화하기
   ⑤ 학생회장 선거 출마하기

09

W: Hi, Paul. What are you doing?

M: Hi, Ellen. I'm practicing a _____ for the school election.

W: You're _____ _____ president, right? Good luck with that.

M: Thanks. I want to look calm and _____. I'm not sure I'm doing it right, though.

W: Then, how about taking a video of yourself giving a speech and _____ it?

M: That's brilliant. I'll give it a try right away.

10. 대화를 듣고, 무엇에 관한 내용인지 가장
    적절한 것을 고르시오.
    ① 자원 절약 방법
    ② 여름철 보양 음식
    ③ 여름철 식중독 예방
    ④ 인터넷 사용 예절
    ⑤ 예방 접종 안내

10

W: Ted, here are some _____ _____ _____ for summer.

M: What are they, Mom?

W: First, always wash your hands before you eat.

M: I already know that. What else?

W: Don't keep food at _____ _____ for more than one hour on hot summer days.

M: Why is that?

W: Food _____ _____ in summer because the increase in temperature causes bacteria to multiply.

11. 대화를 듣고, 두 사람이 함께 이동할 방법으로 가장 적절한 것을 고르시오.
① 택시   ② 도보
③ 기차   ④ 버스
⑤ 지하철

11
W: Min, do you want to go to this new café in Seongsu-dong with me?

M: Yeah, sure. How can we get there?

W: Well, we can _____ _____ _____, the subway, or a taxi.

M: If we take a taxi, it will _____ _____ _____.

W: Then, should we take the bus?

M: I _____ _____ _____. So, I think we should take the subway.

W: Sounds good.

12. 대화를 듣고, 여자가 도서관에 가는 이유로 가장 적절한 것을 고르시오.
① 책을 기증하려고
② 봉사활동을 하려고
③ 자료를 검색하려고
④ 그림책을 구매하려고
⑤ 무료 강좌를 수강하려고

12
M: Wonjee, where are you going?

W: I'm going to the library to _____ _____ _____.

M: Oh, are they selling used books?

W: Yes, they sell old books at a very _____ _____. I want to buy a _____ _____ for my cousin.

M: That's nice. Can I join you?

W: Of course. It'll be fun.

다음 페이지에 계속 ➡

22
회
딕
테
이
션

13. 대화를 듣고, 두 사람이 대화하는 장소로
    가장 적절한 곳을 고르시오.

   ① 공원
   ② 꽃집
   ③ 동물 병원
   ④ 과일 가게
   ⑤ 핸드폰 수리점

13

M: I'd like to _____ _____ _____ about some apples I bought here yesterday.

W: What's the problem?

M: I found that some of them _____ _____ when I got home.

W: Oh, could you show them to me, please?

M: Here you go.

W: I'm sorry for the _____. Would you like a refund?

M: Yes, please.

---

14. 대화를 듣고, 편의점의 위치로 가장 알맞
    은 곳을 고르시오.

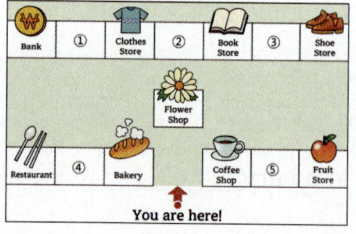

14

W: Excuse me, I'm trying to find a _____ _____. Where can I find one?

M: Do you see the flower shop over there?

W: Yes, I see it.

M: _____ _____ to the flower shop and _____ _____.

W: Go straight and then turn left?

M: That's right. It will be _____ _____ _____. It's between the restaurant and the bakery.

W: Thank you.

15. 대화를 듣고, 남자가 여자에게 부탁한 일로 가장 적절한 것을 고르시오.

① 옷 수선하기
② 서랍장 옮기기
③ 선물 포장하기
④ 옷장 정리하기
⑤ 세탁물 찾아오기

15

W: Paul, what are you _____ _____?

M: My favorite blue shirt, Mom.

W: It's in the top drawer.

M: Found it! Oh, Mom, _____ _____ _____

_____ this.

W: One of the buttons is _____.

M: Can you put a new button on the shirt?

W: Sure. I'll do it right away.

16. 대화를 듣고, 남자가 여자에게 제안한 것으로 가장 적절한 것을 고르시오.

① 베이킹 수업 듣기
② 제과점에서 일하기
③ 조리 도구 구입하기
④ 수제 과자 판매하기
⑤ 요리 자격증 취득하기

16

W: Ben, do you have a hobby?

M: Yes, I bake _____ _____. How about you?

W: I don't have a hobby, but I'd like to have one.

M: Do you like bread and cookies?

W: Yes, I love them.

M: Then why don't you _____ _____ _____

_____?

W: Sure, that sounds fun!

22
회
딕
테
이
션

다음 페이지에 계속 ➡

17. 대화를 듣고, 여자가 주말에 한 일로 가장 적절한 것을 고르시오.

① 미술 수업 듣기
② 목도리 뜨개질하기
③ 극장에서 영화 보기
④ 친구들과 쇼핑하기
⑤ 아빠 생신 파티 하기

17
W: Hajun, how was your weekend?

M: It was fun. I went to the movies with my friends. How about you?

W: I _____ _____ _____ for my dad. It's his birthday next week.

M: Sounds wonderful! Where did you learn _____ _____ _____?

W: At the community center. I _____ _____ _____ for three months last year.

18. 대화를 듣고, 여자의 직업으로 가장 적절한 것을 고르시오.

① 간호사
② 요리사
③ 학원 강사
④ 뮤지컬 배우
⑤ 신발 가게 점원

18
W: How can I help you?

M: I'd like to try on those _____ _____.

W: Of course. What size are you?

M: I _____ wear 270 mm for sneakers.

W: Okay. These are size 270. Would you like to _____ _____ _____?

M: Sure. [pause] They fit great! Is there a mirror _____?

W: Yes, there's one over there.

19. 대화를 듣고, 남자의 마지막 말에 이어질 여자의 말로 가장 적절한 것을 고르시오.

Woman: _____

① I like running.
② It's raining outside.
③ It's 8 dollars in total.
④ They look good on you.
⑤ You can collect them on Friday.

19

W: How can I help you?

M: I'd like to get this jacket _____-_____, please.

W: Sure. What's your name?

M: Eric Kim. Can I also get these trainers _____?

W: Of course. Is there anything else?

M: No. When can I _____ _____ _____?

W: You can collect them on Friday.

20. 대화를 듣고, 남자의 마지막 말에 이어질 여자의 말로 가장 적절한 것을 고르시오.

Woman: _____

① I have to finish my homework.
② Let's go swimming tomorrow.
③ I'm free in the afternoon.
④ I had a good time.
⑤ It's snowing.

20

W: It's _____ _____ today.

M: I'm _____ _____ the beach this afternoon. Do you want to come with me?

W: Sorry. I would love to, but I can't.

M: Why not? Are you going somewhere?

W: No, I have _____ _____ to do.

M: What is it?

W: I have to finish my homework.

22회 딕테이션

Words & Expressions Review 22

● 다음 단어를 암기하세요.

문제	번호	단어	뜻
1	□1	closet	옷장
	□2	shoulder	어깨
	□3	hang	걸다
	□4	prevent	막다, 예방하다
	□5	wrinkle	주름
2	□6	look for	~을 찾다
	□7	another	다른
3	□8	fireworks	불꽃놀이
	□9	shower	소나기, 샤워
	□10	west	서쪽
	□11	breeze	산들바람
	□12	nightfall	해질녘
4	□13	call for ~	~을 필요로 하다, 요구하다
	□14	celebration	축하
5	□15	schedule	예정하다
	□16	take place	열리다, 개최되다
	□17	competition	대회
	□18	department	부, 부서
7	□19	be interested in ~	~에 관심이 있다
	□20	medical science	의학
8	□21	be late for ~	~에 늦다
	□22	broken	고장 난, 부서진

문제	번호	단어	뜻
9	□23	run for ~	~에 출마하다
	□24	president	회장, 대통령
	□25	give a speech	연설하다
	□26	review	확인하다, 검토하다
	□27	room temperature	상온, 평상시 온도
10	□28	spoil	상하다, 썩다
	□29	multiply	증식시키다, 늘리다
12	□30	used	중고의
13	□31	rotten	썩은, 부패한
	□32	inconvenience	불편, 애로
14	□33	restaurant	음식점, 식당
15	□34	missing	없어진
	□35	right away	즉시
16	□36	join	함께 하다
17	□37	knit	뜨개질하다
18	□38	try ~ on	~을 신어 보다, 입어 보다
	□39	running shoes	운동화
	□40	nearby	근처에, 가까이에
19	□41	trainers	운동화
	□42	collect	가지러 가다
20	□43	something else	다른 무언가
	□44	finish	끝마치다, 끝내다

M1(17)_W_22

● 왼쪽 단어장의 뜻이 보이지 않게 반으로 접고, 학습한 단어의 뜻을 아래 빈칸에 적어주세요.

1	be interested in ~		23	missing
2	try ~ on		24	president
3	right away		25	look for
4	rotten		26	call for ~
5	department		27	schedule
6	restaurant		28	celebration
7	wrinkle		29	broken
8	medical science		30	room temperature
9	trainers		31	inconvenience
10	multiply		32	finish
11	used		33	prevent
12	running shoes		34	hang
13	another		35	review
14	give a speech		36	closet
15	shoulder		37	knit
16	fireworks		38	breeze
17	west		39	be late for ~
18	something else		40	join
19	run for ~		41	spoil
20	nearby		42	competition
21	take place		43	shower
22	collect		44	nightfall

22
회
단
어

전국 15개 시·도 교육청 공동주관 및 서울시 연합 내신

23회 중학영어듣기 모의고사

M1(17)_23_US
모두 **미국식 발음(US)**
으로 녹음

M1(17)_23_UK
20문제 중 5문제에 **영국식 발음**
(US+UK)을 포함하여 녹음

정답 및 해석 p. 95

1 다음을 듣고, 'this'가 가리키는 것으로 가장 적절한 것을 고르시오.

①  ② 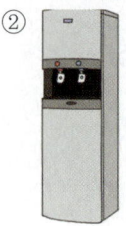 ③ 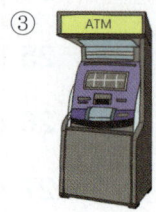 ④  ⑤

2 대화를 듣고, 여자가 구입할 인형으로 가장 적절한 것을 고르시오.

①  ②  ③  ④  ⑤

3 다음을 듣고, 일요일의 날씨로 적절한 것을 고르시오.

①  ②  ③  ④  ⑤

4 대화를 듣고, 남자가 한 마지막 말의 의도로 가장 적절한 것을 고르시오.

① 거절　　　② 사과　　　③ 불평　　　④ 승낙　　　⑤ 후회

5 다음을 듣고, 남자가 작가에 대해 언급하지 <u>않은</u> 것을 고르시오.

① 이름   ② 출생지   ③ 출신 학교   ④ 나이   ⑤ 대표작

6 대화를 듣고, 두 사람이 이야기를 나누는 현재 시각을 고르시오.

① 7:00 p.m.   ② 7:30 p.m.   ③ 8:00 p.m.   ④ 8:30 p.m.   ⑤ 9:00 p.m.

7 대화를 듣고, 남자의 장래 희망으로 가장 적절한 것을 고르시오.

① 작가   ② 과학자   ③ 영화 감독
④ 운동 선수   ⑤ 우주 비행사

8 대화를 듣고, 여자의 심정으로 가장 적절한 것을 고르시오.

① 걱정스러움   ② 즐거움   ③ 슬픔   ④ 뿌듯함   ⑤ 실망스러움

9 대화를 듣고, 남자가 대화 직후에 할 일로 가장 적절한 것을 고르시오.

① 온라인 수업 듣기   ② 친구 병문안 가기
③ 그룹 채팅 방 만들기   ④ 디자인대회 참가하기
⑤ 선생님에게 질문하기

10 대화를 듣고, 무엇에 관한 내용인지 가장 적절한 것을 고르시오.

① 병원 예약   ② TV 드라마   ③ 의료 봉사
④ 교실 청소   ⑤ 컴퓨터 수리

11번~20번 문제는 다음 페이지에 ➡

11 대화를 듣고, 두 사람이 함께 이동할 방법으로 가장 적절한 것을 고르시오.

① 택시　　　　　② 도보　　　　　③ 기차
④ 버스　　　　　⑤ 자전거

12 대화를 듣고, 여자에게 당근이 필요한 이유로 가장 적절한 것을 고르시오.

① 케이크를 만들기 위해서　　　　② 다이어트를 하기 위해서
③ 토끼 먹이로 주기 위해서　　　　④ 갈아서 주스로 마시기 위해서
⑤ 샐러드 재료로 사용하기 위해서

13 대화를 듣고, 두 사람이 대화하는 장소로 가장 적절한 것을 고르시오.

① 부엌　　　　　② 식당　　　　　③ 주차장
④ 슈퍼마켓　　　⑤ 동물 병원

14 대화를 듣고, 남자가 가려고 하는 장소를 고르시오.

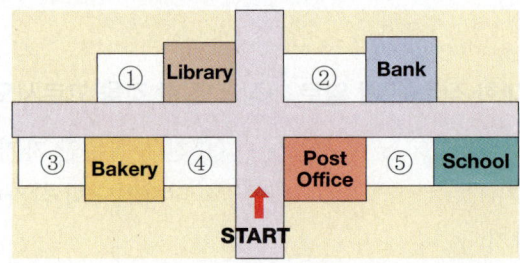

15 대화를 듣고, 남자가 여자에게 부탁한 일을 고르시오.

① 우산 가져오기　　　② 빨래 걷기　　　③ 일기 예보 확인하기
④ 과학 숙제 도와주기　　⑤ 화분 내놓기

16 대화를 듣고, 여자가 남자에게 제안한 것으로 가장 적절한 것을 고르시오.

① 눈을 쉬게 하기   ② 병원 가기
③ 진통제 복용하기   ④ 스트레칭 하기
⑤ 따뜻한 음료 마시기

17 대화를 듣고, 두 사람이 토요일에 할 일로 가장 적절한 것을 고르시오.

① 요리하기   ② 집 꾸미기
③ 아이들 돌보기   ④ 친구들 초대하기
⑤ 생일 선물 고르기

18 대화를 듣고, 남자의 직업으로 가장 적절한 것을 고르시오.

① 소방관   ② 기타리스트   ③ 에어컨 수리 기사
④ 건축가   ⑤ 택시 기사

19 대화를 듣고, 남자의 마지막 말에 이어질 여자의 응답으로 가장 적절한 것을 고르시오.

Woman: _____

① I will look for some science books at the library.
② Sure. Let's go there on Saturday.
③ I can help you to write a book.
④ I will go there by subway.
⑤ I'm glad that my vacation has just started.

20 대화를 듣고, 여자의 마지막 말에 이어질 남자의 응답으로 가장 적절한 것을 고르시오.

Man: _____

① I don't like pasta.   ② I just followed the recipe.
③ I'll bring your dessert.   ④ I found it on the internet.
⑤ You can make me pasta later.

Dictation Test 23

녹음을 다시 듣으면서 빈칸을 채워주세요

M1(17)_23_D

Dictation(받아쓰기)은 본문을 받아쓰면서 영어듣기의 집중력을 향상시키고 다양한 표현을 정리하기 위한 영어듣기 학습법입니다. 녹음을 다시 듣고, 빈칸에 알맞은 단어를 써 보세요.
※Dictation의 정답은 듣기 대본의 밑줄 친 부분을 확인하세요.

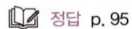 정답 p. 95

맞은 개수 / 총137개

고난도 그림정보파악(담화)

1. 다음을 듣고, 'this'가 가리키는 것으로 가장 적절한 것을 고르시오.

①
②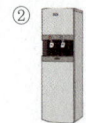
③
④
⑤

01 W: You can find this in many places like the subway station or the movie theater. You put some money into this and _____ _____ _____ under the drink of your choice. Then, you _____ _____ _____ out of this. You may also get _____ _____ back. What is this?

2025 영어듣기능력평가 1회 2번 변형

그림정보파악(대화)

2. 대화를 듣고, 여자가 구입할 인형으로 가장 적절한 것을 고르시오.

①
②
③
④
⑤

02 W: I'm looking for a _____ _____ for my three-year-old niece.

M: We have lions and deer in different styles.

W: She likes beautiful deer with big eyes.

M: How about this one _____ anything on its head?

W: That's perfect! The _____ deer looks cute. I'll take it.

3. 다음을 듣고, 일요일의 날씨로 적절한 것을 고르시오.

① 　②
③ 　④
⑤

03 W: This is Jenny Brown, from Weather Central. This is the weather report for Friday, November 17th. It will be sunny with _____ _____ today and tomorrow. But, the _____ _____ _____, we are expecting snow. It will be the first snow of the year. Thank you for _____ _____.

4. 대화를 듣고, 남자가 한 마지막 말의 의도로 가장 적절한 것을 고르시오.

① 거절　② 사과
③ 불평　④ 승낙
⑤ 후회

04 W: Rick, can you help me _____ basketball?

M: Sure. I have time on Sunday.

W: I need to practice _____ _____.

M: But I'm watching TV!

W: Come on. I _____ you with math before.

M: Then, it'll be just this _____.

다음 페이지에 계속 ➡

5. 다음을 듣고, 남자가 작가에 대해 언급하지 않은 것을 고르시오.

① 이름   ② 출생지
③ 출신 학교   ④ 나이
⑤ 대표작

05 M: Hello, everyone. Today, I'm going to tell you about a great writer of our time. His name is John Hamilton. He lives in New York, but he _____ _____ in London. He is 90 years old, but he _____ _____ every day. His most famous book _____ _____ *Wind from the West*.

6. 대화를 듣고, 두 사람이 이야기를 나누는 현재 시각을 고르시오.

① 7:00 p.m.   ② 7:30 p.m.
③ 8:00 p.m.   ④ 8:30 p.m.
⑤ 9:00 p.m.

06 W: Hi, Oliver. Did you watch the soccer game on TV last night?

M: Of course. David Lee is my favorite player.

W: Then, shall we watch the _____ on him together?

M: Sure. It's tomorrow, right?

W: No, it's tonight at 8 p.m.

M: Really? It's going to start in 30 minutes, then!

W: Are you saying it's 7:30 p.m. now? _____ _____ _____ _____!

7. 대화를 듣고, 남자의 장래 희망으로 가장 적절한 것을 고르시오.

① 작가
② 과학자
③ 영화 감독
④ 운동 선수
⑤ 우주 비행사

07 W: Jim, what are you reading?

M: I'm reading a science fiction novel. It's called *Life on Mars*.

W: You seem to read a lot of books _____ _____ _____.

M: Yeah! Actually my favorite book is *2001: A Space Odyssey*.

W: Wow! Do you want to go to space one day?

M: Yes, I want to become _____ _____ when I grow up.

W: I hope you achieve your dream!

---

8. 대화를 듣고, 여자의 심정으로 가장 적절한 것을 고르시오.

① 걱정스러움   ② 즐거움
③ 슬픔   ④ 뿌듯함
⑤ 실망스러움

08 M: Hi, Susie. Where are you going?

W: I'm going to the _____.

M: You have an exam tomorrow, don't you?

W: Yes, I do. I'm worried that I won't _____ _____ on the exam.

M: Why?

W: I didn't study that much.

M: I _____ _____ _____.

다음 페이지에 계속 ➡

23회 딕테이션

9. 대화를 듣고, 남자가 대화 직후에 할 일로 가장 적절한 것을 고르시오.

① 온라인 수업 듣기
② 친구 병문안 가기
③ 그룹 채팅 방 만들기
④ 디자인대회 참가하기
⑤ 선생님에게 질문하기

09 W: Jiho, we need to start preparing for the Google Science Fair that our team is _____ _____.

M: But our team member Andrew is sick. He didn't come to school today.

W: Then how should we _____ our project?

M: _____ _____ _____ make a group chat room online?

W: Good idea. Then, Andrew will be able to talk with us.

M: Okay. I'll make a _____ _____ room right now.

---

10. 대화를 듣고, 무엇에 관한 내용인지 가장 적절한 것을 고르시오.

① 병원 예약
② TV 드라마
③ 의료 봉사
④ 교실 청소
⑤ 컴퓨터 수리

10 W: Kyle, did you catch _____ _____ _____ of *Doctor Park*?

M: Of course! I never miss the show.

W: _____ _____ _____. Last night's ending was a bit _____ _____, wasn't it?

M: Yeah, it really was. Why would Park ignore his patients?

W: Exactly! I think the plot is _____ _____ _____.

M: I hope they make up for it on the next episode.

11. 대화를 듣고, 두 사람이 함께 이동할 방법으로 가장 적절한 것을 고르시오.
① 택시 ② 도보
③ 기차 ④ 버스
⑤ 자전거

11
W: Brock, do you want to go see the cherry blossoms this weekend?

M: _____ _____ _____! Where should we go?

W: Let's go to Jinhae! There will be a cherry blossom festival there.

M: Sounds good! Should we _____ _____ _____?

W: Why don't we take the bus? It's _____.

M: Alright. I'll check the bus schedule.

12. 대화를 듣고, 여자에게 당근이 필요한 이유로 가장 적절한 것을 고르시오.
① 케이크를 만들기 위해서
② 다이어트를 하기 위해서
③ 토끼 먹이로 주기 위해서
④ 갈아서 주스로 마시기 위해서
⑤ 샐러드 재료로 사용하기 위해서

12
M: Jisu, I'm going to order some _____ online. Do you need anything?

W: Yes, Dad. Please order some carrots for me.

M: Okay. What do you _____ _____ for?

W: Mom's birthday is coming up. So I want to bake her favorite carrot cake.

M: Oh, that's very _____ _____ _____. I'll order them right now.

W: Thank you.

다음 페이지에 계속 ➡

13. 대화를 듣고, 두 사람이 대화하는 장소로 가장 적절한 것을 고르시오.

① 부엌　　② 식당
③ 주차장　④ 슈퍼마켓
⑤ 동물 병원

13

M: Honey, do we need anything else before we go to the checkout counter?

W: Wait a minute. Let's check the grocery list and _____ _____ _____ what's in our shopping cart.

M: Let's see. Hmm… we forgot to buy dog food.

W: I'll _____ _____ _____. Do you know which _____ it is in?

M: It's in the aisle right next to us. Check the pet food section.

W: Okay, I'll be back in a minute.

14. 대화를 듣고, 남자가 가려고 하는 장소를 고르시오.

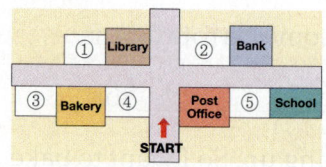

14

M: Excuse me. _____ _____ _____ _____ _____ the hospital?

W: The hospital? Go straight one block and turn left.

M: Go straight one block and turn left?

W: Yes. It will be on your right.

M: I see.

W: It's _____ _____ the bakery. You can't miss it.

M: Thanks.

15. 대화를 듣고, 남자가 여자에게 부탁한 일을 고르시오.

① 우산 가져오기
② 빨래 걷기
③ 일기 예보 확인하기
④ 과학 숙제 도와주기
⑤ 화분 내놓기

15 (Telephone rings.)

M: Mom, it's me. Are you home?

W: Not yet. I'm _____ _____ _____ home from the market.

M: Good! Could you _____ _____ _____ _____?

W: Ah, that plant you are growing for the science class?

M: Yes. It needs to be exposed to the sun. The weather forecast says _____ _____ _____ _____ in the afternoon.

W: OK. Don't worry about it.

16. 대화를 듣고, 여자가 남자에게 제안한 것으로 가장 적절한 것을 고르시오.

① 눈을 쉬게 하기
② 병원 가기
③ 진통제 복용하기
④ 스트레칭 하기
⑤ 따뜻한 음료 마시기

16 W: Hey, John, are you okay?

M: No, I have a _____ _____.

W: I'm sorry to hear that. Do you know what's _____ _____?

M: I think it's because I've been working on my computer all day.

W: Why don't you _____ _____ _____ for a few minutes?

M: Good idea. Maybe that will help.

23
회
딕
테
이
션

다음 페이지에 계속 ➡

17. 대화를 듣고, 두 사람이 토요일에 할 일로 가장 적절한 것을 고르시오.

① 요리하기
② 집 꾸미기
③ 아이들 돌보기
④ 친구들 초대하기
⑤ 생일 선물 고르기

17

M: Kelly, what are you doing this Saturday?

W: _____ _____. How about you?

M: I'm having a birthday party for my little brother

　　Greg, and I _____ _____ _____.

W: I'll help. What can I do?

M: Greg invited a lot of friends, and I'm worried about

　　_____ _____ _____ all the kids.

W: Oh, don't worry. Let's do it together.

18. 대화를 듣고, 남자의 직업으로 가장 적절한 것을 고르시오.

① 소방관
② 기타리스트
③ 에어컨 수리 기사
④ 건축가
⑤ 택시 기사

18

M: Where _____, ma'am?

W: 102 Main Street, please.

M: Edison Road is very busy _____ _____

　　_____ _____ the day. Shall I take Elm Road

　　instead?

W: Sure, how long will it take?

M: It will take about 15 minutes.

W: Great. It's quite hot today. Could you _____

　　_____ the air conditioner, please?

M: Of course.

19. 대화를 듣고, 남자의 마지막 말에 이어질 여자의 응답으로 가장 적절한 것을 고르시오.

Woman: _____

① I will look for some science books at the library.
② Sure. Let's go there on Saturday.
③ I can help you to write a book.
④ I will go there by subway.
⑤ I'm glad that my vacation has just started.

19

W: Hey, Paul! Have you finished your vacation homework?

M: No, not yet. There is too much homework… a science report, a book report…

W: _____ _____ _____ _____ _____. I haven't written a single word on my science report.

M: Me, neither. I don't know _____ _____ _____.

W: I'm thinking about going to the National Science Center.

M: That's a good idea. Can I join you?

W: Sure. Let's go there on Saturday.

20. 대화를 듣고, 여자의 마지막 말에 이어질 남자의 응답으로 가장 적절한 것을 고르시오.

Man: _____

① I don't like pasta.
② I just followed the recipe.
③ I'll bring your dessert.
④ I found it on the internet.
⑤ You can make me pasta later.

20

M: How was your meal, Mom?

W: It was _____. You are a great cook! Thank you, Paul.

M: It's _____ _____. What did you like the most?

W: Everything was so good. Especially the pasta; it was fantastic.

M: Good! I thought you'd like it when I saw the _____.

W: Oh, where did you get the recipe?

M: I found it on the internet.

Words & Expressions Review 23

● 다음 단어를 암기하세요.

문제	번호	단어	뜻
1	☐ 1	press	누르다
	☐ 2	out of ~	~에서, ~으로부터
	☐ 3	change	거스름돈, 잔돈
2	☐ 4	stuffed animal	봉제 동물 인형
	☐ 5	niece	조카딸
3	☐ 6	weather report	일기 예보
	☐ 7	the day after tomorrow	모레
	☐ 8	expect	~을 예상하다, 기대하다
4	☐ 9	practice	연습하다
	☐ 10	help A with B	A가 B하는 것을 돕다
5	☐ 11	still	여전히
6	☐ 12	favorite	가장 좋아하는
	☐ 13	documentary	다큐멘터리, 기록물
	☐ 14	had better + 동사	~하는 게 좋다
	☐ 15	hurry up	서두르다
7	☐ 16	seem to + 동사	~하는 것 같다
	☐ 17	related to ~	~과 관련된
	☐ 18	astronaut	우주비행사
	☐ 19	achieve	이루다, 달성하다
9	☐ 20	discuss	논의하다, 의논하다
	☐ 21	be able to + 동사	~할 수 있다
10	☐ 22	weird	이상한, 기이한

문제	번호	단어	뜻
10	☐ 23	ignore	무시하다
	☐ 24	mess up	엉망으로 만들다, 망치다
11	☐ 25	cherry blossom	벚꽃
	☐ 26	cheaper	(값이) 더 싼
12	☐ 27	grocery	식료품
13	☐ 28	compare	비교하다
	☐ 29	go get	가서 가져오다
14	☐ 30	across from ~	~의 건너편에
	☐ 31	You can't miss it.	틀림없이 찾을 겁니다.
15	☐ 32	expose	노출시키다
16	☐ 33	terrible	심한, 지독한
	☐ 34	cause	~을 야기하다
	☐ 35	rest	쉬게 하다
	☐ 36	for a few minutes	잠시
17	☐ 37	invite	초대하다
	☐ 38	be worried about ~	~을 걱정하다, 염려하다
	☐ 39	take care of ~	~를 돌보다
	☐ 40	instead	대신에
18	☐ 41	quite	아주, 꽤, 상당히
	☐ 42	turn on	켜다
19	☐ 43	You can say that again.	네 말이 맞아.
20	☐ 44	meal	식사

M1(17)_W_23

● 왼쪽 단어장의 뜻이 보이지 않게 반으로 접고, 학습한 단어의 뜻을 아래 빈칸에 적어주세요.

1	practice		23	achieve
2	turn on		24	expect
3	related to ~		25	ignore
4	niece		26	mess up
5	still		27	across from ~
6	weather report		28	instead
7	invite		29	the day after tomorrow
8	change		30	quite
9	be worried about ~		31	astronaut
10	You can say that again.		32	go get
11	seem to + 동사		33	meal
12	grocery		34	for a few minutes
13	rest		35	favorite
14	cheaper		36	hurry up
15	press		37	had better + 동사
16	terrible		38	weird
17	cherry blossom		39	discuss
18	stuffed animal		40	cause
19	out of ~		41	documentary
20	compare		42	expose
21	be able to + 동사		43	help A with B
22	take care of ~		44	You can't miss it.

23회 단어

24회 중학영어듣기 High Level 고난도 모의고사

정답 및 해석 p. 99

M1(17)_24_US
모두 **미국식 발음(US)**으로 녹음

M1(17)_24_UK
20문제 중 5문제에 **영국식 발음 (US+UK)**을 포함하여 녹음

1 다음을 듣고, 'I'가 무엇인지 가장 적절한 것을 고르시오.

①  ②  ③ 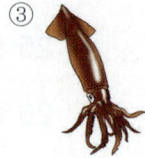 ④  ⑤

2 대화를 듣고, 남자가 구입할 좌식 테이블로 가장 적절한 것을 고르시오.

①  ②  ③

④  ⑤

3 다음을 듣고, 시카고의 날씨로 가장 적절한 것을 고르시오.

①  ②  ③  ④  ⑤

4 대화를 듣고, 남자가 한 마지막 말의 의도로 가장 적절한 것을 고르시오.

① 사과   ② 거절   ③ 후회   ④ 설득   ⑤ 칭찬

5 다음을 듣고, 남자가 환경 동아리에 대해 언급하지 <u>않은</u> 것을 고르시오.

① 이름   ② 인원수   ③ 모임 일정
④ 지도교사   ⑤ 활동 내용

6 대화를 듣고, 두 사람이 만날 시각을 고르시오.

① 1:30 p.m.   ② 2:00 p.m.   ③ 2:30 p.m.   ④ 3:00 p.m.   ⑤ 3:30 p.m.

7 대화를 듣고, 남자의 장래 희망으로 가장 적절한 것을 고르시오.

① 드러머   ② 의사   ③ 선생님   ④ 감독   ⑤ 작곡가

8 대화를 듣고, 남자의 심정으로 가장 적절한 것을 고르시오.

① relaxed   ② upset   ③ surprised
④ excited   ⑤ bored

9 대화를 듣고, 여자가 대화 직후에 할 일로 가장 적절한 것을 고르시오.

① 시험 범위 확인하기   ② 역사시험 공부하기   ③ 책 반납하기
④ 도서관 카드 만들기   ⑤ 문자 메시지 보내기

10 대화를 듣고, 무엇에 관한 내용인지 가장 적절한 것을 고르시오.

① 피아노 연주 영상 만들기   ② 생일 선물 고르기   ③ 결혼 축가 연습하기
④ 노래 경연대회 나가기   ⑤ 결혼 사진 찍기

11번~20번 문제는 다음 페이지에 ➡

11 대화를 듣고, 여자가 이용할 교통수단으로 가장 적절한 것을 고르시오.

① 비행기　　② 기차　　③ 배　　④ 버스　　⑤ 자전거

12 대화를 듣고, 남자가 지금 책을 빌릴 수 없는 이유로 가장 적절한 것을 고르시오.

① 학생증을 안 가져와서　　② 연체료를 안 내서
③ 대출 가능 횟수를 넘어서　　④ 다른 사람이 먼저 예약한 책이어서
⑤ 대출이 불가능한 책이어서

13 대화를 듣고, 두 사람이 대화하는 장소로 가장 적절한 곳을 고르시오.

① 은행　　② 병원　　③ 영화관　　④ 농구장　　⑤ 헬스장

14 Handmade Soap Workshop for Kids에 관한 다음 내용을 듣고, 표에서 일치하지 않는 것을 고르시오.

Handmade Soap Workshop for Kids	
① 일시	this Sunday, 2 p.m.
② 행사 내용	make their own soaps
③ 행사 시간	1 hour
④ 참가비	$5
⑤ 등록 장소	front desk at the community center

15 대화를 듣고, 남자가 여자에게 부탁한 일로 가장 적절한 것을 고르시오.

① 청소하기　　② 음악 소리 줄이기　　③ 이사 도와주기
④ 같이 식사하기　　⑤ 음식점 정보 알려주기

16 대화를 듣고, 남자가 여자에게 제안한 것으로 가장 적절한 것을 고르시오.

① 앱 다운받기　　　　② 도서관 방문하기　　　　③ 책 빌리기
④ 친구에게 전화하기　　⑤ 휴대전화 꾸미기

17 대화를 듣고, 남자가 지난 여름방학에 한 일로 가장 적절한 것을 고르시오.

① 수영 배우기　　　　② 모형 비행기 만들기　　③ 과학 숙제하기
④ 캠핑 가기　　　　　⑤ 친척 방문하기

18 대화를 듣고, 남자의 직업으로 가장 적절한 것을 고르시오.

① 아나운서　　　　　② 축구 선수　　　　　③ 요리 강사
④ 호텔 지배인　　　　⑤ 추리소설 작가

[19~20]　대화를 듣고, 여자의 마지막 말에 이어질 남자의 말로 가장 적절한 것을 고르시오.

19 Man: _____

① I'll visit you there in the hospital.　② It was nice seeing you at the store.
③ I'll bring the groceries to you.　④ I hope you get better soon.
⑤ I received the hospital bill.

20 Man: _____

① Congratulations!　② She likes cheese.
③ I'll come at 5 o'clock.　④ I pick her up from work.
⑤ It's her birthday tomorrow.

Dictation Test 24

M1(17)_24_D

Dictation(받아쓰기)은 본문을 받아쓰면서 영어듣기의 집중력을 향상시키고 다양한 표현을 정리하기 위한 영어듣기 학습법입니다. **녹음을 다시 듣고, 빈칸에 알맞은 단어를 써 보세요.**
※Dictation의 정답은 듣기 대본의 밑줄 친 부분을 확인하세요.

정답 p. 99

맞은 개수 / 총128개

그림정보파악(담화)

1. 다음을 듣고, 'I'가 무엇인지 가장 적절한 것을 고르시오.

①  ②

③   ④

⑤

01 W: I live in the ocean. I have _____ _____, heart or bones. I look like _____ _____ _____ in the water. I sometimes _____ people when they touch me. What am I?

그림정보파악(대화)

2. 대화를 듣고, 남자가 구입할 좌식 테이블로 가장 적절한 것을 고르시오.

①  ②

③  ④

⑤

02 W: May I help you?

M: I'm _____ _____ a mini table.

W: How about this oval table with hearts on it?

M: I don't like hearts. _____, I think rectangular tables are _____.

W: Then, how is this one? It's rectangular and the stars look cool.

M: I like stars. I'll _____ it.

---

3. 다음을 듣고, 시카고의 날씨로 가장 적절한 것을 고르시오.

① 　②

③ 　④

⑤

03 M: Good morning! This is your local weather update. Today, it will be sunny in New York City. But watch out for _____ in Miami. In Boston, there might be some _____ _____. And in Chicago, it's going to be very windy. If you're in Chicago, make sure to _____ _____ your hat!

4. 대화를 듣고, 남자가 한 마지막 말의 의도로 가장 적절한 것을 고르시오.
① 사과　　② 거절
③ 후회　　④ 설득
⑤ 칭찬

04 M: Jane, do you have any plans after school?

W: Nothing special. Why?

M: I'm planning to go downtown with our classmates. Do you want to join us?

W: Thanks for _____ me, but I think I'll just stay home tonight.

M: Are you sure? _____ _____ _____ the new bowling alley. It'll be fun!

W: I don't know. I'm a bit tired. I _____ _____ _____ doing homework last night.

M: Oh, come on! It's Friday! You can rest all day tomorrow!

다음 페이지에 계속 ➡

5. 다음을 듣고, 남자가 환경 동아리에 대해 언급하지 않은 것을 고르시오.

① 이름
② 인원수
③ 모임 일정
④ 지도교사
⑤ 활동 내용

05 M: Let me tell you about our school's environmental club. It's _____ the Green Team. We have twelve members. We _____ _____ _____ after school at 3 p.m. in the library. We _____ _____ like a recycling competition and a community clean-up day. If you care about the environment, you should come check us out!

6. 대화를 듣고, 두 사람이 만날 시각을 고르시오.

① 1:30 p.m.   ② 2:00 p.m.
③ 2:30 p.m.   ④ 3:00 p.m.
⑤ 3:30 p.m.

06 W: Dan, if you're not busy today, can you help me _____ _____ my physics exam?

M: _____ _____ you promise to help me with my chemistry exam.

W: It's a deal! Can we meet at 2 o'clock at the school library then?

M: Hmm… I have a _____ _____ at 2.

W: Okay, come see me at the library after you're finished. I'll be there studying.

M: Okay. I'll be there by 3.

W: Great! See you then!

7. 대화를 듣고, 남자의 장래 희망으로 가장 적절한 것을 고르시오.
   ① 드러머 ② 의사
   ③ 선생님 ④ 감독
   ⑤ 작곡가

07
W: What do you want to be in the future?

M: I want to _____ _____ _____ sick people.

W: I thought you _____ _____ _____ music.

M: Yes, I've played the drums _____ _____, but that's just a hobby.

W: So, do you want to be a doctor?

M: Yes, that's my dream.

W: A doctor _____ can play the drums? How wonderful!

8. 대화를 듣고, 남자의 심정으로 가장 적절한 것을 고르시오.
   ① relaxed ② upset
   ③ surprised ④ excited
   ⑤ bored

08
W: Hey, what are you doing this Saturday?

M: Nothing special. Why?

W: Stacy and I are going on a picnic to _____ _____ _____. Why don't you _____ us?

M: Sounds fun! I'm _____. I'll bring some snacks!

W: Good. Let's meet at the main gate of the park at 2 p.m.

M: Okay. It'll be fun! I can _____ wait!

다음 페이지에 계속 ➡

9. 대화를 듣고, 여자가 대화 직후에 할 일로 가장 적절한 것을 고르시오.
   ① 시험 범위 확인하기
   ② 역사시험 공부하기
   ③ 책 반납하기
   ④ 도서관 카드 만들기
   ⑤ 문자 메시지 보내기

09

M: Jessica, what are you doing this Saturday?

W: I'll be _____ _____. Why?

M: Why don't we go to the library to study for our midterm exam together?

W: Sure! I'm _____ _____ _____ history. Maybe you can help me.

M: Um... _____ _____ _____ _____, I'm not good at history, either.

W: Then, why don't we invite someone else to study with us?

M: Good idea. How about Lidia? She is a history genius.

W: I have her number. I'll text her right now.

10. 대화를 듣고, 무엇에 관한 내용인지 가장 적절한 것을 고르시오.
    ① 피아노 연주 영상 만들기
    ② 생일선물 고르기
    ③ 결혼 축가 연습하기
    ④ 노래 경연대회 나가기
    ⑤ 결혼 사진 찍기

10

M: What a beautiful song! Are you preparing for a singing contest?

W: No, actually I'm singing at my uncle's wedding this Saturday.

M: Amazing! What is the title of the song? It _____ _____.

W: It is a popular song called *The Luckiest*.

M: Yeah, I know that song. I'm sure _____ _____ a special gift for your uncle.

W: I hope so. But I'm a little nervous to sing in front of so many people.

M: You'll do fine. _____ _____ everyone will love your song.

W: Thank you.

11. 대화를 듣고, 여자가 이용할 교통수단으로 가장 적절한 것을 고르시오.

① 비행기   ② 기차
③ 배   ④ 버스
⑤ 자전거

11
M: Honey, when are we _____ _____ Busan?

W: This Saturday!

M: Okay. Are we going to drive our car?

W: Well... *(pause)* It's a _____-_____ _____

and I don't want to get car sickness. Why don't we

take the train?

M: Good idea. I prefer to travel by train.

W: Thank you.

12. 대화를 듣고, 남자가 지금 책을 빌릴 수 없는 이유로 가장 적절한 것을 고르시오.

① 학생증을 안 가져와서
② 연체료를 안 내서
③ 대출 가능 횟수를 넘어서
④ 다른 사람이 먼저 예약한 책이어서
⑤ 대출이 불가능한 책이어서

12
W: Welcome to Southwest University Library. How

can I help you?

M: Hi, I want to _____ _____ _____.

W: Alright. Your student ID, please?

M: 200531, Ma'am.

W: Oh, I'm sorry to say that you can't borrow them

right now.

M: Excuse me?

W: The book you borrowed last month was overdue,

so you owe 2,000 won _____ _____

_____.

M: Oh, I didn't know that.

W: You can't borrow books until you pay the fees.

M: OK, I'll get back to you later.

24
회
딕
테
이
션

다음 페이지에 계속 ➡

13. 대화를 듣고, 두 사람이 대화하는 장소로 가장 적절한 곳을 고르시오.

① 은행
② 병원
③ 영화관
④ 농구장
⑤ 헬스장

13

M: Excuse me, can you show me _____ _____ _____ this exercise machine?

W: Sure. First, put your hands on the horizontal bar.

M: Okay.

W: Next, _____ _____ right foot on the foot pad and push!

M: How many times should I do this?

W: Repeat 15 times and then _____ _____ _____ with your other leg.

M: I think I've got it. Thanks.

표불일치 🇺🇸🇬🇧

신유형 2025 영어듣기능력평가 1회 14번 변형

14. Handmade Soap Workshop for Kids에 관한 다음 내용을 듣고, 표에서 일치하지 않는 것을 고르시오.

Handmade Soap Workshop for Kids		
①	일시	this Sunday, 2 p.m.
②	행사 내용	make their own soaps
③	행사 시간	1 hour
④	참가비	$5
⑤	등록 장소	front desk at the community center

14

W: Hello, everyone! Let me tell you about our _____ Soap Workshop for Kids. It'll be held this Sunday at 2 p.m. at the community center. In this workshop, kids will make their own colorful and _____ _____ in fun shapes. The event will be 1 hour _____ _____. This is a free event, and spots are first come, first served. Those who want to join should visit the front desk at the community center to _____. Thanks!

15. 대화를 듣고, 남자가 여자에게 부탁한 일
로 가장 적절한 것을 고르시오.

① 청소하기
② 음악 소리 줄이기
③ 이사 도와주기
④ 같이 식사하기
⑤ 음식점 정보 알려주기

15

M: Hi, I'm your neighbor, Kim Jay. I live _____

_____.

W: Oh, hi. I'm Kate May.

M: So, you just _____ _____? Do you need

anything?

W: Not now. But thanks.

M: Well, let me know if you do. Umm, by the way,

_____ _____ _____ turning down the

music? The walls are really thin.

W: Oh, I'm sorry. I didn't realize that. I'll make sure

to _____ _____ _____. By the way, is there

a good restaurant near here?

M: Yes, there's a good Italian restaurant named Molto

Bene. It's across the street.

W: Thank you.

16. 대화를 듣고, 남자가 여자에게 제안한 것
으로 가장 적절한 것을 고르시오.

① 앱 다운받기
② 도서관 방문하기
③ 책 빌리기
④ 친구에게 전화하기
⑤ 휴대전화 꾸미기

16

W: Terry, what are you doing?

M: I'm reading a book on my phone.

W: On your phone? Can you do that?

M: Yes, I'm using a library app.

W: That's nice. I _____ _____ _____ more.

M: Then, why don't you download this app, too?

W: Good idea. Is it _____ _____?

M: Yes, it is.

다음 페이지에 계속 ➡

17. 대화를 듣고, 남자가 지난 여름방학에 한 일로 가장 적절한 것을 고르시오.

① 수영 배우기
② 모형 비행기 만들기
③ 과학 숙제하기
④ 캠핑 가기
⑤ 친척 방문하기

17
M: Eva, did you have a good vacation?

W: Yeah, I went to _____ _____ _____.

M: Oh, what did you do there?

W: I went swimming with my cousins. We went camping, too.

M: That sounds fun. You had a nice summer.

W: What about you?

M: I made a _____ _____ _____. It took me weeks.

W: That's amazing!

18. 대화를 듣고, 남자의 직업으로 가장 적절한 것을 고르시오.

① 아나운서
② 축구 선수
③ 요리 강사
④ 호텔 지배인
⑤ 추리소설 작가

18
M: How is it going, Ms. White?

W: I'm making the sauce now. Will you taste it?

M: Sure. (pause) Hmm, it's tasty, but a little _____.

W: Oh, what should I do?

M: Just put in some more oil. You are doing great.

W: Thank you. _____ _____ _____ your excellent teaching.

M: My pleasure. You cooked this fish very well, too.

W: Thank you.

19. 대화를 듣고, 여자의 마지막 말에 이어질 남자의 말로 가장 적절한 것을 고르시오.

Man: _____

① I'll visit you there in the hospital.
② It was nice seeing you at the store.
③ I'll bring the groceries to you.
④ I hope you get better soon.
⑤ I received the hospital bill.

19 (*Telephone rings.*)

M: Hello. Brittany? This is Dennis.

W: Oh, hi, Dennis. How are you?

M: I'm fine. I _____ _____ your mom at the store. She said you were in the hospital.

W: I was, yes. It was just a really bad case _____ _____ _____.

M: I'm sorry to hear that. How are you doing?

W: I'm still _____. I'll be resting at home for the next day or so.

M: I hope you get better soon.

20. 대화를 듣고, 여자의 마지막 말에 이어질 남자의 말로 가장 적절한 것을 고르시오.

Man: _____

① Congratulations!
② She likes cheese.
③ I'll come at 5 o'clock.
④ I pick her up from work.
⑤ It's her birthday tomorrow.

20 W: How can I help you?

M: I'd like to _____ a cake for tomorrow afternoon.

W: Sure. Which cake would you like?

M: Can you _____ one? It's for my wife.

W: _____ _____ the cheesecake or the strawberry cream cake?

M: Hmm… I'll take the cheesecake.

W: OK. When would you like to _____ _____ _____?

M: I'll come at 5 o'clock.

24
회
딕
테
이
션

Words & Expressions Review 24

● 다음 단어를 암기하세요.

문제	번호	단어	뜻
1	□ 1	float	떠다니다
	□ 2	sting	쏘다
2	□ 3	oval	타원형의
	□ 4	local	지역의
3	□ 5	update	최신 정보, 갱신
	□ 6	thunderstorm	천둥번개, 뇌우
4	□ 7	invite	초대하다
5	□ 8	environmental	환경의, 환경과 관련된
	□ 9	recycling	재활용
	□ 10	community	지역 사회
	□ 11	care about	~에 대해 걱정하다, 마음을 쓰다
6	□ 12	physics	물리학
	□ 13	appointment	예약, 약속
7	□ 14	take care of ~	~를 돌보다
	□ 15	be into ~	~에 관심이 많다
8	□ 16	go on a picnic	소풍을 가다
	□ 17	fly a kite	연을 날리다
	□ 18	join	함께 하다
	□ 19	main gate	정문
	□ 20	hardly	도저히 ~할 수 없다
9	□ 21	truth	사실, 진실
	□ 22	genius	천재

문제	번호	단어	뜻
9	□ 23	text	문자를 보내다
10	□ 24	familiar	익숙한, 친숙한
11	□ 25	prefer	~을 더 좋아하다, 선호하다
12	□ 26	overdue	연체된, 기한이 지난
14	□ 27	handmade	수제의
	□ 28	scented	향기로운
15	□ 29	neighbor	이웃
	□ 30	thin	얇은
	□ 31	realize	깨닫다
16	□ 32	app	앱, 애플리케이션
	□ 33	download	다운로드하다, 내려받다
17	□ 34	huge	커다란, 거대한, 막대한
	□ 35	model	모형
	□ 36	taste	맛보다
	□ 37	tasty	맛있는
18	□ 38	salty	짠, 짭짤한, 소금이 든
	□ 39	excellent	훌륭한, 탁월한
	□ 40	My pleasure.	천만에요.
	□ 41	run into ~	~를 우연히 만나다
19	□ 42	recover	회복하다
	□ 43	get better	회복하다, 나아지다
20	□ 44	recommend	추천하다, 권하다

● 왼쪽 단어장의 뜻이 보이지 않게 반으로 접고, 학습한 단어의 뜻을 아래 빈칸에 적어주세요.

1	realize		23	tasty	
2	float		24	physics	
3	text		25	salty	
4	be into ~		26	neighbor	
5	go on a picnic		27	sting	
6	recover		28	recommend	
7	care about		29	thunderstorm	
8	overdue		30	get better	
9	local		31	download	
10	appointment		32	community	
11	truth		33	scented	
12	take care of ~		34	update	
13	fly a kite		35	app	
14	huge		36	taste	
15	run into ~		37	prefer	
16	join		38	handmade	
17	main gate		39	excellent	
18	recycling		40	environmental	
19	My pleasure.		41	familiar	
20	genius		42	oval	
21	hardly		43	model	
22	thin		44	invite	

24회 단어

2026 17차 개정판

마더텅 100%실전대비
MP3 중학 영어듣기
24회 모의고사 1학년

MOTHERTONGUE
마더텅출판사
since1999.4.1.

발행 17차 개정판 3쇄(2026년 1월 31일)

Chief Editorial Director 서은숙 **Editorial Directors** 박상우, 이혜빈, 최민정, 최은조, 신준기, 김현수, 이윤정, 강수민, 김다영

English Editors Christopher Swafford, Jordan Sanders **책임 원고 검수** 서은숙

Writers 신재진, 김경미, 박선주, 유예슬, 이용진, 박새미, 박상우, 김다영, 장정문, 남현정, 신주희, 박헌준, 배기현, 최동렬, 홍유진, 김선혜, 이장원, 김두리, 김유한, 김창범, 노영선, 민희성, 박근혜, 박재민, 손은진, 이찬희, 이상미, 조아라, 허혜경, 손필현, 호현, 박희나, 정수지, 신은경, 김지야, 권주연, 하은옥, Steve McLeod, Arvin Adams, Janine Davis, Iris James, Lorelei Rivers, Tristan Hughes, Liz Stewart

단어 및 해석 집필 정하은, 김현수, 이은영, 임혜영, 박상우, 유지원, 선대훈, 황희진, 송현석, 권은정, 신진실, 이한주

원어민 감수 Kathy O'Handley **감수** 강산(EBSi 수능 영어강사)

Audio 녹음 김지야, 이영재, 백찬솔, 손정은, 이승아, 이승민, 정하은 **Audio 편집** 와이알미디어, Netiline, 이형구

Audio 감수 신소미, 이미경, 이윤정, 김다영, 이은영, 선대훈, 변선영, 신의진, 조수성, 박새미, 신재진, 한기범, 장지현, 허은혜, 황혜진, 손정은, 이혜경, 김수정, 김주현, 조재윤, 이상미, 백경빈, 장시은, 정다혜, 문은아, 이슬기, 이한주, 신진실, 유윤정

Voice Actors 임승미, April Lynn, Laura-Leigh, Margaret Chung, Tony Ruse, Peter Bint, Monique Dami Lee, Janet Lee, Shane Hahm, Josh Smith, Anna Sue, 이지나, Alexander Jensen, Josh Schwartzy

교정 신재진, 이은영, 정하은, 신소미, 이혜빈, 최은조, 최민정, 박혜미, 임미진, 김다영, 정은주, 윤숙경, 김효진, 김하나, 김단, 장정문, 임홍일, 이영재, 임하람, 장지현, 김현, 하은옥, 김주현, 선대훈, 이승민, 신영은, 최소영, 오정훈, 성은혜, 홍성경, 남현정, 양희송, 정새로나, 이한주, 신진실, 장신혜, 이옥현, 변선영, 유윤정, 정현희, 신순화

표지디자인 김연실 **내지디자인** 김연실, 양은선 **인디자인편집** 고연화, 최송실, 양은선, 정은영, 박경아

Illustrators 정제욱, 박주혜, 이혜승, 박현주, 이은경, 이지은, 박우선, 양은선

제작 이주영 **발행인** 문숙영 **발행처** ㈜ 마더텅 (Mother Tongue Co., Ltd.)

주소 서울시 금천구 가마산로 96 708호 **팩스** 02-3142-9126 **홈페이지** www.toptutor.co.kr

등록번호 제1-2423호 (1999년 1월 8일)

마더텅 교재를 풀면서 궁금한 점이 생기셨나요?

교재 관련 내용 문의나 오류신고 사항이 있으면 아래 문의처로 보내 주세요!

문의하신 내용에 대해 성성성의껏 답변해 드리겠습니다.

또한 교재의 **내용 오류** 또는 **오·탈자, 그 외 수정이 필요한 사항**에 대해 가장 먼저 신고해 주신 분께는 감사의 마음을 담아 네이버페이 포인트 1천 원 을 보내 드립니다!

＊기한: 2026년 12월 31일 ＊오류신고 이벤트는 당사 사정에 따라 조기 종료될 수 있습니다. ＊홈페이지에 게시된 정오표 기준으로 최초 신고된 오류에 한하여 상품권을 보내 드립니다.

● **카카오톡** mothertongue ● **이메일** mothert1004@toptutor.co.kr ● **홈페이지** www.toptutor.co.kr ● **교재Q&A게시판**

● **고객센터 전화** 1661-1064(07:00~22:00) ● **문자** 010-6640-1064(문자수신전용)

권○지 님
2020년 2학기 중간고사 국영수 ALL 100점

설명이 자세한 교재로 공부하고 싶었고, 다양한 유형의 문제들을 최대한 많이 풀어보고 싶었습니다. 마더텅 교재가 설명이 자세히 잘되어 있고, 문제 문항 수도 많아서 선택하게 되었습니다. 저는 아침에 집중력이 제일 좋기 때문에 오전에 영어 듣기 모의고사처럼 높은 집중력이 있어야 하는 과목을 공부하고, 오후에는 암기 위주로 공부했습니다.

중학영문법 3800제는 문법 설명과 함께 다양한 예문이 있어서 이해가 잘됩니다. 단원 끝부분의 중간·기말고사 대비 문제를 풀면서 배운 문법을 완전히 숙지할 수 있습니다.

중학영문법 3800제 워크북은 중학영문법 3800제에서 배운 문법 개념을 다시 정리하고, 완벽하게 익히는 데 도움이 많이 됩니다.

중학영어듣기 24회 모의고사는 듣기 평가를 준비할 때 도움이 많이 되었습니다. 실전처럼 모의고사를 풀고, 다시 들으며 지문의 빈칸을 채우는 방법으로 공부했더니 지문을 완벽하게 익힐 수 있었습니다. 특히 미국식, 미+영국식 발음 이렇게 두 가지가 수록된 점이 좋았습니다. 마더텅 교재는 혼자서 공부하는 제게 정말 큰 도움이 되었습니다.

길○정 님
2023년 1학기 중간&기말고사 국어, 수학, 영어 100점

저에게 가장 큰 도움을 준 교재인 중학영문법 3800제 활용법을 말씀드리겠습니다. 일주일에 4번 공부했는데, 한 챕터에 들어있는 한 개의 PSS를 하루에 푸는 것을 목표로 삼았습니다. 그 분량이 매일 달라서 내용이 많은 날도 있었지만, 최대한 세웠던 계획을 지키려고 노력했습니다. 또한 총 세 번의 복습을 해서 내용을 잊지 않고 기억하려고 했습니다.

처음 공부할 때는 먼저 정리되어 있는 개념들을 읽으면서 꼼꼼히 공부했습니다. 제가 약한 부분이나 이해가 안 되는 부분만 골라서 EBS 중학프리미엄 인터넷강좌를 들었습니다. 그렇게 개념 공부를 하고, 딸려 있는 문제들을 모두 풀고 채점, 오답까지 했습니다. 문제들은 개념 공부를 하자마자 바로 한 번 더 머릿속에 내용을 각인시키는 용도로 활용했습니다.

복습의 경우 첫 번째 복습은 문제를 푼 후에 A4용지에 백지 복습을 하는 것이었습니다. 한 PSS에 들어있는 내용들은 백지 복습을 충분히 할 수 있는 정도의 분량이었습니다. 아무것도 없는 A4용지에 공부했던 내용을 큰 개념부터 적어나가며 세부 내용까지 채워나는 방법으로 복습하였습니다. 두 번째 복습은 중학영문법 3800제 워크북이었습니다. 워크북은 본책 공부와 시간을 두고 밤에 잠에 들기 바로 전에 공부해서 내가 어느 정도를 아직까지 기억하고 있는지를 확인했습니다. 기억이 정확히 나지 않았거나 몰라서 틀렸던 문제들의 내용은 본책에 다시 빨간펜으로 표시해 두었습니다. 세 번째 복습은 빨간펜으로 표시해 두었던 내용 위주로 한 번 더 확인한 후 그 날의 공부를 시작하는 것이었습니다. 덕분에 내용들이 더 길게 장기기억으로 남을 수 있었던 것 같습니다.

한편 오답노트에는 문제, 문제의 답과 풀이, 문제를 틀린 이유, 관련 개념도 적어놓아 나중에 복습하기에 종도록 정리해 두었고, 오답노트는 세 개의 단원이 끝날 때마다 한 번에 복습했습니다.

이○우 님
2021년 1학기 기말고사 국영수 ALL 100점

중학생이 되면서 제대로 된 영어 공부의 필요성을 느꼈습니다. 주변 친구들과 선생님의 추천으로 중학영문법 3800제 시리즈를 알게 되었습니다. 친절한 설명을 읽고 유형별 문제를 풀며 공부를 하다 보니 어렵게 느껴졌던 문법 개념들이 머릿속에 잘 정리되었습니다. 중학영문법 3800제는 여태껏 사용했던 책들 중 가장 완성도 높고 만족스러운 교재였기에 지금까지 중학영문법 3800제 시리즈로 공부를 하고 있습니다.

공부를 할 때 가장 중요한 건 '직접 소리 내어 말하기'라고 생각합니다. 항상 공부를 할 때 교과서나 문제집의 개념 설명을 소리 내서 읽는 방법을 사용했습니다. 또한, 구체적인 목표를 세워서 공부하는 것이 좋습니다. 시간표를 만들어

서 일정한 공부 패턴을 만들고 유지하는 방법을 사용했습니다.

중학영문법 3800제는 문법을 쉽게 이해하고 공부할 수 있도록 도와 주는 기본서이자 필수적인 교재입니다. 이해하기 쉬운 설명과 다양한 예문이 실려 있어서 크고 작은 개념들을 모두 잘 이해할 수 있습니다. 개념을 이해한 후에는 각 개념에 대한 풍부한 문제를 풀게 되는데, 이 점이 가장 큰 장점이라고 생각합니다. 또한 중간·기말고사 대비 문제를 통해 그 챕터에서 공부한 내용을 총정리하면 문법 실력을 더 단단하게 다지고 학교 시험도 대비할 수 있습니다. 중학영문법 3800제는 문법을 공부하는 학생이라면 한 번쯤 꼭 풀어 보아야 완성도 높은 교재입니다.

임○연 님
2020년 2학기 기말고사 국영수 ALL 100점

영어 공부를 기초부터 탄탄히 하기 위해 두껍고 문제 수가 많은 마더텅을 고르게 되었습니다. 중간·기말고사 대비문제가 있어서 한번에 연습을 하는 데 굉장히 좋고 해설도 잘 되어 있어서 이해하기가 편했습니다. 디자인도 보기 편하고 예문도 많아서 보고 이해하기 쉬웠습니다. 지금도 중학영문법 3800제 3학년으로 공부를 하고 있습니다.

헷갈리는 부분은 인강을 통해 공부하여 큰 도움이 되었습니다. 공부 방법은 혼자 누구에게 이야기하듯이 말하면서 하는 방법입니다. 영어 같은 경우는 이해가 안되는 문장을 소리를 내어서 계속 읽어 보았고, 암기 과목들은 교과서에 있는 문장을 계속 읽으면서 제가 이해한 대로 바로 정리한 다음 누구에게 설명해 주듯이 하면서 공부했습니다.

중학영문법 3800제에는 앞에 핵심 문법 사항 암기표가 있는데, 꼭 외워야 할 부분을 한 장에 정리한 것이어서 편리하고 좋았습니다. 그리고 많은 문제 양도 매우 좋은 장점이라고 생각합니다. 문법을 공부하는 데 있어서 가장 핵심은 반복적인 학습이라고 생각합니다. 때문에 여러 번 쓰고 문제를 풀 수 있는 것이 이 책의 주요 장점이라고 생각했습니다. 교과서 활용 진도표도 있어서 학교에서 배울 것을 미리 공부해 볼 수 있었습니다.

정○린 님
2024년 1학기 중간고사 국어, 수학, 영어 100점

국어는 뿌리깊은 중학국어 독해력으로 독해력을 향상하는 데 사용하고, 영어는 중학영문법 3800제로 영어 문법 개념을 정리하는데 사용하였고, 수학은 중학수학 뜀틀로 내신을 대비하였습니다.

영어와 국어를 공부할 때는 조금 어렵거나 헷갈리는 부분에 포스트잇을 붙여 여기서는 어떤 부분이 주의한지, 어떤 요점이 나를 헷갈리게 하였는지 정리 해놓았는데, 덕분에 다음날 다시 공부할 때 중요한 부분을 잊지 않고 복습할 수 있었습니다. 또한 틀린 문제는 정답과 해설에 정리된 내용을 토대로 오답노트를 만들어서 다시 한번 풀이해보곤 했습니다. 그러다 보니 친구들에게 개념을 직접 설명할 수 있는 수준까지 이르게 되었습니다.

중학영문법 3800제의 장점은 꼼꼼한 해설과 깔끔하게 정리되어 있는 개념 내용이라고 생각합니다. 답만 나와 있는 교재로 공부할 때에는 해설이 자세하지 않아 이해하기가 어려웠던 적이 있는데, 중학영문법 3800제는 자세한 해설이 있어서 이해하기가 정말 쉬웠습니다.

나○재 님
2021년 1학기 중간고사 영어 100점

학원 영어 선생님께서 중학영문법 3800제 시리즈가 중학생 영어 문법 기초를 다지는데 큰 도움이 되는 교재라고 말씀해주셔서 사용하게 되었습니다.

저는 포스트잇에 그 날 학습하는 매 Problem Solving Skill 에서의 주제나 내용물을 정리하면서 복습하고 문제를 푸는 방식으로 공부했습니다. 중간에 포스트잇으로 내용 정리를 하니 머리 속에 더 오래 남아 더 효율적인 것 같습니다. 중간·기말고사 대비 문제를 풀면서 오답이 나오면 포스트잇에다가 문제를 다시 쓰고 왜 틀렸는지 오답정리를 하였습니다.

영어바다의 세계를 알기 쉽게 자세히 PSS로 개념을 설명해 주는 장점을 중학영문법 3800제가 가지고 있고 중간·

기말고사 대비문제는 그동안 배운 영문법 개념을 다시 한번 다지는 계기가 되고 학교 내신 준비하는데 많은 도움이 되었습니다.

유○인 님
2021년 1학기 기말고사 영어 100점

과외선생님의 추천으로 기초를 다지면서 공부하게 되었고, 무엇보다 개념문제와 실전문제가 많아 중학영문법 3800제로 공부하게 되었습니다. 중학영문법 3800제는 문법의 기초를 탄탄하게 배우지 못하여 문법이 많이 미숙했던 저에게 큰 도움이 되었습니다.

문법을 많이 어려워했지만 이 교재는 작은 개념이라도 쉽게 자세히 설명하고 예문도 들어 있어서 풀기 훨씬 수월했던 것 같습니다. 풀고 나서 답지에도 풀이가 자세히 되어있어서 제가 어느 부분에서 틀렸는지 다시 한 번 볼 수 있어서 좋았습니다. 문법 개념을 바로바로 익히고 그 문법에 대한 연습문제들을 풀어보아서 더 이해가 잘 되었습니다. 무엇보다 차근차근 설명된 개념을 통해 기초를 다진 후, 실력 문제들을 볼 수 있었고 설명도 쉽게 되어있어서 여러 번 각각의 문제의 유형을 풀면서 그 유형문제들에 대해서 자세히 알 수 있어 좋았습니다.

이○우 님
2024년 1학기 중간&기말고사 영어 100점

저는 중학영문법 3800제로 시험 대비를 했습니다. 먼저 PSS를 풀고, 각 chapter 맨 앞에 있는 성취도 기준에 맞춰 스스로 평가하고, 날짜를 기록했습니다. 그리고 시험이 다가왔을 때 성취도가 낮은 부분을 다시 보고 복습하였습니다. 또한 chapter마다 중간·기말고사 대비 문제를 풀어서 제가 배운 문법이 학교 시험에서 어떤 형식으로 나오는지를 확인할 수 있었습니다.

이처럼 중학영문법 3800제는 그 이름에 걸맞게 방대한 문제 수를 수록하고 있어 다양한 유형과 문제풀이 능력기를 수 있었습니다. 물론 다양한 문제를 풀면서 문법 실력 또한 키울 수 있었습니다. 중학영문법 3800제는 PSS (Problem Solving Skill) 개념을 도입하여, 한 번에 한 가지 문제해결 능력을 익히고 다음 단계로 넘어갈 수 있도록 구성되어 있습니다. 이를 통해 문제해결 능력을 키울 수 있었습니다. 더불어 매년 최신 개정판이 나오기 때문에, 내용이 매년 업그레이드되는 점도 좋았습니다.

우○찬 님
토셀 제 72회 정기시험 Basic 2등급

평소 영어에 관심이 있어서 마더텅 100% 실전대비 MP3 중학영어듣기 24회 모의고사를 선택해 공부했습니다. 매주 월요일마다 마더텅 100% 실전대비 MP3 중학영어듣기 24회 모의고사를 풀었습니다. 30분씩 듣고 문제를 풀었습니다. 월요일에는 1번부터 10번까지 문제를 듣고 푼 뒤, 3번씩 다시 들으며 영어 문장을 받아쓰기했습니다. 수요일에는 11번부터 20번까지 문제를 듣고 풀었으며, 20번까지 다 풀고 난 다음 본문에 나왔던 단어들을 정리했습니다. 마더텅 100% 실전대비 MP3 중학영어듣기 24회 모의고사는 책이 두꺼워서 공부를 많이 할 수 있어 좋았습니다.

류○환 님
토셀 제 72회 정기시험 Basic 2등급

영어 과외 수업에서 초등 교재로만 공부를 하다가 중학교 교재인 마더텅 100% 실전대비 MP3 중학영어듣기 24회 모의고사를 접하게 되었는데 학습이 너무 재미있었고 꼭 중학생이 된 거 같아 기분이 좋았습니다.

일주일 중 3번을 마더텅 100% 실전대비 MP3 중학영어듣기 24회 모의고사 교재로 학습하는데, 첫째 날에는 1번부터 10번까지 듣고 푼 뒤, 다시 들어보며 받아쓰기를 합니다. 둘째 날에는 11번부터 20번까지 듣고 풉니다. 셋째 날에는 한 단원을 총정리하며 단어장 정리를 합니다. 처음부터 끝까지 단어를 다 읽고 노트에 스펠링을 찾아서 적은 후, 뜻을 보고 영어 말하기 테스트를 합니다. 처음에는 영어가 잘 안 들리고 힘들었지만, 교재를 풀수록 실력이 향상되었습니다. 마더텅 100% 실전대비 MP3 중학영어듣기 24회 모의고사는 영어 듣기도 여러 번 들을 수 있고 단어도 많이 있어서 좋았습니다.

📱》 모바일로 교재 MP3 재생 방법 마더텅의 교재 MP3는 모바일 스트리밍/다운로드를 지원합니다.

1 아래의 QR 코드 접속

2 스타플레이어 어플 설치

▶▶ SKIP (특정 부분을 건너 뛰어 뒤로 가거나 앞으로 다시 가서 듣고 싶은 경우)

1
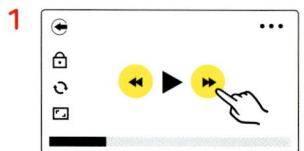
재생 버튼 양쪽의 화살표를 누르면 앞으로 가거나 뒤로 갈 수 있습니다.

2
REW/FF시간 설정 (안드로이드)
건너 뛰기 설정 (iOS)
우측 상단의 점 세 개 버튼을 누르면 REW/FF시간 설정 (안드로이드) 건너 뛰기 설정 (iOS) 가능

🔂 구간반복 (특정 구간을 반복 재생하고 싶은 경우)

좌우 이동 가능

1. 좌측 또는 우측 하단 구간반복 아이콘 누르면 빨간 선 활성화
2. 선의 양쪽 끝점을 이동하여 원하는 반복재생 구간 설정 가능

마더텅 학습 교재 이벤트에 참여해 주세요. 참여해 주신 분께 선물을 드립니다.

이벤트 1 1분 간단 교재 사용 후기 이벤트

마더텅은 고객님의 소중한 의견을 반영하여 보다 좋은 책을 만들고자 합니다.
교재 구매 후, <교재 사용 후기 이벤트>에 참여해 주신 모든 분께는 감사의 마음을 담아
네이버페이 포인트 1천 원 을 보내 드립니다. 지금 바로 QR 코드를 스캔해 소중한 의견을 보내 주세요!

이벤트 2 중학영어듣기 인증샷 이벤트

SNS에 <중학영어듣기> 인증샷을 올려 주시면 참여해 주신 모든 분께 감사의 마음을 담아
네이버페이 포인트 2천 원 을 보내 드립니다. 지금 바로 QR 코드를 스캔해 작성한 게시물의 URL을 입력해 주세요!

필수 태그 #마더텅 #중학영어듣기

이벤트 3 마더텅 우편 이벤트

본 교재의 24회 고난도 모의고사 페이지를 오려서 마더텅으로 보내 주세요!
추첨을 통해 소정의 상품을 보내 드립니다.

참여 방법 24회 고난도 모의고사(p.368~371) 풀이 및 채점 완료
→ 해당 페이지를 모두 오려서 마더텅에 발송(우편, 택배 등) → QR 코드를 스캔하고 발송 인증

주소 (08501) 서울특별시 금천구 가마산로 96, 대륭테크노타운 8차 708호, 마더텅 이벤트 담당자 앞 / 010 - 6640 - 1064

※ 이벤트 기간: 2026년 12월 31일까지 (●해당 이벤트는 당사 사정에 따라 조기 종료될 수 있습니다.) ※ 자세한 사항은 해당 QR 코드를 스캔하거나 홈페이지 이벤트 공지 글을 참고해 주세요. ※ 당사 사정에 따라 이벤트의 내용이나 상품이 변경될 수 있으며 변경 시 홈페이지에 공지합니다. ※ 만 14세 미만은 부모님께서 신청해 주셔야 합니다. ※ 상품은 이벤트 참여일로부터 4~5일(영업일 기준) 내에 발송됩니다. (단, 이벤트 3은 예외) ※ 동일 교재로 세 가지 이벤트 모두 참여 가능합니다. (단, 같은 이벤트 중복 참여는 불가합니다.)

2026 17차 개정판

마더텅 100%실전대비
MP3 중학 영어듣기
24회 모의고사 1학년
정답과 해석

MOTHERTONGUE
마더텅출판사
since1999.4.1.

학습계획표 24회 완성

✓ 100% 실전대비 MP3 중학영어듣기 24회 모의고사를 100% 활용할 수 있도록 도와주는 학습계획표입니다. 계획표를 활용하여 학습 일정을 계획하고
자신의 성적을 체크해 보세요. 스스로 학습 현황을 체크하면서 공부하는 습관은 문제집을 끝까지 푸는 데 도움을 줍니다.

✓ 계획은 도중에 틀어질 수 있습니다. 하지만 계획을 세우고 지키는 과정은 그 자체로 효율적인 학습에 큰 도움이 됩니다.
학습 중 계획이 변경될 경우에 대비해 마더텅 홈페이지에서 학습계획표 PDF 파일을 제공하고 있습니다.

회	학습날짜	문항수	학습결과		딕테이션 맞은 갯수
1회		20	맞음	개	
2회		20	맞음	개	
3회		20	맞음	개	
4회		20	맞음	개	
5회		20	맞음	개	
6회		20	맞음	개	
7회		20	맞음	개	
8회		20	맞음	개	
9회		20	맞음	개	
10회		20	맞음	개	
11회		20	맞음	개	
12회		20	맞음	개	
13회		20	맞음	개	
14회		20	맞음	개	
15회		20	맞음	개	
16회		20	맞음	개	
17회		20	맞음	개	
18회		20	맞음	개	
19회		20	맞음	개	
20회		20	맞음	개	
21회		20	맞음	개	
22회		20	맞음	개	
23회		20	맞음	개	
24회		20	맞음	개	

Listening Test

영어듣기 모의고사 01 회

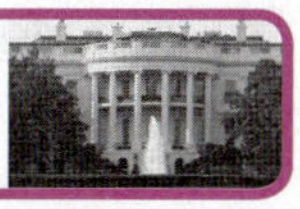

| 정 | 답 |

01 ④	02 ①	03 ③	04 ④	05 ④
06 ③	07 ④	08 ①	09 ④	10 ②
11 ③	12 ④	13 ③	14 ②	15 ④
16 ①	17 ②	18 ④	19 ⑤	20 ③

01 그림정보파악(담화) ▶ 정답 ④

듣•기•대•본

M: I have two hands, two legs and a long tail. I live in trees, and I use my hands and tail to climb trees. I also have a red bottom. I am very clever. What am I?

우•리•말•해•석

남: 나는 두 개의 손과 두 개의 다리, 그리고 한 개의 긴 꼬리가 있다. 나는 나무에서 살고, 나무에 오르기 위해 나의 손과 꼬리를 사용한다. 나는 또한 빨간 엉덩이를 가지고 있다. 나는 매우 영리하다. 나는 무엇일까?

단•어•및•표•현

climb [klaim] [동] 오르다
bottom [bátəm] [명] 엉덩이
clever [klévər] [형] 영리한

02 그림정보파악(대화) ▶ 정답 ①

듣•기•대•본

W: Excuse me. I want to buy a toy figure for my six-year-old son.
M: Sure. Astronauts and pilots are popular.
W: He wants to be an astronaut one day.
M: Then, how about this one with a flag?
W: Great! The astronaut holding a flag looks cute. I'll take it.

우•리•말•해•석

여: 실례합니다. 저는 제 여섯 살 아들을 위해 장난감 피규어를 사고 싶어요.
남: 알겠습니다. 우주 비행사와 조종사가 인기가 많습니다.
여: 그는 언젠가 우주 비행사가 되고 싶어해요.
남: 그럼, 깃발을 든 이건 어떠세요?
여: 좋아요! 깃발을 든 우주 비행사가 귀여워 보여요. 이걸로 할게요.

단•어•및•표•현

toy figure 장난감 피규어
astronaut [ǽstrənɔ̀:t] [명] 우주 비행사
pilot [páilət] [명] 조종사
flag [flæg] [명] 깃발

03 날씨파악–그림 ▶ 정답 ③

듣•기•대•본

W: Good afternoon. This is Sejong's weather report. The light snow stopped this morning, but now heavy rain is falling. It'll be rainy until this evening. So, bring an umbrella if you're going out. But it'll be sunny tomorrow. Thanks for checking out the weather update.

우•리•말•해•석

여: 좋은 오후입니다. 세종 일기예보입니다. 가벼운 눈은 오늘 아침에 그쳤지만, 지금은 거센 비가 내리고 있습니다. 오늘 저녁까지 비가 올 예정입니다. 그러니 만약 외출하신다면 우산을 챙기세요. 하지만 내일은 맑겠습니다. 일기예보를 확인해 주셔서 감사합니다.

단•어•및•표•현

light [lait] [형] 가벼운, (양 · 정도가) 적은
fall [fɔ:l] [동] 내리다, 떨어지다
until [əntíl] [전] ~까지

04 마지막말의도파악 ▶ 정답 ④

듣•기•대•본

W: Grandpa, can I talk to you?
M: Sure. What is it, Eva?
W: My pet hamster, Coco passed away last night.
M: Oh, I'm so sorry to hear that. How are you feeling?
W: I'm really sad.
M: It's fine to feel sad. Let's remember the happy times you had with Coco.

우•리•말•해•석

여: 할아버지, 제가 할아버지께 얘기를 할 수 있을까요?
남: 물론이지. 그게 무엇이니, Eva?
여: 제 반려 햄스터인 Coco가 어젯밤에 죽었어요.
남: 오, 그 말을 들으니 유감이구나. 네 기분은 어떠니?
여: 전 정말 슬퍼요.
남: 슬픔을 느껴도 괜찮아. 네가 Coco와 가졌던 행복한 시간들을 기억하자.

단•어•및•표•현

pass away 죽다
remember [rimémbər] [동] 기억하다

05 담화미언급 ▶ 정답 ④

듣•기•대•본

M: Hi, everyone. I'd like to introduce my younger sister. Her name is Lucy Kim. She's 9 years old. She's very cheerful and friendly. Her favorite food is pizza, and she really likes chocolate ice cream. She always makes me laugh when I feel sad.

우•리•말•해•석

남: 안녕하세요, 여러분. 저는 제 여동생을 소개하고 싶습니다. 그녀의 이름은 Lucy Kim입니다. 그녀는 9살입니다. 그녀는 아주 명랑하고 친근합니다. 그녀가 가장 좋아하는 음식은 피자이고, 초콜릿 아이스크림을 정말 좋아합니다. 제가 슬플 때 그녀는 항상 저를 웃게 만들어 줍니다.

단•어•및•표•현

cheerful [tʃíərfəl] [형] 명랑한
friendly [fréndli] [형] 친근한

06 수치파악 ▶ 정답 ③

듣•기•대•본

M: I'm so excited about the Andong Mask Dance Festival tomorrow.
W: Me too. We're going to meet at the Daejeon Bus Terminal tomorrow morning, right?
M: Yes, we'll be taking the 7:30 bus. What time should we meet?
W: How about 6:30?
M: Hmm, I think that's too early.
W: Then, how about 7:00?
M: Sounds good. See you tomorrow!

우•리•말•해•석

남: 난 내일 (열릴) 안동 탈춤 축제가 너무 기대돼.
여: 나도. 우리는 내일 아침에 대전 버스 터미널에서 만나는 거야, 맞지?
남: 응, 우리는 7시 30분 버스를 탈 거야. 우리 몇 시에 만나야 할까?
여: 6시 30분 어때?
남: 음, 내 생각에 그건 너무 이른 것 같아.
여: 그러면, 7시 어때?
남: 좋아. 내일 보자!

단•어•및•표•현

be going to + 동사원형 ~할 것이다, ~할 셈이다
take [teik] [동] (교통수단, 도로 등을) 타다, 이용하다
early [ə́ːrli] [형] 빠른, 이른

07 장래희망추론 ▶ 정답 ④

듣•기•대•본

W: Hey, how was your family trip?
M: It was great. We went to Gyeongju.
W: Did you have a lot of fun?
M: Yes. I filmed videos to make a video clip. I'll show you.
W: Wow, that's awesome! You're so good at editing videos.
M: I'm really into video editing. I want to become a video editor in the future.

우•리•말•해•석

여: 안녕, 가족 여행은 어땠어?
남: 정말 좋았어. 우리는 경주에 갔어.
여: 많이 재밌었어?
남: 응. 나는 동영상 클립을 만들려고 영상을 찍었어. 보여줄게.
여: 와, 멋지다! 너 영상 편집을 정말 잘한다.
남: 나는 영상 편집에 엄청 빠져 있어. 나는 미래에 영상 편집자가 되고 싶어.

단•어•및•표•현

trip [trip] [명] 여행
film [film] [동] 찍다, 촬영하다
awesome [ɔ́ːsəm] [형] 멋있는, 최고의
editing [éditiŋ] [명] 편집
be into ~ ~에 빠져 있다, ~을 좋아하다

08 심정추론 ▶ 정답 ①

듣•기•대•본

M: Sujin, why do you look so down?
W: I lost my muffler yesterday.
M: You mean the red one?
W: Yes. It was my favorite muffler.
M: That's too bad. I thought it looked good on you.
W: I know. My mother made it for me as a birthday present.
M: Oh, no. I'm sorry to hear that.

우•리•말•해•석

남: 수진아, 왜 이렇게 의기소침해 보여?
여: 나 어제 내 목도리를 잃어버렸어.
남: 그 빨간색 말하는 거야?
여: 응. 그건 내가 가장 좋아하는 목도리였어.
남: 안됐다. 너랑 잘 어울린다고 생각했어.
여: 그러니까. 내 생일 선물로 우리 엄마가 만들어주신 거야.
남: 오, 이런. 안됐다.

단•어•및•표•현

look down 의기소침해 보이다
muffler [mʌ́flər] [명] 목도리

09 할일파악(대화직후) ▶ 정답 ④

듣•기•대•본

W: Mark, we should get going.
M: Hmm... How much time do we have left?
W: About 30 minutes. Is something wrong?
M: Yes, I can't find my cell phone.
W: Have you looked under the bed?
M: Yes, it's not there. Can I use your cell phone for a minute? I'll have to call my phone.
W: Sure, here you go.

우•리•말•해•석

여: Mark, 우리는 가야 해.
남: 음… 우리 시간이 얼마나 남았니?
여: 약 30분. 뭐가 잘못됐니?
남: 응, 나는 내 핸드폰을 찾을 수가 없어.
여: 너는 침대 밑을 봤니?
남: 응, 그것은 거기에 없어. 네 핸드폰을 잠깐 쓸 수 있을까? 내 핸드폰에 전화를 걸어봐야겠어.
여: 물론이지, 여기 있어.

단•어•및•표•현

get going 가다, 출발하다
have ~ left ~이 남아 있다

10 대화화제추론 ▶ 정답 ②

듣•기•대•본

M: Jenny, why are you wearing your sports uniform?
W: I got changed for PE class. Don't we have PE class now, Minjun?
M: No, today's timetable has been changed. We have music class now.
W: Really? I didn't know that.
M: Mrs. Kim told us about it yesterday.
W: Oh, I see. I'll get changed then.

우•리•말•해•석

남: Jenny, 왜 체육복을 입고 있니?
여: 체육 수업을 위해 갈아 입었어. 우리는 지금 체육 수업이 있지 않니, 민준아?
남: 아니, 오늘의 시간표가 변경되었어. 우리는 지금 음악 수업이 있어.
여: 정말? 나 몰랐어.
남: 어제 김 선생님이 그것(시간표 변경)에 대해 말씀하셨어.
여: 오, 그렇구나. 그럼 갈아입어야겠다.

단•어•및•표•현

wear [wɛər] [동] 입다, 착용하다
sports uniform 체육복
PE class 체육 수업
timetable [táimtèibl] [명] 시간표

11 특정정보파악(교통수단) ▶ 정답 ③

듣•기•대•본

W: Why is the traffic so heavy today?
M: I think there is a car accident up ahead. I heard about it on the radio before you turned it off.
W: Oh, really? I didn't hear that. Anyway, we have to hurry to get there on time.
M: How about leaving the car at that parking lot and taking the subway?

W: I agree. Taking the subway will be faster than driving.

우·리·말·해·석

여: 오늘 교통량이 왜 이렇게 많지?

남: 나는 앞에 차 사고가 났다고 생각해. 나는 네가 라디오를 끄기 전에 라디오에서 그것에 대해 들었어.

여: 오, 정말? 나는 그것을 듣지 못했어. 어쨌든, 우리는 제시간에 거기에 도착하기 위해 서둘러야만 해.

남: 저 주차장에 차를 두고 지하철을 타는 것은 어때?

여: 나도 동의해. 지하철을 타는 게 운전하는 것보다 빠를 거야.

단·어·및·표·현

traffic[trǽfik] 명 교통량, 교통
heavy[hévi] 형 많은, 심한
turn off 끄다
on time 제시간에

12 이유파악 ▶ 정답 ④

듣·기·대·본

W: David, where are you going?

M: I'm going to the community center to volunteer for the Youth Mentorship Program.

W: What's that all about?

M: It's a program where I mentor young students, helping them with their homework and offering guidance.

W: That's wonderful! You've always been great with kids.

M: Thanks! I'm excited to help them.

우·리·말·해·석

여: David, 넌 어디 가고 있어?

남: 나는 청년 멘토십 프로그램에 자원봉사하려고 커뮤니티센터에 가는 중이야.

여: 그게 다 뭐야?

남: 그것은 그들(학생들)의 숙제를 도와주고 지도를 제공하여 어린 학생들에게 조언하는 프로그램이야.

여: 멋진걸! 넌 항상 아이들과 잘 지내왔지.

남: 고마워! 난 그들을 도울 수 있어서 기뻐.

단·어·및·표·현

volunteer[vὰləntíər] 동 자원봉사하다
mentor[méntɔːr] 동 지도하다, 조언하다
guidance[gáidəns] 명 지도, 가르침

13 대화장소추론 ▶ 정답 ③

듣·기·대·본

W: Hello, I'd like you to take a photo of me.

M: Sure. May I ask what the photo is for?

W: It's for my passport.

M: Okay. Then, I need to make the background white.

W: Is there anything I need to do?

M: Just make sure your ears are showing.

W: Okay. Shall I sit down here?

우·리·말·해·석

여: 안녕하세요, 저는 당신이 제 사진을 찍어주셨으면 해요.

남: 그럼요. 사진이 어떤 용도인지 물어봐도 될까요?

여: 제 여권을 위한 것이에요.

남: 좋아요. 그러면, 배경을 하얗게 만들 필요가 있네요.

여: 제가 해야 할 것이 있나요?

남: 귀가 꼭 보이도록만 하세요.

여: 알겠어요. 제가 여기에 앉을까요?

단·어·및·표·현

take a photo of ~ ~의 사진을 찍다

14 표불일치 ▶ 정답 ②

듣·기·대·본

W: Hello, everyone! Let me introduce our Kids' Baking Class. It'll be held this Saturday at 2 p.m. In this class, kids will learn how to bake their own cupcakes and decorate them with fun toppings. The class will last 2 hours. The fee is 10 dollars, including all ingredients. Please bring your own apron. The class will take place at the community center.

우·리·말·해·석

어린이 제빵 수업		
①	일시	이번 주 토요일, 오후 2시
②	주제	피자를 만드는 방법
③	수업 시간	2시간
④	참가비	10달러
⑤	장소	지역 주민 회관

여: 안녕하세요, 여러분! 저희 Kids' Baking Class(어린이 제빵 수업)를 소개하겠습니다. 이번 주 토요일 오후 2시에 진행됩니다. 이 수업에서 아이들은 자신만의 컵케이크를 굽고 그것을 재미있는 토핑들로 꾸미는 법을 배울 것입니다. 수업은 2시간 동안 진행됩니다. 요금은 모든 재료를 포함하여 10달러입니다. 개인 앞치마를 가져오시기 바랍니다. 수업은 지역 주민 회관에서 열립니다.

단·어·및·표·현

bake[beik] 동 굽다
decorate[dékərèit] 동 꾸미다, 장식하다
topping[tápiŋ] 명 토핑, 고명
last[læst] 동 계속되다, 지속되다
fee[fiː] 명 요금
include[inklúːd] 동 포함하다
ingredient[ingríːdiənt] 명 재료
apron[éiprən] 명 앞치마
take place 개최되다

15 부탁(요청)한일파악 ▶ 정답 ④

듣·기·대·본

W: What are you doing, honey?

M: I'm making some spaghetti. I learned the recipe at the cooking club.

W: I see. Wow! You have all the vegetables ready.

M: Yes, but I forgot to buy some cheese.

W: I think there's some in the refrigerator.

M: No, there isn't. Actually, could you go and buy some for me?

W: Sure. No problem.

우·리·말·해·석

여: 뭐 하고 있어요, 여보?

남: 저는 스파게티를 좀 만들고 있어요. 저는 요리 동호회에서 요리법을 배웠어요.

여: 그렇군요. 와! 당신이 모든 채소들을 준비해 뒀네요.

남: 네, 하지만 약간의 치즈를 사는 것을 잊었어요.

여: 제 생각에는 냉장고에 좀 있을 거에요.

남: 아니요, 없어요. 실은, 당신이 저를 위해 가서 좀 사다 줄래요?

여: 물론이지요. 문제없어요.

단·어·및·표·현

have ~ ready ~을 준비해 두다

forget to + 동사원형 ~할 것을 잊다

16 제안파악 ▶ 정답 ①

듣·기·대·본

W: This is a beautiful drawing. Did you make it?

M: Yes, I'm practicing for the art contest next month.

W: I didn't know you were interested in art.

M: I joined the art club this year. It's really fun.

W: Oh, then how about going to an art museum together? I like art, too.

M: That sounds exciting!

우·리·말·해·석

여: 이것은 아름다운 그림이다. 네가 그것을 만들었니?

남: 응, 나는 다음 달 미술 대회를 위해 연습하고 있어.

여: 나는 네가 미술에 관심이 있는 줄 몰랐어.

남: 나는 미술 동아리에 올해 가입했어. 그것은 정말 재미있어.

여: 아, 그러면 미술관에 같이 가는 게 어때? 나도 미술을 좋아해.

남: 그거 신나겠다!

단·어·및·표·현

be interested in ~ ~에 관심이 있다

17 할일파악 ▶ 정답 ②

듣·기·대·본

M: Mom, can we go to the K-Pop concert this Saturday?

W: I'm sorry, honey. But I don't think we can.

M: Why?

W: It's too late to get tickets.

M: Oh, okay. Then, how about going to the water park instead?

W: That's a good idea. You did say you wanted to try the new water slide.

우·리·말·해·석

남: 엄마, 우리 이번 주 토요일에 K-Pop 콘서트에 갈 수 있나요?

여: 미안해, 얘야. 하지만 우리는 못 갈 것 같아.

남: 왜요?

여: 표를 사기에는 너무 늦었단다.

남: 아, 알겠어요. 그럼 대신 워터파크에 가는 건 어때요?

여: 그거 좋은 생각이네. 너는 새로 생긴 워터 슬라이드를 타보고 싶다고 했었잖니.

단·어·및·표·현

instead [instéd] [부] 대신에

18 직업추론 ▶ 정답 ④

듣·기·대·본

W: Welcome to Bulguksa! I'm Jinny from Mother Tongue Travel.

M: Wow! It's so beautiful. How old is it?

W: It's about one thousand, two hundred years old.

M: (*pause*) Oh, look! There are two towers. What are those?

W: They are Seokkatap and Dabotap. Please come this way and I'll explain their history.

우·리·말·해·석

여: 불국사에 오신 걸 환영합니다! 저는 마더텅 여행사의 Jinny입니다.

남: 와! 무척 아름답네요. 얼마나 오래된 거죠?

여: 약 1,200년 되었어요.

남: (잠시 후) 오, 보세요! 두 개의 탑이 있네요. 저것들은 뭐죠?

여: 저것들은 석가탑과 다보탑입니다. 이쪽으로 오시면 제가 그것들의 역사를 설명해 드릴게요.

단·어·및·표·현

explain [iksplé in] [동] 설명하다

19 알맞은응답찾기 ▶ 정답 ⑤

듣·기·대·본

W: Kevin, how are you doing?

M: Hi, Ms. Lee. Classes are fine, but I still need to complete some volunteer hours.

W: Then, would you like to join my community service club? You can get volunteer hours there.

M: Oh, really? What kind of community service do you do?

W: We keep the streets and neighborhoods clean by picking up litter.

M: I'm interested. When does your club meet?

W: **Every Friday after school.**

우·리·말·해·석

① 나중에 보자.

② 천만에.

③ 나는 이해가 안 돼.

④ 네가 즐겁기를 바라.

⑤ 매주 금요일 방과 후에.

여: Kevin, 어떻게 지내니?

남: 안녕하세요, 이 선생님. 수업들은 좋아요, 그렇지만 저는 아직도 약간의 봉사 시간들을 채울 필요가 있어요.

여: 그러면, 너는 나의 지역 봉사 활동 동아리에 참여할래? 너는 거기서 봉사 시간들을 얻을 수 있어.

남: 오, 정말요? 선생님은 어떤 종류의 지역 봉사 활동을 하나요?

여: 우리는 쓰레기를 주워서 도로와 인근 지역을 깨끗하게 해.

남: 저 관심있어요. 선생님의 동아리는 언제 만나나요?

여: **매주 금요일 방과 후에.**

단·어·및·표·현

How are you doing? 어떻게 지내니?

Would you like to + 동사원형? ~할래?

neighborhood [néibərhùd] [명] 지역, 인근

20 알맞은응답찾기 ▶ 정답 ③

듣·기·대·본

W: Edward, whose violin is this?

M: It's mine.

W: Can you play the violin?

M: Yes, I can. What about you?

W: I can't play the violin. But, I like to listen to music a lot.

M: Oh, really? What's your favorite genre?

W: **I like classical music.**

우·리·말·해·석

① 나는 TV 보는 것을 좋아해.

② 그거 내가 제일 좋아하는 건데.

③ 나는 고전음악을 좋아해.

④ 괜찮아.

⑤ 정말 고마워.

여: Edward, 이건 누구 바이올린이니?

남: 내 거야.

여: 너 바이올린 연주할 줄 알아?

남: 응, 할 수 있어. 넌 어때?

여: 바이올린은 연주 못 해. 하지만 음악 듣는 것을 매우 좋아해.

남: 어, 정말? 어떤 장르를 가장 좋아하니?

여: **나는 고전음악을 좋아해.**

단·어·및·표·현

favorite[féivərit] 웹 제일 좋아하는

Words & Expressions Review

1. 가벼운, (양·정도가) 적은	2. 잠깐	3. 의기소침해 보이다
4. 음악을 듣다	5. 끄다	6. ~에 관심이 있다
7. 앞치마	8. ~할 것을 잊다	9. 연습하다
10. 계속되다, 지속되다	11. 엉덩이	12. 입다, 착용하다
13. 가장 좋아하는	14. 여행	15. 지역, 인근
16. 목도리	17. 친근한	18. ~할 것이다, ~할 셈이다
19. 오르다	20. 시간표	21. 영리한
22. 제시간에	23. 어떻게 지내니?	24. 죽다
25. 대신에	26. 빠른, 이른	27. 우주 비행사
28. 채소	29. 내리다, 떨어지다	30. 찾다
31. 자원봉사하다	32. (교통수단, 도로 등을) 타다, 이용하다	33. 지도하다, 조언하다
34. 기억하다	35. 설명하다	36. 재료
37. 여기 있어.	38. ~을 준비해 두다	39. 교통량, 교통
40. 가입하다, 함께 하다	41. 많은, 심한	42. 명랑한
43. 이쪽으로 오세요.	44. 냉장고	

Listening Test

영어듣기 모의고사 02회

|정|답|

01 ⑤	02 ②	03 ②	04 ①	05 ③
06 ⑤	07 ③	08 ⑤	09 ④	10 ⑤
11 ③	12 ⑤	13 ③	14 ④	15 ④
16 ⑤	17 ①	18 ③	19 ⑤	20 ⑤

01 그림정보파악(담화)   ▶ 정답 ⑤

듣·기·대·본

M: This is small and has buttons with numbers and symbols. When you press the buttons, you can solve math problems quickly. Students and adults use it for calculations. What is this?

우·리·말·해·석

남: 이것은 작고, 숫자와 부호가 적힌 버튼들이 있습니다. 버튼을 누르면 수학 문제를 빠르게 풀 수 있습니다. 학생들과 어른들은 계산할 때 이것을 사용합니다. 이것은 무엇일까요?

단·어·및·표·현

symbol[símbəl] 웹 부호, 기호

press[pres] 통 누르다

solve[salv] 통 (문제 등을) 풀다, 해결하다

calculation[kæ̀lkjuléiʃən] 웹 계산

02 그림정보파악(대화)   ▶ 정답 ②

듣·기·대·본

M: What can I do for you?

W: I want to buy rain boots for my daughter.

M: How about these ones with a cloud on them?

W: Hmm. Do you have shorter rain boots?

M: Sure. What about these ones with a duck on them? They are shorter.

W: I'll buy those ones. I hope my daughter likes them.

우·리·말·해·석

남: 무엇을 도와드릴까요?

여: 저는 제 딸을 위해 장화를 사고 싶어요.

남: 장화에 구름이 그려진 이것들은 어떤가요?

여: 음. 더 짧은 장화가 있나요?

남: 물론이죠. 장화에 오리 한 마리가 그려진 이것들은 어떤가요? 그것들은 더 짧아요.

여: 저는 그것들을 살게요. 저는 제 딸이 그것들을 좋아하길 바라요.

단·어·및·표·현

rain boots 장화

03 날씨파악-그림   ▶ 정답 ②

듣·기·대·본

W: Good evening. Here is today's weather report. In Seoul, it's cloudy with a chance of light rain later tonight. Busan is warm and sunny, perfect for outdoor activities. In Jeju, strong winds will be blowing throughout the day. Temperatures will drop tonight, so bring a light jacket if you go out!

우·리·말·해·석

여: 좋은 저녁입니다. 여기 오늘의 일기예보입니다. 서울은 흐리고 오늘 밤 늦게 약한 비가 올 가능성이 있습니다. 부산은 따뜻하고 맑아 야외 활동에 완벽합니다. 제주도는 하루 종일 강한 바람이 불겠습니다. 오늘 밤에는 기온이 내려갈 예정이니 만약 외출하신다면 가벼운 재킷을 챙기시기 바랍니다!

단·어·및·표·현

with a chance of ~의 가능성이 있는

perfect for ~에 완벽한

outdoor[áutdɔ̀ːr] 웹 야외의

blow[blou] 통 (바람이) 불다

throughout[θru(ː)áut] 전 ~동안 쭉

temperature[témpərətʃər] 웹 온도, 기온

drop[drap] 통 떨어지다

04 마지막말의도파악   ▶ 정답 ①

듣·기·대·본

W: So, did you do what I said?

M: Yes, Mom. I just finished my homework.

W: Good. How about your piano practice?

M: I finished that, too.

W: Great job. Always do what you have to do first.

M: OK, Mom. May I go out and play with Michael now?

W: Of course, you may.

우·리·말·해·석

여: 그래서, 너는 내가 말한 것을 했니?
남: 네, 엄마. 저는 막 제 숙제를 마쳤어요.
여: 잘했구나. 너의 피아노 연습은 어떻게 됐니?
남: 그것도 끝냈어요.
여: 잘했다. 항상 네가 해야 할 일을 먼저 하렴.
남: 네, 엄마. 이제 나가서 Michael과 놀아도 돼요?
여: 물론이지, 그렇게 해.

단·어·및·표·현

finish [fíniʃ] [동] 끝내다, 마무리 짓다
practice [prǽktis] [명] 연습
have to + 동사원형 (의무) ~해야 하다
may [mei] [동] (허락) ~해도 좋다

05 담화미언급 ▶ 정답 ③

듣·기·대·본

M: Hello, students. Let me remind you about our upcoming field trip to the Museum of Natural History. Don't forget that we are going on February 28th. We will leave at 9:50 in the morning. A bus will take us to the museum. I hope you're excited about the trip!

우·리·말·해·석

남: 안녕하세요, 학생 여러분. 제가 여러분에게 곧 있을 자연사 박물관으로의 현장학습에 대해 상기시켜드리고자 합니다. 우리가 2월 28일에 간다는 것을 잊지 마세요. 우리는 아침 9시 50분에 떠날 것입니다. 버스가 우리를 박물관으로 데려다 줄 것입니다. 저는 여러분이 현장학습에 대해 많이 기대하기를 바랍니다!

단·어·및·표·현

upcoming [ʌ́pkʌ̀miŋ] [형] 곧 있을, 다가오는
field trip 현장학습, 견학

06 수치파악 ▶ 정답 ⑤

듣·기·대·본

M: Hey, Jiyoung! Do you want to go to Burger Bites tonight?
W: Sure! I'm craving a burger!
M: Same here.
W: What time?
M: They start serving at 5 p.m. How about 5:30 p.m.?
W: I have piano practice until 5:15. Can we make it 6 p.m.?
M: Sounds good. See you at Burger Bites.

우·리·말·해·석

남: 이봐, 지영아! 너는 오늘 밤 Burger Bites에 가고 싶니?
여: 물론이지! 난 햄버거를 간절히 원해!
남: 나도 마찬가지야.
여: 몇 시에?
남: 그들은 오후 5시에 식사를 제공하기 시작해. 오후 5시 30분은 어때?
여: 난 오후 5시 15분까지 피아노 연습이 있어. 우리 오후 6시에 갈 수 있을까?
남: 좋아. Burger Bites에서 보자.

단·어·및·표·현

crave [kreiv] [동] 간절히 원하다, 갈망하다
Same here. 나도 마찬가지야.
serve [səːrv] [동] (식사 등을) 제공하다
make it (모임 등에) 가다

07 장래희망추론 ▶ 정답 ③

듣·기·대·본

W: Daniel, what's on your mind?
M: I'm thinking about what job to do in the future.
W: Any ideas?
M: I like how teachers help kids learn.
W: Teachers do make a big difference.
M: Exactly. I want to be like my favorite teachers who helped me learn.
W: That's a great goal!

우·리·말·해·석

여: Daniel, 무슨 생각해?
남: 난 미래에 어떤 일을 할지에 대해 생각하고 있었어.
여: 어떤 생각이 있니?
남: 나는 선생님들이 아이들이 배우도록 돕는 방식을 좋아해.
여: 선생님들은 큰 변화를 일으켜.
남: 정확해. 나는 내가 배우게 도와주셨던 내가 가장 좋아하는 선생님들처럼 되고 싶어.
여: 멋진 목표다!

단·어·및·표·현

make a difference 변화를 일으키다, 차이를 낳다, 도움이 되다
goal [goul] [명] 목표

08 심정추론 ▶ 정답 ⑤

듣·기·대·본

M: Kelly, guess what! I'm going to Japan during summer vacation.
W: Sounds great! What are you going to do there?
M: I'm going to Disney World. I can't wait!
W: Really? I'm so jealous of you!
M: I'm really looking forward to my trip.

우·리·말·해·석

① 걱정스러운 ② 지루한 ③ 부러운 ④ 수줍은 ⑤ 들뜬

남: Kelly, 있잖아! 나는 여름 방학에 일본에 갈 거야.
여: 좋겠다! 거기서 뭐 할 거야?
남: 나는 디즈니월드에 갈 거야. 정말 기다려져!
여: 정말? 나는 네가 무척 부럽다!
남: 내 여행이 정말 기대돼.

단·어·및·표·현

Guess what! 있잖아!
jealous of ~ ~가 부러운, ~을 질투하는

09 할일파악(대화직후) ▶ 정답 ④

듣·기·대·본

M: Good morning, Mom. I woke up late.
W: Good morning, Steve. How about going out for breakfast?
M: Now? What's up?
W: The water supply is down.
M: On Sunday?
W: Just for a couple of hours. Can you make your bed before we go?
M: Sure. I'll do it right now.

우·리·말·해·석

남: 좋은 아침이에요, 엄마. 전 늦게 일어났어요.
여: 좋은 아침이란다, Steve. 아침 먹으러 나가는 거 어때?

남: 지금요? 무슨 일이에요?
여: 수돗물 공급이 끊겼어. (단수됐어.)
남: 일요일에요?
여: 몇 시간 동안만이야. 우리가 가기 전에 네 잠자리를 정돈할 수 있겠니?
남: 물론이죠. 지금 바로 그것을 할게요.

단·어·및·표·현
wake up 일어나다
go out 나가다, 외출하다
supply[səplái] 옝 공급
be down (기계 따위가) 고장 나다, 작동이 멎다
make one's bed (자고 나서) 잠자리를 정돈하다, 이불을 개다

10 대화화제추론 ▶ 정답 ⑤

듣·기·대·본
W: Have you checked the new posting on the school website?
M: You mean the one about the new name for the school library?
W: Yes. There were three options. Which one did you pick?
M: I chose number two, 'Forest of Wisdom.' I like the meaning of the name.
W: Me, too! The name is also catchy.
M: You're right.

우·리·말·해·석
여: 너 학교 웹사이트에 올라온 새로운 게시물 확인했니?
남: 학교 도서관을 위한 새로운 이름에 관한 것 말이니?
여: 응. 3가지 선택지가 있었어. 너는 어느 것을 골랐니?
남: 나는 2번, '지혜의 숲'을 골랐어. 나는 그 이름의 의미가 마음에 들어.
여: 나도 그래! 그 이름은 또한 기억하기도 쉬워.
남: 네 말이 맞아.

단·어·및·표·현
forest[fɔ́(ː)rist] 옝 숲, 삼림
wisdom[wízdəm] 옝 지혜, 슬기
catchy[kǽtʃi] 옝 기억하기 쉬운

11 특정정보파악(교통수단) ▶ 정답 ③

듣·기·대·본
W: John, I got a call from the airline. We cannot fly today.
M: Why? Bad weather?
W: Yes. Should we stay here one more night?
M: Well, there's an express bus. If we leave now, we can be back tonight.
W: Let's hurry, then.

우·리·말·해·석
여: John, 항공사에서 전화를 받았어. 오늘 비행기를 못 탄대.
남: 왜? 날씨가 나빠서?
여: 응. 우리 여기서 하룻밤 더 있어야 하나?
남: 글쎄, 고속버스가 있어. 지금 출발하면, 오늘 밤에 돌아갈 수 있어.
여: 그럼 서두르자.

단·어·및·표·현
get a call 전화를 받다

12 이유파악 ▶ 정답 ⑤

듣·기·대·본
W: Hey, Daniel. Where are you going?
M: Hi, Mia. I'm going to the city park.
W: Oh, are you going to jog there?

M: No, I'm meeting my science group there. We're observing insects for our project.
W: That's cool! I hope you find something interesting.

우·리·말·해·석
여: 안녕, Daniel. 너 어디 가니?
남: 안녕, Mia. 나는 시립 공원에 가.
여: 오, 거기서 조깅할 거야?
남: 아니, 나는 거기서 우리 과학 조를 만날 거야. 우리는 우리 과제를 위해 곤충을 관찰할 거야.
여: 멋지다! 재미있는 걸 찾길 바랄게.

단·어·및·표·현
jog[dʒɑg] 통 조깅하다
observe[əbzə́ːrv] 통 관찰하다
insect[ínsekt] 옝 곤충
hope[houp] 통 바라다

13 대화장소추론 ▶ 정답 ③

듣·기·대·본
W: Dad! I'm so excited right now.
M: Calm down, honey. Don't run near the water.
W: Okay. Can we go on that water slide?
M: Of course, but let's do some warm-ups before we go in the water.
W: Sure. I can't wait to try it out!
M: I'm glad that you like it here.

우·리·말·해·석
여: 아빠! 나 지금 엄청 흥분돼요.
남: 진정해라, 얘야. 물가에서 뛰지 마라.
여: 알았어요. 우리 저 물 미끄럼틀을 타러 갈 수 있어요?
남: 물론이지, 하지만 우리가 물에 들어가기 전에 준비운동을 좀 하자.
여: 그럼요. 저는 몹시 그것을 해보고 싶어요!
남: 네가 여기를 좋아하니 기쁘다.

단·어·및·표·현
calm down 진정하다
can't wait to + 동사원형 몹시 ~하고 싶다, ~하는 것이 무척 기다려지다

14 그림정보파악-위치 ▶ 정답 ④

듣·기·대·본
W: Kevin, can you help me find my watch?
M: Sure. Where did you last see it?
W: I think I saw it on the bed, but it's not there now.
M: It's not on the desk, either. Oh, look! Isn't that your watch on the bookshelf?
W: Ah, there it is! I forgot that I had put it there.

우·리·말·해·석
여: Kevin, 내가 손목시계 찾는 것을 도와줄 수 있어?
남: 물론이지. 네가 그것을 어디서 마지막으로 봤어?
여: 침대에서 봤다고 생각했는데, 지금 거기에 없어.
남: 책상에도 없어. 오, 봐봐! 책장에 있는 저거 네 손목시계 아니야?
여: 아, 저기 있었네! 거기다 올려놓은 걸 잊고 있었어.

단·어·및·표·현
watch[wɑtʃ] 옝 손목시계
bookshelf[búkʃelf] 옝 책장

15 부탁(요청)한일파악 ▶ 정답 ④

듣·기·대·본

M: Maya, did you join any of the school clubs?
W: I'm on my way to join one now. Today is the deadline, remember?
M: Yes, but I'm late for my piano lesson, so I need a favor.
W: You want me to sign you up?
M: Yes. Can you please sign me up for the table tennis club?
W: Sure. See you later!

우·리·말·해·석

남: Maya, 학교 동아리 중 어느 것에라도 가입했어?
여: 지금 가입하러 가는 중이야. 오늘 마감이야, 기억해?
남: 응, 하지만 피아노 수업에 늦어서 그러는데 부탁이 있어.
여: 내가 너를 등록해 줄까?
남: 응, 나를 탁구 동아리에 등록해 줄래?
여: 좋아. 나중에 보자!

단·어·및·표·현

sign ~ up ~을 등록하다

16 제안파악 ▶ 정답 ⑤

듣·기·대·본

M: Tanya, are you okay?
W: No. The rain leaked into my room last night. I was up all night dealing with it.
M: Oh, no. Did you forget to close the windows?
W: The windows were all closed. The water still came in, though.
M: Why don't you call the owner of the house?
W: Yeah, I should ask the owner to repair the leaky windows.

우·리·말·해·석

남: Tanya, 너 괜찮니?
여: 아니. 어젯밤 비가 내 방으로 새어 들어왔어. 나는 그것을 처리하느라 밤을 새웠어.
남: 오, 이런. 너 창문 닫는 것을 잊었니?
여: 창문은 모두 닫혀 있었어. 하지만 물이 계속 들어왔어.
남: 집주인에게 전화해 보는 건 어때?
여: 응, 나는 물이 새는 창문을 수리해달라고 주인에게 부탁해야겠어.

단·어·및·표·현

leak [li:k] [동] (액체 · 기체 등이) 새다
be up all night 밤을 새다
deal with ~ ~을 처리하다, 다루다
though [ðou] [부] (문장 끝에 와서) 하지만, 그렇지만
repair [ripέər] [동] 수리하다
leaky [lí:ki] [형] (물 · 가스가) 새는, 구멍이 난

17 한일파악 ▶ 정답 ①

듣·기·대·본

(Cellphone rings.)
M: Hey, Yejin!
W: Hello, Daniel. Are you coming to the charity bake sale this Saturday?
M: Of course. Do you need me to bring anything?
W: No need. I baked all the treats this afternoon.
M: That's wonderful! What did you make?
W: I made some cookies and brownies.
M: Sounds delicious! Then, I'll come with many friends.

우·리·말·해·석

(휴대전화가 울린다.)
남: 이봐, 예진아!
여: 안녕, Daniel. 너는 이번 주 토요일에 자선 빵 판매 행사에 오니?
남: 물론이지. 너는 내가 뭔가 가져가길 원하니?
여: (그럴) 필요 없어. 난 오늘 오후에 모든 간식들을 구웠어.
남: 멋지다! 너는 무엇을 만들었니?
여: 나는 쿠키들과 브라우니들을 좀 만들었어.
남: 맛있겠다! 그러면, 나는 많은 친구들과 갈게.

단·어·및·표·현

charity [tʃǽrəti] [명] 자선
bake sale 빵 판매 행사
treat [tri:t] [명] 간식

18 직업추론 ▶ 정답 ③

듣·기·대·본

(Telephone rings.)
W: Green Beans.
M: Ms. Carter, I'm delivering your order now. 40kg of coffee beans, right?
W: That's right. I'm expecting many customers this week.
M: Well, your coffee is the best in town.
W: It's thanks to your beans. I'll have a cup ready for you.
M: That's very kind. I'll be there in an hour.

우·리·말·해·석

(전화벨이 울린다.)
여: Green Beans입니다.
남: Carter 씨, 주문하신 것을 지금 배달하려고 합니다. 커피 원두 40kg 맞지요?
여: 맞습니다. 이번 주에 손님이 많을 거라고 예상해요.
남: 음, 당신의 커피는 동네에서 최고예요.
여: 당신의 원두 덕분입니다. 한 잔 준비해 드릴게요.
남: 정말 친절하시네요. 한 시간 후에 가겠습니다.

단·어·및·표·현

thanks to ~ ~ 덕분에

19 알맞은응답찾기 ▶ 정답 ⑤

듣·기·대·본

W: What would you like to order?
M: Can I have a cheese and tomato sandwich, please?
W: Sure. Would you like white bread or brown bread?
M: Brown, please.
W: Is it for here or to go?
M: To go. And I'll also have a bottle of water.
W: OK. It's 7 dollars. How would you like to pay?
M: Here is my credit card.

우·리·말·해·석

① 아뇨, 그게 다예요. ② 저는 치즈를 안 좋아해요.
③ 오늘은 비가 올 거예요. ④ 당신은 매우 친절하군요.
⑤ 여기 제 신용카드요.

여: 무엇을 주문하시겠습니까?
남: 치즈와 토마토 샌드위치로 주시겠어요?
여: 네. 하얀 빵이 좋으세요, 아니면 갈색 빵이 좋으세요?
남: 갈색으로 주세요.
여: 드시고 가시나요, 아니면 가져가시나요?
남: 가져갈 거예요. 그리고 물도 한 병 주세요.

여: 네. 7달러입니다. 어떻게 결제하시겠어요?
남: 여기 제 신용카드요.

단·어·및·표·현

order [ɔ́ːrdər] [동] 주문하다
for here or to go 여기서 드실 건가요, 가져가실 건가요
a bottle of + 명사 ~ 한 병

20 알맞은응답찾기 ▶ 정답 ⑤

듣·기·대·본

M: Laura, where were you yesterday? I didn't see you at Matthew's birthday party.
W: Oh, no! Was that yesterday? I thought it was today.
M: Matthew is disappointed because you didn't come.
W: I completely forgot. How can I make up for it?
M: Well, you should apologize first.
W: Should I send him a text message?
M: No, you should talk to him directly.

우·리·말·해·석

① 많은 사람들이 파티에 있었어.
② 그녀는 항상 실망스러워.
③ 미안, 나 어제 핸드폰을 잃어버렸어.
④ 우리는 내일 바쁠 예정이야.
⑤ 아니, 너는 그와 직접 얘기해야 돼.

남: Laura, 어제 어디 있었어? Matthew의 생일 파티에서 너를 못 봤어.
여: 오, 안 돼! 그게 어제였어? 나는 오늘이라고 생각했어.
남: 네가 안 와서 Matthew가 실망했어.
여: 완전히 잊었어. 어떻게 만회하지?
남: 음, 우선 사과를 해야 돼.
여: 그에게 문자 메시지를 보내야 할까?
남: 아니, 너는 그와 직접 얘기해야 돼.

단·어·및·표·현

completely [kəmplíːtli] [부] 완전히, 전적으로
make up for ~ ~을 만회하다, 보상하다
apologize [əpɑ́lədʒàiz] [동] 사과하다, 사죄하다

Words & Expressions Review

1. 온도, 기온	2. 손님, 고객	3. 부탁이 있다
4. (바람이) 불다	5. 관찰하다	6. 계산
7. 몹시 ~하고 싶다	8. (액체 · 기체 등이) 새다	9. 고속버스
10. 연습	11. 곤충	12. 밤을 새다
13. 숲, 삼림	14. 부호, 기호	15. 수리하다
16. 장화	17. ~하는 중에	18. 곧 있을, 다가오는
19. 진정하다	20. 목표	21. 박물관
22. 끝내다, 마무리 짓다	23. ~을 처리하다, 다루다	24. ~을 만회하다
25. ~을 등록하다	26. ~이 기대되다	27. 현장학습, 견학
28. 변화를 일으키다, 차이를 낳다, 도움이 되다	29. 책장	30. 전화를 받다
31. ~가 부러운, ~를 질투하는	32. ~ 덕분에, ~ 때문에	33. 자선
34. 공급	35. (문제 등을) 풀다, 해결하다	36. 마감, 기한
37. 나가다, 외출하다	38. ~동안, 쭉	39. 기억하기 쉬운
40. 주문하다	41. 누르다	42. 야외의
43. 일어나다	44. 사과하다	

Listening Test

영어듣기 모의고사 03회

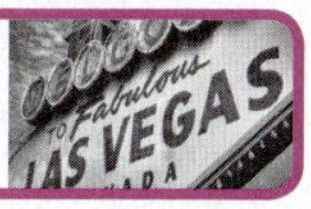

|정|답|

01 ②	02 ②	03 ④	04 ①	05 ⑤
06 ③	07 ②	08 ④	09 ③	10 ①
11 ③	12 ④	13 ③	14 ⑤	15 ①
16 ④	17 ②	18 ⑤	19 ③	20 ④

01 그림정보파악(담화) ▶ 정답 ②

듣·기·대·본

M: I have four legs and a long tail. I have yellow fur with small black spots. I eat mostly meat. I can run faster than any other land animal. What am I?

우·리·말·해·석

남: 나는 4개의 다리와 한 개의 긴 꼬리가 있다. 나는 작고 검은 반점이 있는 노란색 털을 가지고 있다. 나는 주로 고기를 먹는다. 나는 어느 다른 육지 동물들보다 빨리 달릴 수 있다. 나는 뭘까?

단·어·및·표·현

mostly [móustli] [부] 주로, 대부분
land animal 육지 동물

02 그림정보파악(대화) ▶ 정답 ②

듣·기·대·본

M: How can I help you?
W: I'm looking for a poncho towel for my 5-year-old son.
M: How about this one with sharks on it?
W: It's nice, but he really likes dinosaurs these days.
M: What about this one with little dinosaurs on it? It has a hood, too.
W: I love it. I'll buy that one.

우·리·말·해·석

남: 어떻게 도와드릴까요?
여: 저는 제 다섯 살 아들을 위해 망토 타월을 찾고 있어요.
남: 상어 그림이 있는 이건 어떠세요?
여: 그것은 괜찮긴 하지만, 요즘 그는 공룡을 정말 좋아해요.
남: 그럼 작은 공룡이 그려져 있는 이건 어떠세요? 모자도 있어요.
여: 마음에 들어요. 이걸로 살게요.

단·어·및·표·현

look for ~을 찾다
poncho towel 망토 타월
these days 요즘에
hood [hud] [명] 모자

03 날씨파악-그림 ▶ 정답 ④

듣·기·대·본

M: Good morning. This is the weather forecast. We can enjoy the beautiful clear sky now, but it will be cloudy in the afternoon. Tomorrow, we will have the first snow of this winter. So, put on warm clothes and gloves.

우·리·말·해·석

남: 좋은 아침입니다. 일기 예보입니다. 우리는 지금 화창하고 맑은 하늘을 즐길 수 있지만, 오후에는 흐려질 예정입니다. 내일, 우리는 이번 겨울의 첫 눈을 맞을 것입니다. 그러니, 따뜻한 옷을 입고 장갑을 끼세요.

단·어·및·표·현

cloudy [kláudi] 형 흐린
put on 입다, 끼다

04 마지막말의도파악 ▶ 정답 ①

듣·기·대·본

W: Are you OK, Mike? You don't look very well.
M: Mom, I stayed home all day and I feel bored.
W: OK. How about doing some exercise?
M: I don't feel like it.
W: Then, shall we go outside and take a walk?
M: Sure. I think getting some fresh air will help.

우·리·말·해·석

여: 괜찮니, Mike? 너 안 좋아 보여.
남: 엄마, 저는 하루 종일 집에 있었고 지루해요.
여: 그렇구나. 운동을 좀 하는 게 어떻겠니?
남: 그럴 기분이 아니에요.
여: 그러면, 우리 밖에 나가서 산책할까?
남: 좋아요. 신선한 공기를 쐬는 것이 도움될 거라 생각해요.

단·어·및·표·현

bored [bɔːrd] 형 지루해하는, 따분해하는
take a walk 산책하다

05 담화미언급 ▶ 정답 ⑤

듣·기·대·본

M: Hello, students. This is your science teacher, Bill Jones. Let me tell you about the upcoming science camp. It'll be from January 20 to 22. It'll take place at the National Science Museum. The topic for this camp is smart cities, which are cities that use various ways to collect data. The fee is 100,000 won. This will be a great chance for students to learn about smart cities.

우·리·말·해·석

남: 학생 여러분, 안녕하세요. 저는 여러분의 과학 선생님인 Bill Jones입니다. 여러분에게 다가올 과학 캠프에 대해 말씀드릴게요. 그건 1월 20일부터 22일까지 진행될 겁니다. 그건 국립 과학 박물관에서 개최될 예정입니다. 이 캠프의 주제는 스마트 시티인데, 그것은 데이터를 수집하는 다양한 방법을 활용하는 도시입니다. 요금은 10만 원입니다. 이것은 학생들이 스마트 시티에 대해 배울 수 있는 좋은 기회가 될 것입니다.

단·어·및·표·현

upcoming [ʌ́pkʌ̀miŋ] 형 다가오는
take place 개최되다, 일어나다
various [vέ(ː)əriəs] 형 다양한

06 수치파악 ▶ 정답 ③

듣·기·대·본

M: Lily, would you like to help me buy Kenny's birthday present?
W: Sure. Is this afternoon OK?
M: Yes. Shall we meet at 3 at the mall?

W: How about 4? I have to finish my homework.
M: Oh, I forgot. I have to do my homework, too. Let's meet at 5.
W: All right!

우·리·말·해·석

남: Lily, 내가 Kenny의 생일 선물 사는 것을 도와줄래?
여: 물론이지. 오늘 오후 괜찮아?
남: 응. 쇼핑몰에서 3시에 만날까?
여: 4시는 어때? 나 숙제를 끝내야 해.
남: 아, 깜빡했다. 나도 숙제를 해야 해. 5시에 만나자.
여: 좋아!

단·어·및·표·현

Shall we ~? ~할까요?

👂 🎧 LISTENING ADVICE

영국식 영어는 미국식 영어와는 달리 [a]를 [애]가 아닌 [아]로 발음합니다. 예를 들어 'afternoon'이라는 단어는 미국에서는 [애프털눈]이라고 발음하지만 영국에서는 [아프터눈]이라고 발음합니다.

07 장래희망추론 ▶ 정답 ②

듣·기·대·본

M: How did you like the movie?
W: I thought it was awesome. The lead actor was great.
M: Wasn't he? He was very believable in that role.
W: You are really into him. Have you seen any of his other movies?
M: I've seen most of them. I want to be an actor like him.
W: Really? I believe you will be one day.
M: Thanks. That's very kind of you.

우·리·말·해·석

남: 그 영화 어땠어?
여: 나는 그것이 굉장하다고 생각했어. 주연 배우가 훌륭했어.
남: 그렇지 않니? 그는 그 역할에서 매우 그럴듯했어.
여: 너 정말 그에게 푹 빠졌구나. 너는 그의 다른 영화들을 본 적이 있니?
남: 나는 그것들을 대부분 다 봤어. 나는 그와 같은 배우가 되고 싶어.
여: 정말? 나는 네가 언젠가 될 거라고 생각해.
남: 고마워. 너는 참 친절하구나.

단·어·및·표·현

lead actor 주연 배우
believable [bilíːvəbl] 형 그럴듯한
be into ~ ~에 빠져있다
one day 언젠가

08 심정추론 ▶ 정답 ④

듣·기·대·본

M: Hey, Emily.
W: Hi, Huey. Do you know that Ebony moved last week?
M: What? I didn't know that.
W: She moved to San Francisco.
M: Oh, I am so sorry to hear that. Ebony is your best friend, right?
W: Yes. I miss her very much.

우·리·말·해·석

남: 안녕, Emily.
여: 안녕, Huey. 너 Ebony가 지난주에 이사 간 것 알고 있어?
남: 뭐라고? 난 몰랐어.

여: 그녀는 샌프란시스코로 이사 갔어.

남: 오, 정말 유감이다. Ebony는 네 가장 친한 친구잖아, 맞지?

여: 응. 나는 그녀가 정말 그리워.

단·어·및·표·현

move[muːv] 통 이사하다

09 할일파악(대화직후) ▶ 정답 ③

듣·기·대·본

M: Hey, Linda! I like your profile picture.

W: You mean the one on SNS? Thanks, I took it yesterday.

M: It's a nice photo. You look a little different, though.

W: That's because I used a special app to edit it.

M: Really? I didn't notice. Which app did you use?

W: Here, I'll show it to you. It's really handy.

우·리·말·해·석

남: 안녕, Linda! 나는 네 프로필 사진이 마음에 들어.

여: SNS에 있는 거 말하는 거야? 고마워, 그거 어제 찍었어.

남: 그것은 멋진 사진이야. 그런데 너는 조금 달라 보이기는 해.

여: 그것은 내가 편집하기 위해 특별한 앱을 썼기 때문이야.

남: 정말? 알아채지 못했어. 어떤 앱을 썼니?

여: 여기, 내가 너에게 보여줄게. 그것은 정말 편리해.

단·어·및·표·현

edit[édit] 통 편집하다

notice[nóutis] 통 알아채다

handy[hǽndi] 형 편리한

10 대화화제추론 ▶ 정답 ①

듣·기·대·본

W: Mr. Choi, we really want to win the relay race at the sports day.

M: That's great! Let me give you some tips.

W: Yes, please! What's the most important thing?

M: You need to pass the baton smoothly.

W: How can we do that?

M: Practice handing it over while running at full speed.

W: Should we think about the order of the runners, too?

M: Absolutely. Put your fastest runner at the end to finish strong!

우·리·말·해·석

여: 최 선생님, 저희는 운동회에서 계주 경기를 꼭 이기고 싶어요.

남: 좋아! 내가 몇 가지 조언을 줄게.

여: 네, 꼭 알려주세요! 가장 중요한 것은 무엇인가요?

남: 바통을 순조롭게 전달해야 해.

여: 그건 어떻게 할 수 있나요?

남: 전속력으로 달리면서 바통을 넘기는 연습을 하렴.

여: 주자 순서도 생각해야 하나요?

남: 당연하지. 힘 있게 마무리하기 위해 가장 빠른 주자를 마지막에 배치하렴!

단·어·및·표·현

win[win] 통 이기다

sports day 운동회, 체육대회

tip[tip] 명 조언

baton[bætán] 명 바통, 배턴

hand over 넘겨주다

order[ɔ́ːrdər] 명 순서

11 특정정보파악(교통수단) ▶ 정답 ③

듣·기·대·본

W: How are you enjoying your stay?

M: I'm enjoying it very much. The beach here is really nice.

W: There's another nice beach a few kilometers away called Higgs Beach.

M: Really? How do I get there?

W: There's a bus, but I can call you a taxi if you want.

M: The bus will be fine. Thank you.

우·리·말·해·석

여: 즐겁게 머무르고 계시나요?

남: 아주 즐겁게 지내고 있습니다. 여기 해변이 정말 멋집니다.

여: Higgs 해변이라고 불리는 다른 멋진 해변이 몇 킬로미터 떨어진 곳에 있습니다.

남: 정말입니까? 어떻게 갈 수 있나요?

여: 버스가 있지만 원하시면 택시를 불러드릴 수 있습니다.

남: 버스가 좋을 것 같습니다. 고맙습니다.

단·어·및·표·현

another[ənʌ́ðər] 형 다른, 또 하나의 명 또 하나의 것

12 이유파악 ▶ 정답 ④

듣·기·대·본

M: Jina, do you need anything from the supermarket?

W: Yes, honey. I need a bag of ice.

M: Okay. What do you need it for?

W: I sprained my ankle this morning, so I want to use it to reduce the pain.

M: I see. I'll make sure to buy it.

W: Thank you.

우·리·말·해·석

남: Jina, 당신 슈퍼마켓에서 필요한 것이 있나요?

여: 네, 여보. 저는 얼음 한 봉지가 필요해요.

남: 알겠어요. 당신은 그것이 무엇에 필요한가요?

여: 저는 오늘 아침에 발목을 삐어서 통증을 줄이기 위해 그것을 사용하고 싶어요.

남: 그렇군요. 제가 그것을 꼭 사올게요.

여: 고마워요.

단·어·및·표·현

sprain[sprein] 통 삐다, 접지르다

ankle[ǽŋkl] 명 발목

reduce[ridjúːs] 통 줄이다

pain[pein] 명 고통

make sure to + 동사원형 꼭 ~하다

13 대화장소추론 ▶ 정답 ③

듣·기·대·본

M: Can I see your passport, please?

W: Here it is.

M: Why are you visiting Chicago?

W: I have a business meeting here.

M: How long will you stay?

W: For three days.

M: OK. Enjoy your stay in Chicago.

우·리·말·해·석

남: 여권 좀 보여주시겠습니까?

여: 여기요.
남: 왜 시카고를 방문하시는 거죠?
여: 여기에서 업무상 회의가 있어요.
남: 얼마나 머무르실 겁니까?
여: 사흘 동안이요.
남: 좋습니다. 시카고에서 즐거운 시간 보내십시오.

단·어·및·표·현
passport [pǽspɔːrt] 명 여권

> 🗣 **LISTENING ADVICE**
> 't'는 강세를 받는 강모음과 강세를 받지 않는 약모음 사이에 오면, 부드러운 [r] 소리로 발음됩니다. 따라서 'visiting'은 [비지링], 'meeting'은 [미링]으로 발음됩니다.

14 표불일치 ▶ 정답 ⑤

듣·기·대·본
W: Hello, Urban Heights Mall shoppers! Join our Family Drawing Class this Sunday at 1 p.m. Kids will draw a picture of their family, and then their drawing will be printed on a T-shirt for them to keep. The class lasts 2 hours. You can join for free. Spots are first come, first served. To register, visit the information desk on the first floor. Thanks!

우·리·말·해·석

	가족 그림 그리기 수업	
①	일시	이번 주 일요일, 오후 1시
②	행사 내용	자신의 가족을 그림으로 그리면 그 그림이 티셔츠에 인쇄됨
③	소요 시간	2시간
④	참가비	무료
⑤	접수 방법	온라인으로 신청

여: 안녕하세요, Urban Heights Mall 고객 여러분! 이번 주 일요일 오후 1시에 저희 가족 그림 그리기 수업에 참여해 보세요. 아이들은 가족 그림을 그리고, 그들이 직접 가질 수 있도록 그들의 그림은 티셔츠에 인쇄될 것입니다. 수업은 2시간 동안 진행됩니다. 무료로 참여하실 수 있습니다. 자리는 선착순입니다. 등록하시려면 1층 안내 데스크를 방문해 주세요. 감사합니다!

단·어·및·표·현
print [print] 동 인쇄하다
keep [kiːp] 동 (자기 것으로) 갖다, 보유하다
for free 무료로
first come, first served 선착순
register [rédʒistər] 동 등록하다
sign up 신청하다

15 부탁(요청)한일파악 ▶ 정답 ①

듣·기·대·본
[Cellphone rings.]
M: Hi, Jessica.
W: Hey, Ha-jun. Today we're going on a school field trip to the forest.
M: Yes! I've got my lunchbox and trainers ready.
W: I'll bring sun cream. But I don't have a hat.
M: I have two hats.
W: Can I borrow one? It's so sunny outside.

M: Sure. I'll bring them both to school.

우·리·말·해·석
[휴대전화가 울린다.]
남: 여보세요, Jessica.
여: 안녕, 하준아. 오늘 우리는 숲으로 학교 현장학습을 갈 거야.
남: 응! 나는 내 점심 도시락과 운동화를 준비해놨지.
여: 내가 선크림을 가져갈게. 하지만 나는 모자가 없어.
남: 나는 모자가 두 개 있어.
여: 내가 하나 빌려도 될까? 밝은 햇빛이 너무 강해.
남: 물론이지. 내가 그것들 둘 다 학교에 가져갈게.

단·어·및·표·현
field trip 현장학습
lunchbox [lʌntʃbáks] 명 도시락
trainer [tréinər] 명 운동화

16 제안파악 ▶ 정답 ④

듣·기·대·본
M: Hey, look out the window. It's raining!
W: That's true. Did you bring an umbrella?
M: No. My mom is picking me up after school. Did you?
W: No, I totally forgot.
M: Then, why don't you let my mom drive you home, as well?
W: Thanks. That's very kind of you.

우·리·말·해·석
남: 저기, 창문 밖을 봐. 비가 오고 있어!
여: 진짜네. 너 우산 가져왔어?
남: 아니, 엄마가 방과 후에 나를 데리러 오실 거야. 너는 가져왔어?
여: 아니, 나는 (우산 가져오는 것을) 완전히 깜빡했어.
남: 그러면, 우리 엄마께 너도 집에 태워다 달라고 하는 게 어때?
여: 고마워. 정말 친절하구나.

단·어·및·표·현
totally [tóutəli] 부 완전히
let [let] 동 ~하게 하다

17 한일파악 ▶ 정답 ②

듣·기·대·본
M: Sarah, how was your holiday?
W: Great. I relaxed at home watching my favorite movies. How about you?
M: I went on a tour of the fire station.
W: Sounds interesting. Did you learn anything?
M: Yes. The firemen taught us what to do in a fire emergency.

우·리·말·해·석
남: Sarah, 너의 휴일은 어땠어?
여: 아주 좋았어. 나는 내가 가장 좋아하는 영화들을 보면서 집에서 쉬었어. 너는 어땠어?
남: 나는 소방서로 견학을 갔어.
여: 흥미롭게 들리네. 너는 무언가를 배웠어?
남: 응. 소방관들이 우리에게 화재 응급상황에서 무엇을 해야 할지 가르쳐 주었어.

단·어·및·표·현
relax [rilǽks] 동 쉬다, 휴식을 취하다
go on a tour of ~ ~을 견학 가다
fire station 소방서

18 직업추론 ▶ 정답 ⑤

듣·기·대·본

W: Hi, Mike. You look tired.
M: I had to work all night.
W: Are you still working on the web page?
M: Yes. They liked my design, but I needed to make some changes.
W: What kind of changes?
M: Mostly colors. Now the page is more blue-based.

우·리·말·해·석

여: 안녕, Mike. 너 피곤해 보여.
남: 나는 밤새 일해야 했어.
여: 아직도 웹페이지 작업하고 있니?
남: 응. 그 사람들이 내 디자인을 좋아했지만, 몇 가지를 수정할 필요가 있었어.
여: 어떤 수정?
남: 주로 색깔이야. 이제 웹페이지가 더 파란색 기반이야.

단·어·및·표·현

mostly [móustli] ⑪ 주로, 대개

19 알맞은응답찾기 ▶ 정답 ③

듣·기·대·본

W: Next Friday is my grandfather's birthday.
M: Did you get anything for him?
W: Not yet. Do you have any recommendations?
M: How about buying him a birthday cake?
W: I don't think he likes sweets.
M: How about a hat, then? Your grandfather wears a hat all the time.
W: That's a good idea.

우·리·말·해·석

① 토요일이야.　　　　② 나 100점 맞았어.
③ 좋은 생각이야.　　　④ 그분은 70세야.
⑤ 그는 우리 할머니보다 연세가 많아서.

여: 다음 주 금요일은 우리 할아버지 생신이야.
남: 할아버지를 위한 무언가를 마련했니?
여: 아직 못했어. 추천할 만한 게 있어?
남: 할아버지께 생일 케이크를 사 드리는 건 어때?
여: 할아버지는 단것을 좋아하시는 것 같진 않아.
남: 그럼, 모자는 어때? 너희 할아버지는 늘 모자를 쓰고 계시잖아.
여: 좋은 생각이야.

단·어·및·표·현

How about ~? ~은 어때?

20 알맞은응답찾기 ▶ 정답 ④

듣·기·대·본

W: Andy, I heard you're interested in fashion.
M: I am. I want to be a fashion designer in the future.
W: Then, can you help me choose a dress?
M: Sure. What do you need it for?
W: I have to wear a dress for my violin concert.
M: Okay. What kind of style do you want?
W: I'd like a simple and smart one.

우·리·말·해·석

① 너를 도울 수 있어서 기뻐.
② 그들은 내 사이즈를 가지고 있지 않아.
③ 걱정 마, 나는 그것을 스스로 할 수 있어.
④ 나는 장식이 없고 세련된 것을 원해.
⑤ 나는 미래에 바이올린 연주자가 되고 싶어.

여: Andy, 나는 네가 패션에 흥미가 있다고 들었어.
남: 맞아. 나는 미래에 패션 디자이너가 되고 싶어.
여: 그러면 너는 내가 드레스 고르는 것을 도와줄 수 있어?
남: 물론이야. 너는 뭘 위해 그것(드레스)이 필요해?
여: 나는 내 바이올린 콘서트를 위해 드레스를 입어야 해.
남: 알겠어. 너는 무슨 종류의 스타일을 원해?
여: **나는 장식이 없고 세련된 것을 원해.**

단·어·및·표·현

be interested in ~ ~에 흥미가 있다

Words & Expressions Review

1. 여권	2. 개최되다, 일어나다	3. 필요로 하다
4. 발목	5. 인쇄하다	6. 산책하다
7. 편리한	8. 우산	9. 운동화
10. 삐다, 접지르다	11. 그럴듯한	12. 부르다, ~에게 전화하다
13. 순서	14. 소방서	15. 반점
16. 지루해하는	17. 육지 동물	18. 흐린
19. 모자	20. 추천	21. 주로, 대부분
22. 고르다	23. 언젠가	24. 알아채다
25. 다양한	26. 운동	27. 몇, 조금
28. 그리워하다	29. ~하고 싶다	30. 편집하다
31. 입다, 끼다	32. (자기 것으로) 갖다, 보유하다	33. 주연 배우
34. 다가오는	35. 조언	36. 가장 친한 친구
37. 꼬리	38. 털	39. ~에 빠져있다
40. 줄이다	41. 쉬다, 휴식을 취하다	42. ~하게 하다
43. 밤새	44. 현장학습	

Listening Test
영어듣기 모의고사 04회

|정|답|

01 ③	02 ④	03 ②	04 ①	05 ③
06 ③	07 ⑤	08 ②	09 ①	10 ④
11 ①	12 ⑤	13 ②	14 ④	15 ④
16 ④	17 ⑤	18 ⑤	19 ②	20 ⑤

01 그림정보파악(담화) ▶ 정답 ③

듣·기·대·본

W: I live in humid and dark places. You may find me on rainy days. I'm small and move slowly. I have a soft body so I carry a shell on my back to protect my body. What am I?

우·리·말·해·석

여: 나는 습하고 어두운 곳에서 살아요. 당신은 나를 비 오는 날에 발견할

수 있을지도 몰라요. 나는 작고 천천히 움직여요. 나는 부드러운 몸을 가지고 있어서 내 몸을 보호하기 위해 내 등에 (딱딱한) 껍데기를 가지고 다녀요. 나는 무엇일까요?

단·어·및·표·현
humid [hjúːmid] 휑 습한
shell [ʃel] 휑 (딱딱한) 껍데기, 단단한 외피

02 그림정보파악(대화) ▶ 정답 ④

듣·기·대·본
M: Hi, I am looking for a cake for my friend's birthday party.
W: We have square-shaped and round-shaped cakes.
M: I would like a round one, please.
W: Would you like a cake with strawberries on top or just a plain cake? Oh, we have cakes with chocolate on top, too.
M: I will take the one with strawberries on top.

우·리·말·해·석
남: 안녕하세요. 저는 제 친구의 생일 파티를 위한 케이크를 찾고 있어요.
여: 저희는 네모난 모양과 둥근 모양의 케이크가 있어요.
남: 저는 둥근 것을 원해요.
여: 당신은 위에 딸기가 있는 케이크를 원하나요, 아니면 꾸미지 않은 (딸기가 없는) 케이크를 원하나요? 오, 우리는 위에 초콜릿이 있는 케이크들도 있어요.
남: 저는 위에 딸기가 있는 케이크로 할게요.

단·어·및·표·현
square-shaped 네모난 모양의
round-shaped 둥근 모양의
plain [plein] 휑 꾸미지 않은, 무늬가 없는

03 날씨파악-그림 ▶ 정답 ②

듣·기·대·본
W: Good morning, Paris. This is your daily weather forecast. Yesterday, it was sunny all day. It's a little cloudy this morning. This evening, it will start to rain. Tomorrow is also going to be a rainy day, so don't forget to bring your umbrella.

우·리·말·해·석
여: 좋은 아침입니다. 파리. 당신의 일일 일기예보입니다. 어제는 하루 종일 화창했습니다. 오늘 아침은 약간 흐립니다. 오늘 저녁에는, 비가 내리기 시작할 것입니다. 내일도 역시 비 내리는 날이 될 것이므로, 당신의 우산을 챙기는 것을 잊지 마세요.

단·어·및·표·현
bring [briŋ] 통 챙기다, 가져오다

04 마지막말의도파악 ▶ 정답 ①

듣·기·대·본
W: Hajun, can you help me with my homework?
M: OK. What is it?
W: I have to go to the science museum and write a report.
M: That sounds fun. I love science.
W: I'm going on Friday. Can you come with me?
M: I'm afraid not. I have a swimming lesson on Friday.

우·리·말·해·석
여: 하준아, 내가 숙제하는 것을 도와줄 수 있니?
남: 좋아. 뭔데?

여: 나는 과학 박물관에 가서 보고서를 써야 해.
남: 재미있겠다. 나는 과학을 좋아해.
여: 나는 금요일에 갈 거야. 나와 같이 갈 수 있니?
남: 아쉽지만 안 되겠어. 나는 금요일에 수영 수업이 있어.

단·어·및·표·현
help A with B A가 B하는 것을 돕다
I'm afraid not. 아쉽지만 안 되겠어.

05 담화미언급 ▶ 정답 ③

듣·기·대·본
W: Let me tell you about the World Food Festival which will be held on September 5. You can taste food from different countries at the festival. You can also experience different cultures through special events, like playing traditional games. The food will be priced at 4 to 8 dollars per dish. Come to Parkview Gardens and enjoy the day!

우·리·말·해·석
여: 여러분께 9월 5일에 개최되는 세계 음식 축제에 대해 말씀드리겠습니다. 여러분들은 축제에서 다양한 국가의 음식을 맛볼 수 있습니다. 전통 게임을 하는 것 같은 특별한 이벤트를 통해 여러분들은 또한 다른 문화를 경험하실 수 있습니다. 음식은 한 접시당 가격이 4~8달러로 매겨질 것입니다. Parkview Gardens에 오셔서 그날을 즐기세요!

단·어·및·표·현
taste [teist] 통 맛보다, 먹다
traditional [trədíʃənəl] 휑 전통의, 전통적인

06 수치파악 ▶ 정답 ③

듣·기·대·본
W: You look like you're in a good mood.
M: I'm just really excited for the baseball game tonight.
W: Me, too. The game starts at 6:00 p.m., right?
M: Yes, I'll pick you up at your place at 5:30 p.m. How's that?
W: Can you come at 5? Let's buy some fried chicken before we go to the game.
M: No problem. See you later.

우·리·말·해·석
여: 너 기분이 좋아 보여.
남: 나는 그저 오늘 밤 야구 경기에 정말로 신이 났어.
여: 나도. 경기는 오후 6시에 시작해, 맞지?
남: 응, 내가 오후 5시 30분에 너희 집으로 데리러 갈게. 그러면 어때?
여: 5시에 올 수 있어? 경기에 가기 전에 프라이드 치킨을 좀 사자.
남: 문제없어. 이따가 보자.

단·어·및·표·현
in a good mood 기분이 좋은
pick ~ up ~를 (차로) 데리러 가다

07 장래희망추론 ▶ 정답 ⑤

듣·기·대·본
W: Peter, what is your dream?
M: Well, I want to make people happy.
W: Then, you can be a singer since you're good at singing.
M: But I like to draw and build things.
W: Oh, I see. Then, what do you want to be when you grow up?

M: I'm thinking of becoming an architect like my dad.
W: That sounds great! I'm sure your dad would be so happy.

우·리·말·해·석

여: Peter, 너의 꿈은 무엇이니?
남: 음, 나는 사람들을 행복하게 만들고 싶어.
여: 그러면, 너는 노래를 잘하기 때문에 가수가 되면 되겠다.
남: 하지만 나는 그림을 그리고 물건들을 만드는 것을 좋아해.
여: 아, 알겠어. 그러면, 너는 커서 무엇이 되고 싶어?
남: 나는 우리 아빠처럼 건축가가 되는 것을 생각 중이야.
여: 멋지다! 나는 네 아빠가 매우 기뻐하실 거라고 확신해.

단·어·및·표·현

be good at -ing ~을 잘하다
architect [ɑ́ːrkətèkt] 명 건축가

08 심정추론　　　　　▶ 정답 ②

듣·기·대·본

W: Rodney, why are you wearing an eye-patch?
M: I hurt my eye playing basketball yesterday.
W: Sorry to hear that. That must hurt.
M: Yeah, it's all red and puffy.
W: We have a class photo shoot tomorrow.
M: I know. I feel so bad that I have to wear this patch.

우·리·말·해·석

① 수줍어하는　　② 속상한　　③ 자랑스러운
④ 행복한　　　　⑤ 감사한

여: Rodney, 왜 안대를 쓰고 있어?
남: 어제 농구하다가 눈을 다쳤어.
여: 안됐다. 아프겠어.
남: 응, 빨갛고 부었어.
여: 우리 내일 학급 사진 촬영이 있잖아.
남: 알아. 안대를 써야 해서 기분이 안 좋아.

단·어·및·표·현

eye-patch [áipætʃ] 명 안대
puffy [pʌ́fi] 형 부어 있는

09 할일파악(대화직후)　　　　▶ 정답 ①

듣·기·대·본

M: Wow! That roller coaster was so fun!
W: I know! It was scary but really exciting.
M: Do you want to get a drink now?
W: No, I'm not thirsty yet.
M: Then what do you want to do?
W: I want to buy something special from here.
M: How about getting a keychain or a mug?
W: Great idea. I'll go to the souvenir shop now.

우·리·말·해·석

남: 와! 저 롤러코스터 진짜 재미있었어!
여: 맞아! 무서웠지만 정말 신났어.
남: 너 지금 마실 것 좀 원하니?
여: 아니, 난 아직 목 안 말라.
남: 그럼 넌 뭐 하고 싶어?
여: 난 여기서 특별한 걸 사고 싶어.
남: 열쇠고리나 머그잔을 사는 건 어때?
여: 좋은 생각이야. 지금 기념품 가게에 가야겠다.

단·어·및·표·현

keychain [kíːtʃein] 명 열쇠고리
souvenir [sùːvəníər] 명 기념품

10 대화화제추론　　　　　▶ 정답 ④

듣·기·대·본

W: Kevin, what are you looking at?
M: I'm searching for club activities on our school website.
W: Which club do you have in mind?
M: I'm interested in the book club and the volunteer service club.
W: Sounds good!
M: Yeah, but I can't decide between the two. What about you?
W: I'm thinking of joining one of the school sports teams.

우·리·말·해·석

여: Kevin, 너 뭐 보고 있니?
남: 나는 우리 학교 웹사이트에서 동아리 활동을 찾아보고 있어.
여: 너는 어떤 동아리를 생각해 두고 있니?
남: 나는 독서 동아리와 자원봉사 활동 동아리에 관심이 있어.
여: 좋은 생각이다!
남: 응, 하지만 나는 그 둘 중에서 결정을 못 하겠어. 너는 어떠니?
여: 나는 학교 스포츠 팀들 중 하나에 가입할 생각이야.

단·어·및·표·현

search for ~을 찾다
have in mind 생각해 두다, 염두에 두다

11 특정정보파악(교통수단)　　▶ 정답 ①

듣·기·대·본

W: Hey, how are we going to get to the concert downtown?
M: Hmm, I'm not sure. Maybe we'll take the subway or grab a taxi.
W: Why don't we ride our bikes instead?
M: Really? Do you want to bike to the concert?
W: Yeah, it would be faster and more fun.
M: Okay, let's ride our bikes then.

우·리·말·해·석

여: 이봐, 시내에 있는 콘서트장에 어떻게 갈 거야?
남: 음, 난 확실하지 않아. 아마 우리는 지하철을 타거나 택시를 잡겠지.
여: 대신 우리의 자전거를 타는 건 어때?
남: 정말? 너는 콘서트장에 자전거로 가고 싶어?
여: 응, 더 빠르고 더 재밌을 거야.
남: 그래, 그럼 우리 자전거를 타자.

단·어·및·표·현

downtown [dàuntáun] 부 시내에, 시내로
sure [ʃuər] 형 확신하는
grab a taxi 택시를 잡다
Why don't we ~? ~하는 게 어때?
bike [baik] 명 자전거 동 자전거로 가다

12 이유파악　　　　　▶ 정답 ⑤

듣·기·대·본

W: Hey, David. Where are you going after school?
M: I'm going to the shopping mall.
W: Are you going there to buy new clothes?
M: No, I'm going there to join the video game tournament.
W: That sounds fun! Can I come and watch you play?

M: Sure. Let's meet in front of the school at 3:30.

우·리·말·해·석

여: 안녕, David. 방과 후에 어디 가?
남: 나 쇼핑몰 가.
여: 너는 거기에 새 옷을 사러 가는 거야?
남: 아니, 나는 비디오 게임 경기에 참가하기 위해 그곳에 가.
여: 재밌겠다! 내가 가서 너 게임하는 거 봐도 돼?
남: 그럼. 학교 앞에서 3시 30분에 만나자.

단·어·및·표·현

after school 방과 후
join [dʒɔin] [동] 참가하다
tournament [túərnəmənt] [명] 경기, 시합

13 대화장소추론 ▶ 정답 ②

듣·기·대·본

M: Hi, Miranda. Where are you going?
W: Hi, Sam. I'm on my way to the nursing home.
M: Do you do volunteer work there?
W: Yes. What about you? Where are you heading?
M: I'm going to the movies. Oh, here comes my bus.
W: OK. Have a good time. See you at school.
M: You, too!

우·리·말·해·석

남: 안녕, Miranda. 너 어디 가고 있니?
여: 안녕, Sam. 나는 양로원에 가는 중이야.
남: 너는 거기에서 봉사활동을 하니?
여: 응. 너는? 어디 가고 있어?
남: 나는 영화 보러 가고 있어. 오, 내가 타야 할 버스가 왔어.
여: 알겠어. 좋은 시간 보내. 학교에서 보자.
남: 너도!

단·어·및·표·현

on one's way to ~로 가는 길에
nursing home 양로원
head [hed] [동] 가다, 향하다

14 그림정보파악–지도 ▶ 정답 ④

듣·기·대·본

M: Hello. Can you tell me where the ice cream shop is?
W: Sure. Do you see the hot dog cart over there?
M: Yes.
W: Go straight to the hot dog cart and turn left.
M: Go straight and then turn left?
W: Yes. Then, you should see it on your left. It's between the bakery and the coffee house.
M: Thank you.

우·리·말·해·석

남: 안녕하세요. 아이스크림 매장이 어디에 있는지 말해주실 수 있나요?
여: 그럼요. 저쪽의 핫도그 카트 보이세요?
남: 네.
여: 핫도그 카트로 쭉 가서 왼쪽으로 도세요.
남: 쭉 가서 왼쪽으로 돌라고요?
여: 네. 그러면 당신의 왼편에 보일 거예요. 그것은 빵집과 커피 전문점 사이에 있어요.
남: 감사합니다.

단·어·및·표·현

cart [kɑːrt] [명] 카트, 수레

15 부탁(요청)한일파악 ▶ 정답 ④

듣·기·대·본

W: Did you finish your homework?
M: Yes, Mom. I'm done with my homework.
W: That's awesome! Are you ready for your violin lesson?
M: Yes, I've been practicing all week.
W: Great job! Please don't forget to bring your music book.
M: Thanks for reminding me, Mom.

우·리·말·해·석

여: 너는 네 숙제를 다 마쳤니?
남: 네, 엄마. 저는 제 숙제를 마쳤어요.
여: 멋지구나! 너는 네 바이올린 강습을 위해 준비됐니?
남: 네, 저는 일주일 내내 연습해 왔어요.
여: 잘했어! 네 음악 교재 챙기는 것을 부디 잊지 마렴.
남: 상기시켜줘서 고마워요, 엄마.

단·어·및·표·현

be done with ~을 마치다
be ready for ~할 준비가 되다
practice [prǽktis] [동] 연습하다
all week 일주일 내내
bring [briŋ] [동] ~을 챙기다, 갖고 가다
remind [rimáind] [동] 상기시키다

16 제안파악 ▶ 정답 ④

듣·기·대·본

W: What shall we do for Mom's birthday?
M: Hmm... She didn't like the party very much last year, did she?
W: No, she likes to keep quiet. Do you think she would like a present?
M: Yes, but it doesn't have to be anything expensive. She liked our homemade cookies, remember?
W: Then how about writing a letter to her? I think she would like it even better than flowers.
M: Sounds good!

우·리·말·해·석

여: 엄마 생일을 위해 우리 무엇을 할까?
남: 흠… 그녀는 작년에 파티를 별로 좋아하지 않으셨어, 그렇지?
여: 응, 그녀는 조용히 있는 것을 좋아하셔. 너는 그녀가 선물은 원하실 거라고 생각하니?
남: 응, 하지만 그것이 비싼 것일 필요는 없어. 그녀는 우리가 집에서 만든 쿠키를 좋아하셨어, 기억나?
여: 그러면 그녀에게 편지를 쓰는 것은 어때? 나는 그녀가 꽃보다 그것을 훨씬 더 좋아하실 거라고 생각해.
남: 좋은 생각이야!

단·어·및·표·현

would like ~ ~을 원하다
even [íːvən] [부] (비교급 앞에서) 훨씬 더

17 한일파악 ▶ 정답 ⑤

듣·기·대·본

W: Tom, what did you do on your vacation?
M: I just played computer games. What about you?
W: I learned how to scuba dive.
M: That sounds interesting. Tell me more about it.

W: I saw lots of beautiful fish underwater. It was amazing.
M: Good for you.

우•리•말•해•석

여: Tom, 방학 때 무엇을 했니?
남: 나는 그저 컴퓨터 게임을 했어. 너는?
여: 나는 스쿠버 다이빙 하는 법을 배웠어.
남: 재미있게 들린다. 그것에 대해 더 얘기해줘.
여: 나는 물속에서 많은 아름다운 물고기들을 봤어. 그것은 놀라웠어.
남: 좋았겠다.

단•어•및•표•현

lots of 많은
underwater [ʌ̀ndərwɔ́:tər] [부] 물속에서

18 직업추론 ▶ 정답 ⑤

듣•기•대•본

M: Hello, how can I help you?
W: Hi, I dropped my phone this morning and my screen broke. Can I get it fixed?
M: May I take a look?
W: Sure, here you go.
M: Hmm… I cannot fix this, but I can replace your screen with a new one if you'd like.
W: Yes, please. I'd like that.

우•리•말•해•석

남: 안녕하세요, 어떻게 도와드릴까요?
여: 안녕하세요, 제가 오늘 아침에 제 휴대폰을 떨어뜨려서 화면이 깨졌어요. 제가 그것을 수리 맡길 수 있을까요?
남: 제가 한번 봐도 될까요?
여: 물론이죠, 여기 있어요.
남: 흠… 저는 이것을 고칠 수 없지만, 만약 당신이 원하면 제가 화면을 새 것으로 교체해드릴 수 있어요.
여: 네, 해주세요. 저는 그러길 원해요.

단•어•및•표•현

drop [drɑp] [동] 떨어뜨리다
fix [fiks] [동] 고치다
replace A with B A를 B로 교체(대체)하다

19 알맞은응답찾기 ▶ 정답 ②

듣•기•대•본

W: Have you been to the new restaurant down the road?
M: No, I haven't. How about you?
W: Me neither. Shall we have lunch there today?
M: That would be nice. What do they have?
W: They mainly sell organic sandwiches and salads.
M: I see. They sound healthy, but they're not my favorites.
W: Why don't you try anyway? You might like it.
M: **Okay, I'll try this once.**

우•리•말•해•석

① 물론이죠! 저는 샐러드를 아주 좋아해요.
② 알겠어요, 이걸 한번 시도해 볼게요.
③ 아니요, 그 식당은 별로였어요.
④ 네, 저는 중국 음식을 먹을 거예요.
⑤ 고맙지만 오늘 점심은 제가 살게요.

여: 길 아래 새로 생긴 식당에 가 봤어요?
남: 아뇨, 안 가봤어요. 당신은요?
여: 저도요. 오늘 점심 거기서 먹을래요?
남: 그게 좋겠네요. 그들은 뭘 팔고 있나요?
여: 그들은 주로 유기농 샌드위치와 샐러드를 팔아요.
남: 그렇군요. 건강하게 들리지만, 제가 좋아하는 것은 아니네요.
여: 어쨌든 시도해보는 건 어때요? 당신은 아마 좋아할 거예요.
남: **알았어요, 이걸 한번 시도해 볼게요.**

단•어•및•표•현

organic [ɔːrgǽnik] [형] 유기농의
favorite [féivərit] [명] 좋아하는 것[사람]

20 알맞은응답찾기 ▶ 정답 ⑤

듣•기•대•본

M: This museum is a huge place!
W: Yes, we've been here for two hours and we still have many things to see.
M: I want to check out the Egyptian exhibit.
W: This floor plan says that it is on the second floor.
M: Before we go, how about taking a break and having a snack?
W: Good idea. Where is the cafeteria?
M: **The map says it's on the third floor.**

우•리•말•해•석

① 5시에 만나자.
② 나는 샌드위치 먹을래.
③ 나는 더 이상 못 걷겠어.
④ 나는 표를 잃어버린 것 같아.
⑤ 지도에는 그것이 3층에 있다고 나와.

남: 이 박물관은 거대한 곳이야!
여: 그래, 우리는 여기에 두 시간 동안 있었는데 아직도 볼 것이 많아.
남: 나는 이집트 전시회를 보길 원해.
여: 이 평면도에는 그것이 2층에 있다고 나와.
남: 우리가 가기 전에 쉬면서 간식을 먹는 게 어때?
여: 좋은 생각이야. 카페테리아가 어디에 있지?
남: **지도에는 그것이 3층에 있다고 나와.**

단•어•및•표•현

exhibit [igzíbit] [명] 전시회, 전시품
floor plan 평면도
snack [snæk] [명] 간식

Words & Expressions Review

1. ~때문에, ~이므로	2. ~로 가는 길에	3. 많은
4. 보호하다	5. 건축가	6. 습한
7. 양로원	8. 집에서 만든	9. 가다, 향하다
10. 참가하다	11. ~을 챙기다, 갖고 가다	12. 집, 장소
13. 경기, 시합	14. (비교급 앞에서) 훨씬 더	15. 가지고 다니다
16. 전통의, 전통적인	17. 간식	18. 방과 후
19. ~을 찾다	20. 맛보다, 먹다	21. ~을 잘하다
22. A가 B하는 것을 돕다	23. 천천히	24. 연습하다
25. 상기시키다	26. 매일 일어나는, 나날의	27. 생각해 두다, 염두에 두다
28. 기념품	29. 네모난 모양의	30. 꾸미지 않은, 무늬가 없는

31. A를 (차로) 데리러 가다	32. 카트, 수레	33. 껍데기
34. ~에 관심이 있다	35. 사진 촬영	36. 물속에서
37. 부어 있는	38. 고치다	39. 기분이 좋은
40. (다) 크다, 성장하다	41. 유기농의	42. 평면도
43. 잊다, 잊어버리다	44. 만들다, 짓다	

Listening Test
영어듣기 모의고사 05회

|정|답|

01 ①	02 ④	03 ⑤	04 ③	05 ⑤
06 ③	07 ⑤	08 ③	09 ⑤	10 ③
11 ⑤	12 ③	13 ②	14 ⑤	15 ①
16 ④	17 ①	18 ④	19 ②	20 ②

01 그림정보파악(담화) ▶ 정답 ①

듣·기·대·본

M: This is a round vegetable that grows underground. This has a strong smell and taste. This has many white layers. This can make you cry when you cut this. What is this?

우·리·말·해·석

남: 이것은 땅 아래에서 자라는 둥근 모양의 채소예요. 이것은 강한 냄새와 맛을 갖고 있어요. 이것은 많은 흰색의 층들을 가지고 있어요. 이것은 당신이 이것을 자를 때 당신을 울게 만들 수 있어요. 이것은 무엇일까요?

단·어·및·표·현

layer[léiər] 몡 막, 층, 겹

02 그림정보파악(대화) ▶ 정답 ④

듣·기·대·본

W: Hello, can I help you?
M: Hi, I'm looking for a door mat.
W: How about this round one?
M: Well, I like the rectangular one better.
W: Okay. We have this one with a duck on it.
M: Oh, that's nice. It's very cute.
W: Yes, and it will make you feel cozy.
M: Great! I'll take it.

우·리·말·해·석

여: 안녕하세요, 무엇을 도와드릴까요?
남: 안녕하세요, 현관 매트를 찾고 있는데요.
여: 이 동그란 것은 어떠세요?
남: 음, 저는 직사각형의 것을 더 좋아해요.
여: 알겠습니다. 오리 한 마리가 그려져 있는 것이 있어요.
남: 오, 그거 좋네요. 매우 귀여워요.
여: 네, 그리고 그것은 당신이 포근함을 느끼게 해줄 거예요.
남: 좋아요! 그걸로 할게요.

단·어·및·표·현

look for + 명사 ~을 찾다

round[raund] 몡 둥근, 동그란
rectangular[rektǽŋgjulər] 몡 직사각형의, 직사각형 모양의
cozy[kóuzi] 몡 포근한, 안락한

03 날씨파악-그림 ▶ 정답 ⑤

듣·기·대·본

W: Good morning! It's time for your Sunday weather forecast. If you are living in Seoul, you will need an umbrella because it is going to rain. In Gwangju, it will be cloudy but there is no chance of rain. Busan, on the other hand, will be very sunny, so enjoy the sun.

우·리·말·해·석

여: 좋은 아침입니다! 일요일 일기예보 시간입니다. 만약 당신이 서울에 살고 계신다면, 비가 올 것이기 때문에 우산이 필요할 것입니다. 광주는 흐리겠지만 비가 올 가능성은 없습니다. 반면 부산은 매우 화창하겠으니, 햇빛을 즐기시기 바랍니다.

단·어·및·표·현

there is no chance ~ ~할 가능성이 없다
on the other hand 반면에

04 마지막말의도파악 ▶ 정답 ③

듣·기·대·본

M: Mom, you look unwell.
W: Oh, I'm fine, honey. My throat just hurts a little.
M: Why does it hurt?
W: The wind was pretty cold when I was outside.
M: Can I get you anything?
W: Well, can you please get me a glass of water?

우·리·말·해·석

남: 엄마, 아파 보이세요.
여: 오, 난 괜찮단다. 얘야. 그저 목이 약간 아플 뿐이야.
남: 그것이 왜 아픈가요?
여: 내가 밖에 있었을 때 바람이 꽤 차가웠어.
남: 제가 무언가 가져다 드릴까요?
여: 음, 나에게 물 한 잔 가져다 주겠니?

단·어·및·표·현

unwell[ʌnwél] 몡 아픈, 몸이 편치 않은
honey[hʌ́ni] 몡 (좋아하거나 사랑하는 사람에 대한 호칭) 얘, 자기, 여보

05 담화미언급 ▶ 정답 ⑤

듣·기·대·본

W: We'll have a clean-up event at our school soon. It will take place on May 10th. We'll walk around our neighborhood for an hour picking up trash. You should wear comfortable shoes and clothing. Please bring a trash bag and gloves. Let's work together to make our community cleaner and greener!

우·리·말·해·석

여: 우리 학교에서 대청소 행사가 곧 있을 예정입니다. 그것은 5월 10일에 개최될 것입니다. 우리는 한 시간 동안 쓰레기를 주우며 우리 동네 주변을 걸을 것입니다. 여러분은 편안한 신발과 옷을 착용하셔야 합니다. 부디 쓰레기 봉투와 장갑을 가져오십시오. 우리 지역 사회를 더 깨끗하고 더 푸르게 만들도록 함께 작업합시다!

단·어·및·표·현

clean-up 대청소

take place 개최되다, 일어나다
neighborhood [néibərhùd] 명 근처, 인근 지역
pick up 줍다
trash [træʃ] 명 쓰레기
comfortable [kʌ́mfərtəbl] 형 편안한
community [kəmjúːnəti] 명 지역 사회, 공동체

06 수치파악(시각) ▶ 정답 ③

듣·기·대·본
[Cellphone rings.]
W: Hi, Kevin. Are you almost here?
M: Yeah. I got on the bus at 4:30 p.m.
W: Okay. How's the traffic?
M: It's a bit slow today. I think it'll take about 30 more minutes to get there.
W: So, you'll arrive around 5:30?
M: Yes. It's 5:00 now, so I should be there by then.

우·리·말·해·석
[휴대폰이 울린다.]
여: 안녕, Kevin. 너 거의 다 왔니?
남: 응. 나는 오후 4시 30분에 버스를 탔어.
여: 알겠어. 교통량은 어때?
남: 오늘은 좀 느려. 거기에 도착하려면 30분 정도는 더 걸릴 것 같아.
여: 그럼 5시 30분쯤에 도착하겠네?
남: 응. 지금이 5시니까 그때쯤이면 도착할 거야.

단·어·및·표·현
almost [ɔ́ːlmoust] 부 거의
get on (버스, 지하철 등을) 타다
traffic [trǽfik] 명 교통(량)
around [əráund] 부 약, ~쯤

07 장래희망추론 ▶ 정답 ⑤

듣·기·대·본
W: What do you want to be when you grow up, Craig?
M: I like all kinds of animals. I want to help them when they are sick.
W: You mean you want to be a vet?
M: Yes. A doctor for animals.
W: I think you will be a good vet.

우·리·말·해·석
여: 너는 커서 뭐가 되고 싶니, Craig?
남: 나는 모든 종류의 동물들을 좋아해. 나는 그들이 아플 때 그들을 돕고 싶어.
여: 수의사가 되고 싶다는 말이니?
남: 응. 동물들을 위한 의사 말이야.
여: 너는 좋은 수의사가 될 것 같아.

단·어·및·표·현
grow up 크다, 자라다

08 심정추론 ▶ 정답 ③

듣·기·대·본
W: James, I've found my puppy!
M: Really? That's good news!
W: Yes. I've been looking for the puppy for two days since I lost it at the park.
M: How did you find it?

W: I put photos of it all over the park. One woman called me.
M: That's great! I know how much you love your puppy.

우·리·말·해·석
여: James, 내 강아지를 찾았어!
남: 정말? 좋은 소식이구나!
여: 응. 공원에서 강아지를 잃어버리고 난 후 이틀 동안 강아지를 찾고 있었어.
남: 어떻게 찾았니?
여: 공원 곳곳에 강아지 사진을 붙여 놨거든. 어떤 여자가 전화했어.
남: 잘됐다! 나는 네가 얼마나 네 강아지를 사랑하는지 알아.

단·어·및·표·현
find [faind] 동 찾다 (find-found-found)
lose [luːz] 동 잃어버리다, 분실하다 (lose-lost-lost)

09 할일파악(대화직후) ▶ 정답 ⑤

듣·기·대·본
M: Jenny, have you seen this video online?
W: What is it about?
M: It's a video of adorable puppies and babies playing together. It has more than three million views on YouTube.
W: Oh! That sounds so cute!
M: It sure is.
W: I want to see it.
M: Okay. I'll show it to you right away.

우·리·말·해·석
남: Jenny, 너는 이 동영상을 인터넷으로 본 적이 있니?
여: 그것은 무엇에 관한 거야?
남: 그것은 함께 노는 사랑스러운 강아지들과 아기들의 동영상이야. 그것은 유튜브에서 삼백만이 넘는 조회수를 갖고 있어.
여: 오! 그것은 매우 귀여울 것 같아!
남: 확실히 그래.
여: 나 그걸 보고 싶어.
남: 좋아. 지금 바로 너에게 보여줄게.

단·어·및·표·현
adorable [ədɔ́ːrəbl] 형 사랑스러운

10 대화화제추론 ▶ 정답 ③

듣·기·대·본
W: Steve, what are you doing?
M: I'm checking the library website on how to return books.
W: The library is closed because of renovations.
M: Yes, but there's a return box outside the building.
W: Oh, then you can just toss the books in.
M: Yes!

우·리·말·해·석
여: Steve, 뭐하고 있어?
남: 도서관 홈페이지에서 책을 반납하는 방법을 확인하고 있어.
여: 도서관은 수리 때문에 닫았잖아.
남: 맞아, 하지만 건물 밖에 반납함이 있어.
여: 오, 그러면 너는 거기다 책을 그냥 던져서 넣을 수 있네.
남: 맞아!

단·어·및·표·현
return [ritə́ːrn] 동 반납하다, 되돌려주다

renovation[renəvéiʃən] 몡 수리, 수선
toss[tɔ(ː)s] 통 던지다, 내던지다

11 특정정보파악(교통수단) ▶ 정답 ⑤

듣·기·대·본

M: Honey, I have a business trip next week.
W: Again? Are you going overseas this time, as well?
M: Not this time. I have a meeting to attend in Busan.
W: That's great, considering it's only a three-hour drive from here.
M: Yeah, but I'm planning on taking the train. Driving makes me tired.
W: Sure. Do whatever suits you best!

우·리·말·해·석

남: 여보, 나 다음 주에 출장 가요.
여: 또요? 이번에도 역시 해외로 가나요?
남: 이번에는 아니에요. 부산에서 참석할 회의가 있어요.
여: 여기서 차로 겨우 3시간 걸린다는 것을 고려해볼 때 잘됐네요.
남: 그래요, 하지만 나는 기차를 타려고 계획하고 있어요. 운전은 나를 피곤하게 해요.
여: 물론이죠. 무엇이든 당신에게 가장 적합한 것으로 하세요!

단·어·및·표·현

as well 역시
plan on -ing ~할 계획이다

12 이유파악 ▶ 정답 ③

듣·기·대·본

M: Kate, where are you going?
W: I'm going to the town festival.
M: Are you going there to enjoy the local food?
W: No, I'm going to do a taekwondo performance.
M: Really? So you'll show some taekwondo moves on stage?
W: Yes! I hope lots of people come and watch us.

우·리·말·해·석

남: Kate, 너 어디 가니?
여: 나는 지역 축제에 가고 있어.
남: 거기에 현지음식을 먹으러 가는 거야?
여: 아니, 나는 태권도 시범을 하러 가.
남: 진짜? 그림 너는 무대에서 태권도 동작들을 보여주는 거야?
여: 응! 나는 많은 사람들이 와서 우리를 봐주면 좋겠어.

단·어·및·표·현

town[taun] 몡 소도시
festival[féstəvəl] 몡 축제
local food 현지 음식, 지역 음식
performance[pərfɔ́ːrməns] 몡 공연, 시범
stage[steidʒ] 몡 무대

13 대화장소추론 ▶ 정답 ②

듣·기·대·본

W: Hi, how can I help you?
M: Hi, I'll be going on a road trip soon. And…
W: Are you worried about car sickness?
M: Yes. Can you give me something that will help?
W: Sure. Take this medicine half an hour before you get in the car.

M: Thank you. I'll buy four packages of them.

우·리·말·해·석

여: 안녕하세요. 어떻게 도와드릴까요?
남: 안녕하세요. 저는 곧 자동차 여행을 갈 거예요. 그리고…
여: 차멀미에 대해 걱정하시나요?
남: 네. 제게 도움이 되는 뭔가를 주실 수 있나요?
여: 그럼요. 차에 타기 30분 전에 이 약을 드세요.
남: 고맙습니다. 저는 그것들을 네 팩을 살게요.

단·어·및·표·현

car sickness 차멀미
medicine[médisin] 몡 약

14 그림정보파악-위치 ▶ 정답 ⑤

듣·기·대·본

W: We have to leave now or we're going to miss our flight.
M: I just need to find my passport.
W: Isn't it on your desk?
M: I remember putting it there, but I can't find it.
W: Oh, I see it! It's on the carpet on the floor. You must have dropped it.
M: Thanks. Let's go now.

우·리·말·해·석

여: 우리는 지금 출발하지 않으면 항공편을 놓칠 거야.
남: 저는 여권을 찾아야 해요.
여: 네 책상 위에 있지 않아?
남: 그곳에 놓아둔 것은 기억나는데 못 찾겠어요.
여: 오, 보인다! 바닥의 카펫 위에 있어. 네가 그것을 떨어뜨린 게 틀림없어.
남: 고마워요. 이제 가요.

단·어·및·표·현

miss[mis] 통 놓치다
flight[flait] 몡 항공편, 비행
drop[drɑp] 통 떨어뜨리다, 떨어지다

15 부탁(요청)한일파악 ▶ 정답 ①

듣·기·대·본

M: What's that smell? Did something burn?
W: Yeah, I burnt the toast.
M: Did you take it out of the toaster?
W: I did. I ruined a good piece of bread.
M: Don't worry about it. Let's just get rid of the smell.
W: Oh, right. Could you open the window for me?
M: Sure. I'll open it right now.

우·리·말·해·석

남: 저게 무슨 냄새야? 뭔가 탔나?
여: 응, 나는 토스트를 태웠어.
남: 너는 토스터에서 그것을 꺼냈어?
여: 그랬지. 나는 좋은 빵 한 조각을 망쳤어.
남: 걱정하지 마. 냄새를 좀 없애자.
여: 아, 그래. 나를 위해 창문을 열어줄 수 있니?
남: 물론이지. 나는 지금 바로 그것을 열게.

단·어·및·표·현

burn[bəːrn] 통 불에 타다
ruin[rú(ː)in] 통 망치다, 엉망으로 만들다
get rid of ~을 없애다, 제거하다

16 제안파악　　　　　　　　▶ 정답 ④

듣·기·대·본

M: Anna, why the long face?
W: I had a fight with my sister this morning.
M: Why?
W: I wore her jeans the other day without her permission, and she was upset.
M: Oh, I'm sorry to hear that. How about sending her an apology text?
W: Yeah, texting sounds good.

우·리·말·해·석

남: Anna, 왜 그렇게 시무룩한 얼굴이니?
여: 나는 오늘 아침에 나의 언니랑 싸웠어.
남: 왜?
여: 며칠 전에 내가 그녀의 청바지를 그녀의 허락 없이 입었고, 그녀는 화가 났어.
남: 아, 안됐구나. 그녀에게 사과 문자를 보내는 것은 어때?
여: 응, 문자를 보내는 게 좋겠다.

단·어·및·표·현

long face 시무룩한 얼굴
the other day 며칠 전에
permission [pərmíʃən] 몡 허락, 허가
apology [əpάlədʒi] 몡 사과

17 한일파악　　　　　　　　▶ 정답 ①

듣·기·대·본

W: Did you watch the documentary last Saturday?
M: No, I missed it. How was it?
W: It was very interesting. I learned new things about AI.
M: Well, I couldn't miss soccer practice.
W: Oh, did you have a soccer practice on Saturday?
M: Yeah. I'll watch a rerun of the documentary on the Internet.

우·리·말·해·석

여: 너 지난 토요일에 그 다큐멘터리 봤니?
남: 아니, 난 그것을 놓쳤어. 어땠어?
여: 그것은 매우 흥미로웠어. 나는 AI에 관한 새로운 것들을 알게 됐어.
남: 음, 나는 축구 연습을 빠질 수 없었어.
여: 오, 너는 토요일에 축구 연습이 있었니?
남: 응. 나는 인터넷에서 다큐멘터리 재방송을 볼 거야.

단·어·및·표·현

miss [mis] 동 놓치다, 빠지다
rerun [ríːrʌ̀n] 몡 재방송

18 직업추론　　　　　　　　▶ 정답 ④

듣·기·대·본

W: Thank you for coming on such short notice.
M: No problem. I was in the neighborhood. What seems to be the problem?
W: The air conditioner isn't working properly. Customers are complaining that our restaurant is too hot.
M: Hmm… There seems to be some leakage from the pipe.
W: How long will it take to get it fixed?
M: I can fix it within an hour.

우·리·말·해·석

여: 그런 갑작스러운 통지에도 와 주셔서 감사합니다.

남: 괜찮습니다. 저는 근처에 있었어요. 뭐가 문제인 것 같나요?
여: 에어컨이 제대로 작동하지 않아요. 손님들이 저희 식당이 너무 덥다고 불평하고 있어요.
남: 흠… 파이프에서 새는 것이 좀 있는 것 같네요.
여: 고치는 데 얼마나 걸리나요?
남: 한 시간 내로 고칠 수 있어요.

단·어·및·표·현

properly [prάpərli] 閉 제대로, 적절하게
it takes A to + 동사원형 ～하는 데 A(시간)가 걸리다

19 알맞은응답찾기　　　　　　　　▶ 정답 ②

듣·기·대·본

W: Joel, we've decided on the place to have your birthday party.
M: Where is it going to be, Mom?
W: It will be at your favorite restaurant.
M: You mean at Jamie's Burgers?
W: That's right.
M: Thank you so much, Mom! I love that restaurant.
W: How many friends do you want to invite?
M: Five friends, please.

우·리·말·해·석

① 포장할게요.
② 다섯 명의 친구요.
③ 나중에 주문해도 될까요?
④ 그들은 버스를 타고 올 거예요.
⑤ 버거 한 개로 충분해요.

여: Joel, 우리는 너의 생일 파티를 열 장소를 결정했어.
남: 그곳은 어디가 될까요, 엄마?
여: 그곳은 네가 제일 좋아하는 식당일 거야.
남: Jamie's Burgers에서 말씀이세요?
여: 맞아.
남: 정말 감사해요, 엄마! 저는 그 식당이 정말 좋아요.
여: 친구들은 몇 명 초대하고 싶니?
남: 다섯 명의 친구요.

단·어·및·표·현

decide on ~ ～으로 정하다
favorite [féivərit] 톙 제일 좋아하는
take-out 가지고 가는 음식

20 알맞은응답찾기　　　　　　　　▶ 정답 ②

듣·기·대·본

W: Honey, are you going to work?
M: Yes, I'm leaving in a minute. Why?
W: Can you drop me off at the subway station on your way there?
M: Of course. Where are you going?
W: I need to go to the bookstore.
M: Okay, I'll be waiting in the car. Can you be down in five minutes?
W: Sure, no problem.

우·리·말·해·석

① 전 직장에 늦었어요.
② 물론이죠, 문제없어요.
③ 만나서 반가워요.
④ 저는 책 읽는 것을 좋아해요.
⑤ 버스 정류장은 근처에 있어요.

여: 여보, 출근해요?
남: 네, 곧 떠나요. 왜요?
여: 거기 가는 길에 나를 지하철역에 내려줄 수 있어요?
남: 그럼요. 어디 가요?
여: 나는 서점에 가야 해요.
남: 그래요, 나는 차에서 기다리고 있을게요. 5분 후에 내려올 수 있어요?
여: **물론이죠, 문제없어요.**

단·어·및·표·현
drop ~ off ~를 내려 주다

Words & Expressions Review

1. 직사각형의	2. ~을 고치다	3. 모든 종류의
4. 포근한	5. 아픈, 몸이 편치 않은	6. 쓰레기
7. 반면에	8. 곧, 즉시	9. 지하에
10. 제대로, 적절하게	11. 둥근	12. ~을 찾다
13. 재방송	14. 사과	15. 손님
16. 채소	17. 공연, 시범	18. A를 내려 주다
19. 가지고 가는 음식	20. 100만	21. 무대
22. 항공편, 비행	23. 근처, 인근 지역	24. 수의사
25. 불에 타다	26. 놓치다, 빠지다	27. 거의
28. 시무룩한 얼굴	29. 약	30. 찾다
31. 대청소	32. 얘, 자기, 여보	33. 반납하다
34. 적합하다, 어울리다	35. ~할 가능성이 없다	36. 차멀미
37. 던지다	38. 자라다	39. ~이라는 말이니?
40. 허락, 허가	41. 수리, 수선	42. 막, 층, 겹
43. 잃어버리다, 분실하다	44. 사랑스러운	

Listening Test

영어듣기 모의고사 06회

|정|답|

01 ②	02 ①	03 ③	04 ④	05 ⑤
06 ③	07 ④	08 ③	09 ②	10 ④
11 ③	12 ⑤	13 ④	14 ②	15 ④
16 ②	17 ②	18 ①	19 ⑤	20 ③

01 그림정보파악(담화) ▶ 정답 ②

들·기·대·본
M: You can find this in a kitchen. It has one door. You put food on the plate inside. The plate turns around and heats up the food. What is this?

우·리·말·해·석
남: 당신은 부엌에서 이것을 발견할 수 있습니다. 그것은 한 개의 문을 갖고 있습니다. 당신은 안에 있는 접시 위에 음식을 놓습니다. 접시가 돌아가고 음식을 데웁니다. 이것은 무엇일까요?

단·어·및·표·현
plate[pleit] 영 (둥근) 접시, 그릇
inside[ínsáid] 부 안에

turn around 회전하다
heat up ~을 데우다, 뜨겁게 만들다

02 그림정보파악(대화) ▶ 정답 ①

들·기·대·본
M: Hi, Erin. What's that?
W: It's a fridge magnet for my friend.
M: The ice cream shape looks cute. Did you make it?
W: Yes, I made it myself.
M: Wow, I want to have one, too. Can you make a bird-shaped magnet for me?
W: Okay, I will.

우·리·말·해·석
남: 안녕, Erin. 그게 뭐야?
여: 그것은 내 친구를 위한 냉장고 자석이야.
남: 아이스크림 모양이 귀엽다. 네가 그것을 만들었어?
여: 응, 내가 직접 만들었어.
남: 와, 나도 하나 갖고 싶어. 너는 나에게 새 모양의 자석을 만들어줄 수 있니?
여: 그래, 만들어줄게.

단·어·및·표·현
fridge magnet 냉장고 자석
bird-shaped 새 모양의

03 날씨파악-그림 ▶ 정답 ③

들·기·대·본
W: Hello! This is the weather report for Pohang. Yesterday, it was cloudy, but the clouds cleared by late afternoon. This morning, it will be nice outside with a light breeze. It will be mostly sunny and warm this afternoon. Enjoy the beautiful weather in Pohang today!

우·리·말·해·석
여: 안녕하세요! 포항의 일기 예보입니다. 어제는 구름이 끼었지만, 늦은 오후에는 구름이 걷혔습니다. 오늘 아침은, 가벼운 산들바람과 함께 바깥 날씨가 좋을 것입니다. 오늘 오후에는 대체로 맑고 따뜻할 것입니다. 오늘 포항의 아름다운 날씨를 즐기세요!

단·어·및·표·현
clear[kliər] 통 (안개 등이) 걷히다
breeze[briːz] 명 산들바람
mostly[móustli] 부 대체로, 주로, 대개

04 마지막말의도파악 ▶ 정답 ④

들·기·대·본
M: Jessica, are you alright? You look like you're in pain.
W: I have a toothache. It hurts so much!
M: I think you'd better see a dentist right away.
W: Right. But to be honest, I'm afraid of the dentist.
M: Do you want me to come with you?
W: Thanks, but I can handle it on my own.

우·리·말·해·석
남: Jessica, 너 괜찮아? 너는 아픈 것처럼 보여.
여: 나는 치통이 있어. 그것은 많이 아파!
남: 나는 네가 당장 치과에 가야 한다고 생각해.
여: 맞아. 하지만 솔직히, 나는 치과 의사가 무서워.
남: 너는 내가 너와 같이 가길 원하니?
여: 고마워, 하지만 나는 혼자 힘으로 처리할 수 있어.

단·어·및·표·현
to be honest 솔직히 (말해서)

handle [hǽndl] [동] 처리하다, 다루다
on one's own 혼자 힘으로

05 담화미언급 ▶ 정답 ⑤

듣·기·대·본

W: Hello, music lovers. The London Jazz & Blues Music Festival is back. It will take place from July 8th to the 10th. Tickets are priced at £10 for each day. Come and enjoy live music performances at Hyde Park in London. Hope to see you there!

우·리·말·해·석

여: 안녕하세요, 음악 애호가 여러분. 런던 재즈&블루스 음악 축제가 돌아왔습니다. 그것은 7월 8일부터 10일까지 열릴 것입니다. 표는 각 날마다 10파운드로 가격이 정해졌습니다. 오셔서 런던 하이드 파크에서의 라이브 음악 공연을 즐기세요. 그곳에서 만나기를 희망합니다!

단·어·및·표·현

take place (행사가) 열리다
performance [pərfɔ́:rməns] [명] 공연, 행사

06 수치파악 ▶ 정답 ③

듣·기·대·본

M: Sophia, there's a free classical concert at the community center tonight.
W: Great! Why don't we go together and check it out?
M: Okay. The concert starts at 7:00 p.m.
W: Then, I'll come by your place at 6:30.
M: If we're late, we won't be able to get good seats. How about 6?
W: 6 o'clock? Got it. See you then.

우·리·말·해·석

남: Sophia, 오늘 밤 주민 센터에서 무료 클래식 콘서트가 있어.
여: 멋지다! 우리 같이 가서 그것을 살펴보는 게 어때?
남: 좋아. 그 콘서트는 오후 7시에 시작해.
여: 그러면, 나는 6시 반에 너희 집에 들를게.
남: 만약 우리가 늦는다면, 우리는 좋은 자리를 얻을 수가 없을 거야. 6시는 어때?
여: 6시? 알겠어. 그때 보자.

단·어·및·표·현

free [fri:] [형] 무료의
community center 주민 센터
check out (흥미로운 것을) 살펴보다[보다]
come by 잠깐 들르다
be able to + 동사원형 ~할 수 있다
seat [si:t] [명] 자리, 좌석

07 장래희망추론 ▶ 정답 ④

듣·기·대·본

W: Ted, what are you watching on your phone?
M: I'm watching a documentary about a famous basketball player, Stephen Curry.
W: Oh, that looks fun. Do you like basketball?
M: Yes. In fact, I want to become a basketball player when I grow up.
W: I hope you achieve your dreams.
M: Thank you.

우·리·말·해·석

여: Ted, 너 휴대폰으로 무엇을 보고 있니?
남: 나는 유명한 농구 선수인 Stephen Curry의 다큐멘터리를 보고 있어.
여: 오, 그거 재미있어 보인다. 너는 농구를 좋아하니?
남: 응, 사실, 나는 커서 농구 선수가 되고 싶어.
여: 나는 네가 꿈을 이루길 바라.
남: 고마워.

단·어·및·표·현

achieve [ətʃí:v] [동] 이루다, 성취하다

08 심정추론 ▶ 정답 ③

듣·기·대·본

M: Jane, you're so talented at yoga!
W: I wasn't good at it in the beginning.
M: You must have trained hard.
W: Yes, I've gotten better little by little, and now I'm able to stay calm in difficult poses.
M: You must feel so good about yourself.
W: I do. I feel more confident now.

우·리·말·해·석

① 수줍은 ② 속상한 ③ 자랑스러운 ④ 걱정하는 ⑤ 감사하는

남: Jane, 너는 요가에 매우 재능이 있네!
여: 나는 처음에는 잘하지 못했어.
남: 너는 틀림없이 열심히 훈련했겠다.
여: 응, 나는 조금씩 좋아졌고, 이제 어려운 자세에서 안정적으로 있을 수 있어.
남: 너는 네 자신에 대해 무척 기분이 좋겠다.
여: 그래. 나는 이제 더 자신감이 있어.

단·어·및·표·현

talented [tǽləntid] [형] 재능이 있는
little by little 조금씩

09 할일파악(대화직후) ▶ 정답 ②

듣·기·대·본

M: Whoa, your eyes are all red, Olivia.
W: Really? Well, I was just rubbing them.
M: Do you want eye drops? I have some.
W: That's okay, thanks. I probably just had something in my eyes.
M: Are you sure? You should at least wash them with clean water.
W: That's a good idea. I'll do it now.

우·리·말·해·석

남: 우와, 네 눈이 온통 빨갛게 충혈됐어, Olivia.
여: 정말? 음, 내가 방금 그것들을(눈을) 비볐어.
남: 너는 안약을 원하니? 내가 좀 갖고 있어.
여: 괜찮아, 고마워. 방금 내 눈 안에 뭐가 들어갔나봐.
남: 확실해? 너는 적어도 그것들을(눈을) 깨끗한 물로 씻어야 해.
여: 좋은 생각이야. 나는 지금 그것을 할게.

단·어·및·표·현

rub [rʌb] [동] 비비다, 문지르다
eye drop 안약
at least 적어도, 최소한

10 대화화제추론 ▶ 정답 ④

듣·기·대·본

M: Do you live in this apartment?
W: Yes, I do. I moved in a few days ago.

M: Oh, I see. Well, please separate the trash before throwing it away.
W: Okay. Where do I put the used paper and cans?
M: There are recycling bins over there.
W: Oh, thank you.

우•리•말•해•석

남: 이 아파트에 사세요?
여: 네, 그래요. 며칠 전에 이사 왔어요.
남: 아, 그렇군요. 저기, 쓰레기를 버리기 전에 그것들을 분리해 주세요.
여: 알았어요. 사용한 종이와 캔은 어디에 넣죠?
남: 저쪽에 재활용 수거함이 있어요.
여: 아, 고맙습니다.

단•어•및•표•현

separate [sépəreit] [동] 분리하다, 나누다
throw ~ away ~을 버리다
recycling [risáikliŋ] [명] 재활용

11 특정정보파악(교통수단) ▶ 정답 ③

듣•기•대•본

W: Evan, aren't you excited about the concert tomorrow?
M: I am! My favorite band is playing.
W: Mine, too. How will you get to the concert?
M: I'll take the subway. My bike is broken. You?
W: I'll be on foot. It's not far from my house.

우•리•말•해•석

여: Evan, 내일 콘서트 갈 생각에 신나지 않니?
남: 맞아! 내가 제일 좋아하는 밴드가 연주해.
여: 내가 제일 좋아하는 밴드도. 콘서트에 어떻게 갈 거야?
남: 지하철 타고 갈 거야. 내 자전거가 고장 났거든. 너는?
여: 나는 걸어갈 거야. 우리 집에서 별로 멀지 않거든.

단•어•및•표•현

on foot 걸어서

12 이유파악 ▶ 정답 ⑤

듣•기•대•본

M: Hey, Lily. Are you going out?
W: Yes. I'm going to the bookstore near the station.
M: Are you going to buy a new comic book again?
W: No. My favorite writer is coming to the store today. She will sign books for her readers.
M: Wow, I hope you get it!

우•리•말•해•석

남: 안녕, Lily. 나가니?
여: 응. 나는 역 근처에 있는 서점에 가.
남: 너 또 새 만화책 사러 가는 거야?
여: 아니. 내가 제일 좋아하는 작가가 오늘 가게에 와. 그녀는 독자들을 위해 책에 사인해 줄 거야.
남: 와, 네가 꼭 받길 바라!

단•어•및•표•현

near [niər] [전] ~에 가까운
station [stéiʃən] [명] 역, 정류장
sign [sain] [동] 사인하다

13 대화장소추론 ▶ 정답 ④

듣•기•대•본

M: I'm happy to see so many sea animals that I love!
W: You must be really happy to see your favorite sea animal, the beluga. Now, let's go touch some starfishes in that touch pool.
M: Okay, Mom! I'm so excited to touch some starfishes!
W: But, David, before you touch them, you need to wash your hands first.
M: Okay! I will go wash my hands.
W: Don't run, David!

우•리•말•해•석

남: 저는 제가 너무 좋아하는 바다 동물들을 아주 많이 보게 되어서 기뻐요!
여: 너는 네가 가장 좋아하는 바다 동물인 벨루가(흰돌고래)를 보게 되어서 정말 행복하겠구나. 자, 우리 가서 저 터치풀 안에 있는 불가사리들을 만져보자.
남: 좋아요, 엄마! 저는 불가사리들을 만진다니 정말 신이 나요!
여: 그렇지만, David, 그것들을 만지기 전에 너는 먼저 네 손을 씻어야 해.
남: 좋아요! 저는 가서 제 손을 씻을게요.
여: 뛰지 마라, David!

단•어•및•표•현

favorite [féivərit] [형] 가장 좋아하는, 마음에 드는
beluga [bəlúːgə] [명] 흰돌고래
starfish [stáːrfiʃ] [명] 불가사리
touch pool 어린이들이 물에 살고 있는 생물들을 직접 손으로 만지고 체험해 볼 수 있는 대형 수조
be excited to + 동사원형 ~하게 되어서 신나다

14 그림정보파악-위치 ▶ 정답 ②

듣•기•대•본

W: Honey, look. I framed our new family photo.
M: Oh, it's beautiful. The photo came out so nice.
W: I think so, too. Where should we put it?
M: We can put it on the bookshelf.
W: It's kind of crowded there. How about right next to the TV?
M: That would be nice.

우•리•말•해•석

여: 여보, 봐요. 저는 우리의 새로운 가족 사진을 액자에 넣었어요.
남: 오, 아름답네요. 사진이 너무 멋지게 나왔어요.
여: 저도 그렇게 생각해요. 우리는 그것을 어디에 둬야 할까요?
남: 우리는 그것을 책꽂이 선반 위에 둘 수 있어요.
여: 그곳은 약간 복잡해요. TV 바로 옆은 어때요?
남: 그게 좋겠네요.

단•어•및•표•현

frame [freim] [동] 액자에 넣다
come out 나오다
bookshelf [búkʃèlf] [명] 책꽂이
kind of 약간, 어느 정도
crowded [kráudid] [형] 붐비는

15 부탁(요청)한일파악 ▶ 정답 ④

듣•기•대•본

W: Jamie, did you do the dishes in the sink?
M: Of course, Mom. I even cleaned my room.
W: Wow, I'm impressed.
M: Anyway, when is Dad coming home?
W: He should be here by now. Will you give him a phone call?

M: Okay, I will. I'm so hungry. What are we having for dinner?

W: We're having roast chicken and baked beans.

우·리·말·해·석

여: Jamie, 싱크대에 있는 그릇들 설거지했니?

남: 물론이에요, 엄마. 저는 제 방도 청소했어요.

여: 와, 나 감동 받았다.

남: 그런데 아빠는 언제 집에 오세요?

여: 지금쯤이면 집에 오실 텐데. 그에게 전화 걸어 주겠니?

남: 좋아요, 그럴게요. 저는 무척 배고파요. 우리 저녁으로 무엇을 먹나요?

여: 우리는 통닭구이와 삶은 콩을 먹을 거야.

단·어·및·표·현

do the dishes 설거지하다

impressed [imprést] 혱 감동받은

16 제안파악 ▶ 정답 ②

듣·기·대·본

W: Congratulations on winning the basketball game yesterday.

M: Thanks. I owe it all to my coach, Mr. Snaders.

W: He must be a great coach.

M: He is. I'd like to get him a gift as a thank-you.

W: How about a basketball signed by everyone on the team?

M: That's a great idea.

우·리·말·해·석

여: 어제 농구 경기 이긴 것 축하해.

남: 고마워. 모든 건 나의 코치님인 Snaders 선생님 덕분이야.

여: 그분은 훌륭한 코치임에 틀림없어.

남: 맞아. 그분에게 감사의 의미로 선물을 드리고 싶어.

여: 팀 모두의 사인이 담긴 농구공을 드리는 게 어때?

남: 그거 좋은 생각이다.

단·어·및·표·현

owe A to B A는 B의 덕분이다

How about ~? ~는 어때?

17 할일파악 ▶ 정답 ②

듣·기·대·본

M: Hey, let's have a picnic in the park this Saturday.

W: I don't think that's a good idea.

M: Why not?

W: The weather forecast says it might rain, and picnicking in the rain isn't fun.

M: True. How about trying some new sweets at a café instead?

W: Great idea! We can enjoy some tasty treats together.

우·리·말·해·석

남: 이봐, 이번 주 토요일에 공원으로 소풍 가자.

여: 난 그게 좋은 생각일 것 같진 않아.

남: 왜 아닌데?

여: 일기 예보에서 말하길 비가 올 수도 있다는데, 빗속에서 소풍 가는 건 재미있지 않아.

남: 맞아. 대신에 카페에서 새로운 디저트들을 좀 시도해 보는 건 어때?

여: 좋은 생각이야! 우리는 함께 맛있는 몇몇 간식들을 즐길 수 있어.

단·어·및·표·현

picnic [píknik] 혱 소풍, 피크닉 동 소풍[피크닉] 가다

weather forecast 일기 예보

sweet [swi:t] 혱 디저트

instead [instéd] 윗 대신에

tasty [téisti] 혱 맛있는

treat [tri:t] 혱 간식

18 직업추론 ▶ 정답 ①

듣·기·대·본

M: Hello, how can I help you?

W: Hi, I'm here to have an ID photo taken.

M: Sure. What's the photo for?

W: I need the photo for my driver's license.

M: Okay. Please sit over here and look at the camera.

W: Sure. Shall I sit like this?

M: Perfect! Now stay still for a moment, please.

우·리·말·해·석

남: 안녕하세요, 어떻게 도와드릴까요?

여: 안녕하세요, 저는 신분증 사진을 찍으러 왔어요.

남: 알겠어요. 사진이 어떤 용도인가요?

여: 저는 제 운전면허증용 사진이 필요해요.

남: 좋아요. 여기에 앉으시고 카메라를 보세요.

여: 알겠어요. 제가 이렇게 앉을까요?

남: 완벽합니다! 이제 잠깐 동안 가만히 계세요.

단·어·및·표·현

Shall I ~? 내가 ~할까요? (상대방의 의사를 물음)

still [stil] 혱 가만히 있는

19 알맞은응답찾기 ▶ 정답 ⑤

듣·기·대·본

M: What's the matter, Sujin?

W: I'm worried about my math test tomorrow.

M: Do you want some help?

W: It's okay. I studied all day today.

M: Then why are you so worried?

W: I got a really bad grade on my last exam.

M: You'll do better this time.

우·리·말·해·석

① 아마도 다음번에.   ② 그거 좋은 생각이야.

③ 그렇다니 기쁘다.   ④ 도와줘서 고마워.

⑤ 이번엔 더 잘할 거야.

남: 무슨 일 있니, 수진아?

여: 내일 내 수학 시험이 걱정돼.

남: 좀 도와줄까?

여: 괜찮아. 나는 오늘 하루 종일 공부했어.

남: 그런데 왜 그렇게 걱정하는 거야?

여: 내 지난 시험에서 정말로 나쁜 점수를 받았거든.

남: 이번엔 더 잘할 거야.

단·어·및·표·현

What's the matter? 무슨 일 있니?

20 알맞은응답찾기 ▶ 정답 ③

듣·기·대·본

M: Nancy, do you want to play badminton tomorrow evening?

W: I'd love to, but I don't have a racket.

M: You can use mine. I have a spare one.

W: Great. Thanks! What time shall we meet?

M: Is 7 o'clock okay? I have two other friends coming.
W: Oh, that's fine. How long are you planning to play?
M: We'll play for about an hour.

우·리·말·해·석

① 네 명이 있을 거야.
② 난 7시 정각에 맞춰 갈 수 없어.
③ 우리는 대략 한 시간 동안 칠 거야.
④ 그곳에 도착하는 데 10분이 걸려.
⑤ 너는 돈을 전혀 지불할 필요가 없어.

남: Nancy, 너 내일 저녁에 배드민턴 치고 싶니?
여: 그러고 싶지만 난 라켓을 갖고 있지 않아.
남: 넌 내 것을 사용해도 돼. 내가 여분의 것(라켓)을 가지고 있어.
여: 좋아. 고마워! 우리 몇 시에 만날까?
남: 7시 정각 괜찮아? 다른 친구 두 명이 올 거야.
여: 아, 그건 괜찮아. 얼마나 오래 칠 계획이야?
남: 우리는 대략 한 시간 동안 칠 거야.

단·어·및·표·현

spare[spεər] 형 여분의, 예비용의
be planning to + 동사원형 ~할 계획이다

Words & Expressions Review

1. 가만히 있는, 아직도	2. 내가 ~할까요?	3. 공연, 행사
4. 액자에 넣다	5. ~을 데우다, 뜨겁게 만들다	6. 여분의, 예비용의
7. 솔직히 (말해서)	8. 안에	9. 며칠 전에
10. 비비다, 문지르다	11. 적어도, 최소한	12. 재능이 있는
13. 고장 난, 부서진	14. 불가사리	15. 혼자 힘으로
16. A는 B의 덕분이다	17. ~하게 되어서 신나는	18. 재활용
19. ~할 수 있다	20. (행사가) 열리다	21. ~은 어때?
22. 이루다, 성취하다	23. 조금씩	24. 걸어서
25. 대신에	26. 주민 센터	27. 처리하다, 다루다
28. ~에 가까운	29. 사인하다	30. ~을 버리다
31. 새 모양의	32. 감동받은	33. 잠깐 들르다
34. 회전하다	35. 붐비는	36. 쓰레기
37. (둥근) 접시, 그릇	38. (흥미로운 것을) 살펴보다[보다]	39. 역, 정류장
40. 산들바람	41. 냉장고 자석	42. 분리하다, 나누다
43. 디저트	44. 소풍, 피크닉 / 소풍[피크닉] 가다	

|정|답|

01 ⑤	02 ⑤	03 ①	04 ①	05 ⑤
06 ⑤	07 ⑤	08 ③	09 ③	10 ①
11 ②	12 ③	13 ⑤	14 ④	15 ④
16 ③	17 ④	18 ④	19 ②	20 ①

---

01 그림정보파악(담화) ▶ 정답 ⑤

듣·기·대·본

W: I live in Africa. I have spots on my body. I have four long legs. I am tall and I have a very long neck. I eat leaves and twigs. What am I?

우·리·말·해·석

여: 나는 아프리카에 살아. 나는 내 몸에 반점들이 있어. 나는 네 개의 긴 다리가 있어. 나는 키가 크고 매우 긴 목을 갖고 있어. 나는 나뭇잎들과 잔가지들을 먹어. 나는 무엇일까?

단·어·및·표·현

spot[spɑt] 명 반점
twig[twig] 명 잔가지

02 그림정보파악(대화) ▶ 정답 ⑤

듣·기·대·본

W: Hello, I'd like to buy a coin purse.
M: We have round ones and square ones.
W: Could you show me the round ones?
M: Sure, how about this one with stripes?
W: Hmm… Do you have any other designs?
M: We have this round one with hearts on it.
W: I like hearts. I'll take that one.

우·리·말·해·석

여: 안녕하세요, 저는 동전 지갑을 하나 사고 싶어요.
남: 저희는 둥근 것과 네모난 것이 있습니다.
여: 제게 둥근 것 좀 보여주시겠어요?
남: 네, 줄무늬가 있는 이건 어떠세요?
여: 흠… 다른 디자인도 있나요?
남: 저희는 하트 무늬가 있는 둥근 것도 있습니다.
여: 저는 하트를 좋아해요. 그걸로 할게요.

단·어·및·표·현

coin purse 동전지갑
round[raund] 형 둥근
stripe[straip] 명 줄무늬

03 날씨파악-그림 ▶ 정답 ①

듣·기·대·본

W: Good morning! Let's check the weather for today. In Seoul, it will be cloudy. There will be heavy rain in Daegu. Busan will be very windy. If you're in Busan, don't forget to wear a jacket when you go outside.

우·리·말·해·석

여: 좋은 아침입니다! 오늘의 날씨를 확인해 보죠. 서울은 구름이 많이 끼겠습니다. 대구에는 많은 비가 내리겠습니다. 부산은 바람이 매우 많이 불겠습니다. 만약 부산에 계신다면, 밖에 나갈 때 재킷을 입는 것을 잊지 마세요.

단·어·및·표·현

check[tʃek] 동 확인하다, 알아보다
heavy[hévi] 형 (양·정도 등이 보통보다) 많은, 심한
windy[wíndi] 형 바람이 많이 부는

04 마지막말의도파악 ▶ 정답 ①

듣·기·대·본

M: Hey, Emily. Who's that you're with?
W: Hey, Roger. She's a new student. I'm showing her

around the school.

M: But aren't you busy with the student council?

W: It's okay. I like helping people.

M: You're always there for others. That's amazing!

우·리·말·해·석

남: 안녕, Emily. 같이 있는 사람은 누구야?

여: 안녕, Roger. 그녀는 전학생이야. 내가 학교를 구경시켜 주고 있어.

남: 근데 너 학생회 일로 바쁘지 않아?

여: 괜찮아. 나는 사람들 도와주는 게 좋아.

남: 너는 항상 다른 사람들을 위해주네. 진짜 대단하다!

단·어·및·표·현

new student 전학생, 새 학생

show around 구경시켜주다

be busy with ~하느라 바쁘다

student council 학생회

amazing [əméiziŋ] 혱 놀라운

05 담화미언급 ▶ 정답 ⑤

듣·기·대·본

M: I want to tell you about a nice store in our town. It's called Jeremy's Best Subs. It is on Elm Street, right next to the subway station. They sell many kinds of sandwiches, but ham and egg is my favorite. I love this place because they always give discounts at the beginning of the semester!

우·리·말·해·석

남: 저는 당신에게 우리 도시에 있는 좋은 가게에 대해 말해주고 싶습니다. 그것은 Jeremy's Best Subs라고 불립니다. 그것은 지하철역 바로 옆 Elm Street에 있습니다. 그들은 많은 종류의 샌드위치를 팔지만, 햄에 그(샌드위치)가 제가 가장 좋아하는 것입니다. 그들은 학기 초에 항상 할인을 해주기 때문에 저는 이곳을 매우 좋아합니다!

단·어·및·표·현

right [rait] 흰 바로, 정확히

give a discount 할인하다

semester [siméstər] 혱 학기

06 수치파악 ▶ 정답 ⑤

듣·기·대·본

(Telephone rings.)

M: Hello?

W: Dad, it's me. You are coming to pick me up, right?

M: Of course, sweetheart. I'll be at the station by 2:00 p.m.

W: No, I'm taking the next train. It arrives one and a half hours later.

M: No problem. I'll see you at 3:30.

W: Thanks, Dad. See you soon.

우·리·말·해·석

(전화벨이 울린다.)

남: 여보세요?

여: 아빠, 저예요. 저를 데리러 오실 거죠, 그렇죠?

남: 물론이지, 얘야. 오후 2시까지 역에 갈 거야.

여: 안 돼요, 저 다음 기차 탈 거예요. 그건 1시간 30분 더 늦게 도착해요.

남: 문제없다. 3시 30분에 보자.

여: 고마워요, 아빠. 조금 있다 봐요.

단·어·및·표·현

pick ~ up ~를 (차로) 데리러 가다

07 장래희망추론 ▶ 정답 ⑤

듣·기·대·본

W: Brad, what are you working on?

M: I'm writing a sports article for our school newspaper.

W: That sounds interesting. You must like sports very much.

M: Yes, I want to become a sports journalist in the future.

W: I'm sure you'll make it!

M: Thank you!

우·리·말·해·석

여: Brad, 너 무슨 일을 하고 있는 거야?

남: 난 우리 학교 신문을 위해 스포츠 기사를 쓰고 있어.

여: 흥미롭게 들린다. 너는 스포츠를 아주 많이 좋아하는 게 틀림없어.

남: 그래, 나는 미래에 스포츠 기자가 되고 싶어.

여: 난 네가 해낼 거라고 확신해!

남: 고마워!

단·어·및·표·현

work on ~에 애쓰다, 공들이다

article [áːrtikl] 혱 (신문, 잡지의) 기사, 글

journalist [dʒə́ːrnəlist] 혱 기자, 저널리스트

make it (바라던 일을) 해내다, 이루다

08 심정추론 ▶ 정답 ③

듣·기·대·본

M: What are you reading?

W: I'm reading the school newspaper. My sister is on the front page.

M: Your sister?

W: Yes. She won first prize in the piano competition. I'm so proud of her.

M: Wow, that's great!

W: I'm really happy for her. She did a great job.

우·리·말·해·석

남: 너 뭐 읽고 있는 거니?

여: 난 학교 신문을 읽고 있어. 내 여동생이 제1면에 났어.

남: 네 여동생?

여: 응. 그녀가 피아노 경연에서 1등을 했거든. 난 그녀가 정말 자랑스러워.

남: 우와, 굉장하다!

여: 난 정말 기뻐. 그녀는 아주 잘해줬어.

단·어·및·표·현

competition [kὰmpitíʃən] 혱 경연, 대회, 경쟁

be proud of ~ ~를 자랑스러워하다

09 할일파악(대화직후) ▶ 정답 ③

듣·기·대·본

W: Chris, can you help me with these boxes?

M: Sure! What are they?

W: They're used clothes that I'm sending to people in developing countries.

M: How did you collect them?

W: I called all my friends and asked for help.

M: I have some clothes at home that I don't wear anymore.

W: Then can you give them to me?

M: Sure! I'll go get them right now.

우·리·말·해·석

여: Chris, 이 상자들을 (옮기는 것을) 도와줄 수 있니?

남: 물론! 그것들은 무엇이야?
여: 내가 개발도상국의 사람들에게 보내는 헌 옷이야.
남: 너는 그것들을 어떻게 모았니?
여: 내 모든 친구들에게 전화해서 도움을 요청했어.
남: 나는 더 이상 입지 않는 옷이 집에 좀 있어.
여: 그러면 그것들을 나에게 줄 수 있니?
남: 물론이지! 바로 가서 그것들을 가져올게.

단·어·및·표·현

used [ju:zd] [형] 헌, 중고의
ask for ~ ~을 요청하다

10 대화화제추론 ▶ 정답 ①

듣·기·대·본

M: What are you looking at, Sojin?
W: I'm looking at how to get a refund from this website.
M: What did you buy?
W: A T-shirt. But the sleeves are different from the pictures.
M: Okay. But it says you need to pay for return postage.
W: That's fine. This T-shirt doesn't suit me.

우·리·말·해·석

남: 소진아, 넌 무엇을 보고 있니?
여: 난 이 웹사이트에서 환불을 받는 방법을 보고 있어.
남: 네가 무엇을 샀는데?
여: 티셔츠. 하지만 소매가 사진과 달라.
남: 그렇구나. 하지만 네가 반송료를 지불해야 한다고 쓰여 있어.
여: 그건 괜찮아. 이 티셔츠는 나한테 어울리지 않아.

단·어·및·표·현

get a refund 환불받다
different from ~ ~와 다른
return postage 반송료, 반송용 우편 요금
suit [su:t] [동] (~에게) 어울리다, 맞다

11 특정정보파악(교통수단) ▶ 정답 ②

듣·기·대·본

W: Honey, how did you like the movie?
M: It was really great, especially the train scene. That was amazing.
W: It really was. By the way, it's 11:15. Do you think the subway is still running?
M: No, the subway only runs until 11:00 p.m.
W: Then, I guess we should take a taxi to get home.
M: Right! Look, there's an empty taxi coming.
W: All right, let's take that one.

우·리·말·해·석

여: 여보, 영화 어땠어요?
남: 정말 훌륭했어요, 특히 열차 장면이요. 그건 아주 놀라웠어요.
여: 정말 그랬어요. 그런데 시간이 11시 15분이네요. 아직도 지하철이 운행할까요?
남: 아니요. 지하철은 밤 11시까지만 운행해요.
여: 그럼 집에 가려면 택시를 타야겠네요.
남: 맞아요! 봐요, 저기 빈 택시가 오고 있어요.
여: 잘됐네요. 우리 저 차를 타요.

단·어·및·표·현

take a taxi 택시를 타다
empty [émpti] [형] 빈, 비어 있는

12 이유파악 ▶ 정답 ③

듣·기·대·본

W: Jay! You look so nice! Did you buy another shirt?
M: Yes, I bought this red shirt.
W: It's really great. However, you already have a lot of shirts.
M: But I didn't have a red one and I like this color so much.
W: Oh, okay. Anyway, I think it goes best with your new jeans.

우·리·말·해·석

여: Jay! 너 정말 멋져 보인다! 또 다른 셔츠를 샀니?
남: 응, 난 이 빨간 셔츠를 샀어.
여: 정말 멋지다. 그런데, 너는 이미 많은 셔츠를 갖고 있잖아.
남: 그렇지만 난 빨간색은 없었고 이 색이 매우 좋아.
여: 아, 그래. 아무튼, 내 생각에 그 셔츠가 너의 새 청바지와 가장 잘 어울리는 것 같아.

단·어·및·표·현

a lot of 많은
go best with ~ ~와 가장 잘 어울리다

13 대화장소추론 ▶ 정답 ⑤

듣·기·대·본

W: Hi there! How can I help you?
M: I want to know when the animals get fed.
W: Sure! Just look for the signs around the zoo showing feeding times.
M: Thanks! I'll check them out.
W: We also have special times when you can help our staff feed the animals.
M: Cool! How can I join?
W: You can sign up at the zoo entrance.

우·리·말·해·석

여: 안녕하세요! 어떻게 도와드릴까요?
남: 저는 동물들에게 언제 먹이가 주어지는지 알고 싶어요.
여: 네! 동물원 곳곳에 먹이 주는 시간을 알려주는 표지판을 찾아보세요.
남: 감사합니다! 찾아볼게요.
여: 저희 직원들이 동물에게 먹이 주는 것을 당신이 도울 수 있는 특별한 시간도 있어요.
남: 멋지네요! 어떻게 참여할 수 있나요?
여: 동물원 입구에서 신청하실 수 있습니다.

단·어·및·표·현

feed [fi:d] [동] 먹이를 주다
look for ~을 찾다
check ~ out ~을 확인하다
sign up 신청하다

14 그림정보파악-지도 ▶ 정답 ④

듣·기·대·본

M: Excuse me. Is there a supermarket nearby?
W: Yes, there is one not too far from here.
M: Good! Can you tell me where it is?
W: Sure. Go straight one block and turn left on Parker Street.
M: On Parker Street?
W: Yes, it's on your left. It's between the library and the movie theater.

M: Thank you.

우·리·말·해·석

남: 실례합니다. 가까운 곳에 슈퍼마켓이 있나요?

여: 네, 여기서 멀지 않은 곳에 한 군데 있어요.

남: 잘됐군요! 그것이 어디 있는지 말해주실 수 있나요?

여: 그럼요. 한 블럭을 똑바로 가다가 Parker 가에서 왼쪽으로 도세요.

남: Parker 가에서요?

여: 네, 그것은 당신의 왼쪽에 있어요. 그것은 도서관과 영화관 사이에 있어요.

남: 고맙습니다.

단·어·및·표·현

nearby [nìərbái] ⓟ 가까운 곳에, 인근에

straight [streit] ⓟ 똑바로, 일직선으로

turn [təːrn] ⓥ 몸을 돌리다

movie theater 영화관

15 부탁(요청)한일파악 ▶ 정답 ④

듣·기·대·본

W: Sam, did you feed the dog?

M: Yes, Mom. I fed him half an hour ago.

W: Good. Then, can you take him for a walk?

M: Okay, I'll take him to the park.

W: Thank you.

우·리·말·해·석

여: Sam, 너 개에게 먹이를 줬니?

남: 네, 엄마. 30분 전에 개에게 먹이를 줬어요.

여: 잘했다. 그러면, 너 개 산책을 시킬 수 있니?

남: 알겠어요, 제가 개를 공원으로 데려갈게요.

여: 고맙구나.

단·어·및·표·현

take ~ for a walk ~를 산책시키다

16 제안파악 ▶ 정답 ③

듣·기·대·본

W: I'm going to make orange juice. Do you want some?

M: We're out of oranges. Mom will buy some later. But, we have lemons.

W: Then, I'll make some lemonade.

M: Why don't we make it together? I'm thirsty, too.

W: Sounds good.

우·리·말·해·석

여: 나는 오렌지 주스를 만들 거야. 너도 좀 먹을래?

남: 우리 오렌지가 다 떨어졌어. 이따가 엄마가 좀 사오실 거야. 하지만 우리는 레몬이 있어.

여: 그러면, 레모네이드를 좀 만들어야겠다.

남: 우리 같이 만드는 것이 어때? 나도 목이 말라.

여: 좋은 생각이야.

단·어·및·표·현

Why don't we ~? 우리 ~하는 게 어때?

17 한일파악 ▶ 정답 ④

듣·기·대·본

M: Lisa, what did you do over the weekend?

W: I baked cookies with my mom at home. How was your weekend?

M: I helped my dad wash his car at the car wash.

W: That sounds like hard work.

M: Yeah, I'm a bit tired today.

W: Still, I think it's sweet of you to help your dad.

우·리·말·해·석

남: Lisa, 넌 주말 동안 무엇을 했니?

여: 난 집에서 우리 엄마와 쿠키를 구웠어. 너의 주말은 어땠어?

남: 난 세차장에서 우리 아빠가 세차하시는 걸 도왔어.

여: 그건 힘든 일처럼 들려.

남: 그래, 난 오늘 조금 피곤해.

여: 그래도, 너희 아빠를 도와드리다니 넌 참 다정한 것 같아.

단·어·및·표·현

car wash 세차장

a bit 조금, 약간

still [stil] ⓟ 그래도, 그럼에도 불구하고

18 직업추론 ▶ 정답 ④

듣·기·대·본

W: Hello. Do you go to Bakersville?

M: We stop at the entrance to the village. It's easy walking from there.

W: Oh, good. How long does it take?

M: About 40 minutes. There are four stops in between.

W: I see. Which bus should I take to get back?

M: Bus 402. The same number. Would you like to hop on?

W: Yes! How much is the fare?

M: It's 4 dollars.

우·리·말·해·석

여: 안녕하세요. Bakersville로 가세요?

남: 저희는 그 마을의 입구에서 섭니다. 거기서 걸어가기 쉽습니다.

여: 아, 좋네요. 얼마나 걸리나요?

남: 약 40분입니다. 그 사이에 4개의 정류장이 있습니다.

여: 알겠습니다. 돌아오려면 어느 버스를 타야 하나요?

남: 402번 버스입니다. 같은 번호죠. 타시겠습니까?

여: 네! 요금이 얼마입니까?

남: 4달러입니다.

단·어·및·표·현

in between 그 사이에, 중간에

hop on (버스, 기차 등에) 타다

19 알맞은응답찾기 ▶ 정답 ②

듣·기·대·본

W: Hey, Jinwoo.

M: Hi, Yujin. Did you see the new poster on the notice board?

W: Which one do you mean?

M: The one about the online lecture on art.

W: Oh, yes. It looks very interesting. I love art.

M: Then shall we register for the lecture? I'm interested in art, too.

W: Sure, let's do it together now.

우·리·말·해·석

① 그 온라인 강의는 무료야.

② 물론이야, 지금 같이 하자.

③ 내 취미는 그림을 그리는 거야.

④ 새로운 포스터는 흥미로워 보여.

⑤ 학교 마치고 강의 들으러 가자.

07 회 모의고사

여: 야, 진우야.
남: 안녕, 유진아. 게시판에 있는 새로운 포스터 봤어?
여: 어떤 걸 말하는 거야?
남: 예술에 관한 온라인 강의에 대한 거 말이야.
여: 아, 맞아. 그거 매우 흥미로워 보이더라. 난 예술을 좋아하거든.
남: 그러면 우리 강의에 등록할래? 나도 예술에 관심이 있어.
여: **물론이야. 지금 같이 하자.**

단·어·및·표·현
notice board 게시판
lecture [léktʃər] 몡 강의
register [rédʒistər] 됭 등록하다
be interested in ~에 관심이 있다

20 알맞은응답찾기 ▶ 정답 ①

듣·기·대·본
M: Hi, Harin. Did you have a good weekend?
W: Yes. I took a soap making class.
M: That's nice. I love making soap.
W: It was really fun. How was your weekend?
M: It was great. I went to a strawberry farm.
W: Did you pick many strawberries?
M: Yes, I did. Do you want to try some?
W: Yes, I'd love to.

우·리·말·해·석
① 응, 그리고 싶어.
② 아니, 나는 그것을 먹지 않았어.
③ 응, 나는 네 비누를 사용해볼게.
④ 아니, 나는 요리를 잘 못해.
⑤ 글쎄, 나는 수업을 듣는 걸 좋아하지 않아.

남: 안녕, 하린아. 주말 잘 보냈어?
여: 응. 난 비누 만들기 수업을 들었어.
남: 좋다. 나도 비누 만드는 거 좋아해.
여: 정말 재미있었어. 네 주말은 어땠어?
남: 좋았어. 나는 딸기 농장에 갔어.
여: 너는 딸기를 많이 땄니?
남: 응, 많이 땄어. 좀 먹어볼래?
여: 응, 그리고 싶어.

단·어·및·표·현
take [teik] 됭 (수업·강의 등을) 듣다, 수강하다
soap [soup] 몡 비누
pick [pik] 됭 (과일 등을) 따다

Words & Expressions Review

1. 택시를 타다	2. 역, 정류장	3. 몸을 돌리다
4. 반점	5. 학기	6. 빈, 비어 있는
7. 바람이 많이 부는	8. 기자, 저널리스트	9. (바라던 일을) 해내다
10. 환불받다	11. 잔가지	12. 아무튼, 어쨌든
13. ~과 다른	14. ~을 확인하다	15. ~을 찾다
16. 반송료	17. 놀라운	18. ~를 자랑스러워하다
19. 많은, 심한	20. 바로, 정확히	21. 신청하다
22. 운행하다, 운영하다	23. 그런데	24. (~에게) 어울리다
25. 가까운 곳에, 인근에	26. 30분	27. 도착하다
28. 강의	29. (신문, 잡지의) 기사, 글	30. (버스, 기차 등에) 타다
31. A를 산책시키다	32. 헌, 중고의	33. 먹이를 주다, 먹이
34. 세차장	35. 제1면	36. 조금, 약간
37. 특히	38. 그래도, 그럼에도 불구하고	39. 경연, 대회
40. (수업·강의 등을) 듣다, 수강하다	41. ~과 가장 잘 어울리다	42. 비누
43. ~을 요청하다	44. (과일 등을) 따다	

영어듣기 모의고사 **08**회

|정|답|

01 ④	02 ③	03 ④	04 ②	05 ④
06 ②	07 ③	08 ②	09 ⑤	10 ⑤
11 ④	12 ②	13 ①	14 ④	15 ④
16 ②	17 ②	18 ③	19 ②	20 ⑤

01 그림정보파악(담화) ▶ 정답 ④

듣·기·대·본
M: I live in the forest. I have large eyes, a flat face, and broad wings. I hunt for small animals like mice mostly at night using powerful claws. I can turn my head and neck up to 270 degrees. I make a unique "hooting" sound. What am I?

우·리·말·해·석
남: 나는 숲에 살아요. 나는 큰 눈, 평평한 얼굴, 그리고 넓은 날개가 있어요. 나는 대부분 밤에 강력한 발톱을 이용해서 쥐 같은 작은 동물을 사냥해요. 나는 내 머리와 목을 270도까지 돌릴 수 있어요. 나는 독특한 "부엉부엉"하는 소리를 내요. 나는 무엇일까요?

단·어·및·표·현
flat [flæt] 웽 평평한
broad [brɔːd] 웽 넓은
claw [klɔː] 몡 (동물의) 발톱
up to ~까지
hoot [huːt] 됭 (부엉이가) 부엉부엉 울다

02 그림정보파악(대화) ▶ 정답 ③

듣·기·대·본
M: How can I help you?
W: Hi. I want to buy pajamas for my son.
M: Okay. How about these ones with circles on them?
W: Hmm... I don't think he'll like those ones.
M: Then, how about these ones with stars?
W: Great! He loves stars.
M: I'm sure he'll like them.
W: Right. I'll take them.

우·리·말·해·석
남: 어떻게 도와드릴까요?
여: 안녕하세요. 저는 제 아들을 위한 잠옷을 사고 싶어요.

남: 알겠습니다. 그것들(잠옷) 위에 동그라미가 있는 이것들은 어떠세요?
여: 흠… 그가 그것들을 좋아할 거라고 생각하지 않아요.
남: 그럼, 별이 있는 이것들은 어떠세요?
여: 좋아요! 그는 별을 아주 좋아해요.
남: 그가 그것들을 좋아할 거라고 확신합니다.
여: 맞아요. 그것들로 할게요.

단·어·및·표·현
pajamas [pədʒɑ́:məz] [명] 잠옷
How about ~? ~은 어때요?
be sure 확신하다

03 날씨파악-그림 ▶ 정답 ④

듣·기·대·본
W: Good morning! It's Friday, February 12th. This is the weather report. It's sunny and warm all over the country now, but tomorrow will be colder than today. Seoul will have very strong winds. In Jeju and Daegu, there will be showers in the afternoon.

우·리·말·해·석
여: 안녕하세요! 오늘은 2월 12일 금요일입니다. 일기 예보입니다. 지금은 전국적으로 화창하고 따뜻하지만, 내일은 오늘보다 더 춥겠습니다. 서울은 매우 강한 바람이 불겠습니다. 제주도와 대구에서는 오후에 소나기가 오겠습니다.

단·어·및·표·현
all over the country 전국적으로, 전국에

04 마지막말의도파악 ▶ 정답 ②

듣·기·대·본
W: Hey, do you have a biology textbook?
M: Yes, I do. Why?
W: Can I borrow your book today? I forgot to bring mine today.
M: Hmm. You tore my book last time.
W: Oh, that was my mistake. I promise I will be careful this time.
M: Okay. Just this once.

우·리·말·해·석
여: 얘, 너 생물 교과서 있니?
남: 응, 있어. 왜?
여: 나 오늘 네 책 좀 빌릴 수 있어? 오늘 내 것을 가지고 오는 것을 깜빡했어.
남: 흠. 너 지난번에 내 책을 찢었잖아.
여: 아, 그건 내 실수였어. 이번에는 조심하겠다고 약속할게.
남: 알겠어. 이번 한 번만이야.

단·어·및·표·현
tear [tɛər] [동] 찢다(tear-tore-torn)

05 담화미언급 ▶ 정답 ④

듣·기·대·본
M: Hello, everyone. I'd like to talk about my pet dog. His name is Max. He's three years old. I got him when he was a puppy. He has soft, golden fur and loves meeting new people. He's very friendly and loves to play outside. He's like a little brother to me.

우·리·말·해·석
남: 안녕하세요, 여러분. 저는 제 반려견에 대해 이야기하고 싶습니다. 그의 이름은 Max입니다. 그는 세 살입니다. 저는 그가 강아지였을 때 그를 얻었습니다. 그는 부드러운 금빛 털을 가지고 있고 새로운 사람들을 만나는 것을 좋아합니다. 그는 아주 친근하고, 밖에서 노는 것을 정말 좋아합니다. 그는 저에게 동생과 같습니다.

단·어·및·표·현
soft [sɔ(:)ft] [형] 부드러운, 푹신한
golden [góuldən] [형] 금빛의
friendly [fréndli] [형] 친근한

06 수치파악 ▶ 정답 ②

듣·기·대·본
M: Hi, Sophie. I have an extra ticket to the basketball game.
W: Really? Can I come?
M: Sure. It starts at 5 p.m. tomorrow.
W: Then, I'll come to your house at 4:00. Let's grab a snack on the way.
M: In that case, let's meet 30 minutes earlier.
W: 3:30 at your house? Okay. I'll see you then.

우·리·말·해·석
남: 안녕, Sophie. 내가 여분의 농구 경기 표를 한 장 가지고 있어.
여: 정말? 내가 가도 돼?
남: 물론. 내일 오후 5시에 시작해.
여: 그럼, 내가 너희 집에 4시에 갈게. 가는 길에 간식을 먹자.
남: 그렇다면, 30분 더 일찍 만나자.
여: 3시 30분에 너희 집에서? 알았어. 그때 봐.

단·어·및·표·현
extra [ékstrə] [형] 여분의
grab a snack 간식을 먹다
on the way 가는 길에
earlier [ə́:rliər] [부] 더 일찍

07 장래희망추론 ▶ 정답 ③

듣·기·대·본
W: What are you doing, David?
M: I'm studying English. I want to speak English well.
W: Why? Do you want to become an English teacher?
M: No, I want to design clothes. I want to go abroad and study fashion.
W: I see. Is that why you always practice drawing?
M: That's right. I have to study art and draw pictures well.
W: Wow. You're working really hard to achieve your dream!

우·리·말·해·석
여: 뭐하고 있니, David?
남: 나는 영어 공부를 하고 있어. 나는 영어를 잘하고 싶어.
여: 왜? 너는 영어 선생님이 되고 싶니?
남: 아니, 나는 옷을 디자인하고 싶어. 나는 외국에 가서 패션을 공부하고 싶어.
여: 그렇구나. 그게 네가 항상 그림 그리기를 연습하는 이유니?
남: 맞아. 나는 미술을 공부하고 그림을 잘 그려야 해.
여: 와. 너는 너의 꿈을 이루기 위해 정말 열심히 노력하는구나!

단·어·및·표·현
go abroad 외국에 가다

08 심정추론 ▶ 정답 ②

듣·기·대·본
M: Vacation time! Are you excited, Claire?

W: I would be… But our <u>principal</u> has been talking for 20 minutes <u>already</u>…

M: Yeah… He is making a particularly <u>long announcement</u> today.

W: <mark>It is <u>way too long</u>.</mark> All I want to do is get out of here.

M: Just <u>hang in there</u>. Let's hope that he will be done soon.

W: Okay…

우·리·말·해·석

① 수줍은   ② 지루한   ③ 침착한   ④ 신난   ⑤ 초조한

남: 방학 기간이다! 너 신나니, Claire?

여: 그렇다면 좋을텐데… 하지만 우리 교장 선생님은 이미 20분째 말씀 하고 계셔…

남: 그래… 오늘은 특별히 긴 공지사항을 전하시네.

여: 지나치게 너무 길어. 내가 하고 싶은 것은 여기서 나가는 거야.

남: 참고 견뎌봐. 그가 곧 끝내기를 바라자.

여: 그래…

단·어·및·표·현

principal [prínsəpəl] 명 교장 선생님

already [ɔ:lrédi] 부 이미, 벌써

make an announcement 소식을 전하다, 발표를 하다

particularly [pərtíkjələrli] 부 특히, 특별히

way too long 지나치게 너무 긴

Just hang in there. 참고 견뎌봐.

09 할일파악(대화직후)   ▶ 정답 ⑤

들·기·대·본

W: Lorrie, who's your group project partner?

M: It's Patrick. Why do you ask?

W: My partner Margaret is moving to another school, so I <u>no longer</u> have a partner.

M: Do you want to <u>join</u> us?

W: Can I?

M: Sure. Patrick will be glad to have you, too.

W: Just to <u>make sure</u>, I'll call and ask him right now.

우·리·말·해·석

여: Lorrie, 너의 그룹 과제 동료는 누구야?

남: Patrick이야. 왜 물어보니?

여: 내 동료 Margaret이 다른 학교로 전학가게 되어서 난 더 이상 동료 가 없어.

남: 우리와 함께 하기를 원하니?

여: 그래도 돼?

남: 물론이야. Patrick도 너와 함께 하는 걸 기뻐할 거야.

여: 확실히 하기 위해서, 내가 지금 그에게 전화해서 물어볼게.

단·어·및·표·현

project [prádʒekt] 명 과제, 연구 프로젝트

no longer 더 이상 ~하지 않는

join [dʒɔin] 동 함께 하다, 합류하다

make sure 확실하게 하다

10 대화화제추론   ▶ 정답 ⑤

들·기·대·본

W: James, did you see this new <u>notice</u> on the school website?

M: No, what is it about?

W: <mark>It's about the <u>open house</u></mark> next Wednesday. It says that our parents should come.

M: Then, what are we doing on that day?

W: <mark>We just <u>take classes</u> as usual <u>while</u> our parents are watching.</mark> And then, they will have some time with our teacher to talk about us.

우·리·말·해·석

여: James, 학교 홈페이지에 올라온 이 새로운 공지사항 봤니?

남: 아니, 무엇에 관한 거야?

여: 다음 주 수요일에 있을 공개 수업의 날에 관한 내용이야. 우리 부모님 들이 오셔야 한다고 나와 있어.

남: 그러면, 우리는 그날에 무엇을 하는 거니?

여: 우리는 부모님들이 보고 계시는 동안 그냥 평소처럼 수업을 듣는 거 야. 그리고 나서, 그들은 선생님과 우리에 관해서 이야기하는 시간을 좀 가지실 거야.

단·어·및·표·현

notice [nóutis] 명 공지사항, 공고문

open house 공개 수업의 날

as usual 평소처럼, 늘 그렇듯이

while [wail] 접 ~하는 동안

11 특정정보파악(교통수단)   ▶ 정답 ④

들·기·대·본

M: Where do you want to go today?

W: Let's go to Gyeongbokgung Palace.

M: Okay. Shall we <u>take the subway</u>? There's a subway station near the palace.

W: Hmm… I was hoping to do some sightseeing on our way there.

M: <mark>Why don't we <u>borrow</u> bicycles then?</mark>

W: <mark>Great idea! Let's <u>ride bicycles</u> to the palace.</mark>

우·리·말·해·석

남: 넌 오늘 어디에 가기를 원하니?

여: 경복궁에 가자.

남: 좋아. 우리 지하철을 탈까? 그 궁 근처에 지하철역이 있어.

여: 흠… 난 그곳에 가는 길에 관광을 좀 하기를 바라고 있었어.

남: 그러면 자전거를 빌리는 게 어때?

여: 좋은 생각이야! 자전거를 타고 그 궁에 가자.

단·어·및·표·현

sightseeing [sáitsì:iŋ] 명 관광

on one's way + 장소 ~에 가는 길에

Why don't we ~? ~하는 게 어때?

borrow [bárou] 동 빌리다

12 이유파악   ▶ 정답 ⑤

들·기·대·본

M: Mom, can I go to the movies with my friends today?

W: Today? No, <u>I'm afraid</u> you can't.

M: Why not?

W: <mark>You promised to go shopping</mark> with me today so we could buy you a new coat.

M: Oh, I'm sorry. I forgot about that.

W: Why don't you go to the movies <u>another day</u>?

M: Okay, I will.

우·리·말·해·석

남: 엄마, 제가 오늘 제 친구들과 영화를 보러 가도 될까요?

여: 오늘? 아니, 안 될 것 같구나.

남: 왜 안 돼요?

여: 우리가 너의 새 코트를 살 수 있도록 너는 오늘 나와 쇼핑을 가기로 약속했어.
남: 오, 죄송해요. 제가 그것에 대해 잊었어요.
여: 다른 날에 영화를 보러 가는 것이 어떠니?
남: 좋아요, 그럴게요.

단•어•및•표•현

another day 다른 날

13 대화장소추론 ▶ 정답 ①

듣•기•대•본

M: Hi, how can I help you?
W: I'd like to buy a ticket to Seoul, please.
M: Sure. What time would you like to depart?
W: I'd like to leave as soon as possible.
M: There's a premium bus that leaves in 10 minutes.
W: I'll take that one. Thank you.

우•리•말•해•석

남: 안녕하세요, 어떻게 도와드릴까요?
여: 저는 서울로 가는 승차권을 사려고 합니다.
남: 알겠습니다. 몇 시에 출발하고 싶으십니까?
여: 저는 가능한 한 빨리 떠나려고 합니다.
남: 10분 뒤에 떠나는 우등 버스가 있습니다.
여: 그것으로 하겠습니다. 감사합니다.

단•어•및•표•현

depart [dipɑ́ːrt] [동] 출발하다, 떠나다
as soon as possible 가능한 한 빨리
premium bus 우등버스

14 표불일치 ▶ 정답 ④

듣•기•대•본

W: Hello, everyone! Let me tell you about our Kids' DIY Workshop. It'll be held this Saturday at 1 p.m. In this workshop, kids will build their own kites, and then test them outside. The event will be 2 hours in length. The fee is 10 dollars, including all materials. The workshop will take place at Central Park. Thanks.

우•리•말•해•석

	키즈 DIY 워크숍	
①	일시	이번 주 토요일, 오후 1시
②	내용	연 만들고 날리기
③	소요 시간	2시간
④	참가비	5달러
⑤	장소	센트럴 파크

여: 안녕하세요, 여러분! 저희 키즈 DIY 워크숍에 대해 말씀드리겠습니다. 그것은 이번 주 토요일 오후 1시에 개최될 것입니다. 이 워크숍에서 아이들은 자신의 연을 만들고, 그것들을 밖에서 시험할 것입니다. 그 행사는 2시간일 것입니다. 참가비는 모든 재료를 포함하여 10달러입니다. 그 워크숍은 센트럴 파크에서 열릴 것입니다. 감사합니다.

단•어•및•표•현

DIY 소비자가 직접 하기(do-it-yourself의 약어)
build [bild] [동] 만들다
length [leŋkθ] [명] 길이, (무엇이 계속되는) 시간[기간]
include [inklúːd] [동] 포함하다
material [mətí(ː)əriəl] [명] 재료
take place 열리다, 개최되다

15 부탁(요청)한일파악 ▶ 정답 ④

듣•기•대•본

(*Telephone rings.*)
M: Hello.
W: Hi, Jamie. This is Hailey.
M: Hi, Hailey. Are you back from your trip?
W: No, my flight has been cancel(l)ed because of bad weather.
M: Oh, I'm sorry to hear that.
W: I won't be home until tomorrow. So, could you feed my cat for one more day?
M: No problem. She's in good hands, so don't worry.

우•리•말•해•석

(전화벨이 울린다.)
남: 여보세요.
여: 안녕, Jamie. 나 Hailey야.
남: 안녕, Hailey. 너 여행에서 돌아왔니?
여: 아니, 나쁜 날씨 때문에 내 비행편이 취소되었어.
남: 오, 그렇다니 안됐다.
여: 나는 내일까지는 집에 못 갈 거야. 그래서 네가 내 고양이에게 하루 더 먹이를 줄래?
남: 문제없어. 그녀는 잘 관리되고 있으니, 걱정 마.

단•어•및•표•현

cancel [kǽnsəl] [동] 취소하다
in good hands 잘 관리되는

16 제안파악 ▶ 정답 ②

듣•기•대•본

M: Hailey, nice jeans!
W: Thank you. I bought them yesterday.
M: Where did you get them?
W: A new store just opened in my town. It has all kinds of clothes.
M: Good for you! Does it have jeans for men, too? I really need to buy some.
W: Yes. Why don't we go shopping together?
M: That sounds great!

우•리•말•해•석

남: Hailey, 청바지 멋지다!
여: 고마워. 나는 그것을 어제 샀어.
남: 어디서 샀어?
여: 새 가게가 우리 동네에 막 열었어. 모든 종류의 옷들이 있어.
남: 잘됐다! 남자 청바지도 있어? 나 정말로 좀 사야 하거든.
여: 응. 우리 같이 쇼핑 가는 게 어때?
남: 그거 좋은데!

단•어•및•표•현

Good for you! (너에게) 잘됐다!

17 한일파악 ▶ 정답 ②

듣•기•대•본

W: Fred, how did you spend your weekend?
M: I watched a movie with my friends. How was your weekend?
W: I went fishing with my Dad.
M: Wow, that sounds awesome! Did you catch many fish?
W: No, I couldn't catch any, but I still had fun.

08회 모의고사

M: Great! I'd like to give fishing a try as well.

우·리·말·해·석

여: Fred, 너는 주말을 어떻게 보냈니?
남: 나는 내 친구들과 함께 영화를 봤어. 네 주말은 어땠니?
여: 나는 아빠랑 낚시하러 갔어.
남: 우와, 멋진 것 같아! 물고기를 많이 잡았니?
여: 아니, 나는 아무것도 잡을 수 없었지만, 그런데도 재미있었어.
남: 대단해! 나도 낚시 한번 해보고 싶어.

단·어·및·표·현

go fishing 낚시하러 가다
still [stil] [부] 그런데도, 그럼에도 불구하고
would like to + 동사원형 ~하고 싶다
as well ~도, 또한, 역시

18 직업추론 ▶ 정답 ③

듣·기·대·본

W: How can I help you today?
M: My dog, Rocky, hasn't been able to walk properly since yesterday.
W: Let's take a look. [*Pause*] He has a sharp piece of wood stuck in his paw.
M: Oh, can you take it out?
W: Sure. I'll also clean his wound and put a bandage on it.
M: Thank you.

우·리·말·해·석

여: 오늘 어떻게 도와드릴까요?
남: 제 개, Rocky가, 어제 이후로 제대로 걷지 못하고 있어요.
여: 한번 보죠. [잠시 후] 그의 발에 날카로운 나무 조각이 박혀 있네요.
남: 오, 당신은 그걸 빼낼 수 있나요?
여: 물론이죠. 저는 또한 그의 상처도 깨끗이 닦아내고, 그 위에 붕대를 감아줄게요.
남: 감사합니다.

단·어·및·표·현

properly [prápərli] [부] 제대로
stick [stik] [동] 찔리다, 박히다
paw [pɔː] [명] (동물의 발톱이 달린) 발
wound [wuːnd; waund] [명] 상처, 부상
bandage [bǽndidʒ] [명] 붕대

19 알맞은응답찾기 ▶ 정답 ②

듣·기·대·본

W: Jake, have you started studying for the math quiz?
M: No, not yet. How about you?
W: Me, neither. Why don't we study together?
M: Sounds good. The quiz is next week, isn't it?
W: Yes, it's next Friday. Let's start studying tomorrow after school.
M: Great idea! Where shall we meet?
W: Let's meet at the library.

우·리·말·해·석

① 수영하러 가자.
② 도서관에서 만나자.
③ 나는 시험 치는 것을 좋아하지 않아.
④ 수학은 내가 가장 좋아하는 과목이야.
⑤ 내일이 벌써 금요일이야!

여: Jake, 수학 시험 공부를 시작했어?
남: 아니, 아직. 너는?
여: 나도 아니야. 우리 같이 공부하는 게 어때?
남: 좋은 것 같아. 시험은 다음주야, 그렇지 않아?
여: 그래, 다음 금요일이야. 내일 학교 끝나고 공부하기 시작하자.
남: 좋은 생각이야! 우리 어디서 만날까?
여: 도서관에서 만나자.

단·어·및·표·현

quiz [kwiz] [명] (간단한) 시험

20 알맞은응답찾기 ▶ 정답 ⑤

듣·기·대·본

M: Who is that girl? She's so good at tennis.
W: She's a new student in my class.
M: What do you think of her?
W: She's very nice. By the way, aren't you good at tennis, too?
M: Yes, I am.
W: Then why don't you play with her?
M: That sounds good.

우·리·말·해·석

① 테니스 치자.
② 특별한 건 없어.
③ 천만에.
④ 난 테니스 못 쳐.
⑤ 그거 좋겠다.

남: 저 여자애는 누구야? 테니스를 정말 잘하네.
여: 우리 반에 새로 온 학생이야.
남: 그녀에 대해 어떻게 생각해?
여: 아주 괜찮아. 그런데 너도 테니스 잘 치지 않니?
남: 응, 잘해.
여: 그러면 저 애랑 같이 하는 게 어때?
남: 그거 좋겠다.

단·어·및·표·현

What do you think of ~? ~에 대해 어떻게 생각해?

Words & Expressionss Review

1. 평소처럼, 늘 그렇듯이	2. 부드러운, 푹신한	3. 관광
4. 너에게 잘됐다!	5. ~하는 동안	6. 잠옷
7. 교장 선생님	8. 출발하다, 떠나다	9. 과제, 연구 프로젝트
10. 확신하다	11. ~도, 또한	12. 친근한
13. 소식을 전하다, 발표를 하다	14. ~하는 게 어때?	15. 외국에 가다
16. 이미, 벌써	17. 잘 관리되는	18. ~에 가는 중에
19. 넓은	20. 금빛의	21. 공지사항, 공고문
22. 더 이상 ~하지 않는	23. 만들다	24. 포함하다
25. 확실하게 하다	26. 가는 길에	27. 여분의
28. 다른 날	29. 찔리다, 박히다	30. 빌리다
31. 찢다	32. 제대로	33. 재료
34. 취소하다	35. 평평한	36. 모든 종류의
37. 더 일찍	38. 간식을 먹다	39. ~하고 싶다
40. 가능한 한 빨리	41. 그런데도, 그럼에도 불구하고	42. 전국적으로, 전국에
43. (간단한) 시험	44. ~에 대해 어떻게 생각해?	

영어듣기 모의고사 09회

|정|답|

01 ③	02 ④	03 ④	04 ③	05 ②
06 ③	07 ⑤	08 ④	09 ②	10 ④
11 ⑤	12 ⑤	13 ①	14 ①	15 ④
16 ②	17 ⑤	18 ②	19 ②	20 ①

01   그림정보파악(담화)   ▶ 정답 ③

듣·기·대·본

W: I am an insect. I have large eyes. I have six legs and I also have <u>wings</u>. I am yellow and black. I fly around from flower to flower and make honey. What am I?

우·리·말·해·석

여: 나는 곤충이야. 나는 큰 눈이 있어. 나는 여섯 개의 다리가 있고 또한 날개들도 있어. 나는 노란색이고 검은색이야. 나는 꽃에서 꽃으로 이리 저리 날아다니고 꿀을 만들어. 나는 무엇일까?

단·어·및·표·현

insect[ínsekt] 몡 곤충
from A to B A에서 B로

02   그림정보파악(대화)   ▶ 정답 ④

듣·기·대·본

M: Can I help you?
W: Yes. I'm looking to buy a sofa cushion.
M: How about this one with the <u>butterfly</u> picture?
W: Hmm… Do you have anything else?
M: We have this one with a cat on it.
W: Oh… I like that one!
M: I'm glad that you like it.
W: Great! I'll take it.

우·리·말·해·석

남: 도와드릴까요?
여: 네. 소파 쿠션을 사기 위해 보고 있어요.
남: 나비 사진이 있는 이것은 어떠신가요?
여: 음… 다른 거 있나요?
남: 고양이가 그려져 있는 이것도 있어요.
여: 오… 그게 마음에 드네요!
남: 좋아하시니 기쁩니다.
여: 좋네요! 그걸로 할게요.

단·어·및·표·현

cushion[kúʃən] 몡 쿠션, 방석
butterfly[bʌ́tərflài] 몡 나비

03   날씨파악-그림   ▶ 정답 ④

듣·기·대·본

W: Good morning. Here's the <u>weather forecast</u>. We are having a little bit of rain right now. The rain will turn into snow this afternoon. The snow will continue until tomorrow morning. So, please be careful on the road.

우·리·말·해·석

여: 안녕하세요. 일기 예보입니다. 지금 약간의 비가 내리고 있습니다. 그

비가 오늘 오후에는 눈이 되겠습니다. 눈은 내일 아침까지 계속될 것입니다. 그러니 부디 도로에서 조심하시기 바랍니다.

단·어·및·표·현

weather forecast 일기 예보
a little bit of 약간의, 조금의
turn into ~으로 변하다
until[əntíl] 쩐 ~(때)까지

04   마지막말의도파악   ▶ 정답 ③

듣·기·대·본

M: Kelly! What happened to the camera?
W: I'm sorry, Dad. I <u>broke</u> it.
M: How did it happen?
W: I <u>slipped</u> on the floor when I tried to take a photo of our puppy yesterday.
M: Oh, didn't you <u>get hurt</u>?
W: I'm OK. I <u>apologize</u> for the camera trouble again.

우·리·말·해·석

남: Kelly! 카메라가 어떻게 된 거니?
여: 죄송해요, 아빠. 제가 부셨어요.
남: 어쩌다 이렇게 됐어?
여: 어제 우리 강아지 사진을 찍으려다가 제가 바닥에서 미끄러졌어요.
남: 오, 다치지는 않았니?
여: 저는 괜찮아요. 카메라 문제에 대해 다시 한번 사과드려요.

단·어·및·표·현

break[breik] 통 부수다, 고장 내다
slip[slip] 통 미끄러지다

05   담화미언급   ▶ 정답 ②

듣·기·대·본

M: Hello, everyone. Let me tell you about my best friend. His name is John. He is my <u>elementary school</u> friend. He likes to play soccer and video games for fun. He is kind and <u>outgoing</u>. He likes to eat everything, <u>except for</u> vegetables.

우·리·말·해·석

남: 안녕하세요, 여러분. 저의 가장 친한 친구에 대해서 말씀드리겠습니다. 그의 이름은 John입니다. 그는 저의 초등학교 친구입니다. 그는 취미로 축구와 비디오 게임 하는 것을 좋아합니다. 그는 친절하고 외향적입니다. 그는 채소를 제외한 모든 걸 먹는 것을 좋아합니다.

단·어·및·표·현

elementary school 초등학교
for fun 취미로
outgoing[áutgòuiŋ] 몡 외향적인, 사교적인
except for ~을 제외하고

06   수치파악   ▶ 정답 ③

듣·기·대·본

W: Sam, did you do the reading and writing homework?
M: No, I can't decide which book I want to read.
W: <u>Me, neither</u>. Why don't we go to the library together?
M: Okay. Let's meet tomorrow morning at 9.
W: Um… That's a little <u>early for me</u>. Can we meet at 10 a.m.?
M: No problem. See you tomorrow.

우·리·말·해·석
여: Sam, 너 읽기와 쓰기 숙제했어?
남: 아니, 나는 내가 어느 책을 읽고 싶은지 결정하지 못하겠어.
여: 나도, 우리 같이 도서관에 가는 게 어때?
남: 좋아. 내일 아침 9시에 만나자.
여: 음… 그건 나에게 좀 일러. 우리 오전 10시에 만날 수 있어?
남: 문제없어. 내일 보자.

단·어·및·표·현
neither[níːðər] 🔊 (부정문에서) ~도 아니다

07 장래희망추론 ▶ 정답 ⑤

듣·기·대·본
M: I love these videos on your blog. Did you make them?
W: Yes. I used my cell phone. Which video is your favorite?
M: The one with your sister dancing. It's like a movie.
W: Really? You know what? I want to become a movie director.
M: Wow. That's wonderful!

우·리·말·해·석
남: 나는 너의 블로그에 있는 이 영상들이 정말 마음에 들어. 네가 그것들을 만든 거니?
여: 응. 내 핸드폰을 이용했어. 너는 어떤 영상이 가장 마음에 드니?
남: 너의 여동생이 춤추고 있는 영상. 그건 영화 같아.
여: 정말? 그거 알아? 나는 영화감독이 되고 싶어.
남: 와. 정말 멋있다!

단·어·및·표·현
movie director 영화감독

08 심정추론 ▶ 정답 ④

듣·기·대·본
M: Mary, these are for you.
W: Oh, new shoes! I love them, Dad. But, it's not my birthday.
M: Your shoes are worn out. And, I saw you looking at these ones at the shop.
W: Really? Dad, you are amazing!
M: Also, they are green, your favorite color.
W: Thank you so much, Dad. I love you.

우·리·말·해·석
남: Mary, 이것들은 너를 위한 거야.
여: 오, 새 신발이네요! 저는 그것들이 너무 좋아요, 아빠. 그렇지만, 오늘은 제 생일이 아닌데요.
남: 너의 신발은 닳았잖아. 그리고, 나는 네가 가게에서 이것들을 보는 모습을 보았어.
여: 정말요? 아빠, 아빠는 놀라워요!
남: 게다가, 그것들은 초록색으로 네가 가장 좋아하는 색이야.
여: 정말 감사해요, 아빠. 사랑해요.

단·어·및·표·현
worn out 닳아서 못 쓰게 된
amazing[əméiziŋ] 🔊 놀라운

09 할일파악(대화직후) ▶ 정답 ②

듣·기·대·본
W: Dad, I need to go to the bookstore and buy some new workbooks.
M: Sure, take my credit card with you.

W: I can't find your wallet, Dad!
M: It's in the front pocket of my coat.
W: I don't know which coat you're talking about.
M: Oh, I'll go find it for you.
W: Thank you, Dad!

우·리·말·해·석
여: 아빠, 저 서점에 가서 새로운 참고서들을 사야 해요.
남: 그래, 내 신용카드를 가져가렴.
여: 아빠의 지갑을 못 찾겠어요, 아빠!
남: 그건 내 코트의 앞 주머니에 있단다.
여: 저는 아빠가 어떤 코트를 말씀하시고 있는지 모르겠어요.
남: 아, 내가 너를 위해서 가서 찾아줄게.
여: 고마워요, 아빠!

단·어·및·표·현
credit card 신용카드
wallet[wálit] 🔊 지갑
pocket[pákit] 🔊 주머니
talk about ~에 대해서 이야기하다

10 대화화제추론 ▶ 정답 ④

듣·기·대·본
M: Amy, when you're on public transit, always keep these rules in mind.
W: What rules, Dad?
M: Keep your voice down, line up in an orderly fashion, and no food allowed.
W: I understand the first two, but why can't I eat?
M: Because the smell can be disturbing to others.
W: Okay. I will always keep those things in mind.

우·리·말·해·석
남: Amy, 네가 대중교통을 이용할 때는 항상 이 규칙들을 명심해야 한단다.
여: 어떤 규칙이요, 아빠?
남: 목소리를 작게 하고, 줄은 질서 있게 서고, 음식은 허용되지 않아.
여: 앞의 두 가지는 이해가 가는데요, 하지만 왜 먹는 것은 안 되나요?
남: 왜냐하면 냄새가 다른 사람들에게 방해가 될 수 있기 때문이란다.
여: 알겠어요. 저는 항상 그것들을 염두에 둘 거예요.

단·어·및·표·현
public transit 대중교통
keep A in mind A를 명심하다, 염두에 두다
in an orderly fashion 질서 있게
allowed[əláud] 🔊 허용된
disturbing[distə́ːrbiŋ] 🔊 방해가 되는

11 특정정보파악(교통수단) ▶ 정답 ⑤

듣·기·대·본
W: How should we get to the airport tomorrow?
M: Since we have some luggage, why don't we grab a taxi?
W: I'm not sure about that. Isn't it too expensive?
M: Then let's take the airport bus instead.
W: Hmm... Is the bus stop near our house?
M: Yes, and it'll take us straight to the airport.
W: Great!

우·리·말·해·석
여: 우리 내일 공항에 어떻게 가야 할까?

남: 우리에게 짐이 좀 있으니까 택시를 잡는 게 어때?
여: 나는 잘 모르겠어. 그건 너무 비싸지 않을까?
남: 그럼 대신에 공항 버스를 타자.
여: 흠… 버스 정류장이 우리 집 근처에 있어?
남: 응, 그리고 그건 우리를 바로 공항으로 데려갈 거야.
여: 좋아!

단·어·및·표·현
luggage[lʌ́gidʒ] 명 짐, 수하물
grab a taxi 택시를 잡다
straight[streit] 부 바로, 곧장

12 이유파악　　▶ 정답 ⑤

듣·기·대·본
W: Hi, Victor. Those flowers are so pretty! Where did you get them from?
M: I bought them from the flower shop down the road.
W: Oh, what are they for?
M: They're for my parents' wedding anniversary. It's today.
W: I see. How nice of you to buy flowers for them!
M: Well, I just hope they'll like them.
W: I'm sure they will.

우·리·말·해·석
여: 안녕, Victor. 그 꽃들 정말 예쁘다! 넌 그것들을 어디서 구했어?
남: 난 길 아래에 있는 꽃 가게에서 그것들을 샀어.
여: 아, 그것들은 무엇을 위한 거야?
남: 그것들은 우리 부모님의 결혼기념일을 위한 거야. 오늘이거든.
여: 그렇구나. 그분들을 위해 꽃을 사다니 넌 참 다정하구나!
남: 글쎄, 난 그저 그분들이 그것들(꽃)을 좋아하시기를 바라.
여: 그러실 거라고 확신해.

단·어·및·표·현
anniversary[æ̀nəvə́ːrsəri] 명 기념일

13 대화장소추론　　▶ 정답 ①

듣·기·대·본
W: Good morning, sir. May I help you?
M: Yes, please. I made a reservation two days ago.
W: Okay. What is your name?
M: Thomas Boyles.
W: You booked a double room for three days, right?
M: Yes.
W: Here is the key. Please leave your key at the front desk when you go out.

우·리·말·해·석
여: 안녕하세요, 손님. 무엇을 도와드릴까요?
남: 네. 이틀 전에 예약을 했는데요.
여: 알겠습니다. 성함이 어떻게 되시죠?
남: Thomas Boyles입니다.
여: 3일 동안 2인실을 예약하셨네요, 맞습니까?
남: 맞아요.
여: 여기 열쇠 있습니다. 외출하실 때에는 안내데스크에 열쇠를 맡겨 주세요.

단·어·및·표·현
make a reservation 예약하다
book[buk] 동 예약하다

09
회
모
의
고
사

🎧 LISTENING ADVICE
'예약하다'라는 의미를 가진 동사 'book'은 명사로 쓰일 때에는 '책'이라는 의미를 갖게 됩니다. 동사 'book'과 명사 'book'은 단어 철자도 같고 발음도 동일하지만 의미는 전혀 다르게 쓰이는 동음이의어인 셈이지요. 이럴 때에는 앞뒤 단어를 모두 잘 듣고 문맥에 따라 뜻을 유추해야 합니다.

14 그림정보파악-위치　　▶ 정답 ①

듣·기·대·본
W: Ted, did you see my letter from Sarah?
M: Didn't you put it on top of the books?
W: I did, but it's not there.
M: Then look under the table or on the chairs.
W: I still can't find it. Can you look between the flower vases?
M: It's not there. Wait a minute. Oh, it's next to the left one in the corner!

우·리·말·해·석
여: Ted, 너 Sarah에게서 온 내 편지 봤어?
남: 너 그것을 책들 위에 두지 않았어?
여: 그랬어, 하지만 그것이 거기에 없어.
남: 그러면 테이블 밑이나 의자 위를 봐.
여: 나는 여전히 찾을 수가 없어. 네가 꽃병들 사이를 봐 줄래?
남: 거기에 없어. 잠깐만. 아, 그것은 모퉁이에 있는 왼쪽 것 옆에 있어!

단·어·및·표·현
on top of ~ ~ 위에

15 부탁한일파악　　▶ 정답 ④

듣·기·대·본
W: Happy anniversary, Dad. Have a great dinner with Mom.
M: Thanks, sweetie. You know what to eat for dinner, right?
W: Yes, Mom told me how to warm up the food.
M: And your little sister needs help with her homework after dinner.
W: Her math homework?
M: Yes. Could you give her a hand?
W: Sure, no problem.

우·리·말·해·석
여: 결혼기념일 축하드려요, 아빠. 엄마랑 멋진 저녁식사 하세요.
남: 고맙다, 얘야. 너는 저녁으로 뭘 먹어야 할지 알지, 맞지?
여: 네, 엄마가 저한테 음식 데우는 법을 알려주셨어요.
남: 그리고 저녁 식사 후에 네 여동생은 숙제(를 하는데)에 도움이 필요해.
여: 그녀의 수학 숙제 말인가요?
남: 그래. 네가 그녀를 좀 도와줄 수 있겠니?
여: 네, 문제없어요.

단·어·및·표·현
anniversary[æ̀nəvə́ːrsəri] 명 (결혼)기념일
warm up (식은 음식을) 데우다
give ~ a hand ~를 도와주다

16 제안파악　　▶ 정답 ②

듣·기·대·본
M: Rebecca, when are you leaving for Pohang?
W: Tomorrow. I'll stay just for one night.
M: Did you book a room?
W: Not yet. I'll do that on my cellphone on the way.

M: Why don't you do it now? It can be hard to find a room.
W: Okay, I will. That's a good idea.

우·리·말·해·석

남: Rebecca, 너 언제 포항으로 떠나니?
여: 내일. 난 딱 하룻밤 동안만 머물 거야.
남: 너 방은 예약했어?
여: 아직 안 했어. 가면서 휴대폰으로 그것을 할 거야.
남: 지금 그것을 하는 게 어때? 방을 찾기 어려울 수도 있어.
여: 알겠어, 그럴게. 그거 좋은 생각이다.

단·어·및·표·현

leave for ~로 떠나다
book [buk] 图 예약하다

17 할일파악   ▶ 정답 ⑤

듣·기·대·본

W: What do you think of this t-shirt?
M: It's nice, but I don't think it suits you very well.
W: Don't worry. I bought it for my brother. It's his birthday this weekend.
M: Oh, okay. Do you have any plans?
W: We're planning to watch a baseball game at the stadium this Saturday.
M: Sounds fantastic! Have fun.

우·리·말·해·석

여: 이 티셔츠 어떻게 생각하세요?
남: 멋지네요, 하지만 당신에게 아주 잘 어울린다고 생각하지 않아요.
여: 걱정 마세요. 저는 제 남동생을 위해 그것을 샀어요. 이번 주말이 그의 생일이에요.
남: 오, 알겠습니다. 계획이 있으신가요?
여: 저희는 이번 주 토요일에 경기장에서 야구 경기를 볼 계획이에요.
남: 정말 멋지네요! 즐거운 시간 보내세요.

단·어·및·표·현

suit [s(j)uːt] 图 어울리다
plan [plæn] 图 계획
stadium [stéidiəm] 图 경기장

18 직업추론   ▶ 정답 ②

듣·기·대·본

M: Hello. What can I help you with?
W: I made an appointment to get my hair colored today.
M: Sure. Sit here, please. So what color were you thinking?
W: Can you color my hair light brown?
M: Okay. Do you want to get your hair cut, too?
W: Yes. Just a trim, please.
M: Alright. Let's begin.

우·리·말·해·석

남: 안녕하세요. 무엇을 도와드릴까요?
여: 오늘 제 머리를 염색하기로 예약했습니다.
남: 그러시군요. 여기 앉으세요. 그러면 어떤 색상을 생각하고 계셨나요?
여: 제 머리를 밝은 갈색으로 염색해 주시겠어요?
남: 알겠습니다. 머리도 자르길 원하시나요?
여: 네. 그냥 다듬어주세요.
남: 좋습니다. 시작하죠.

단·어·및·표·현

make an appointment 예약하다
color [kʌ́lər] 图 염색하다 图 색, 빛깔

trim [trim] 图 (머리를) 다듬기, 약간 자르기

19 알맞은응답찾기   ▶ 정답 ②

듣·기·대·본

W: Hi, Mark. You're coming to tonight's dance practice, right?
M: Oh, Sally, I'm afraid I can't.
W: Why not? Our contest is next week.
M: I know. I have to go visit my grandpa in the hospital.
W: Oh, I see. Is he very sick?
M: I think so. I'd better go and see how he is.
W: I hope he gets better soon.

우·리·말·해·석

① 넌 정말 잘했어!
② 나는 그가 곧 좋아지시길 바라.
③ 나는 그가 우리의 춤을 좋아해서 기뻐.
④ 걱정하지 마, 너는 아주 잘할 거야.
⑤ 이해해줘서 고마워.

여: 안녕, Mark. 너 오늘 밤의 춤 연습에 오지, 맞지?
남: 오, Sally, 유감이지만 나는 못 갈 것 같아.
여: 왜 못 와? 우리 대회가 다음 주야.
남: 나도 알아. 나는 병원에 계신 내 할아버지를 방문하러 가봐야 해.
여: 아, 그렇구나. 그는 매우 편찮으시니?
남: 그런 것 같아. 나는 가서 그가 어떤지 보는 편이 낫겠어.
여: **나는 그가 곧 좋아지시길 바라.**

단·어·및·표·현

practice [præktis] 图 연습
had better + 동사원형 ~하는 편이 낫다, ~해야 하다

20 알맞은응답찾기   ▶ 정답 ①

듣·기·대·본

W: May I help you?
M: I'm looking for a baseball cap for my daughter.
W: OK. How old is she?
M: She's 14. Can you recommend one for me?
W: Sure. This one is very popular among girls that age.
M: That looks nice. I'll take it.
W: Would you like it gift-wrapped?
M: Is there an extra charge?
W: No, it's free.

우·리·말·해·석

① 아뇨, 그건 공짜예요.
② 그것은 판매하지 않아요.
③ 나는 야구를 하지 않아요.
④ 그것은 좋은 선택이에요.
⑤ 네, 써 보실 수 있어요.

여: 제가 도와드릴까요?
남: 저는 제 딸을 위한 야구 모자를 찾고 있어요.
여: 그렇군요. 그녀는 몇 살인가요?
남: 그녀는 14살이에요. 절 위해 하나 추천해 주실 수 있을까요?
여: 물론이죠. 이건 그 나이 여자아이들 사이에서 아주 인기가 많아요.
남: 좋아 보이네요. 저는 그걸로 할게요.
여: 선물 포장해서 드릴까요?
남: 추가 비용이 있나요?
여: **아뇨, 그건 공짜예요.**

단·어·및·표·현

look for ~ ~을 찾다
recommend [rèkəménd] 통 추천하다

Words & Expressions Review

1. 바로, 곧장	2. 계획	3. 나비
4. 약간의, 조금의	5. 방해가 되는	6. 어울리다
7. ~으로 변하다	8. 초등학교	9. 예약, 약속
10. 미끄러지다	11. 예약하다	12. 바닥, 층
13. ~로 떠나다	14. 취미로	15. 기념일
16. 외향적인, 사교적인	17. 닳아서 못 쓰게 된	18. 무엇을 도와드릴까요?
19. 택시를 잡다	20. 경기장	21. (부정문에서) ~도 아니다
22. 안내데스크	23. ~의 사진을 찍다	24. ~을 제외하고
25. 질서 있게	26. 곤충	27. 영화감독
28. ~를 도와주다	29. 놀라운	30. 허용된
31. 아주 멋진, 훌륭한	32. ~ 위에	33. 예약하다
34. 대중교통	35. 신용카드	36. 주머니
37. (식은 음식을) 데우다	38. 숙제	39. 외출하다
40. 지갑	41. 공항	42. ~에 대해서 이야기하다
43. A에서 B로	44. 바라다	

Listening Test

영어듣기 모의고사 10회

|정|답|

01	③	02	⑤	03	②	04	②	05	③
06	②	07	③	08	⑤	09	②	10	①
11	③	12	③	13	①	14	④	15	⑤
16	④	17	④	18	③	19	①	20	④

01 그림정보파악(담화) ▶ 정답 ③

듣·기·대·본

W: You can find this <u>either on</u> a desk or on the wall. <u>This is a system for dividing time into</u> days, months, or years. You can use this to <u>write down</u> important events, like friends' birthdays, so you don't forget them. What is this?

우·리·말·해·석

여: 당신은 책상 위나 벽 위에서 이것을 볼 수 있습니다. 이것은 시간을 일, 월, 또는 년으로 나누는 체계입니다. 당신은 친구들의 생일과 같은 중요한 행사들을 적어서 그것들을 잊지 않도록 하기 위해 이것을 사용할 수 있습니다. 이것은 무엇일까요?

단·어·및·표·현

either A or B A나 B

02 그림정보파악(대화) ▶ 정답 ⑤

듣·기·대·본

W: Hi, I am looking for a lunch box for my daughter.
M: We have <u>rectangular</u> ones and <u>round</u> ones.
W: I think a round one would be nice.
M: Okay. Any <u>preferred pattern</u> for the lunch box?
W: My daughter likes cats. Do you have one with <u>cats on it?</u>
M: Yes, we do! This one would be perfect! Isn't it cute?
W: Great! I will take it. Thank you.

우·리·말·해·석

여: 안녕하세요, 저는 제 딸을 위한 도시락통을 찾고 있어요.
남: 저희는 직사각형인 것들과 원형인 것들이 있습니다.
여: 제 생각에 원형의 것이 좋을 것 같아요.
남: 알겠습니다. 도시락통에 선호하는 무늬가 있나요?
여: 제 딸은 고양이를 좋아해요. 고양이가 그려진 것이 있나요?
남: 네, 있습니다! 이게 완벽하겠네요! 귀엽지 않나요?
여: 좋아요! 그걸로 할게요. 고맙습니다.

단·어·및·표·현

lunch box 도시락통
rectangular [rektǽŋgjulər] 형 직사각형의
round [raund] 형 원형의
preferred [priːfə́ːrd] 형 선호하는

03 날씨파악-그림 ▶ 정답 ②

듣·기·대·본

W: Here is the weather forecast for next week. It will be rainy until next Wednesday evening and start to <u>clear up</u> Wednesday night. It will be <u>warm</u> and <u>sunny</u> Thursday and Friday. However, we will have very cloudy skies again and be <u>caught in showers</u> this weekend.

우·리·말·해·석

여: 다음 주 일기 예보입니다. 다음 주 수요일 저녁까지 비가 오겠고, 수요일 밤에 개기 시작하겠습니다. 목요일과 금요일은 따뜻하고 맑겠습니다. 그러나, 이번 주말에는 다시 매우 흐린 하늘에 소나기를 만나게 될 것입니다.

단·어·및·표·현

be caught in a shower 소나기를 만나다

04 마지막말의도파악 ▶ 정답 ②

듣·기·대·본

M: Mom, can I <u>sleep over</u> at David's house?
W: Why?
M: He has got an awesome toy robot. It's very <u>hard to assemble</u> alone.
W: I guess it can be fun.
M: Yes! And he asked for my help.
W: OK. Don't forget to <u>leave his address</u> and phone number.

우·리·말·해·석

남: 엄마, 제가 David네 가서 자도 될까요?
여: 왜 그러니?
남: David가 멋진 로봇 장난감을 받았어요. 그건 혼자서 조립하기가 매우 어려워요.
여: 내 생각에 그건 재미있겠구나.

남: 네! 그리고 그가 제 도움을 요청했어요.
여: 좋아. 그 애 주소와 전화번호 남기는 것을 잊지 마라.

단•어•및•표•현

sleep over (남의 집에서) 자다
assemble [əsémbl] [동] 조립하다

05 담화미언급 ▶ 정답 ③

듣•기•대•본

M: Good morning, students! Let me remind you about tomorrow's Sports Day. The events will begin at 9 a.m. Please gather at the soccer field before then. The weather will be very hot tomorrow. Don't forget to bring a water bottle, hat, and sunscreen.

우•리•말•해•석

남: 좋은 아침입니다, 학생 여러분! 제가 내일 있을 체육대회에 대하여 여러분에게 상기시켜드리려고 합니다. 행사는 오전 9시에 시작할 예정입니다. 그 이전에 축구장으로 모여주시기 바랍니다. 내일 날씨가 매우 더울 것입니다. 물병, 모자, 그리고 자외선 차단제를 가져오시는 걸 잊지 마세요.

단•어•및•표•현

remind [rimáind] [동] 상기시키다
gather [gǽðər] [동] 모이다

06 수치파악 ▶ 정답 ②

듣•기•대•본

M: Esther, I've got two tickets to a concert tonight at Lincoln Center. Would you like to come?
W: Sounds great! When does the concert start?
M: It starts at 7 p.m.
W: Then we should get there by 6:30 p.m.
M: Right. So we have to get going. It's 6 p.m. now.
W: Is it 6 already? Let's hurry!

우•리•말•해•석

남: Esther, 나에게 오늘 밤 링컨 센터에서 열리는 콘서트 티켓이 두 장 있어. 너도 갈래?
여: 좋아! 콘서트는 언제 시작해?
남: 오후 7시에 시작해.
여: 그러면 우리는 오후 6시 30분까지 그곳에 도착해야겠네.
남: 맞아. 그래서 우리는 출발해야 해. 지금 오후 6시야.
여: 벌써 6시야? 서두르자!

단•어•및•표•현

tonight [tənáit] [부] 오늘 밤(에)
Would you like to + 동사원형? ~할래?, ~하시겠습니까?
get going 출발하다, 시작하다

07 장래희망추론 ▶ 정답 ③

듣•기•대•본

W: Daniel, what are you watching?
M: I'm watching game-playing videos.
W: But don't you enjoy playing the actual game more than watching it?
M: I enjoy both. I want to be a pro gamer someday.
W: I believe you will be a great pro gamer.
M: Thank you!

우•리•말•해•석

여: Daniel, 넌 뭘 보고 있니?
남: 나는 게임하는 영상을 보고 있어.
여: 근데 너는 게임을 보는 것보다 실제 게임을 하는 것을 더 즐기지 않니?
남: 난 둘 다 즐겨. 나는 언젠간 프로 게이머가 되고 싶어.
여: 나는 네가 훌륭한 프로 게이머가 될 거라 믿어.
남: 고마워!

단•어•및•표•현

actual [ǽktʃuəl] [형] 실제의
someday [sʌ́mdèi] [부] 언젠가, 훗날

08 심정추론 ▶ 정답 ⑤

듣•기•대•본

W: Tony, what's wrong?
M: I got a bad score on my math test.
W: Well, you will do better next time.
M: But my mom will be so angry.
W: I'm sure your mom will understand.
M: No, you don't know my mom. She will be mad for weeks.

우•리•말•해•석

① 지루한 ② 안심한 ③ 신난
④ 화가 난 ⑤ 걱정스러운

여: Tony, 뭐가 잘못됐니?
남: 수학 시험에서 나쁜 점수를 받았어.
여: 저런, 다음에는 더 잘할 거야.
남: 하지만 엄마가 정말 화내실 거야.
여: 너의 엄마가 이해하실 것이라고 확신해.
남: 아니, 너는 우리 엄마를 몰라. 몇 주 동안 화를 내실 거야.

단•어•및•표•현

What's wrong? 뭐가 잘못됐니?
I'm sure ~ ~라고 확신하다

09 할일파악(대화직후) ▶ 정답 ②

듣•기•대•본

M: Isn't the weather lovely, Annie?
W: Yes, Dad. It's beautiful and I love this park.
M: I'm glad you like it. Look! There are people riding bicycles.
W: It looks so fun. Can we ride bicycles, too? There's a rental shop over there.
M: Sure. I'll go and rent two bicycles now.
W: Great! Thanks, Dad.

우•리•말•해•석

남: 날씨가 참 좋지 않니, Annie?
여: 네, 아빠. 날씨는 화창하고 저는 이 공원이 매우 좋아요.
남: 네가 좋아한다니 기쁘구나. 봐! 자전거를 타고 있는 사람들이 있어.
여: 정말 재밌어 보여요. 우리도 자전거를 탈 수 있어요? 저기에 대여점이 있어요.
남: 물론이지. 내가 지금 가서 자전거 두 대를 빌려올게.
여: 좋아요! 감사해요, 아빠.

단•어•및•표•현

beautiful [bjúːtəfəl] [형] (날씨가) 화창한
rental shop 대여점
rent [rent] [동] (사용료를 내고 단기간) 빌리다

10 대화화제추론 ▶ 정답 ①

듣•기•대•본

M: Sandy, here are some safety rules for your school bus.
W: What are they, Dad?
M: First, you should always wear your seatbelt.
W: I already know that. What else?
M: Also, don't leave your seat before the bus stops.
W: Why not?
M: It's dangerous to stand up on a moving bus.
W: Okay. I'll remember the rules.

우·리·말·해·석

남: Sandy, 여기 네 통학 버스를 위한 몇 가지 안전 수칙이 있어.
여: 그게 뭔데요, 아빠?
남: 우선, 너는 항상 안전벨트를 착용해야 해.
여: 전 그건 이미 알고 있어요. 그 밖에 다른 것은요?
남: 또, 버스가 멈추기 전에는 자리를 떠나지 마.
여: 왜 안 돼요?
남: 움직이는 버스에서 일어서는 건 위험해.
여: 알겠어요. 그 수칙들을 기억할게요.

단·어·및·표·현

safety rules 안전 수칙
seatbelt [síːtbèlt] 명 안전벨트, 안전띠

11 특정정보파악(교통수단) ▶ 정답 ③

듣·기·대·본

W: Ed, aren't you late for the dentist?
M: No, Mom. My appointment is at 5 p.m. It's only 4:30.
W: That's my point. It'll take more than 30 minutes to get there by bus.
M: Ah, Dad's going to drive me there by car.
W: Oh, that's good. It'll save a lot of time.

우·리·말·해·석

여: Ed, 치과에 늦지 않았니?
남: 아니에요, 엄마. 제 예약 시간은 오후 다섯 시예요. 아직 4시 30분밖에 안 됐어요.
여: 내 말이 바로 그거야. 버스 타고 거기까지 가는 데 30분 넘게 걸릴 거야.
남: 아, 아빠가 차로 거기까지 데려다 주실 거예요.
여: 오, 잘됐다. 그러면 시간이 많이 절약될 거야.

단·어·및·표·현

appointment [əpɔ́intmənt] 명 예약, 약속
save [seiv] 동 절약하다

12 이유파악 ▶ 정답 ③

듣·기·대·본

M: Hi, Ella! Where are you going?
W: Hi! I'm going to a café.
M: Are you going to meet a friend there?
W: Actually, no. They sell delicious cookies there, and I'm going to buy some.
M: Sounds good! Can I come with you?
W: Of course you can!

우·리·말·해·석

남: 안녕, 티나! 너는 어디에 가니?
여: 안녕! 나는 카페에 가.
남: 너는 거기에 친구를 만나러 가니?
여: 사실, 아니야. 거기에서 맛있는 쿠키를 팔아서 나는 쿠키를 좀 사러 가.
남: 좋다! 내가 너랑 같이 가도 돼?
여: 물론이지!

단·어·및·표·현

delicious [dilíʃəs] 형 아주 맛있는

13 대화장소추론 ▶ 정답 ①

듣·기·대·본

M: Wow, let's ride the roller coaster! It looks so exciting!
W: It looks scary. I'm afraid it's too fast.
M: Come on. It's safe. It's the most popular ride in this park.
W: Let's try the merry-go-round first.
M: Okay. First, ride the merry-go-round, and then we'll try the roller coaster.

우·리·말·해·석

남: 와, 롤러코스터 타러 가자! 정말 신나 보인다!
여: 무서워 보여. 너무 빠를까 봐 걱정이야.
남: 괜찮아. 안전하다니까. 이 공원에서 가장 인기 있는 놀이기구야.
여: 회전목마 먼저 타자.
남: 좋아. 먼저 회전목마를 타고, 그 다음에 롤러코스터를 타 보자.

단·어·및·표·현

ride [raid] 명 놀이기구, 탈 것 동 타다

14 그림정보파악-지도 ▶ 정답 ④

듣·기·대·본

M: Excuse me. How can I get to the art gallery?
W: Oh, it's not far. Go straight for two blocks, and then turn left.
M: Turn left?
W: Yes. Walk down a few meters, and you'll see it on your left. It's right next to the coffee house.
M: Okay, thanks a lot.

우·리·말·해·석

남: 실례합니다. 미술관까지 어떻게 가야 하나요?
여: 오, 멀지 않아요. 두 블록을 곧장 가서, 그 다음에 왼쪽으로 도세요.
남: 왼쪽으로 돌라고요?
여: 네. 몇 미터를 걸어 내려가면, 당신의 왼편에 그것이 보일 거예요. 커피 전문점 바로 옆에 있어요.
남: 알겠습니다, 정말 고맙습니다.

단·어·및·표·현

far [fɑːr] 부 멀리

15 부탁(요청)한일파악 ▶ 정답 ⑤

듣·기·대·본

M: Mary, can I talk to you?
W: Sure, Mr. Johnson.
M: Are you going to practice the piano in the music room?
W: Yes. The school festival is next week.
M: Then, can you lock the door when you leave the room?
W: Yes, I'll do that.

우·리·말·해·석

남: Mary, 이야기 좀 할 수 있을까?
여: 물론이죠, Johnson 선생님.
남: 너는 음악실에서 피아노 연습을 할 예정이니?
여: 네. 학교 축제가 다음 주거든요.
남: 그러면, 방에서 나갈 때 문을 잠가 줄 수 있겠니?
여: 네, 그렇게 할게요.

단·어·및·표·현

be going to + 동사원형 ~할 예정이다

16 제안파악 ▶ 정답 ④

들·기·대·본

W: Tony, are you okay?
M: Not really. It's so hot in here. Is the air conditioner not working?
W: I'm afraid not. It'll be fixed this afternoon.
M: Oh, no. I can't study in this heat. What can I do?
W: Well, how about going to the library?
M: Sounds good. It won't be so hot in the library.

우·리·말·해·석

여: Tony, 너 괜찮니?
남: 아니 안 괜찮아. 여기 안은 너무 더워. 에어컨이 작동하지 않니?
여: 유감스럽게도 작동하지 않아. 그것은 오늘 오후에 고쳐질 거야.
남: 오, 안돼. 나는 이 더위에서 공부할 수 없어. 내가 무엇을 할 수 있지?
여: 음, 도서관에 가는 것이 어때?
남: 좋아. 도서관 안은 그렇게 덥지 않을 거야.

단·어·및·표·현

work [wəːrk] [동] 작동되다, 기능하다
fix [fiks] [동] 수리하다, 고치다
heat [hiːt] [명] 더위, 열기

17 한일파악 ▶ 정답 ④

들·기·대·본

M: Rose, did you have a good summer vacation?
W: Yes, I went camping with my cousins.
M: That sounds fun! What did you do together?
W: We sang around the fire. What about you?
M: I learned to play the drums at the community center.
W: Wow! That sounds wonderful.

우·리·말·해·석

남: Rose, 좋은 여름 방학을 보냈니?
여: 응, 나는 사촌들과 캠핑을 갔어.
남: 재미있었겠다! 너희들은 무엇을 함께 했니?
여: 우리는 모닥불 주변에서 노래를 불렀어. 너는?
남: 나는 주민센터에서 드럼을 연주하는 법을 배웠어.
여: 우와! 정말 멋지다.

단·어·및·표·현

go camping 캠핑 가다
sound + 형용사 ~하게 들리다
learn to + 동사원형 ~하는 것을 배우다

18 직업추론 ▶ 정답 ③

들·기·대·본

M: Tiffany, how was the event with your fans?
W: It was amazing. They all congratulated me on winning the MVP award.
M: Great! You played really well this season.
W: I hope they'll keep supporting me next season as well.
M: I'm sure they will. You're the best player in the women's volleyball league.
W: Thank you for saying that.

우·리·말·해·석

남: Tiffany, 너의 팬들과 함께한 그 이벤트는 어땠어?
여: 그건 놀라웠어. 그들은 모두 내가 MVP 상을 받은 걸 축하해줬어.
남: 대단한데! 넌 이번 시즌에 정말 경기를 잘했어.
여: 나는 그들이 다음 시즌에도 나를 계속 지지해 주길 바라.
남: 그들이 그럴 거라 확신해. 너는 여자 배구 리그에서 최고의 선수잖아.
여: 그렇게 말해줘서 고마워.

단·어·및·표·현

congratulate [kəngrǽtʃulèit] [동] 축하하다
win an award 상을 받다
keep ~ing 계속해서 ~하다
volleyball [válibɔ̀ːl] [명] 배구

19 알맞은응답찾기 ▶ 정답 ①

들·기·대·본

W: Have you heard about the peach festival happening next weekend?
M: Yeah, it'll be a lot of fun. Are you thinking of going?
W: I'm considering entering the peach pie eating contest. I love peaches!
M: That's awesome! You'll have so much fun!
W: Thanks!
M: How many pies do you think you can eat?
W: I'll try for ten.

우·리·말·해·석

① 나는 10개에 도전해 볼 거야.
② 너는 그것을 시도해봐야 해.
③ 그거 맛있어 보인다.
④ 난 충분히 먹었어.
⑤ 사과 파이 두 개 주세요.

여: 너는 다음 주말에 열리는 복숭아 축제에 대해 들었어?
남: 응, 엄청 재밌을 거야. 너는 가려고 생각 중이야?
여: 나는 복숭아 파이 먹기 대회에 참가할까 고려 중이야. 난 복숭아를 좋아해!
남: 굉장한걸! 너는 아주 즐거울 거야!
여: 고마워!
남: 너는 네가 몇 개의 파이를 먹을 수 있을 거라고 생각해?
여: 나는 10개에 도전해 볼 거야.

단·어·및·표·현

consider [kənsídər] [동] 고려하다, 숙고하다
enter [éntər] [동] (대회 등에) 참가하다, 출전하다
try [trai] [동] 도전해 보다, 노력하다

20 알맞은응답찾기 ▶ 정답 ④

들·기·대·본

M: It's getting hotter these days.
W: Yeah. Summer is coming up.
M: Do you like summer?
W: Not really. It's too hot in summer.
M: What season do you like most, then?
W: Winter is my favorite season.

우·리·말·해·석

① 나는 여름에 수영하는 것을 즐겨.
② 바람이 세다.
③ 바깥은 날씨가 맑아.
④ 겨울이 내가 가장 좋아하는 계절이야.
⑤ 꽃은 봄에 활짝 펴.

남: 요즘 점점 더워지네.
여: 그러게. 여름이 다가오고 있어.
남: 너 여름 좋아하니?
여: 별로. 여름에는 너무 더워.

남: 그럼, 넌 어떤 계절을 가장 좋아하니?
여: **겨울이 내가 가장 좋아하는 계절이야.**

단·어·및·표·현

come up 다가오다
most [moust] ⊕ 가장

Words & Expressions Review

1. 오늘 밤, 오늘 밤에	2. (날씨가) 화창한	3. 걱정하는, 두려워하는
4. 대여점	5. 절약하다, 구하다	6. 조립하다
7. 실제의	8. 더위, 열기	9. 주소
10. 상기시키다	11. 멋진, 굉장한	12. 선호하는
13. 축하하다	14. ~할래?, ~하시겠습니까?	15. 상을 받다
16. 혼자서, 혼자	17. 언젠가, 훗날	18. 치과, 치과의사
19. ~을 요청하다	20. (사용료를 내고 단기간) 빌리다	21. 예약, 약속
22. 수리하다, 고치다	23. 직사각형의	24. 꽃이 피다, 꽃
25. 계속해서 ~하다	26. 만나다	27. ~하게 들리다
28. 출발하다, 시작하다	29. 회전목마	30. 소나기
31. 잠그다, 자물쇠	32. 지지하다	33. A나 B
34. ~하는 것을 배우다	35. 원형의	36. (남의 집에서) 자다
37. 안전벨트, 안전띠	38. 안전 수칙	39. 배구
40. 고려하다, 숙고하다	41. 아주 맛있는	42. 인기 있는, 대중적인
43. 사실은	44. ~을 만나다	

Listening Test

영어듣기 모의고사 11회

|정답|

01 ②	02 ②	03 ③	04 ④	05 ④
06 ②	07 ①	08 ②	09 ⑤	10 ④
11 ④	12 ②	13 ④	14 ③	15 ④
16 ⑤	17 ④	18 ②	19 ④	20 ⑤

01 그림정보파악(담화) ▶ 정답 ②

듣·기·대·본

W: I have four legs and a long tail. I can jump very far and high. I eat plants. I live in Australia. I have a pouch on my stomach and carry my baby in it. What am I?

우·리·말·해·석

여: 나는 네 개의 다리와 하나의 긴 꼬리가 있다. 나는 매우 멀리 그리고 높이 뛸 수 있다. 나는 식물을 먹는다. 나는 호주에 산다. 나는 배에 한 개의 주머니가 있고 나의 새끼를 그 안에 넣고 다닌다. 나는 무엇일까?

단·어·및·표·현

pouch [pautʃ] ⊕ (캥거루 같은 동물의) 새끼 주머니
carry [kǽri] ⊛ 가지고 다니다

02 그림정보파악(대화) ▶ 정답 ②

듣·기·대·본

M: Can I help you?
W: Hello. I'd like to buy a cup for my little brother.
M: OK. How about this one with a star on it?
W: It's nice, but my brother really likes animals.
M: Then how about this one with a pig on it? It's very popular.
W: He'll like it very much. I'll take it.

우·리·말·해·석

남: 무엇을 도와드릴까요?
여: 안녕하세요, 제 남동생을 위한 컵을 사고 싶은데요.
남: 알겠습니다. 별이 그려진 이 제품은 어떠세요?
여: 좋아요, 하지만 제 남동생은 동물을 정말 좋아해요.
남: 그렇다면 돼지가 그려진 이 제품은 어떠세요? 이것은 정말 인기가 있어요.
여: 그가 정말 좋아할 거예요. 그걸로 할게요.

단·어·및·표·현

popular [pɑ́pjulər] ⊚ 인기 있는

03 날씨파악-그림 ▶ 정답 ③

듣·기·대·본

M: Good morning. This is your weather report. In Boston, it's sunny and clear. New York is experiencing light rain and strong winds. In Chicago, it's not raining, but it is cloudy. Expect cooler temperatures in the evening. Be prepared for changing weather!

우·리·말·해·석

남: 좋은 아침입니다. 이것은 여러분의 일기예보입니다. 보스턴은 맑고 청명합니다. 뉴욕은 약한 비와 강한 바람을 겪고 있습니다. 시카고는 비가 오지 않지만 흐립니다. 저녁에는 더 시원한 기온을 예상합니다. 변하는 날씨에 대비하시기 바랍니다!

단·어·및·표·현

experience [ikspíəriəns] ⊛ 겪다, 경험하다
expect [ikspékt] ⊛ 예상하다
temperature [témpərətʃər] ⊚ 기온, 온도
prepare [pripέər] ⊛ 준비하다

04 마지막말의도파악 ▶ 정답 ④

듣·기·대·본

W: What's wrong, Frank?
M: I am so tired. I want to sleep right now.
W: Why? Didn't you sleep well last night?
M: No. I had to do my homework all night long because I played computer games until late.
W: So, did you finish your homework?
M: No. I didn't have enough time.
W: I think you should always do your homework first.

우·리·말·해·석

여: 무슨 일이야, Frank?
남: 나 너무 피곤해. 지금 당장 자고 싶어.
여: 왜? 어젯밤에 잘 못 잤니?

남: 응. 늦게까지 컴퓨터 게임을 했기 때문에 밤새도록 숙제를 해야 했어.
여: 그래서 숙제는 다 했니?
남: 아니. 시간이 충분하지 않았어.
여: 내 생각엔 넌 항상 숙제부터 먼저 해야겠다.

단·어·및·표·현

until late 늦게까지

05 담화미언급 ▶ 정답 ④

듣·기·대·본

M: This spring, we're organizing a tree planting event. It will take place on April 22nd. We'll be planting trees in the local park to celebrate Earth Day. The meeting point will be near the park entrance. We'll give volunteers shovels and small trees to plant. You can register to participate in the event on our website.

우·리·말·해·석

남: 이번 봄에, 저희는 나무 심기 행사를 준비하고 있습니다. 그것은 4월 22일에 개최될 것입니다. 저희는 지구의 날을 기념하기 위해 지역 공원에 나무들을 심을 것입니다. 모임 장소는 공원 입구 근처일 것입니다. 저희는 자원봉사자들에게 (나무를) 심을 삽들과 작은 나무들을 줄 것입니다. 여러분은 저희 웹사이트에서 행사에 참여하기 위해 등록하실 수 있습니다.

단·어·및·표·현

organize [ɔ́ːrgənàiz] [동] 준비하다
plant [plænt] [동] 심다
take place 개최되다, 일어나다
celebrate [séləbrèit] [동] 기념하다
entrance [éntrəns] [명] 입구, 문
volunteer [vɑ̀ləntíər] [명] 자원봉사자
shovel [ʃʌ́vəl] [명] 삽
register [rédʒistər] [동] 등록하다
participate in ~에 참여하다

06 수치파악 ▶ 정답 ②

듣·기·대·본

W: How about playing tennis this afternoon?
M: OK. What time shall we meet?
W: How about at five?
M: I think that's too late. Why don't we meet a little earlier?
W: What time do you say?
M: Let's meet up at three.
W: All right. See you then.

우·리·말·해·석

여: 오늘 오후에 테니스 치는 게 어때?
남: 그래. 몇 시에 만날까?
여: 5시는 어때?
남: 그건 너무 늦은 것 같아. 우리 조금 더 일찍 만나는 게 어때?
여: 몇 시가 좋을까?
남: 3시에 만나자.
여: 좋아. 그때 봐.

단·어·및·표·현

earlier [ə́ːrliər] [부] 더 일찍 [형] 더 이른

07 장래희망추론 ▶ 정답 ①

듣·기·대·본

W: What's this notebook for? May I take a look?
M: Sure. I practice writing poetry in that notebook.
W: Wow! Did you really write these poems by yourself? They're amazing.
M: Thanks. I'm practicing to become a poet in the future.
W: I'm sure you'll become an amazing poet.
M: Thank you.

우·리·말·해·석

여: 이 공책은 무엇을 위한 거니? 내가 좀 봐도 될까?
남: 물론이지. 나는 그 공책에 시 쓰는 것을 연습해.
여: 우와! 정말 이 시들을 너 스스로 쓴 거야? 이것들은 굉장한걸.
남: 고마워. 나는 미래에 시인이 되기 위해서 연습하고 있어.
여: 나는 네가 훌륭한 시인이 될 거라고 확신해.
남: 고마워.

단·어·및·표·현

poetry [póuitri] [명] (집합적으로) 시
poem [póuəm] [명] (한 편의) 시
by oneself (도움을 받지 않고) 스스로, 혼자
poet [póuit] [명] 시인

08 심정추론 ▶ 정답 ②

듣·기·대·본

M: Grace, guess what!
W: You look really excited. What's the news?
M: I got tickets to my favorite band's concert!
W: No way! Can I see the tickets?
M: Sure. Now I can finally see them perform live!
W: I'm so jealous! I've been wanting to see them for ages.

우·리·말·해·석

남: Grace, 맞혀봐!
여: 너 정말 신나 보인다. 무슨 소식이야?
남: 나는 내가 제일 좋아하는 밴드의 콘서트 티켓을 얻었어!
여: 말도 안 돼! 내가 티켓을 봐도 될까?
남: 물론이지. 이제 난 드디어 그들이 라이브 공연을 하는 걸 볼 수 있게 됐어!
여: 정말 부럽다! 나는 오랫동안 그들을 보길 원해 왔어.

단·어·및·표·현

finally [fáinəli] [부] 드디어, 마침내
jealous [dʒéləs] [형] 부러워하는, 질투하는
for ages 오랫동안

09 할일파악(대화직후) ▶ 정답 ⑤

듣·기·대·본

M: I'm home, honey. Something smells delicious!
W: I'm making spaghetti. It's your favorite.
M: Do you need any help?
W: No, thanks. I'm almost finished.
M: Then, do you want me to set the table?
W: That would be great. The spaghetti will be done in a minute.
M: I'll go wash my hands first.

우·리·말·해·석

남: 여보, 나 왔어요. 맛있는 냄새가 나요!
여: 스파게티를 만들고 있어요. 당신이 제일 좋아하는 거잖아요.
남: 도움이 필요해요?
여: 아니요, 괜찮아요. 거의 다 했어요.
남: 그럼, 상을 차릴까요?

여: 그러면 좋죠. 스파게티는 금방 될 거예요.
남: 난 가서 손부터 씻고 올게요.

단•어•및•표•현
delicious [dilíʃəs] [형] 맛있는

> **LISTENING ADVICE**
> 불규칙동사를 제외한 모든 동사들의 과거형에는 단어의 끝에 '-ed'가 붙습니다. 하지만 동사 뒤에 붙은 모든 'ed'가 동일하게 소리 나는 것은 아니지요. [p], [k], [f], [s], [ʃ], [tʃ]와 같이 성대를 울리지 않는 소리들 뒤에 'ed'가 붙는 때에는 [t] 소리가 납니다. 따라서 'I'm almost finished'에서 'finished'는 [피니쉬이드]가 아닌 [피니쉬트]로 발음됩니다.

10 대화화제추론 ▶ 정답 ④

듣•기•대•본
W: Hey, James. What are you looking at?
M: I'm looking at this poster. It's about an event called the Untact Donation Run.
W: What's that?
M: It's a marathon to raise money to help those in need.
W: That's wonderful!
M: Isn't it? And to avoid large crowds, runners can choose their own course and date.

우•리•말•해•석
여: 야, James. 너 뭘 보고 있어?
남: 난 이 포스터를 보고 있어. '비대면 기부 달리기'라고 하는 행사에 관한 거야.
여: 그게 뭔데?
남: 어려움에 처한 사람들을 돕기 위해 모금을 하기 위한 마라톤이야.
여: 그거 멋지다!
남: 그렇지? 그리고 많은 사람들이 몰리는 걸 피하기 위해서 주자들은 자기만의 코스와 날짜를 선택할 수 있어.

단•어•및•표•현
untact [ʌntækt] [명] 비대면, 비접촉
donation [dounéiʃən] [명] 기부, 기증
raise money 모금하다, 돈을 마련하다
in need 어려움에 처한, 궁핍한

11 특정정보파악(교통수단) ▶ 정답 ④

듣•기•대•본
W: Gary, let's go home. This library will close soon.
M: Okay. How are you getting home, Amy?
W: I'll take the subway.
M: Why don't you take the bus? The stop is right outside the library, but the subway station is far away.
W: Okay, I'll do that. How about you?
M: I brought my bike.

우•리•말•해•석
여: Gary, 집에 가자. 이 도서관은 곧 닫을 거야.
남: 그래. 너는 집에 어떻게 가니, Amy?
여: 나는 지하철을 탈 거야.
남: 버스를 타는 게 어때? 정류장은 도서관 바로 밖에 있지만, 지하철역은 멀리 떨어져 있어.
여: 그래, 그렇게 할게. 너는 어떻게 가니?
남: 나는 자전거를 가져왔어.

단•어•및•표•현
take the subway 지하철을 타다
take the bus 버스를 타다
stop [stap] [명] 정류장
bike [baik] [명] 자전거

12 이유파악 ▶ 정답 ②

듣•기•대•본
M: Mom, what are you looking for?
W: I'm trying to find the new gloves I bought yesterday.
M: The black ones? I saw them on the kitchen table.
W: Oh, there they are! I need to return them to the store.
M: Why? Are they too small?
W: Yes, and there's a small hole in one of them.

우•리•말•해•석
남: 엄마, 무엇을 찾고 계세요?
여: 나는 어제 산 새 장갑을 찾으려고 하고 있어.
남: 그 검은색 장갑이요? 저는 그걸 부엌 식탁 위에서 봤어요.
여: 아, 저기 있네! 나는 저걸 가게에 반품해야 해.
남: 왜요? 그게 너무 작아요?
여: 응, 그리고 그 중 하나에 작은 구멍이 있어.

단•어•및•표•현
look for ~을 찾다
return [ritə́ːrn] [동] 반품하다, 반납하다
hole [houl] [명] 구멍

13 대화장소추론 ▶ 정답 ④

듣•기•대•본
M: Hi, Sally. What can I do for you today?
W: I would like to have a haircut.
M: Haircut? How short?
W: Just trim it, please.
M: Around your neck?
W: No, not too short.
M: Just let me know when you'd like to stop.
W: Okay.

우•리•말•해•석
남: 안녕하세요, Sally. 오늘은 어떻게 해드릴까요?
여: 머리를 자르고 싶어서요.
남: 머리를 자르려고요? 얼마나 짧게요?
여: 그냥 다듬어 주세요.
남: 목 정도까지요?
여: 아니요, 너무 짧지 않게요.
남: 그만 자르고 싶을 때 제게 알려 주세요.
여: 알겠어요.

단•어•및•표•현
would like to + 동사원형 ~하고 싶다

14 그림정보파악–지도 ▶ 정답 ③

듣•기•대•본
M: Amy, is there a flower shop around here? I need to buy some flowers for my sister's birthday.
W: Yes, I know a good one. First, walk straight for two blocks and turn right.
M: OK.
W: Then, go straight for one more block and turn left.

M: Turn left?
W: That's right. You'll see it on your right, next to the gas station.
M: I see. Thanks!

우·리·말·해·석

남: Amy, 이 주위에 꽃가게가 있니? 나는 내 누이의 생일을 위해 꽃을 좀 살 필요가 있어.
여: 응, 나는 좋은 데를 알아. 먼저, 두 블록을 똑바로 걸어가서 오른쪽으로 돌아.
남: 응.
여: 그리고 나서, 한 블록 더 직진해서 왼쪽으로 돌아.
남: 왼쪽으로 돌아가?
여: 맞아. 너는 네 오른편에, 주유소 옆에서 그것을 볼 거야.
남: 알겠어. 고마워!

단·어·및·표·현
around [əráund] 전 주위에

15 부탁(요청)한일파악 ▶ 정답 ④

듣·기·대·본

W: This campsite is great. What do you think, Kevin?
M: I really like it, Mom.
W: I'll take the grill out and make some barbecue now.
M: So soon? I'm not hungry, yet.
W: It'll take time. Your dad is still putting up the tent. Can you go help him?
M: Sure. I'll do that.

우·리·말·해·석

여: 이 야영지는 멋지구나. 너는 어떻게 생각하니, Kevin?
남: 정말 마음에 들어요, 엄마.
여: 나는 이제 석쇠를 꺼내서 바비큐를 만들어야겠다.
남: 이렇게 빨리요? 저는 아직 배 안 고파요.
여: 시간이 걸릴 거야. 너희 아버지는 아직 텐트를 치고 계시는구나. 가서 그를 도와주겠니?
남: 그럼요. 그렇게 할게요.

단·어·및·표·현
campsite [kǽmpsàit] 명 야영지
take out ~을 꺼내다
take time 시간이 걸리다
put up (텐트 등을 어디에) 세우다

16 제안파악 ▶ 정답 ⑤

듣·기·대·본

M: Amy, are you okay? You don't look well.
W: I have a sore throat.
M: Did you drink some water?
W: A little bit. But my throat still hurts.
M: How about drinking some warm tea?
W: That sounds nice. I'll make some now.

우·리·말·해·석

남: Amy, 너 괜찮아? 너는 상태가 안 좋아 보여.
여: 나는 목이 아파.
남: 너는 물을 좀 마셨니?
여: 조금. 하지만 내 목은 여전히 아파.
남: 따뜻한 차를 좀 마시는 건 어때?
여: 그거 좋겠다. 나는 지금 차를 좀 끓일게.

단·어·및·표·현
look well 건강해 보이다, 안색이 좋다
have a sore throat 목이 아프다
throat [θrout] 명 목, 목구멍
still [stil] 부 여전히
hurt [həːrt] 동 아프다
warm [wɔːrm] 형 따뜻한
tea [tiː] 명 차

17 한일파악 ▶ 정답 ④

듣·기·대·본

W: James, did you have a good weekend?
M: Yes, I spent time with my baby brother. How about you?
W: I took care of my friend's dog. Her family went away for the weekend.
M: Oh, did you enjoy it?
W: Yeah. I enjoyed walking him.
M: Sounds like you had fun!

우·리·말·해·석

여: James, 너 주말 잘 보냈니?
남: 응, 나는 내 남동생이랑 시간을 보냈어. 너는 어때?
여: 나는 내 친구의 강아지를 돌봐줬어. 그녀의 가족이 주말 동안 집을 떠났거든.
남: 오, 너는 그것을 즐겼니?
여: 응, 나는 그를 산책시키는 것을 즐겼어.
남: 너는 재미있었겠구나!

단·어·및·표·현
take care of ~을 돌보다
go away (특히 휴가를 맞아) 집을 떠나다

18 직업추론 ▶ 정답 ②

듣·기·대·본

W: How was your day, dear?
M: I'm feeling quite tired.
W: Did you have to deliver a lot of packages today?
M: No, but there was heavy traffic all day. It was hard to drive through it.
W: You're really good at making sure the packages get there on time.
M: Thanks. I feel proud of what I do.

우·리·말·해·석

여: 당신의 하루는 어땠나요, 여보?
남: 저는 꽤 피곤함을 느껴요.
여: 당신은 오늘 많은 택배를 배달해야 했어요?
남: 아뇨, 하지만 하루 종일 교통 체증이 있었어요. 그걸 뚫고 운전하는 게 힘들었어요.
여: 당신은 소포가 제 시간에 그곳에 반드시 도착하도록 하는 것을 정말 잘하잖아요.
남: 고마워요. 저는 제가 하는 일이 자랑스러워요.

단·어·및·표·현
quite [kwait] 부 꽤
deliver [dilívər] 동 배달하다
package [pǽkidʒ] 명 택배
heavy traffic 교통 체증
be good at ~을 잘하다
make sure 반드시 (~하도록) 하다

on time 제 시간에, 시간을 어기지 않고
feel proud of ~을 자랑스러워하다

19 알맞은응답찾기 ▶ 정답 ④

듣·기·대·본

M: Riley, there's a new <u>horror movie coming out</u> tomorrow.
W: Oh really? I hope it's good.
M: I heard it's really scary. The reviews are <u>good as well</u>.
W: It sounds great. We should go see it.
M: Okay. Why don't we go see it next week?
W: Let's do that! <u>How is Thursday for you?</u>
M: <u>Thursday is fine with me.</u>

우·리·말·해·석

① 10시야.
② 우리는 거기에 버스를 타고 갈 수 있어.
③ 나는 팝콘 먹는 것을 좋아해.
④ 나는 목요일 괜찮아.
⑤ 우리는 서둘러야 해, 아니면 우리는 늦을 거야.

남: Riley, 내일 나오는 새 공포 영화가 있어.
여: 오 정말? 재미있으면 좋겠다.
남: 나는 그것이 정말 무섭다고 들었어. 후기들 또한 좋아.
여: 좋은 것 같다. 우리는 가서 그것을 봐야 해.
남: 좋아. 우리 다음주에 가서 보는 게 어때?
여: 그러자! 너에게 목요일은 어때?
남: <u>나는 목요일 괜찮아.</u>

단·어·및·표·현

as well 또한, 역시

20 알맞은응답찾기 ▶ 정답 ⑤

듣·기·대·본

W: Dad, let's buy some ice cream there.
M: Okay, sweetie.[pause] Is this an <u>unmanned</u> store?
W: Yes.
M: Then how do we pay?
W: We use the <u>kiosk</u> here.
M: Oh, do you know <u>how to</u> use it?
W: It's easy. Just scan the barcode and <u>press</u> the pay button on the screen.
M: <u>Where is the pay button?</u>
W: <u>It's the big blue one at the bottom.</u>

우·리·말·해·석

① 키오스크가 뭐예요?
② 저건 큰 화면이에요.
③ 저는 아이스크림보다 과자가 더 좋아요.
④ 옆쪽에 스캐너가 있어요.
⑤ 아래쪽에 있는 크고 파란 거예요.

여: 아빠, 우리 저기서 아이스크림을 좀 사요.
남: 그러자, 얘야. [잠시 후] 이곳은 무인 가게이니?
여: 네.
남: 그러면 우리는 어떻게 계산을 하지?
여: 우리는 여기에 있는 키오스크를 사용해요.
남: 아, 너는 그것을 사용하는 방법을 알고 있니?
여: 쉬워요. 그냥 바코드를 스캔하고 화면에 있는 결제 버튼을 누르면 돼요.
남: 결제 버튼이 어디에 있니?
여: <u>아래쪽에 있는 크고 파란 거예요.</u>

단·어·및·표·현

unmanned [ʌnmǽnd] 형 무인의
kiosk [kíːásk] 명 키오스크(무인 주문 및 결제 기계)
how to + 동사원형 ~하는 방법, 어떻게 ~하는지
press [pres] 동 누르다

Words & Expressions Review

1. ~을 꺼내다	2. 야영지	3. 준비하다
4. ~을 찾다	5. 배달하다	6. 상을 차리다
7. 인기 있는	8. 오랫동안	9. 주위에
10. 맛있는	11. ~를 돌보다	12. 꽤
13. 기온, 온도	14. 시간이 걸리다	15. 여전히
16. (집합적으로) 시	17. (특히 휴가를 맞아) 집을 떠나다	18. 비대면, 비접촉
19. 어려움에 처한, 궁핍한	20. 시인	21. 드디어, 마침내
22. 다 하다, 끝내다	23. 무인의	24. 모금하다, 돈을 마련하다
25. 목, 목구멍	26. 예상하다	27. 들고 있다, 나르다
28. 다듬다, 손질하다	29. 구멍	30. 심다
31. 키오스크(무인 주문 및 결제 기계)	32. (작은) 주머니	33. ~와 시간을 보내다
34. 충분한	35. 기부, 기증	36. (한 편의) 시
37. 거의	38. 부러워하는, 질투하는	39. (텐트 등을) 세우다
40. 변화하는	41. 겪다, 경험하다	42. 준비하다
43. 테니스를 치다	44. 반품하다, 반납하다	

Listening Test
영어듣기 모의고사 12회

|정|답|

01 ②	02 ③	03 ③	04 ④	05 ③
06 ②	07 ③	08 ①	09 ③	10 ③
11 ④	12 ④	13 ⑤	14 ②	15 ①
16 ⑤	17 ⑤	18 ②	19 ⑤	20 ②

01 그림정보파악(담화) ▶ 정답 ②

듣·기·대·본

M: This can be worn <u>on your face</u>. <u>This covers your mouth and nose. This can protect you from getting sick.</u> You can also use this on a smoggy day. What is this?

우·리·말·해·석

남: 이것은 당신의 얼굴 위에 씌워질 수 있습니다. 이것은 당신의 입과 코를 덮습니다. 이것은 아프게 되는 것으로부터 당신을 보호할 수 있습니다. 당신은 또한 이것을 스모그가 많은 날에 사용할 수 있습니다. 이것은 무엇입니까?

단·어·및·표·현
cover[kʌ́vər] 통 덮다, 가리다
protect A from B A를 B로부터 보호하다
smoggy[smɑ́gi] 형 스모그가 많은

02 그림정보파악(대화) ▶ 정답 ③

듣·기·대·본

W: Minho, what's that?
M: It's a brooch for my mom. It's a Parents' Day gift.
W: The brooch looks like your mom's face. I like it.
M: Thanks. I hope she likes it, too.
W: I thought you were going to make a flower brooch.
M: Yes, but I changed my mind.

우·리·말·해·석

여: 민호야, 저게 뭐니?
남: 우리 엄마를 위한 브로치야. 그것은 어버이날 선물이야.
여: 브로치가 너희 어머니의 얼굴처럼 보여. 맘에 들어.
남: 고마워. 어머니도 좋아하셨으면 좋겠다.
여: 나는 네가 꽃 브로치를 만들 거라고 생각했어.
남: 맞아, 하지만 마음을 바꿨어.

단·어·및·표·현

brooch[broutʃ] 명 브로치
Parents' Day 어버이날
look like + 명사 ~인 것처럼 보이다

03 날씨파악-그림 ▶ 정답 ③

듣·기·대·본

W: Hi, I'm Jenny Lee for the world weather update. Let's take a look at the weather in Europe. Stormy weather and thunderstorms throughout the day is forecasted in London. Paris is expected to be warm, but it will be very cloudy today. Berlin is mostly cloudy this morning but clearing later on, so it will be sunny after around noon.

우·리·말·해·석

여: 안녕하세요. 세계 일기 예보의 Jenny Lee입니다. 유럽 지역의 날씨를 살펴보겠습니다. 런던은 온종일 폭풍우가 치는 날씨와 뇌우가 있을 것으로 예상됩니다. 파리는 오늘 따뜻하리라 예상되지만, 매우 구름 낀 날씨가 되겠습니다. 베를린은 아침에 대부분 구름이 끼겠으나 점차 맑아져 정오쯤 이후에는 맑겠습니다.

단·어·및·표·현

take a look at ~ ~을 살펴보다
thunderstorm[θʌ́ndərstɔ̀ːrm] 명 뇌우

04 마지막말의의도파악 ▶ 정답 ④

듣·기·대·본

W: Hey, Andy! What are you doing at the park?
M: I'm trying to fly this kite, but I can't get it up.
W: Let me help you. Which way is the wind blowing?
M: It's coming from the east.
W: Let's change how we're holding the kite to make it fly better.
M: Thanks for helping out.

우·리·말·해·석

여: 이봐, Andy! 너는 공원에서 뭐 하고 있니?
남: 나는 이 연을 날리려고 하고 있어, 하지만 나는 그걸 일으킬(띄울) 수가 없어.

여: 내가 너를 도와줄게. 바람이 불어오는 게 어느 방향이야?
남: 그건 동쪽에서 오고 있어.
여: 그것이 더 잘 날 수 있도록 우리 연을 잡는 방법을 바꿔보자.
남: 도와줘서 고마워.

단·어·및·표·현

try to ~하려고 노력하다
way[wei] 명 방향, 쪽
hold[hould] 통 잡다, 쥐다

05 담화미언급 ▶ 정답 ③

듣·기·대·본

M: Hello, students. Our school is starting a new drone class starting next week. It's from 9 a.m. to 12:00 p.m. every Saturday. The class will be held in the computer room. You must bring your own smartphone or tablet PC. There is no fee to participate. In this class, you can learn what a drone is and how to control it. Hope to see you there!

우·리·말·해·석

남: 학생 여러분, 안녕하세요. 우리 학교는 다음 주부터 새로운 드론 수업을 시작합니다. 수업 시간은 매주 토요일 오전 9시부터 오후 12시까지입니다. 수업은 컴퓨터실에서 진행할 예정입니다. 여러분들은 반드시 자신의 스마트폰이나 태블릿 PC를 가져오셔야 합니다. 참여하기 위해 드는 비용은 없습니다. 이 수업에서, 여러분들은 드론이 무엇인지, 그리고 그것을 어떻게 조종하는지에 대해서 배우실 수 있습니다. 수업에서 뵙기를 기대하겠습니다!

단·어·및·표·현

hold[hould] 통 (회의 등을) 하다, 개최하다, 열다
fee[fiː] 명 요금
participate[pɑːrtísəpèit] 통 참가하다

06 수치파악 ▶ 정답 ②

듣·기·대·본

M: Jane, what are you going to do tonight?
W: I'm going to watch my favorite TV show. Shall we watch it together?
M: Sure. What time does it begin?
W: It begins at 7 o'clock. Come to my house at 6:30.
M: Okay. See you then.

우·리·말·해·석

남: Jane, 오늘 밤에 너 뭐할 거니?
여: 내가 제일 좋아하는 TV 쇼를 보려고 해. 같이 볼까?
남: 그래. 몇 시에 시작하는데?
여: 7시에 시작해. 6시 반에 우리 집으로 와.
남: 좋아. 그때 보자.

단·어·및·표·현

favorite[féivərit] 형 제일 좋아하는

07 장래희망추론 ▶ 정답 ③

듣·기·대·본

M: Tina, what are you doing in front of the mirror?
W: I was just practicing some of my ballet moves.
M: Wow, you're amazing! Do you like ballet?
W: Yeah, I want to become a ballerina when I grow up.
M: You're definitely going to make it.
W: Thanks, Paul.

남: Tina, 거울 앞에서 무엇을 하고 있니?
여: 나는 그저 몇 가지 발레 동작을 연습하는 중이었어.
남: 우와, 너 정말 멋지다! 너는 발레를 좋아하니?
여: 응, 나는 커서 발레리나가 되고 싶어.
남: 너는 분명히 해낼 거야.
여: 고마워, Paul.

단·어·및·표·현

in front of ~의 앞에서
ballet move 발레 동작
definitely [défənitli] ⅋ (강조의 의미로 쓰여) 분명히, 틀림없이
make it (바라던 일을) 해내다

08 심정추론 ▶ 정답 ①

듣·기·대·본

M: Mom, I'm home.
W: How was your day? Did you do anything interesting at school today?
M: I made too many mistakes on my math quiz. I feel like I've let you down.
W: Don't say that! I know that you studied hard for the quiz. Chin up! You'll do better next time.
M: Thanks, but I still feel bad about myself.

우·리·말·해·석

① 슬픈   ② 수줍은   ③ 침착한   ④ 신이 난   ⑤ 초조한

남: 엄마, 저 집에 왔어요.
여: 오늘 하루가 어땠니? 오늘 학교에서 어떤 재미있는 일을 했니?
남: 저는 수학 시험에서 너무 많은 실수를 했어요. 제가 엄마를 실망시킨 것처럼 느껴져요.
여: 그런 말 하지 마라! 나는 네가 시험을 위해 열심히 공부한 것을 알아. 기운 내! 다음에는 더 잘 할 거야.
남: 고마워요, 하지만 저는 여전히 제 자신에 대해 기분이 좋지 않아요.

단·어·및·표·현

let ~ down ~를 실망시키다
Chin up! 기운 내!

09 할일파악(대화직후) ▶ 정답 ③

듣·기·대·본

W: Hurry up, Mike! We're going to miss the train.
M: I'm sorry. I just can't find my wallet.
W: It's on the sofa.
M: Oh, thanks. Now let's go.
W: Wait. Isn't it going to rain this evening?
M: I think you're right.
W: Then we should close the windows before we go.
M: I'll do it right now.

우·리·말·해·석

여: 서둘러, Mike! 우리 기차를 놓치겠어.
남: 미안해. 나는 내 지갑을 찾을 수가 없어.
여: 그것은 소파 위에 있어.
남: 아, 고마워. 이제 가자.
여: 잠깐만. 오늘 저녁에 비가 오지 않니?
남: 네 말이 맞는 것 같아.
여: 그러면 우리는 가기 전에 창문들을 닫아야 해.
남: 내가 바로 그것을 할게.

단·어·및·표·현

Hurry up. 서둘러.

10 대화화제추론 ▶ 정답 ③

듣·기·대·본

M: Look! That robot is bringing our food!
W: Yeah, it's my first time seeing a service robot in a restaurant.
M: Do we need to do anything?
W: When the robot stops, take your tray from it and press "Done."
M: Haha! Can it talk to us, too?
W: I wish! It just plays a short message and then leaves.

우·리·말·해·석

남: 봐! 저 로봇이 우리 음식을 가져오고 있어!
여: 응, 나는 식당에서 서빙 로봇을 보는 게 처음이야.
남: 우리가 무엇을 해야 돼?
여: 로봇이 멈추면 그것에서 네 쟁반을 가져오고 "완료" 버튼을 눌러.
남: 하하! 그게 우리한테 말도 할 수 있어?
여: 그랬으면 좋겠다! 그것은 그냥 짧은 메시지만 재생하고 나서 가버려.

단·어·및·표·현

bring [briŋ] ⅋ 가져오다
restaurant [réstərənt] ⅋ 식당
tray [trei] ⅋ 쟁반
press [pres] ⅋ 누르다
leave [liːv] ⅋ 떠나다

11 특정정보파악(교통수단) ▶ 정답 ④

듣·기·대·본

W: Hey, Paul. I heard that you're going to China next week.
M: Yes. I always wanted to go there.
W: Did you buy a plane ticket?
M: No. That's too expensive for me.
W: Then how are you going to China?
M: I'm taking a ship from Incheon.
W: I see. I hope you have a good trip!

우·리·말·해·석

여: 안녕, Paul. 네가 다음 주에 중국에 간다고 들었어.
남: 맞아. 난 언제나 거기에 가고 싶었어.
여: 비행기 표는 샀니?
남: 아니. 그건 나한텐 너무 비싸.
여: 그럼 중국엔 어떻게 가려고?
남: 인천에서 배를 탈 거야.
여: 그렇구나. 즐거운 여행이 되길 바라!

단·어·및·표·현

expensive [ikspénsiv] ⅋ 비싼

12 이유파악 ▶ 정답 ④

듣·기·대·본

M: Wendy, your hair is wet. Did you go swimming?
W: Yes, but I couldn't dry my hair there.
M: Was the dryer broken?
W: No. Before I could dry my hair, the fire alarm went off.
M: Oh, no. Was there a fire?
W: Just a small one, but I had to leave right away.

be held 열리다, 개최되다
community hall 주민센터 다목적실

남: Wendy, 네 머리가 젖었어. 수영하러 갔었니?
여: 응, 하지만 거기서 내 머리를 말릴 수 없었어.
남: 드라이기가 고장 났었니?
여: 아니. 머리를 말리기 전에, 화재 경보가 울렸어.
남: 오, 이런. 불이 났었니?
여: 작은 불이었어. 하지만 나는 곧바로 떠나야 했어.

단·어·및·표·현
right away 곧바로

13 대화장소추론   ▶ 정답 ⑤

듣·기·대·본

M: I lost my bag in the subway station.
W: We have three bags here. Please tell me what your bag looks like.
M: My bag is big, green, and has a name tag.
W: What is your name?
M: James Benson.
W: Oh, you're lucky. Here is your bag.

우·리·말·해·석

남: 지하철역에서 제 가방을 잃어버렸어요.
여: 여기에 가방이 세 개 있습니다. 당신 가방이 어떻게 생겼는지 말씀해 주세요.
남: 제 가방은 크고, 녹색이고, 이름표가 달려 있어요.
여: 성함이 어떻게 되시죠?
남: James Benson입니다.
여: 오, 운이 좋으시네요. 여기 당신 가방이 있네요.

단·어·및·표·현
lucky[lʌ́ki] 📖 운이 좋은

14 표불일치   ▶ 정답 ②

듣·기·대·본

W: Hello, everyone in Maplewood Village. Let me tell you about our Weekly Art Workshop. It'll be this Sunday at 2 p.m. In this workshop, you'll learn how to paint with watercolors. The workshop will be 2 hours in length. You need to pay 18 dollars to join. The workshop will be held at the community hall. Thanks.

우·리·말·해·석

주간 미술 워크숍		
①	일시	이번 주 일요일, 오후 2시
②	주제	유화 물감으로 그림을 그리는 방법
③	소요 시간	2시간
④	참가비	18 달러
⑤	장소	주민센터 다목적실

여: Maplewood Village에 계신 여러분, 안녕하세요. 저희 주간 미술 워크숍에 대해 말씀드리겠습니다. 그것은 이번 주 일요일 오후 2시입니다. 이 워크숍에서 여러분은 수채화 그림물감으로 그림을 그리는 방법을 배우실 것입니다. 이 워크숍은 2시간 동안 진행될 것입니다. 여러분은 참가하시려면 18달러를 내셔야 합니다. 이 워크숍은 주민센터 다목적실에서 열릴 것입니다. 감사합니다.

단·어·및·표·현
paint[peint] 📖 그리다
watercolor[wɔ́:tərkλ̀lər] 📖 수채화 그림물감

15 부탁(요청)한일파악   ▶ 정답 ①

듣·기·대·본

(Telephone rings.)
M: Hello?
W: Hello. This is Rina. May I speak to Karl?
M: Speaking. What's up, Rina?
W: You have the book "Charlie and the Chocolate Factory," don't you?
M: Yes, I do. Why?
W: I have to read it for my homework. Can you lend it to me for three days?
M: Sure.

우·리·말·해·석

(전화벨이 울린다.)
남: 여보세요?
여: 여보세요. 전 Rina인데요. Karl과 통화할 수 있을까요?
남: 나야. 무슨 일이야, Rina?
여: 너 "찰리와 초콜릿 공장" 책 있지, 그렇지 않니?
남: 응, 있어. 왜?
여: 나 숙제 때문에 그것을 읽어야 하거든. 사흘 동안 나한테 그것을 빌려 줄 수 있니?
남: 그래.

단·어·및·표·현
lend[lend] 📖 빌려주다

16 제안파악   ▶ 정답 ⑤

듣·기·대·본

M: Tia, what's wrong? You look so tired.
W: I got up too early this morning.
M: Why?
W: Well, the birds in the trees outside my window started singing so early this morning.
M: Oh, really? Then why don't you try using earplugs?
W: Yeah, using earplugs sounds like a great idea.

우·리·말·해·석

남: Tia, 무슨 일이야? 너 엄청 피곤해 보여.
여: 나는 오늘 아침에 너무 일찍 일어났어.
남: 왜?
여: 음, 내 창문 밖 나무에 있는 새들이 오늘 아침에 너무 일찍 지저귀기 시작했어.
남: 오, 정말? 그럼 너는 귀마개를 사용해보는 게 어때?
여: 응, 귀마개를 사용하는 것은 좋은 생각처럼 들려.

단·어·및·표·현
tired[taiərd] 📖 피곤한, 지친
get up (잠자리에서) 일어나다, 깨다
earplug[íərplʌ̀g] 📖 귀마개

17 한일파악   ▶ 정답 ⑤

듣·기·대·본

W: Oliver, did you do anything fun last weekend?
M: Yes, I went to the movies. What about you?
W: I went to the amusement park with my friends.

M: That's great! Did you have fun?
W: Some of the <u>rides were too scary</u> for me, but it was fun.
M: I should go there with my friends as well.

우·리·말·해·석

여: Oliver, 지난 주말에 뭐 재미있는 거 했어?
남: 응. 난 영화 보러 갔어. 너는 뭐했어?
여: 나는 나의 친구들과 놀이공원에 갔어.
남: 좋았겠다! 재미있었어?
여: 몇몇 놀이 기구들은 나에게 너무 무서웠지만, 재미있었어.
남: 나도 내 친구들과 거기에 가야겠다.

단·어·및·표·현

go to the movies 영화 보러 가다
amusement park 놀이공원
ride[raid] 명 놀이 기구
as well 또한, 역시

18 직업추론 ▶ 정답 ②

듣·기·대·본

W: Owen, are you going to the countryside again?
M: Yes, Mia. I need some quiet time to write.
W: Are you <u>working on</u> your next book?
M: Yes. <u>I'm writing about my experiences</u> in nature.
W: That sounds great. <u>I love your essays.</u>
M: Thank you! I hope you enjoy the new one, too.

우·리·말·해·석

여: Owen, 너는 또 시골에 가니?
남: 응, Mia. 나는 글을 쓰기 위해서 조용한 시간이 좀 필요해.
여: 너 다음 책 작업하고 있는 거야?
남: 응. 나는 자연 속에서의 내 경험에 대해서 쓰고 있어.
여: 멋지다. 나는 네 수필 정말 좋아해.
남: 고마워! 나는 네가 이번 새 책도 즐기길 바라.

단·어·및·표·현

countryside[kʌ́ntrisàid] 명 시골
experience[ikspíəriəns] 명 경험
nature[néitʃər] 명 자연
essay[ései] 명 수필
enjoy[indʒɔ́i] 동 즐기다

19 알맞은응답찾기 ▶ 정답 ⑤

듣·기·대·본

M: Emma, are you going to <u>take the bus</u> now?
W: Yes, Jake. I have to go downtown.
M: Be careful. There's <u>road work</u> on Main Street.
W: Really? I didn't know that.
M: <u>The bus might get stuck</u> in traffic. Why don't you take the subway instead?
W: <u>Thanks for telling me.</u>

우·리·말·해·석

① 택시 타자.
② 너는 이미 늦었어.
③ 나는 걷는 것을 좋아하지 않아.
④ 너는 여기에서 기다려야 해.
⑤ 내게 말해줘서 고마워.

남: Emma, 너는 지금 버스를 탈 거니?
여: 응, Jake. 나는 시내에 가야 해.
남: 조심해. Main가에 도로 공사가 있어.

여: 정말? 몰랐어.
남: 버스가 교통 체증에 갇힐 수도 있어. 대신 지하철을 타는 게 어때?
여: <u>내게 말해줘서 고마워.</u>

단·어·및·표·현

downtown[dàuntáun] 부 시내에[로]
Be careful. 조심해.
road work 도로 공사
get stuck in traffic 교통 체증에 갇히다
subway[sʌ́bwèi] 명 지하철
instead[instéd] 부 대신에

20 알맞은응답찾기 ▶ 정답 ②

듣·기·대·본

W: It's a <u>beautiful</u> day.
M: Hey, how about going to the zoo?
W: That's a <u>great idea</u>. What time shall we meet?
M: I have something to do in the morning. Let's go in the afternoon.
W: <u>You set the time.</u>
M: <u>How about three o'clock?</u>

우·리·말·해·석

① 어제 그걸 했어.
② 3시는 어때?
③ 그거 안됐구나.
④ 가고 싶어.
⑤ 그건 너무 늦어.

여: 날씨가 좋은 날이구나.
남: 야, 동물원에 가는 게 어때?
여: 그거 좋은 생각이다. 몇 시에 만날까?
남: 난 오전엔 할 일이 좀 있어. 오후에 가자.
여: 네가 시간을 정해.
남: <u>3시는 어때?</u>

단·어·및·표·현

set the time 시간을 정하다

Words & Expressions Review

1. 오후에	2. 운이 좋은	3. 놀이 기구
4. 놓치다	5. 이름표	6. 제일 좋아하는
7. 귀마개	8. 시작하다	9. 초조한
10. 뇌우	11. 피곤한, 지친	12. 열리다, 개최되다
13. 놀이공원	14. 동물원	15. 브로치
16. 자연	17. 어버이날	18. ~를 실망시키다
19. ~의 앞에서	20. 온종일	21. 시간을 정하다
22. 그리다	23. 누르다	24. 영화 보러 가다
25. 수필	26. 방향, 쪽	27. 스모그가 많은
28. ~을 살펴보다	29. 떠나다	30. 수채화 그림물감
31. 분명히, 틀림없이	32. 비싼	33. (바라던 일을) 해내다
34. 덮다, 가리다	35. 오전에	36. 쟁반
37. 또한, 역시	38. 참가하다	39. 시골
40. 도로 공사	41. 바로, 지금 당장	42. 빌려주다
43. 지하철역	44. (잠자리에서) 일어나다, 깨다	

정	답			
01 ①	02 ③	03 ③	04 ④	05 ④
06 ③	07 ④	08 ①	09 ③	10 ⑤
11 ⑤	12 ②	13 ①	14 ⑤	15 ④
16 ⑤	17 ⑤	18 ③	19 ②	20 ④

01 그림정보파악(담화) ▶ 정답 ①

들·기·대·본

W: This is usually rectangular. You can open this, put tissues inside, and then close it. This has a hole on its top. You can pull tissues out through the hole. What is this?

우·리·말·해·석

여: 이것은 보통 직사각형입니다. 여러분은 이것을 열어서, 안에 화장지를 넣고, 그런 다음 그것을 닫습니다. 그것의 윗면에는 구멍이 하나 있습니다. 여러분은 그 구멍을 통해 화장지를 뽑을 수 있습니다. 이것은 무엇일까요?

단·어·및·표·현

rectangular [rektǽŋgjulər] 형 직사각형의
hole [houl] 명 구멍
pull [pul] 동 뽑다, 빼다, 잡아당기다

02 그림정보파악(대화) ▶ 정답 ③

들·기·대·본

W: Hello. I am looking for a vase for my grandmother.
M: How about this one with a big heart on it? It is our best seller.
W: That heart is way too big. I would like a vase with a smaller pattern.
M: Okay. How about this one with smaller hearts?
W: That's nice. But I think my grandmother would prefer that one with flowers on it.
M: That's a good choice!
W: Thank you. I'll take it.

우·리·말·해·석

여: 안녕하세요. 저희 할머니께 드릴 꽃병을 하나 찾고 있습니다.
남: 위에 큰 하트가 그려진 이건 어떠세요? 저희의 가장 잘 나가는 상품입니다.
여: 저 하트는 너무 많이 커요. 저는 더 작은 무늬가 있는 꽃병을 원해요.
남: 알겠습니다. 더 작은 하트들이 있는 이건 어떠세요?
여: 좋아요. 하지만 제 생각에 저희 할머니는 위에 꽃이 그려진 저것을 더 좋아하실 것 같아요.
남: 좋은 선택이십니다!
여: 고마워요. 이걸로 할게요.

단·어·및·표·현

vase [veis] 명 꽃병
How about ~? ~은 어때요?
way [wei] 부 (부사, 전치사를 강조하여) 너무, 훨씬

03 날씨파악-그림 ▶ 정답 ③

들·기·대·본

W: Happy weekend! This is Carrie. It's Saturday, the 14th of March. It was rainy all day long yesterday but it stopped this morning. Today's weather condition is perfect for outdoor activities. Don't forget sunscreen, though. We can't enjoy clear skies tomorrow, because there's an eighty percent chance of showers.

우·리·말·해·석

여: 즐거운 주말입니다! 저는 Carrie입니다. 오늘은 3월 14일, 토요일입니다. 어제는 하루 종일 비가 왔지만, 오늘 아침에 그쳤습니다. 오늘 날씨 상태는 야외 활동하기에 아주 좋습니다. 그래도 자외선 차단제를 잊지 마세요. 내일은 소나기 가능성이 80퍼센트이므로 맑은 하늘을 즐기실 수는 없습니다.

단·어·및·표·현

all day long 하루 종일
condition [kəndíʃən] 명 상태
outdoor [áutdɔ̀ːr] 형 야외의

04 마지막말의도파악 ▶ 정답 ④

들·기·대·본

M: You look upset, Jisu. What happened?
W: Dad, you know I really wanted to win the speaking contest. But my friend Hojin won first prize.
M: I see. Did he do a good job?
W: He actually did. But I feel so jealous, and I don't even want to speak to him.
M: I understand why you are upset, but I think you should congratulate him.

우·리·말·해·석

남: 너 속상해 보여, 지수야. 무슨 일이니?
여: 아빠, 제가 말하기 대회에서 우승하기를 정말로 원했던 거 아시죠. 하지만 제 친구 호진이가 일등을 했어요.
남: 그랬구나. 그 애가 잘했니?
여: 그는 실제로 잘했어요. 하지만 저는 무척 질투가 나고 그에게 말조차 걸고 싶지 않아요.
남: 네가 왜 속상해하는지 이해하지만, 나는 네가 그를 축하해주어야 한다고 생각한다.

단·어·및·표·현

do a good job 잘 해내다
speak to ~ ~에게 말을 걸다

05 담화미언급 ▶ 정답 ④

들·기·대·본

W: This is one of the most famous and historic buildings in New York City. It is called the Flatiron Building. Its triangular shape makes it different from other buildings. The building was built in 1902. It is about 97 meters tall.

우·리·말·해·석

여: 이것은 뉴욕시에서 가장 유명하고 역사적인 건물들 중에 하나입니다. 그것은 플랫아이언 빌딩(건물 모양이 다리미를 닮았다고 해서 붙여진 이름)이라고 불립니다. 그것의 삼각형 모양은 그것을 다른 건물들과 차이가 나도록 만듭니다. 그 건물은 1902년에 지어졌습니다. 그것은 약 97미터 높이입니다.

단·어·및·표·현

triangular [traiǽŋgjulər] 형 삼각형의
about [əbáut] 부 약, 대략

06 수치파악 ▶ 정답 ③

듣·기·대·본

W: Sam, let's go see the new <u>animated movie</u> tomorrow.
M: Sounds good. Let's see the earliest show.
W: Um... It's at 9 in the morning. Isn't that <u>too early</u>?
M: It is. Hey, there is one at 10:30.
W: Good. <u>How about meeting at 10</u> at the theater?
M: Great. See you tomorrow.

우·리·말·해·석

여: Sam, 내일 같이 새로운 애니메이션 영화를 보러 가자.
남: 좋은데. 가장 이른 영화를 보자.
여: 음… 그것은 아침 9시에 있는데. 그건 너무 이르지 않아?
남: 그러네. 이봐, 10시 30분에 하나가 있네.
여: 좋아. 극장에서 10시에 만나는 게 어때?
남: 아주 좋아. 내일 보자.

단·어·및·표·현

animated movie 애니메이션 영화
show[ʃou] 뗑 (극장에서 하는) 영화, 쇼

07 장래희망추론 ▶ 정답 ④

듣·기·대·본

[Orchestra sound]
M: I'm excited to be at a symphony concert.
W: Me, too. All the different musical instruments <u>come together</u> to make a beautiful harmony.
M: What are those <u>instruments</u>? The players are all blowing on them.
W: They're flutes, oboes, and clarinets.
M: How do you know their names?
W: I'm studying classical music. <u>I want to become a flutist.</u>
M: That's fantastic!

우·리·말·해·석

[오케스트라 소리]
남: 난 심포니 콘서트에 참석하게 돼서 신나.
여: 나도. 모두 다른 악기들이 (하나로) 합쳐져 아름다운 하모니를 만들어내.
남: 저 악기들은 뭐야? 연주자들은 온통 그것들을 불고 있어.
여: 그것들은 플루트, 오보에, 그리고 클라리넷이야.
남: 너는 어떻게 그것들의 이름들을 알아?
여: 난 클래식 음악을 공부하고 있어. 나는 플루트 연주자가 되고 싶어.
남: 멋지네!

단·어·및·표·현

orchestra[ɔ́ːrkəstrə] 뗑 오케스트라, 관현악단
symphony[símfəni] 뗑 심포니, 교향곡
musical instrument 악기
come together (하나로) 합치다, 모이다
oboe[óubou] 뗑 오보에
clarinet[klæ̀rənét] 뗑 클라리넷

08 심정추론 ▶ 정답 ①

듣·기·대·본

M: Amy, what's wrong?
W: Dad, Kevin <u>tore up</u> my notes again.
M: I'm sorry to hear that. I'll tell him to <u>apologize</u> to you.
W: No. <u>I don't even want to talk to him anymore.</u>
M: But sweetie, he's only three years old. I hope you

understand.
W: I'm trying. But <u>he really gets on my nerves!</u>

우·리·말·해·석

① 화난 ② 행복한 ③ 걱정하는 ④ 자랑스러운 ⑤ 신이 난

남: Amy, 무슨 일이야?
여: 아빠, Kevin이 제 공책을 또 갈기갈기 찢었어요.
남: 안됐구나. 내가 너에게 사과하라고 그에게 이야기할게.
여: 아니요. 저는 심지어 더이상 그에게 말도 하고 싶지 않아요.
남: 하지만 얘야, 그는 고작 세 살이잖니. 네가 이해를 해주면 좋겠구나.
여: 노력하고 있어요. 하지만 그는 정말 제 신경을 건드린다구요!

단·어·및·표·현

tear up 갈기갈기 찢다
apologize[əpálədʒàiz] 뗑 사과하다
get on one's nerves 신경을 건드리다

09 할일파악(대화직후) ▶ 정답 ③

듣·기·대·본

M: It's Heesu's birthday today. Did you know that?
W: Oh, I <u>forgot about</u> that.
M: How about buying a cake <u>for him</u>?
W: That's a good idea. <u>Should we go to the bakery now?</u>
M: Sure. There's one <u>next to</u> the bookstore.
W: Okay. Let's go.

우·리·말·해·석

남: 오늘은 희수의 생일이야. 넌 그걸 알고 있었니?
여: 오, 내가 그걸 잊어버렸네.
남: 그를 위해 케이크를 사는 건 어때?
여: 좋은 생각이야. 지금 우리가 제과점에 가야 할까?
남: 물론이지. 서점 옆에 제과점이 하나 있어.
여: 좋아. 가자.

단·어·및·표·현

forget about ~ ~을 잊다

10 대화화제추론 ▶ 정답 ⑤

듣·기·대·본

W: <u>What are your plans for the weekend?</u>
M: I'm going to Gapyung to see my aunt. How about you?
W: I'm going to a hospital with some friends. <u>We'll sing to the sick kids.</u>
M: That's nice! <u>Have a good time.</u>
W: Thanks. You, too.

우·리·말·해·석

여: 네 주말 계획은 뭐야?
남: 나는 가평에 이모를 뵈러 갈 거야. 너는?
여: 나는 친구 몇 명과 병원에 갈 거야. 우리는 아픈 아이들에게 노래를 불러줄 거야.
남: 그거 멋지다! 좋은 시간 보내.
여: 고마워. 너도.

단·어·및·표·현

plan[plæn] 뗑 계획

11 특정정보파악(교통수단) ▶ 정답 ⑤

듣·기·대·본

W: Jihoon, how will you get to the ski resort this weekend?
M: I'm not sure, Mom.

W: How about taking a train?
M: The resort is quite far from the train station.
W: Then, why don't you take a shuttle bus? It'll get you right at the door.
M: A shuttle bus? That sounds good.

우•리•말•해•석

여: 지훈아, 이번 주말에 스키 리조트에 어떻게 갈 거니?
남: 잘 모르겠어요, 엄마.
여: 기차를 타는 건 어떠니?
남: 그 리조트는 기차역에서 꽤 멀어요.
여: 그러면, 셔틀버스를 타지 그러니? 그것은 너를 문 바로 앞까지 데려다 줄 거야.
남: 셔틀버스요? 그게 좋겠어요.

단•어•및•표•현

get to ~에 도착하다
far [fɑːr] [형] 먼, 멀리 떨어진

12 이유파악 ▶ 정답 ②

듣•기•대•본

W: You look sad. What happened?
M: Something terrible happened to me.
W: Did you mess up on your English exam?
M: Yes, but it's not because of that.
W: What's the matter with you, then?
M: I lost my dog yesterday. He ran away from home. I can't find him.

우•리•말•해•석

여: 너 슬퍼 보인다. 무슨 일이야?
남: 끔찍한 일이 내게 일어났어.
여: 너 영어 시험을 망쳤니?
남: 응, 그렇지만 그것 때문은 아니야.
여: 그럼, 무슨 일인데?
남: 나 어제 우리 집 개를 잃어버렸어. 개가 집에서 도망갔어. 개를 못 찾겠어.

단•어•및•표•현

mess up 망치다, 엉망으로 만들다
run away 도망치다, 달아나다

13 대화장소추론 ▶ 정답 ①

듣•기•대•본

W: Hello. I have an appointment under the name Grace Lim.
M: Oh, yes! For 4 o'clock, right? Please, have a seat.
W: Thank you.
M: So, do you have any particular design in mind? If not, we have monthly designs you could choose from.
W: I was thinking of just getting a manicure and using one solid-color for my nails.
M: Sounds good. Let me see your nails.

우•리•말•해•석

여: 안녕하세요. 저는 Grace Lim이라는 이름으로 예약이 되어 있어요.
남: 오, 네! 4시, 맞죠? 자리에 앉으세요.
여: 감사합니다.
남: 자, 당신은 생각하고 계신 어떤 특정 디자인이 있나요? 만약 없으시다면, 저희는 당신이 선택할 수 있는 이달의 디자인을 가지고 있습니다.
여: 저는 단지 손톱 관리를 받는 것과 저의 손톱에 한 가지 단색을 사용할 것을 생각하고 있었어요.
남: 좋습니다. 당신의 손톱을 보여주세요.

단•어•및•표•현

have an appointment 예약이 되어 있다
have a seat 자리에 앉다
have ~ in mind ~을 생각하다, 염두에 두다
get a manicure 손톱 관리를 받다
solid-color 단색

14 그림정보파악–위치 ▶ 정답 ⑤

듣•기•대•본

M: Mom, can I go and ride my bicycle?
W: Sure. It's sunny outside, so don't forget your cap.
M: OK. I put it on my bicycle this morning.
W: But it's not there. Can you check on the table?
M: It isn't there. Oh! Here it is under the table.
W: Great. Have fun.

우•리•말•해•석

남: 엄마, 제가 나가서 자전거를 타도 될까요?
여: 물론이지. 밖은 화창하니 모자를 잊지 말렴.
남: 네. 전 오늘 아침에 제 자전거 위에 그것을 뒀어요.
여: 하지만 그건 거기 없어. 테이블 위를 확인해줄 수 있니?
남: 그건 거기 없어요. 오! 테이블 아래 여기에 있네요.
여: 좋아. 재밌게 놀아.

단•어•및•표•현

forget [fərgét] [동] 잊다

15 부탁(요청)한일파악 ▶ 정답 ④

듣•기•대•본

W: Honey, let's clean the house today.
M: Since we don't have any plans today, that's a good idea.
W: It's about time. We haven't done any cleaning for a while.
M: You're right. We have so many other things to do.
W: First of all, can you separate the trash?
M: No problem.

우•리•말•해•석

여: 여보, 오늘 집을 청소합시다.
남: 오늘 우리는 아무 계획도 없으니, 좋은 생각이네요.
여: 때가 됐어요. 우리는 한동안 전혀 청소를 하지 않았어요.
남: 당신이 맞아요. 우리는 다른 할 일이 너무 많아요.
여: 우선, 당신은 쓰레기를 분리해줄 수 있나요?
남: 문제없어요.

단•어•및•표•현

It's about time. 때가 됐다.
for a while 한동안
separate [sépəreit] [동] 분리하다, 나누다
trash [træʃ] [명] 쓰레기

16 제안파악 ▶ 정답 ⑤

듣•기•대•본

M: Vicky, you are such a good cook.
W: Thank you. I'm glad you like my cupcakes.
M: Can you give me the recipe? I want to try it someday.
W: Sure. It's not difficult to follow.
M: I'm sure everyone would love your recipe. Why don't

you upload it on your blog?

W: OK, I'll give it a try.

우·리·말·해·석

남: Vicky, 너는 정말 훌륭한 요리사야.

여: 고마워. 나는 네가 내 컵케이크를 좋아해서 기뻐.

남: 나에게 요리법을 줄 수 있니? 나는 언젠가 그것을 해보길 원해.

여: 그럼. 그것은 따라하기 어렵지 않아.

남: 나는 모든 사람들이 네 요리법을 좋아할 것이라고 확신해. 네 블로그에 그것을 올리는 게 어때?

여: 좋아, 한번 해볼게.

단·어·및·표·현

recipe [résəpì:] 몡 요리법

give it a try 한번 해보다

17 한일파악 ▶ 정답 ⑤

듣·기·대·본

W: Alfie, how was your holiday?

M: It was good. I practiced basketball with my brother at the park. What about you?

W: I went to the board game café with my friends.

M: That sounds nice! What games did you play?

W: We played Clue for an hour. It was fun.

우·리·말·해·석

여: Alfie, 네 휴일이 어땠니?

남: 그것은 좋았어. 나는 공원에서 나의 형과 농구 연습을 했어. 너는?

여: 나는 내 친구들과 보드 게임 카페에 갔어.

남: 그것 멋지다! 너는 무슨 게임들을 했니?

여: 우리는 Clue(대저택 안에서 벌어진 살인사건의 용의자를 추리하는 게임)를 한 시간 동안 했어. 그것은 재미있었어.

단·어·및·표·현

fun [fʌn] 혱 재미있는

18 직업추론 ▶ 정답 ③

듣·기·대·본

M: What brings you here today?

W: I've been having headaches lately.

M: For how long?

W: About two weeks. It's only when I wear my glasses.

M: Hmm. Have you been having trouble seeing clearly when wearing them?

W: Not really. But I notice my eyes get tired more easily than before.

M: I see. Well, let's start off with the eye chart again, just to check.

우·리·말·해·석

남: 오늘은 무슨 일로 오셨어요?

여: 최근에 두통이 있어서요.

남: 얼마나 오랫동안 그러셨어요?

여: 2주 정도요. 제가 제 안경을 쓸 때만요.

남: 음. 당신은 안경을 썼을 때 또렷하게 보는 데 어려움이 있나요?

여: 그렇지는 않아요. 그런데 전보다 제 눈이 더 쉽게 피로해지는 걸 알았어요.

남: 그렇군요. 그럼, 확인하기 위해 다시 시력 검사표부터 시작해보죠.

단·어·및·표·현

have trouble V-ing ~하는 데 어려움이 있다

clearly [klíərli] 閉 또렷하게

start off with ~부터 시작하다

eye chart 시력 검사표

19 알맞은응답찾기 ▶ 정답 ②

듣·기·대·본

W: Tony, we should get started on our group project.

M: I agree. We should choose a topic first.

W: Yeah. Do you have any good ideas?

M: Why don't we do a presentation about K-pop?

W: That's a great idea! Let's start doing some research.

M: Okay. Can you search for some K-pop photos online?

W: Sure, leave it to me.

우·리·말·해·석

① 나는 K-pop 음악을 정말 좋아해.

② 물론이야, 나에게 맡겨.

③ 나는 콘서트에 가고 싶어.

④ 나는 네가 최선을 다했다고 확신해.

⑤ 우리 발표는 내일이야.

여: Tony, 우리는 우리 그룹 과제를 시작해야 해.

남: 동의해. 우리는 먼저 주제를 골라야 해.

여: 응. 좋은 생각 있어?

남: 우리 K-pop에 대한 발표를 하는 게 어때?

여: 그거 좋은 생각이야! 조사를 시작하자.

남: 좋아. 인터넷으로 K-pop 사진을 좀 찾아줄 수 있어?

여: **물론이야, 나에게 맡겨.**

단·어·및·표·현

get started 시작하다

presentation [prì:zəntéiʃən] 몡 발표

20 알맞은응답찾기 ▶ 정답 ④

듣·기·대·본

W: Dad, I need a dress to wear to uncle's wedding.

M: I know. Do you want to go shopping on Saturday?

W: Of course! Is Mom coming with us, too?

M: Yes. She'll help you pick a dress.

W: Great. Can we have dinner on the way back?

M: Sure. What do you want to eat?

W: I want Vietnamese noodles.

우·리·말·해·석

① 당신은 요리를 정말 잘하네요!

② 파란색 드레스면 괜찮을 거예요.

③ 결혼식은 일요일이에요.

④ 저는 베트남식 국수를 원해요.

⑤ 우리는 집에 버스를 타고 갈 수 있어요.

여: 아빠, 저 삼촌의 결혼식에 입고 갈 드레스가 필요해요.

남: 맞아. 토요일에 쇼핑하러 가겠니?

여: 당연하죠! 엄마도 같이 가시나요?

남: 그래. 네가 드레스를 고르는 것을 그녀가 도와줄 거야.

여: 좋아요, 우리 돌아오는 길에 저녁 먹어도 되나요?

남: 그럼. 무엇을 먹고 싶니?

여: **저는 베트남식 국수를 원해요.**

단·어·및·표·현

wedding [wédiŋ] 몡 결혼식

pick [pik] 통 고르다

have dinner 저녁 식사하다
on the way back 돌아오는 길에

Words & Expressions Review

1. (하나로) 합치다, 모이다	2. ~은 어때요?	3. 직사각형의
4. 꽃병	5. 끔찍한	6. 심포니, 교향곡
7. 결혼식	8. 뽑다, 빼다, 잡아당기다	9. ~에 도착하다
10. ~을 생각하다, 염두에 두다	11. 돌아오는 길에	12. 제과점, 빵집
13. 너무, 훨씬	14. 타다	15. 갈기갈기 찢다
16. 주말	17. 한번 해보다	18. 망치다, 엉망으로 만들다
19. 이해하다	20. 자리에 앉다	21. 잘 해내다
22. 계획	23. 구멍	24. 상태, 상황
25. 먼, 멀리 떨어진	26. 약, 대략	27. ~ 옆에
28. 아픈, 병든	29. 하루 종일	30. 또렷하게
31. 사과하다	32. 신경을 건드리다	33. 예약이 되어 있다
34. 때가 됐다.	35. ~하는 데 어려움이 있다	36. ~을 잊다
37. 고르다	38. 삼각형의	39. (극장에서 하는) 쇼, 영화
40. 이모, 고모	41. 발표	42. 도망치다, 달아나다
43. 시작하다	44. 한동안	

Listening Test
영어듣기 모의고사 14회

|정|답|

01 ①	02 ②	03 ③	04 ④	05 ④
06 ④	07 ④	08 ①	09 ②	10 ②
11 ③	12 ②	13 ⑤	14 ④	15 ⑤
16 ③	17 ④	18 ④	19 ③	20 ⑤

01 그림정보파악(담화) ▶ 정답 ①

듣·기·대·본

M: I am large and very heavy. I have four short legs and two small ears. I have thick, dark colored skin. I also have two horns on top of my nose. What am I?

우·리·말·해·석

남: 나는 크고 매우 무거워. 나는 네 개의 짧은 다리가 있고 두 개의 작은 귀가 있어. 나는 두껍고, 어두운 색의 피부가 있어. 나는 또한 내 코 위에 두 개의 뿔이 있어. 나는 무엇일까?

단·어·및·표·현

thick [θik] 혱 두꺼운

02 그림정보파악(대화) ▶ 정답 ②

듣·기·대·본

M: Hello, I want to buy a bookbag for my daughter.

W: Sure, we have square ones and round ones.

M: I think she would prefer a round one.

W: Okay, then how about this one with the stripes?

M: Hmm… Is there anything else?

W: Yes, of course. There is this one with a unicorn.

M: She will love it! I'll take this one.

우·리·말·해·석

남: 안녕하세요, 저는 제 딸에게 줄 책가방을 사고 싶어요.

여: 그렇군요, 저희는 네모난 것들과 둥근 것들을 가지고 있습니다.

남: 제 생각에 그녀는 둥근 걸 더 좋아할 것 같아요.

여: 네, 그러면 줄무늬가 그려진 이건 어떠세요?

남: 흠… 그 밖에 또 다른 것도 있나요?

여: 네, 물론이죠. 유니콘이 있는 이것도 있어요.

남: 그녀는 그것을 좋아할 거예요! 저는 이걸로 살게요.

단·어·및·표·현

bookbag [búkbæg] 혱 책가방
stripe [straip] 혱 줄무늬
anything else 그 밖에 또 다른 것

03 날씨파악-그림 ▶ 정답 ③

듣·기·대·본

W: Good morning! This is the weather report. Right now, it is snowing outside. And it looks like we will get more snow throughout the day. Fortunately, by tomorrow morning, the snow will have stopped but it will be very windy. So, make sure to wear a jacket when you go outside.

우·리·말·해·석

여: 좋은 아침입니다! 일기예보입니다. 바로 지금, 밖에는 눈이 내리고 있습니다. 그리고 온종일 더 많은 눈이 내릴 것으로 보입니다. 다행히도, 내일 아침이면 눈은 그치겠지만 바람이 매우 많이 불 것입니다. 그러니, 외출하실 때 반드시 외투를 입으세요.

단·어·및·표·현

throughout [θru:áut] 젠 ~동안, 내내
make sure 반드시 ~하다, 확실히 하다
go outside 외출하다, 밖으로 나가다

04 마지막말의도파악 ▶ 정답 ④

듣·기·대·본

W: Excuse me, can I get a different table?

M: Of course. Is there something wrong?

W: Yes, this table is too close to the kitchen, and it isn't quiet.

M: I understand. Let me find you a table in a quieter section right away.

W: Thank you.

M: My apologies for the trouble.

우·리·말·해·석

여: 실례합니다, 다른 테이블로 옮길 수 있을까요?

남: 물론입니다. 혹시 무슨 문제라도 있나요?

여: 네, 이 테이블은 주방과 너무 가깝고 조용하지 않아요.

남: 알겠습니다. 제가 바로 손님께 더 조용한 구역에 있는 테이블을 찾아드리겠습니다.

여: 감사합니다.

남: 불편을 드려 죄송합니다.

W: Yes. So I am practicing every day.
M: Great!

우·리·말·해·석

남: Emma, 네 책상 위에 멋진 포스터가 있구나.

여: 고마워. 그건 내가 가장 좋아하는 예술가, Leona Wilson이 그린 작품의 복사본이야.

남: 멋져. 그럼, 그녀는 화가야?

여: 응. 나도 언젠가 저렇게 아름다운 걸 만들어낼 수 있기를 원해.

남: 우와! 그러면, 너는 미래에 그녀처럼 되고 싶은 거야?

여: 맞아. 그래서 나는 매일 연습을 하고 있어.

남: 훌륭해!

단·어·및·표·현

photocopy [fóutoukàpi] 명 복사본

work [wə:rk] 명 작품

painter [péintər] 명 화가

someday [sʌ́mdèi] 부 (미래의) 언젠가

단·어·및·표·현

wrong [rɔːŋ] 형 문제가 있는

close [klous] 형 가까운

understand [ʌ̀ndərstǽnd] 동 이해하다, 알아듣다

section [sékʃən] 명 구역, 부분

right away 바로, 즉시

apology [əpálədʒi] 명 사과

trouble [trʌ́bl] 명 불편, 문제

05 담화미언급 ▶ 정답 ④

듣·기·대·본

M: Let me tell you about my plans for a family trip. My family will go to Gyeongju and visit historical sites. We'll be there for 3 days. We'll take trains and buses to get around. My family will stay at a hotel built in a traditional Korean style.

우·리·말·해·석

남: 가족 여행에 대한 나의 계획을 얘기해 줄게. 나의 가족은 경주에 갈 거고 역사적인 유적지에 방문할 거야. 우리는 3일 동안 거기에 있을 거야. 우리는 돌아다니기 위해 기차와 버스를 탈 거야. 나의 가족은 전통적인 한국의 방식으로 지어진 호텔에서 머물 거야.

단·어·및·표·현

historical [histɔ́:rikəl] 형 역사적인, 역사의

site [sait] 명 유적, 장소, 위치

get around (여기 저기) 돌아다니다

traditional [trədíʃənl] 형 전통적인, 전통의

06 수치파악 ▶ 정답 ④

듣·기·대·본

M: It's really hot today. Let's go swimming this afternoon.

W: Okay. Let's meet at the indoor pool.

M: Can we meet at 1:30?

W: I have lunch at 1.

M: Then, let's meet at 2:30. We shouldn't go into the water right after lunch.

W: Okay. See you then.

우·리·말·해·석

남: 오늘 진짜 덥네. 오늘 오후에 같이 수영하러 가자.

여: 그래. 실내 수영장에서 만나자.

남: 우리 1시 30분에 만날 수 있어?

여: 나는 1시에 점심을 먹어.

남: 그러면, 2시 30분에 만나자. 우리는 점심 식사 후에 바로 물에 들어가서는 안 돼.

여: 알겠어. 그때 보자.

단·어·및·표·현

indoor [índɔ̀:r] 형 실내의

07 장래희망추론 ▶ 정답 ④

듣·기·대·본

M: Emma, that's a nice poster on your desk.

W: Thanks. It's a photocopy of a work by Leona Wilson, my favorite artist.

M: Cool. So, she's a painter?

W: Yes. I want to be able to create something that beautiful someday.

M: Wow! So, do you want to be like her in the future?

08 심정추론 ▶ 정답 ①

듣·기·대·본

M: Mom, the rock festival was cancel(l)ed.

W: What? Are you sure? But you really wanted to go to it.

M: I know. How could they do that? I've already saved money for the ticket.

W: I'm so sorry, honey.

M: This is so bad.

우·리·말·해·석

남: 엄마, 록 페스티벌이 취소됐어요.

여: 뭐라고? 확실하니? 하지만 너는 정말로 거기 가고 싶어 했잖아.

남: 그러니까요. 그들이 어떻게 그럴 수가 있죠? 저는 벌써 표를 위해서 돈을 모았단 말이에요.

여: 정말 안됐구나, 얘야.

남: 이건 너무 나빠요.

단·어·및·표·현

already [ɔːlrédi] 부 벌써

09 할일파악(대화직후) ▶ 정답 ②

듣·기·대·본

W: What's wrong, Isaac?

M: My eyes are sore.

W: You are watching videos on your phone too much.

M: Maybe. I put eye drops in, but they're not working.

W: How about closing your eyes and giving them some rest?

M: That sounds good. Could you turn the light off for me?

W: Sure. I'll do it right now.

우·리·말·해·석

여: 무슨 일이야, Issac?

남: 내 눈이 아파.

여: 너는 네 핸드폰으로 영상을 너무 많이 보고 있어.

남: 그럴지도. 나는 안약을 넣었는데, 효과가 없어.

여: 눈을 감고 눈을 좀 쉬게 하는 건 어때?

남: 좋아. 넌 날 위해 불을 좀 꺼줄 수 있니?

여: 물론이지. 지금 바로 할게.

단·어·및·표·현

sore [sɔ:r] 형 아픈, 따가운

eye drops 안약, 점안액

work[wə:rk] 동 효과가 있다

10 대화화제추론 ▶ 정답 ②

듣·기·대·본

W: Did you hear about the school book sale?
M: You mean the school charity event?
W: Yes. We can buy used books at a cheap price there.
M: Sounds great. When is it?
W: It starts this Friday and will continue all week.
M: Why don't we go together this Saturday?
W: Sure. I'd love to.

우·리·말·해·석

여: 학교 도서 판매에 대해 들었어?
남: 학교 자선 행사를 말하는 거야?
여: 응. 우리는 그곳에서 싼 가격에 중고 책을 살 수 있어.
남: 좋아, 언제야?
여: 이번 주 금요일에 시작해서 일주일 내내 계속될 거야.
남: 이번 주 토요일에 같이 가는 거 어때?
여: 그래. 좋아.

단·어·및·표·현

sale[seil] 명 판매, 매매
charity[tʃǽrəti] 명 자선, 자선 단체
used[ju:zd] 형 중고의
cheap[tʃi:p] 형 싼, 저렴한

11 특정정보파악(교통수단) ▶ 정답 ③

듣·기·대·본

M: Amy, do you want to go to the cinema today?
W: Sure. What movie do you want to see?
M: I'm thinking of watching The Flying Man.
W: Oh, I'd love to watch it! Shall we walk there?
M: It's too hot outside. Why don't we take a taxi?
W: A taxi sounds better.

우·리·말·해·석

남: Amy, 오늘 영화 보러 갈래?
여: 그래. 너는 무슨 영화를 보고 싶어?
남: 난 "The Flying Man"을 보려고 생각 중이야.
여: 오, 난 그것이 너무 보고 싶어! 우리 거기에 걸어갈까?
남: 밖은 너무 더워. 택시를 타는 게 어때?
여: 택시가 더 낫겠다.

단·어·및·표·현

go to the cinema 영화를 보러 가다
think of ~을 생각하다
would love to + 동사원형 너무 ~하고 싶다

12 이유파악 ▶ 정답 ②

듣·기·대·본

M: Sarah, do you need anything from the supermarket?
W: Yes, Dad. Can you buy me a mat?
M: Sure. What for?
W: My friends and I are going on a picnic this weekend.
   Karen and Sophia will bring food and I will bring a mat.
M: I see. I'll buy one for you.
W: Thank you.

우·리·말·해·석

남: Sarah, 슈퍼마켓에서 필요한 것 있니?

여: 네, 아빠. 저에게 매트 하나 사 주실 수 있어요?
남: 물론이지. 뭐 하려고?
여: 제 친구들과 제가 이번 주말에 소풍을 가요. Karen과 Sophia는 음식을
   가져올 것이고 저는 매트를 가져갈 거예요.
남: 알겠어. 내가 너를 위해 하나 살게.
여: 감사해요.

단·어·및·표·현

What for? 왜(뭐 하러)? (목적, 이유를 물음)
go on a picnic 소풍가다
bring[briŋ] 동 가져오다, 데려오다

13 대화장소추론 ▶ 정답 ⑤

듣·기·대·본

M: Excuse me. I'd like to borrow some books.
W: OK. May I see your library card, please?
M: Here it is. And these are the books I want to borrow.
W: Oh, you can't borrow all these books.
M: Why?
W: You can borrow only three books at a time.
M: OK. I'll borrow these three books.

우·리·말·해·석

남: 실례합니다. 책을 좀 빌리고 싶은데요.
여: 알겠습니다. 당신의 도서관 카드를 볼 수 있을까요?
남: 여기요. 그리고 이것들은 제가 빌려 가고 싶은 책이에요.
여: 오, 이 책 모두를 빌려갈 수는 없어요.
남: 왜요?
여: 한 번에 세 권씩만 빌려갈 수 있거든요.
남: 알았어요. 이 세 권을 빌려갈게요.

단·어·및·표·현

at a time 한 번에

14 그림정보파악-위치 ▶ 정답 ④

듣·기·대·본

M: Maria, have you seen my cellphone?
W: I think it is on the table.
M: No, it's not there.
W: Well, look on the bed.
M: It's not there, either.
W: Hmm, that's weird. What about on the piano?
M: Oh, there it is.

우·리·말·해·석

남: Maria, 내 휴대전화 봤어?
여: 탁자 위에 있는 것 같은데.
남: 아니, 거기 없어.
여: 음, 침대 위에 봐봐.
남: 거기도 없어.
여: 흠, 그거 이상하네. 피아노 위에는?
남: 오, 거기 있네.

단·어·및·표·현

weird[wiərd] 형 이상한, 수상한

15 부탁(요청)한일파악 ▶ 정답 ⑤

듣·기·대·본

W: David, you look tired.
M: It's so hot in here.
W: That's true. I think the air conditioner is broken.

M: Would you do me a favor?
W: Sure, what is it?
M: Please leave the door wide open on your way out.

우·리·말·해·석

여: David, 너 피곤해 보인다.
남: 여기는 너무 더워.
여: 맞아. 에어컨이 고장 난 것 같아.
남: 내 부탁 좀 들어줄래?
여: 물론이지, 뭔데?
남: 네가 나가는 길에 문을 활짝 열어놔 줘.

단·어·및·표·현

wide open 활짝 열린

16 제안파악 ▶ 정답 ③

듣·기·대·본

M: Sally, my neck hurts.
W: You must have text neck!
M: Text neck? What is that?
W: It is neck pain caused by looking down at your phone for too long.
M: Oh, what should I do?
W: Why don't you stretch your neck more often?
M: Okay, I will. Thank you.

우·리·말·해·석

남: Sally, 제 목이 아파요.
여: 거북목이 있는 게 틀림없어요!
남: 거북목이요? 그게 뭐예요?
여: 너무 오랫동안 당신의 휴대전화를 내려다봐서 생긴 목 통증이에요.
남: 오, 제가 뭘 해야 하죠?
여: 당신의 목을 더 자주 스트레칭 하는 게 어때요?
남: 알겠어요, 그럴게요. 고마워요.

단·어·및·표·현

text neck 거북목
look down 내려보다, 내려다보다
stretch [stretʃ] [동] 스트레칭 하다, 펴다

17 할일파악 ▶ 정답 ④

듣·기·대·본

W: Hi, Brian. Do you have any plans for the weekend?
M: Yes, Amy. I'm going to practice the guitar at home.
W: Oh, are you learning a new song?
M: Yeah! I want to make sure I play it well for my school festival.
W: That's cool. I'd love to hear you play someday.
M: Sure! I'll play for you when I get better.

우·리·말·해·석

여: 안녕, Brian. 너는 이번 주말에 무슨 계획 있니?
남: 응, Amy. 나는 집에서 기타 연습을 할 거야.
여: 오, 너 새로운 노래를 익히고 있는 거야?
남: 응! 나는 학교 축제에서 그것을 잘 연주하게 확실히 하고 싶어.
여: 멋지다. 언젠가 나는 네가 연주하는 것을 들어보고 싶어.
남: 좋아! 내가 더 잘하게 되면 너한테 연주해 줄게.

단·어·및·표·현

practice [prǽktis] [동] 연습하다
learn [ləːrn] [동] 익히다, 배우다
make sure 확실하게 하다

18 직업추론 ▶ 정답 ④

듣·기·대·본

W: How was your day, honey?
M: I'm quite tired.
W: Were there many visitors at the zoo today?
M: No, but we had to move some animals to their winter homes. It was a lot of work.
W: Your effort to keep the animals safe and healthy is impressive.
M: Thank you. I feel good knowing they're happy and safe.

우·리·말·해·석

여: 당신의 하루는 어땠어요, 여보?
남: 저는 꽤 지쳤어요.
여: 오늘 동물원에 많은 방문객들이 있었나요?
남: 아뇨, 하지만 저희는 몇몇 동물들을 그들의 겨울용 시설로 옮겨야 했어요. 많은 일이었죠(정말 힘들었죠).
여: 동물들을 안전하고 건강하게 유지하는 당신의 노력은 인상적이에요.
남: 고마워요. 저는 그들이 행복하고 안전하다는 것을 알게 되어 기뻐요.

단·어·및·표·현

quite [kwait] [부] 꽤
visitor [vízitər] [명] 방문객
home [houm] [명] 시설
effort [éfərt] [명] 노력
impressive [imprésiv] [형] 인상적인, 감명 깊은

19 알맞은응답찾기 ▶ 정답 ③

듣·기·대·본

W: Paul, did you go to your grandparents' house last New Year's Day?
M: Yes, I did. Did you?
W: No, I couldn't go, because I was sick.
M: Oh, no! That's too bad.
W: So, what did you do there?
M: I ate a lot of food and played games. It was fun.
W: Good for you.

우·리·말·해·석

① 정말 안됐다. ② 절대 안 돼! ③ 좋았겠다.
④ 마음껏 먹어. ⑤ 조심해라.

여: Paul, 지난 설에 조부모님 댁에 갔었니?
남: 응, 갔었어. 너는?
여: 아니, 갈 수 없었어, 왜냐하면 아팠거든.
남: 저런! 안됐구나.
여: 그래서, 거기서 넌 뭘 했어?
남: 나는 많은 음식을 먹고 게임도 했어. 재미있었어.
여: 좋았겠다.

단·어·및·표·현

sick [sik] [형] 아픈
fun [fʌn] [형] 재미있는 [명] 재미

20 알맞은응답찾기 ▶ 정답 ⑤

듣·기·대·본

M: Do you enjoy cooking?
W: I love cooking! Here's a photo of a dish I made yesterday.
M: Amazing! What is it?

W: Homemade lasagna with meat sauce.
M: Looks so yummy! Did you follow a recipe?
W: Yes. It's a family recipe that I've been using for years.
M: Looks tasty! I want to try it someday.
W: Sure, I'll cook it for you sometime!

우·리·말·해·석

① 좋은 시도였어.
② 너는 좋은 요리사야! (너는 요리를 잘하는구나!)
③ 내가 음식의 사진을 찍어 줄게.
④ 내가 너의 요리법을 받을 수 있을까?
⑤ 물론이지, 내가 언젠가 너를 위해 그것을 요리해줄게!

남: 넌 요리하는 걸 즐기니?
여: 나는 요리하는 게 좋아! 여기 내가 어제 만든 요리의 사진이야.
남: 놀라운걸! 이게 뭐야?
여: 집에서 만든 미트 소스 라자냐야.
남: 엄청 맛있어 보인다! 너는 요리법을 따라했니?
여: 응, 내가 다년간 이용해 온 가족 요리법이야.
남: 맛있어 보인다! 나는 언젠가 그걸 먹어보고 싶어.
여: 물론이지, 내가 언젠가 너를 위해 그것을 요리해줄게!

단·어·및·표·현

homemade [hóumméid] [형] 집에서 만든, 손수 만든
yummy [jʌ́mi] [형] 맛있는
follow [fálou] [동] 따라하다, 따르다
recipe [résəpìː] [명] 요리법
try [trai] [동] 먹어보다

Words & Expressions Review

1. (여기 저기) 돌아다니다	2. 고장 난, 부서진	3. 스트레칭 하다, 펴다
4. 사과	5. 외출하다, 밖으로 나가다	6. 실내의
7. 연습하다	8. 책가방	9. 반드시 ~하다, 확실히 하다
10. 수영하러 가다	11. 줄무늬	12. 시설
13. 수영장	14. (미래의) 언젠가	15. 그 밖에 또 다른 것
16. 전통적인, 전통의	17. 이상한	18. 먹어보다
19. ~을 생각하다	20. 안약, 점안액	21. 축제
22. 활짝 열린	23. 설날	24. 복사본
25. 노력	26. 한 번에	27. 작품
28. 싼, 저렴한	29. ~동안, 내내	30. 아픈, 따가운
31. 따라하다, 따르다	32. 에어컨	33. 두꺼운
34. 역사적인, 역사의	35. 문제가 있는	36. 자선, 자선 단체
37. 인상적인, 감명 깊은	38. 요리법	39. 중고의
40. 유적, 장소, 위치	41. 내려보다, 내려다보다	42. 너무 ~하고 싶다
43. 화가	44. 가져오다, 데려오다	

Listening Test

영어듣기 모의고사 15회

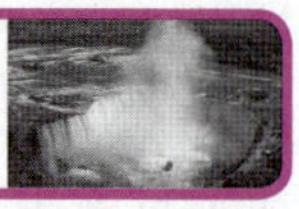

|정|답|

01 ④	02 ②	03 ④	04 ①	05 ⑤
06 ③	07 ④	08 ④	09 ②	10 ③
11 ⑤	12 ②	13 ②	14 ②	15 ④
16 ①	17 ④	18 ③	19 ④	20 ①

01 그림정보파악(담화) ▶ 정답 ④

듣·기·대·본

W: You can use this when you drink something. This is usually long and thin. You suck the drink into your mouth with this. This is a tube usually made of plastic or waterproof paper. What is this?

우·리·말·해·석

여: 당신은 당신이 무언가를 마실 때 이것을 사용할 수 있습니다. 이것은 보통 길고 얇습니다. 당신은 이것으로 음료를 당신의 입으로 빨아들입니다. 이것은 보통 플라스틱이나 방수 종이로 만든 관입니다. 이것은 무엇일까요?

단·어·및·표·현

drink [driŋk] [동] 마시다 [명] 음료
suck [sʌk] [동] 빨아 마시다[먹다]
made of ~로 만든
waterproof [wɔ́ːtərprùːf] [형] 방수의

02 그림정보파악(대화) ▶ 정답 ②

듣·기·대·본

M: Hi, I am looking for a teddy bear for my daughter's birthday.
W: Oh, okay. How about this one with a big heart?
M: She already has that one.
W: Okay. How about this one with a moon on it? It's a new design.
M: That's cute. But do you have one with flowers on it?
W: We do! Here it is.
M: It's lovely! I'll take it.

우·리·말·해·석

남: 안녕하세요, 저는 제 딸의 생일선물로 줄 곰 인형을 찾고 있어요.
여: 오, 알겠어요. 큰 하트 하나가 있는 이것은 어떠세요?
남: 그녀는 이미 그것을 가지고 있어요.
여: 그렇군요. 달 하나가 그려져 있는 이것은 어떠신가요? 새로운 디자인이에요.
남: 그거 귀엽네요. 그런데 그것에 꽃들이 그려진 것이 있나요?
여: 있습니다! 여기 있어요.
남: 너무 사랑스럽네요! 저는 그걸로 선택할게요.

단·어·및·표·현

daughter [dɔ́ːtər] [명] 딸
lovely [lʌ́vli] [형] 사랑스러운, 아름다운
take [teik] [동] 선택하다, 사다

03 날씨파악-그림 ▶ 정답 ④

듣·기·대·본

W: Taking a look at today's weather, we have cloudy skies

this morning with a <u>seventy percent chance</u> of showers this afternoon. <u>Tomorrow is expected to be warmer</u> than today with clear, sunny skies. Please prepare an umbrella when you go out today.

우·리·말·해·석

여: 오늘 날씨를 보시면, 오늘 아침은 하늘에 구름이 끼겠으며 오후에는 소나기가 올 가능성이 70퍼센트가 되겠습니다. 내일은 오늘보다 더 따뜻하며 맑고 청명한 하늘이 예상됩니다. 오늘 외출 시에는 우산을 준비하시기 바랍니다.

단·어·및·표·현

take a look at ~ ~을 보다
be expected to + 동사원형 ~할 것으로 예상되다
prepare[pripέər] 동 준비하다

04 마지막말의도파악 ▶ 정답 ①

듣·기·대·본

M: Did you say something, Nina?
W: Yes. I said, "<u>Turn down</u> the music a little."
M: Oh, I didn't hear that. Sorry.
W: You didn't hear what I said because the music was too loud. I'm <u>trying to study</u> here.
M: Sorry again. I <u>lowered</u> the volume.
W: Thank you. <u>Just try not to play the music too loudly.</u>

우·리·말·해·석

남: 너 무슨 말 했니, Nina?
여: 응. 나는 "음악 소리 좀 줄여."라고 말했어.
남: 아, 못 들었어. 미안해.
여: 그 음악이 너무 시끄러워서 너는 내가 말한 걸 못 들었잖아. 나 지금 공부하려고 해.
남: 다시 한번 미안해. 나는 볼륨을 줄였어.
여: 고마워. 그냥 음악을 너무 크게 틀지 않도록 해 줘.

단·어·및·표·현

turn down (소리·온도 등을) 낮추다
here[hiər] 부 지금, 이 순간에, 여기에
lower[lóuər] 동 ~을 내리다[낮추다]

05 담화미언급 ▶ 정답 ⑤

듣·기·대·본

M: Hi, everyone. I'm Minsu. I'm pleased to meet you. Today is my first day at this school. I've just moved here from Daegu. I live with my parents and an older brother. I like math. My hobby is playing baseball. I think we are going to be good friends. Thank you.

우·리·말·해·석

남: 안녕, 얘들아. 나는 민수야. 너희를 만나게 돼서 기뻐. 오늘은 내가 이 학교에서 보내는 첫날이야. 나는 대구에서 막 여기로 이사 왔어. 나는 부모님과 형이랑 함께 살고 있어. 나는 수학을 좋아해. 취미는 야구를 하는 거야. 나는 우리가 좋은 친구가 될 거라고 생각해. 고마워.

단·어·및·표·현

hobby[hάbi] 명 취미

🦻 LISTENING ADVICE

'd'나 't'가 연속되는 두 단어의 자음 사이에 올 때, [d] 소리와 [t] 소리는 종종 탈락되곤 합니다. 'I'm pleased to meet you'에서 'pleased to'를 살펴보면 자음 's'와 't'사이에 'd'가 있으므로 [플리즈드 투]가 아닌 [플리즈투]와 같이 자연스럽게 연결되어 들립니다.

06 수치파악 ▶ 정답 ③

듣·기·대·본

[Cellphone rings.]
W: Tyler, are you at the airport now?
M: Yes, I <u>got here</u> at 1 p.m.
W: What time is your <u>flight</u>?
M: It's at 3 p.m.
W: It's 2 p.m. now. So, you have about an hour before you <u>take off</u>.
M: That's right. I'm just <u>relaxing</u> at the gate now.

우·리·말·해·석

[휴대폰이 울린다.]
여: Tyler, 너 지금 공항에 있어?
남: 응, 나는 여기에 오후 1시에 도착했어.
여: 너의 항공편은 몇 시야?
남: 오후 3시야.
여: 지금은 오후 2시야. 그러니까, 너는 이륙하기 전에 한 시간 정도 있네.
남: 맞아. 나는 지금 그냥 게이트에서 쉬고 있어.

단·어·및·표·현

airport[έərpɔ̀:rt] 명 공항
flight[flait] 명 항공편
take off 이륙하다
relax[rilǽks] 동 느긋이 쉬다, 휴식을 취하다
gate[geit] 명 (공항의) 게이트, 탑승구

07 장래희망추론 ▶ 정답 ④

듣·기·대·본

W: What do you want to be in the future?
M: You know that I <u>love singing</u>. I'd like to be a singer. What about you?
W: When I was young, I wanted to be a ballerina. However, now I like traveling, so I've <u>changed my mind</u>.
M: You mean you want to be <u>a tour guide</u>?
W: No, <u>I want to be a flight attendant.</u>

우·리·말·해·석

여: 너 장래에 무엇이 되고 싶니?
남: 너는 내가 노래 부르는 것을 무지 좋아한다는 것 알잖아. 나는 가수가 되고 싶어. 너는 어때?
여: 어렸을 때는 나는 발레리나가 되고 싶었어. 하지만 지금은 여행하는 걸 좋아해서 마음을 바꿨어.
남: 너 관광 가이드가 되고 싶다는 거니?
여: 아니, 나는 비행기 승무원이 되고 싶어.

단·어·및·표·현

change one's mind 마음·생각을 바꾸다
flight attendant 비행기 승무원

08 심정추론 ▶ 정답 ④

듣·기·대·본

M: What's up? <u>You keep smiling.</u>
W: My dad is back! It's his first day home from the hospital.
M: Oh, that's good. How's your dad feeling?
W: He is <u>much better</u>. I can't wait to have dinner all together at home.
M: You must be <u>thrilled</u>! Have a wonderful evening with your family.
W: Thanks! I will.

우·리·말·해·석

① 지루한　② 걱정스러운　③ 무서운
④ 행복한　⑤ 당황스러운

남: 무슨 일이야? 너 계속 웃고 있잖아.
여: 우리 아버지가 돌아오셨어! 병원에서 퇴원하신 첫날이야.
남: 오, 잘됐구나. 아버지는 어떠시니?
여: 훨씬 더 나아지셨어. 빨리 집에서 다 함께 저녁을 먹고 싶어.
남: 너 분명 설레겠다! 가족과 멋진 저녁을 보내.
여: 고마워! 그럴게.

단·어·및·표·현

keep -ing 계속 ~하다

09 할일파악(대화직후) ▶ 정답 ②

듣·기·대·본

M: Honey, do you remember where we keep our spare batteries?
W: They're in our bedroom drawer.
M: I checked the drawer, but they weren't there.
W: I guess we've run out of spare batteries, then.
M: Hmm… That's not good.
W: Let's buy some next time we're at the store.
M: It's urgent. I'll head out and buy some right now.

우·리·말·해·석

남: 여보, 당신은 우리가 우리의 여분의 건전지를 어디에 보관하는지 기억해요?
여: 그것들은 우리 침실 서랍에 있어요.
남: 제가 서랍을 확인했는데, 그것들은 거기에 없었어요.
여: 그러면 우리는 여분의 건전지를 다 써버린 것 같네요.
남: 음… 그건 좋지 않군요.
여: 다음 번에 우리가 가게에 가면 좀 사죠.
남: 시급해요. 저는 지금 당장 나가서 좀 사 올게요.

단·어·및·표·현

drawer [drɔːr] [명] 서랍
run out of ~ ~을 다 써버리다, ~이 고갈되다
urgent [ə́ːrdʒənt] [형] 시급한, 긴급한
head out 나가다, 출발하다

10 대화화제추론 ▶ 정답 ③

듣·기·대·본

W: Did you see the poster on the wall?
M: You mean the one about the new school lunch menu?
W: Yeah, we have to choose a dessert menu for Christmas Eve.
M: Yes, I saw it. There are two options on the menu, chocolate cake and banana waffles.
W: I want the chocolate cake. I love sweet dessert.
M: I haven't decided yet. They both look delicious.

우·리·말·해·석

여: 너 벽에 붙은 포스터 봤니?
남: 새로운 학교 점심 메뉴에 관한 것 말이니?
여: 응, 우리는 크리스마스 이브의 디저트 메뉴를 선택해야 해.
남: 응, 나는 그것을 봤어. 메뉴에는 초콜릿 케이크와 바나나 와플 두 가지 선택지가 있어.
여: 나는 초콜릿 케이크를 원해. 나는 달콤한 디저트를 정말 좋아해.
남: 나는 아직 결정하지 못했어. 그것들은 둘 다 맛있어 보여.

단·어·및·표·현

have to + 동사원형 ~해야 한다
option [ɑ́pʃən] [명] 선택지, 선택

11 특정정보파악(교통수단) ▶ 정답 ⑤

듣·기·대·본

W: Why don't we go to 'Happy Beach' this weekend?
M: Great idea. I'll book our train tickets.
W: It takes four hours by train, right? That's quite a long trip.
M: Do you want to take an airplane, then? It's only a one-hour flight and tickets are cheap these days.
W: Really? Let's take the plane then.

우·리·말·해·석

여: 우리 이번 주말에 'Happy Beach'에 가는 거 어때?
남: 좋은 생각이다. 나는 우리의 기차 표들을 예약할게.
여: 기차로 4시간 걸리지, 맞지? 그건 꽤 긴 여행이야.
남: 그러면 너는 비행기를 타기를 원해? 그건 겨우 한 시간짜리 비행이고 요즘엔 표들이 싸.
여: 정말? 그러면 비행기를 타자.

단·어·및·표·현

book [buk] [동] 예약하다
take [teik] [동] (얼마의 시간이) 걸리다, (교통수단 · 도로 등을) 타다
flight [flait] [명] 비행, 여행
cheap [tʃiːp] [형] 싼, 저렴한

12 이유파악 ▶ 정답 ②

듣·기·대·본

W: Dad, can I go to the swimming pool with my friends on Friday?
M: On Friday? No, I'm afraid you can't.
W: Why not?
M: You have to go to the dentist on Friday.
W: Do I? I thought it was Wednesday.
M: Your mom couldn't make it on Wednesday so she changed your appointment to Friday.
W: Oh, I forgot. Then I'll have to go to the swimming pool on another day.
M: Yes.

우·리·말·해·석

여: 아빠, 저 금요일에 제 친구들과 수영장에 가도 돼요?
남: 금요일에? 아니, 안 될 것 같구나.
여: 왜 안 돼요?
남: 너는 금요일에 치과에 가야해.
여: 제가요? 저는 (치과 예약이) 수요일이었다고 생각했어요.
남: 네 엄마가 수요일에 갈 수 없어서 그녀가 네 예약을 금요일로 바꿨어.
여: 아, 제가 잊었어요. 그러면 저는 다른 날에 수영장에 가야겠네요.
남: 그래.

단·어·및·표·현

appointment [əpɔ́intmənt] [명] 예약, 약속

13 대화장소추론 ▶ 정답 ②

듣·기·대·본

M: Can I take your order, ma'am?
W: Yes. I'll have the vegetable soup and the beef steak.
M: How do you want your steak?

W: I want it well-done.
M: Okay. Do you need something to drink?
W: Just water, please.

우·리·말·해·석
남: 주문하시겠습니까, 손님?
여: 네. 채소 수프와 쇠고기 스테이크로 하겠어요.
남: 스테이크는 어떻게 익혀 드릴까요?
여: 완전히 익혀 주세요.
남: 알겠습니다. 마실 것이 필요하십니까?
여: 그냥 물 주세요.

단·어·및·표·현
order[ɔ́ːrdər] 명 주문

14 그림정보파악–지도 ▶ 정답 ②

듣·기·대·본
M: Excuse me. Is there a movie theater near here?
W: Yes, there is one nearby.
M: How can I get there from here?
W: Go straight for one block and then turn left on Green Street.
M: On Green Street?
W: Yes. The movie theater will be on your right. It's next to the police station.

우·리·말·해·석
남: 실례합니다. 여기 근처에 영화관이 있나요?
여: 네, 근처에 하나 있어요.
남: 여기서 거기에 어떻게 가나요?
여: 한 블록 직진한 다음 Green Street에서 왼쪽으로 도세요.
남: Green Street에서요?
여: 네. 그 영화관은 당신의 오른쪽에 있을 거예요. 그것은 경찰서 옆에 있어요.

단·어·및·표·현
movie theater 영화관
nearby[níərbái] 부 근처에, 가까이에

15 부탁(요청)한일파악 ▶ 정답 ④

듣·기·대·본
M: Excuse me. Can you help me?
W: Sure. What do you need?
M: Would you take a picture of me in front of the museum?
W: Okay. Do you want the whole building in the picture?
M: That would be great. Thank you.

우·리·말·해·석
남: 실례합니다. 절 도와주실 수 있나요?
여: 물론이죠. 무엇이 필요하시죠?
남: 박물관 앞에서 제 사진을 찍어 주시겠어요?
여: 알겠어요. 사진에 건물 전체가 나오길 바라시나요?
남: 그러면 좋겠네요. 감사합니다.

단·어·및·표·현
Would you ~? ~해 주시겠어요?

16 제안파악 ▶ 정답 ①

듣·기·대·본
M: Look. My new neighbors left these at the door.
W: Fresh oranges! How kind of them!

M: There's this note saying hi, too.
W: They must be nice people.
M: I should do something. What can I buy them?
W: Instead of buying something, how about making cookies? You're good at baking.
M: That's a good idea.

우·리·말·해·석
남: 봐. 내 새 이웃이 이것들을 문 앞에 뒀어.
여: 신선한 오렌지네! 정말 친절하다!
남: 인사말을 건네는 쪽지도 있어.
여: 그들은 착한 사람들임이 틀림없어.
남: 나는 뭔가를 해야겠어. 내가 그들에게 무엇을 사줄 수 있을까?
여: 무언가를 사는 대신에 쿠키를 만드는 건 어때? 너는 (과자) 굽는 것을 잘하잖아.
남: 그거 좋은 생각이다.

단·어·및·표·현
neighbor[néibər] 명 이웃, 가까이 있는 사람
instead of ~ 대신에
be good at ~을 잘하다

17 한일파악 ▶ 정답 ④

듣·기·대·본
W: Phil, what did you do last weekend?
M: I did some spring cleaning in my room last weekend.
W: Nice! How was it?
M: It was worth it. I even found some photos of me when I was a baby.
W: Cool! It must be refreshing to have a clean room.
M: Yeah. I'm glad I did the cleaning.

우·리·말·해·석
여: Phil, 너는 지난 주말에 뭐했니?
남: 나는 지난 주말에 내 방에서 봄맞이 대청소를 좀 했어.
여: 잘했다! 그것은 어땠어?
남: 그것은 그만한 가치가 있었어. 나는 심지어 내가 아기였을 때 사진들도 몇 장 발견했어.
여: 멋진데! 깨끗한 방을 갖는 것은 틀림없이 상쾌할 거야.
남: 응. 내가 청소를 했다는 것이 기뻐.

단·어·및·표·현
spring cleaning (봄에 하는) 대청소
worth[wəːrθ] 형 ~할 가치가 있는
refreshing[rifréʃiŋ] 형 상쾌한, 산뜻한

18 직업추론 ▶ 정답 ③

듣·기·대·본
M: Hello, Ms. Blake. What seems to be the problem today?
W: I have a severe toothache.
M: Okay, let me take a look first. Open your mouth, please.
W: Sure. Ah...
M: Hmm... It seems that you've got a bad tooth here.
W: Oh no! Do you have to pull the tooth out?
M: No need for that. It does need treatment, though.

우·리·말·해·석
남: 안녕하세요, Blake씨. 오늘 무엇이 문제인 것 같은가요?
여: 저는 심한 치통이 있어요.
남: 네, 제가 먼저 보겠습니다. 입을 벌리세요.
여: 그럼요. 아…

남: 흠… 여기에 충치가 하나 있는 것 같아요.
여: 아, 안 돼요! 이를 뽑아야 하나요?
남: 그럴 필요는 없습니다. 하지만 치료가 필요합니다.

단·어·및·표·현
severe [sivíər] 휑 심한, 심각한
treatment [trí:tmənt] 휑 치료

19 알맞은응답찾기 ▶ 정답 ④

듣·기·대·본
[Cellphone rings.]
M: Hello.
W: Hello, Troy. This is McKenzie.
M: Hey, what's up?
W: We should <u>meet up</u> for our group project.
M: Right. Did you talk to the others?
W: Yes. They are all <u>free</u> on Saturday afternoon. Can you come?
M: Of course, I can. Where are we going to meet?
W: My place, at 2 p.m.

우·리·말·해·석
① 나는 이미 내 과제를 끝냈어.
② 내 취미는 독서야.
③ 미안하지만, 그럴 수 없어.
④ 우리 집에서, 오후 2시에.
⑤ 그것은 내 잘못이 아니야.

[휴대전화가 울린다.]
남: 여보세요.
여: 여보세요, Troy. 나는 McKenzie야.
남: 야, 무슨 일이야?
여: 우리는 우리의 조별 과제를 위해 만나야 해.
남: 맞아. 너는 나머지 사람들과 얘기했어?
여: 응. 그들은 모두 토요일 오후에 한가해. 너도 올 수 있어?
남: 물론, 갈 수 있지. 우리는 어디서 만날까?
여: 우리 집에서, 오후 2시에.

단·어·및·표·현
meet up (~와) 만나다
group project 조별 과제
free [fri:] 휑 한가한, 다른 계획이 없는

20 알맞은응답찾기 ▶ 정답 ①

듣·기·대·본
M: It was delicious.
W: Yes, it really was. Excuse me, can I <u>have the check</u>, please?
M: Oh, no!
W: What's wrong, Larry?
M: I <u>forgot</u> to bring my wallet!
W: Don't worry. I'll treat you this time.
M: I'm so sorry. I'll pay next time.

우·리·말·해·석
① 정말 미안해. 다음엔 내가 낼게.　② 천만에. 다음에 봐.
③ 그 음식 어떻게 생각해?　④ 나 배고파. 지금 주문하자.
⑤ 나 늦을 거야.

남: 맛있었어.
여: 응. 정말 맛있었어. 저기요, 계산서 가져다주시겠어요?

남: 오, 이런!
여: 무슨 일이야, Larry?
남: 지갑 가져오는 걸 잊어버렸어!
여: 걱정하지 마. 이번엔 내가 대접할게.
남: 정말 미안해. 다음엔 내가 낼게.

단·어·및·표·현
What's wrong? 무슨 일이야?

Words & Expressions Review

1. 마음을 바꾸다	2. 사랑스러운, 아름다운	3. 훨씬 나은
4. 치통	5. 준비하다	6. 지금, 이 순간에, 여기에
7. 선택하다, 사다, (시간이) 걸리다, (교통수단·도로 등을) 타다	8. 치과 의사	9. 시급한, 긴급한
10. 영화관	11. 예약, 약속	12. 예약하다
13. ~ 대신에	14. 서랍	15. 채소
16. 완전히 익힌	17. 전체의, 완전히	18. 선택지, 선택
19. ~을 잘하다	20. ~할 가치가 있는	21. (공항의) 게이트, 탑승구
22. 치료	23. 마시다, 음료	24. ~할 것으로 예상되다
25. 기쁜	26. (소리·온도 등을) 낮추다	27. 비행, 여행
28. 주문	29. 공항	30. 심한, 심각한
31. ~와 만나다	32. 꽤, 상당히	33. 대접하다
34. 이륙하다	35. 박물관	36. ~으로 만든
37. ~을 다 써버리다, ~이 고갈되다	38. 조별 과제	39. 방수의
40. 이웃, 가까이 있는 사람	41. (돈을) 내다	42. (봄에 하는) 대청소
43. 느긋이 쉬다, 휴식을 취하다	44. 상쾌한, 산뜻한	

Listening Test
영어듣기 모의고사 16회

|정|답|

01 ①	02 ③	03 ②	04 ⑤	05 ④
06 ④	07 ①	08 ⑤	09 ④	10 ②
11 ③	12 ⑤	13 ②	14 ①	15 ②
16 ③	17 ③	18 ⑤	19 ④	20 ②

01 그림정보파악(담화) ▶ 정답 ①

듣·기·대·본
M: I have six legs and <u>two pairs of wings</u>. I'm brown, but there are others who are grey. I am active at night and fly around bright lights. I look a lot like a butterfly. What am I?

우·리·말·해·석

남: 나는 여섯 개의 다리와 두 쌍의 날개가 있다. 나는 갈색이지만, 회색인 다른 것들도 있다. 나는 밤에 활동적이고 밝은 빛 주변을 날아다닌다. 나는 나비와 굉장히 비슷하게 생겼다. 나는 무엇일까?

단·어·및·표·현

active [ǽktiv] [형] 활동적인
look like ~와 비슷하게 생기다
a lot 굉장히

02 그림정보파악(대화) ▶ 정답 ③

듣·기·대·본

M: How can I help you?
W: I'm looking for cargo shorts for my son.
M: How about these checkered ones?
W: I think he would prefer something simpler. Do you have any plain ones?
M: Yes, how about these plain cargo shorts with extra pockets?
W: Perfect! I'll take them.

우·리·말·해·석

남: 어떻게 도와드릴까요?
여: 전 제 아들을 위한 카고 반바지를 찾고 있어요.
남: 이 체크무늬는 어떠세요?
여: 제 아들은 더 단순한 걸 더 좋아할 것 같아요. 무늬 없는 거 있나요?
남: 네, 주머니가 추가로 있는 이 무늬 없는 카고 반바지는 어떠세요?
여: 완벽하네요! 이걸로 할게요.

단·어·및·표·현

shorts [ʃɔːrts] [명] 반바지
prefer [prifə́ːr] [동] 선호하다, 좋아하다
plain [plein] [형] 무늬가 없는, 수수한
extra [ékstrə] [형] 추가의, 여분의

03 날씨파악-그림 ▶ 정답 ②

듣·기·대·본

W: Good morning. This is the daily weather report. Yesterday, it was cloudy and windy. But today, the sky will be sunny and clear with no clouds. Starting tomorrow, it'll be rainy for the rest of the week. Have a great day!

우·리·말·해·석

여: 좋은 아침입니다. 일일 일기예보입니다. 어제, 흐리고 바람이 많이 불었습니다. 하지만 오늘, 하늘은 화창하고 구름 한 점 없이 맑을 것입니다. 내일부터, 이번 주 내내 비가 올 것입니다. 좋은 하루 보내세요!

단·어·및·표·현

weather report 일기예보
for the rest of ~내내, ~의 나머지 동안

04 마지막말의도파악 ▶ 정답 ⑤

듣·기·대·본

M: Congratulations, Somin. I heard your basketball team came in second at the championship game.
W: Thanks, Juho. But we nearly won the championship.
M: What do you mean?
W: I made a huge mistake at the end of the game. I didn't know what to say to my teammates.
M: Well, everyone makes mistakes and second place is still something to be proud of.

우·리·말·해·석

남: 축하해, 소민아. 나는 너의 농구 팀이 챔피언전에서 준우승했다고 들었어.
여: 고마워, 주호야. 하지만 우리는 거의 우승할 뻔했어.
남: 무슨 말이야?
여: 내가 경기 끝 무렵에 큰 실수를 했어. 나는 내 팀 동료들에게 뭐라고 말해야 할지 몰랐어.
남: 음, 모든 사람은 실수를 하고 2등은 여전히 자랑스러워할 만한 거야.

단·어·및·표·현

make a mistake 실수하다
second place 2등

05 담화미언급 ▶ 정답 ④

듣·기·대·본

M: Let me tell you about the Summer Dance Contest at West Hill Park. It'll be on July 2. Twenty people are participating and will put on wonderful performances. The contest will last for three hours between 5 p.m. and 8 p.m. It will be a great event, so don't miss out on it!

우·리·말·해·석

남: West Hill 공원에서의 여름 댄스 대회에 대해 말씀드리겠습니다. 그것은 7월 2일에 있을 예정입니다. 20명의 사람들이 참가하고 훌륭한 공연을 보여줄 것입니다. 대회는 오후 5시에서 8시 사이에 세 시간 동안 계속될 것입니다. 그것은 굉장한 행사가 될 것이니, 그것을 놓치지 마세요!

단·어·및·표·현

participate [pɑːrtísəpèit] [동] 참가하다
put on 상연하다
miss out on ~ ~을 놓치다

06 수치파악 ▶ 정답 ④

듣·기·대·본

M: Anna, Mac's Smoothies opened a store in our town!
W: Really? Their smoothies are famous!
M: Do you want to go there on Saturday?
W: Sure! I get up at 9 a.m. on weekends. So, let's meet at 10 a.m.
M: But they open at 11 a.m.
W: Let's make it 11 then.
M: Okay. See you at the shop on Saturday.

우·리·말·해·석

남: Anna, Mac's Smoothies가 우리 동네에 가게를 열었대!
여: 정말? 그들의 스무디는 유명하잖아!
남: 너는 토요일에 그곳에 가고 싶어?
여: 물론이지! 나는 주말에 오전 9시에 일어나. 그러니, 오전 10시에 만나자.
남: 하지만 그들은 오전 11시에 열어.
여: 그러면 11시에 맞춰 가자.
남: 그래. 토요일에 가게에서 보자.

단·어·및·표·현

famous [féiməs] [형] 유명한
get up 일어나다
make it 시간 맞춰 가다

07 장래희망추론 ▶ 정답 ①

듣·기·대·본

W: Tommy, what do you want to be when you <u>grow up</u>?
M: Well, I want to help other people, just like my dad.
W: Oh, you want to be a <u>police officer</u> like your dad?
M: I'd like to. What about you, Lisa?
W: I want to help other people, just <u>like you</u>. I want to be a doctor.
M: You'll be a wonderful doctor.

우·리·말·해·석

여: Tommy, 넌 커서 뭐가 되고 싶니?
남: 음, 나는 우리 아버지처럼 다른 사람들을 돕고 싶어.
여: 아, 너의 아버지처럼 경찰관이 되고 싶은 거야?
남: 그러고 싶어. Lisa 너는?
여: 나도 너처럼 다른 사람들을 돕고 싶어. 난 의사가 되고 싶어.
남: 넌 훌륭한 의사가 될 거야.

단·어·및·표·현

like [laik] 전 ~처럼

08 심정추론 ▶ 정답 ⑤

듣·기·대·본

W: Excuse me, sir. You cannot go into the pool without a swimming cap.
M: Oh, but I <u>forgot to bring</u> it here today. Can I borrow one?
W: I'm sorry. We <u>only sell them</u>.
M: How much is it?
W: It's $50.
M: What! <u>That's too expensive</u>. And I already have lots of them at home.

우·리·말·해·석

여: 실례합니다, 선생님. 수영모 없이는 풀장에 들어가실 수 없습니다.
남: 오, 하지만 오늘 제가 그것을 가져오는 걸 잊었어요. 하나 대여할 수 있을까요?
여: 죄송합니다. 저희는 판매만 합니다.
남: 얼마요?
여: 50달러입니다.
남: 뭐라고요! 너무 비싸네요. 그리고 저는 집에 이미 수영모를 많이 가지고 있다고요.

단·어·및·표·현

borrow [bárou] 동 대여하다, 빌리다

09 할일파악(대화직후) ▶ 정답 ④

듣·기·대·본

M: Oh no, the bakery is closed, Christine.
W: That's <u>disappointing</u>. What should we do for dessert?
M: How about making some cookies?
W: That sounds <u>delicious</u>! Do you have a good recipe?
M: Yes, but I'm not sure if we have all the <u>ingredients</u>.
W: <u>Let's check</u> the kitchen and see what we have.

우·리·말·해·석

남: 오 안돼, 제과점이 문을 닫았어, Christine.
여: 그거 실망스러운걸. 우리는 디저트로 무엇을 해야 하지?
남: 쿠키를 좀 만드는 건 어때?
여: 그거 맛있겠다! 너는 좋은 요리법이 있니?
남: 응, 하지만 우리가 모든 재료를 가지고 있는지 확실하지 않아.
여: 부엌을 확인해보고 우리가 가지고 있는 것을 보자.

단·어·및·표·현

disappointing [dìsəpɔ́intiŋ] 형 실망스러운
delicious [dilíʃəs] 형 맛있는
recipe [résəpì:] 명 요리법
ingredient [ingrí:diənt] 명 재료

10 대화화제추론 ▶ 정답 ②

듣·기·대·본

W: Kevin, why are you <u>collecting</u> all these plastic bottles?
M: I'm helping with the <u>school recycling campaign</u>, Mom.
W: Oh, that's great! What are you going to do with the bottles?
M: We're going to make a big <u>art piece</u> with recycled materials.
W: That sounds fun. Do you need any help cleaning the bottles?
M: Yes, please. Thanks for helping me!

우·리·말·해·석

여: Kevin, 넌 왜 이 플라스틱 병들을 다 모으고 있니?
남: 전 학교 재활용 캠페인을 돕고 있어요, 엄마.
여: 오, 그거 좋네! 너희들은 그 병들로 뭐 할 거니?
남: 저흰 재활용 재료로 큰 예술 작품을 만들 거예요.
여: 재미있겠다. 너는 병을 닦는 데 도움이 필요하니?
남: 네, 부탁드려요. 도와주셔서 고마워요!

단·어·및·표·현

collect [kəlékt] 동 모으다
bottle [bátl] 명 병
recycle [ri:sáikl] 동 재활용하다
piece [pi:s] 명 작품
material [mətí:əriəl] 명 재료

11 특정정보파악(교통수단) ▶ 정답 ③

듣·기·대·본

M: Mom, how are we getting to the restaurant this evening?
W: Well, we can't go <u>by car</u>. Dad took it.
M: Then, let's go by bus.
W: In fact, I was thinking of getting there <u>on foot</u>.
M: Really?
W: It's only a 30-minute walk, and you need <u>exercise</u>.
M: All right, then.

우·리·말·해·석

남: 엄마, 우리 오늘 저녁에 식당에 어떻게 가요?
여: 음, 우리는 차로 못 가. 아빠가 그것을 가져가셨어.
남: 그러면, 버스로 가죠.
여: 사실, 나는 그곳에 걸어서 가려고 생각했었어.
남: 정말요?
여: 걸어서 단 30분 거리에 있고, 너는 운동이 필요해.
남: 그러면, 알겠어요.

단·어·및·표·현

take [teik] 동 가지고 가다
on foot 걸어서, 도보로
exercise [éksərsàiz] 명 운동

12 이유파악 ▶ 정답 ⑤

듣·기·대·본

W: I'm going shopping now. Will you come with me?
M: Okay. What do you need to buy?
W: I want to buy a birthday present for Carol. But I don't know what to buy.
M: How about earrings? She's always wearing accessories. I think she'll like it.
W: That's a great idea! Thank you.
M: It's my pleasure.

우·리·말·해·석

여: 나 지금 쇼핑 가려고 하는데. 같이 갈래?
남: 좋아. 뭘 사야 하는데?
여: Carol에게 줄 생일 선물을 사고 싶어. 하지만 뭘 사야 할지 모르겠어.
남: 귀걸이는 어때? 그녀는 늘 액세서리를 하고 있잖아. 그녀가 좋아할 것 같은데.
여: 그거 좋은 생각이야! 고마워.
남: 천만에.

단·어·및·표·현

what to + 동사원형 무엇을 ~해야 할지

LISTENING ADVICE

'I want to buy a birthday present for Carol.'에서 'present'는 '선물'의 의미로 쓰였지만 다양한 뜻을 가진 다의어입니다. present는 명사로는 '선물, 현재'라는 의미를, 동사로는 '주다, 제시하다, 보여주다'라는 의미를 가집니다. 다의어는 앞뒤 문맥 및 문장의 흐름을 통해 그 뜻을 파악해야 합니다. 또한 동일한 단어일지라도 강세를 다르게 두는데 present가 명사일 때는 [préznt], 즉 첫 번째 e에 강세를 두어 [프레즌ㅌ]로 발음되고, 동사일 때는 [prizént], 즉 두 번째 e에 강세를 두어 [프리젠ㅌ]로 발음됩니다.

13 대화장소추론 ▶ 정답 ②

듣·기·대·본

M: Hi, how can I help you?
W: I'm looking for an apartment to rent.
M: Have a seat here. What area are you interested in?
W: I'm interested in the Seocho-dong area.
M: Can you tell me what kind of place you are looking for?
W: I need a two-bedroom apartment.
M: Okay, let me see what we have.

우·리·말·해·석

남: 안녕하세요, 무엇을 도와드릴까요?
여: 저는 임대할 아파트 한 채를 찾고 있어요.
남: 여기 앉으세요. 당신은 어느 지역에 관심이 있으세요?
여: 저는 서초동 지역에 관심이 있어요.
남: 당신은 어떤 종류의 장소를 찾고 있는지 저에게 말해주실 수 있나요?
여: 저는 방 두 개짜리 아파트가 필요해요.
남: 네, 저희가 가지고 있는 걸 확인해볼게요.

단·어·및·표·현

look for ~ ~을 찾다
rent [rent] [동] 임대하다, 빌리다
be interested in ~ ~에 관심이 있다

14 그림정보파악-지도 ▶ 정답 ①

듣·기·대·본

W: Oliver, I found this purse on the sidewalk. What should I do?
M: You should take it to the police station. There's one nearby.
W: Good idea. Can you give me directions?
M: Sure. Go straight two blocks and turn left on Oak Street.
W: Got it. Turn left on Oak Street.
M: Yes. It will be on your right. It's next to the post office.
W: Thanks!

우·리·말·해·석

여: Oliver, 나는 이 지갑을 인도에서 (우연히) 발견했어. 내가 무엇을 해야 할까?
남: 너는 그것을 경찰서로 갖다줘야 해. 근처에 한 군데가 있어.
여: 좋은 생각이야. 네가 나에게 길을 알려줄 수 있어?
남: 물론이지. 두 블록을 곧장 간 다음에 Oak Street에서 왼쪽으로 돌아.
여: 알겠어. Oak Street에서 왼쪽으로 도는 거구나.
남: 맞아. 그것은 너의 오른편에 있을 거야. 그것은 우체국 옆에 있어.
여: 고마워!

단·어·및·표·현

purse [pəːrs] [명] 지갑
sidewalk [sáidwɔ̀ːk] [명] 인도, 보도
give A directions A에게 길을 알려주다

15 부탁(요청)한일파악 ▶ 정답 ②

듣·기·대·본

[Knock knock]
M: Come in.
W: Hello, Mr. Kim.
M: Hi, Yuna. What brings you here?
W: I have a favor to ask. It's about our sports day next week.
M: Oh, I see. How can I help you?
W: Can you be the referee for the relay race?
M: Sure! I'd be glad to help.
W: Thank you so much. It means a lot to us.

우·리·말·해·석

[똑똑]
남: 들어오렴.
여: 안녕하세요, 김 선생님.
남: 안녕, 유나야. 무슨 일로 왔니?
여: 부탁드릴 일이 있어요. 다음 주 저희 운동회에 관한 거예요.
남: 오, 그렇구나. 어떻게 도와줄까?
여: 계주의 심판을 해 주실 수 있나요?
남: 물론이지! 도울 수 있어 기쁘구나.
여: 정말 감사해요. 저희에게 큰 의미가 있어요.

단·어·및·표·현

sports day 운동회
referee [rèfəríː] [명] 심판

16 제안파악 ▶ 정답 ③

듣·기·대·본

M: I don't feel good today.
W: Why? What's wrong?
M: I played soccer in the rain yesterday and now I keep sneezing and coughing.
W: Oh no! You might have a cold.
M: Yeah, I think so, too.
W: Why don't you see a doctor after school?

우·리·말·해·석

남: 나 오늘 몸이 아픈 것 같아.

여: 왜? 뭐가 잘못됐어?
남: 나는 어제 빗속에서 축구를 했는데 지금 계속 재채기하고 기침을 해.
여: 오, 안 돼! 너는 감기에 걸렸을지도 몰라.
남: 응, 나도 그렇게 생각해.
여: 학교 끝나고 병원에 가보는 게 어때?

단·어·및·표·현

keep -ing 계속 ~하다
sneeze [sniːz] [동] 재채기하다

17 할일파악 ▶ 정답 ③

듣·기·대·본

M: What are you doing this Saturday, Kate?
W: I invited Tammy and In-su to my house. We're having a small party for my birthday.
M: Oh, really? I didn't know this Saturday was your birthday.
W: It's OK.
M: Can I join you? I want to celebrate with you.
W: Sure. I'd be happy if you came.

우·리·말·해·석

남: 너는 이번주 토요일에 뭐하니, Kate?
여: 나는 Tammy와 인수를 내 집에 초대했어. 우리는 내 생일을 위해 작은 파티를 할 거야.
남: 오, 정말? 나는 이번 주 토요일이 네 생일인지 몰랐어.
여: 괜찮아.
남: 나도 함께 해도 돼? 나도 너희들과 함께 축하하고 싶어.
여: 물론이지. 네가 오면 나는 기쁠 거야.

단·어·및·표·현

invite [inváit] [동] 초대하다
join [dʒɔin] [동] 함께 하다, 합류하다
celebrate [séləbrèit] [동] 축하하다, 기념하다

18 직업추론 ▶ 정답 ⑤

듣·기·대·본

W: Can you help me with my backhand?
M: Sure, let's see how you hit the ball.
W: Like this?
M: You need to hold your racket a bit higher.
W: Oh, I get it.
M: Yes, that's it! Now try hitting the ball again.
W: Wow, it feels much better!
M: Good job!

우·리·말·해·석

여: 제가 백핸드를 하는 것을 도와주실 수 있나요?
남: 물론이죠, 당신이 어떻게 공을 치는지 봅시다.
여: 이렇게요?
남: 당신은 라켓을 조금 더 높이 쥐어야 해요.
여: 아, 알겠어요.
남: 그렇죠, 바로 그것입니다! 이제 다시 한번 공을 쳐보세요.
여: 우와, 훨씬 더 나아진 거 같아요!
남: 잘했어요!

단·어·및·표·현

help A with B A가 B하는 것을 돕다
backhand [bǽkhæ̀nd] [명] 백핸드(손등을 공쪽으로 향하게 해서 치는 것)
try -ing 한번 ~해보다

19 알맞은응답찾기 ▶ 정답 ④

듣·기·대·본

M: Excuse me. How can I get to the museum?
W: You can take a bus or the subway.
M: Can't I just walk there?
W: No. It's too far to walk.
M: I see. How long will it take by bus?
W: **It will take half an hour.**

우·리·말·해·석

① 저는 10개를 가질게요. ② 꼭 찾으실 겁니다.
③ 3번을 타세요. ④ 30분 걸릴 거예요.
⑤ 저쪽에 있습니다.

남: 실례합니다. 박물관에 어떻게 가나요?
여: 버스나 지하철을 타고 갈 수 있습니다.
남: 그냥 거기까지 걸어갈 수 없을까요?
여: 아니요. 걷기엔 너무 멀어요.
남: 알겠습니다. 버스로 시간이 얼마나 걸릴까요?
여: 30분 걸릴 거예요.

단·어·및·표·현

take + 시간 (시간이) 걸리다

20 알맞은응답찾기 ▶ 정답 ②

듣·기·대·본

W: Hello. May I help you?
M: Yes, please. I'm looking for these pants in black.
W: Oh, they are on this rack. What size do you need?
M: I wear a size 6.
W: Here they are.
M: Thank you. Can I try them on?
W: **Sure! Come this way.**

우·리·말·해·석

① 물론이죠! 제가 해볼게요. ② 그럼요! 이리로 오세요.
③ 당신은 아무 때나 와도 돼요. ④ 아니요, 우리는 그것들이 없어요.
⑤ 네, 계산대는 저쪽에 있어요.

여: 안녕하세요. 도와드릴까요?
남: 네, 부탁드려요. 저는 이 바지를 검은색으로 찾고 있어요.
여: 오, 그것들은 이 선반에 있어요. 어떤 사이즈가 필요하세요?
남: 저는 사이즈 6을 입어요.
여: 여기 있습니다.
남: 고맙습니다. 제가 입어볼 수 있나요?
여: 그럼요! 이리로 오세요.

단·어·및·표·현

rack [ræk] [명] 선반, 받침대

Words & Expressions Review

1. 운동회	2. A에게 길을 알려주다	3. 무늬가 없는, 수수한
4. 선호하다, 좋아하다	5. (시간이) 걸리다	6. (손으로) 쥐고 있다
7. 활동적인	8. 상연하다	9. 초대하다
10.참가하다	11. 일기예보	12. ~할 필요가 있다
13. 실수하다	14. 작품	15. 액세서리
16. 계속 ~하다	17. 공을 치다	18. 추가의, 여분의
19. (테니스 등의) 라켓	20. 한번 ~해보다	21. ~할 것을 잊다

22. 버스를 타다	23. 축하하다, 기념하다	24. 재료
25. 무엇을 ~해야 할지	26. A가 B하는 것을 돕다	27. 2등
28. 선반, 받침대	29. 함께 하다, 합류하다	30. 지갑
31. ~와 비슷하게 생기다	32. 맛있는	33. 반바지
34. 굉장히	35. ~에 관심이 있다	36. ~처럼
37. 인도, 보도	38. 모으다	39. 가지고 가다
40. ~을 찾다	41. 심판	42. 재채기하다
43. 실망스러운	44. ~내내, ~의 나머지 동안	

Listening Test

영어듣기 모의고사 17회

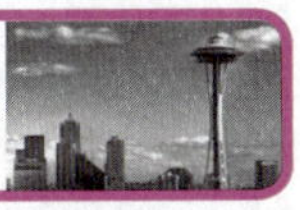

| 정 | 답 |

01 ④	02 ②	03 ①	04 ④	05 ④
06 ②	07 ②	08 ④	09 ⑤	10 ⑤
11 ⑤	12 ⑤	13 ③	14 ⑤	15 ③
16 ②	17 ④	18 ③	19 ①	20 ③

01 그림정보파악(담화) ▶ 정답 ④

듣·기·대·본

M: People's lives became much easier when this was invented. This is an electronic device used with televisions and air conditioners. You can turn on the TV and turn up the volume wirelessly from a short distance with this. What is this?

우·리·말·해·석

남: 이것이 발명되었을 때 사람들의 삶은 훨씬 더 수월해졌습니다. 이것은 텔레비전 그리고 에어컨과 함께 사용되는 전자 기기입니다. 당신은 이것을 가지고 가까운 거리에서 무선으로 TV를 켜고 소리를 키울 수 있습니다. 이것은 무엇일까요?

단·어·및·표·현

electronic [ilektránik] [형] 전자의
device [diváis] [명] 기기

02 그림정보파악(대화) ▶ 정답 ②

듣·기·대·본

W: Can I help you, sir?
M: Yes, I need a diary for my daughter.
W: What about this one with the heart on it? Girls like hearts.
M: Well, she's really into mermaids these days. I'll take this one.
W: Good choice, sir.

우·리·말·해·석

여: 도와드릴까요, 손님?
남: 네, 딸에게 줄 일기장이 필요합니다.
여: 위에 하트가 있는 이것은 어떠세요? 여자아이들은 하트를 좋아해요.
남: 글쎄요, 그 아이는 요즘 인어에 푹 빠져있어요. 이걸로 할게요.
여: 잘 선택하셨습니다, 손님.

단·어·및·표·현

be into ~ ~에 빠지다, ~에 관심이 많다

03 날씨파악-그림 ▶ 정답 ①

듣·기·대·본

W: Here is the weather forecast for next week. It will be cloudy until next Wednesday and start to be clear from Thursday morning. We can see blue skies on Thursday and Friday. But the weather condition for the weekend won't be good. There will be strong winds this weekend.

우·리·말·해·석

여: 다음 주 일기 예보입니다. 다음 주 수요일까지 날씨가 흐리고, 목요일 아침부터 개기 시작하겠습니다. 목요일과 금요일에는 푸른 하늘을 볼 수 있을 것입니다. 그러나 주말 기상 상황은 좋지 않을 것입니다. 이번 주말에는 강한 바람이 불겠습니다.

단·어·및·표·현

clear [kliər] [형] (날씨가) 갠, 맑은

04 마지막말의도파악 ▶ 정답 ④

듣·기·대·본

W: At last, my online shopping mall opens tomorrow.
M: I know you have put so much effort in this business. Congratulations!
W: Thank you.
M: I believe that it will be a huge success!
W: I couldn't launch it without your advice about online business.

우·리·말·해·석

여: 마침내, 내 온라인 쇼핑몰을 내일 열어.
남: 나는 네가 이 사업을 위해 얼마나 많이 노력했는지 알아. 축하해!
여: 고마워.
남: 나는 이 사업이 큰 성공을 거둘 것이라고 믿어!
여: 온라인 사업에 대한 너의 조언 없이는 이 쇼핑몰을 시작할 수 없었을 거야.

단·어·및·표·현

at last 마침내
launch [lɔːntʃ] [동] 시작하다, 출시하다
advice [ədváis] [명] 조언, 충고

05 담화미언급 ▶ 정답 ④

듣·기·대·본

M: Let me introduce a famous statue in my town. It is in the middle of Central Park. It is in the shape of a tiger, the mascot of our town. It is 3 meters tall. The statue was designed by Laura Hopkins, the famous architect. Many visitors take photos in front of it.

우·리·말·해·석

남: 제가 우리 마을의 유명한 조각상을 소개하겠습니다. 그것은 Central Park의 중앙에 있습니다. 그것은 우리 마을의 마스코트인 호랑이 모양입니다. 그것은 3m 높이입니다. 그 조각상은 유명한 건축가인 Laura Hopkins에 의해 설계되었습니다. 많은 방문객들이 그것의 앞에서 사진을 찍습니다.

단·어·및·표·현
statue [stǽtʃuː] 명 조각상
in the middle of ~ ~의 중앙에
mascot [mǽskət] 명 마스코트
architect [ɑ́ːrkitèkt] 명 건축가

06 수치파악 ▶ 정답 ②

듣·기·대·본

M: All our friends are meeting at the restaurant tonight. Can you make it at six?
W: No. I won't be able to be there until a half past seven.
M: Why? Do you have to work late?
W: No. I always work out from six to seven.
M: That's very impressive. No wonder you are always in shape.
W: I'm sorry, I'll be late. I'll see you then!

우·리·말·해·석

남: 우리 친구들 모두 오늘 저녁에 식당에서 모이기로 했어. 6시까지 올 수 있겠니?
여: 아니. 7시 반까지는 거기에 갈 수 없어.
남: 왜? 늦게까지 일해야 하니?
여: 아니. 나는 항상 6시부터 7시까지 운동을 해.
남: 그거 상당히 멋진데. 그러니 항상 건강한 게 당연하지.
여: 늦게 돼서 미안해. 그럼 그때 봐!

단·어·및·표·현

impressive [imprésiv] 형 멋진, 감명 깊은
in shape 건강한

07 장래희망추론 ▶ 정답 ②

듣·기·대·본

W: Look how fast he is!
M: He is the fastest runner on that baseball team.
W: Is running important in baseball games?
M: Of course. Not only hitting the ball but also running fast is important.
W: You know a lot about baseball.
M: I'm a big fan of baseball. I want to be a baseball player in the future.
W: I believe you can be.

우·리·말·해·석

여: 그가 얼마나 빠른지 봐!
남: 그는 저 야구팀에서 가장 빠르게 달리는 사람이야.
여: 야구 경기에서 달리기가 중요하니?
남: 물론이지. 공을 치는 것뿐만 아니라 빠르게 달리는 것 또한 중요해.
여: 너는 야구에 대해 많이 아는구나.
남: 나는 야구의 열혈 팬이야. 난 미래에 야구 선수가 되고 싶어.
여: 난 네가 될 수 있을 거라 믿어.

단·어·및·표·현

runner [rʌ́nər] 명 달리는 사람, 주자
important [impɔ́ːrtənt] 형 중요한
not only A but also B A뿐만 아니라 B도

08 심정추론 ▶ 정답 ④

듣·기·대·본

M: Hey, Rosie. What's up?
W: Hey, Mark. I have to give a presentation next class.
M: Oh, right. You have a presentation in science class today.
W: I'm so worried because I'm not good at speaking in front of a lot of people.
M: Relax. You'll do just fine.
W: Will I? My heart is racing and my palms are starting to sweat.

우·리·말·해·석

남: 이봐, Rosie. 무슨 일이야?
여: 안녕, Mark. 나는 다음 수업 시간에 발표를 해야 해.
남: 오, 맞아. 너 오늘 과학 수업 시간에 발표하지.
여: 나는 많은 사람 앞에서 말하는 것에 능숙하지 않기 때문에 너무 걱정돼.
남: 긴장 풀어. 너는 잘할 거야.
여: 그럴까? 내 가슴은 두근거리고 내 손바닥에서는 땀이 나기 시작했어.

단·어·및·표·현

give a presentation 발표하다, 보고하다
be good at ~에 능숙하다
My heart is racing. 가슴이 두근거린다.
sweat [swet] 동 땀을 흘리다

09 할일파악(대화직후) ▶ 정답 ⑤

듣·기·대·본

W: What happened here? This place is a mess!
M: I'm sorry. I spilled soda on the floor.
W: Oh, that's why the floor is sticky.
M: I'll clean it up before we open the store.
W: I'll help you clean this up. Can you go get some cleaning supplies?
M: Okay, I'll go get them.

우·리·말·해·석

여: 여기서 무슨 일이 일어났어? 이곳이 엉망이야!
남: 미안해. 내가 바닥에 탄산음료를 쏟았어.
여: 오, 그것이 바닥이 끈적거리는 이유구나.
남: 우리가 가게를 열기 전에 내가 청소할게.
여: 네가 이곳을 청소하는 것을 내가 도울게. 가서 청소 도구들을 가져올 수 있어?
남: 알았어, 내가 가서 그것들을 가져올게.

단·어·및·표·현

mess [mes] 명 엉망인 상황
sticky [stíki] 형 끈적거리는

10 대화화제추론 ▶ 정답 ⑤

듣·기·대·본

W: Aaron, you and your team should join the school festival.
M: What are you talking about?
W: They are looking for a dance team for the opening.
M: Really? Isn't there already a team performing?
W: It's a singing group. They need dancers, too.
M: Then, I can't miss this chance. I should go see the teacher now.

우·리·말·해·석

여: Aaron, 너와 네 팀은 학교 축제에 참가해야 돼.
남: 넌 무슨 말을 하는 거야?
여: 그들은 개막식을 위한 댄스팀을 찾고 있어.
남: 정말이야? 이미 공연하는 팀이 있지 않니?
여: 그건 노래하는 그룹이야. 그들은 댄서들도 필요해.

남: 그럼, 난 이 기회를 놓칠 수 없지. 난 지금 선생님을 만나러 가야겠어.

단·어·및·표·현
look for ~을 찾다
opening [óupəniŋ] 명 개막식
perform [pərfɔ́ːrm] 동 공연하다, 연주하다

11 특정정보파악(교통수단)　　　▶ 정답 ⑤

듣·기·대·본
W: Mike, how should we get to the library?
M: Why don't we ride our bikes? It will only take about 20 minutes.
W: But it's raining outside.
M: Oh, really? I didn't know that.
W: Let's take the bus instead.
M: Sure. Taking the bus seems like a better idea.
W: Good. Let's leave in ten minutes.

우·리·말·해·석
여: Mike, 우리는 도서관에 어떻게 가야 해?
남: 우리 자전거를 타는 건 어때? 20분 정도밖에 안 걸려.
여: 하지만 밖에 비가 오고 있어.
남: 아, 그래? 그건 몰랐어.
여: 대신 버스 타자.
남: 그래. 버스 타는 게 더 좋은 생각인 것 같다.
여: 좋아. 10분 후에 떠나자.

단·어·및·표·현
instead [instéd] 부 대신에
seem like ~인 것 같다, ~처럼 보이다

12 이유파악　　　▶ 정답 ⑤

듣·기·대·본
W: Dad, can you give me a ride to the shoe store, The Shoe Factory?
M: Sure, Lizzy, but I thought you liked to shop online.
W: I do, but I have to go to the store today.
M: Why? Do you need to try the shoes on?
W: No, they are having a huge sale today. It is even cheaper than online shopping.
M: Really?
W: Yes. I can't miss it.

우·리·말·해·석
여: 아빠, 저를 The Shoe Factory라는 신발 가게로 태워 줄 수 있어요?
남: 물론이지, Lizzy, 하지만 나는 네가 온라인에서 쇼핑하는 걸 좋아한다고 생각했어.
여: 맞아요, 하지만 저는 오늘 가게로 가야 해요.
남: 왜? 너는 신발들을 신어 봐야 하니?
여: 아뇨, 그들은 오늘 큰 세일을 해요. 온라인 쇼핑보다 훨씬 더 싸요.
남: 정말?
여: 네. 저는 그것을 놓칠 수 없어요.

단·어·및·표·현
give A a ride A를 태워 주다
shop [ʃɑp] 동 쇼핑하다, 사다
try ~ on ~를 (시험 삼아) 신어 보다, 입어 보다
have a sale 세일하다

13 대화장소추론　　　▶ 정답 ③

듣·기·대·본
W: Hello! How can I help you?

M: Hi, I'm here to get my dog groomed.
W: What services are you interested in?
M: I think my dog needs a bath and a haircut.
W: Excellent! What's your dog's name?
M: Her name is Daisy.
W: OK. Daisy is in good hands. Would you like to wait here or come back later?
M: I'll wait, thank you.

우·리·말·해·석
여: 안녕하세요! 어떻게 도와드릴까요?
남: 안녕하세요, 저는 제 개의 미용을 받으려 왔어요.
여: 고객은 무슨 서비스에 관심이 있으신가요?
남: 저는 제 개에게 목욕과 이발이 필요하다고 생각해요.
여: 좋아요! 고객님의 개의 이름이 무엇인가요?
남: 그녀의 이름은 Daisy입니다.
여: 알겠습니다. Daisy에 대해서는 안심하셔도 됩니다. 고객님께서는 여기서 기다리시겠습니까, 아니면 나중에 다시 돌아오시겠습니까?
남: 기다릴게요, 감사합니다.

단·어·및·표·현
groom [gru(ː)m] 동 (머리, 털 등을) 다듬다
interested in ~에 관심이 있는
bath [bæθ] 명 목욕
haircut [héərkʌt] 명 이발, 미용
be in good hands 안심해도 되다, 잘 관리되고 있다

14 그림정보파악–위치　　　▶ 정답 ⑤

듣·기·대·본
W: Dad, there was a ring on my desk. Have you seen it?
M: No, nothing was on your desk.
W: I thought that I left it on the desk…
M: Did you look under the bed? Maybe you dropped it.
W: I checked everywhere! I can't find it.
M: Well, did you also look on the bookshelf?
W: Ah, I found it. You were right.

우·리·말·해·석
여: 아빠, 제 책상 위에 반지가 하나 있었어요. 그것을 보셨나요?
남: 아니, 네 책상 위에는 아무것도 없었어.
여: 저는 제 책상 위에 그것을 뒀다고 생각했는데…
남: 침대 밑을 찾아봤니? 아마도 네가 그것을 떨어트렸을 거야.
여: 저는 모든 곳을 확인해 봤어요! 저는 못 찾겠어요.
남: 음, 너는 책장 위도 찾아봤니?
여: 아, 찾았어요. 아빠가 맞았어요.

단·어·및·표·현
leave [liːv] 동 ~을 두고 오다, 남기다
drop [drɑp] 동 떨어트리다, 떨어지다
check [tʃek] 동 확인하다, 조사하다

15 부탁(요청)한일파악　　　▶ 정답 ③

듣·기·대·본
M: Mom, I'm going to an amusement park tomorrow.
W: I know. Are you excited?
M: Of course! But I'm worried about the weather. It's going to rain.
W: Do you want to take your raincoat?
M: No. Can you just put an umbrella in my bag?
W: No problem.

우·리·말·해·석

남: 엄마, 저 내일 놀이공원에 가요.
여: 알고 있어. 신나니?
남: 물론이죠! 하지만 날씨가 걱정돼요. 비가 올 거래요.
여: 우비를 챙겨가는 걸 원하니?
남: 아니요. 그냥 제 가방에 우산 좀 넣어주실래요?
여: 그럴게.

단·어·및·표·현

put A in B A를 B에 넣다

16 제안파악 ▶ 정답 ②

듣·기·대·본

M: Congratulations, Sumi! I heard you won a prize at a writing contest.
W: Yes. Thanks, Jiho.
M: I wish I was good at writing, too.
W: Well, I believe anyone can have better writing skills.
M: Really? How?
W: Why don't you try reading the newspaper? It really helps.
M: Okay. I'll try it.

우·리·말·해·석

남: 축하해, 수미야! 나는 네가 글쓰기 대회에서 상을 탔다고 들었어.
여: 응. 고마워, 지호야.
남: 나는 나도 글쓰기를 잘했으면 해.
여: 음, 나는 누구나 더 나은 글쓰기 기술을 가질 수 있다고 생각해.
남: 정말? 어떻게?
여: 신문 읽기를 해보는 게 어때? 그것은 정말 도움이 돼.
남: 좋아. 내가 그것을 해볼게.

단·어·및·표·현

win [win] [동] 타다, 획득하다

17 할일파악 ▶ 정답 ④

듣·기·대·본

W: Hi, Tom. Any plans for the weekend?
M: Yes, Lucy. I'm going to ride my bike along the river.
W: That sounds refreshing. Do you often go cycling?
M: Not really. I just bought a new bike, so I want to try it out.
W: Nice! Have fun and be careful.
M: Thanks! I'm really excited.

우·리·말·해·석

여: 안녕, Tom. 주말에 계획 있어?
남: 응, Lucy. 난 강을 따라 자전거를 탈 거야.
여: 상쾌하겠다. 넌 자주 자전거를 타니?
남: 그렇진 않아. 난 막 새 자전거를 사서 한번 타 보고 싶어.
여: 좋네! 재밌게 즐기고 조심해.
남: 고마워! 정말 기대돼.

단·어·및·표·현

along [əlɔ́(:)ŋ] [전] ~을 따라
refreshing [rifréʃiŋ] [형] 상쾌하게 하는
just [dʒʌst] [부] 막, 이제 방금
try ~ out (시험 삼아) 해 보다

18 직업추론 ▶ 정답 ③

듣·기·대·본

M: Sarah, I've tried your pilot version of the game. It was so much fun!
W: Really? Are you sure the game wasn't too easy?
M: Not at all. I enjoyed playing it.
W: How were the new characters?
M: They were well-designed.
W: I'm glad to hear it. Now I have to work on some graphics.
M: Good luck with the launch.

우·리·말·해·석

남: Sarah, 나는 네 게임의 체험판을 해봤어. 엄청 재밌었어!
여: 정말? 너는 확실히 그 게임이 너무 쉽지는 않았니?
남: 전혀. 나는 그것을 플레이하는 걸 즐겼어.
여: 새로운 캐릭터들은 어땠어?
남: 그들은 잘 설계됐었어.
여: 그 말을 들으니 기뻐. 이제 나는 그래픽을 좀 작업해야 해.
남: 출시에 행운을 빌게.

단·어·및·표·현

try [trai] [동] 해보다, 써보다
pilot [páilət] [형] 시험하는, 시험적인
enjoy [indʒɔ́i] [동] 즐기다
well-designed 잘 설계된
work on 작업하다, 착수하다
launch [lɔ:ntʃ] [명] 출시, 출간

19 알맞은응답찾기 ▶ 정답 ①

듣·기·대·본

(Cellphone rings.)
M: Hello, Lily. What's up?
W: Hey, did you finish your math homework?
M: No, I haven't even started. What about you?
W: Me neither. I'll do it with Andy this afternoon.
M: That's a good idea. Can I join you?
W: Sure. That's why I called you. Come to Andy's house.
M: Okay. What time should I be there?
W: Let's meet at four.

우·리·말·해·석

① 네 시에 만나자.
② 그것에 대해서는 걱정하지 마.
③ 두 시간이 걸려.
④ 그가 너를 많이 도와줄 거야.
⑤ 늦어서 미안해.

(휴대폰이 울린다.)
남: 여보세요, Lily. 무슨 일이야?
여: 야, 너 수학 숙제 끝냈어?
남: 아니, 난 시작하지도 않았어. 너는?
여: 나도 마찬가지야. 나는 오늘 오후에 Andy와 함께 그것을 할 거야.
남: 그거 좋은 생각이야. 내가 너희와 함께 해도 될까?
여: 물론이지. 그래서 내가 너에게 전화한 거야. Andy네 집으로 와.
남: 좋아. 내가 거기에 몇 시에 가야 해?
여: 네 시에 만나자.

단·어·및·표·현

neither [ní:ðər] [부] (부정문을 만들며) ~도 마찬가지다
join [dʒɔin] [동] (~에) 함께 하다, 합류하다
that's why ~ 그래서 ~한 것이다

20 알맞은응답찾기 ▶ 정답 ③

듣·기·대·본

W: Dale, are you okay? You don't <u>look</u> so well.
M: I'm okay. I think I can <u>manage</u> until school ends.
W: Are you sure? If you're not feeling well, you should go see a doctor.
M: Actually, you're right. I think I should go.
W: Did you <u>catch a cold</u>?
M: No, <u>I have a stomachache</u>. I think I ate something <u>bad</u>.
W: <u>That's too bad.</u>

우·리·말·해·석

① 좋은 생각이야!   ② 네가 옳아.
③ 그것 참 안됐구나.   ④ 괜찮아.
⑤ 축하해!

여: Dale, 너 괜찮니? 안색이 안 좋아 보여.
남: 난 괜찮아. 난 학교가 끝날 때까지는 버틸 수 있을 거라고 생각해.
여: 정말이야? 너 몸이 안 좋으면, 병원에 가야 해.
남: 사실은, 네 말이 맞구나. 난 (병원에) 가야 할 것 같아.
여: 너 감기에 걸렸니?
남: 아니, 난 배가 아파. 내가 상한 것을 먹은 것 같아.
여: <u>그것 참 안됐구나.</u>

단·어·및·표·현

look well 안색이 좋다, 건강해 보이다
stomachache[stʌ́məkeik] 몡 배탈, 복통

Words & Expressions Review

1. 발표하다, 보고하다	2. A를 태워 주다	3. 운동하다
4. 쏟다, 흘리다	5. 인어	6. 개막식
7. ~을 두고 오다, 남기다	8. ~에 관심이 있는	9. 땀을 흘리다
10. 조각상	11. ~에 빠지다, ~에 관심이 많다	12. 대신에
13. 떨어뜨리다, 떨어지다	14. 안심해도 되다, 잘 관리되고 있다	15. 선택
16. 발명하다	17. 중요한	18. 조언, 충고
19. 소리를 키우다	20. 멋진, 감명 깊은	21. 일기 예보
22. (날씨가) 갠, 맑은	23. ~을 따라	24. 일기장
25. (머리, 털 등을) 다듬다	26. ~하는 게 당연하다	27. (전등, 기계 등을) 켜다
28. ~에 능숙하다	29. ~을 찾다	30. 시작하다, 출시하다
31. 노력	32. 전자의	33. 공연하다, 연주하다
34. ~인 것 같다, ~처럼 보이다	35. A를 B에 넣다	36. 마침내
37. 이발, 미용	38. 확인하다, 조사하다	39. 배탈, 복통
40. 그래서 ~한 것이다	41. 목욕	42. 병원에 가다
43. ~에 대해 걱정하다	44. 시험하는, 시험적인	

영어듣기 모의고사 18^회

|정|답|

01 ⑤	02 ④	03 ⑤	04 ③	05 ③
06 ③	07 ③	08 ④	09 ④	10 ③
11 ③	12 ②	13 ⑤	14 ①	15 ②
16 ②	17 ②	18 ②	19 ①	20 ①

01 그림정보파악(담화) ▶ 정답 ⑤

듣·기·대·본

W: You can see this in the kitchen. It has <u>a special container</u>. You put different types of food in this to mix and <u>chop them up</u> really fast. You can make smoothies or soups with this. What is this?

우·리·말·해·석

여: 당신은 이것을 부엌에서 볼 수 있습니다. 그것은 특별한 용기를 가지고 있습니다. 당신은 다양한 종류의 음식을 정말 빠르게 섞거나 다지기 위해 이것에 넣습니다. 당신은 이것으로 스무디나 수프를 만들 수 있습니다. 이것은 무엇일까요?

단·어·및·표·현

container[kəntéinər] 몡 용기, 그릇
chop up (잘게) 다지다, 썰다

02 그림정보파악(대화) ▶ 정답 ④

듣·기·대·본

M: What can I do for you?
W: I need a skirt.
M: What about this <u>striped one</u>?
W: I'm not a fan of stripes. <u>I prefer a plain skirt</u>.
M: Okay. How about this <u>blue jean</u> skirt with pockets?
W: I love it. I'll buy that one.

우·리·말·해·석

남: 무엇을 도와드릴까요?
여: 저는 치마가 필요해요.
남: 이 줄무늬가 있는 것은 어떠신가요?
여: 저는 줄무늬를 좋아하지 않아요. 저는 민무늬 치마를 선호해요.
남: 알겠습니다. 주머니가 있는 이 청치마는 어떠신가요?
여: 너무 좋네요. 그것으로 살게요.

단·어·및·표·현

striped[straipt] 혱 줄무늬가 있는
prefer[prifə́:r] 됭 선호하다
plain[plein] 혱 민무늬의
blue jean skirt 청치마
pocket[pάkit] 몡 주머니

03 날씨파악-그림 ▶ 정답 ⑤

듣·기·대·본

W: Hello, New York. Here is the weather forecast for this week. It looks like a rainy week is <u>ahead of</u> us. It will rain on Monday and Tuesday. But, <u>thankfully</u>, the rain will stop and <u>the sun will come out</u> on Wednesday. It will be sunny but a little cloudy on Thursday. And then, on

---

18 회 모 의 고 사

Friday, we will get rain again.

우·리·말·해·석
여: 안녕하세요, 뉴욕. 이번 주 일기예보입니다. 비 오는 한 주가 다가오고 있는 것 같습니다. 월요일과 화요일에 비가 올 것입니다. 그러나, 다행스럽게도, 수요일에는 비가 그칠 것이고 해가 나올 것입니다. 목요일에는 화창할 것이나 약간의 구름이 있을 것입니다. 그러고는, 금요일에 다시 비가 올 것입니다.

단·어·및·표·현
ahead of ~ (공간·시간상으로) ~앞에
thankfully [θǽŋkfəli] ⓑ 다행스럽게도, 고맙게도
come out (해·달·별이) 나오다
get rain 비가 오다

04 마지막말의도파악   ▶ 정답 ③

듣·기·대·본
(Cell phone rings.)
W: Hi, Ben. Are you home?
M: Yes. What's up?
W: Do you have any plans tonight?
M: No, nothing special. Why do you ask?
W: I have one extra ticket for the Cardinals' basketball game tonight. Do you want to come?
M: Are you kidding? I wouldn't miss it for the world!

우·리·말·해·석
(휴대전화가 울린다.)
여: 안녕, Ben. 너 집에 있니?
남: 응, 무슨 일이야?
여: 오늘 밤에 계획 있어?
남: 아니, 특별히 없어. 왜 물어보는 거야?
여: 나한테 오늘 밤 Cardinals의 농구 경기에 남는 표가 한 장 있어. 너 가고 싶니?
남: 농담해? 무슨 일이 있어도 가야지!

단·어·및·표·현
What's up? 무슨 일이야?, 잘 지냈어?

05 담화미언급   ▶ 정답 ③

듣·기·대·본
M: Hello. I'm Sandy Marks. I'd like to tell you about a new Korean learning app called Easy Korean. I created it with my friends. You can learn basic Korean expressions and test yourself with this app. You can download the app for free from the application market now.

우·리·말·해·석
남: 안녕하세요. 저는 Sandy Marks입니다. 저는 여러분에게 Easy Korean(쉬운 한국어)이라고 불리는 새로운 한국어 학습 앱에 대해 말하고 싶습니다. 저는 저의 친구들과 그것을 만들었습니다. 이 앱으로 여러분은 기본적인 한국어 표현들을 배울 수 있고 여러분 스스로를 테스트할 수 있습니다. 여러분은 애플리케이션 마켓에서 지금 그 앱을 무료로 다운로드할 수 있습니다.

단·어·및·표·현
would like to + 동사원형 ~하고 싶다
expression [ikspréʃən] ⓝ 표현
for free 무료로, 공짜로

06 수치파악   ▶ 정답 ③

듣·기·대·본
M: Let's go fishing tomorrow.
W: OK. What time shall we meet?
M: How about at noon?
W: But my class ends at one.
M: Then let's meet at 1:20 in front of the school.
W: OK.

우·리·말·해·석
남: 내일 낚시하러 가자.
여: 그래. 몇 시에 만날까?
남: 정오는 어때?
여: 그런데 난 수업이 1시에 끝나.
남: 그러면 1시 20분에 학교 앞에서 만나자.
여: 좋아.

단·어·및·표·현
in front of ~ ~의 앞에서

07 장래희망추론   ▶ 정답 ③

듣·기·대·본
M: Mom, would you take a look at this movie character?
W: Wow! Did you draw this?
M: Yes, I did. I can't wait to show it to my friends.
W: I'm sure they will love it. You're really good at drawing.
M: Thanks, Mom. I want to be a cartoonist someday.
W: I believe you can be.

우·리·말·해·석
남: 엄마, 이 영화 캐릭터를 한번 봐주실래요?
여: 우와! 네가 이것을 그렸니?
남: 네, 제가 그렸어요. 저는 제 친구들에게 그것을 빨리 보여주고 싶어요.
여: 나는 그들이 그것을 좋아할 거라고 확신해. 너는 정말 그림을 잘 그리는구나.
남: 고마워요, 엄마. 저는 언젠가 만화가가 되고 싶어요.
여: 나는 네가 될 수 있을 거라 믿어.

단·어·및·표·현
take a look at ~을 (한번) 보다
can't wait to + 동사원형 빨리 ~하고 싶다, ~가 기대된다
be good at ~을 잘하다, ~에 능숙하다
cartoonist [ka:rtúːnist] ⓝ 만화가
someday [sʌ́mdèi] ⓑ 언젠가, 훗날

08 심정추론   ▶ 정답 ④

듣·기·대·본
M: Minji, do you have a special plan for this weekend?
W: Yes, Dad. I'm going to visit a nursing home.
M: Really? Are you going to do volunteer work?
W: Yes. I want to do something good for others.
M: Oh! It's very important to help others. You are a wonderful girl!

우·리·말·해·석
남: 민지야, 이번 주말에 특별한 계획이 있니?
여: 네, 아빠. 요양원을 방문할 거예요.
남: 정말? 너는 자원봉사를 하러 갈 거니?
여: 네. 저는 다른 사람들을 위해서 좋은 일을 하고 싶어요.
남: 오! 다른 사람을 돕는 것은 매우 중요하단다. 너는 멋진 소녀구나!

단·어·및·표·현

nursing home 요양원

09 할일파악(대화직후) ▶ 정답 ④

듣·기·대·본

W: Harry, what are you doing this weekend?
M: I'm going to go watch *The Good Guys* in the theater.
W: By yourself?
M: Yes. I asked my friend Jack to go with me, but he said that he had another appointment.
W: If you want, I can go with you.
M: That would be great. Thank you. Let me book two movie tickets online right away.

우·리·말·해·석

여: Harry, 이번 주말에 뭐해?
남: 나는 영화관에 가서 "The Good Guys"를 볼 거야.
여: 너 혼자?
남: 응. 나는 내 친구 Jack에게 나와 함께 가자고 물어봤는데, 그가 다른 약속이 있다고 말했어.
여: 네가 원하면, 나는 너와 함께 갈 수 있어.
남: 그거 좋겠다. 고마워. 내가 곧바로 온라인으로 영화 티켓 두 장을 예매할게.

단·어·및·표·현

by yourself 너 혼자서
have another appointment 다른 약속이 있다
book a ticket 티켓을 예매하다

10 대화화제추론 ▶ 정답 ③

듣·기·대·본

W: David, what are you looking at?
M: I'm checking the fire safety rules.
W: What are they?
M: First, when a fire breaks out, get out fast.
W: We shouldn't use the elevators, right?
M: You're right! And it's important to cover your mouth.
W: Cover my mouth?
M: Yes. You need to avoid breathing in too much smoke.

우·리·말·해·석

여: David, 뭐를 보고 있어?
남: 나는 화재 안전 수칙을 확인하고 있어.
여: 그게 뭐야?
남: 우선, 화재가 발생했을 때, 빨리 나가야 해.
여: 우리는 엘리베이터를 사용하면 안 돼, 맞지?
남: 맞아! 그리고 입을 가리는 것이 중요해.
여: 입을 가려?
남: 응. 연기를 너무 많이 마시는 것을 피해야 해.

단·어·및·표·현

safety rule 안전 수칙
break out 발생하다, 발발하다
cover [kʌ́vər] [동] 가리다, 씌우다
avoid [əvɔ́id] [동] 피하다
breathe in (숨을) 들이마시다

11 특정정보파악(교통수단) ▶ 정답 ③

듣·기·대·본

W: Tom, how should we get to Seoul next week?
M: How about taking the train?
W: It sounds fun, but the train station is too far away.
M: You're right. Then what shall we do?
W: Why don't we take the bus?
M: Good idea. The bus terminal is close to here.
W: Yes. I'll check the schedule, then.

우·리·말·해·석

여: Tom, 다음 주에 우리 서울에 어떻게 갈까?
남: 기차 타는 건 어때?
여: 재밌을 것 같지만, 기차역은 너무 멀리 떨어져 있어.
남: 네 말이 맞아. 그럼 우리 어떻게 할까?
여: 버스 타는 건 어때?
남: 좋은 생각이야. 버스 터미널은 여기서 가까워.
여: 응. 그럼 내가 일정을 확인해 볼게.

단·어·및·표·현

far away 멀리 떨어진
close [klous] [형] 가까운, 근접한

12 이유파악 ▶ 정답 ②

듣·기·대·본

M: Lucy, what are you baking?
W: I'm baking cookies for Mrs. Brown, Dad.
M: Mrs. Brown? Our neighbor?
W: Yes, she's always been so kind to us, so I'm baking her cookies to thank her.
M: That's thoughtful of you! Why are you baking for her today?
W: She's moving away next week, so I want to give her something to remember us by.

우·리·말·해·석

남: Lucy, 너는 무엇을 굽고 있니?
여: 저는 Brown 부인을 위해 쿠키를 굽고 있어요, 아빠.
남: Brown 부인? 우리 이웃 말이니?
여: 네, 그녀는 항상 우리에게 너무 친절했어서 전 그녀에게 감사를 전하기 위해 그녀에게 줄 쿠키를 굽고 있어요.
남: 너는 사려 깊구나! 너는 왜 오늘 그녀를 위해 굽는 거니?
여: 그녀는 다음 주에 이사를 가서, 저는 그녀에게 우리를 기억할 무언가를 주고 싶어요.

단·어·및·표·현

bake [beik] [동] 굽다
neighbor [néibər] [명] 이웃(사람)
thank [θæŋk] [동] 감사를 전하다
thoughtful [θɔ́:tfəl] [형] 사려 깊은, 친절한
move away 이사 가다

13 대화장소추론 ▶ 정답 ⑤

듣·기·대·본

M: What can I do for you?
W: I'm looking for running shoes. Do you have any?
M: Yes. How about these? They are very light and comfortable.
W: Hmm, can I try them on?
M: Of course. What size do you wear?
W: I wear size six.

우·리·말·해·석

남: 무엇을 도와드릴까요?

여: 운동화를 사려고 하는데요. 있나요?
남: 네. 이것은 어떠세요? 굉장히 가볍고 편하답니다.
여: 음, 신어 볼 수 있을까요?
남: 물론이죠. 사이즈 몇 신으세요?
여: 전 사이즈 6을 신어요.

단·어·및·표·현

light [lait] [형] 가벼운
comfortable [kʌ́mfərtəbl] [형] 편안한
try ~ on ~을 신어 보다, 입어 보다

14 그림정보파악–위치 ▶ 정답 ①

듣·기·대·본

W: What are you doing, Jack? It's time for bed.
M: Mom, I can't find my earphone case. Did you see it?
W: No. Did you check the table?
M: I did. It's not there. I checked the sofa too, but I don't see it.
W: Then, did you look through the shelves?
M: [*Pause*] Oh, I found it. It's on the second shelf from the top.

우·리·말·해·석

여: 뭐 하고 있니, Jack? 잘 시간이란다.
남: 엄마, 저는 제 이어폰 케이스를 찾을 수가 없어요. 그것을 보셨나요?
여: 아니. 탁자를 확인해 봤니?
남: 했어요. 그것은 거기 없어요. 저는 소파도 확인해 봤지만, 안 보여요.
여: 그러면 너는 선반들을 살펴봤니?
남: [잠시 후] 오, 찾았어요. 그것은 위에서 두 번째 선반에 있어요.

단·어·및·표·현

It's time for ~ ~할 시간이다
look through 살펴보다, 훑어보다
shelf [ʃelf] [명] 선반, 책꽂이

15 부탁(요청)한일파악 ▶ 정답 ②

듣·기·대·본

W: I am so sleepy today.
M: Come on. We have a math test tomorrow.
W: I know. But I went to bed at 2 a.m. last night.
M: Wow, you really studied hard yesterday.
W: Not really. Ted, could you wake me up in 30 minutes?
M: Sure.
W: Thank you!

우·리·말·해·석

여: 난 오늘 너무 졸려.
남: 이봐. 우리는 내일 수학 시험이 있잖아.
여: 알아. 하지만 나 지난밤에 새벽 2시에 잤어.
남: 와, 넌 어제 정말 열심히 공부했구나.
여: 꼭 그런 건 아냐. Ted, 나를 30분 후에 깨워 줄 수 있어?
남: 물론이지.
여: 고마워!

단·어·및·표·현

wake up (잠을) 깨우다, 일어나다

16 제안파악 ▶ 정답 ②

듣·기·대·본

M: Hey, Jane. What are you doing?
W: I'm just throwing my old clothes away.
M: Why? It looks like they are still in great condition.
W: I know, but they don't fit me anymore.
M: Why don't you donate them instead?
W: That's a good idea.

우·리·말·해·석

남: 안녕, Jane. 너 뭘 하고 있니?
여: 그냥 내 오래된 옷들을 버리고 있어.
남: 왜? 상태가 아직도 아주 좋아 보이는데.
여: 알아, 하지만 그것들이 더 이상 나한테 맞지 않아.
남: 대신 옷들을 기부하는 게 어떠니?
여: 좋은 생각이네.

단·어·및·표·현

throw away 버리다
fit [fit] [동] (모양 · 크기가) 맞다
donate [dóuneit] [동] 기부하다, 기증하다

17 한일파악 ▶ 정답 ②

듣·기·대·본

W: Hi, John. How was your weekend?
M: It was terrible. I had to go to the hospital because I had a cold.
W: Oh no! That's too bad.
M: Don't worry. I'm better now. What did you do last weekend, Jane?
W: I went shopping with my friends.
M: That sounds great.

우·리·말·해·석

여: 안녕, John. 주말 어땠어?
남: 그것은 끔찍했어. 나는 감기에 걸려서 병원에 가야 했어.
여: 오 이런! 너무 안됐다.
남: 걱정 마. 나 지금은 나아졌어. 너는 지난 주말에 무엇을 했니, Jane?
여: 나는 내 친구들과 쇼핑을 갔어.
남: 좋았겠다.

단·어·및·표·현

terrible [térəbl] [형] 끔찍한

18 직업추론 ▶ 정답 ②

듣·기·대·본

M: You did that very well. How do you feel?
W: My legs are burning!
M: Keep your back straight when you do your squat next time.
W: Okay. What do I do next?
M: Some stretches to relax your muscles.
W: I'm glad I started to exercise. I feel so energetic.
M: I'm glad to help you out.

우·리·말·해·석

남: 당신은 그것을 아주 잘하셨어요. 기분이 어때요?
여: 제 다리가 화끈거려요!
남: 다음 번에 스쿼트를 할 때는 등을 곧게 펴세요.
여: 알겠어요. 다음에는 제가 뭘 하나요?
남: 당신의 근육을 이완시키기 위해 스트레칭을 좀 하죠.
여: 운동을 시작해서 기뻐요. 매우 활기찬 기분이 들어요.
남: 당신을 돕게 되어서 기뻐요.

단·어·및·표·현

keep ~ straight ~을 곧게 유지하다
squat [skwɑt] [명] 쪼그리고 앉은 자세, 스쿼트 동작
relax [rilǽks] [동] (근육 등의) 긴장을 풀다
energetic [ènərdʒétik] [형] 활기에 찬, 정력적인

19 알맞은응답찾기 ▶ 정답 ①

듣·기·대·본

W: Hurry up! We are late.
M: Let's cross the street here.
W: No. This is not a crosswalk.
M: Come on, Audrey. We don't have much time.
W: Watch out! George, that car almost hit you.
M: Oh, my goodness!
W: **You should be more careful.**

우·리·말·해·석

① 너는 더 조심해야 해. ② 행운을 빌어!
③ 그렇다니 유감이야. ④ 우리가 제시간에 와서 기뻐.
⑤ 그거 재미있겠는걸.

여: 서둘러! 우리 늦었어.
남: 여기서 길을 건너자.
여: 안 돼. 여기는 횡단보도가 아니란 말이야.
남: 이봐, Audrey. 우린 시간이 많지 않아.
여: 조심해! George, 저 차가 너를 거의 칠 뻔했잖아.
남: 오, 맙소사!
여: **너는 더 조심해야 해.**

단·어·및·표·현

watch out 조심하다

20 알맞은응답찾기 ▶ 정답 ①

듣·기·대·본

M: Alyssa, I'm going grocery shopping. Do you want to come?
W: Okay, Dad. Can we buy some chocolate, too?
M: Sure.
W: Great! And can we also get some fruit?
M: Of course. I was going to buy some bananas.
W: Hmm. I don't feel like eating bananas.
M: Okay. Then what fruit do you want to eat?
W: **I want oranges.**

우·리·말·해·석

① 저는 오렌지를 원해요.
② 우리는 택시를 탈 수 있어요.
③ 그것들은 맛있어 보여요.
④ 30분 걸릴 거예요.
⑤ 식당에서 먹어요.

남: Alyssa, 나는 장보러 갈 거야. 너도 가고 싶니?
여: 네, 아빠. 초콜릿도 좀 사도 되나요?
남: 물론이지.
여: 좋아요! 그리고 우리 과일도 좀 사도 돼요?
남: 물론이지. 나는 바나나를 좀 사려고 했어.
여: 음. 저는 바나나를 먹고 싶지 않아요.
남: 알겠다. 그러면 어떤 과일을 먹고 싶니?
여: **저는 오렌지를 원해요.**

단·어·및·표·현

grocery shopping 장보기, 식료품점 쇼핑
get [get] [동] 사다, 얻다

Words & Expressions Review

1. ~할 시간이다	2. 무료로, 공짜로	3. 가벼운
4. 자원봉사	5. ~하고 싶다	6. 선반, 책꽂이
7. 남는, 여분의	8. 표현	9. (잘게) 다지다, 썰다
10. 장보기	11. 조심하다	12. 사려 깊은, 친절한
13. (잠을) 깨우다, 일어나다	14. 버리다	15. 줄무늬가 있는
16. 만화가	17. 멀리 떨어진	18. 살펴보다, 훑어보다
19. (모양·크기가) 맞다	20. 활기에 찬, 정력적인	21. 무슨 일이야?, 잘 지냈어?
22. 횡단보도	23. 민무늬의	24. ~하고 싶다
25. 다행스럽게도, 고맙게도	26. 요양원	27. 용기, 그릇
28. 가까운, 근접한	29. 쪼그리고 앉은 자세, 스쿼트 동작	30. 굽다
31. 감사를 전하다	32. 이사 가다	33. 발생하다, 발발하다
34. (시간, 공간상으로) ~앞에	35. 비가 오다	36. 상태, 상황
37. 중요한	38. ~을 곧게 유지하다	39. (숨을) 들이마시다
40. 특별한	41. 언젠가, 훗날	42. 편안한
43. 너 혼자서	44. 멋진, 훌륭한	

Listening Test

영어듣기 모의고사 19회

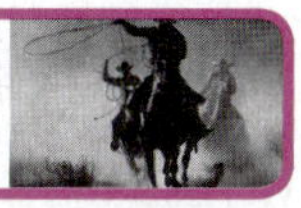

|정|답|

01 ②	02 ③	03 ④	04 ④	05 ④
06 ③	07 ④	08 ①	09 ③	10 ②
11 ④	12 ③	13 ④	14 ③	15 ②
16 ③	17 ①	18 ①	19 ⑤	20 ⑤

01 그림정보파악(담화) ▶ 정답 ②

듣·기·대·본

M: I live in the desert and eat plants. I help people cross the desert and carry baggage. I have humps on my back and there is a lot of fat in them. So, I can keep going without food and water for a long period.

우·리·말·해·석

남: 저는 사막에 살며 식물을 먹습니다. 저는 사람들이 사막을 건너고 짐을 나르는 것을 돕습니다. 저는 등에 혹이 있고 그것들 안에는 많은 지방이 있습니다. 그래서 저는 오랜 기간 음식과 물 없이 견딜 수 있습니다.

단·어·및·표·현

cross [krɔ(:)s] [동] 건너다, 가로지르다
hump [hʌmp] [명] 혹, 툭 솟아 오른 것

02 그림정보파악(대화) ▶ 정답 ③

듣·기·대·본

M: May I help you?
W: I want to buy a lock.
M: We have 3-digit locks and 4-digit locks.
W: I want a 3-digit lock.
M: Okay, how about this 3-digit square lock?
W: Do you have anything else?
M: How about this heart-shaped one?
W: I like hearts. I'll take it.

우·리·말·해·석

남: 무엇을 도와드릴까요?
여: 저는 자물쇠를 하나 사고 싶어요.
남: 저희는 세 자릿수 자물쇠와 네 자릿수 자물쇠가 있어요.
여: 저는 세 자릿수 자물쇠를 원해요.
남: 네, 이 사각형 모양의 세 자릿수 자물쇠는 어떠세요?
여: 다른 게 있나요?
남: 이 하트 모양의 것은 어떠세요?
여: 저는 하트가 좋아요. 그걸로 살게요.

단·어·및·표·현

lock [lɑk] 몡 자물쇠
digit [dídʒit] 몡 자릿수, 숫자
square [skwɛər] 혱 사각형 모양의
heart-shaped 하트 모양의

03 날씨파악-그림 ▶ 정답 ④

듣·기·대·본

W: Hello! This is the Gyeongju weather report. Yesterday, we had some light snow here and there, but by evening, the sky cleared. Today, it's a cold but sunny day outside. Later in the afternoon, we might experience some strong winds. So, dress warmly if you're going out.

우·리·말·해·석

여: 안녕하세요! 경주 일기 예보입니다. 어제, 이곳저곳에 약한 눈이 내렸는데요, 하지만 저녁 즈음 하늘이 맑게 개었습니다. 오늘은, 밝은 춥지만 화창한 날입니다. 나중에 오후에는, 우리는 아마도 좀 강한 바람을 경험할 것입니다. 그러니, 만약 밖에 나가신다면 따뜻하게 입으세요.

단·어·및·표·현

light [lait] 혱 약한, 가벼운
outside [ὰutsáid] 閉 밖에, 외부에
experience [ikspí(ː)əriəns] 동 경험하다

04 마지막말의도파악 ▶ 정답 ④

듣·기·대·본

W: Eric, what are you doing?
M: I'm making a thank-you card for our school bus driver.
W: That's thoughtful of you. What made you want to do that?

M: He's always so kind, and I wanted to show my thanks.
W: I'm sure he'll love it. You're so sweet.

우·리·말·해·석

여: Eric, 뭐 하고 있어?
남: 학교 버스 기사님을 위한 감사 카드를 만들고 있어.
여: 참 사려 깊구나. 무엇이 네가 감사 카드를 만들고 싶게 했어?
남: 그분은 항상 매우 친절하셔서 내 감사한 마음을 보이고 싶었어.
여: 분명히 그분이 좋아하실 거야. 너 정말 다정하구나.

단·어·및·표·현

thank-you card 감사 카드
thoughtful [θɔ́ːtfəl] 혱 사려 깊은, 친절한

05 담화미언급 ▶ 정답 ④

듣·기·대·본

W: This spring we'll have a school camping event. It will take place on April 27th. You will learn to set up a tent, make a fire, and more. The school grounds will be our camping site. The event will run from the evening of April 27th until the next morning. You can sign up for the event on the school website.

우·리·말·해·석

여: 이번 봄에 학교 캠핑 행사가 있을 것입니다. 그것은 4월 27일에 열릴 겁니다. 여러분은 텐트를 설치하고, 불을 피우고, 그 외 여러 가지를 배울 것입니다. 학교 운동장이 우리의 캠핑 장소일 것입니다. 그 행사는 4월 27일 저녁부터 다음 날 아침까지 진행될 것입니다. 여러분은 학교 웹사이트에서 그 행사를 신청할 수 있습니다.

단·어·및·표·현

take place 열리다, 개최되다
set up 설치하다
make a fire 불을 피우다
ground [graund] 몡 운동장
camping site 캠핑 장소
run [rʌn] 동 (언급된 시간에) 진행되다
sign up for ~을 신청하다

06 수치파악 ▶ 정답 ③

듣·기·대·본

M: Hey, Jennifer. Did you know that there is a free lecture at the community center today?
W: Yes, it's about jobs of the future, isn't it?
M: Right. It starts at 5 p.m. Let's go together.
W: Sure, then I'll see you in front of the school at 4:30.
M: That'll be too tight. How about 4:00?
W: All right. See you then.

우·리·말·해·석

남: 이봐, Jennifer. 너는 오늘 주민센터에 무료 강의가 있는 거 알고 있었어?
여: 응, 그것은 미래의 직업에 관한 거잖아, 그렇지 않아?
남: 맞아. 오후 5시에 시작해. 같이 가자.
여: 물론이지, 그러면 4시 30분에 학교 앞에서 만나자.
남: 그건 너무 빠듯할 것 같아. 4시는 어때?
여: 좋아. 그때 보자.

단·어·및·표·현

free [friː] 혱 무료의
lecture [léktʃər] 몡 강의, 강연

community center 주민 센터
tight [tait] 형 (여유가 없이) 빠듯한, 빡빡한

07 장래희망추론 ▶ 정답 ④

듣·기·대·본
M: Kathy, what do you usually do on the weekend?
W: I spend time with my dogs and my hamsters.
M: Oh, you must love animals.
W: Yes, I want to become a zookeeper when I grow up.
M: Great. I'm sure your dream will come true.
W: Thanks, Mike. I will do my best.

우·리·말·해·석
남: Kathy, 너는 보통 주말에 무엇을 하니?
여: 나는 내 개들과 햄스터들과 함께 시간을 보내.
남: 오, 너는 동물들을 무척 좋아하는 게 틀림없어.
여: 응, 나는 커서 동물원 사육사가 되고 싶어.
남: 좋아. 나는 네 꿈이 이루어질 거라 확신해.
여: 고마워, Mike. 난 최선을 다할 거야.

단·어·및·표·현
zookeeper [zú:kì:pər] 명 동물원 사육사
come true 이루어지다, 실현되다
do one's best 최선을 다하다

08 심정추론 ▶ 정답 ①

듣·기·대·본
M: Finally, our exams are all over!
W: Yay! The best thing is that we don't have to study today!
M: You're right. What should we do today?
W: Why don't we go to the new coin noraebang?
M: Great idea! Let's go have some fun.

우·리·말·해·석
남: 드디어 모든 시험이 끝났어!
여: 오예! 가장 좋은 점은 오늘 공부할 필요가 없다는 거야!
남: 맞아. 우리 오늘 뭘 하면 좋을까?
여: 우리 새로 생긴 동전 노래방에 가는 게 어때?
남: 좋은 생각이야! 가서 재미있게 놀자.

단·어·및·표·현
Why don't we ~? 우리 ~하는 게 어때?

09 할일파악(대화직후) ▶ 정답 ③

듣·기·대·본
M: Did you decide what to make for the science fair?
W: Not yet. I'm thinking about making a model of a volcano.
M: Have you read any books about how to make one?
W: I did, but I still don't know what materials to use.
M: Why don't you ask the science teacher?
W: That's a good idea. I'll go ask her now.

우·리·말·해·석
남: 너 과학 박람회에 무엇을 만들지 결정했어?
여: 아직. 난 화산 모형을 만들까 생각 중이야.
남: 그것을 만드는 법에 대한 어떤 책이라도 읽어봤어?
여: 읽어봤는데, 나는 어떤 재료를 써야 할지 아직 잘 모르겠어.
남: 과학 선생님께 여쭤보는 건 어때?
여: 좋은 생각이야. 지금 가서 여쭤볼게.

단·어·및·표·현
fair [fɛər] 명 박람회
volcano [vɑlkéinou] 명 화산
material [mətí(:)əriəl] 명 재료

10 대화화제추론 ▶ 정답 ②

듣·기·대·본
M: Can I ask you something?
W: Sure, sir.
M: Can I machine wash this T-shirt?
W: No, you have to wash it by hand in cold water with a gentle detergent.
M: What happens if I machine wash it?
W: All the color will come out.

우·리·말·해·석
남: 뭘 좀 물어봐도 될까요?
여: 물론이죠, 손님.
남: 이 티셔츠를 세탁기로 빨아도 되나요?
여: 아니요, 그것은 찬물에서 순한 세제로 손빨래해야 합니다.
남: 그것을 세탁기로 빨면 어떻게 되나요?
여: 색이 다 빠질 거예요.

단·어·및·표·현
machine wash 세탁기로 빨다
gentle [dʒéntl] 형 순한, 온화한
detergent [ditə́:rdʒənt] 명 세제
come out 빠지다, 빠져나오다

🔊 LISTENING ADVICE
영어에서의 'ch'는 대개 우리말 [ㅊ]나 [ㅋ]와 비슷한 소리가 납니다. 'chair'[체어ㄹ], 'school'[스쿨]과 같은 단어들이 그러합니다. 하지만 'machine'이라는 단어에서는 이례적으로 'ch'가 [sh]와 같이 발음됩니다. 따라서 'machine'은 [머친]이나 [머킨]이 아닌 [머쉰]으로 들리게 됩니다.

● How to pronounce [sh]
'sh' 소리는 발음기호로는 [ʃ]로 표기하며, '쉿!'이라고 말할 때와 같이 소리 냅니다.

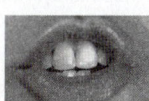

11 특정정보파악(교통수단) ▶ 정답 ④

듣·기·대·본
W: Dad, how are we going to Busan this weekend?
M: I was thinking of going in our car.
W: But it's the weekend. There'll be heavy traffic!
M: That's true.
W: Can't we take the plane?
M: Sure, why not? Let's take the plane.
W: Great! I'll check the flight schedule.

우·리·말·해·석
여: 아빠, 이번 주말에 우리 부산에 어떻게 가요?
남: 우리 차를 타고 가려고 생각하고 있었단다.
여: 하지만 주말이잖아요. 심한 교통 체증이 있을 거예요!
남: 그건 사실이야.
여: 우리가 비행기를 타도 되지 않을까요?
남: 물론이지, 왜 안되겠어? 비행기를 타자꾸나.
여: 좋아요! 제가 비행기 시간표를 확인할게요.

heavy traffic 교통 체증, 극심한 교통량
schedule [skédʒuːl] 명 시간표, 일정

12 이유파악 ▶ 정답 ③

듣·기·대·본

M: You look annoyed. What's wrong?
W: I ordered a new dress online, but I haven't gotten it yet.
M: What happened?
W: I wanted a red one, but they were all sold out. I have to wait for another week.
M: That must be annoying.
W: I wanted to wear it on my date this Friday, but now my plans are ruined.

우·리·말·해·석

남: 너 짜증난 것 같은데. 무슨 일이야?
여: 내가 새 옷을 온라인으로 주문했는데 아직 받지 못했어.
남: 무슨 일이 일어난 거야?
여: 나는 빨간색을 원했는데 빨간색은 다 팔렸대. 나는 한 주를 더 기다려야 해.
남: 그것 참 짜증 나겠어.
여: 이번주 금요일 데이트에 그걸 입기를 원했는데, 이제 내 계획이 망쳐졌어.

단·어·및·표·현

sold out 다 팔린, 매진된

13 대화장소추론 ▶ 정답 ④

듣·기·대·본

M: How can I help you?
W: I bought this subway pass yesterday, but I want to exchange it for a monthly pass.
M: Sure, do you want the monthly pass for the same area?
W: Yes, please. Can I also get a receipt?
M: Absolutely! I'll do that for you.
W: Thanks a lot.

우·리·말·해·석

남: 어떻게 도와드릴까요?
여: 저는 이 지하철 승차권을 어제 샀는데, 이것을 월간 정기권으로 교환하고 싶어요.
남: 알겠습니다, 같은 구역의 월간 정기권을 원하시나요?
여: 네. 영수증 또한 받을 수 있을까요?
남: 그럼요! 그렇게 해드리겠습니다.
여: 감사합니다.

단·어·및·표·현

subway [sʌ́bwèi] 명 지하철
pass [pæs] 명 승차권
exchange [ikstʃéindʒ] 동 교환하다
monthly [mʌ́nθli] 형 한 달 동안의
area [ɛ́əriə] 명 구역, 지역
receipt [risíːt] 명 영수증

14 표불일치 ▶ 정답 ③

듣·기·대·본

W: Hello, Moonberry shoppers! Let me tell you about our Kids' Baking Event. It'll be held this Saturday at 11 a.m. During the event, kids will learn how to make tasty and colorful rice cakes with fun designs. The event will be 2 hours in length. The fee is 30 dollars, including all ingredients. It will take place at Moonberry Mall in the event space on the first floor. Thanks!

우·리·말·해·석

아이들을 위한 베이킹 행사		
①	일시	이번 주 토요일, 오전 11시
②	행사 내용	떡을 만드는 법
③	소요 시간	1.5시간
④	비용	30달러
⑤	장소	Moonberry 쇼핑몰 행사장

여: 안녕하세요, Moonberry 쇼핑몰 고객 여러분! 우리 아이들을 위한 베이킹 행사에 대해 알려드리겠습니다. 그것은 이번 주 토요일 오전 11시에 열릴 거예요. 행사 동안 아이들은 재미있는 형태의 맛있고 알록달록한 떡을 만드는 법을 배울 거예요. 이 행사는 2시간 동안 진행될 것입니다. 참가비는 모든 재료비를 포함해서 30달러입니다. 행사는 Moonberry 쇼핑몰 1층 행사장에서 열릴 거예요. 감사합니다!

단·어·및·표·현

during [djú(ː)əriŋ] 전 ~동안
fee [fiː] 명 요금
include [inklúːd] 동 포함하다
ingredient [ingríːdiənt] 명 재료
take place 열리다, 개최되다

15 부탁(요청)한일파악 ▶ 정답 ②

듣·기·대·본

M: Honey, I'm so happy. Rachel is finally coming home with us.
W: I know. She was in the hospital for too long.
M: We should celebrate.
W: I think so, too. Shall we get her a present?
M: Yes! How about new clothes?
W: Good idea. Can you go and buy them today?
M: Yes, I can.

우·리·말·해·석

남: 여보, 전 정말 행복해요. Rachel이 마침내 우리와 함께 집으로 돌아오네요.
여: 맞아요. 그녀는 너무 오랫동안 입원해 있었어요.
남: 우리는 축하해야 해요.
여: 저도 그렇게 생각해요. 우리 그녀에게 선물을 줄까요?
남: 그래요! 새 옷은 어때요?
여: 좋은 생각이에요. 당신이 오늘 가서 그것들을 살 수 있어요?
남: 네, 할 수 있어요.

단·어·및·표·현

be in the hospital 입원해 있다
celebrate [séləbrèit] 동 축하하다, 기념하다

16 제안파악 ▶ 정답 ③

듣·기·대·본

W: Tommy, you look stressed out.
M: I have so many things to do today.
W: Like what?
M: I have to write a report, clean my room, visit the dentist, walk my dog, and... Oh, I forget what else.
W: Why don't you try making a list of all the things you have

to do today?

우·리·말·해·석

여: Tommy, 너 스트레스 받은 것 같아 보여.

남: 오늘 해야 할 일이 너무 많아.

여: 어떤 거?

남: 나는 리포트를 써야 하고, 방 청소도 해야 하고, 치과에도 가야 하고, 강아지도 산책시켜야 하고… 오, 그 밖의 다른 것들은 잊어버렸어.

여: 네가 오늘 해야 할 모든 일들의 목록을 만드는 게 어때?

단·어·및·표·현

stressed out 스트레스를 받은

dentist [déntist] 명 치과, 치과의사

17 한일파악 ▶ 정답 ①

듣·기·대·본

W: Ken, how was your weekend?

M: It was awful. My computer broke down, so I had to fix it.

W: Oh, that sounds terrible. Did you manage to fix it?

M: Yeah, I did. How did you spend your weekend?

W: I went camping with my family.

M: That sounds great.

우·리·말·해·석

여: Ken, 네 주말은 어땠어?

남: 그것은 끔찍했어. 내 컴퓨터가 고장 났고, 그래서 나는 그것을 고쳐야 했어.

여: 아, 그것은 끔찍했겠다. 너는 그것을 어떻게든 고쳤니?

남: 응, 그랬어. 너는 너의 주말을 어떻게 보냈니?

여: 나는 내 가족과 캠핑을 갔어.

남: 좋았겠다.

단·어·및·표·현

awful [ɔ́ːfəl] 형 끔찍한

break down 고장 나다

manage to + 동사원형 어떻게든 ~하다, 그럭저럭 ~하다

18 직업추론 ▶ 정답 ①

듣·기·대·본

M: Good morning. May I help you?

W: Yes. My car makes strange sounds when I'm driving.

M: I see. Hmm, I think there is something wrong with the engine.

W: Oh, no. Is it serious?

M: I don't know yet. I'll have to look inside.

W: Can you finish by tomorrow?

M: I'm not sure, but I'll do my best.

우·리·말·해·석

남: 안녕하세요. 무엇을 도와드릴까요?

여: 네. 운전할 때 차에서 이상한 소리가 나요.

남: 알겠습니다. 음, 제 생각에는 엔진이 뭔가 잘못된 것 같은데요.

여: 오, 이런. 심각한가요?

남: 아직은 모릅니다. 안을 들여다봐야 해요.

여: 내일까지 끝내실 수 있나요?

남: 확실하진 않지만 최선을 다하겠습니다.

단·어·및·표·현

make a sound 소리가 나다, 소리를 내다

do one's best 최선을 다하다

19 알맞은응답찾기 ▶ 정답 ⑤

듣·기·대·본

M: Emma, we're going camping in Gangwondo next week.

W: Really, Dad? Are we going to have a campfire?

M: Yes.

W: Awesome! Can we also have a barbecue?

M: Sure. What do you want to eat?

W: I want sausages and sweet potatoes.

M: OK. Let's have them both.

W: Great! How long are we going to stay there?

M: We'll be there for 3 days.

우·리·말·해·석

① 그거 맛있겠구나.　　② 근처에 화장실이 있어.

③ 차로 한 시간 걸려.　　④ 불조심해.

⑤ 우리는 3일 동안 그곳에 있을 거야.

남: Emma, 우리 다음 주에 강원도에 캠핑 갈 거야.

여: 정말이요, 아빠? 우리 캠프파이어 할 거예요?

남: 그래.

여: 멋져요! 우리 바비큐도 할 수 있어요?

남: 물론이지. 넌 뭘 먹고 싶니?

여: 저는 소시지와 고구마를 원해요.

남: 좋아. 그것들을 둘 다 먹자.

여: 아주 좋아요! 우리 거기서 얼마나 오래 머무를 거예요?

남: 우리는 3일 동안 그곳에 있을 거야.

단·어·및·표·현

go camping 캠핑 가다

have a campfire 캠프파이어를 하다, 모닥불을 피우다

sweet potato 고구마

20 알맞은응답찾기 ▶ 정답 ⑤

듣·기·대·본

M: Maggie, how are you doing these days?

W: Hi, Mr. Baker. My classes are fine, but it's kind of hard to make friends.

M: Then, why don't you join a club? Many students make friends there.

W: Really?

M: Really. And you play the guitar, don't you?

W: I do. Is there a guitar club?

M: Yes. And they take new members.

우·리·말·해·석

① 나는 널 믿어.

② 나는 그렇게 잘 연주하지 못해.

③ 너는 언제나 환영이야.

④ 학교 축제가 열릴 거야.

⑤ 응. 그리고 그들은 새로운 회원을 받아.

남: Maggie, 넌 요즘 어떻게 지내?

여: 안녕하세요, Baker 선생님. 제 수업들은 좋지만, 친구들을 사귀는 것은 약간 어려워요.

남: 그러면 동아리에 가입하는 것은 어떠니? 많은 학생들이 거기서 친구들을 사귄단다.

여: 정말요?

남: 정말. 그리고 너는 기타를 치잖아, 그렇지 않니?

여: 맞아요. 기타 동아리도 있나요?

남: 응. 그리고 그들은 새로운 회원들을 받아.

단·어·및·표·현

kind of 약간, 어느 정도
join [dʒɔin] [동] 가입하다, 합류하다
believe in ~ ~을 믿다
take [teik] [동] (고객 · 환자 · 학생 등으로) 받다

Words & Expressions Review

1. 입원해 있다	2. 이상한	3. 순한, 온화한
4. 어떻게든 ~하다	5. 짜증난	6. 시간표, 일정
7. 교통 체증, 극심한 교통량	8. 강의, 강연	9. 화산
10. ~을 믿다	11. 캠핑 가다	12. 주민 센터
13. 이루어지다, 실현되다	14. 하트 모양의	15. 운동장
16. 엔진	17. 고구마	18. 동물원 사육사
19. 약간, 어느 정도	20. 보여 주다	21. 고장 나다
22. 사각형 모양의	23. 자릿수, 숫자	24. 최선을 다하다
25. ~동안	26. 다 팔린, 매진된	27. 자물쇠
28. 주, 일주일	29. 심각한	30. 스트레스를 받은
31. 리포트, 보고서	32. 소리가 나다, 소리를 내다	33. 혹, 툭 솟아 오른 것
34. 세제	35. (여유가 없이) 빠듯한, 빡빡한	36. 짐
37. 교환하다	38. 그 밖의 다른 것	39. 나르다
40. 목록을 만들다	41. 치과, 치과 의사	42. 건너다, 가로지르다
43. 재미있게 놀다, 즐기다	44. 사려 깊은, 친절한	

Listening Test

영어듣기 모의고사 20회

| 정 | 답 |

01 ⑤	02 ③	03 ①	04 ⑤	05 ③
06 ③	07 ⑤	08 ③	09 ①	10 ①
11 ④	12 ③	13 ②	14 ③	15 ③
16 ④	17 ③	18 ③	19 ②	20 ⑤

01 그림정보파악(담화) ▶ 정답 ⑤

듣·기·대·본

M: I live in a very cold area. I am black and white. I have small wings but I can't fly. I can swim and hunt fish very well. What am I?

우·리·말·해·석

남: 나는 매우 추운 지역에 살아요. 나는 검은색과 흰색이에요. 나는 작은 날개가 있지만 날 수는 없어요. 나는 헤엄치고 물고기를 사냥하는 것을 아주 잘해요. 나는 무엇일까요?

단·어·및·표·현

area [ɛ́əriə] [명] 지역
hunt [hʌnt] [동] 사냥하다

02 그림정보파악(대화) ▶ 정답 ③

듣·기·대·본

M: May I help you?
W: Yes, I am looking for a new EarPods case.
M: We have several different choices. How about this one with a heart on it?
W: No thanks. Do you have anything related to animals?
M: Oh, we have one with a bear and one with a rabbit.
W: The one with the rabbit on it sounds good. I will take that one.

우·리·말·해·석

남: (무엇을) 도와드릴까요?
여: 네, 저는 새 이어폰 케이스를 찾고 있어요.
남: 저희에게는 (선택 가능한) 여러 가지 종류가 있습니다. 위에 하트가 그려진 이 제품은 어떠세요?
여: 괜찮습니다. 동물들과 관련된 것이 있나요?
남: 오, 저희는 곰이 그려진 것과 토끼가 그려진 것이 있습니다.
여: 위에 토끼가 그려진 것이 좋겠네요. 저는 그걸로 선택할게요.

단·어·및·표·현

look for ~을 찾다
several [sévərəl] [형] 여러 가지의, 몇몇의
related to + 명사 ~과 관련된
take [teik] [동] 선택하다, 사다

03 날씨파악-그림 ▶ 정답 ①

듣·기·대·본

M: Good morning. It rained heavily yesterday. But today, you don't have to take your umbrella with you. It will be sunny and warm all day. You'd better wear light clothes. Have a nice day.

우·리·말·해·석

남: 안녕하세요. 어제는 비가 많이 내렸습니다. 그러나 오늘은 우산을 가지고 가실 필요가 없습니다. 온종일 맑고 따뜻하겠습니다. 얇은 옷을 입는 게 좋겠습니다. 좋은 하루 보내세요.

단·어·및·표·현

had better + 동사원형 ~하는 게 좋다, ~하는 게 낫다

04 마지막말의도파악 ▶ 정답 ⑤

듣·기·대·본

W: Jake, do you have any plans for tomorrow?
M: Hi, Kate. I am going to the mall to buy a birthday gift for Emily.
W: Oh, I forgot to buy her a gift!
M: Her birthday is this Sunday.
W: Right, there's not much time. Can I go with you?
M: Sure. Let's go and shop together.

우·리·말·해·석

여: Jake, 너는 내일 어떤 계획이 있니?
남: 안녕, Kate. 나는 Emily의 생일 선물을 사기 위해 쇼핑몰에 갈 예정이야.
여: 오, 나는 그녀에게 선물을 사줄 것을 잊었어!

남: 그녀의 생일은 이번 주 일요일이야.

여: 맞아, 시간이 많지 않아. 내가 너랑 같이 가도 될까?

남: 물론이지. 같이 가서 쇼핑하자.

단·어·및·표·현

forget to + 동사원형 ~할 것을 잊다

shop[ʃɑp] 동 쇼핑하다, 사다

05 담화미언급 ▶ 정답 ③

듣·기·대·본

W: Hi, everyone. Today, I will tell you about an amazing hat designer. Her name is Marylin Chung. She was born in Canada, but now she lives in the UK. She is only 28 years old, but her hats are already very famous. Her customers include members of the European royal families.

우·리·말·해·석

여: 안녕하세요, 여러분. 오늘, 저는 여러분께 놀라운 모자 디자이너에 대해 말씀드릴 겁니다. 그녀의 이름은 Marylin Chung입니다. 그녀는 캐나다에서 태어났지만, 지금 그녀는 영국에서 살고 있습니다. 그녀는 28살밖에 되지 않았지만, 그녀의 모자는 이미 매우 유명합니다. 그녀의 고객들에는 유럽의 왕실도 포함되어 있습니다.

단·어·및·표·현

amazing[əméiziŋ] 형 놀라운

famous[féiməs] 형 유명한

customer[kʌ́stəmər] 명 고객, 손님

include[inklú:d] 동 포함하다

European[jùərəpí(:)ən] 형 유럽의

royal family 왕실, 황족

06 수치파악 ▶ 정답 ③

듣·기·대·본

M: Are you ready to leave, sweetie?

W: Yes, Dad. How long will it take to get to the resort?

M: It's a one-hour ride, but it'll take longer this morning.

W: Why is that?

M: There was an accident on the road at 8:00 a.m.

W: It's 9:00 a.m. now. The road should be cleared.

M: I hope so. Let's go.

우·리·말·해·석

남: 떠날 준비 됐니, 얘야?

여: 네, 아빠. 리조트까지 얼마나 걸릴까요?

남: 차로 한 시간 걸리지만 오늘 아침에는 더 오래 걸릴 거야.

여: 왜 그렇죠?

남: 오전 8시에 도로에서 사고가 있었어.

여: 지금은 오전 9시예요. 도로가 치워져야 하는데요.

남: 나도 그러기를 바란다. 가자.

단·어·및·표·현

be ready to + 동사원형 ~할 준비가 되다

accident[ǽksidənt] 명 사고

should[ʃəd] 동 (아마) ~일 것이다

clear[kliər] 동 (장애물을) 치우다, 제거하다

07 장래희망추론 ▶ 정답 ⑤

듣·기·대·본

M: Wow, you have a lot of classical albums in your room.

W: Yes. I love listening to classical music.

M: Cool! Do you play a musical instrument as well?

W: I play the piano. I actually want to become a pianist when I grow up.

M: Great! I'm sure you'll become a famous pianist one day.

W: Thanks!

우·리·말·해·석

남: 와, 넌 네 방에 클래식 앨범을 많이 가지고 있구나.

여: 응. 나는 클래식 음악을 듣는 걸 아주 좋아해.

남: 멋지다! 너는 악기도 연주하니?

여: 나는 피아노를 쳐. 나는 사실 어른이 되면 피아니스트가 되고 싶어.

남: 굉장하다! 분명히 너는 언젠가 유명한 피아니스트가 될 거야.

여: 고마워!

단·어·및·표·현

classical[klǽsikəl] 형 (음악이) 클래식의, 고전적인

musical instrument 악기

grow up 어른이 되다, 자라다

I'm sure (that) 분명히 ~이다

08 심정추론 ▶ 정답 ③

듣·기·대·본

M: Hey, Jane! What are you doing here alone?

W: I'm waiting for Emma. By the way, what time is it?

M: It's 2 o'clock.

W: Not again! She's 30 minutes late. She's always late.

M: Calm down! Why don't you sit down here and wait for her?

우·리·말·해·석

① 흥분한   ② 행복한   ③ 화난   ④ 걱정스러운   ⑤ 침착한

남: 이봐, Jane! 너 여기서 혼자 뭘 하고 있니?

여: Emma를 기다리고 있어. 그나저나, 몇 시야?

남: 2시야.

여: 또야! 그녀가 30분이나 늦네. 그녀는 항상 늦어.

남: 진정해! 여기 앉아서 그녀를 기다리는 게 어떻겠니?

단·어·및·표·현

wait for ~ ~을 기다리다

Not again! 또야!

calm down 진정하다, 진정시키다

09 할일파악(대화직후) ▶ 정답 ①

듣·기·대·본

M: Honey, are we almost ready for the camping trip?

W: Almost! Did you pack the sleeping bags?

M: Yes, they're already in the car.

W: Great. What about the cooler?

M: It's ready, too.

W: Perfect. Oh! I forgot about the lanterns.

M: Don't worry. I'll put them in the car right now.

우·리·말·해·석

남: 여보, 우리 캠핑 여행 준비 거의 다 됐어요?

여: 거의요! 당신은 침낭을 챙겼나요?

남: 네, 그것들은 벌써 차에 있어요.

여: 잘했어요. 아이스박스는요?

남: 그것도 준비됐어요.

여: 완벽해요. 아! 랜턴을 잊었네요.

남: 걱정 마요. 제가 그것들을 지금 당장 차에 넣어둘게요.

단·어·및·표·현

pack [pæk] [동] (여행) 짐을 챙기다, 싸다
sleeping bag 침낭
cooler [kúːlər] [명] 아이스박스
forget [fərgét] [동] 잊다
lantern [lǽntərn] [명] 랜턴, 손전등

10 대화화제추론 ▶ 정답 ①

듣·기·대·본

W: Sir, you can't take pictures inside the museum.
M: I have to take a picture of this old dish. This is my history homework.
W: The camera flash can damage the artwork.
M: Then, what should I do?
W: There is a photo book. We sell it in the gift shop.
M: Okay.

우·리·말·해·석

여: 손님, 박물관 안에서는 사진을 찍으실 수 없습니다.
남: 저는 이 오래된 접시의 사진을 찍어야 해요. 이건 제 역사 숙제라고요.
여: 카메라의 플래시가 예술품들을 손상시킬 수 있어요.
남: 그러면 저는 어떻게 해야 하죠?
여: 사진책자가 있어요. 기념품점에서 팔고 있죠.
남: 알았어요.

단·어·및·표·현

take a picture 사진을 찍다
damage [dǽmidʒ] [동] 손상시키다

11 특정정보파악(교통수단) ▶ 정답 ④

듣·기·대·본

W: Jake, how are you going to get home? Your car is at the repair shop, isn't it?
M: Yeah. I'll have to take the subway today.
W: I can give you a ride home if you'd like.
M: Really? I'd appreciate that.
W: Great! Meet me downstairs in 10 minutes.
M: Okay. Thanks, Rina!

우·리·말·해·석

여: Jake, 너 집에 어떻게 갈 거야? 네 차는 정비소에 있잖아, 그렇지 않니?
남: 응. 나는 오늘 지하철을 타야 할 거야.
여: 네가 원한다면 내가 너를 집에 태워줄 수 있어.
남: 정말? 그렇게 해주면 고맙겠어.
여: 좋아! 10분 후에 아래층에서 만나.
남: 알았어. 고마워, Rina!

단·어·및·표·현

repair shop 정비소, 수리점
give + 사람 + a ride (차 등으로) ~을 태워주다
appreciate [əpríːʃièit] [동] 고마워하다, 환영하다

12 이유파악 ▶ 정답 ③

듣·기·대·본

M: Megan, where are you going?
W: I'm going to the museum to help with the history tour.
M: That sounds interesting. What do you do on the tour?
W: I guide students and explain the history of Korean artifacts.
M: That's great! You really like history, right?
W: Yes. I'm so happy to volunteer as a tour guide.

우·리·말·해·석

남: Megan, 너 어디 가는 거야?
여: 난 역사 투어를 도우러 박물관에 가는 중이야.
남: 재미있겠다. 그 투어에서 너는 무슨 일을 해?
여: 난 학생들을 안내하고 한국 유물들의 역사를 설명해.
남: 멋지다! 넌 역사를 정말 좋아하는구나, 그렇지?
여: 응. 투어 가이드로 자원 봉사할 수 있어서 정말 행복해.

단·어·및·표·현

museum [mju(ː)zí(ː)əm] [명] 박물관
guide [gaid] [동] 안내하다 [명] 안내(원)
explain [ikspléin] [동] 설명하다
artifact [áːrtəfæ̀kt] [명] 유물
volunteer [vɑ̀ləntíər] [동] 자원 봉사로 하다

13 대화장소추론 ▶ 정답 ②

듣·기·대·본

W: Can I help you?
M: Yes, please. I'm looking for a book. It's about Beethoven.
W: Do you know the title of the book?
M: It's *The Life of Beethoven*.
W: Oh, sorry. It's sold out right now. But we'll have more on Monday.
M: Really? Thanks.

우·리·말·해·석

① 음반 가게 ② 서점 ③ 식당 ④ 도서관 ⑤ 박물관

여: 도와드릴까요?
남: 네. 책을 하나 찾고 있는데요. 베토벤에 관한 책이에요.
여: 책 제목을 아세요?
남: "베토벤의 일생"이에요.
여: 아, 죄송합니다. 그건 지금 다 팔렸어요. 하지만 월요일에 책이 더 들어올 거예요.
남: 정말요? 고맙습니다.

단·어·및·표·현

sold out 다 팔린, 매진된

LISTENING ADVICE

'I'm looking for a book. It's about Beethoven.'에서 'Beethoven'의 [b] 발음과 [v] 발음의 차이에 주의하며 잘 들어보세요.

● **How to pronounce [b], [v]**

[b]는 우리말 [ㅂ] 발음과 같고, [v] 발음은 [f] 발음과 같이 윗니로 아랫입술을 살짝 물었다가 [브]라고 발음하면 됩니다.

14 그림정보파악–지도 ▶ 정답 ③

듣·기·대·본

M: Excuse me. How do I get to the department store?
W: Go straight to Main Street and turn left.
M: Go straight and turn left?
W: Yes. Then, walk straight a little further. You'll see it on your left next to the restaurant.
M: It will be on my left?

W: Yes. It's across from the bank.
M: Thank you.

우·리·말·해·석

남: 실례합니다. 백화점까지 어떻게 가죠?
여: Main Street까지 쭉 가서 왼쪽으로 도세요.
남: 쭉 가서 왼쪽으로 돌라고요?
여: 네. 그런 다음, 조금 더 쭉 걸어가세요. 당신의 왼쪽으로 식당 옆에 그
것이 보일 겁니다.
남: 제 왼쪽에 있을 거라고요?
여: 네. 은행 건너편이에요.
남: 감사합니다.

단·어·및·표·현
further [fə́ːrðər] ᄝ 더, 더 멀리

15 부탁(요청)한일파악 ▶ 정답 ③

듣·기·대·본

M: Grace, what time is my flight supposed to leave tomorrow?
W: 11:50, sir.
M: I think I can't make it. The meeting in the morning won't finish on time.
W: Do you want me to reschedule it?
M: Yes, please. One would be good for me.

우·리·말·해·석

남: Grace, 내일 내 항공편이 몇 시에 출발하기로 돼 있죠?
여: 11시 50분입니다.
남: 그 시간에 맞추기 어려울 것 같아요. 아침 회의가 제시간에 끝나지 않
을 거예요.
여: 제가 일정을 변경할까요?
남: 네, 그렇게 해주세요. 1시가 좋을 것 같아요.

단·어·및·표·현
reschedule [rìːskédʒuːl] ᄝ 일정을 변경하다

📢 **LISTENING ADVICE**

'What time is my flight supposed to leave tomorrow?'에서
'flight'는 'gh'가 묵음으로 소리가 나지 않아 [플라잍]이라고 발음되고,
'supposed to'는 'd'가 탈락되어 [서포즈투]라고 발음됩니다.

---

16 제안파악 ▶ 정답 ④

듣·기·대·본

M: Taylor, you look sad! What's wrong?
W: Well, I got a new cat last weekend, but she doesn't seem to like me.
M: Why do you think so?
W: Whenever she sees me, she tries to hide or escape.
M: You should try using a cat toy. Why don't you buy one?
W: Good idea! I'll go buy a toy today.

우·리·말·해·석

남: Taylor, 슬퍼 보여! 무슨 일이야?
여: 음, 나는 지난 주말에 새 고양이를 얻었는데, 고양이가 나를 좋아하지
않는 것 같아.
남: 왜 그렇게 생각해?
여: 그녀는 나를 볼 때마다, 숨거나 도망치려고 해.
남: 너 고양이 장난감을 사용해 봐. 하나 사는 게 어때?
여: 좋은 생각이네! 오늘 가서 장난감을 사야겠어.

단·어·및·표·현
wrong [rɔ(ː)ŋ] ᄒ (잘못된) 일이 있는, 이상이 있는
weekend [wíːkènd] ᄝ 주말
seem [siːm] ᄝ ~인 것 같다, ~처럼 보이다
whenever [hwenévər] ᄌ ~할 때마다
hide [haid] ᄝ 숨다
escape [iskéip] ᄝ 달아나다, 탈출하다

17 한일파악 ▶ 정답 ③

듣·기·대·본

W: Harry, what did you do yesterday?
M: I went to the bookstore near Central Park. What about you, Linda?
W: I went to a flea market.
M: Cool! Did you buy anything interesting?
W: I bought a used camera. I love taking pictures.
M: Really? Can you take a picture of me?
W: Sure. I will bring my camera tomorrow.

우·리·말·해·석

여: Harry, 너는 어제 무엇을 했니?
남: 나는 센트럴파크 근처에 있는 서점에 갔어. 너는 무엇을 했니, Linda?
여: 나는 벼룩시장에 갔어.
남: 멋지다! 너는 무언가 흥미로운 걸 샀니?
여: 나는 중고 카메라 한 대를 샀어. 나는 사진 찍는 것을 아주 좋아해.
남: 정말로? 나의 사진도 찍어 줄 수 있니?
여: 물론이지. 내가 내일 내 카메라를 가지고 올게.

단·어·및·표·현
flea market 벼룩시장
used [juːzd] ᄒ 중고의
take a picture 사진을 찍다

18 직업추론 ▶ 정답 ③

듣·기·대·본

M: May I help you?
W: Yes. I'd like to buy some medicine for a stomachache.
M: Here you are. Take two pills three times a day.
W: Do I have to take them after meals?
M: Yes. If you start to feel better, take one pill at a time.
W: Okay. And can I get some bandages, too?
M: Sure.

우·리·말·해·석

남: (무엇을) 도와드릴까요?
여: 네. 배탈에 듣는 약을 좀 사고 싶어요.
남: 여기 있습니다. 하루 세 번 두 알씩 복용하세요.
여: 제가 그것들을 식후에 복용해야 하나요?
남: 네. 만약 나아지기 시작하면, 한 번에 한 알씩 복용하세요.
여: 알겠습니다. 그리고 붕대도 좀 살 수 있을까요?
남: 물론이죠.

단·어·및·표·현
medicine [médisin] ᄝ 약
stomachache [stʌ́məkèik] ᄝ 배탈, 복통
take [teik] ᄝ (약을) 복용하다
bandage [bǽndidʒ] ᄝ 붕대

19 알맞은응답찾기 ▶ 정답 ②

듣·기·대·본

M: Hi, Michelle. How was your weekend?
W: It was terrible.
M: Oh, why? You were supposed to go camping with your friends, weren't you?
W: Yes, I was, but we couldn't go.
M: What happened?
W: It was pouring, so we had to cancel the trip.
M: You must have been disappointed.

우·리·말·해·석

① 그거 좋네.
② 너는 틀림없이 실망했겠구나.
③ 부산에 사는 친구를 방문했어.
④ 도서관에 가는 중이야.
⑤ 모든 게 괜찮을 거야.

남: 안녕, Michelle. 주말 어땠니?
여: 정말 안 좋았어.
남: 오, 왜? 너 친구들이랑 캠핑 가기로 되어 있었잖아, 안 그래?
여: 응, 맞아. 그렇지만 우린 갈 수 없었어.
남: 무슨 일 있었어?
여: 비가 쏟아져서 우리는 여행을 취소해야만 했어.
남: 너는 틀림없이 실망했겠구나.

단·어·및·표·현

be supposed to + 동사원형 ~하기로 되어 있다
cancel [kǽnsəl] [동] 취소하다

20 일맞은응답찾기 ▶ 정답 ⑤

듣·기·대·본

W: Do you have any plans for this afternoon?
M: Yes, I am going to the pet shop.
W: Wow, are you getting a pet?
M: Yes, I am. Will you come with me?
W: Of course, I will. What kind of pet do you want?
M: A goldfish.

우·리·말·해·석

① 나 배고파. ② 아니, 안 했어. ③ 수의사.
④ 재미있겠다. ⑤ 금붕어.

여: 오늘 오후에 계획 있니?
남: 응, 반려동물 가게에 갈 거야.
여: 와, 반려동물 살 거니?
남: 응, 그래. 나랑 같이 갈래?
여: 물론이지, 같이 갈게. 어떤 종류의 반려동물을 원하는데?
남: 금붕어.

단·어·및·표·현

pet [pet] [명] 반려동물

Words & Expressions Review

1. 반려동물	2. 붕대	3. 선택하다, 사다
4. ~하기로 되어있다	5. ~할 준비가 되다	6. 손상시키다
7. 더	8. (아마) ~일 것이다	9. 사고
10. 악기	11. 더, 더 멀리	12. 다 팔린, 매진된
13. 온종일	14. ~하는 게 좋다	15. 역사
16. 고마워하다	17. 팔다	18. ~하는 게 어때?
19. ~과 관련된	20. 지역	21. (여행) 짐을 챙기다, 싸다
22. 정비소, 수리점	23. 약	24. 또야!
25. 벼룩시장	26. 아이스박스	27. 실망한
28. 유물	29. 일정을 변경하다	30. 진정하다, 진정시키다
31. ~할 것을 잊다	32. (장애물을) 제거하다, 치우다	33. 유명한
34. 박물관	35. ~을 찾다	36. 많이, 심하게, 세게
37. 기념품점	38. 사냥하다	39. 조금
40. 여러 가지의, 몇몇의	41. 예술품	42. 취소하다
43. 클래식의, 고전적인	44. 숙제	

Listening Test

영어듣기 모의고사 21회

|정|답|

01 ①	02 ④	03 ③	04 ③	05 ②
06 ③	07 ②	08 ①	09 ④	10 ④
11 ①	12 ⑤	13 ③	14 ④	15 ⑤
16 ④	17 ③	18 ④	19 ②	20 ③

01 그림정보파악(담화) ▶ 정답 ①

듣·기·대·본

W: I am a bird. I have wings, but I cannot fly. Instead, I can run very fast. I can run at speeds of over 70 kilometers per hour. My legs are long and very strong. My neck is very long, too. What am I?

우·리·말·해·석

여: 나는 새입니다. 나는 날개가 있지만 날 수는 없습니다. 대신에 나는 빨리 달릴 수 있습니다. 나는 시간당 70킬로미터 이상의 속도로 달릴 수 있습니다. 나의 다리는 길고 매우 튼튼합니다. 나의 목도 아주 깁니다. 나는 무엇인가요?

단·어·및·표·현

per hour 시간당

02 그림정보파악(대화) ▶ 정답 ④

듣·기·대·본

M: May I help you?
W: Yes, I'm looking for a mug for a friend.
M: What about this one with a big heart on it? It's our most popular one.
W: I like the heart, but I think it's too big.
M: Then, you may like this one. It has many small hearts on it.
W: It's great! I'll take it.

우·리·말·해·석

남: (무엇을) 도와드릴까요?
여: 네, 저는 친구에게 줄 머그잔 하나를 찾고 있어요.
남: 위에 큰 하트가 그려진 이것은 어떠세요? 그것은 저희의 가장 인기 있는 제품이에요.

여: 저는 하트 모양은 맘에 들지만, 그게 너무 크다고 생각해요.
남: 그러면, 당신은 아마 이것을 좋아하실 거예요. 그것은 위에 작은 하트들이 많이 그려져 있어요.
여: 좋네요! 전 그걸로 할게요.

look for ~ ~을 찾다
popular[pápjulər] 형 인기 있는
take[teik] 동 사다, 선택하다

03 날씨파악-그림 ▶ 정답 ③

듣·기·대·본

M: Good morning, everyone! This is the weekly weather report. There will be strong winds on Monday, but on Tuesday, we will have clear skies. On Wednesday, it will rain in the morning, but the rain will stop in the afternoon.

우·리·말·해·석

남: 좋은 아침입니다, 여러분! 주간 일기예보입니다. 월요일에는 강풍이 있겠습니다만, 화요일에는 하늘이 맑겠습니다. 수요일에는 오전에 비가 오겠지만 오후에는 비가 그칠 것입니다.

단·어·및·표·현

weekly[wíːkli] 형 주간의, 매주의
weather report 일기예보
strong wind 강풍

04 마지막말의도파악 ▶ 정답 ③

듣·기·대·본

W: Hey, Kevin, what's up?
M: Hi, Wendy. Do you want to go bowling after school?
W: Oh, I don't think I can.
M: Why not?
W: I have an awards ceremony to attend. I won first prize in a writing competition.
M: Good for you! That's an amazing achievement.

우·리·말·해·석

여: 이봐, Kevin, 잘 지내?
남: 안녕, Wendy. 오늘 방과 후에 볼링 치러 갈래?
여: 오, 나는 못 갈 것 같아.
남: 왜 못 가?
여: 나는 참석해야 할 시상식이 있어. 내가 글쓰기 대회에서 1등 상을 받았거든.
남: 잘했다! 놀라운 성취구나.

단·어·및·표·현

What's up? 잘 지냈어?, 요즘 어때?
awards ceremony 시상식
win first prize 1등 상을 타다
competition[kàmpətíʃən] 명 대회, 시합
achievement[ətʃíːvmənt] 명 성취, 업적

05 담화미언급 ▶ 정답 ②

듣·기·대·본

W: Hi, class. Let me introduce my best friend to you. Her name is Da-won Kim. She goes to Suwon Middle School. She is very tall and I like her short hair very much. Her hobby is dancing to pop music. She is popular among her classmates because she is kind and gentle.

우·리·말·해·석

여: 안녕하세요, 급우 여러분. 저의 가장 친한 친구를 여러분에게 소개하겠습니다. 그녀의 이름은 김다원입니다. 그녀는 수원 중학교에 다닙니다. 그녀는 매우 키가 크고, 저는 그녀의 짧은 머리를 아주 좋아합니다. 그녀의 취미는 대중 음악에 맞춰 춤추는 것입니다. 그녀는 그녀의 반 친구들 사이에서 인기가 많은데, 왜냐하면 그녀가 친절하고 온화하기 때문입니다.

단·어·및·표·현

introduce[ìntrədjúːs] 동 ~를 소개하다
hobby[hábi] 명 취미
dance to + 명사 ~에 맞추어 춤추다
pop music 대중 음악
among[əmʌ́ŋ] 전 ~사이에서, ~중에서
gentle[dʒéntl] 형 온화한, 순한

06 수치파악 ▶ 정답 ③

듣·기·대·본

W: Welcome, Josh. Was it hard to find my place?
M: Not at all. I'm late because I missed the 5 p.m. bus. Sorry.
W: No worries. Dinner will be ready at 6:30 p.m., so you got here in time.
M: That's a relief. And what a nice smell!
W: I have a pie in the oven. It'll be done at 6 p.m.
M: It's 6 p.m. now. You should take it out.

우·리·말·해·석

여: 어서 와, Josh. 내 집을 찾는 것이 어려웠어?
남: 전혀 아냐. 내가 오후 5시 버스를 놓쳐서 늦었어. 미안해.
여: 걱정 마. 저녁은 오후 6시 반에 준비가 다 될 거니까, 너는 시간 맞춰 여기 왔어.
남: 그거 안심되네. 그리고 정말 좋은 냄새가 난다!
여: 오븐 안에 파이가 있어. 그건 오후 6시에 다 될 거야.
남: 지금 오후 6시야. 너는 그것을 꺼내야 해.

단·어·및·표·현

place[pleis] 명 집
miss[mis] 동 놓치다
in time 시간 맞춰
relief[rilíːf] 명 안심

07 장래희망추론 ▶ 정답 ②

듣·기·대·본

W: What would you like to be when you grow up?
M: I'm very interested in music. I want to be a musician.
W: It will be difficult to succeed in that field.
M: I know, but I really enjoy playing the piano and listening to music.
W: I understand. I feel the same when I write something. My dream is to write screenplays.
M: That sounds wonderful! I look forward to seeing your stories on screen.

우·리·말·해·석

여: 넌 커서 뭐가 되고 싶니?
남: 난 음악에 매우 관심이 있어. 음악가가 되고 싶어.
여: 그 분야에서 성공하는 건 어려울 텐데.

남: 알아. 하지만 난 피아노를 치는 것과 음악을 듣는 것을 정말 즐겨.
여: 이해해. 나도 뭔가를 쓸 때 같은 느낌이 들거든. 내 꿈은 시나리오를 쓰는 거야.
남: 멋지구나! 네 작품을 영화에서 볼 수 있길 기대해.

단•어•및•표•현

succeed[səksíːd] [동] 성공하다
screenplay[skrínplei] [명] 시나리오, 영화 대본

08 심정추론 ▶ 정답 ①

듣•기•대•본

M: Mona, what's up? You look different today.
W: Well, it's because of the audition.
M: You mean, the dance audition?
W: Yeah, I made it through the first round!
M: Really? I'm so happy for you. When is the second round?
W: Next week. I'm practicing really hard. I can't wait for it!

우•리•말•해•석

남: Mona, 무슨 일이야? 너 오늘 다르게 보인다.
여: 음, 오디션 때문이야.
남: 댄스 오디션 말하는 거니?
여: 응, 내가 첫 번째 라운드를 통과했어!
남: 정말이야? 정말 기쁘다. 두 번째 라운드는 언제야?
여: 다음 주야. 난 정말 열심히 연습하고 있어. 그날이 정말 기대돼!

단•어•및•표•현

audition[ɔːdíʃən] [명] (가수 · 배우 등의) 오디션
make it through ~을 통과하다
round[raund] [명] (토너먼트 경기의) 라운드, 승부, 시합
practice[prǽktis] [동] 연습하다
can't wait for ~이 정말 기대되다

09 할일파악(대화직후) ▶ 정답 ④

듣•기•대•본

M: Did you finish writing the script for the school broadcast?
W: Not yet. I still need some comments from the event organizer.
M: Did you find any information on the school website?
W: I did, but it doesn't have any quotes.
M: Then why don't you go and interview Mr. Kim? He planned the whole event.
W: That's a good idea. I'll go and interview him now.

우•리•말•해•석

남: 너는 학교 방송의 대본 쓰는 것을 끝냈니?
여: 아직. 난 아직 행사 주최자에게 의견을 좀 더 받아야 해.
남: 학교 홈페이지에서 정보는 찾아봤어?
여: 찾아봤는데, 어떤 인용문도 없어.
남: 그럼 김 선생님께 가서 인터뷰하는 건 어때? 그가 전체 행사를 계획하셨어.
여: 좋은 생각이야. 지금 그에게 가서 인터뷰할게.

단•어•및•표•현

broadcast[brɔ́ːdkæ̀st] [명] 방송
comment[kάment] [명] 의견
organizer[ɔ́ːrgənàizər] [명] 주최자
quote[kwout] [명] 인용문, 인용 어구
whole[houl] [형] 전체의, 전부의

10 대화화제추론 ▶ 정답 ④

듣•기•대•본

W: Minsu, I heard about your environment club. Can I join?
M: Anyone interested in protecting the environment is welcome.
W: What kind of activities do you guys do?
M: We meet every Saturday to clean up the neighborhood.
W: Okay. I'll see you on Saturday then.

우•리•말•해•석

여: 민수야, 나 네 환경 동아리에 대해 들었어. 내가 가입할 수 있을까?
남: 환경을 보호하는 데 관심 있는 사람이라면 누구든지 환영이야.
여: 너희는 어떤 종류의 활동을 하니?
남: 우리는 매주 토요일에 동네 청소를 하려고 만나.
여: 알겠어. 그럼 토요일에 보자.

단•어•및•표•현

environment[inváirənmənt] [명] 환경
protect[prətékt] [동] 보호하다

11 특정정보파악(교통수단) ▶ 정답 ①

듣•기•대•본

(Cell phone rings.)
M: Hey, Gina!
W: Hey, Minho! Do you want to go to Island Park?
M: Sure. How do we get there?
W: We can ride our bikes.
M: Hey, there's a new ferry service. How about trying it?
W: A ferry sounds a little scary.
M: It's perfectly safe. Trust me.
W: Okay, then. Let's go now!

우•리•말•해•석

(휴대폰이 울린다.)
남: 안녕, Gina!
여: 안녕, 민호! 너 아일랜드 공원에 가기 원해?
남: 물론이지. 거기에 어떻게 가?
여: 우리는 우리의 자전거를 타고 갈 수 있어.
남: 이봐, 새로운 연락선 운항편이 있어. 그거 타보는 거 어때?
여: 연락선은 조금 무섭게 들리는데.
남: 그건 완전히 안전해. 날 믿어.
여: 그래, 그럼. 지금 가자!

단•어•및•표•현

ferry service 연락선 운항
perfectly[pə́ːrfiktli] [부] 완전히, 지극히

12 이유파악 ▶ 정답 ⑤

듣•기•대•본

M: Hyomin, what are you doing?
W: I'm writing a card to Ms. Newman, Dad.
M: You mean your English teacher?
W: Yes. She is moving to a different school, so the whole class is leaving her a message.
M: The whole class? That's why the card is so big.
W: Yes, we are saying our thanks and good-byes.

우•리•말•해•석

남: 효민아, 너 뭐하고 있니?
여: 저는 Newman 선생님께 드릴 카드를 쓰고 있어요, 아빠.

남: 너는 네 영어 선생님 말하는 거니?
여: 네. 그녀는 다른 학교로 옮기셔서 (전근 가셔서), 반 전체가 그녀에게 메시지를 남기고 있어요.
남: 반 전체가? 그래서 카드가 엄청 큰 거구나.
여: 네, 저희는 (선생님에 대한) 저희의 감사와 작별 인사를 전하고 있어요.

단·어·및·표·현
move[muːv] 동 (집, 근무지 등을) 옮기다, 이사하다
leave[liːv] 동 남기다

13 대화장소추론 ▶ 정답 ③

듣·기·대·본
M: Do you see that big statue over there?
W: Yeah, and look at all those paintings on the wall.
M: They're really beautiful. But we have to be quiet, okay?
W: Okay. There are so many people here.
M: Right, but I'm still glad we came today.
W: Yeah, me too.
M: Let's go check out the next exhibit.

우·리·말·해·석
남: 저기에 있는 저 큰 조각상이 보이니?
여: 응, 그리고 벽에 있는 모든 그림들을 봐.
남: 그것들은 정말 아름다워. 하지만 우린 조용히 해야 해, 알았지?
여: 응, 여긴 정말 많은 사람들이 있어.
남: 맞아, 하지만 난 우리가 오늘 왔다는 게 여전히 기뻐.
여: 응, 나도 그래.
남: 다음 전시품을 보러 가자.

단·어·및·표·현
statue[stǽtʃuː] 명 조각상
check out (흥미로운 것을) 보다, 살펴보다
exhibit[igzíbit] 명 전시품

14 그림정보파악-위치 ▶ 정답 ④

듣·기·대·본
W: Mark, can you turn down the TV volume, please?
M: Sure, but I don't know where the TV remote control is.
W: I think I saw it on the sofa.
M: It's not there. It must be somewhere else.
W: Oh, it's right there, next to the flower vase.
M: I see it! I'll turn down the volume now.

우·리·말·해·석
여: Mark, TV 음량을 낮춰주겠니?
남: 물론이지, 하지만 난 TV 리모컨이 어디 있는지 모르겠어.
여: 내가 소파 위에서 그것을 본 것 같아.
남: 그건 거기에 없어. 그건 어딘가 다른 곳에 있는 게 틀림없어.
여: 아, 바로 저기에 있어, 꽃병 옆에.
남: 난 그것이 보여! 내가 지금 소리를 낮출게.

단·어·및·표·현
turn down (소리, 온도 등을) 낮추다
volume[váljuːm] 명 (TV · 라디오 등의) 음량, 용량

15 부탁(요청)한일파악 ▶ 정답 ⑤

듣·기·대·본
(Cell phone rings.)
M: Hi, Kate. I'm at the supermarket. Do you need anything?
W: No, but can I ask you a favor?
M: Sure, what can I do for you?

W: Can you pick up my shirt at the cleaner's on your way home?
M: Sure, no problem.

우·리·말·해·석
(휴대전화가 울린다.)
남: 안녕, Kate. 난 슈퍼마켓에 있어. 뭐 필요한 거라도 있어?
여: 아니, 하지만 나 너한테 부탁 좀 해도 될까?
남: 물론이야, 뭘 도와줄까?
여: 집에 오는 길에 세탁소에서 내 셔츠 좀 찾아다 줄 수 있니?
남: 물론이지, 문제없어.

단·어·및·표·현
ask A a favor A에게 부탁하다

🦻 LISTENING ADVICE
연음이란 단어와 단어를 연결하여 마치 한 단어처럼 발음하는 것을 말합니다. 특히 앞 단어가 자음으로 끝나고 뒤 단어가 모음으로 시작할 때 이러한 연음현상이 종종 발생합니다. 예를 들면 'pick up'은 [픽업]으로 소리 나기보다는 [피컵]으로 자연스럽게 연결되어 소리 납니다. 마찬가지로 'ask you' 또한 [애스크 유]가 아닌 [애스큐]라고 발음됩니다.

16 제안파악 ▶ 정답 ④

듣·기·대·본
W: Joel, what are you doing here?
M: I'm waiting for a bus to go home. But it's taking so long.
W: Oh, the buses aren't running as usual. There's a big parade today.
M: Really? I didn't know that. What should I do?
W: How about walking home?
M: Yeah, walking home will be better.

우·리·말·해·석
여: Joel, 너 여기서 뭐 하고 있니?
남: 나는 집에 가기 위해 버스를 기다리고 있어. 근데 너무 오래 걸려.
여: 오, 버스들은 평소처럼 운행하지 않고 있어. 오늘 큰 퍼레이드가 있거든.
남: 정말? 난 그것을 몰랐어. 어떡하지?
여: 집에 걸어가는 것이 어때?
남: 그래, 집에 걸어가는 게 더 나을 거야.

단·어·및·표·현
run[rʌn] 동 (버스 · 기차 등이) 운행하다, 다니다
as usual 평소처럼, 늘 그렇듯이

17 한일파악 ▶ 정답 ③

듣·기·대·본
M: Jessie, how was your holiday?
W: It was great. I went on a trip with my family.
M: Oh, where did you go?
W: We went to Jeju Island. I had so much fun! How did you spend your holiday?
M: I learned how to play the piano.
W: That's wonderful!

우·리·말·해·석
남: Jessie, 너의 휴일은 어땠어?
여: 그것은 훌륭했어. 나는 내 가족과 여행을 갔어.
남: 오, 어디에 갔니?

여: 우리는 제주도에 갔어. 나는 많이 재미있었어! 너는 너의 휴일을 어떻게 보냈니?
남: 나는 피아노 치는 법을 배웠어.
여: 그거 멋진데!

단·어·및·표·현
holiday [hάlədèi] 명 휴일, 휴가
spend [spend] 동 (시간을) 보내다

18 직업추론 ▶ 정답 ④

듣·기·대·본
M: You look tired. Did you work late last night?
W: Yes. I only got three hours of sleep because I had to work.
M: Oh, how's your work going?
W: Actually, very good. My team just finished developing a new educational software program.
M: Good for you. You are a very brilliant programmer.
W: Thank you. This new computer software will help students to learn math more easily.

우·리·말·해·석
① 요리사　　　　　② 선생님　　　　　③ 관광 안내원
④ 컴퓨터 프로그래머　　　⑤ 의사

남: 피곤해 보이세요. 어젯밤에 야근했어요?
여: 네. 일을 해야 해서 3시간밖에 못 잤어요.
남: 오, 일은 잘 돼 가요?
여: 사실, 아주 잘되고 있어요. 우리 팀이 새로운 교육용 소프트웨어 프로그램 개발을 막 끝냈어요.
남: 잘됐군요. 당신은 정말 능력이 뛰어난 프로그래머예요.
여: 고마워요. 이 새로운 컴퓨터 소프트웨어는 학생들이 수학을 더 쉽게 배우도록 해줄 거예요.

단·어·및·표·현
develop [divéləp] 동 개발하다

19 알맞은응답찾기 ▶ 정답 ②

듣·기·대·본
W: Dad, when does the movie start?
M: In 10 minutes.
W: Oh, no! We still have to buy the tickets.
M: And we need to get some popcorn, too.
W: Okay! Let's go now!
M: Let's hurry up.

우·리·말·해·석
① 나는 너무 피곤해.
② 서두르자.
③ 그건 날 위한 것이 아냐.
④ 너는 쉬는 게 좋겠어.
⑤ 나는 액션 영화를 안 좋아해.

여: 아빠, 영화는 언제 시작해요?
남: 10분 후에.
여: 오, 안돼! 저희는 아직 표를 사야 해요.
남: 그리고 우리는 팝콘도 좀 사야 해.
여: 알겠어요! 지금 가요!
남: 서두르자.

단·어·및·표·현
have to + 동사원형 ~해야 한다

20 알맞은응답찾기 ▶ 정답 ③

듣·기·대·본
M: Mom, can we go get some ice cream later?
W: Sure, Sam. But why do you want to go later?
M: I want to finish watching this movie first.
W: Well, you know it's going to get hotter in the afternoon.
M: Oh, I didn't think about that. I guess it's much cooler in the morning.
W: Yes. So, shall we go now?
M: Okay. I'll be ready in 5 minutes.

우·리·말·해·석
① 아뇨, 저는 조깅을 좋아하지 않아요.
② 문제없어요. 나중에 전화할게요.
③ 알겠어요. 5분 안에 준비할게요.
④ 제 노트북을 사용하셔도 돼요.
⑤ 저는 바닐라 아이스크림을 좋아하지 않아요.

남: 엄마, 나중에 아이스크림 사갈까요?
여: 물론이지, Sam. 근데 왜 나중에 가고 싶어 하는 거니?
남: 우선 이 영화 보는 것을 마치고 싶어요.
여: 음, 오후에 더 더워진다는 것을 너도 알잖니.
남: 오, 그건 생각 안 했어요. 아침이 훨씬 더 시원한 것 같아요.
여: 맞아. 그래서, 우리 지금 갈까?
남: 알겠어요. 5분 안에 준비할게요.

단·어·및·표·현
later [léitər] 부 나중에, 후에
finish [fíniʃ] 동 마치다, 끝내다
get + 비교급 점점 더 ~해지다

Words & Expressions Review

1. 온화한, 순한	2. ~를 소개하다	3. ~에 관심이 있는
4. 평소처럼	5. 잘 지냈어?, 요즘 어때?	6. 분야, 들판
7. 시상식	8. ~을 기대하다	9. 교육용의
10. 날개	11. (가수·배우 등의) 오디션	12. 음량, 용량
13. 1등상을 타다	14. 휴일, 휴가	15. 보호하다
16. 남기다	17. ~을 통과하다	18. 집
19. (토너먼트 경기의) 라운드	20. ~이 정말 기대되다	21. 취미
22. 전체의, 전부의	23. (버스·기차 등이) 운행하다, 다니다	24. 놓치다
25. (소리를) 낮추다	26. 완전히, 지극히	27. 전시품
28. 성공하다	29. 연습하다	30. 개발하다
31. 대신에	32. 안심	33. 성취, 업적
34. 점점 더 ~해지다	35. A에게 부탁하다	36. 꽃병
37. 환경	38. 능력 있는, 뛰어난	39. 방송
40. 인용문, 인용 어구	41. 의견	42. 조각상
43. 튼튼한	44. 대회, 시합	

Listening Test

영어듣기 모의고사 22회

| 정 | 답 |

01 ④	02 ⑤	03 ②	04 ②	05 ⑤
06 ③	07 ④	08 ③	09 ④	10 ③
11 ⑤	12 ④	13 ④	14 ④	15 ①
16 ①	17 ②	18 ⑤	19 ⑤	20 ①

01 그림정보파악(담화) ▶ 정답 ④

듣·기·대·본

W: You can find this in your closet. This is in the shape of human shoulders. This is used to hang a coat, jacket, or dress. This prevents wrinkles in clothing. Sometimes, this has clips to hang skirts and pants. What is this?

우·리·말·해·석

여: 당신은 옷장에서 이것을 찾을 수 있습니다. 이것은 사람의 어깨 모양을 하고 있습니다. 이것은 코트, 재킷, 혹은 드레스를 거는 데 사용됩니다. 이것은 옷에 주름이 가는 것을 막아줍니다. 때때로, 이것에는 치마나 바지를 걸기 위한 집게가 달려 있습니다. 이것은 무엇일까요?

단·어·및·표·현

hang [hæŋ] [동] 걸다

02 그림정보파악(대화) ▶ 정답 ⑤

듣·기·대·본

W: Hi, I'm looking for a coin purse.
M: We have round ones and square ones.
W: I like square ones more.
M: Okay, how about this one with a duck on it?
W: Hmm… Do you have another one?
M: Sure, we also have this square one with a rabbit on it.
W: I like rabbits. I'll take it.

우·리·말·해·석

여: 안녕하세요, 저는 동전 지갑을 찾고 있어요.
남: 저희는 둥근 것들과 네모난 것들이 있습니다.
여: 저는 네모난 것들을 더 좋아해요.
남: 네, 위에 오리가 그려진 이것은 어떠세요?
여: 음… 다른 것이 있나요?
남: 물론이죠, 저희는 위에 토끼가 그려진 이 네모난 것도 있습니다.
여: 저는 토끼들을 좋아해요. 그걸로 할게요.

단·어·및·표·현

look for ~을 찾다
another [ənʌ́ðər] [형] 다른

03 날씨파악-그림 ▶ 정답 ②

듣·기·대·본

W: If you were planning to see the fireworks in the park this July 4th, don't worry because the weather will be beautiful. There will be early morning showers that will give way to sunny, clear skies in the afternoon. There will be winds coming in from the west to provide a nice, cool breeze by nightfall.

우·리·말·해·석

여: 이번 7월 4일에 공원에서 불꽃놀이를 구경할 계획이셨다면, 날씨가 매우 좋을 것이니 걱정하지 마세요. 아침 일찍 소나기가 온 후 오후에는 햇빛이 나고 맑은 하늘로 바뀌겠습니다. 서쪽에서 불어오는 기분 좋고 시원한 산들바람이 해질녘까지 불겠습니다.

단·어·및·표·현

fireworks [fáiərwə̀ːrks] [명] 불꽃놀이
shower [ʃáuər] [명] 소나기, 샤워
breeze [briːz] [명] 산들바람

04 마지막말의도파악 ▶ 정답 ②

듣·기·대·본

W: What did you do last night?
M: I watched the soccer game against Japan.
W: It must have been exciting.
M: Yes, I cheered for our victory with all my heart.
W: So, how did it go?
M: We won! I am so happy.
W: Congratulations! This calls for a celebration.

우·리·말·해·석

여: 너 어젯밤에 뭘 했니?
남: 나는 일본과의 축구 경기를 봤어.
여: 정말 흥미진진했겠다.
남: 응, 나는 우리의 승리를 위해 진심으로 응원했어.
여: 그래서, 어떻게 됐어?
남: 우리가 이겼어! 나는 너무 기뻐.
여: 축하해! 이건 축하할 일이야.

단·어·및·표·현

with all one's heart 진심으로
call for ~ ~을 필요로 하다, 요구하다
celebration [sèləbréiʃən] [명] 축하, 기념

05 담화미언급 ▶ 정답 ⑤

듣·기·대·본

W: This summer, we're having a swimming race for middle school students. It's scheduled for July 20th. There will be different swimming races like freestyle and backstroke. The competition will take place at the community pool. Students can sign up for the competition through their school's sports department or on the community center's website.

우·리·말·해·석

여: 이번 여름, 저희는 중학생들을 위한 수영 경기를 가질 것입니다. 그것은 7월 20일로 예정되어 있습니다. 자유형이나 배영 같은 다양한 수영 경기들이 있을 것입니다. 대회는 주민센터 수영장에서 열릴 것입니다. 학생들은 그들의 학교 운동부를 통하거나 혹은 주민센터 웹사이트 상에서 대회에 등록할 수 있습니다.

단·어·및·표·현

swimming race 수영 경기
schedule [skédʒuːl] [동] 예정하다
backstroke [bǽkstròuk] [명] (수영의) 배영
take place 열리다, 개최되다
sign up 등록하다, 신청하다
competition [kɑ̀mpətíʃən] [명] 대회
department [dipɑ́ːrtmənt] [명] 부, 부서

06 수치파악　　　　　　▶ 정답 ③

듣·기·대·본

M: Let's go to Disneyland.
W: That's a good idea. What time shall we meet?
M: How about meeting at 9:30 tomorrow?
W: 9:30? I think that is too early. I have something to do in the morning.
M: Then how about two hours later?
W: At 11:30? That will be fine.

우·리·말·해·석

남: 디즈니랜드에 가자.
여: 그거 좋은 생각이네. 몇 시에 만날까?
남: 내일 9시 30분에 만나는 게 어때?
여: 9시 30분? 그건 너무 이른 것 같아. 오전에 할 일이 있어.
남: 그럼, 두 시간 후는 어때?
여: 11시 30분에? 그게 좋겠어.

단·어·및·표·현

How about -ing? ~하는 게 어때?

07 장래희망추론　　　　　▶ 정답 ④

듣·기·대·본

W: Bill, what do you want to be when you grow up?
M: Well, when I was little, I wanted to be a doctor.
W: Really? I didn't know that you were interested in medical science.
M: I'm not interested in that anymore. Now, I want to become a singer.
W: I'm sure you will be a good singer. You sing very well.

우·리·말·해·석

여: Bill, 너는 커서 뭐가 되고 싶어?
남: 음, 어렸을 때는 의사가 되고 싶었어.
여: 정말? 난 네가 의학에 관심이 있는지 몰랐는데.
남: 더 이상 그것에 관심이 없어. 이제는 난 가수가 되고 싶어.
여: 난 네가 훌륭한 가수가 될 거라고 확신해. 넌 노래를 매우 잘하잖아.

단·어·및·표·현

medical science 의학

> 🦻 **LISTENING ADVICE**
>
> 첫 번째 단어 끝 자음과 두 번째 단어 첫 자음이 만나면 앞의 자음 소리가 탈락합니다. 'I want to become a singer'에서, 첫 번째 단어인 'want'의 [t]와 두 번째 단어인 'to'의 [t]가 만나면 'want'의 [t] 소리가 탈락합니다. 따라서 [원트]와 [투]가 만나 [트]가 탈락하여 [원투]로 발음됩니다.

08 심정추론　　　　　　▶ 정답 ③

듣·기·대·본

W: Wake up, Brian! You're late for school! It's already 9:30.
M: No, it's seven o'clock. Look at the clock.
W: The clock is broken. Look at my watch. It's 9:30.
M: Oh, no! I'm so late for school. It's embarrassing!
W: Come on. Don't cry over spilled milk. I'll drive you to school now.

우·리·말·해·석

여: 일어나, Brian! 학교에 늦었잖아! 벌써 9시 30분이야.
남: 아니에요, 7시예요. 시계를 보세요.

여: 그 시계는 고장 났어. 내 시계를 보렴. 9시 30분이야.
남: 오, 안 돼! 학교에 너무 늦었어요. 당혹스러워요!
여: 괜찮아. 지나간 일에 후회하지 마렴. 내가 지금 학교에 차로 데려다 줄게.

단·어·및·표·현

already [ɔːlrédi] ⓟ 벌써, 이미

09 할일파악(대화직후)　　　▶ 정답 ④

듣·기·대·본

W: Hi, Paul. What are you doing?
M: Hi, Ellen. I'm practicing a speech for the school election.
W: You're running for president, right? Good luck with that.
M: Thanks. I want to look calm and confident. I'm not sure I'm doing it right, though.
W: Then, how about taking a video of yourself giving a speech and reviewing it?
M: That's brilliant. I'll give it a try right away.

우·리·말·해·석

여: 안녕, Paul. 넌 뭐 하는 중이야?
남: 안녕, Ellen. 나는 학교 선거를 위해 연설을 연습하는 중이었어.
여: 너는 회장(선거)에 출마하지, 맞지? 행운을 빌게.
남: 고마워. 나는 차분하고 자신감 있어 보이고 싶어. 하지만 나는 내가 제대로 하고 있는지 확신할 수 없어.
여: 그러면, 너는 연설하는 너의 모습을 직접 동영상으로 찍어서 그것을 확인하는 건 어때?
남: 그거 아주 좋다. 나는 당장 한번 해봐야겠어.

단·어·및·표·현

run for ~ ~에 출마하다, 입후보하다
president [prézidənt] ⓝ 회장, 대통령
give a speech 연설하다
review [rivjúː] ⓥ 확인하다, 검토하다
give it a try 한번 해보다, 시도하다

10 대화화제추론　　　　　▶ 정답 ③

듣·기·대·본

W: Ted, here are some food safety tips for summer.
M: What are they, Mom?
W: First, always wash your hands before you eat.
M: I already know that. What else?
W: Don't keep food at room temperature for more than one hour on hot summer days.
M: Why is that?
W: Food spoils quickly in summer because the increase in temperature causes bacteria to multiply.

우·리·말·해·석

여: Ted, 몇 가지 여름철 식품 안전 관련 정보를 알려줄게.
남: 그게 뭐예요, 엄마?
여: 우선, 먹기 전에 항상 손을 씻어야 해.
남: 그건 이미 알고 있어요. 다른 건요?
여: 더운 여름날에는 한 시간 이상 상온에 음식을 두면 안 돼.
남: 왜요?
여: 여름에는 온도의 상승이 박테리아의 증식을 유발하기 때문에 음식이 빨리 상하거든.

단·어·및·표·현

room temperature 상온, 평상시 온도
spoil [spɔil] ⓥ 상하다, 썩다, 못 쓰게 되다
cause [kɔːz] ⓥ 유발하다, 야기하다

multiply [mʌ́ltəplài] [동] 증식시키다, 늘리다

11 특정정보파악(교통수단) ▶ 정답 ⑤

듣·기·대·본

W: Min, do you want to go to this new café in Seongsu-dong with me?
M: Yeah, sure. How can we get there?
W: Well, we can take the bus, the subway, or a taxi.
M: If we take a taxi, it will cost too much.
W: Then, should we take the bus?
M: I get car sick. So, I think we should take the subway.
W: Sounds good.

우·리·말·해·석

여: 민아, 너는 성수동에 있는 이 새로운 카페에 나와 함께 가고 싶니?
남: 응, 물론이지. 우리는 그곳에 어떻게 가지?
여: 음, 우리는 버스나 지하철, 또는 택시를 탈 수 있어.
남: 만약 우리가 택시를 타면, 비용이 너무 많이 들 거야.
여: 그러면, 우리는 버스를 타야 하나?
남: 나는 차멀미가 있어. 그래서, 우리는 지하철을 타야 할 것 같아.
여: 좋아.

단·어·및·표·현

take [teik] [동] (교통수단 · 도로 등을) 타다[이용하다]
cost [kɔ(:)st] [동] (값, 비용이) ~ 들다
car sick 차멀미

12 이유파악 ▶ 정답 ④

듣·기·대·본

M: Wonjee, where are you going?
W: I'm going to the library to buy some books.
M: Oh, are they selling used books?
W: Yes, they sell old books at a very low price. I want to buy a picture book for my cousin.
M: That's nice. Can I join you?
W: Of course. It'll be fun.

우·리·말·해·석

남: 원지야, 너 어디 가는 중이야?
여: 난 책들을 좀 사기 위해 도서관에 가는 중이야.
남: 아, 그들이 중고 서적들을 팔고 있니?
여: 응, 그들은 매우 저렴한 가격으로 오래된 책들을 팔아. 나는 나의 사촌을 위해 그림책을 사고 싶어.
남: 좋은걸. 내가 너와 함께 해도 돼?
여: 물론이지. 재밌을 거야.

단·어·및·표·현

sell [sel] [동] 팔다
used [ju:zd] [형] 중고의
at a low price 저렴한 가격으로, 저가로
picture book 그림책
cousin [kʌ́zən] [명] 사촌
join [dʒɔin] [동] 함께 하다, 합류하다

13 대화장소추론 ▶ 정답 ④

듣·기·대·본

M: I'd like to make a complaint about some apples I bought here yesterday.
W: What's the problem?
M: I found that some of them were rotten when I got home.
W: Oh, could you show them to me, please?
M: Here you go.
W: I'm sorry for the inconvenience. Would you like a refund?
M: Yes, please.

우·리·말·해·석

남: 저는 어제 제가 여기서 산 사과 몇 개에 대해 항의하고 싶어요.
여: 무엇이 문제일까요?
남: 집에 가서 저는 그것들 중 몇 개가 썩은 것을 발견했습니다.
여: 이런, 저에게 그것들을 보여주실 수 있을까요?
남: 여기 있습니다.
여: 불편을 끼쳐드려 죄송합니다. 환불하시겠습니까?
남: 네, 해주세요.

단·어·및·표·현

would like to + 동사원형 ~하고 싶다
make a complaint about ~에 대해 항의하다, 클레임을 걸다
rotten [rɑ́tn] [형] 썩은, 부패한
inconvenience [ìnkənví:njəns] [명] 불편, 애로

14 그림정보파악-지도 ▶ 정답 ④

듣·기·대·본

W: Excuse me, I'm trying to find a convenience store. Where can I find one?
M: Do you see the flower shop over there?
W: Yes, I see it.
M: Go straight to the flower shop and turn left.
W: Go straight and then turn left?
M: That's right. It will be on your left. It's between the restaurant and the bakery.
W: Thank you.

우·리·말·해·석

여: 실례합니다, 저는 편의점을 찾고 있어요. 제가 어디에서 찾을 수 있을까요?
남: 저쪽의 꽃집 보이세요?
여: 네, 보여요.
남: 꽃집으로 쭉 가서 왼쪽으로 도세요.
여: 쭉 가서 왼쪽으로 돌라고요?
남: 맞아요. 그것은 당신의 왼편에 있을 거예요. 그것은 음식점과 빵집 사이에 있어요.
여: 감사합니다.

단·어·및·표·현

convenience store 편의점
restaurant [réstərənt] [명] 음식점, 식당
bakery [béikəri] [명] 빵집

15 부탁(요청)한일파악 ▶ 정답 ①

듣·기·대·본

W: Paul, what are you looking for?
M: My favorite blue shirt, Mom.
W: It's in the top drawer.
M: Found it! Oh, Mom, take a look at this.
W: One of the buttons is missing.
M: Can you put a new button on the shirt?
W: Sure. I'll do it right away.

우·리·말·해·석

여: Paul, 넌 무엇을 찾고 있니?

남: 제가 가장 좋아하는 파란색 셔츠요, 엄마.
여: 그건 맨 위 서랍에 있단다.
남: 찾았어요! 오, 엄마, 이것 좀 보세요.
여: 단추 하나가 없어졌구나.
남: 셔츠에 새 단추를 달아 주실 수 있어요?
여: 물론이지. 곧바로 해 줄게.

단•어•및•표•현

take a look at ~을 보다
missing [mísiŋ] [형] 없어진
right away 곧바로, 즉시

16 제안파악 ▶ 정답 ①

듣•기•대•본

W: Ben, do you have a hobby?
M: Yes, I bake for fun. How about you?
W: I don't have a hobby, but I'd like to have one.
M: Do you like bread and cookies?
W: Yes, I love them.
M: Then why don't you join my baking class?
W: Sure, that sounds fun!

우•리•말•해•석

여: Ben, 너는 취미가 있어?
남: 응, 나는 재미로 빵을 구워. 너는?
여: 나는 취미가 없지만, 하나 있으면 좋겠어.
남: 너는 빵과 쿠키를 좋아하니?
여: 응, 나는 그것들을 좋아해.
남: 그러면 나의 빵 굽기 수업에 함께하는 게 어때?
여: 그래, 그것 재미있겠다!

단•어•및•표•현

for fun 재미로
join [dʒɔin] [동] 함께하다

17 한일파악 ▶ 정답 ②

듣•기•대•본

W: Hajun, how was your weekend?
M: It was fun. I went to the movies with my friends. How about you?
W: I knitted a scarf for my dad. It's his birthday next week.
M: Sounds wonderful! Where did you learn how to knit?
W: At the community center. I took a class for three months last year.

우•리•말•해•석

여: 하준아, 네 주말은 어땠어?
남: 재미있었어. 나는 내 친구들과 영화 보러 갔어. 너는 어땠어?
여: 나는 우리 아빠를 위해 목도리를 뜨개질했어. 다음 주가 아빠 생신이야.
남: 훌륭해! 너 뜨개질하는 법은 어디서 배웠어?
여: 커뮤니티 센터에서. 나는 작년에 세 달 동안 강좌를 들었어.

단•어•및•표•현

knit [nit] [동] 뜨개질하다
scarf [skɑːrf] [명] 목도리

18 직업추론 ▶ 정답 ⑤

듣•기•대•본

W: How can I help you?
M: I'd like to try on those running shoes.
W: Of course. What size are you?
M: I normally wear 270 mm for sneakers.
W: Okay. These are size 270. Would you like to try them on?
M: Sure. [*pause*] They fit great! Is there a mirror nearby?
W: Yes, there's one over there.

우•리•말•해•석

여: 어떻게 도와드릴까요?
남: 저는 저 운동화들을 신어 보고 싶어요.
여: 그럼요. 사이즈가 어떻게 되세요?
남: 전 운동화는 보통 270 mm를 신어요.
여: 네. 이것들이 270 사이즈예요. 당신은 그것들을 신어 보고 싶으세요?
남: 물론이죠. [잠시 후] 그것들은 잘 맞네요! 근처에 거울이 있나요?
여: 네, 저기 하나 있어요.

단•어•및•표•현

try ~ on ~을 신어 보다, 입어 보다
running shoes 운동화
fit [fit] [동] (모양, 크기가 어떤 사람 · 사물에) 맞다
nearby [nìərbái] [부] 근처에, 가까이에

19 알맞은응답찾기 ▶ 정답 ⑤

듣•기•대•본

W: How can I help you?
M: I'd like to get this jacket dry-cleaned, please.
W: Sure. What's your name?
M: Eric Kim. Can I also get these trainers cleaned?
W: Of course. Is there anything else?
M: No. When can I get them back?
W: You can collect them on Friday.

우•리•말•해•석

① 저는 달리는 것을 좋아해요.
② 밖에 비가 오고 있어요.
③ 총 8달러입니다.
④ 당신과 잘 어울려요.
⑤ 당신은 금요일에 가지러 오실 수 있어요.

여: 어떻게 도와드릴까요?
남: 이 재킷을 드라이 클리닝하고 싶어요.
여: 네. 성함이 어떻게 되시죠?
남: Eric Kim입니다. 이 운동화도 세탁할 수 있을까요?
여: 물론이죠. 또 다른 것도 있나요?
남: 아뇨. 언제 다시 가지러 오면 될까요?
여: 당신은 금요일에 가지러 오실 수 있어요.

단•어•및•표•현

trainer [tréinər] [명] 운동화(주로 복수형), 트레이너
collect [kəlékt] [동] 가지러 가다, 데리러 가다

20 알맞은응답찾기 ▶ 정답 ①

듣•기•대•본

W: It's so hot today.
M: I'm going to the beach this afternoon. Do you want to come with me?
W: Sorry. I would love to, but I can't.
M: Why not? Are you going somewhere?
W: No, I have something else to do.
M: What is it?
W: I have to finish my homework.

우·리·말·해·석

① 숙제를 끝마쳐야만 해. ② 내일 수영하러 가자.
③ 오후에는 한가해. ④ 즐겁게 지냈어.
⑤ 눈이 와.

여: 오늘 무척 덥구나.
남: 나는 오늘 오후에 해변에 갈 거야. 너도 같이 가고 싶어?
여: 미안해. 가고 싶지만, 갈 수 없어.
남: 왜 안 돼? 어디 가?
여: 아니, 다른 해야 할 것이 있어.
남: 그게 뭔데?
여: 숙제를 끝마쳐야만 해.

단·어·및·표·현

something else 다른 무언가
finish[fíniʃ] [동] 끝마치다

Words & Expressions Review

1. ~에 관심이 있다	2. ~을 신어 보다, 입어 보다	3. 즉시
4. 썩은, 부패한	5. 부, 부서	6. 음식점, 식당
7. 주름	8. 의학	9. 운동화
10. 증식시키다, 늘리다	11. 중고의	12. 운동화
13. 다른	14. 연설하다	15. 어깨
16. 불꽃놀이	17. 서쪽	18. 다른 무언가
19. ~에 출마하다	20. 근처에, 가까이에	21. 열리다, 개최되다
22. 가지러 가다	23. 없어진	24. 회장, 대통령
25. ~을 찾다	26. ~을 필요로 하다, 요구하다	27. 예정하다
28. 축하	29. 고장 난, 부서진	30. 상온, 평상시 온도
31. 불편, 애로	32. 끝마치다, 끝내다	33. 막다, 예방하다
34. 걸다	35. 확인하다, 검토하다	36. 옷장
37. 뜨개질하다	38. 산들바람	39. ~에 늦다
40. 함께 하다	41. 상하다, 썩다	42. 대회
43. 소나기, 샤워	44. 해질녘	

Listening Test

영어듣기 모의고사 23회

| 정 | 답 |

01 ①	02 ④	03 ④	04 ④	05 ③
06 ②	07 ⑤	08 ①	09 ③	10 ②
11 ④	12 ①	13 ④	14 ①	15 ⑤
16 ①	17 ③	18 ⑤	19 ②	20 ④

01 그림정보파악(담화) ▶ 정답 ①

듣·기·대·본

W: You can find this in many places like the subway station or the movie theater. You put some money into this and press the button under the drink of your choice. Then, you take the drink out of this. You may also get some change back. What is this?

우·리·말·해·석

여: 당신은 이것을 지하철역이나 영화관과 같은 많은 장소에서 찾을 수 있습니다. 당신은 이것에 약간의 돈을 넣고 당신이 선택한 음료 아래의 버튼을 누릅니다. 그 다음에, 당신은 이것에서 그 음료를 꺼냅니다. 당신은 또한 약간의 거스름돈을 받을지도 모릅니다. 이것은 무엇일까요?

단·어·및·표·현

press[pres] [동] 누르다
take out of ~ ~에서 꺼내다
change[tʃeindʒ] [명] 거스름돈

02 그림정보파악(대화) ▶ 정답 ④

듣·기·대·본

W: I'm looking for a stuffed animal for my three-year-old niece.
M: We have lions and deer in different styles.
W: She likes beautiful deer with big eyes.
M: How about this one without anything on its head?
W: That's perfect! The female deer looks cute. I'll take it.

우·리·말·해·석

여: 저는 제 세 살짜리 조카딸을 위한 봉제 동물 인형을 찾고 있어요.
남: 저희는 다양한 형태의 사자들과 사슴들이 있어요.
여: 그녀는 큰 눈을 가진 예쁜 사슴을 좋아해요.
남: 머리 위에 아무것도 없는 이건 어때요?
여: 완벽해요! 암사슴이 귀엽네요. 이걸로 할게요.

단·어·및·표·현

stuffed animal 봉제 동물 인형
niece[niːs] [명] 조카딸
female[fíːmèil] [형] 암컷의, 여성의

03 날씨파악-그림 ▶ 정답 ④

듣·기·대·본

W: This is Jenny Brown, from Weather Central. This is the weather report for Friday, November 17th. It will be sunny with beautiful skies today and tomorrow. But, the day after tomorrow, we are expecting snow. It will be the first snow of the year. Thank you for joining us.

우·리·말·해·석

여: Weather Central의 Jenny Brown입니다. 11월 17일 금요일 일기 예보입니다. 오늘과 내일은 아름다운 하늘의 맑은 날씨가 되겠습니다. 그러나 모레는 눈이 예상됩니다. 올해 들어 첫눈이 되겠습니다. 함께해 주셔서 감사합니다.

단·어·및·표·현

expect[ikspékt] [동] 예상하다, 기대하다

04 마지막말의도파악 ▶ 정답 ④

듣·기·대·본

W: Rick, can you help me practice basketball?
M: Sure. I have time on Sunday.
W: I need to practice right now.
M: But I'm watching TV!
W: Come on. I helped you with math before.
M: Then, it'll be just this once.

우·리·말·해·석

여: Rick, 너 내가 농구 연습하는 걸 도와줄 수 있니?

남: 물론이지. 난 일요일에 시간이 있어.

여: 난 지금 당장 연습해야 해.

남: 하지만 나는 TV를 보고 있는 중이야!

여: 어서. 내가 전에 수학 공부 도와줬잖아.

남: 그럼, 딱 이번 한 번만이야.

단·어·및·표·현

practice [prǽktis] [동] 연습하다

right now 지금 당장

help A with B A가 B하는 것을 돕다

05 담화미언급 ▶ 정답 ③

듣·기·대·본

M: Hello, everyone. Today, I'm going to tell you about a great writer of our time. His name is John Hamilton. He lives in New York, but he was born in London. He is 90 years old, but he still writes every day. His most famous book is titled *Wind from the West*.

우·리·말·해·석

남: 안녕하세요, 여러분. 오늘, 저는 우리 시대의 훌륭한 작가에 대해 여러분들에게 이야기할 것입니다. 그의 이름은 John Hamilton입니다. 그는 뉴욕에 살지만, 그는 런던에서 태어났습니다. 그는 90세이지만, 그는 여전히 매일 (글을) 씁니다. 그의 가장 유명한 책은 〈Wind from the West(서쪽으로부터의 바람)〉라는 제목이 붙여졌습니다.

단·어·및·표·현

time [taim] [명] 시대, 시기

be born 태어나다

still [stil] [부] 여전히

title [táitl] [동] 제목을 붙이다

06 수치파악 ▶ 정답 ②

듣·기·대·본

W: Hi, Oliver. Did you watch the soccer game on TV last night?

M: Of course. David Lee is my favorite player.

W: Then, shall we watch the documentary on him together?

M: Sure. It's tomorrow, right?

W: No, it's tonight at 8 p.m.

M: Really? It's going to start in 30 minutes, then!

W: Are you saying it's 7:30 p.m. now? We'd better hurry up!

우·리·말·해·석

여: 안녕, Oliver. 너 어젯밤 TV에서 축구 경기 봤어?

남: 당연하지. David Lee는 내가 가장 좋아하는 선수야.

여: 그럼, 그에 관한 다큐멘터리를 같이 볼래?

남: 물론이지. 그건 내일이야, 그렇지?

여: 아니, 오늘 밤 8시야.

남: 정말? 그럼 30분 후에 시작하겠네!

여: 지금이 오후 7시 30분이라는 말이야? 우리 서두르는 게 좋겠어!

단·어·및·표·현

favorite [féivərit] [형] 가장 좋아하는

documentary [dɑ̀kjuméntəri] [명] 다큐멘터리, 기록물

had better + 동사원형 ~하는 게 좋다, ~하는 게 낫다

hurry up 서두르다

07 장래희망추론 ▶ 정답 ⑤

듣·기·대·본

W: Jim, what are you reading?

M: I'm reading a science fiction novel. It's called *Life on Mars*.

W: You seem to read a lot of books related to space.

M: Yeah! Actually my favorite book is *2001: A Space Odyssey*.

W: Wow! Do you want to go to space one day?

M: Yes, I want to become an astronaut when I grow up.

W: I hope you achieve your dream!

우·리·말·해·석

여: Jim, 무엇을 읽고 있니?

남: 나는 공상 과학 소설을 읽고 있어. 그것은 "화성의 생명체"라고 해.

여: 너는 우주와 관련된 많은 책들을 읽는 것 같아.

남: 응! 사실 내가 가장 좋아하는 책은 "2001: 스페이스 오디세이"야.

여: 와! 너는 언젠가 우주에 가보고 싶니?

남: 응, 나는 커서 우주비행사가 되고 싶어.

여: 나는 네가 네 꿈을 이루길 바라!

단·어·및·표·현

related to ~ ~에 관련된

astronaut [ǽstrənɔ̀ːt] [명] 우주 비행사

08 심정추론 ▶ 정답 ①

듣·기·대·본

M: Hi, Susie. Where are you going?

W: I'm going to the library.

M: You have an exam tomorrow, don't you?

W: Yes, I do. I'm worried that I won't do well on the exam.

M: Why?

W: I didn't study that much.

M: I wish you luck.

우·리·말·해·석

남: 안녕, Susie. 어디 가니?

여: 도서관에 가는 중이야.

남: 너 내일 시험이 있지, 그렇지 않니?

여: 응, 있어. 시험을 잘 못 볼까 봐 걱정이 돼.

남: 왜?

여: 공부를 그리 많이 못했거든.

남: 행운을 빌어.

단·어·및·표·현

exam [igzǽm] [명] 시험

worried [wə́ːrid] [형] 걱정하는

LISTENING ADVICE

미국식 영어에서 단어가 'nd' 혹은 'nt'로 끝날 때 끝소리 [d]와 [t]는 탈락되거나 약하게 발음되어 거의 들리지 않습니다. 따라서 'don't'는 [돈]과 같이 들립니다. 그러나 영국식 영어에서는 이러한 경우에 [t] 발음이 탈락되지 않고 끝까지 발음되기도 합니다. 따라서 'won't'는 [원트], 'didn't'는 [디든트]와 같이 들립니다.

09 할일파악(대화직후) ▶ 정답 ③

듣·기·대·본

W: Jiho, we need to start preparing for the Google Science

Fair that our team is participating in.
M: But our team member Andrew is sick. He didn't come to school today.
W: Then how should we discuss our project?
M: Why don't we make a group chat room online?
W: Good idea. Then, Andrew will be able to talk with us.
M: Okay. I'll make a group chat room right now.

우·리·말·해·석

여: 지호야, 우리는 우리 팀이 참가하는 Google Science Fair 준비를 시작해야 해.
남: 하지만 우리 팀원 Andrew가 아파. 그는 오늘 학교에 오지 않았어.
여: 그러면 우리는 어떻게 우리의 과제를 논의해야 할까?
남: 우리 온라인으로 단체 채팅 방을 만드는 게 어때?
여: 좋은 생각이다. 그러면, Andrew도 우리와 이야기할 수 있을 거야.
남: 응. 내가 지금 바로 단체 채팅 방을 만들게.

단·어·및·표·현

participate in ~ ~에 참가하다, 참여하다
discuss [diskʌ́s] [동] 논의하다, 의논하다
be able to + 동사원형 ~할 수 있다

10 대화화제추론 ▶ 정답 ②

들·기·대·본

W: Kyle, did you catch last night's episode of *Doctor Park?*
M: Of course! I never miss the show.
W: Neither do I. Last night's ending was a bit weird though, wasn't it?
M: Yeah, it really was. Why would Park ignore his patients?
W: Exactly! I think the plot is getting messed up.
M: I hope they make up for it on the next episode.

우·리·말·해·석

여: Kyle, 너 지난밤 편 "Doctor Park" 봤어?
남: 물론이지! 나는 그 프로그램을 절대 놓치지 않아.
여: 나도 그래. 하지만 어젯밤의 결말은 조금 이상했어, 그렇지 않았어?
남: 응, 정말 그랬어. Park이 왜 그의 환자들을 무시하려고 했을까?
여: 내 말이! 나는 줄거리가 점점 엉망이 되고 있다고 생각해.
남: 나는 다음 회에서 그들이 만회하기를 바라.

단·어·및·표·현

Neither do I. 나도 그래. (부정문의 동의)
though [ðou] [부] 하지만(문장의 끝에 붙임)

11 특정정보파악(교통수단) ▶ 정답 ④

들·기·대·본

W: Brock, do you want to go see the cherry blossoms this weekend?
M: I'd love to! Where should we go?
W: Let's go to Jinhae! There will be a cherry blossom festival there.
M: Sounds good! Should we take the train?
W: Why don't we take the bus? It's cheaper.
M: Alright. I'll check the bus schedule.

우·리·말·해·석

여: Brock, 너 이번 주말에 벚꽃 보러 갈래?
남: 그러고 싶어! 어디로 가야 할까?
여: 진해로 가자! 거기에서 벚꽃 축제가 열릴 거야.
남: 좋은 생각이야! 우리가 기차를 타야 할까?
여: 버스를 타는 게 어때? 그게 더 싸.
남: 좋아. 내가 버스 시간표를 확인해 볼게.

단·어·및·표·현

cherry blossom 벚꽃
cheaper [tʃíːpər] [형] (값이) 더 싼

12 이유파악 ▶ 정답 ①

들·기·대·본

M: Jisu, I'm going to order some groceries online. Do you need anything?
W: Yes, Dad. Please order some carrots for me.
M: Okay. What do you need them for?
W: Mom's birthday is coming up. So I want to bake her favorite carrot cake.
M: Oh, that's very thoughtful of you. I'll order them right now.
W: Thank you.

우·리·말·해·석

남: 지수야, 나는 인터넷으로 식료품을 좀 주문하려고 해. 너는 필요한 것이 있니?
여: 네, 아빠. 저를 위해 당근을 좀 주문해 주세요.
남: 알았다. 너는 그것들이 무엇에 필요하니?
여: 엄마의 생신이 다가오고 있어요. 그래서 저는 엄마가 가장 좋아하는 당근 케이크를 굽고 싶어요.
남: 오, 너는 정말 사려 깊구나. 내가 그것들을 지금 당장 주문할게.
여: 고맙습니다.

단·어·및·표·현

order [ɔ́ːrdər] [동] 주문하다
grocery [gróusəri] [명] 식료품
thoughtful [θɔ́ːtfəl] [형] 사려 깊은

13 대화장소추론 ▶ 정답 ④

들·기·대·본

M: Honey, do we need anything else before we go to the checkout counter?
W: Wait a minute. Let's check the grocery list and compare it with what's in our shopping cart.
M: Let's see. Hmm… we forgot to buy dog food.
W: I'll go get it. Do you know which aisle it is in?
M: It's in the aisle right next to us. Check the pet food section.
W: Okay, I'll be back in a minute.

우·리·말·해·석

남: 여보, 우리가 계산대로 가기 전에 그 밖에 다른 게 필요한가요?
여: 잠깐만요. 식료품 목록을 확인하고 그것을 우리 쇼핑 카트 안에 있는 것과 비교해요.
남: 봅시다. 흠… 우리는 개 사료를 사는 것을 잊었어요.
여: 내가 가서 가져올게요. 그것이 어느 통로에 있는지 알아요?
남: 우리 바로 옆에 있는 통로에 있어요. 반려동물 사료 구역을 확인해봐요.
여: 좋아요, 곧 돌아올게요.

단·어·및·표·현

aisle [ail] [명] 통로
in a minute 곧

14 그림정보파악-지도 ▶ 정답 ①

듣·기·대·본

M: Excuse me. How do I get to the hospital?
W: The hospital? Go straight one block and turn left.
M: Go straight one block and turn left?
W: Yes. It will be on your right.
M: I see.
W: It's across from the bakery. You can't miss it.
M: Thanks.

우·리·말·해·석

남: 실례합니다. 병원까지 어떻게 가죠?
여: 병원이요? 한 블록 쭉 가서 왼쪽으로 도세요.
남: 한 블록 쭉 가서 왼쪽으로 돌라고요?
여: 네. 당신의 오른쪽에 있을 거예요.
남: 그렇군요.
여: 제과점 건너편이에요. 틀림없이 찾을 겁니다.
남: 감사합니다.

단·어·및·표·현

You can't miss it. 틀림없이 찾을 겁니다.

15 부탁(요청)한일파악 ▶ 정답 ⑤

듣·기·대·본

(*Telephone rings.*)
M: Mom, it's me. Are you home?
W: Not yet. I'm on my way home from the market.
M: Good! Could you put my flowerpot outside?
W: Ah, that plant you are growing for the science class?
M: Yes. It needs to be exposed to the sun. The weather forecast says the rain will stop in the afternoon.
W: OK. Don't worry about it.

우·리·말·해·석

(전화벨이 울린다.)
남: 엄마, 저예요. 집에 계세요?
여: 아직 아니야. 지금 시장에서 집으로 가는 길이야.
남: 잘됐네요! 제 화분을 밖에다 내놓아 주시겠어요?
여: 아, 네가 과학 수업을 위해 키우는 그 식물 말이지?
남: 네. 그것은 햇빛에 노출되어야 해요. 일기 예보에서 오후에는 비가 그칠 거라고 하네요.
여: 알았어. 걱정하지 마.

단·어·및·표·현

expose [ikspóuz] [동] 노출시키다
weather forecast 일기 예보

16 제안파악 ▶ 정답 ①

듣·기·대·본

W: Hey, John, are you okay?
M: No, I have a terrible headache.
W: I'm sorry to hear that. Do you know what's causing it?
M: I think it's because I've been working on my computer all day.
W: Why don't you rest your eyes for a few minutes?
M: Good idea. Maybe that will help.

우·리·말·해·석

여: 이봐, John, 너 괜찮아?
남: 아니, 나는 아주 심한 두통이 있어.
여: 그렇다니 유감이야. 무엇 때문에 그러는 건지 아니?
남: 내 생각에 내가 하루 종일 컴퓨터로 일을 해서 그런 것 같아.
여: 네 눈을 잠시 쉬게 해주는 게 어때?
남: 좋은 생각이야. 그게 도움이 될지도 모르겠어.

단·어·및·표·현

terrible [térəbl] [형] 심한, 지독한
cause [kɔːz] [동] ~을 야기하다, ~의 원인이 되다
rest [rest] [동] 쉬게 하다
for a few minutes 잠시

17 할일파악 ▶ 정답 ③

듣·기·대·본

M: Kelly, what are you doing this Saturday?
W: Nothing much. How about you?
M: I'm having a birthday party for my little brother Greg, and I need some help.
W: I'll help. What can I do?
M: Greg invited a lot of friends, and I'm worried about taking care of all the kids.
W: Oh, don't worry. Let's do it together.

우·리·말·해·석

남: Kelly, 이번 주 토요일에 뭐해?
여: 별일 없어. 너는?
남: 나는 남동생 Greg의 생일파티를 하는데, 도움이 좀 필요해.
여: 내가 도와줄게. 뭘 하면 되는데?
남: Greg이 친구들을 많이 초대했는데 그 모든 아이들을 돌보는 게 걱정돼.
여: 오, 걱정 마. 같이 하자.

단·어·및·표·현

be worried about ~ ~을 걱정하다, 염려하다
take care of ~ ~을 돌보다, ~에 신경을 쓰다

18 직업추론 ▶ 정답 ⑤

듣·기·대·본

M: Where to, ma'am?
W: 102 Main Street, please.
M: Edison Road is very busy at this time of the day. Shall I take Elm Road instead?
W: Sure, how long will it take?
M: It will take about 15 minutes.
W: Great. It's quite hot today. Could you turn on the air conditioner, please?
M: Of course.

우·리·말·해·석

남: 어디로 갈까요, 손님?
여: Main Street 102번지로요.
남: 하루 중 지금 이 시간에는 Edison Road가 아주 붐벼요. 대신 Elm Road를 타도 될까요?
여: 물론이죠, 얼마나 오래 걸릴까요?
남: 15분 정도 걸릴 거예요.
여: 좋아요. 오늘 아주 덥네요. 에어컨 좀 틀어주시겠어요?
남: 물론입니다.

단·어·및·표·현

instead [instéd] [부] 대신에
quite [kwait] [부] 아주, 꽤, 상당히
turn on (라디오, TV, 전기, 가스 따위를) 켜다

19 알맞은응답찾기 ▶ 정답 ②

들·기·대·본

W: Hey, Paul! Have you finished your vacation homework?

M: No, not yet. There is too much homework… a science report, a book report…

W: You can say that again. I haven't written a single word on my science report.

M: Me, neither. I don't know what to write.

W: I'm thinking about going to the National Science Center.

M: That's a good idea. Can I join you?

W: Sure. Let's go there on Saturday.

우·리·말·해·석

① 나는 도서관에서 과학책을 좀 찾아볼 거야.
② 물론이지. 토요일에 그곳에 가자.
③ 나는 네가 책을 쓰는 걸 도와줄 수 있어.
④ 나는 지하철을 타고 그곳에 갈 거야.
⑤ 나는 방학이 막 시작되어 기뻐.

여: 이봐, Paul! 너 방학 숙제 다 했어?
남: 아니, 아직, 숙제가 너무 많아… 과학 보고서에, 독후감에…
여: 네 말이 맞아. 나는 아직 과학 보고서에 한 글자도 못 썼어.
남: 나도. 나는 뭘 써야 할지 모르겠어.
여: 나는 국립 과학관에 가려고 생각 중이야.
남: 좋은 생각이야. 내가 같이 가도 될까?
여: **물론이지. 토요일에 그곳에 가자.**

단·어·및·표·현

book report 독후감
You can say that again. 네 말이 맞아., 동감이야.

20 알맞은응답찾기 ▶ 정답 ④

들·기·대·본

M: How was your meal, Mom?

W: It was delicious. You are a great cook! Thank you, Paul.

M: It's my pleasure. What did you like the most?

W: Everything was so good. Especially the pasta; it was fantastic.

M: Good! I thought you'd like it when I saw the recipe.

W: Oh, where did you get the recipe?

M: I found it on the internet.

우·리·말·해·석

① 저는 파스타를 안 좋아해요.
② 저는 단지 조리법을 따라 했어요.
③ 제가 디저트를 가져올게요.
④ 저는 그것을 인터넷에서 발견했어요.
⑤ 나중에 저에게 파스타를 만들어주세요.

남: 식사는 어땠어요, 엄마?
여: 맛있었어. 너는 훌륭한 요리사야! 고마워, Paul.
남: 별말씀을요. 무엇이 가장 좋았나요?
여: 모든 것이 정말 좋았어. 특히 파스타인데, 그것은 환상적이었어.
남: 좋아요! 저는 조리법을 봤을 때 엄마가 좋아하실 거라 생각했어요.
여: 오, 어디에서 조리법을 구했니?
남: **저는 그것을 인터넷에서 (우연히) 찾았어요.**

단·어·및·표·현

meal[miːl] 명 식사
delicious[dilíʃəs] 형 맛있는
It's one's pleasure. (감사에 대한 정중한 대답으로) 별말씀을요.

---

fantastic[fæntǽstik] 형 환상적인
recipe[résəpìː] 명 조리법

Words & Expressions Review

1. 연습하다	2. 켜다	3. ~과 관련된
4. 조카딸	5. 여전히	6. 일기 예보
7. 초대하다	8. 거스름돈, 잔돈	9. ~을 걱정하다, 염려하다
10. 네 말이 맞아.	11. ~하는 것 같다	12. 식료품
13. 쉽게 하다	14. (값이) 더 싼	15. 누르다
16. 심한, 지독한	17. 벚꽃	18. 봉제 동물 인형
19. ~에서, ~으로부터	20. 비교하다	21. ~할 수 있다
22. ~를 돌보다	23. 이루다, 달성하다	24. ~을 예상하다, 기대하다
25. 무시하다	26. 엉망으로 만들다, 망치다	27. ~의 건너편에
28. 대신에	29. 모레	30. 아주, 꽤, 상당히
31. 우주비행사	32. 가서 가져오다	33. 식사
34. 잠시	35. 가장 좋아하는	36. 서두르다
37. ~하는 게 좋다	38. 이상한, 기이한	39. 논의하다, 의논하다
40. ~을 야기하다	41. 다큐멘터리, 기록물	42. 노출시키다
43. A가 B하는 것을 돕다	44. 틀림없이 찾을 겁니다.	

Listening Test

영어듣기 고난도 모의고사 High Level 24회

|정답|

01 ⑤	02 ④	03 ②	04 ④	05 ④
06 ④	07 ②	08 ④	09 ⑤	10 ③
11 ②	12 ②	13 ⑤	14 ④	15 ②
16 ①	17 ②	18 ③	19 ④	20 ③

01 그림정보파악(담화) ▶ 정답 ⑤

들·기·대·본

W: I live in the ocean. I have no brain, heart or bones. I look like an umbrella floating in the water. I sometimes sting people when they touch me. What am I?

우·리·말·해·석

여: 나는 바다에서 살아요. 나는 뇌, 심장, 혹은 뼈들이 없어요. 나는 물 속에서 떠다니는 우산처럼 보여요. 나는 가끔 사람들이 나를 만질 때 그들을 쏘기도 해요. 나는 무엇일까요?

단·어·및·표·현

float[flout] 동 (물 위나 공중에서) 떠다니다
sting[stiŋ] 동 쏘다

02 그림정보파악(대화) ▶ 정답 ④

듣•기•대•본

W: May I help you?
M: I'm looking for a mini table.
W: How about this oval table with hearts on it?
M: I don't like hearts. Besides, I think rectangular tables are better.
W: Then, how is this one? It's rectangular and the stars look cool.
M: I like stars. I'll take it.

우•리•말•해•석

여: 도와드릴까요?
남: 저는 작은 좌식 테이블을 찾고 있어요.
여: 그것 위에 하트들이 있는 이 타원형 테이블은 어떠세요?
남: 저는 하트를 좋아하지 않아요. 게다가, 저는 직사각형 테이블이 더 좋은 것 같아요.
여: 그러면, 이건 어떠세요? 이건 직사각형이고 별들이 멋져 보여요.
남: 저는 별들을 좋아해요. 이걸로 할게요.

단•어•및•표•현

look for ~을 찾다, 구하다
oval [óuvəl] [형] 타원형의
besides [bisáidz] [부] 게다가

03 날씨파악-그림 ▶ 정답 ②

듣•기•대•본

M: Good morning! This is your local weather update. Today, it will be sunny in New York City. But watch out for thunderstorms in Miami. In Boston, there might be some light snow. And in Chicago, it's going to be very windy. If you're in Chicago, make sure to hold onto your hat!

우•리•말•해•석

남: 좋은 아침입니다! 지역 날씨 최신 정보입니다. 오늘, 뉴욕은 맑을 것입니다. 그러나 마이애미에서는 천둥번개를 조심하세요. 보스턴에는, 약간의 약한 눈이 내릴 것입니다. 그리고 시카고는, 바람이 아주 많이 불 것입니다. 만약 당신이 시카고에 있다면, 당신의 모자를 꼭 붙잡으세요!

단•어•및•표•현

local [lóukəl] [형] 지역의
update [ʌ́pdèit] [명] 최신 정보, 갱신
thunderstorm [θʌ́ndərstɔ̀ːrm] [명] 천둥번개, 뇌우
make sure 확실히 하다
hold onto 붙잡다, 쥐다

04 마지막말의도파악 ▶ 정답 ④

듣•기•대•본

M: Jane, do you have any plans after school?
W: Nothing special. Why?
M: I'm planning to go downtown with our classmates. Do you want to join us?
W: Thanks for inviting me, but I think I'll just stay home tonight.
M: Are you sure? We're going to the new bowling alley. It'll be fun!
W: I don't know. I'm a bit tired. I stayed up late doing homework last night.
M: Oh, come on! It's Friday! You can rest all day tomorrow!

우•리•말•해•석

남: Jane, 학교 끝나고 무슨 계획이 있니?
여: 특별한 일은 없어. 왜?
남: 나는 우리 반 친구들과 시내에 갈 계획이야. 우리랑 같이 갈래?
여: 나를 초대해줘서 고맙기는 한데, 나는 오늘 밤에는 그냥 집에 있을게.
남: 진심이야? 우리는 새로운 볼링장에 갈 거야. 재미있을 텐데!
여: 모르겠어. 나는 좀 피곤해. 나는 어젯밤에 숙제를 하느라 늦게까지 깨어있었거든.
남: 아, 그러지 말고! 오늘 금요일이야! 너 내일 하루 종일 쉴 수 있잖아!

단•어•및•표•현

invite [inváit] [동] 초대하다

LISTENING ADVICE

단어의 가운데에 위치한 't'는 대체로 소리가 약화되거나 생략됩니다. 따라서 'Thanks for inviting me ~'에서의 'inviting'은 [인바이팅]보다는 부드럽게 약화된 소리인 [인바이링]으로 들리게 됩니다. 이러한 [t] 소리의 약화는 미국식 영어에서 흔히 발생합니다.

05 담화미언급 ▶ 정답 ④

듣•기•대•본

M: Let me tell you about our school's environmental club. It's called the Green Team. We have twelve members. We meet every Friday after school at 3 p.m. in the library. We organize events like a recycling competition and a community clean-up day. If you care about the environment, you should come check us out!

우•리•말•해•석

남: 여러분에게 우리 학교의 환경 동아리에 대해 말씀드리겠습니다. 그것은 Green Team이라고 불립니다. 우리는 열두 명의 회원이 있습니다. 우리는 매주 금요일 방과 후 3시에 도서관에서 만납니다. 우리는 재활용 대회와 지역 사회 청소의 날과 같은 행사들을 준비합니다. 만약 당신이 환경에 대해 걱정하신다면, 찾아와서 우리를 확인해 보셔야 합니다!

단•어•및•표•현

environmental [invàirənméntəl] [형] (자연, 주위) 환경의, 환경과 관련된
organize [ɔ́ːrgənàiz] [동] (어떤 일을) 준비하다, 조직하다
recycling [risaikəliŋ] [명] 재활용
competition [kɑ̀mpətíʃən] [명] 대회, 경쟁, 시합
community [kəmjúːnəti] [명] 지역 사회
clean-up day 청소하는 날
care about ~에 대해 걱정하다, 마음을 쓰다

06 수치파악 ▶ 정답 ④

듣•기•대•본

W: Dan, if you're not busy today, can you help me prepare for my physics exam?
M: Only if you promise to help me with my chemistry exam.
W: It's a deal! Can we meet at 2 o'clock at the school library then?
M: Hmm… I have a dentist appointment at 2.
W: Okay, come see me at the library after you're finished. I'll be there studying.
M: Okay. I'll be there by 3.
W: Great! See you then!

우•리•말•해•석

여: Dan, 오늘 바쁘지 않다면, 내가 물리 시험 준비하는 것 도와줄 수 있어?
남: 네가 내 화학 시험을 도와준다고 약속하면.
여: 좋아! 그러면 우리 학교 도서관에서 2시에 만날 수 있어?
남: 흠… 나는 2시에 치과 예약이 있어.
여: 좋아, 끝나고 나서 도서관에 날 보러와. 거기서 공부하고 있을게.
남: 응, 3시까지 갈게.
여: 좋아! 그때 보자!

단•어•및•표•현

prepare for ~ ~을 준비하다, 대비하다
It's a deal! 좋아!, 그렇게 하자!

07 장래희망추론 ▶ 정답 ②

듣•기•대•본

W: What do you want to be in the future?
M: I want to take care of sick people.
W: I thought you were really into music.
M: Yes, I've played the drums for years, but that's just a hobby.
W: So, do you want to be a doctor?
M: Yes, that's my dream.
W: A doctor who can play the drums? How wonderful!

우•리•말•해•석

여: 너 미래에 뭐가 되고 싶니?
남: 나는 아픈 사람들을 돌보고 싶어.
여: 나는 네가 음악에 매우 관심이 많다고 생각했는데.
남: 응, 나는 수년간 드럼을 연주해왔지만 그것은 단지 취미야.
여: 그래서 너는 의사가 되고 싶니?
남: 응, 그것이 나의 꿈이야.
여: 드럼을 연주할 수 있는 의사? 정말 멋지다!

단•어•및•표•현

be into ~ ~에 관심이 많다

08 심정추론 ▶ 정답 ④

듣•기•대•본

W: Hey, what are you doing this Saturday?
M: Nothing special. Why?
W: Stacy and I are going on a picnic to fly a kite. Why don't you join us?
M: Sounds fun! I'm in. I'll bring some snacks!
W: Good. Let's meet at the main gate of the park at 2 p.m.
M: Okay. It'll be fun! I can hardly wait!

우•리•말•해•석

① 편안한 ② 속상한 ③ 놀란 ④ 신이 난 ⑤ 지루한

여: 얘, 너는 이번 주 토요일에 뭐 할 거니?
남: 특별한 건 없어. 왜?
여: Stacy와 나는 연을 날리기 위해 소풍을 갈 거야. 너도 우리와 함께하는 거 어때?
남: 재밌겠다! 나도 할래. 내가 간식을 좀 가져갈게!
여: 좋아. 오후 2시에 공원 정문에서 만나자.
남: 알겠어. 재미있겠다! 나는 도저히 기다릴 수 없어! (빨리 가고 싶어!)

단•어•및•표•현

go on a picnic 소풍을 가다
fly a kite 연을 날리다
join [dʒɔin] [동] 함께 하다, 합류하다
hardly [hɑ́ːrdli] [부] [can, could와 함께] 도저히 ~할 수 없다

09 할일파악(대화직후) ▶ 정답 ⑤

듣•기•대•본

M: Jessica, what are you doing this Saturday?
W: I'll be at home. Why?
M: Why don't we go to the library to study for our midterm exam together?
W: Sure! I'm having trouble studying history. Maybe you can help me.
M: Um... To tell the truth, I'm not good at history, either.
W: Then, why don't we invite someone else to study with us?
M: Good idea. How about Lidia? She is a history genius.
W: I have her number. I'll text her right now.

우•리•말•해•석

남: Jessica, 너는 이번 토요일에 무엇을 할 거야?
여: 나는 집에 있을 거야. 왜?
남: 중간고사를 위해 같이 공부하러 도서관에 가는 게 어때?
여: 좋아! 나는 역사를 공부하는 데 어려움이 있어. 아마도 네가 날 도와줄 수 있을 것 같아.
남: 음… 사실은, 나도 역사를 잘하진 않아.
여: 그러면, 우리와 같이 공부할 다른 누군가를 초대하는 것은 어때?
남: 좋은 생각이야. Lidia는 어때? 그녀는 역사 천재야.
여: 나는 그녀의 번호가 있어. 내가 바로 지금 그녀에게 문자를 보낼게.

단•어•및•표•현

have trouble -ing ~하는 데 어려움이 있다
to tell the truth 사실은, 진실을 말하자면
genius [dʒíːnjəs] [명] 천재

10 대화화제추론 ▶ 정답 ③

듣•기•대•본

M: What a beautiful song! Are you preparing for a singing contest?
W: No, actually I'm singing at my uncle's wedding this Saturday.
M: Amazing! What is the title of the song? It sounds familiar.
W: It is a popular song called *The Luckiest*.
M: Yeah, I know that song. I'm sure it'll be a special gift for your uncle.
W: I hope so. But I'm a little nervous to sing in front of so many people.
M: You'll do fine. I bet everyone will love your song.
W: Thank you.

우•리•말•해•석

남: 정말 아름다운 노래야! 너는 노래 대회를 준비하고 있니?
여: 아니, 사실 나는 이번 주 토요일에 삼촌의 결혼식에서 노래할 거야.
남: 놀라워! 노래 제목이 뭐야? 그것은 익숙하게 들려.
여: 그것은 "The Luckiest"라는 유명한 노래야.
남: 그래, 나 그 노래를 알아. 나는 그것이 네 삼촌에게 특별한 선물일 거라고 확신해.
여: 나는 그러길 바라. 하지만 너무 많은 사람들 앞에서 노래를 부르려니 약간 긴장돼.
남: 너는 잘할 거야. 나는 모든 사람들이 네 노래를 좋아할 거라고 확신해.
여: 고마워.

단•어•및•표•현

familiar [fəmíljər] [형] 익숙한
I bet ~. 나는 ~라고 확신해., 틀림없이 ~야.

11 특정정보파악(교통수단) ▶ 정답 ②

듣·기·대·본

M: Honey, when are we leaving for Busan?
W: This Saturday!
M: Okay. Are we going to drive our car?
W: Well... (pause) It's a five-hour ride and I don't want to get car sickness. Why don't we take the train?
M: Good idea. I prefer to travel by train.
W: Thank you.

우·리·말·해·석

남: 여보, 우리 언제 부산으로 떠나요?
여: 이번 토요일요!
남: 알았어요. 우리는 우리 차를 운전할 거예요?
여: 글쎄요… (잠시 후) 그것은 차로 5시간 걸리고 나는 차멀미를 하고 싶지 않아요. 우리 기차를 타는 게 어때요?
남: 좋은 생각이에요. 나는 기차로 여행하는 게 더 좋아요.
여: 고마워요.

단·어·및·표·현

ride[raid] 명 타고 가는 시간
prefer[prifə́:r] 동 ~을 더 좋아하다

12 이유파악 ▶ 정답 ②

듣·기·대·본

W: Welcome to Southwest University Library. How can I help you?
M: Hi, I want to borrow these books.
W: Alright. Your student ID, please?
M: 200531, Ma'am.
W: Oh, I'm sorry to say that you can't borrow them right now.
M: Excuse me?
W: The book you borrowed last month was overdue, so you owe 2,000 won in overdue fees.
M: Oh, I didn't know that.
W: You can't borrow books until you pay the fees.
M: OK, I'll get back to you later.

우·리·말·해·석

여: Southwest 대학 도서관에 오신 것을 환영합니다. 어떻게 도와드릴까요?
남: 안녕하세요, 저는 이 책들을 빌리고 싶어요.
여: 좋습니다. 학생증 번호는요?
남: 200531입니다.
여: 오, 말씀드리기 죄송하지만 당신은 지금 당장은 그것들을 빌릴 수 없어요.
남: 네?
여: 지난달에 빌린 책이 연체되어서 연체료로 2,000원을 내야 해요.
남: 오, 그것을 몰랐어요.
여: 연체료를 내기 전까진 책을 빌릴 수 없어요.
남: 알겠어요. 나중에 다시 올게요.

단·어·및·표·현

overdue[òuvərdjú:] 형 연체된, 기한이 지난

13 대화장소추론 ▶ 정답 ⑤

듣·기·대·본

M: Excuse me, can you show me how to use this exercise machine?
W: Sure. First, put your hands on the horizontal bar.

M: Okay.
W: Next, place your right foot on the foot pad and push!
M: How many times should I do this?
W: Repeat 15 times and then do the same with your other leg.
M: I think I've got it. Thanks.

우·리·말·해·석

남: 실례지만, 이 운동 기구를 어떻게 이용하는지 알려 주시겠어요?
여: 그러죠. 먼저, 손을 수평 바에 올려 놓으세요.
남: 네.
여: 다음으로 오른발을 발판에 놓고 미세요!
남: 몇 번이나 이걸 해야 하죠?
여: 15번 반복하고 나서 다른 다리로도 똑같이 하세요.
남: 알 것 같아요. 고마워요.

단·어·및·표·현

exercise machine 운동 기구
place[pleis] 동 놓다, 두다

14 표불일치 ▶ 정답 ④

듣·기·대·본

W: Hello, everyone! Let me tell you about our Handmade Soap Workshop for Kids. It'll be held this Sunday at 2 p.m. at the community center. In this workshop, kids will make their own colorful and scented soaps in fun shapes. The event will be 1 hour in length. This is a free event, and spots are first come, first served. Those who want to join should visit the front desk at the community center to register. Thanks!

우·리·말·해·석

아이들을 위한 수제 비누 워크숍		
①	일시	이번 주 일요일, 오후 2시
②	행사 내용	자신만의 비누를 만들다
③	행사 시간	1시간
④	참가비	5달러
⑤	신청 장소	커뮤니티 센터의 안내 데스크

여: 안녕하세요, 여러분! 우리 아이들을 위한 수제 비누 워크숍에 대해 알려드리겠습니다. 이번 주 일요일 오후 2시에 커뮤니티 센터에서 열릴 거예요. 이 워크숍에서 아이들은 그들만의 재미있는 모양의 알록달록하고 향기 나는 비누를 직접 만들게 됩니다. 이 행사의 길이는 1시간입니다. 이것은 무료 행사이며, 자리는 선착순입니다. 참가를 원하는 분들은 신청하기 위해 커뮤니티 센터 안내 데스크를 방문하셔야 합니다. 감사합니다!

단·어·및·표·현

handmade[hǽndméid] 형 수제의
scented[séntid] 형 향기로운
shape[ʃeip] 명 모양
in length 길이는
first come, first served 선착순
register[rédʒistər] 동 신청하다, 등록하다

15 부탁(요청)한일파악 ▶ 정답 ②

듣·기·대·본

M: Hi, I'm your neighbor, Kim Jay. I live next door.
W: Oh, hi. I'm Kate May.
M: So, you just moved in? Do you need anything?

W: Not now. But thanks.

M: Well, let me know if you do. Umm, by the way, would you mind turning down the music? The walls are really thin.

W: Oh, I'm sorry. I didn't realize that. I'll make sure to keep it down. By the way, is there a good restaurant near here?

M: Yes, there's a good Italian restaurant named Molto Bene. It's across the street.

W: Thank you.

우·리·말·해·석

남: 안녕하세요, 저는 이웃인 Kim Jay입니다. 저는 옆집에 살아요.

여: 아, 안녕하세요. 저는 Kate May예요.

남: 그러니까 막 이사 오셨죠? 필요한 것이 있나요?

여: 지금은 없어요. 하지만 고맙습니다.

남: 그럼, 필요한 게 있으면 저에게 알려주세요. 음, 그런데, 음악 소리 좀 줄여주시겠어요? 벽이 정말 얇아요.

여: 아, 미안합니다. 그것을 깨닫지 못했어요. 소리를 낮춰놓도록 할게요. 그런데, 이 근처에 좋은 식당이 있나요?

남: 네. Molto Bene라는 좋은 이탈리아 식당이 있어요. 길 건너편에 있어요.

여: 고맙습니다.

단·어·및·표·현

by the way 그런데, 그건 그렇고

mind [maind] 통 ~을 꺼리다

realize [rí(:)əlàiz] 통 깨닫다

16 제안파악 ▶ 정답 ①

듣·기·대·본

W: Terry, what are you doing?

M: I'm reading a book on my phone.

W: On your phone? Can you do that?

M: Yes, I'm using a library app.

W: That's nice. I really should read more.

M: Then, why don't you download this app, too?

W: Good idea. Is it for free?

M: Yes, it is.

우·리·말·해·석

여: Terry, 뭐하고 있어?

남: 내 휴대폰으로 책을 읽고 있어.

여: 휴대폰으로? 그것을 할 수 있어?

남: 응, 나는 도서관 앱을 사용하고 있어.

여: 그거 멋지다. 나는 정말 책을 더 많이 읽어야 해.

남: 그러면, 너도 이 앱을 다운로드하는 게 어때?

여: 좋은 생각이야. 그것은 무료야?

남: 응, 그래.

단·어·및·표·현

for free 무료로

17 한일파악 ▶ 정답 ②

듣·기·대·본

M: Eva, did you have a good vacation?

W: Yeah, I went to visit my aunt.

M: Oh, what did you do there?

W: I went swimming with my cousins. We went camping, too.

M: That sounds fun. You had a nice summer.

W: What about you?

M: I made a huge model airplane. It took me weeks.

W: That's amazing!

우·리·말·해·석

남: Eva, 방학 잘 보냈어?

여: 응, 나는 이모네 방문하러 갔어.

남: 오, 거기서 무엇을 했어?

여: 내 사촌들이랑 수영하러 갔어. 우리는 캠핑도 갔어.

남: 그거 재미있게 들린다. 너는 멋진 여름을 보냈네.

여: 너는 어때?

남: 나는 커다란 모형 비행기를 만들었어. 그것은 여러 주가 걸렸어.

여: 그거 놀랍다!

단·어·및·표·현

huge [hju:dʒ] 형 커다란, 거대한

18 직업추론 ▶ 정답 ③

듣·기·대·본

M: How is it going, Ms. White?

W: I'm making the sauce now. Will you taste it?

M: Sure. (pause) Hmm, it's tasty, but a little salty.

W: Oh, what should I do?

M: Just put in some more oil. You are doing great.

W: Thank you. It's thanks to your excellent teaching.

M: My pleasure. You cooked this fish very well, too.

W: Thank you.

우·리·말·해·석

남: 어떻게 되어가요, White 씨?

여: 저는 지금 소스를 만들고 있어요. 맛보시겠어요?

남: 그럼요. (잠시 후) 흠, 맛있지만 약간 짜요.

여: 오, 제가 무엇을 해야 하죠?

남: 그냥 기름을 조금 더 넣으세요. 잘하고 있어요.

여: 고맙습니다. 당신의 훌륭한 가르침 덕분이에요.

남: 천만에요. 당신도 이 생선을 매우 잘 요리했어요.

여: 고맙습니다.

단·어·및·표·현

How is it going? 어떻게 되어 가고 있습니까?, 어떻게 지내나요?

thanks to ~ ~ 덕분에

19 알맞은응답찾기 ▶ 정답 ④

듣·기·대·본

(Telephone rings.)

M: Hello. Brittany? This is Dennis.

W: Oh, hi, Dennis. How are you?

M: I'm fine. I ran into your mom at the store. She said you were in the hospital.

W: I was, yes. It was just a really bad case of the flu.

M: I'm sorry to hear that. How are you doing?

W: I'm still recovering. I'll be resting at home for the next day or so.

M: I hope you get better soon.

우·리·말·해·석

① 내가 그 병원에서 너를 찾아갈게.

② 너를 가게에서 만나서 좋았어.

③ 내가 너에게 식료품을 가져다줄게.

④ 나는 네가 곧 회복되길 바라.

⑤ 나 병원 청구서를 받았어.

24회 모의고사

(전화벨이 울린다.)
남: 안녕. Brittany? 나 Dennis야.
여: 오, 안녕, Dennis. 어떻게 지내?
남: 좋아. 나 너희 엄마를 가게에서 우연히 만났어. 그녀가 말하길 너 병원에 있었다고 하더라.
여: 응, 그랬어. 그저 정말 심한 독감이었어.
남: 그 말을 들어 유감이다. 지금은 어떠니?
여: 나는 여전히 회복 중이야. 나는 내일 하루 정도 좀 더 집에서 휴식할 거야.
남: 나는 네가 곧 회복되길 바라.

단·어·및·표·현

recover[rikʌ́vər] [동] 회복하다

20 알맞은응답찾기 ▶ 정답 ③

듣·기·대·본

W: How can I help you?
M: I'd like to order a cake for tomorrow afternoon.
W: Sure. Which cake would you like?
M: Can you recommend one? It's for my wife.
W: How about the cheesecake or the strawberry cream cake?
M: Hmm… I'll take the cheesecake.
W: OK. When would you like to pick it up?
M: **I'll come at 5 o'clock.**

우·리·말·해·석

① 축하합니다!
② 그녀는 치즈를 좋아해요.
③ 제가 5시에 올게요.
④ 제가 직장에서 그녀를 태워 옵니다.
⑤ 내일은 그녀의 생일이에요.

여: 어떻게 도와드릴까요?
남: 저는 내일 오후를 위해 케이크를 주문하고 싶습니다.
여: 그러세요. 어떤 케이크로 하시겠어요?
남: 당신이 하나 추천해 주시겠어요? 그건 제 아내를 위한 거예요.
여: 치즈케이크나 딸기 크림 케이크는 어떠세요?
남: 흠… 전 치즈케이크로 할게요.
여: 알겠습니다. 언제 찾아가시겠어요?
남: **제가 5시에 올게요.**

단·어·및·표·현

order[ɔ́ːrdər] [동] 주문하다
recommend[rèkəménd] [동] 추천하다, 권하다
pick ~ up (어디에서) ~을 찾아오다, ~를 (차에) 태우러 가다

Words & Expressions Review

1. 깨닫다	2. 떠다니다	3. 문자를 보내다
4. ~에 관심이 많다	5. 소풍을 가다	6. 회복하다
7. ~에 대해 걱정하다, 마음을 쓰다	8. 연체된, 기한이 지난	9. 지역의
10. 예약, 약속	11. 사실, 진실	12. ~를 돌보다
13. 연을 날리다	14. 커다란, 거대한, 막대한	15. ~를 우연히 만나다
16. 함께 하다	17. 정문	18. 재활용
19. 천만에요.	20. 천재	21. 도저히 ~할 수 없다
22. 얇은	23. 맛있는	24. 물리학
25. 짠, 짭짤한, 소금이 든	26. 이웃	27. 쏘다
28. 추천하다, 권하다	29. 천둥번개, 뇌우	30. 회복하다, 나아지다
31. 다운로드하다, 내려받다	32. 지역 사회	33. 향기로운
34. 최신 정보, 갱신	35. 앱, 애플리케이션	36. 맛보다
37. ~을 더 좋아하다, 선호하다	38. 수제의	39. 훌륭한, 탁월한
40. 환경의, 환경과 관련된	41. 익숙한, 친숙한	42. 타원형의
43. 모형	44. 초대하다	

중학영어듣기 필수 표현 📝

중요도 최상 ★★★ 상 ★★ 중 ★

길 안내하기

중요도	주요표현	해석
★★	(In fact) It's ~	(사실) 그것은 ~에 있습니다.
★★	(In that case,) Go(Cross, Turn, Follow)~.	(그럴 경우엔,) ~가십시오. (~건너십시오, ~도세요, ~따라가십시오.)
★	(Excuse me.) Can you tell me the way ~	(실례합니다.) ~가는 길 좀 알려주시겠어요?
★	Can you tell me where ~ is?	~가 어디인지 알려주시겠어요?
★	Excuse me. Where's the ~?	실례합니다. ~가 어디 있죠?
★	Where can I find ~?	~를 어디에서 찾을 수 있죠?
★	How can I get there?	어떻게 거기에 갈 수 있죠?
★	Is this the right way to ~?	이 길이 ~가는 길 맞죠?
★	It's (just) down the road.	그것은 (바로) 길 아래에 있습니다.
★	That road leads you to ~	저 길로 가면 ~에 도착합니다.
★	Let's go straight. We can walk across ~	직진합시다. 우리는 ~를 건너갈 수 있습니다.
★	You can see it on your ~	당신의 ~에서 그것을 볼 수 있습니다.
★	You have to go straight ~	직진하셔야 합니다.

기억/경험 묻고 말하기

중요도	주요표현	해석
★★	Do you remember ~?	~기억납니까?
★★	I'll never forget ~	나는 ~를 결코 잊지 않을 거야.
★★	I've (actually) never p.p. ~	(사실) 나는 ~한 적이 결코 없습니다.
★	Is that really true?	그게 정말 사실입니까?
★	Have you forgotten ~?	~잊으셨습니까?
★	Sure.	물론이야.
★	I forgot about that.	나 그거 잊어버렸어.
★	I didn't know that. That's amazing!	나는 그거 몰랐어. 놀라워!
★	I find it hard to believe ~.	나는 ~을 믿기 어렵습니다.
★	Have you ever ~ p.p.?	~한 적이 있습니까?
★	I've (actually) p.p. ~	(사실) 나는 ~한 적이 있습니다.
★	(Actually,) I have had (done) the same experience (before).	(사실,) 나는 똑같은 경험이 있습니다.

마더텅 100%실전대비 MP3 중학영어듣기 24회 모의고사 1학년

정답표

1회
1	2	3	4	5	6	7	8	9	10
④	①	③	④	⑤	③	④	①	④	②
11	12	13	14	15	16	17	18	19	20
③	④	③	②	④	①	②	④	⑤	③

2회
1	2	3	4	5	6	7	8	9	10
⑤	②	②	①	③	⑤	③	⑤	④	⑤
11	12	13	14	15	16	17	18	19	20
③	⑤	③	④	④	③	①	③	⑤	⑤

3회
1	2	3	4	5	6	7	8	9	10
②	②	④	①	⑤	②	④	⑤	③	①
11	12	13	14	15	16	17	18	19	20
③	④	⑤	⑤	①	④	③	⑤	②	④

4회
1	2	3	4	5	6	7	8	9	10
③	④	②	①	③	③	⑤	④	①	④
11	12	13	14	15	16	17	18	19	20
①	⑤	②	④	④	④	⑤	⑤	②	⑤

5회
1	2	3	4	5	6	7	8	9	10
①	④	③	④	⑤	③	⑤	③	④	②
11	12	13	14	15	16	17	18	19	20
③	③	④	⑤	①	④	②	⑤	②	②

6회
1	2	3	4	5	6	7	8	9	10
②	①	③	④	⑤	③	④	③	②	④
11	12	13	14	15	16	17	18	19	20
⑤	⑤	②	④	②	②	①	⑤	⑤	③

7회
1	2	3	4	5	6	7	8	9	10
⑤	⑤	①	①	⑤	④	⑤	③	④	①
11	12	13	14	15	16	17	18	19	20
④	③	④	①	②	④	③	④	②	①

8회
1	2	3	4	5	6	7	8	9	10
④	③	④	②	④	④	⑤	③	②	⑤
11	12	13	14	15	16	17	18	19	20
③	④	③	①	②	④	③	②	④	⑤

9회
1	2	3	4	5	6	7	8	9	10
⑤	④	③	③	②	⑤	③	①	②	④
11	12	13	14	15	16	17	18	19	20
⑤	⑤	①	④	③	①	④	⑤	②	①

10회
1	2	3	4	5	6	7	8	9	10
③	⑤	②	②	⑤	②	③	⑤	②	①
11	12	13	14	15	16	17	18	19	20
③	⑤	③	①	④	⑤	④	④	③	④

11회
1	2	3	4	5	6	7	8	9	10
②	②	③	④	④	②	①	②	⑤	④
11	12	13	14	15	16	17	18	19	20
⑤	②	④	③	④	⑤	③	④	⑤	⑤

12회
1	2	3	4	5	6	7	8	9	10
②	③	⑤	④	③	②	③	①	③	③
11	12	13	14	15	16	17	18	19	20
④	④	⑤	②	④	③	②	⑤	⑤	②

13회
1	2	3	4	5	6	7	8	9	10
①	②	③	④	③	④	③	④	①	⑤
11	12	13	14	15	16	17	18	19	20
⑤	②	⑤	③	②	⑤	③	①	③	④

14회
1	2	3	4	5	6	7	8	9	10
①	②	④	④	④	②	④	①	②	⑤
11	12	13	14	15	16	17	18	19	20
③	①	⑤	②	⑤	③	④	④	③	⑤

15회
1	2	3	4	5	6	7	8	9	10
④	②	④	①	⑤	③	④	②	⑤	③
11	12	13	14	15	16	17	18	19	20
②	②	②	④	①	④	⑤	③	④	①

16회
1	2	3	4	5	6	7	8	9	10
①	②	⑤	④	①	④	①	⑤	④	③
11	12	13	14	15	16	17	18	19	20
③	⑤	②	①	②	③	③	⑤	④	②

17회
1	2	3	4	5	6	7	8	9	10
④	②	④	③	④	②	②	④	⑤	⑤
11	12	13	14	15	16	17	18	19	20
⑤	⑤	⑤	③	②	⑤	④	③	①	③

18회
1	2	3	4	5	6	7	8	9	10
②	⑤	⑤	③	②	④	⑤	③	②	④
11	12	13	14	15	16	17	18	19	20
③	②	⑤	①	②	②	②	①	①	①

19회
1	2	3	4	5	6	7	8	9	10
④	②	④	③	④	①	③	②	③	④
11	12	13	14	15	16	17	18	19	20
④	②	④	③	④	③	①	④	②	⑤

20회
1	2	3	4	5	6	7	8	9	10
②	④	⑤	①	③	②	①	④	③	④
11	12	13	14	15	16	17	18	19	20
④	③	②	③	④	②	③	④	⑤	⑤

21회
1	2	3	4	5	6	7	8	9	10
①	③	③	②	③	④	⑤	③	②	③
11	12	13	14	15	16	17	18	19	20
①	⑤	③	④	③	④	③	④	②	③

22회
1	2	3	4	5	6	7	8	9	10
④	⑤	②	⑤	③	④	④	②	⑤	③
11	12	13	14	15	16	17	18	19	20
⑤	④	④	④	①	①	⑤	⑤	⑤	①

23회
1	2	3	4	5	6	7	8	9	10
⑤	④	④	③	②	③	⑤	④	①	②
11	12	13	14	15	16	17	18	19	20
④	①	①	④	③	②	③	⑤	⑤	①

24회
1	2	3	4	5	6	7	8	9	10
④	④	②	④	④	②	⑤	②	④	③
11	12	13	14	15	16	17	18	19	20
②	②	⑤	②	④	①	②	③	④	③

중학영어듣기 필수 표현 📝

중요도 최상 ★★★ 상 ★★ 중 ★

질문/대답하기

중요도	주요표현	해석
★★★	I'm(We're) planning to + 동사원형	나는(우리는) ~할 계획이야.
★★★	I'm going to + 동사원형	나는 ~할 계획이야.
★★★	Have you heard of/about ~?	~에 대해 들어본 적 있어?
★★★	What are you planning to do?	무엇을 할 생각이야? (계획이 뭐야?)
★★★	Could/Can you (please) tell me ~?	~에 대해 말해 줄 수 있어?
★★	What would you like to + 동사원형?	너 무엇을 ~하고 싶어?
★★	Have you (ever) p.p. ~?	너 ~해본 적 있어?
★	What are you going to do?	너 뭐 할거야?
★	Do you know ~?	너 ~에 대해 알아?
★	Do you want to + 동사원형?	너 ~하고 싶어?
★	Are you planning to + 동사원형?	너 ~할 계획이야?
★	Do you have any plans?	어떤 계획이라도 있어?
★	I've never p.p. ~	나는 ~해본 적이 없어.
★	I have to ~	나는 ~해야만 해.
★	How did you + 동사원형?	어떻게 ~했어?
★	What is ~?	~는 무엇이야?
★	Who + 과거동사 ~?	누가 ~했어?
★	What did he + 동사원형 ~?	그가 무엇을 ~했어?
★	When + 동사 ~?	언제 ~야?
★	Why ~?	왜 ~야?
★	Did you + 동사원형 ~?	너 ~했어?
★	What do you do to + 동사원형 ~?	~하기 위해 너는 무엇을 해?
★	What do you call + 명사 ~?	너는 ~를 뭐라고 불러?
★	What A do you want to + 동사원형?	어떤 A를 ~하기 원해?
★	Which A do you like most?	어떤 A를 너는 가장 좋아해?
★	Which A would you like to + 동사원형?	어떤 A를 ~하고 싶어?
★	What do you want to be in the future?	너는 커서 무엇이 되고 싶어?
★	Would you like to + 동사원형 ~?	너 ~하고 싶어?
★	What kind of A do you prefer?	어떤 종류의 A를 너는 선호해?

감사/칭찬

중요도	주요표현	해석
★	I couldn't have p.p. without you.	네가 없었다면 나는 ~할 수 없었을 거야. (정말 고마워.)
★	Thanks (so much).	(매우) 감사합니다.
★	Thank you for + 명사	~에 대해 감사드립니다.
★	I appreciate it.	그것에 대해 감사드립니다.
★	It's (very) nice of you to + 동사원형	~를 해주셔서 (매우) 감사드립니다.
★	Terrific!	정말 멋졌어! (정말 잘했어!)
★	Excellent!	정말 멋졌어! (정말 잘했어!)
★	You did a good(great) job!	너 정말 훌륭했어!
★	I like(liked) your + 명사	나는 너의 ~가 좋아(좋았어).
★	You are such a friendly person.	너는 매우 친절하구나.
★	I'm glad you like it.	네가 그것을 좋아하니 기쁘다.
★	Don't mention it.	별말씀을요. (그렇게 말해 주니 고마워요.)

불가능 표현하기

중요도	주요표현	해석
★★★	I have no idea how ~	나는 어떻게 ~ 하는지 잘 모르겠어. (못하겠어.)
★	It's/That's/A is (almost) impossible!	그것은(A는) 불가능해!
★	I can't.	나는 할 수 없어.
★	That won't be possible.	그것은 불가능해.
★	I don't think I can.	내가 할 수 있다고 생각하지 않아. (못해.)
★	I /We won't be able to + 동사원형	나는(우리는) ~ 할 수 없어요.
★	I'm not good at ~	나는 ~를 잘하지 못해요.
★	There is no/a chance ~	~ 인 가능성은 없어. (있어.)
★	I have no time to + 동사원형	나는 ~ 할 시간이 없어.